KENSAL GREEN CEMETERY

KENSAL GREEN CEMETERY

The Origins and Development of the General Cemetery of All Souls, Kensal Green, London, 1824-2001

edited by

James Stevens Curl

Phillimore

Of this Edition 1,000 copies have been printed

This copy is No. 179

2001

Published by
PHILLIMORE & CO. LTD.
Shopwyke Manor Barn, Chichester, West Sussex

© James Stevens Curl and the other Contributors named within, 2001

ISBN 1 86077 194 7

Printed and bound in Great Britain by
BUTLER & TANNER LTD.
London and Frome

Frontispiece on previous page: Watercolour (*c.*1832) of the General Cemetery of All Souls, Kensal Green, perhaps by Thomas Allom (1804-72) or John Griffith (1796-1888), showing an early version (*unrealised*) of the entrance-gate and lodges (*bottom left*) facing the Harrow Road (*right*), Anglican chapel (*centre, at the end of the main avenue [later Centre Avenue], then lined with cedars*), colonnade over a long range of catacombs (*top right – of much greater extent than the realised terrace catacomb*), and the canal (*left*). The cemetery looks like an English landscaped park, with tombs judiciously placed within it. The Museum of London dates this as *c.*1831, which cannot be correct, as a trawl through the Minutes of the Company shows quite clearly that it was mid-1832 before the layout and sites for the buildings were anything like finalised. The Anglican chapel (the central portico of which looks as though it was intended to be of the Greek Ionic Order [it was built as Doric]) is probably derived from designs by the Hon. Thomas Liddell (1800-56), possibly drawing on an earlier proposal by H. E. Kendall (1776-1875). It seems that Kendall favoured a site for the entrance further west, however, so this image probably reflects a joint scheme envisaged by Liddell and Griffith. Note the tall monument proposed to stand in the centre of the circle of paths in front of the chapel and the extensive architectural treatment proposed for the platform on which the chapel was to sit. The boundary-wall includes a substantial length of railing on the canal-side, which is what was erected, and the clear demarcation between the consecrated and unconsecrated grounds (*behind the entrance-arch*) is shown (*Picture Courtesy of The Museum of London, CLOO/5082, D.181*).

IN MEMORIAM

John Griffith (1796-1888)
Architect

who was largely responsible for the design of the cemetery and its buildings

Si monumentum requiris, circumspice
(If you seek a monument, look around)

Inscription over the grave of Sir Christopher Wren (1632-1723)
in St Paul's Cathedral, attributed to his son, CHRISTOPHER WREN (1765-1747).

... there is a certain frame of mind to which a cemetery is, if not an antidote, at least an alleviation. If you are in a fit of the blues, go nowhere else.

ROBERT LOUIS BALFOUR STEVENSON (1850-94):
Further Memories ('The Wreath of Immortelles')
(London: William Heinemann Ltd., in association with Chatto & Windus, Cassell & Company Ltd.,
and Longmans, Green, & Company, Tusitala Edition, 1924), 166.

Contents

List of Contributors

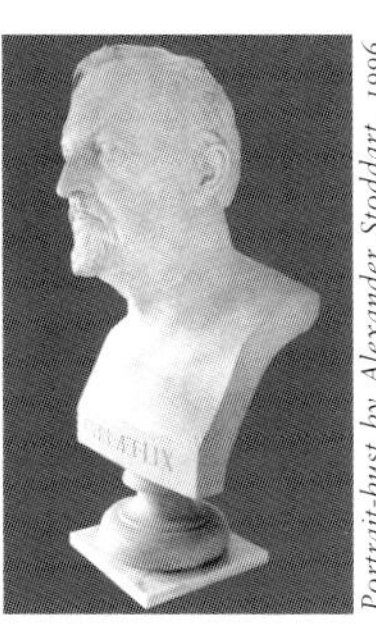

Portrait-bust by Alexander Stoddart, 1996

James Stevens Curl (*Editor*) is Professor of Architectural History and Senior Research Fellow at The Queen's University of Belfast. Among his more recent books are *Classical Architecture: an Introduction to its Vocabulary and Essentials, with a Select Glossary of Terms* (2001); *The Victorian Celebration of Death* (2000); *The Honourable The Irish Society and the Plantation of Ulster, 1608-2000: the City of London and the Colonisation of County Londonderry* (2000); *The Oxford Dictionary of Architecture* (1999 and 2000); *The English Heritage Book of Victorian Churches* (1995); and *Egyptomania* (1994). He was the first Director of the Friends of Kensal Green Cemetery, has been a member of the Friends' Advisory Council since 1989, and a member of the Fabric Committee since 1991.

Roger Bowdler was born in Cambridge in 1962. Educated at Bryanston and Sidney Sussex College, Cambridge, he completed his PhD on 17th-century church monuments (of the macabre variety) in 1991. Since 1989 he has worked as an historian with English Heritage. Among his responsibilities are blue plaques and carrying out surveys of London's burial-grounds. A member of the Friends of Kensal Green Cemetery's Advisory Council, he is a Trustee of the Mausolea and Monuments Trust and a Council Member of the Church Monuments Society.

André Davies joined the permanent staff at the Victoria and Albert Museum in 1984. After an initial period in the Museum's Publications Department, he assisted in the setting up of the Buildings and Estate Department following the demise of the Property Services Agency in 1986-8. Currently he is Estate Manager of the Museum. Involved with the Friends of Kensal Green Cemetery since the foundation of the group in 1989, he was the first Honorary Treasurer, and is now the Director and a Member of the Advisory Council. Recent lecture papers include *The Victoria & Albert Museum – The Early Years*; *The Victoria & Albert Museum – The War Years*; and *The History of the Garden Cemetery Movement*.

Christopher Brooks was born in London in 1949 and educated at Manchester and Oxford, where he wrote his Doctoral thesis on Dickens and mid-Victorian art and architecture. He is Professor of Victorian Culture in Exeter University's School of English, has been a member of the Advisory Council of the Friends of Kensal Green Cemetery since 1990, and Chairman of the Victorian Society since 1993. Among his books are *Mortal Remains. The History and Present State of the Victorian and Edwardian Cemetery* (1989) and *The Gothic*

Revival (1999), and he is the editor of *The Albert Memorial* (2000). He is currently working on a study of Queen Victoria's funeral.

[William] Brent Elliott was born in Vancouver, British Columbia, in 1952. He is the Librarian and Archivist of the Royal Horticultural Society, a member of the Historic Parks and Gardens Advisory Committee of English Heritage, and a long-standing member of the Buildings Sub-Committee of the Victorian Society. Formerly a Council Member of the Garden History Society, he was also Editor (1984-8) of that Society's Journal, *Garden History*. A one-time Chairman of the Cemeteries Committee of the Victorian Society, he contributed to its publication, *Mortal Remains* (1989). Among his books are *Victorian Gardens* (1986) and *The Country House Garden* (1995).

Timothy Hugh Freed was born in London in 1957. He was educated at Eton, Aberdeen University, and the Royal College of Art (where his Doctorate was conferred for research on butterfly ecology in Kensal Green cemetery). He works as a freelance illustrator and ecological consultant. Artwork by him is held at the Natural History Museum and in private collections, and his illustrations appear in *The Moths and Butterflies of Great Britain and Ireland* (1985-96), amongst other publications. Since 1991 he has been a member of the Central Royal Parks Wildlife Group, undertaking consultancies for the Royal Parks Agency and other bodies. He was recently involved with the RHS Wisley Wildlife Area Advisory Group and is currently engaged with the Westminster Biodiversity Partnership.

Jennifer Margaret Freeman was educated at Manchester University and the Architectural Association, London. She worked in New York for the Landmarks Preservation Commission, and later, in London, for the Civic Trust and the Victorian Society. Since 1991 she has chaired the Fabric Committee of the Friends of Kensal Green Cemetery, and has been a member of the Advisory Council of the Friends since its inception. She became the first Director of the Historic Chapels Trust when it was founded in 1993. Her publications include the definitive study of the architect William Douglas Caröe (1857-1938) which appeared in 1990, and frequent contributions to journals on architectural and conservation matters. She also runs a small company that specialises in the repair of Listed Buildings 'at risk'.

Photograph by Ken Jackson

Julian William Sebastian Litten was born in Wolverhampton in 1947. Educated in Wolverhampton, Ilford, and Cardiff, he also had conferred upon him an Honorary Doctor of Art by De Montfort University, Leicester, for his contribution to ecclesiastical conservation. A member of staff of the Victoria and Albert Museum (1966-1999), he is currently Visiting Lecturer in the Theory and Practice of Mediaeval Craftsmanship at Canterbury Christ Church University College. Among his published works is *The English Way of Death: The Common Funeral Since 1450* (1991). He is the founder and President of the Friends of Kensal Green Cemetery.

Robert Moulder was born in Oxford. Educated at Chipping Norton School and North Oxfordshire Technical College and School of Art, he has had much varied experience working in many capacities and locations. Over the last few years he has devoted much of his time to historical research in the cemeteries of All Souls and St Mary, Kensal Green. He has contributed the article on the General Cemetery's founder, George Frederick Carden, to the *New Dictionary of National Biography* (to be published).

John Physick, CBE, is a former Deputy Director of the Victoria and Albert Museum, and was a member of the Advisory Council of the Friends of Kensal Green Cemetery. His publications include *Designs for English Sculpture 1680-1860* (1969) and the second, revised, edition of *Sculpture in Britain 1530-1840* by Margaret Whinney (1988). Since 1966 he has been revising and adding to Rupert Gunnis's *Dictionary of British Sculptors 1660-1851*. He is a contributor to *The Albert Memorial*, edited by Christopher Brooks (2000). His most recent works include the continuing production of the inventory (in Westminster Abbey's Library) of the monuments within the Abbey.

Ruth Richardson is an historian and has published widely on issues surrounding death, funerary culture, and disposal of the dead. She is the author of *Death, Dissection, and the Destitute* (1987), a new edition of which was published in 2001, and was the co-author (with Robert Thorne) of *The Builder Illustrations Index*. She and her husband, Professor Brian Hurwitz, have published the first ever survey-profile of whole-body donors for dissection in *The Lancet* (1995). She is becoming increasingly involved in the study of the aftermath of the unfolding scandal concerning the removal of organs from dead children without consent, and has drawn attention to worrying parallels between global policies of organ procurement and body-snatching in the past.

Eric Robinson is a geologist who read for his first degree at King's College Newcastle in 1950, subsequently having his Doctorate conferred by Durham University in 1953. From 1953 until 1997 he lectured at University College London, and since 1997 has been Research Associate at the same College in which capacity he promotes geology through the study of buildings and building-stones. He is the author of two books on London buildings, and of six illustrated cards (published by the Geological Survey) dealing with focal-points for visitors to London. As Vice-President of the Royal Archaeological Institute he promotes an awareness of the importance of geology among art-historians. He was President of The Geologists' Association, 1991-4, and has been its Librarian since 1970.

David Taylor-Pescod FLS was born in London in 1939. Having read chemistry and biology, he became Head of Science at a school in the Midlands. He has lectured and written on subjects relating to science, philosophy, dying, death, and disposal of the

dead, and is a frequent contributor to television and radio programmes. His family links with Kensal Green cemetery started with the burial there [796/101/3] in January 1837 of his fourth great-uncle, Joseph Charles Taylor (1770-1837), wine merchant and founder of Taylor's Port. In 1991, after the successful launch of the Friends of Kensal Green Cemetery, he was appointed Head Guide, and subsequently became Secretary to the Main Committee of the Friends.

Henry Vivian-Neal was educated at the University of Newcastle upon Tyne. He has been a Member of the Main Committee of the Friends of Kensal Green Cemetery since 1992, Secretary to the Friends since 1994, and Secretary to the Advisory Council of the Friends since 1995. He is the Editor of *Paths of Glory. A Select Alphabetical and Biographical List, illustrated with Line Drawings of their Monuments, of Persons of Note Commemorated at The Cemetery of All Souls at Kensal Green* (1998).

List of Illustrations

Sources for illustrations are given in abbreviated form *in italics* at the end of each caption as follows:

BL	By permission of The British Library
BN	Bibliothèque Nationale, Paris
BTB	B. T. Batsford Ltd
CB	© Christopher Brooks
DO	Dumbarton Oaks, Studies in Landscape Architecture, Photo Archive, Trustees for Harvard University
ECJSC	Editor's Collection © James Stevens Curl
GCC	By courtesy of The General Cemetery Company
GLCL	Corporation of London, Guildhall Library
HFALHC	By courtesy of Hammersmith & Fulham Archives and Local History Centre
JMF	© Jennifer M. Freeman
JSC	© James Stevens Curl
MC	© Martin Charles
NMR	© Crown copyright. National Monuments Record, followed by the NMR photographic reference number
RBKC	By courtesy of the Royal Borough of Kensington & Chelsea Library and Arts Service
SH	Simon Houfe
SJSM	By courtesy of the Trustees of Sir John Soane's Museum, London
THF	© Timothy H. Freed

List of Subscribers

Eddie Adams
Mr Edward J. Addinall
Mr E.J. Addinall
Thomas Aird
Andrew Alpern, Attorney at Law
The Rev'd A.B. Andrews (Vicar)
Nichola Archer
William Arthurs, Esq
John F. Ashby MBIFD
John Ashdown
Dr Mark K. Askey
Claire E.E. Aston
Javier Rodríguez Barberán
Todd C. Bardes
Mr and Mrs Ashley Barker
Beatrice and Robert Barker
Nicholas Barnard
Reginald and Maureen Barton
Freda Ann Bates, MA(Cantab.), PGCE, TESOL
Ray Bateson
George Batten
John Batten
Karin Baye
The Reverend Royston D. Beal, TD, BD, AKC
Marjorie Beaven
Jason Beckett
Keith and Christine Bennett
Glenn Benson
Marion J. Bernard
Luciano Bierti
Mr and Mrs D.A. Bigger
Barry C. Bingham
Dr Carmen Blacker
Richard I. Blake
Sytze de Boer
Thomas Bolton
Mrs Sue Booth
Ronald H. Bond
Professora Maria Elizia Borges
Dr Roger Bowdler
Peter Bowyer
Georgina Brady pp Georgiana Boyd
Charles and Virginia Brand
Julia Brickman
Michael Brook
Dr Chris Brooks
Rindert Brouwer
Mrs Christine Browne
A. Buckley
Buermans Jacques
Sam Bull
Dr Anthony Burch
Peter Burman MBE, FJA
Peter W. Burrowes
Maggie Cahill
Ron Callard
Barbara Card
Carmen
Anthony Rex Cartwright
Eric Cartwright
The Revd David L. Cawley FSA
Marcel M. Celis
Ernest Chaloner
Dilwyn Chambers
Count de Loriol Chandieu
Martin Charles
The Worshipful Company of Chartered Architects
Rachael Chattle
Andrew Philip Cheseldine
John and Lesley Clare
C.E. Clark (Undercliffe Cemetery)
Barry Clarke
Peter A. Clayton FLA, FSA, FRNS
Peter Clifford
Roger Cline
Elizabeth Anne Coleman
H.H. Judge Christopher Compston
Emily Compston
Derek and Gill Connell
Paul Cooke
Susan Cooper
Revd Anthony D. Couchman
Council for the Care of Churches
Andrew Cowser
Alexandra Croft
Michael Curling
Frank Dabell, Esq.
James W. Daniel
Gillian Darby
Mr André P. Davies JP
Anne Davies
Gareth Alban Davies
Mr William Davies
W. Peter Day
William Delafield
P.R. Dennison
P.C. Dineley
Brian Dix
Mr M.J. Drew
Ronald D. Dudley
Sean James Duggan
Sir James Dunbar-Nasmith
Dr Ian Dungavell
Donald K. Eade FCA
Hazel Eagles
Dr Harold Elwood
Siegfried Engelmann
John R.F. Espir
David Farrell
Elizabeth and Ray Faulks
Peter Finch
Robyn H. Firth
Diana FitzGeorge-Balfour
Terence John Fitzgerald
Dr R.J. Flanagan
The Reverend Douglas Fletcher
Daniel and Thomas Ford
Sir Edward Ford
Mr G. Ford
Michael H. Ford
Neal M. Ford
Edward Foxton
Mr T. Foxx-Foy
Caroline Franklyn
Harriet Frazer
Timothy Hugh Freed
Dr Jennifer Freeman
Jennifer M. Freeman
Leslie Freestone MBIFD, Dip.FD
Robert Alan Freidus
Nicholas Friend MA, FRSA
John G. Fryman
Andrew Fuller
Dr William M. Gaynor
General Cemetery Company
Dr Liv Gibbs
Lord Gladwyn
Robert Goddard
Mike Goldmark
John Goodier
Sarah Jane Goodricke-Poole
John Goss
Ralph E. Gough
The Duke of Grafton KG
Janet Gray
Jennie Gray
Jacobus Greetham
Alan C.A. Gregory
Peter Gregory
Richard Griffiths
Leslie Grout
Erna Guttmann
Howard R. Hague
Keith Haines
Janice Edwina Hallett
Dr Gottfried M. Hamernik
Rosamond, Viscountess Hanworth
G.N. Harby (in memory of Dr. R. Buttimore, PhD)
J. Hardy
John F. Harris
Professor Robert Harris
Jacqueline Harrod
David Harvey
Roger Harvey
Ian Hatchman
Dr and Mrs Anthony W. Henfrey
Mr and Mrs John Hess
Miss Lindsay Hewitt
Susan Hibberd (Pixie)
Margaret Carl Hibbs LGSM
Adrian J. Hill
Mr David Charles Marshall Hill
Mr Brian W. Hingston
Hermione Hobhouse
Signe Hoffos
David and Fran Holt
Davyd Foard Hood
Arnold Francis George Hooper
Charles Hooper

J. St Brioc Hooper
Patrick Horsbrugh
Joe Hughes
Karen and John Humpage
Laurence Hunt
Madeline Huxstep
Professor Dorota Iwaniec
Jean Florence Jackson
Dr Astrid James
Henry R. James
Victoria Jebens
Ian Johnson
Revd Malcolm Johnson
Mr D. Jones
David Kaye
E.B. Keeling
Georg Friedrich Kempter
J.D.R. Kewley
Joe Kilner
Stephen King
Sally Kington
Rosemary A. Kinnaird-Smith
Laurence Kinney
Hans C. Kokhuis
Petra Laidlaw
Maureen Lambourne
Lucinda Lambton
Shân Lancaster
Cynthia Langdon-Davies
John Law
Library and Museum of Freemasonry
Library Services, University College London
John F. Lindley
Julian W.S. Litten FSA
Professor Adrian Long
David Lorimer
Peter Luscombe RIBA
David McDonald
John McDowell MA BMus
James Alexander Bain McIntyre
Gordon B. MacIver
Jennifer McKendry
Isobel Mary McMinn
Mr Graham Magness
John A. Mallinson
Brian Marsh
Linda Gwynneth Marsh
Mr Barry J. Martin
Linda D.G. Masters
Sam Matthews
Yoke Matze
Yvonne Meah
Janet M. Meikle
Hugh Meller
Men of the Stones
Wendy S. Mercer
David Merrigan
Maureen D. Merrigan
George Meyrick
Joyce Millard
Alan and Joanna Monckton
Dr Timothy Mowl
John J. Murray
M.J.K. Nodes
N.T.K. Nodes
Nottingham Subscription Library
David and Iris Oakey
Howard Stuart Oldfield
Siobhan O'Leary
Mr C.D. Oxley
Nicholas J. Page
E.S Palmer
Mr and Mrs Neil Parker
Ray Parnell
Andrew McIntosh Patrick
David Pettigrew
I.S. Pettman FRSA
Jonquil Lucia Phelan
John Physick CBE, FSA
Professor J.H.M. Pinkerton
Alan Powers
A. Pugh-Thomas
The Queen's University of Belfast
Carlos Saguar Quer
Lazina Khan Ramdath
Caroline Raphael
Abi Rapley
Piers Edmund Ravensworth
Michael Read
Diana Glenister Redford
Margaret Reed
Miss Rosemary Rendel
Peter F. Reynolds
Anthony Richardson
Hilda and William Richardson
John Richardson
Dr Ruth Richardson and Dr B.S. Hurwitz
W.N.B. Richardson DL
Mr and Mrs Andrew Richmond
Peter James Ridgway
Timothy Robertson
Andy Robson
John Rodgers ARICS
David Roger
Paul and Beryl Rosenbaum
Royal Institute of British Architects Library
James R. Russell
Rex C. Russell
Elizabeth Ryeburn-Gilchrist
Roc Sandford
Leslie W. Sayers
Scott
Mrs Ronald Scrivener
Michael Seeley
Professor and Mrs Vincent Shacklock
C.J. Sharp
Tracy Siggins
John Simmonds
Allan and Jane Smith
Barry S. Smith
Celia Luetchford Smith Dip. FD, A.Inst. BCA
Eric P. Smith
Robin Charnley Smith
Prof. Georg Graf zu Solms
Alan James Spinks
Dawn Squires
Gavin Stamp
Michael Stannard
Rosalind Stanwell-Smith
Robert Stephenson
Mary McKinney Stevenson
Aengus Stewart
Trevor Stewart
Catriona and Sandy Stoddart
Ms R.M. Stoddart and Mr P. Duerden
Professor Peter Swallow
Michael Taylor
Sue Taylor
Mr and Mrs Paul Teesdale
Janet Rendell Thomas
Lord Thomas of Swynnerton
Marjorie Trusted, Victoria and Albert Museum
David Unwin
Kevin Varty
Mr and Mrs G. Vivian-Neal
Henry Vivian-Neal
Wim Vlaanderen
Mr and Mrs F. Wagnall
Robert M. Wall
Robert Wallace
Mr A. Walton
Frances Warburton
Mr N.M. Waring
David Watkin
Jay Weissberg, Esq.
Barbara Westerberg
David S. Whitelegge
Theon Wilkinson
Derek Williams
Martin Williams
Fredric Woodbridge Wilson
Mr and Mrs Hal Wilson
Andrew Wilton
Michael Wolton
Philippa Jane Woodcock
Martin C. Woods
May A. Woods
Ron Woollacott
Jan Woudstra
Nick Wright
Robin Wyatt
Michael C. Wylie
Laurie Macgregor Young

Foreword by the Duke of Grafton KG

The appalling condition of the City of London churchyards at the beginning of the 19th century led private enterprise to establish Kensal Green Cemetery in 1833 as a leafy necropolis for the reverent disposal of the dead. Ratified in 1843 when selected by George III's son, Augustus Frederick, Duke of Sussex, as his place of burial, Kensal Green rapidly became the 'society cemetery' of the metropolis, a status it continues to enjoy. I am pleased to have been associated with the recent regeneration of this national Valhalla, the result of an increasing appreciation of the late-Hanoverian garden-cemetery movement.

As a result of an amicable co-operation between the General Cemetery Company, English Heritage, the Historic Chapels Trust, and the Royal Borough of Kensington and Chelsea, the Friends of Kensal Green Cemetery have established a template for similar heritage societies to follow, in much the same way as Kensal Green itself was emulated by other joint-stock cemeteries in the early 19th century and beyond.

Grafton

The Duke of Grafton KG
Patron of the Friends of Kensal Green Cemetery

From the Chairman of the General Cemetery Company

The establishment of the General Cemetery of All Souls at Kensal Green in 1832 marked a turning-point for London and the disposal of its dead, for, until then, burial was restricted to churches, churchyards, and parochial burial-grounds of the Established Anglican Church, to spaces under Nonconformist chapels and in Dissenters' graveyards, to grounds of limited extent for Jews and other faiths, and to small burial-places run as speculative ventures by private individuals or groups. The appalling state of many of those places created pressures to reform burial in the Metropolis and, after much agitation and a great deal of effort, Kensal Green began to take shape.

Henry John Chetwynd Talbot (1803-68), Viscount Ingestre (from 1826), later (1849) 3rd Earl Talbot of Hensol and (from 1856) 18th Earl of Shrewsbury and Waterford, the first Chairman of the Company, presided over the difficult job of marketing the new venture, the subsequent success of which would probably have surprised him. Today, my Board continues to run Kensal Green Cemetery as a place of dignified and reverent disposal of the dead, and, while most new burials take place at the western end of the grounds, adjacent to the Neoclassical crematorium by Gerald Berkeley Wills (1882-1979), we continue to maintain the historic parts, the landscape, and the wild-life habitats. Some of our tasks are assisted by the Friends of Kensal Green Cemetery, established in 1989, whose fund-raising skills, voluntary labour, and erudite interpretation of the cemetery have re-established the cemetery's fame through their Guided Tours and Publications and through the skilled restoration and extension of the Dissenters' chapel.

My Director colleagues join me in thanking those scholars who have contributed essays to this book, the first publication of its kind devoted entirely to Kensal Green. We wish the venture every success.

Michael J K Nodes
Chairman, The General Cemetery Company

Preface and Acknowledgements

Miremur periisse homines? Monumenta fatiscunt;
Mors etiam saxis nominibusque venit.

(Can we wonder that Man perishes? His monuments decay;
and Death comes even to his marble [memorials] and to the names [upon them].

DECIMUS MAGNUS AUSONIUS (*c.*AD 310-95):
Epitaphia; 'De Nomine Cuiusdam Lucii Sculpto in Marmore'
(On the name of a certain Lucius sculpted in marble), xxxii, 9-10.

Many are those who helped in one way or another with the assembling of the material that is the basis of this book. All the contributors, of course (listed on p.xi), deserve the thanks of the Editor, for without their individual expertise there would have been a lesser book. Mr André Davies, Director of the Friends of Kensal Green Cemetery, has been a staunch ally, and if his support had not been forthcoming, little would have materialised. Especial thanks are also due to Professor Christopher Brooks (for help with the Chapters on monuments);[1] Dr Timothy Freed (for providing evidence and texts concerning the areas of the various parcels of land purchased by the General Cemetery Company, who worked with the Editor to arrive at what is a reasonably precise estimate of the extent of the cemetery ground, and who assisted the Editor to come to conclusions regarding the ownership of the lands before the involvement of the Cemetery Company);[2] Lady Freeman (for many kindnesses, including checking dimensions, photographing many items, helping with recent parliamentary reports, and giving much appreciated support);[3] Mr Ian Johnson (treasurer of the Friends – who dealt briskly and courteously with many problems and other matters); Mr Robert Moulder (who was supremely diligent in providing most of the footnotes giving positions of graves, contributed many of the biographical facts concerning those interred within the cemetery, very kindly corrected many errors of fact in the texts, and gave unstintingly of his time and expertise);[4] Mr Robert Stephenson (who provided facts concerning the programme of lectures); Mr David Taylor-Pescod (who contributed copy dealing with tours and helped with information concerning aspects of the history of the Friends);[5] and Mr Henry Vivian-Neal (Secretary of the Friends – who responded quickly to the Editor's frequent appeals for assistance, photocopied vast numbers of documents, and gave support in many different ways).[6]

Much of the book is based upon documents preserved among the papers of the General Cemetery Company, for the story could not be told without access to those: the Editor therefore records his gratitude to the Chairman (Mr Michael Nodes) and Board of the Company (especially Mr Michael Ford), for allowing him to inspect these papers. Mr David Burkett, Secretary, and the office-staff of the General Cemetery Company put up with his frequent visits to the archives, many questions, and sundry badgerings: the Editor appreciates all the help he has had from the Company, its Directors, and employees.

[1] In addition to the contribution to this volume. [2] Ibid. [3] Ibid. [4] Ibid. [5] Ibid. [6] Ibid.

Mr Martin Charles helped to record the surviving drawings in the Company's archive, and carried out a programme of photography without which this history would have been impoverished: the Editor records his gratitude to Mr Charles for his efficiency, good humour, professionalism, and support. Most of the photographs illustrating Dr Bowdler's chapter were taken by Mr Derek Kendall of English Heritage, whose work is acknowledged with thanks. Acknowledgement for help is also given to the staffs of the Royal Institute of British Architects (RIBA) Library (especially Mr Robert Elwall and Mr Trevor Todd); of the RIBA Drawings Collection (Ms Philippa Martin); of the Society of Antiquaries of London; of the Society of Antiquaries of Scotland, Edinburgh; of the National Monuments Record Centre, English Heritage (especially Miss Anna Eavis, Mrs Anne Woodward, and Mr Ian Leith); of the Bodleian Library, University of Oxford; of the Library of the University of Cambridge; of the British Library; of the Musée Carnavalet, Paris; of the Center for Studies in Landscape Architecture, Dumbarton Oaks, Washington, D.C.; of the Bibliothèque Nationale, Paris; of the Oriental and India Office Collections, The British Library; of the Libraries of the Royal Borough of Kensington and Chelsea (notably Mr Peter Greenwood, Librarian); of Guildhall Library, Corporation of London (especially Mr Ralph Hyde [formerly Keeper of Prints and Maps], Mr John Fisher, Mr Jeremy Smith, and Miss Sarah Ash); of the Linenhall Library, Belfast; of the Museum of London Picture Library (Mr Andrew Batt); of the London Metropolitan Archives (Mr Mick Scott, Senior Librarian); of the Kimberlin Library, De Montfort University, Leicester (notably Mrs Julie Bunyan, Mr Anselm Kersten, and Mrs Ann Perry); of the National Art Library, Victoria and Albert Museum (with warm thanks to Mr Patrick Perratt); of the Natural History Museum, London (notably Mrs Ann Datta, Librarian, and Ms. Judith Magee, Botany Librarian); of the Hammersmith and Fulham Archives Department (Mrs Anne Wheeldon); of the Royal Entomological Society (Ms. Berit Pederson, Librarian); and of the Library of The Queen's University of Belfast (especially Mrs Karen Latimer and Mr Michael Smallman) for dealing courteously with many queries concerning facts, illustrations, bibliographies. Mr Alasdair Black (who kindly transcribed conveyances) and Mrs Maureen Lambourne (John Gould's great-great-granddaughter) have been most helpful.

The Queen's University of Belfast (especially Professor Adrian Long and Mr Lawrence J. G. Johnston) made it possible to have the time to research, edit, and write part of, this book. The genesis of Chapter I was researched when the Editor was Visiting Fellow at Peterhouse, University of Cambridge, and he records his thanks due to the Master, Fellows, and Governing Body of that august College. He is also grateful to Taylor & Francis Ltd. for permission to quote from material published by them (and fully acknowledged in the footnotes and Select Bibliography) in 1994. Thanks are also due to Sutton Publishing Ltd (especially Mrs Jane Crompton) for permission to make use of other matter published in 2000 (and again fully referenced).

In any study such as this, debts accrue to other individuals and societies. To list the precise nature of the many kindnesses and generosity in sharing information or helping in other ways would fill a book, so it is hoped that acknowledgement by name will suffice. To the following persons, therefore, warmest thanks are extended: Dr and Mrs Alan Ahern, the late Dr Philippe Ariès, the late Mr A. H. Buck, Miss Iona Cruickshank, Sir Howard Colvin, Dr Maurice Craig, Dr Brent Elliott,[7] the late Mr Edmund Esdaile, Professor Richard A. Etlin, Herr Christoph Fischer, Mr John

7 In addition to the contribution to this volume.

Greenacombe, Mr Martyn Gregory, the late Mr R. A. Harrison, Mr and Mrs John Humpage, Mr Gordon Johnson, Miss Wendy Johnston, Mr Anthony F. Kersting, Mr Richard Linzey, Dr Julian Litten,[8] Dr Rosie Llewellyn-Jones, Dr Jennifer McKendry, the late Mr John Morley, Professor Dr. Sten Åke Nilsson, Dr Ruth Richardson,[9] Mr Rodney C. Roach, Señor Francisco Javier Rodríguez Barberán, Dr Julie Rugg, Dr Carlos Saguar Quer, Mr Peter Salter, Frau Renate Schein, Dr Melanie Louise Simo, Mr Philip Temple, Dr David Watkin, the late Mrs Eleonore Wetzler, Mr Theon Wilkinson, Mr Ron Woollacott, Mr Michael Wright, and Mr Andrew Wyld.

The Editor's wife, Dorota, helped in a great many ways, and gave the project every support during its gestation. Mrs Margaret Reed transformed the notebooks, handwritten texts, and edited typescripts into coherent form, and helped to create Order out of Chaos (an architectural skill somewhat thin on the ground these days). Last, but not least, Mr Noel Osborne, Miss Nicola Willmot, and Mrs Carolyn Oliver, of Phillimore & Co Ltd, worked with the Editor to produce the book: their enthusiasm and efficiency have been enormously helpful. Miss Frances Mather prepared the Index, and has the Editor's gratitude for taking *that* onerous task off his shoulders.

Without such essential support and collaboration *Kensal Green Cemetery* would never have emerged from the catacomb of wishful thinking.

JAMES STEVENS CURL
Cambridge, Holywood, and London
2000-2001

[8] In addition to the contribution to this volume. [9] Ibid.

The *main object* of a [cemetery is] the disposal of the remains of the dead in such a manner as that their decomposition, and return to the earth from which they sprung, shall not prove injurious to the living; either by affecting their health, or shocking their feelings, opinions, or prejudices.

A *secondary object* is, or ought to be, the improvement of the moral sentiments and general taste of all classes, and more especially of the great masses of society.

JOHN CLAUDIUS LOUDON (1783-1843):
On the Laying Out, Planting, and Managing of Cemeteries; and on the Improvement of Churchyards
(London: Longman, Brown, Green, & Longmans, 1843), 1.

Explanatory Note on the Layout of the Cemetery

JAMES STEVENS CURL

The first point to be attended to ... is to devise a system for *throwing the interior* [of a cemetery] *into imaginary squares or parallelograms*, which shall be indicated by numbers and letters on the boundary fence, and by marks inserted in the ground at their points of intersection.

JOHN CLAUDIUS LOUDON (1783-1843):
On the Laying Out, Planting, and Managing of Cemeteries; and on the Improvement of Churchyards
(London: Longman, Brown, Green, & Longmans, 1843), 16.

Every grave in the General Cemetery of All Souls at Kensal Green has been allocated a number that is issued by the Company in sequence as the first burial (or deposit, as it is sometimes known) in any plot takes place. Some graves, however, were never used, but were sold, and even fitted out as brick-lined shafts (brick graves), in which cases they, too, acquired a number for identification purposes. The problem with this sequential numbering, of course, is that graves can be anywhere in the cemetery, and would be impossible to find without further identification.

The cemetery is divided into imaginary rectangular compartments (called, bizarrely, 'squares'), each with a number. Those compartments are shown on the plan of the cemetery (**Fig. 1**). In this book these compartment-numbers are given in **bold** type, and run from 1 to 241. In order to assist further in the location of graves, letters are added as follows:

RS = road-side
PS = path-side
IC = Inner Circle
1 = first row from a road or path
2 = second row from a road or path, *etc.*
IR = inner row from road or path
BC = by the canal.

Immediately to the east of the Anglican chapel is a circular path (very obvious on the plan, but increasingly difficult to 'read' on site because of the encroachment of new graves and the overgrown nature of the grounds) known as the Circle, with its centre at the junction of two main roads at right angles to each other in 'square' [88]. This Circle, with the roads, thus forms four quadrants: the north-west quadrant (part of rectangles [88, 101, 102, 89, 103, and 90]); the north-east quadrant (part of rectangles [88, 76, 89, 77, 90, and 78]); the south-west quadrant (part of rectangles [88, 101, 100, 87, 86, and 99]); and the south-east quadrant (part of rectangles [88, 76, 75, 87, 86, and 74]).

To give some examples of how to locate a grave, let us select a few prominent monuments. The grave of H.R.H. the Duke of Sussex (5.5) is in front of the Anglican chapel in rectangle [114], and his grave number is 5268, so its location is given as [5268/

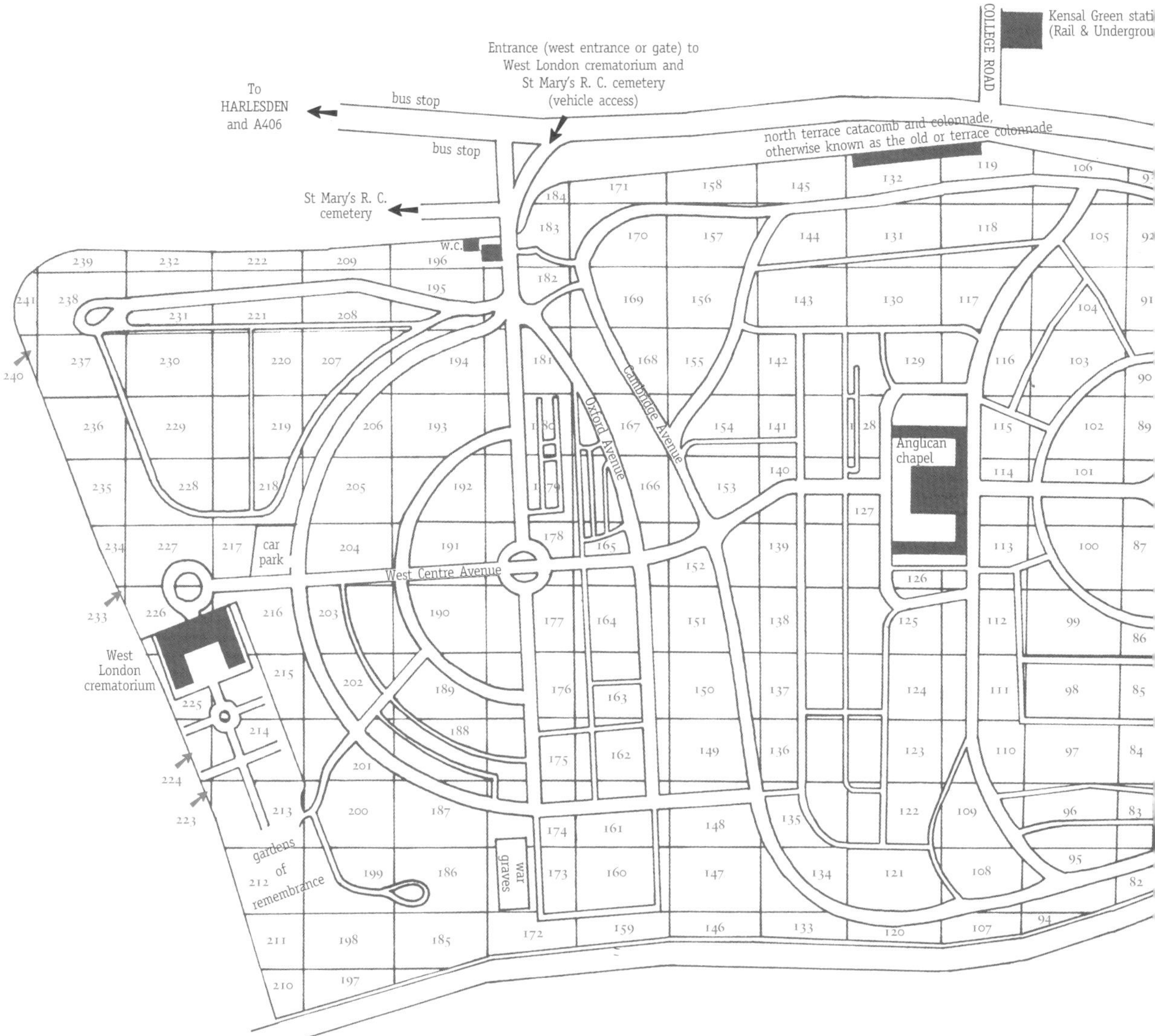

114/PS], where the first number is that of the grave, the second (**bold**) is that of the rectangle, and the third is the position, in this case by a path north of Centre Avenue. The Duke's sister, H.R.H. Princess Sophia, is also entombed (**5.10**) to the east of the Anglican chapel in the same rectangle, but south of Centre Avenue: the location of her monument is [8028/**114**/PS].The Kiralfy temple-tomb (**9.3**) is at [47543/**32**/RS], and the Brunel clan are located at [8590/**41**/PS] (**8.6**).

However, not all deposits are in graves (earth or brick-lined). In the early days of the cemetery there was considerable demand for entombment in vaults or catacombs, partly for reasons of security, and partly because of status. There was also a great fear of being buried in cold, dank earth, and, for those who could afford it, being deposited in an expensive coffin on a shelf in a dry catacomb was preferable to being consigned to the heavy, sticky, London Clay.

There are three sets of catacombs in Kensal Green cemetery. They are located beneath the old or north terrace colonnade attached to the wall that separates the Harrow Road from the cemetery (**Catacomb A**) [**132, 119**]; below the Anglican chapel and its flanking colonnades (**Catacomb B**) [**126, 127, 128, 113, 114, 115**]; and beneath the

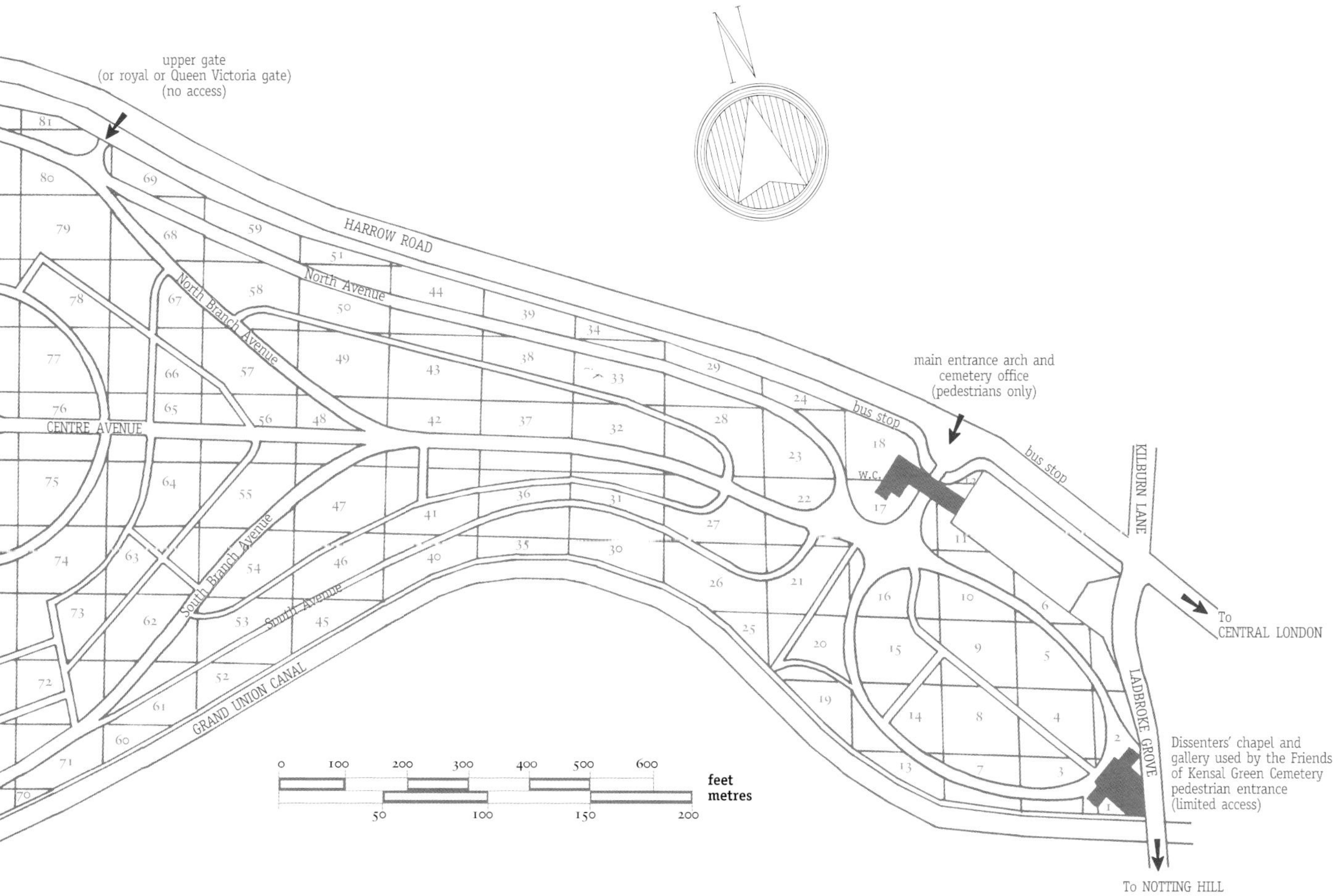

Fig 1 Layout of the General Cemetery of All Souls, Kensal Green, showing the principal roads and paths, buildings, and numbered rectangles (*Mr John Humpage*)

Dissenters' Chapel (**Catacomb Z**). For deposits in these catacombs the same numbering system is used by the General Cemetery Company as for non-catacomb burials. Mr Vivian-Neal[1] lists catacomb deposits as **CAT. A**, **CAT. B**, or **CAT.Z** followed by the vault-number (in Catacomb B the vault-numbers run from 1 to 216, and these numbers are carved and painted on the individual vaults. The plan of these vaults in relation to the Anglican chapel may be seen in Mr Sambrook's drawing (**7.23**).[2] Within each vault are several compartments called *loculi*, and each *loculus*[3] has a number starting from 1 at the bottom left from left to right, and from bottom to top. Thus [**CAT.B**/Vault 65/ Comp 15] identifies the catacomb, vault, and *loculus* where lie the remains of the utterly dissipated[4] and thoroughly disreputable William Pole Tylney Long-Wellesley (1788-1857), 4th Earl of Mornington and 2nd Baron Maryborough, who got through several fortunes and spent his last days subsisting upon 'the bounty of his uncle, the Duke of Wellington'.[5]

1 Vivian-Neal (1999), *passim*. 2 Kindly made available by Mr John Greenacombe, General Editor, *Survey of London*, and reproduced by permission of English Heritage. 3 A *loculus* is literally a small place, chamber, or cell for the reception of a body. 4 *D.N.B.*, **xx** (1917), 1136, goes so far as to record his obituary in the *Morning Chronicle* to the effect that he was 'redeemed by no single virtue, adorned by no single grace'. 5 Ibid.

Unfortunately, only Catacomb B is still in use, and it is the largest operating catacomb in the country: the other two are sealed, and no access is possible to either Catacomb A or Catacomb Z. Those who wished could also build their tombs with *loculi* inside, both above and below ground. The cemetery has several mausolea,[6] some of considerable grandeur and size, where families could be reunited in death. Among the largest is the Huth mausoleum (**8.28**) [2735/77/IC], supposedly capable of holding over forty coffins. The mausoleum of Andrew Ducrow (**4.29**, **8.23**, and **8.24**) [820/76/RS] is perhaps the most outrageously showy, even in its decay: when it was new and brightly coloured it must have been indeed a coxcomb among the more staid sepulchres.

John Claudius Loudon was critical of the way in which cemeteries were artificially subdivided for the purposes of identifying graves. The 'system of laying out a cemetery into imaginary squares is a very unsatisfactory one, for the following reasons:

1. it neither admits of a permanent system of surface drainage, nor of grass paths among the graves;
2. from their being no obvious principle of order or arrangement in conformity with which the graves are placed, the general aspect of the interior of the cemetery is confused and unsatisfactory; the graves and tomb-stones seeming to be put down at random as in common churchyards;
3. a very slight error in mapping the graves may render it difficult, if not impossible, to identify a particular grave, either to point it out to the relations of the deceased; or, when the square is nearly full, for the purpose of avoiding an old grave in digging a new one. Let any one who doubts this examine the map books in the principal London cemeteries, and ask to see one of the graves indicated in the plan;
4. unless a head-stone is put to the grave, or some other permanent mark, it is impossible for any person but the sexton to identify it; which circumstance can by no means be rendered satisfactory to the relations of the deceased;
5. no provision is made for paths among these graves, so that, when the squares are nearly full, there will be no mode of getting to any one grave, but by walking over a number of others; which is not only a species of desecration, but, when there are several of the graves having head-stones, must be exceedingly inconvenient'.[7]

Loudon advocated laying out the ground in double beds with green paths between, which would 'admit of a permanent system of surface drainage', would require no mapping, and would be far more convenient and logical. Loudon made many other valuable suggestions, all of which were sensible, and resolved all the difficulties of identification as at places like Kensal Green cemetery. There can be no doubt that the system adopted by the General Cemetery Company right at the beginning was cumbersome, and bound to lead to problems. Some kind of geometrical layouts, with permanent paths and drainage, would have been more convenient and easier to manage. As usual, Loudon spotted the problems at once, and proposed solutions.

So some degree of perseverance is required when tracking down graves at Kensal Green cemetery. Each grave's location has been checked against the Cemetery Company's records, and the locations given here derive from Mr Moulder's careful researches, carried out at the request of the Editor in 2001: the Editor is profoundly grateful to Mr Moulder for his many corrections, suggestions, and filling in of blanks.

[6] A mausoleum (*pl.* mausolea) is a roofed building used as a tomb, detached or adjoining another building, containing sarcophagi, coffins, or urns, usually on shelves in compartments (*loculi*). The term originated with the fourth-century BC Hellenistic Ionic tomb of King Mausolos of Caria. [7] Loudon (1843), 17.

Introductory Remarks

James Stevens Curl

So live, that when thy summons comes to join
The innumerable caravan, which moves
To that mysterious realm, where each shall take
His chamber in the silent halls of death,
Thou go not, like the quarry-slave at night,
Scourged to his dungeon, but, sustained and soothed
By an unfaltering trust, approach thy grave
Like one who wraps the drapery of his couch
About him, and lies down to pleasant dreams.

WILLIAM CULLEN BRYANT (1794-1878): *Thanatopsis* (1817), l. 73.

A large-scale monograph on a British cemetery may strike some observers as odd, probably because there is still a widespread public attitude that dismisses cemeteries, and refuses to acknowledge their importance in terms of architecture, landscape-design, sculpture, history, education, ecology, habitats for flora and fauna, and much else. Yet the pleasures of visiting cemeteries have long been known to travellers, as many 19th-century texts make clear: visitors to Paris who miss the glories of Père-Lachaise cemetery, and those who fail to wander among the tombs of Italian and German cities, are the poorer for their omissions. As Thomas Tickell (1686-1740) observed, the 'sad luxury' of contemplating memorials is 'to vulgar minds unknown': the General Cemetery of All Souls at Kensal Green has its fair share of

Proud names, who once the reins of empire held;
In arms who triumphed, or in arts excelled.[1]

John Strang (1795-1863) argued that cemeteries were 'beneficial to public morals' and could even contribute to 'the improvement of manners'.[2] John Claudius Loudon (1783-1843), one of the most influential writers of the late-Hanoverian and early-Victorian period, was of the opinion that cemeteries could improve 'the moral sentiments and general taste of all classes', and 'by their botanical riches ... cultivate the intellect'.[3] Even more important, Loudon recognised the significance of cemeteries as historical records, but he was at pains to argue that they 'might become a school of instruction in architecture, sculpture, landscape-gardening, arboriculture, botany, and in those important parts of general gardening, neatness, order, and high keeping'.[4] A graveyard, to Loudon, was 'to the poor man a local history and biography'.[5]

Strang, the promoter of the Glasgow Necropolis, and described as 'a brilliant, super-orthodox luminary burning in a dense cloud of Scotch prejudice and Glasgow smoke',[6] argued that it was from 'funeral monuments that we gather much that is

[1] *To the Earl of Warwick, on the Death of Mr Addison* (1721). [2] Strang (1831), 58-9. [3] Loudon (1843), 1, 13. [4] Ibid., 12-13. [5] Ibid., 13. [6] Blair (1857), 29.

known of ... civil progress and of ... advancement in taste'.[7] 'The tomb has', he robustly declared, 'been the great chronicler of taste throughout the world'. Glasgow Necropolis, by 1857, had a 388-page monograph devoted to it.[8]

Other cemeteries have attracted the attention of authors: Albany Rural Cemetery had a 'hand-book' of 141 pages;[9] Professor Etlin has made a massive study of the origins of Père-Lachaise cemetery in Paris;[10] there are countless pamphlets and guide-books to many cemeteries; Hugh Meller gave us his illustrated guide and gazetteer to London cemeteries;[11] the Parisian cemeteries have several publications concerning them;[12] and the delightful Mount Auburn cemetery was well-served by Blanche Linden-Ward in 1989.[13] More recently, a hefty book on important cemeteries in Dublin, Genoa, Madrid, and Turin has appeared, published under the aegis of the European Commission,[14] and a handsome volume covering the proceedings of what our Iberian colleagues delight in calling an 'Encounter' in Seville[15] in 1991 was published in 1993,[16] co-ordinated by Francisco Javier Rodríguez Barberán.

Professor Etlin has recorded that until 'the emergence of the American "rural" cemeteries in the 1830s', Père-Lachaise 'would enjoy the virtually unqualified praise' of travellers, who 'expatiated ... upon the sentimental, moral, and cultural significance of the cemetery'.[17] It is perhaps interesting to note that one of the earliest modern books on the cemeteries of London was by a Belgian,[18] and that was in the 1970s, before Meller's gazetteer appeared. The Select Bibliography at the end of this present book may be consulted for the titles most relevant to the subject.

So why such a hefty monograph on one of London's necropoleis? First of all, the General Cemetery of All Souls at Kensal Green was the first large cemetery to be established in the vicinity of London, and that alone is of historic interest. Secondly, the cemetery is still owned and managed by the General Cemetery Company, which created it, and the minute-books and other records are unusually complete, offering a marvellous quarry from which the historian may obtain his facts. Unfortunately, none of the Sub-Committee Minute-Books appears to have survived. Thirdly, many of the original design- and contract-drawings of the buildings (by John Griffith of Finsbury) are held by the Company and are reproduced here. Fourthly, the architectural competition of 1831-2 for the cemetery buildings is of some importance, especially as drawings for one of the more interesting entries are still in existence (and are also reproduced in this book, together with some of the less competent submissions). It is not true, as rumour has had it, that *all* the designs entered for the competition still exist. Fourthly, the buildings as realised are architecturally distinguished, and deserve recognition in their own right. Fifthly, there are some very fine mausolea and monuments in the cemetery, many of the first rank, and these should be better known. Sixthly, the landscape and planting are not only historically interesting but, in parts, beautiful too. Finally, this great 19th-century Valhalla, established in the reign of King William IV, contains the mortal remains of many notable people, who contributed to the making of Britain and her Empire, and their resting-place deserves to be cared-for and visited. Kensal Green is worth visiting for its array of inscriptions alone. The cemetery is also the habitat of many creatures and plants, discussed by Dr Freed in Chapter XIV.

There are many other reasons why Kensal Green cemetery should be celebrated, and this book will attempt to give a flavour of its character and historical importance. In addition, there is one very good reason for the publication of a book based on archival research: many earlier publications dealing with the cemetery have been

7 Strang (1857), 62. 8 Blair (1857), *passim*. 9 Fitzgerald (1871), *passim*. 10 Etlin (1984*a*), *passim*. 11 Meller (1981), *passim*. 12 *See*, for example, Saint-A. (1816), *passim*, and Barozzi (1990), *passim*. 13 Linden-Ward (1989), *passim*. 14 Diéguez Patao and Giménez (2000), *passim*. 15 Attended by three of the contributors to the present monograph. 16 Andalucía (1993), *passim*. 17 Etlin (1984*a*), 356. 18 Vaes (1978), *passim*.

inaccurate, even getting the name of the architect responsible for the buildings wrong, and the histories of the ground and its ownership have not been treated with much regard for facts.

Furthermore, recent reports[19] on the future of cemeteries have dealt with the re-use of graves, and in 2001 a Committee of MPs produced a study[20] that investigated a range of issues associated with cemeteries, and published a wide-ranging *Report* in March 2001 that was mainly concerned with the diminishing amount of burial-space available in English cemeteries, but it also directed attention to the dire state of repair, even dereliction, that is characteristic of many of them. This *Report* will be outlined in the Conclusion of the present volume. However, many other studies of British cemeteries have tended to be depressingly short on aspects of the historical landscapes, memorials, mausolea, and cemetery buildings. Kensal Green cemetery is far too significant in architectural, historical, and landscape terms to be viewed from a purely utilitarian point of view. Publication of this book, it is hoped, will make the cemetery's national and international distinction better-known: there can be no doubt that the General Cemetery of All Souls is an irreplaceable part of our heritage, a place of memorability, eminence, nobility, and even greatness.

Note on Decimal Equivalents

Le nouveau système de poids et mesures sera un sujet d'embarras et de difficultés pour plusiers générations ...

(The new system of weights and measures will be a stumbling-block and source of difficulties for several generations ...)

NAPOLÉON I (1769-1821 – Emperor of the French, 1804-15): On the introduction of the metric system, in *Mémoires ... ecrits à Ste-Hélène* (1823-5), iv, Ch. 21, pt. 4.

To translate areas of land from acres to hectares requires a multiple of 0.4047; similarly, conversion of inches to centimetres is achieved by multiplying imperial measures by 2.54, by 0.3048 for feet to metres, and so on. In some cases, those long figures have been printed, partly to demonstrate the problem of changing one well-tried system to another, the limitations of which have long been recognised (not least by Napoléon himself).

Where pounds, shillings and pence have been given, further problems arise. Translation of a labourer's weekly wage of shillings and pence to £0.79 (say) is pointless, as inflation has rendered a wage in the 1840s incomprehensible today. For approximate equivalents see Munby's work listed in the Select Bibliography.

[19] *See*, for example, Davies and Shaw (1995), *passim*, and Dunk and Rugg (1994), *passim*. [20] *Cemeteries. Report and Proceedings of the House of Commons Environment, Transport, and Regional Affairs Committee, Session 2000-2001* (21 March 2001). Volumes I and II. HC 91-1 (London: The Stationery Office Ltd.). *See* Conclusion of the present work.

CHAPTER I

The Historical Background

JAMES STEVENS CURL

Introduction; Literary Influences; The 'Narcissa' Episode; The Arcadian Ideal; Developments in France; The Beginnings of the Modern Cemetery; Conditions in Britain; Some Early Cemeteries

In large towns, and more especially in the metropolis, it has become more difficult to find room for the dead than the living.

The Penny Magazine of the Society for the Diffusion of Useful Knowledge, 150 (2 August 1834), 298.

Introduction

For a long time voices had been raised against the universal custom of burying dead bodies in churches, vaults, and overcrowded graveyards, yet very little had been done to alleviate what had become a scandalous state of affairs (not least in London) by the time the 19th century dawned. John Evelyn (1620-1706), in his *Sylva* (1664), deplored that the burial of the dead had not been banished to the north walls of the City of London, 'where a grated inclosure, of competent breadth for a mile in length, might have served as a universal cemetery to all the parishes, distinguished by the like separations, and with ample walks of trees, the walks adorned with monuments, inscriptions,' and the like, 'apt for contemplation and memory of the defunct'.[1] Sir Christopher Wren (1632-1723) also advocated the establishment of large cemeteries after the Great Fire of London destroyed so much of the medieval fabric in 1666, but things went on very much as before.

During the 18th century, however, a gradual change of sensibility towards the dead could be perceived. The young John Vanbrugh (1664-1726) dealt in silks and cottons on the west coast of India between 1683 and 1685 as an employee of the East India Company (to the Freedom of which he was admitted on 9 October 1682). He knew Surat, where European traders had laid out cemeteries outside the city embellished with handsome and vast mausolea (1.1), something not possible to do in small urban churchyards in London. Vanbrugh sketched a cemetery and argued that churches should no longer be used for burial of the dead, insisting that 'Caemitarys' should be laid out in the 'skirts' of towns where the 'Rich as well as the Poor' would be 'content to ly'. 'If the Caemitarys', he continued, should 'be consecrated, Handsomely and regularly wall'd in, and planted with trees in such form as to make a solemn distinction between one Part and another', the better-off would doubtless prefer to be 'decently interr'd' there in preference to being placed in 'Aisles and under Pews in Churches'. Moreover, they could be more honourably 'remember'd by Lofty and Noble Mausoleums' than by 'little Tawdry Monuments of Marble, stuck up against Walls and Pillars'.[2]

1.1 Mausolea of the English Factors of the East India Company at Surat, from a photograph of *c.*1925 taken by Lt Col L. G. W. Hamber. The largest is that of the Oxenden (or Oxinden) Brothers (d. 1659 and 1669). In the foreground are tombs of other English Factors of the Company. Such grand mausolea would not have been possible in English urban churchyards of the period, and Europeans returning from India would have compared the possibilities for commemoration at home unfavourably with those available in the Sub-Continent (*Archive of the British Association of Cemeteries in South Asia (BACSA) in the Oriental and India Office Collection within The British Library, donated to BACSA by Mr Theon Wilkinson, and kindly made available by him*).

Vanbrugh clearly was profoundly influenced by what he had seen in India, and he made numerous sketches of 'garden temples' which are much more likely designs for

[1] Quoted in *The Penny Magazine of the Society for the Diffusion of Useful Knowledge*, 150 (2 August 1834), 298.
[2] The drawing survives in the Bodleian Library, University of Oxford, among papers entitled 'Mr Vann-Brugg's Proposals about Building ye New Churches', Bodl. MS Rawl. B. 376, ff. 351-2. For Surat *see* Bellasis (1868), *passim*, esp. 6-9. *See also* Rawlinson (1920) which contains some excellent photographs of outstanding funerary monuments. The author owes these references to Mr. Theon Wilkinson. *See also* Wilkinson (1976*a*, 1976*b*, 1976*c*, and 1984), *Chowdikar* (from 1977), and Curl (2000*e*), 29-30.

1.2a and b Two views of South Park Street cemetery, Calcutta, showing the splendid arrays of Classical mausolea and monuments laid out along roads, giving it the appearance of a fine necropolis. Many designs were derived from architectural publications, such as the *Treatise on Architecture* (1759) by Sir William Chambers (1723-96). Such grand funerary display was impossible in contemporary European burial-grounds (*The late Mr K. T. Groves, who kindly took these photographs at the request of the Editor in the 1970s [ECJSC]*).

mausolea (at a time they were virtually unknown) that he advocated should be erected in English landscaped country-house parks and cemeteries. Nicholas Hawksmoor's (1661-1736) noble mausoleum at Castle Howard, Yorkshire (1729-42), is a prime example of a family tomb which also acted as a monumental temple-like funerary structure in the landscaped grounds: its influence was to be immense.

Necessity also dictated that British dead should be buried quickly in India, and, unrestricted by custom, new cemeteries were laid out in the 18th century. One of the grandest was the South Park Street cemetery, Calcutta, established in 1767, which pre-dates burial-reform in Europe. It is celebrated for its numerous stuccoed tombs, built along streets, giving the cemetery the appearance of a veritable city of the dead (**1.2a** and **b**).

Literary Influences

One of the most curious aspects of the many threads that were to be drawn together to become the Cemetery Movement, however, was the importance of literary influences. Apart from the 'Gothic' novels of men like William Beckford (1759-1844), Matthew Gregory Lewis (1775-1818), and Horace Walpole (1717-97) in creating a climate of opinion in which romantic decay and 'gloomths' could be appreciated, the most important published works as catalysts of the reform of burial customs were those of the 'Graveyard Poets': Thomas Gray (1716-71); Robert Blair (1699-1746); and Edward Young (1683-1765). Gray's *Elegy* (published 1750) emphasised death as the leveller, but Blair's *Grave* (1743) celebrated the solitude and horrors of the tomb, the anguish of bereavement, and the frightening, ever-present realities of death. Young's *Night Thoughts* (1742-50), however, was by far the most important, for from the time of its publication it was acclaimed as a masterpiece and translated into every European language. It was a powerful stimulus in Europe, and for more than a century was the most influential, widely praised, and well-known poem in the English language. Even more important, it was a 'seminal work' in the 'secular cult of sepulchral melancholy'.[3]

[3] Curl (1994*a*), *passim*; Forster (1986), *passim*; Young (1989), *passim*. The Editor acknowledges with thanks the permission of Taylor & Francis Ltd. to use material previously published by them, and listed in the Select Bibliography.

In its progress through Europe 'Youngism' went through a transformation of emphasis in different languages. Pierre Prime Félicien Le Tourneur (1737-88) freely adapted and translated Young's work as *Les Nuits d'Young* (1769)[4] so that it became essentially an evocation of the poet's solitary grief as he wandered among the tombs.[5] *Night Thoughts* was translated into German by Johann Arnold Ebert (1723-95) and published in 1751/2, with further editions in 1753 and 1756,[6] and 1752 saw another translation by C. B. Kayser.[7] In 1760/1 Ebert brought out an edition with the original English text facing the German translation, copiously embellished with learned notes, and Kayser also published a revised version of his work around the same time. Young's poem had a considerable influence on the *Sturm und Drang*[8] movement of the German *Aufklärung*,[9] and was admired by many literary figures including Friedrich Gottlieb Klopstock (1724-1803), Gotthold Ephraim Lessing (1729-81 – who regarded *Night Thoughts* as a great work of the Sublime), Johann Gottfried Herder (1744-1803 – the decisive influence on Goethe), and the great man himself, Johann Wolfgang von Goethe (1749-1832 — who used *Night Thoughts* as his English reader). So numerous were the German imitators of *Nachtgedanken* that they were called 'Younglings' (a jest on *Jüngling*, meaning a youth, young man, or stripling). Goethe's *Die Wahlverwandschaften* (1809) and *Die Leiden des jungen Werthers* (1774) were both influenced by Young's work.[10]

The 'Narcissa' Episode

The most significant element in Young's poem was the famous episode of 'Narcissa's burial' in *Night III* which captured the European imagination and created a vogue for burial in gardens that was the single most powerful factor in the nascent movement to create garden-cemeteries.

The story described in *Night III* was based on true events. 'Narcissa' was Elizabeth Lee (*c*.1718-36), who married (1735) Young's friend Henry Temple (*c*.1703-40).[11] The Temples, with Young and his wife, had travelled to France in 1736, seeking a more beneficial climate to alleviate the effects of young Elizabeth's consumption. However, the girl died, and was interred in the cemetery of the *Hôtel-Dieu* in Lyons at eleven at night.[12] Young dramatised this, emphasising the gloom and horror of a burial in the darkness in a grave stealthily dug, and probably already occupied (which explains Young's term 'a stolen grave'). Le Tourneur helpfully provided an illustration showing the poet at midnight secretly laying 'Narcissa' in her 'stolen grave'.

Young described the French as 'Strangers to Kindness', with eyes that 'let fall Inhuman Tears' as they 'deny'd a Grave' to 'Narcissa'. They were fast held in 'blind *Infallibility*'s embrace', and 'Deny'd the Charity of Dust, to spread O'er Dust! a charity their Dogs' enjoyed. 'Half-execration', Young wrote, 'mingled with' his prayers, as he

> Sore grudg'd the Savage land her Sacred Dust,
> Stampt the curst Soil; and with Humanity,
> (Deny'd Narcissa,) wisht them All a Grave.[13]

Young's savage denunciation of the heartless, bigoted, 'Papist' French, who had denied the young 'heretic' Englishwoman what they gladly gave to their dogs, made, perhaps, more memorable by the lugubrious illustration published by Le Tourneur (and liberally

4 Tourneur (1769). 5 Young (1989), 18. 6 Ebert (1753), *passim*. 7 Published in Hanover by Johann Wilhelm Schmidt. 8 Storm and Stress. 9 The Enlightenment in German-speaking lands. 10 Goethe (1774) and (1809), *passim*. *Die Wahlverwandschaften* is usually given in English as *Elective Affinities*, and *Die Leiden* is translated literally as *The Sorrows of Young Werther*. 11 Temple was the elder son of Henry Temple (*c*.1673-1757), 1st Viscount Palmerston (from 1722-3). 12 Forster (1986), 150. 13 Young (1989), iii, 156-7, 167, 169-70, 184-8.

copied thereafter in numerous editions), had an enormous impact throughout Europe, and led many (in positions to lead opinion) to demonstrate their open-mindedness, tender sensibilities, and lack of bigotry by erecting tombs in their own gardens.

The Arcadian Ideal

However, there were other aspects that helped the tombs to enter the Picturesque landscaped garden. Nicolas Poussin (1594-1665), in the second version of his painting of the *et in Arcadia ego* theme (*c.*1635-6), depicted shepherds in an Arcadian landscape studying the inscription on a simple, rather severe Classical tomb: the shadow of one of the shepherds cast on the tomb alludes to the Spirit, or Classical *Manes*, and the inscription was interpreted to mean either 'and I was once an inhabitant of Arcady' or that, even there, in Arcadia, 'I' (meaning Death) was ever-present. Yet, with Poussin's vision, overt references to Death (e.g. skulls, bones, animated skeletons, etc., that had been features of Baroque and earlier art) were expunged. A gentle melancholy pervaded the lovely scene, and all references to the familiar horrors of decay, bones, decomposition, and dank, unwholesome graveyards were banished. Here was the peaceful, beautiful, ideal, a place fit for reflection and memories, where death was civilised.[14]

1.3 The 'Shepherd's Grave' at Shugborough, Staffordshire, showing a version of Poussin's *et in Arcadia ego* (*JSC*).

The image often recurs, perhaps most evocatively in the so-called 'Shepherd's Grave' at Shugborough, Staffordshire (*c.*1758), consisting of two primitivist Greek Doric columns, with the flutes only partly carved, carrying a primitive Doric entablature above which are shell-like antefixa: this ensemble forms an aedicule framing a grotto-like arch taken straight from *Grottos* by Thomas Wright (1711-86) within which is a carved relief by Peter Scheemakers (*c.*1691-1781), the subject being *et in Arcadia ego*, but in a mirror-image of Poussin's painting (1.3). The designers of this haunting 'grave' in an English garden were thus Scheemakers, Wright, and (probably) James 'Athenian' Stuart (1713-88), who was responsible for other garden-buildings at Shugborough, including the 'Lanthorn of Demosthenes' (1770), the 'Doric Temple' (1764), the 'Triumphal Arch' (1764-7), and the 'Tower of the Winds' (1764). The pedestal under Scheemakers's relief is inscribed with the mysterious letters

O · U · O · S · V · A · V · V
D M

[14] Curl (1994*a*), *passim*. *See also* Curl (2000*e*), 11.

which some commentators have suggested may have Freemasonic overtones. The D M probably stands for DIS MANIBUS or DI MANES, a term given to Roman dead as a sort of title. Capital letters with dots between them signify the first letters of words in a sentence, perhaps a line from Virgil, or they may represent the initials of the dead. This tomb, however, clearly suggests loss, longing, and the unattainable ideal of ancient Arcady.

English writers, such as Abraham Cowley (1618-67), had expressed desires to be buried in gardens, away from pain and noise, where the beauties of landscape evoked Paradise.[15] One of the first major landscaped gardens to suggest the Elysian Fields was that at Castle Howard, Yorkshire, where the great mausoleum and pyramid (1728) commemorated the dead. Alexander Pope (1688-1744) created a garden of 'memory and meditation' at Twickenham (1719-44) containing an obelisk set in a grove of cypresses (as a memorial to his mother) which was much admired and publicised, notably by Christian Cajus Lorenz Hirschfeld (1742-92) in his *Theorie der Gartenkunst*,[16] who gave credit to England for introducing memorials such as urns, columns, and buildings into gardens. Pope's obelisk appears to have been one of the first such memorials through which the poet sought to retain the presence of his mother near him by means of allusions, mnemonics, and the artful composition of a landscaped garden.[17]

One of the most significant English figures in the curious transformation of the garden was the English poet, William Shenstone (1714-63), whose elegiac compositions, lamenting lost youth, friendships, lives, or loves, disseminated notions of memorials set in evocative landscapes. Professor Richard Etlin has written that in Shenstone's works the 'connection between the elegiac sentiment and the landscape could not be made more explicit',[18] especially as Shenstone intended that his *Elegies* should be illustrated with scenes from his own garden at The Leasowes, Halesowen, Worcestershire, that was designed to invoke a Virgilian Arcady. For example, in Virgil's fifth *Eclogue*, the building of a monument to Daphnis is mentioned, and this is alluded to in the illustration of a funerary urn set in a grove used as a vignette by Robert Dodsley (1703-64)[19] in his edition of Shenstone's writings (1764). Furthermore, Shenstone celebrated his friends in what was essentially a Garden of Remembrance. Shenstone's creation (of which very little survives) proved to be an exemplar, and the urn, the marker, and the memorial became essential ornaments of the garden, part of an 18th-century attempt to evoke elegiac sentiments and Classical Antiquity in Northern Europe. However, Shenstone transformed the *et in Arcadia ego* phrase so that it signified the dead who had once known the pleasures of a charming landscape. Thus the spirits of the dead remained in the Garden of Allusion, and through death the living passed into an evocation of Arcadia, the land of perpetual Spring.[20]

At Stowe, Buckinghamshire, things were carried further by commemorating not only individuals but virtues and ideas in the celebrated gardens. In the Elysian Fields at Stowe attempts were made to re-create a landscape of agreeable Virgilian groves, sweetly watered meadows, and still, mirror-like lakes. William Kent (*c*.1685-1748) set the elegiac note with his Temple of British Worthies (1733), and the numerous monuments erected in the gently contoured landscape commemorated national figures. Virtues of the British were alluded to in the temples, and many triggers for further contemplation were created. In essence, Stowe was of great importance because it showed how ideas and commemoration could be contained in a pastoral setting that evoked Arcady and Elysium. Hirschfeld perceived Stowe as a powerful exemplar for future developments, inspiring noble thoughts through mnemonic triggers, and linking Classical Antiquity to

15 Etlin (1984*a*), 163, 171. 16 Hirschfeld (1779-85), *passim*. 17 Curl (2000*e*), 12. 18 Etlin (1984*a*), 176.
19 Dodsley also published Young's *Night Thoughts*. 20 Curl (2000*e*), 12.

the recent past, the present, and the future. As more and more Continental visitors began to admire such innovative English landscapes, a potent series of themes began to merge and blossom anew.

Young's *Night Thoughts* proved to be an important influence on Salomon Gessner (1730-88), whose *Idyllen* came out in 1756, with a French edition of 1762.[21] This pastoral poetry enjoyed sensational international success, and Gessner's work was admired by Hirschfeld and many others for whom it greatly surpassed comparable works of Antiquity. Continental landowners, keen to lay out their estates in the English manner, were also profoundly influenced by Gessner's work, which was said to inspire virtuous behaviour through sensibility. Gessner described tombs set in charming, gentle landscapes, arguing that these could be significant catalysts in promoting tender feelings towards the dead and the living, and thereby improve the general tone of society. The *Idylls* helped to promote the idea of the visit to the tomb of a loved one, and tombs in landscapes began to be regarded as essential elements in visions of Arcadia, for they were places where the living could weep moderate tears, recall the dead decorously to mind, reflect, remember, and keep those who had 'gone before' 'alive' in some way in both thought and spirit. In Gessner's world, graves were surrounded with sweet honeysuckle, shaded by willows, and embraced by fresh green ivies: there, in Arcady, the living could pour libations, meditate, and recall their dead in ways that might suggest their continuing presence. Gessnerian tombs were therefore evocative 'markers' between two worlds, either of which, as Young had suggested, could be more 'real' than the other. The living could derive inspiration, happiness, serenity, moral uplift, and even improve their sensibilities by visits to them. Gessner's work also has to be considered in the context of disposal of the dead at the time. Insanitary, malodorous, overcrowded, pestilential, and ugly burial-grounds were not places to be visited at all, and to bury loved ones in such horrible spots was something to be avoided if at all possible. A mourner brave enough to venture into an urban burial-ground to stand by a new grave would have been hard-pressed to summon up improving or tender thoughts: a heaving stomach, horrors, and despair were more likely to be his lot.

Developments in France

Paris acquired (1773-78) a *Bois des Tombeaux*, where pyramids, pedestals, and urns were set among the trees of the Parc Monceau. Designed by Louis Carrogis[22] (1717-1806 – known as 'Carmontelle'), the *Parc* was laid out for the Anglophile Duc de Chartres and Grand Master of the Freemasonic Grand Orient of France, Louis-Phillipe-Joseph (1747-93),[23] and was one of the first 'naturalistic' French gardens. The presence of tomb-like *fabriques*[24] in a garden led Nicolas-Thérèse-Benoist, Comte Frochot (1757-1828), to propose that the *Parc* should be converted into a public cemetery where real tombs would embellish it further, augmenting the cenotaphs in the *Bois des Tombeaux*. Although this was not realised, it is worth tracing how the idea had evolved.

Various themes outlined above began to coalesce in the 1770s. At Ermenonville, René-Louis, Marquis de Girardin (1735-1808) and eminent Freemason, created an *Elysée* modelled on The Leasowes (which he had visited in the 1760s) and on the famous description of Julie's garden in *La Nouvelle Héloïse*, the popular novel by Jean-Jacques Rousseau (1712-78).[25] Rousseau had been born a Protestant, and therefore would have been regarded as a 'heretic' in the France of the *ancien régime*. When he died, Girardin had Rousseau's body buried in the centre of a small island in the *Élysée* lake, and there,

[21] Gessner (1756) and (1762), *passim*. [22] Carrogis (1779), *passim*. [23] Curl (1991), 131-2. [24] Buildings or inventions. [25] Rousseau (1761), *passim*.

surrounded by poplars, a temporary memorial, consisting of a Classical pedestal surmounted by an urn, was erected (1.4).

This celebrated burial was widely reported in the press, and a view of the *Île des Peupliers*, complete with Rousseau's tomb, was published. Soon afterwards, Hubert Robert (1733-1808) designed a permanent stone tomb in the form of an Antique sarcophagus, which again was recorded in illustrations and became familiar throughout Europe.[26] Hirschfeld waxed lyrical about it, finding nothing disagreeable or morbid about Rousseau's burial, for the poet appeared to be 'sleeping' on the island: indeed, Hirschfeld saluted Rousseau's grave as an exemplar of a new type of burial in gardens rather than within urban churchyards and churches. This influential tomb, however, was more than just a memorable image. It evoked English gardens and was certainly influenced by the Leasowes and Stowe; it was a monument to Nature, Friendship, and Truth; and it made a public statement about Girardin's open-mindedness and lack of bigotry by burying a 'heretic' in his own garden. The Marquis was thus responding in an open, dramatic, and practical way to the 'Narcissa' episode in Young's *Night Thoughts*. Soon the *Élysée* became much visited by tourists.

1.4 Tomb of Rousseau (1712-78) on the Île des Peupliers, or *Élysée*, at Ermenonville, from a view by J.-M. Moreau the Younger, of 1778 (*BN*).

Stanislas-Cécile-Xavier-Louis, Comte de Girardin, Vicomte d'Ermenonville (1762-1827), author of the official guide-book to the gardens,[27] suggested that the park at Ermenonville could easily have provided Gessner with many appropriate settings for his *Idylls*. Moreover, the abstractions at Stowe were elaborated upon by celebrating ideas such as Humanity, Justice, Light, Nature, Physics, and Satire by means of monuments to individuals associated with them (e.g. Sir Isaac Newton [1642-1727] for Light, and Voltaire [1694-1778] for Satire). There were many other cenotaphs and memorials to sundry persons, including a truncated pyramid commemorating Theocritus (early 3rd century BC), Virgil (70-19 BC), James Thomson (1700-48), and Gessner, the four poets who had been most influential in the 18th-century celebration of sweet images of Nature. Nearby was a monument inscribed in English to Shenstone's memory.[28]

Ermenonville, therefore, was an influential garden, and recognised as such by many commentators, including Hirschfeld,[29] who also lauded other tombs in gardens, such as those of Johann Georg Sulzer (1720-79 – who had promoted 'English' landscaped gardens in Germany[30]) near Berlin, and of the Landgräfin Henrietta Caroline of Hesse-Darmstadt (1721-74) in the *Herrengarten*, Darmstadt. Sulzer's tomb was marked by an obelisk set on a pedestal placed by a quiet pool surrounded by trees, and that of the Landgräfin by a funerary mound covered with ivy and shaded by willows, yews, and dark conifers. Later, the mound was surmounted by a funerary urn embellished with an inscription by King Frederick II ('the Great') of Prussia (reigned 1740-86).

Other writers helped to change perceptions. The Abbé Jacques Delille (1738-1813) published his poem *Les Jardins* in 1782[31] in which he rhapsodised about Poussin's vision

[26] Girardin (1777) and (1788). [27] Girardin (1788), *passim*. [28] Curl (2000*e*), 16. [29] Hirschfeld (1779-85), *passim*. [30] Sulzer (1771-4), *passim*. [31] Delille (1782), *also called* Jacques Montanier.

of Arcady as an exemplar, and urged the importance of plants, trees, and water to provide appropriate and soothing settings for tombs. Bernardin de Saint-Pierre (1737-1814) proposed further transformations of the commemorative garden in his *Études de la Nature* (1784),[32] for he suggested landscaped *Élysées* as burial-places of the Great and Good, and public cemeteries that would be landscaped gardens embellished, if prosperity permitted, by monuments. Bernardin denounced contemporary churchyards and burials in churches as harmful to the living, aesthetically and hygienically indefensible, and utterly disgusting. He proposed that Paris should follow the examples of Classical Antiquity, the Chinese, and the Ottoman Turks by burying its dead in the countryside in public cemeteries planted with cypresses, pines, and fruit-trees, and argued that monuments erected in such settings would induce profound moral feelings and tender melancholy in the living, who would derive benefits from perambulations of the Arcadian cemeteries, whereas anybody who stumbled into the foetid and revolting churchyards could only experience horror, disgust, and an assault on all sentimental feelings. Bernardin's garden-cemetery was to have its own chapel for funeral services (probably treated as a Classical temple), and the landscaped park (or *Élysée*) would be beautified by means of columns, obelisks, pyramids, urns, statues, pedestals, domed buildings, temples, and sculpture of all sorts, made of varieties of stone in order to ensure varied colouring. Overcrowding of monuments would be avoided and the established principles of 'English' Picturesque landscape-design would be applied to the new cemeteries. Trees and shrubs would be many and varied, and planted with care to achieve the best visual effects.[33]

Many of these ideas and themes were further drawn together in the entry on cemeteries in the *Encyclopédie Méthodique* of 1788 contributed by Antoine-Chrysostôme Quatremère de Quincy (1755-1849), architectural theorist, Freemason, and key figure in the formation of the first landscaped cemeteries.[34] However, literary efforts were one thing, but quite another matter was the impact made by gardens actually realised that looked forward to the Elysian cemetery of the future. Among the most important of these was the extraordinary and evocative elegiac garden at Franconville-la-Garenne created in the 1780s by Claude-Camille-François, Comte d'Albon (1753-89), several views of which were drawn by the Comtesse d'Albon and published.[35] This charming Picturesque garden contained numerous *fabriques*, including a Pantheon-like temple (a common motif in Freemasonic iconography[36]), an obelisk, a Temple of the Muses, a *Bosquet de l'Amitié* (Grove of Tender Affection), a cascade, a Temple of the Dawn, a Primitive Hut (an allusion to theories concerning the origins of architecture), a Priapus, an Isle, a Chinese Kiosk, a *Rocher* (artificial rock, in this case with waterfalls), a fountain, a statue of Pan, a Devil's Bridge, an Asylum for Shepherds (being an evocation of Arcady, an essential shelter in case of foul weather), a column, and a Pyramid (commemorating d'Albon's ancestors). Such wide-ranging allusions[37] to many styles, ideas, and civilisations were not only intended to be mnemonic, but the eclecticism itself was a statement of open-mindedness and intellectual inquiry in the search of knowledge leading to improvements, all very much Freemasonic virtues.[38] There was also a monument to William Tell (an allusion to freedom from oppression, to national aspirations, and to democratic principles).

Three more elements in d'Albon's garden deserve mention. The first was the cenotaph of Swiss botanist Albrecht von Haller (1708-77), consisting of a mound like a truncated pyramid with an urn on top and four poplars planted around the mound. The second was the tomb (1.5) of Court de Gébelin (1725-84), linguist, Protestant, Freemason,

[32] Bernardin de Saint-Pierre (1784), *passim*. [33] Etlin (1984*a*). *See also* Etlin (1984*b*). [34] Etlin (1984*a*), 216.
[35] Lussi (1784). [36] Curl (1991), *passim*. [37] Curl (1997), *passim*. [38] Curl (1991), *passim*.

1.5 Tomb of Court de Gébelin (1725-84) at Franconville-la-Garenne, from de Lussi (1784) (*BL.140[21]*).

1.6 *Caverne d'Young* in the gardens at Franconville-la-Garenne, from de Lussi (1784) (*BL. 140[21]*).

and author of *Monde Primitif*,[39] who had inspired d'Albon with many ideas for his garden. His tomb had four 'ruined' columns standing sentinel around the blocky sarcophagus-like element, a composition similar to that of von Haller's cenotaph. D'Albon therefore had arranged for his friend, a 'heretic' to be buried in his own garden, partly in emulation of Girardin's burial of Rousseau at Ermenonville, and partly to demonstrate an enlightened, civilised outlook in contrast to the unfeeling bigotry exposed by Young in the 'Narcissa episode' in *Night Thoughts*. The third element was the *Caverne d'Young* (1.6), an artificial cave or grotto erected in memory of the English poet, high-priest of the cult of 'Sepulchral Melancholy'. D'Albon's garden was a demonstration of kindness, benevolence, freedom of thought, and rejection of religious bigotry by an enlightened, sensitive, French Freemason, who, by burying and commemorating 'heretics' and fellow-Freemasons on his estate, showed the world he had taken Young's strictures on board. What was clear, however, was that monuments were far more powerful in their impact if they stood over real bodies: cenotaphs were all very well, but tombs were better at getting messages across.

Sometimes, however, it was not possible to acquire bodies, so cenotaphs had to suffice. Anne-Pierre, Marquis de Montesquiou-Fézensac (1739-98) was an influential Freemason, and commissioned Alexandre-Théodore Brongniart (1739-1815) to design the famous 'ruined' pyramid to stand by the lake in the *Élysée* set within the gardens at Maupertuis. The well-known view of this pyramid (1.7) was published (with many views of French gardens) by Alexandre-Louis-Joseph, Comte de Laborde (1773-1842), in his *Descriptions des Nouveaux Jardins de la France* (1808),[40] but very few people seem to have noticed the Neoclassical mausoleum-like building to the left of the pyramid: this was the monumental cenotaph commemorating the Protestant Admiral Gaspard de Coligny (1517-72), who was murdered on St Bartholomew's Day, and whose dead body was displayed on a gibbet where it suffered further indignities. Now this is very significant, for the Marquis was making overt his disapproval of the rabid bigotry that had led to the St Bartholomew's Day Massacre of French Protestants, and demonstrated

39 Court de Gébelin (1776). 40 Laborde (1808-15), *passim*.

1.7 'Ruined' pyramid in the *Élysée* at Maupertuis, designed by Brongniart. The primitive Doric columns and segmented pediment allude to Ancient Egyptian mysteries (the crescent-moon of Isis). On the left is the cenotaph commemorating Admiral Gaspard de Coligny, a Protestant murdered on St Bartholomew's Day, 1572. Drawn by Constant Bourgeois and engraved by Anne Athénes femme Massard, from Laborde (1808-15) (*DO*).

1.8 Rostral column erected in the *Élysée* at Méréville. Drawn by Constant Bourgeois and engraved by Gamble. From Laborde (1808-15) (*DO*).

he could (and would) commemorate 'heretics', and would bury them with decency (if he could) in his own garden, but, if he had no corpse to inter, he would solemnly commemorate the dead by means of cenotaphs to their memory. Thus he responded to the 'Narcissa episode' in Young's *Night Thoughts*.

Jean-Joseph, Marquis de Laborde (1724-94), also a Freemason, erected another evocative *Elysée* in his garden at Méréville and there, by the lake, he erected monuments to two of his sons who perished on the expedition of Jean-François de Galaup, Comte de La Pérouse (1741-88), which came to grief in the Samoan Islands and on reefs north of the New Hebrides (**1.8**). In order to demonstrate his even-handedness and open mind, he also erected a monument to the memory of Captain James Cook (1728-79), who lost his life in Hawaii during his third great voyage of exploration (**1.9**). The gardens at Méréville were designed by Hubert Robert, who succeeded François-Joseph-Bélanger (1744-1818), the architect responsible for the general plan. The siting of the two monuments by the lake, the sea-pine, and other carefully chosen trees and shrubs were intended to allude to the distant sea-shores on which both the French and British expeditions met disaster. Weeping willows and poplars further contributed to the sad, elegiac qualities of the landscape around the *Elysée*.

A.-L.-J. Laborde, in his *Descriptions* ...,[41] listed and illustrated several important French gardens, including Ermenonville, Méréville, Maupertuis, and Morfontaine. The

[41] Laborde (1808-15), *passim*.

1.9 Cenotaph in memory of Captain Cook in the *Élysée* at Méréville, designed by Hubert Robert and François-Joseph Bélanger (1744-1818). Drawn by Constant Bourgeois and engraved by Gamble. From Laborde (1808-15) (*DO*).

1.10 Tomb of the wife of the owner of the garden of Plessis-Chamand. Intended as a place of reflection, this evocative design was the Enlightenment ideal of burial in gardens. Drawn by Constant Bourgeois and engraved by de Villiers the Younger. From Laborde (1808-15) (*SJM*).

last, the property of Louis-Michel Le Peletier de Saint Fargeau (1760-93 – yet another Freemason), had a Weymouth Pine,[42] a black-marble tomb on a high pedestal set on an artificial mound, a *bosquet* and altar-like tomb at the entrance to the Little Park, and rock-work inscribed with an appropriate verse by Delille. Laborde also described the garden at Plessis-Chamand where the wife of the owner was buried in a fine tomb set in the park and surrounded by shrubs and trees (1.10).[43]

The Beginnings of the Modern Cemetery

Thus the garden-cemetery, the Arcadian landscaped garden ornamented with monuments and other *fabriques*, began to emerge as the desirable exemplar for burial of the dead. In the 1780s the large Parisian Cemetery of the Innocents that had been used for many centuries, served many parishes, and was surrounded by *charniers* (charnel-houses), was closed, following years of debate about its scandalous state and putrid ground. In 1785 there began the transfer of bones to underground ossuaries in worked-out quarries under the Plaine de Montrouge in Montparnasse. Contemporary accounts suggest that these were the stuff of nightmares, worlds of darkness and silence broken only when new cartloads of bones from other closed crypts and churchyards were tipped in. This closing and clearance of churchyards and crypts was part of a general move towards improving urban hygiene begun during the *ancien régime*, and has been admirably chronicled by Professor Etlin.[44] Much later, in 1810, Prefect Frochot (who, as has been noted, proposed converting the Parc Monceau into a cemetery) and the Inspector-General of Quarries, Louis-Étienne-François Héricart-Ferrand, Vicomte de Thury (1776-1854), created Order (an architectural and Freemasonic skill) in the Kingdom of Death and Chaos by arranging the bones in carefully constructed walls lining corridors and spaces within the old quarries which became known as the Paris Catacombs.[45]

Quatremère de Quincy also favoured catacombs, and was responsible for transforming the church of Ste-Geneviève[46] (which had been secularised in 1791) into a

[42] The New English larch, introduced to England in 1705, and named after Sir Thomas Thynne, 1st Viscount Weymouth (1640-1714). [43] Villeneuve (1787). [44] Etlin (1984*a*), *passim*. [45] Thury (1815). *See also* Saint-A... (1816). [46] Designed by Jacques-Germain Soufflot (1713-80).

national *Panthéon*: in order to give the building a suitably funereal character he arranged for the windows to be blocked up. In this he was supported by Charles-Michel de la Villette, Marquis du Plessis (1736-93), who argued that the church should be converted into a National Mausoleum for the Great and Good of France, and the body of Rousseau was brought to the *Panthéon* from Ermenonville in 1794. Villette also argued that the remaining Parisian burial-grounds were foul and hideous places, and that they should be replaced by cemeteries as 'sleeping-places', doubtless with the garden at Plessis-Chamand firmly in mind. For a brief period it seemed likely that a large public cemetery would be laid out around the *Panthéon*, but this was never realised, and for many years Soufflot's great building stood alone in a bald open space. Another idea for a new Parisian cemetery was floated when the architect Antoine-Laurent-Thomas Vaudoyer (1756-1846) proposed converting the promenade of the *Champs-Élysées* into a linear cemetery, the precedents for which were those of Roman Antiquity (e.g. the Via Appia Antica outside Rome), but the Parisian cemetery was to be much grander, lined with noble mausolea and statues of illustrious Frenchmen. Vaudoyer flagged the idea of an educational programme in his proposals, where history would be taught, and the places of the dead in that history demonstrated by means of the monuments.[47]

As has been argued elsewhere,[48] the notion of a cemetery as a *Champ de Repos* (Field of Rest) evolved as part of the anti-clericalism and egalitarian ideas of the French Enlightenment. The dead were to be severed from churches, Christian symbols removed, and the new cemeteries would become a means of social engineering: at the secular tomb in the cemetery contracts could be signed, promises sworn, and discord smoothed. Cemeteries were to be the catalysts in the promotion of tender feelings in Elysian Fields that were a considerable improvement on the traditional Church burial-grounds where skulls, bones, foetor, horrors, and loathsomeness were to be found in plenty. Philanthropic idealism and reason were to oust despair, terror, hell-fire, superstition, and disgusting sights and odours. Death, in short, would be tamed, and the garden-cemetery, with its Freemasonic and anti-clerical connotations, would weaken the forces of reaction, superstition, and the *ancien régime*.

The official Decree of 23 Prairial, Year XII (12 June 1804) drew up rules for French cemeteries that have remained in essence the same until our own times. It prohibited burial of the dead in churches and towns and ordered the establishment of cemeteries outside urban limits, planted with trees and shrubs. Regulations were made concerning modes of burial, the erection of monuments, and much else. This Decree was the result of much debate, indecision, and differences of opinion: as Ariès noted,[49] however, it became more than a legal text, and was a sort of 'Ten Commandments' of a new cult, that of the Dead, although the moral aspects of the Decree have been gradually eroded over the years, so that eventually it became more or less a set of regulations for Public Health. A further aspect was that the distant cemetery at first impinged little on the physical realities and awareness of the living: however, within a decade or two not only did the cemeteries become places of resort, but towns could not be regarded as viable social organisations without them.[50]

Four new cemeteries in rural settings were proposed by the Administration of Public Works for Paris, and the concept of large, well-planted cemeteries began to gain acceptance. Nevertheless it was not until 1804 that Frochot was able to give instructions to Brongniart (then Chief Inspector-General of the Second Section of Public Works for the *Département* of the Seine and the City of Paris) to lay out a great cemetery at Mont-Louis to the east of the city. This became the celebrated Père-Lachaise which contained a straight main axis, circuitous carriageways, and formal and naturalistic elements.[51]

[47] Curl (2000*e*), 23-4. [48] Ibid., 24. [49] Ariès (1981), 516. [50] Ibid., *passim*. [51] For the evolution of Père-Lachaise, *see* Etlin (1984*a*), 303-58.

Père-Lachaise was to become world-famous and enormously influential throughout Europe and America. It was visited by many[52] who were concerned with the problems of burying the dead. Its mausolea and monuments became widely known by means of illustrated books[53] and were copied on both sides of the Atlantic. In order to give a kind of secular seal of approval to Père-Lachaise cemetery the bodies of the medieval lovers Pierre Abélard (1079-1142) and Heloïse (d. 1163), and the writers Jean de La Fontaine (1621-95) and Jean-Baptiste Poquelin, called Molière (1622-73), were translated thither (**1.11**). Just as it had once been desirable to be buried in churches near the relics of saints, post-Revolutionary, supposedly rational France sought to bury its dead in Arcadian gardens, somehow made acceptable by the presence of cadavers of the Great and Good.

There were subtle allusions at Père-Lachaise too. The *Grand Rond* (**1.12**), where various paths converged, was originally surrounded by poplars, so deliberately alluded to Rousseau's grave at Ermenonville. Around the *rond-point* were the tombs of several *savants*, including Gaspard Monge (1746-1818), the inventor of descriptive geometry, and Jean-François Champollion (1790-1832), who classified Ancient Egyptian hieroglyphs and formulated a system of grammar, collected in his *Précis du système hiéroglyphique des anciens Égyptiens*[54] (1824). In a quiet glade not far from the *rond-point* are the Classical tombs of two of the begetters of the cemetery, Brongniart and Delille (**1.13**). The latter had envisaged his 'poetic tomb' in a 'place of peace, love, and mourning', and that is what he got: Père-Lachaise was seen as just that, and was contrasted with urban burial-grounds (such as the sordid Innocents, with its stinking *charniers*) that nobody could ever perceive as places 'of peace, love, and mourning'.

Thus nothing short of a revolution had occurred, and Père-Lachaise cemetery became the model for an entirely new culture that transformed the disposal of the dead in many countries. The English Picturesque garden, English literary influences, and the powerful stimulus of both Antiquity and the 'Narcissa episode' in Young's *Night Thoughts* led to the development of 'naturalistic' French gardens embellished with cenotaphs and tombs, and these, in turn, were the begetters of the garden-cemetery.[55]

Conditions in Britain

London acquired a cemetery of limited extent in the 17th century at Bunhill Fields. The City of London enclosed the ground in 1665, and the cemetery was theoretically open to all, but it rapidly became the *Campo Santo* (holy field or cemetery) of Nonconformists sanctified by the burial there of John Bunyan (1628-88), Daniel Defoe (*c*.1660-1731), Isaac Watts (1674-1748), William Blake (1757-1827), and many others.[56] Most burials in England, however, were in parish churches, parish churchyards, or parish burial-grounds not necessarily situated beside a church. Nonconformists (or Dissenters) resented having to be buried in consecrated ground, and, especially, having to pay a fee to clergymen of the Established Anglican Church: they often sought to form their own burial-grounds.

In Scotland the separation of the burial-grounds from churches occurred much earlier than in France, for the Reformed Protestant Church, keen to stamp out any survivals of 'Papist' beliefs and practices, abolished prayers for the dead and all the paraphernalia of chantries (establishments, endowments, or foundations for the daily or frequent saying of Masses on behalf of the souls of the founder, founders, or other persons). In 1581 the Church of Scotland prohibited burial within churches and created a climate in which graveyards had to be created, of which Greyfairs, Edinburgh (opened 1562) is an early

52 *See*, e.g., Fisk (1838). 53 *See*, e.g., Marty, Lassalle, and Rousseau (n.d.), and Normand Fils (1832). 54 Summary of the hieroglyphical system of the Ancient Egyptians, published in Paris by Didot. 55 Curl (1991), 169-204; Curl (1994*a*); Curl (2000*e*), 25-7 and *passim*. 56 Curll (1717); Light (1913); Reed *et al.* (1867).

1.11 Tombs of La Fontaine and Molière in Père-Lachaise cemetery, Paris, designed by Feuchère. The bust and tomb-enclosure (*left*) marks the grave of Louis Savart; the urn on the pedestal commemorates N. Rambourg; the Corinthian column behind the poplars is Pierre Dufrenel's monument; and the obelisk is the Gémon memorial. Drawn by Boisselier and engraved by Normand. From Normand Fils (1832) (*ECJSC*).

1.12 *Rond-Point des Peupliers*, Père-Lachaise cemetery, Paris, with Monge's Egyptianising mausoleum on the left, designed by Clochard. Drawn by Boisselier and engraved by Normand. From Normand Fils (1832) (*ECJSC*).

1.13 Tombs of Brongniart (*left*) by Louis-Hippolyte Lebas (1782-1867) and of Jacques Delille (*right*) by Philippon in Père-Lachaise cemetery, Paris. Drawn by Boisselier and engraved by Normand. From Normand Fils (1832) (*ECJSC*).

and fascinating example.[57] Burial-grounds detached from churches weakened old beliefs: good 18th-century examples include Old Calton Burying-Ground, Edinburgh (opened 1718), and the New Burying-Ground, Clifton Street, Belfast, dating from 1797.[58] Of course, Belfast in the 18th century had a strong radical Dissenting tradition, so it is not surprising that it laid out one of the earliest modern cemeteries, just as the German-speaking countries (inspired by the *Aufklärung*) were also acquiring new, walled cemeteries outside their cities (e.g. Dessau [1787] [1.14], St Marx, Vienna [1784], and the late 18th-century cemeteries in Berlin-Kreuzberg[59]) thanks to an increasing concern for public health and new tenderness towards the dead promoted by the literature of the time.

1.14 Entrance to the public non-denominational cemetery at Dessau, designed (1787) by Friedrich Wilhelm, Freiherr von Erdmannsdorff (1736-1800). The figure on top is Hope (with anchor), and the statues in the niches represent the twin brothers, Sleep and Death (with inverted torches representing the extinguishing of life). The inscription reads 'Death is not Death, only an ennobling of mortal Nature'. Etching by Christian Friedrich Wiegand (1752-1832) (*Staatliche Galerie Dessau, Schloss Georgium, Inv. No. G.660*).

In 18th-century London the population increased, and it was not long before churchyards and vaults under the many new churches were filled. As early as the 1720s there were dire warnings that burial of corpses in churches and churchyards was prejudicial to the health of the living, and that, for the common good, new burial-grounds should be provided outside urban areas.[60] In some instances extra ground was acquired when parish churchyards could no longer cope: an example was the parish of St Giles-in-the-Fields, where a new burial-ground was acquired adjacent to Old St Pancras churchyard; and similar 'overspill' burial-grounds distant from the original church and churchyard could be found in London and other cities such as Paris, Vienna, and Berlin. The original churchyard of St Giles-in-the-Fields was notorious for its disgusting state, and there is plenty of evidence that it was by no means unique. In many (if not most) metropolitan churchyards any burial was impossible without disturbing previous burials, and it was more usual than not to dig up parts of bodies before they had decayed, thus causing great offence to local inhabitants and unbearable horror to relations of these whose graves knew no peace. It is little wonder that in urban burial-grounds relatives very rarely went to the graveside for the committal of the body: to do so would have been too distressing. Dead bodies in most of the urban burial-grounds were certain to be disturbed by gravediggers, rats, and even dogs scavenging for food, but they were prey to others as well: the much-feared 'resurrection-men', or body-snatchers. This topic will be pursued in the following Chapter.

Conditions created a demand for 'burial' in vaults or crypts which were perceived as more secure, though they were nothing of the sort, as palms could be greased. Evidence of the widespread custom of interring bodies in churches may still be seen today in the very large number of ledger-slabs in church-floors and mural tablets recording burials in 'vaults' near by. However, such privileges were available only to those who could afford

57 Gifford, McWilliam, and Walker (1984). 58 Merrick and Clarke (1991); Strain (1961). 59 Fischer and Schein (*Eds.*) (1987), *passim*. 60 Lewis (1721), *passim*.

them, so the less well-off had to entrust their dead to burial-grounds. 'Facilities' began to be offered for 'vault' burial in certain Dissenters' chapels. Persuaded that depositing their loved ones in such places (often little more than basements or cellars of independent chapels) would offer better security, the bereaved would pay, yet there again dishonesty ruled, for the coffins would find their way back to the undertakers or were sold as firewood, and the corpses would be disposed of by any means available. Such chapels (e.g. the infamous Enon and Elim chapels in London) were erected as speculative enterprises by those who aspired to preach, with a 'burial' part of the business bringing in a not insignificant portion of income. However, volumes tend to fill, and once filled, could bring in no more cash, so the only way in which a continuing source of income could be assured was to recycle the coffins and dispose of the bodies.[61] Some parishes, too, it seems, indulged in such vile practices, and during the first three decades of the 19th century, before the founding of the first large commercial cemeteries, about fifteen small private burial-grounds also were established in London.[62] As Dr Ruth Richardson has written, 'high walls and brick-built burial-vaults were accompanied by higher prices, and offered the comforting illusion of security'.[63] Curiously, there may have been some residual pre-Reformation sentiments that survived, for burial in churches was not merely a matter of status and security, but was connected with old beliefs associated with sanctity.[64] Burial in the small, independent, private-enterprise burial-grounds, however, seems to have been prompted by the unsavoury state of parish churchyards, anticlericalism, and a desire to protect the dead from the body-snatchers. Charles Dickens (1812-70) often alluded to the state of London's burial-grounds,[65] including those 'entirely detached from churches, always so pressed upon by houses' that were 'so small, so rank, so silent, so forgotten', and places of 'abomination', infested by rats, where new burials could be uncovered with a 'broom'.

Some Early Cemeteries

So there were small burial-grounds in existence, for parishes, for Dissenters, and as private speculations, but nothing on the scale of Père-Lachaise cemetery in Paris, a place that became famous and was visited by countless travellers. George Hadfield (1787-1879) is credited with the founding of the cemetery in Chorlton Row, Rusholme Road, Manchester, a joint-stock venture for Dissenters, in 1820, and apparently the first of its kind. However, in the previous year (1819), the Rosary Road cemetery, Norwich, was laid out, the first non-denominational public cemetery in England, it has been claimed, promoted by Thomas Drummond, a Nonconformist minister, but not recognised by the Bishop for Anglican burial until 1821. Bunhill Fields in London, though mainly associated with Dissenters, seems to have been used to bury anybody, including Anglicans, so it really has to be seen as an earlier non-denominational cemetery.

Then, in 1825, the Liverpool Necropolis[66] (or Low Hill General Cemetery), West Derby Road, Liverpool, was opened. It cost £8,000 to lay out, but was quite small at only two hectares (4.942 acres) in area. It was again founded by Dissenters desiring burial facilities independent of the Established Church, and was, for a time, remarkably successful, paying *average* dividends of 12½ per cent, a better return than could be obtained from speculative housing, or, later, railway stock. The Necropolis had a handsome Greek Doric entrance (**1.15**) incorporating offices and a dwelling for the

[61] Knight (*Ed.*) (*c*.1870), **iv**, 163. *See also The Builder*, **iii**/105, 107 (1845), 83, 69, 82, 92, 110. [62] Holmes (1896), 138, 194-5. [63] Richardson (1993), 579. [64] Lewis (1721), *passim*; Duffy (1992), 332 and *passim*. [65] For example, in *The Uncommercial Traveller* or *Bleak House*. *See also Household Words*, *passim*. [66] From νεκρός (corpse) and *πόλις* (city), hence νεκρόπλις (city of the dead).

Superintendent,[67] and was designed by John Foster (*c.*1787-1846), who was also responsible for the building-works of the Anglican riposte, the much larger (and spectacular) St James's cemetery, Liverpool, laid out in a disused quarry between 1825 and 1829 (**1.16**). Again, a joint-stock company promoted the cemetery, and buildings included a fine mortuary-chapel (Greek Doric outside and Ionic within) (**1.17**), a Superintendent's house, an arched entrance-gateway, and the circular Greek Corinthian mausoleum (1834) of William Huskisson, MP (1770-1830), who got himself killed at the opening of the Liverpool and Manchester Railway.[68]

1.15 Entrance to the Liverpool Necropolis (or Low Hill General cemetery) designed by Foster. Drawn by Thomas Allom and engraved by Robert Wallis (*ECJSC*).

The idea of using a worked-out quarry as a cemetery had been pioneered in Paris, not only at the catacombs of Montparnasse, but at Montmartre, where a cemetery had been established in 1798, but re-ordered and enlarged, and re-opened in 1825,[69] so its metamorphosis is contemporary with the start of work at St James's cemetery, though any acknowledgements of design or conceptual debts have eluded discovery. At Liverpool Foster constructed great ramps leading to the floor of the quarry, formed chambers by cutting into the rock set behind a battered wall, and drove tunnels through outcrops of stone to create routes and cavernous effects. Landscaping was by John Shepherd (*c.*1764-1836), who had worked with Foster on other projects: the completed cemetery was both Picturesque and Sublime,[70] yet reassuringly private and securely enclosed, with an ensemble ideal for Contemplation of the Tomb, yet was a commercial venture (by 1830 it was paying a gratifying dividend of 8 per cent to its shareholders).

These two Liverpudlian cemeteries were of national importance as stimuli to other cities in providing cemeteries, and had distinguished buildings by a great Neoclassical architect. It is worse than regrettable (indeed it is a local and national disgrace) that both these cemeteries have been largely cleared (of the Necropolis virtually nothing remains) and comprehensively vandalised (both officially and unofficially) by those who were obviously ignorant of the quality and significance of what they once had.

In Glasgow, the Merchants' House owned a rocky eminence known as the Fir Park, east of the great medieval cathedral of St Mungo (or Kentigern), and it was decided in 1828 to establish a cemetery there, partly because the site bore a slight resemblance to Mont-Louis (on which Père-Lachaise cemetery had been laid out earlier), and partly because the 'soil and substrata' rendered it to be 'of all other spots the most eligible for a cemetery', ideal for 'every species of sepulture ... and every sort of sepulchral ornament'.[71] Proposals were invited (1831) for transforming the Fir Park into an 'Ornamental Cemetery ... in [a] manner which should best embrace economy, security, and *picturesque* effect'.[72] Sixteen schemes were submitted, premiums were awarded to five, but none was adopted.

[67] Collinson (1840). [68] Curl (2000*e*), 42. [69] Etlin (1984*a*), 240. [70] Curl (2000*a*), 498, 694. [71] Pagan (1847), 165.
[72] George Blair (1857), 26. Editor's italics.

1.16 View of the cemetery of St James, Liverpool, showing (*left*) the ramps descending to the floor of the disused quarry with entrances to burial-chambers set into the walls, (*right*) the Greek Revival chapel, and (*centre*) the circular mausoleum of Huskisson. Engraved, printed, and published by H. Lacey of Liverpool, as No. 7 of *Lacey's Liverpool Localities*. Note the procession entering the dark tunnel. The great Anglican cathedral now stands to the left of the chapel (*ECJSC*).

1.17 Greek Revival chapel and entrance-gate at St James's cemetery, Liverpool, designed by John Foster (*JSC*).

There was a certain amount of resistance to the formation of any new cemetery, for nothing like it had happened in Scotland for a very long time, and public opinion had to be wooed. In 1831 John Strang (1795-1863) published his *Necropolis Glasguensis; with Osbervations* [sic] *on Ancient and Modern Tombs and Sepulture*,[73] in which he claimed he was 'solely actuated by the desire of awakening the attention of his countrymen to the generally neglected condition of their churchyards, and of furthering ... the many claims ... of converting the Fir Park into a garden cemetery ...'.[74] Strang proposed 'imitating the French in the formation of a Scottish *Père La Chaise*',[75] and his book (though prolix and somewhat unctuous in tone) was important in many ways. Like many of his worthy contemporaries he deplored broken tombstones, the 'disgusting charnel-house ... infected with ... pestilence ..., calculated to call forth ... feelings of aversion', and much else.[76] In Père-Lachaise cemetery, however, 'all the disagreeable sensations' associated with many graveyards were 'dispelled by the beauty of the garden, the variety of its walks, ... and the commanding view of Paris and its environs'. Moreover, in 'that vast grove of the dead', each person had 'his own grave',[77] and the 'contemplative mind' was 'impressed with sentiments ... of the most tender and heart-affecting melancholy'.[78] Should a new Père-Lachaise be created in Scotland, as Strang wished, its effects would be 'beneficial', and Glasgow would gain

73 Strang (1831). 74 Ibid., v. 75 Ibid., vii. 76 Ibid., 24. 77 Ibid., 28. 78 Ibid., 29.

1.18 Glasgow Necropolis, showing (*foreground*) the 'Bridge of Sighs' over the ravine, the Façade (7), and sundry monuments. Engraving by James Mitchell & Co. From George Blair (1857) (*ECJSC*).

'one of the most eloquent advocates of religion and morality…, one of the greatest foes to preternatural terror and superstition, and one of the most convincing arguments for the existence of taste'.[79] Furthermore, the decorations of the 'tomb and garden cemetery' were 'calculated to extend religious, … virtuous, and generous feelings'. 'A garden cemetery', Strang declared, was indicative of 'the most convincing tokens of a nation's progress' in civilisation and the arts.[80]

Many more advantages were to accrue in the polemics of their protagonists: cemeteries were held to stimulate morals, public health, virtue (public and private), education, the development of artistic taste, sentiment, kindness, appreciation of architecture and sculpture, instruction in botany and landscape-gardening, arboriculture, family values, literature (by means of improving texts and allusions to the Bible and Classical texts carved on monuments), emulation of worth (by reference to the lives commemorated on the memorials), and much else besides. Cemeteries provided dictionaries of biographies of the Great and Good, whose lives would be exemplars for impressionable youth,[81] and everywhere one looked something would trigger improving thoughts by allusion. The student of pro-coemeterial literature of the time might be forgiven for speculating if there were any aspects of life on which the beneficial effects of cemeteries would not impinge.

Glasgow Necropolis was one of the most glorious creations of the early British cemetery movement, a remarkable architectural ensemble that constitutes a stunningly memorable composition of townscape (1.18). Its very name, a 'city of the dead', is apposite, for it looks at first glance like a hill-town, embellished with handsome buildings, obelisks, temples, and monuments. Unfortunately, the Glasgow Necropolis has suffered from much erosion of character because kerbs and other elements have been removed for ease of maintenance, and much has been demolished by officialdom terrified that anything might fall on the *unofficial* vandals intent on destroying and defacing the monuments, a deplorable response symptomatic of a widespread malaise.[82]

The exemplars outside London had been created. It was now the turn of the capital to create the first of its metropolitan cemeteries, and it is to this development that we now turn.

79 Strang (1831), 57. 80 Ibid., 62. 81 The youthful vandals of Liverpool and elsewhere have been impervious to such blandishments. 82 See Curl (2000*e*) for the Glasgow Necropolis and other matters in greater detail.

CHAPTER II

George Frederick Carden and the Genesis of the General Cemetery Company

RUTH RICHARDSON
& JAMES STEVENS CURL

Introduction; The General Burial-Grounds Association; Body-Snatchers and the Anatomists; The 'Life, Death, Burial, and Resurrection Company'; The Re-Launch of Carden's Proposals; The Provisional Committee and its Business; The Nascent Company; Acquisition of Land at Kensal Green; Enclosure of the Ground and First Moves towards Planting; Events until early in 1832

> A garden cemetery is the sworn foe to preternatural fear and superstition ... In the mazes of *Père La Chaise*, we feel walking as in the porch of eternity, and our heart is at once impressed with a sense of the evanescence and the value of time. There, the instability of all human affairs is emphatically and eloquently taught by the dread silence of the tomb ...
>
> JOHN STRANG (1795-1863):
> *Necropolis Glasguensis; with Osbervations* [sic] *on Ancient and Modern Tombs and Sepulture* (Glasgow: Atkinson & Company, 1831), 59, 30.

Introduction

Many commentators have perceived the General Cemetery of All Souls at Kensal Green (which it became) as a great Victorian cemetery, forgetting that it opened in 1833, four years before Victoria's accession to the Throne, and that its creation was the result of Georgian preoccupations and Georgian enterprise. Had economic conditions been more favourable in the previous decade, the cemetery might have opened its gates in the 1820s, during the reign of King George IV,[1] instead of being realised during the reign of his brother.[2]

Few visitors to Kensal Green cemetery realise, too, that its early history was profoundly influenced by the evolution of anatomical study.[3] The reasons for the choice of site beside an existing canal, for the magnitude and solidity of the high boundary-walls, for the great gates and tall iron railings, and for the perceived market in providing for secure vaults and catacombs, become apparent when the need for security from body-snatchers is taken fully into account. The heyday of the body-snatchers extended through the Georgian period, and was facing its end as the cemetery opened its massive gates for the interment of the dead in 1833. This Chapter will outline the early history of Kensal Green cemetery in the context of the 1820s and 1830s.

The General Burial-Grounds Association

George Frederick Carden (1798-1874), barrister and philanthropist, appears to have first declared in public his interest in the problem of providing cemeteries for London in 1824.[4] During a visit to Paris in 1821, he was so impressed by Père-Lachaise cemetery that he decided to contact other like-minded persons who would help to determine how an English version of the French model could be realised, at a time when influential opinion began to move towards acceptance that something had to be done. Widespread publicity given to the garden-cemetery of Père-Lachaise helped to shape views, and Carden was not alone in his enthusiasm, although his was an effective voice during the early days of attempts to form cemeteries.

By 1825 Carden had formed an organisation to realise his ideas (which he called The General Burial-Grounds Association), and published a *Prospectus*. He and his colleagues who sought to promote new commercial burial-grounds in the 1820s knew all about the difficulties of disposing of the dead in London. They were well aware that persons of middling or modest means could not afford to carry their dead out of town, and had no access to family mausolea on spacious country estates. Outdoor burial in London, they knew, was both unpleasant and insecure. Church-vaults were becoming full, and were expensive. A new enterprise offering secure burial in beautiful landscaped surroundings at moderate cost, permitting the erection of memorials or mausolea, and providing vaults and catacombs, would be a certain commercial success, especially if modelled on Père-Lachaise cemetery in Paris, which had become quite an attraction for tourists since the end of the Napoleonic Wars (as discussed in the previous Chapter).

In the *Prospectus*, which was issued to launch the new group, The General Burial-Grounds Association stated its aims. It advocated the formation of a cemetery for London similar to the Parisian exemplar, and noted that a suitable site was available at

[1] George Augustus Frederick (1762-1830), reigned as George IV (1820-30). [2] William Henry (1765-1837), Duke of Clarence and St Andrews, and Earl of Munster, reigned as William IV (1830-7). [3] Richardson (1987) tells the entire story of the provenance of corpses for anatomical studies from the Renaissance to the present day. *See also* Ruth Richardson: 'La Compañía de la Vida, la Muerte, el Entierro y la Resurrectión: el entierro metropolitano en el Reino Unido, 1800-1900' and its English translation *in* Andalucía (1993), 74-87, 577-82. Richardson (1993) hereafter. [4] *The Penny Magazine of the Society for the Diffusion of Useful Knowledge*, iii/150 (2 August 1834), 299.

Primrose Hill, north of London.[5] The Association was launched on the London Stock Exchange, and a public meeting was to be held to promote it and its aims.[6]

This 1825 *Prospectus* is interesting because it reveals a great deal about how Carden and his associates were thinking. The intention was to raise venture-capital in the sum of £300,000 (a vast amount then[7]) by means of shares offered at £50 each, in order to establish a commercial 'burial-ground' to be known as *The British Père La Chaise*.[8] Various matters were stressed, including, first of all, the need for vaults and provision for burial secure from the attentions of body-snatchers; the opportunities to create peaceful and beautiful landscapes as a fitting setting for burial and commemoration; the necessity of removing dangers to public health caused by overcrowded and insanitary graveyards within the metropolis; the desirability of Government intervention to facilitate the necessary legislation to allow the establishment of such burial-grounds; the importance of private enterprise in the creation of means by which the dead of London could be decently interred; and the opportunity the scheme offered for adequate returns on investment in commercial provision for burial.[9] It should be noted that the awfulness of churchyards was *not* the prime concern at the time, but that security most certainly was; in fact, the *Prospectus* emphasised *security from violation* by means of conspicuous capital letters.

Included in The General Burial-Grounds Association's *Prospectus* was an *Appendix* entitled *A Brief Description of the Celebrated Cemetery of Père La Chaise, near Paris, and of the General Effect produced upon the Minds of Travellers upon beholding it*, an idealised and sentimental account, which nevertheless successfully emphasised how the proposed new 'burial-ground' would be wholly unlike the dreadful graveyards so familiar to Londoners.

Like many polemical writings of the period, the *Appendix* over-stated its case: it was oleaginous in tone, and the phraseology was often ludicrous. There were references to 'smiling flowers', 'fragrant bowers', and 'costly mausoleums' in the proposed enticing 'burial-ground' where, the public was assured, there would be no 'frightful images' causing the 'willing visitor to withdraw his footsteps'. Artificial flowers would, improbably, 'make a perpetual Spring ..., and render imperceptible .... decay in Nature'. In this terrestrial Paradise 'Nature, Art, and Situation' would 'all combine to render' it the 'proudest spot in Europe'.[10] However, thanks to the unfavourable economic climate of 1825[11] Carden's 'Burial-Ground' (complete with its 'fragrant bowers' and so on) had to be put on ice, and the promotional public meeting never took place.

Body-Snatchers and the Anatomists

Ever since Tudor times there had been only one legal source of corpses for dissection: the gallows. Although capital punishment claimed many lives in Georgian London, the demand for corpses generated by the anatomy-schools could not be met from this source alone. From *c.*1730 until the passing of the Anatomy Act in 1832,[12] grave-robbers had been active in any area where corpses were required for dissection. Body-snatchers were employed to obtain fresh dead bodies to keep the dissecting-tables well supplied with subjects for the anatomists: they were daring, bold, quick, and extremely efficient. Sir Astley Cooper,[13] the leading surgeon-anatomist of Regency London, boasted that he

[5] General Burial-Grounds Association (1825), 1-48. [6] Papers in the archives of the General Cemetery Company. [7] £30,000,000 would probably be insufficient as an equivalent today, so the project was very ambitious. [8] *Sic.* [9] General Burial-Grounds Association (1825), 1-48. [10] Ibid. [11] *See* Ruth Richardson: 'The Life, Death, Burial and Resurrection Company: UK metropolitan burial 1800-1900', *in* Andalucía (1993), 579, 582, and n. 16. See footnote 3 of this Chapter. [12] An Act for Regulating Schools of Anatomy, 2 & 3 Will. IV, c. 75. [13] Sir Astley Paston Cooper (1768-1841).

could obtain *anyone's* body, no matter whose, and from whatever station in life. Ready money was always the key. 'The law', that 'indefatigable dissector' declared, 'only enhances the price and does not prevent the exhumation'.[14]

Thanks to the demand created by Cooper and his many competitors, body-snatchers could make a good living in all the major towns of the Georgian period, but most particularly in London, which (like Edinburgh) was a centre of anatomical tuition, exploration, and demonstration. All the major teaching-hospitals had busy anatomy-schools, and several smaller independent schools offered private anatomical tuition at competitive rates. Every year these establishments educated hundreds of students in the science of anatomy and the art of dissection. All the schools operated on a commercial basis: students paid fees for tuition, and were also obliged to purchase the human materials with which they were taught.

The 'resurrection-men', as the body-snatchers were called, usually worked at night, in churchyards and other open-air burial-grounds. Day-time reconnaissance kept them informed as to where fresh bodies had been buried, how deep were their graves, and whether more than one corpse might be obtained by one spate of digging. The tools of their trade were simple: wooden shovels to lessen noise; a rope with hooks; a crow-bar to pull up the coffin-lid; a few capacious sacks; and (sometimes, but not invariably) a lantern with a shade.

A hole would be dug at the head of a freshly-filled grave. The soil, being uncompacted, would be easy to shift, and would be heaped on the sacking. Once visible, the coffin-lid would be forced: the earth on the rest of the coffin served as a counter-weight, so when the crow-bar or hooks were used, the lid would break across, and the body could be hoisted out with a hook through the shroud. Any clothing on the body would be thrown back into the desecrated grave, and the earth quickly replaced by tipping up the sacking. It was important to leave the grave in good order: if local suspicions were aroused, future attempts on the same graveyard could meet with considerable danger, as public loathing of body-snatchers was great. The body would be sacked up, and the men would make their escape, usually to their look-out who waited nearby with a cart.

Expansion of the population of London and other major cities in the 18th and early 19th centuries was so great that the old parish churchyards, and even the out-of-town fields purchased as additional burial-grounds, had become terribly overcrowded. In many districts, coffins were stacked in deep graves, the topmost lying not far below the surface of the soil.[15] Ordinary people could do little to protect their dead, other than to make work difficult for the body-snatchers by mixing straw with the earth returned to the grave in order to clog the resurrectionists' shovels; or by sharing stints of 'watching' by the graveside.

The better-off could purchase greater security, and the market rose to the occasion. Better-quality coffins were described as 'stout', and extra rows of coffin-nails were signs of social status. Double and triple coffins, with a lead shell, were bought by wealthier members of society, and, of course, lead coffins were often used (but not invariably) in vault or crypt entombment. Ingenious inventors devised and patented special coffin-

[14] *D.N.B.*, iv, (1917), 1062. [15] It was in the 1820s that the population of London increased by about a fifth, and the ghastly conditions prevailing in already crammed burial-grounds could no longer be ignored. It has been estimated (Sheppard [*Ed.*] [1973], 335) that some of the older graveyards in London had absorbed about 3,000 bodies per acre (0.4047 hectares), and the *average* number of new burials per acre was often in excess of 200 per annum. With such high-density burial the problem was that decomposition and dissolution of corpses were incomplete before new interments took place, and in some grossly overcrowded grounds bodies had hardly started to decompose before they were disturbed. Horrible methods involving burning of coffins and bodies, shovelling heaps of quarried flesh aside to make room, and other disgusting practices were much-attested, and make sickening reading (*See Parliamentary Papers* (1843): *Report on the Practice of Interment in Towns*, xii, 27, 133).

bands, locks, screws, and other reinforcements. Cast-iron coffins[16] were also manufactured, but widespread use of these was discouraged by the Church because of the pressure on space, and permanent coffins that would not decay could only exacerbate what was already a major problem.

Private burial-grounds appealed to those who could afford to indulge a desire for burial more secure than anything the churchyards could offer, but whether or not they provided real security is a moot point. It seems that owners of several private-enterprise burial-grounds probably worked in collusion with the 'resurrectionists', and that in at least one instance a profitable private London burial-ground was actually owned by an anatomist, who had a double income from those who paid for the supposedly 'secure' plots *and* from his medical students who paid for the remarkably fresh dead bodies.[17]

Many London burial-grounds were provided with watchers' huts to protect night-watchmen from the elements: the churchyard of St Paul's, Covent Garden, for example, was provided with a sentry-box, as was that of St Mary, Rotherhithe, but watchmen were not well paid and so could be bribed or intimidated by gangs of body-snatchers, who would use force if necessary. At the additional burial-ground at Tyburn belonging to St George's, Hanover Square, double walls were erected, allowing the ground to be patrolled with or without dogs: two walls made a fast escape difficult, and a sacked-up body would have been a serious impediment to a gang if attacked by dogs and armed watchmen.

The well-to-do endeavoured to avoid interment in any open-air burial-ground. Although vaults under churches were expensive, their comparative security meant that entombment in them was very much sought after. The very rich could afford to be carried out of London to be buried in purpose-built mausolea in the grounds of country estates, or entombed in family vaults in country churches where elaborate funerary monuments could afterwards be erected to commemorate the dead. Security and burial locations (as far away from anatomy-schools as possible) were much in demand.

However, as Sir Astley Cooper made clear, whatever efforts were made to protect the dead, nobody could be completely certain of their efficacy. Should a specific body be wanted, the body-snatchers could usually find ways to obtain it. There is no doubt that, on occasion, bodies were stolen to order. One such, a giant[18] whose skeleton was wanted for an anatomical museum, is said to have cost between £500 and £800 to obtain, an enormous sum then. In another case, Cooper wished to know how a specific surgical technique had helped a patient survive an otherwise fatal condition for many years. His men went out to a village in Suffolk and fetched the body back to London.

The widespread horror of body-snatchers and dissection, together with measures taken to ensure that bodies were kept out of the clutches of the anatomists, suggest that a strong residue of pre-Reformation beliefs or feelings had survived. Belief in the after-life was closely associated with the perception that it depended on the resurrection of the body, and the whole, undissected body at that.[19] It is also curious that this was true of most religious persuasions, apart from those of the most aggressively utilitarian hue.

[16] A patent cast-iron coffin survives in the crypt of St Bride's church, Fleet Street, London, where it was found.
[17] *The Lancet* (1828-9), i, 563, quoted in Richardson (1987). *See also* Richardson (1993), 578-9, 582, and footnote 3 of the present Chapter. [18] The Irish Giant's skeleton remains a prize exhibit in the Anatomical Museum at the Royal College of Surgeons in Lincoln's Inn Fields. *See*, for estimates of its cost, Royal College of Surgeons of England (1971): *Descriptive Catalogue of the Physiological Series in the Hunterian Museum* (London: Royal College of Surgeons of England), 199-204. [19] Sentences passed on criminals often specified that their bodies should be 'punished' further by being dissected, so a body 'snatched' from a grave was perceived as suffering further insult by being 'punished' and the dead person 'criminalised' as well as having survival in an after-life jeopardised. This fear survived well into the Victorian period, and there are published accounts of bodies being kept until they were too far decomposed to be of any use to the anatomists. Fear of premature burial also encouraged the keeping of corpses until unmistakable signs of decomposition had occurred: this was true of all classes of society. This custom, in poorer circumstances, did nothing to improve the health of those in close proximity to the bodies. *See* Richardson (1987), *passim*.

The 'Life, Death, Burial, and Resurrection Company'

London's readiness to embrace Carden's vision doubtless was not encouraged by a spoof 'Prospectus' for a fictitious joint-stock Company to be called the 'Life, Death, Burial, and Resurrection Company',[20] clearly a lampoon on Carden's ideas. This spoof purported to raise capital of £100,000,000 by issuing shares of one pound each, in order:

> To rob Death of its Terrors, and make it delightful
> To give up your breath, and abolish the frightful
> Old custom of lying defunct in your shroud
> Surrounded by relatives sobbing aloud ...

Père-Lachaise, as in Carden's first *Prospectus*, was recruited in order to 'make it quite pleasant to die' and be buried in a wondrous cemetery from which even decomposition would be prevented by blasts of steam to:

> boil all worms and grubs in their holes
> And preserve from decay every part but your souls.

The poetaster continued in jocular vein:

> First, then, we propose with the graces of Art,
> Like our Parisian friends, to make ev'ry Tomb smart;
> And, by changing the feelings of funeral terrors,
> Remove what remain'd of old Catholic errors.

There were several allusions in that last line, for, as was explained in Chapter I, those who thought about these matters were very much aware that burial of the dead in France (and Scotland, for that matter) far from churches was prompted by a hidden programme of weakening old beliefs and the power of traditional religion.[21] In England the demand for burial-grounds separated from those of the Anglican Established Church were prompted, not by concern for hygiene and decency, but from the desire of Nonconformists to have their own distinct grounds where Church of England clergy had no jurisdiction. So 'anticlericalism' in England was mostly a phenomenon of antipathy towards the Establishment, and the Established Church in particular, which claimed to be part of the 'Holy, Catholick, and Apostolick Church'. In Dissenting or Nonconformist circles, therefore, 'old Catholic errors' might be seen as not just those lingering from the pre-Reformation past, but within the Anglican Church itself. It should also be remembered that a fair part of the impetus towards establishing *cemeteries* came from Dissenters, and much of the opposition came from the Established clergy.

Of course, the financial aspects were not ignored, for:

> In this age of projectors, when bubbles[22] are spread
> With illusive attractions to bother each head,
> When bulls,[23] bears,[24] and jobbers[25] all quit Capel-court[26]
> To become Speculators, and join in the sport,
> Who can wonder, when Interest with Intellect clashes,
> We should have a new Club to dispose of our ashes?

[20] Anonymous (1825) quoted by Richardson in Andalucía (1993), 577-82. *See* footnote 3 of this Chapter.
[21] Anticlericalism was specifically part of the French programme to found cemeteries. [22] A term signifying a dodgy enterprise, something deceptive or transient. [23] Persons who seek to raise the price of stocks and speculate on a rise: the opposite of *bears*. [24] Persons who sell stocks for delivery at a future date, anticipating a fall in price: the opposite of *bulls*. [25] Persons who buy and sell stocks: also known as *brokers*. [26] A dig at lawyers who gave up their profession to concentrate on financial speculation.

But the anonymous author was well-versed in the literature concerning garden-cemeteries, as the following proves, for the new cemetery would feature:

> A diversified, soothing, commixture of trees,
> Umbrageous and fann'd by the perfumed breeze;
> With alcoves, and bowers, and fish-ponds, and shrubs,
> Select, as in life, from intrusion of scrubs.

The word 'scrubs' may not be as familiar today as it once was, but a 'scrub' means, among other things, a person of mean presence, an insignificant fellow, or a person of little account or poor appearance. The fact that a 'scrub' can also mean a low, stunted tree or shrub might wryly divert attention from the main thrust of the squib; the poetaster was referring to the exclusive nature of Carden's proposals, which addressed only those who could afford burial-fees sufficient to generate a profit. Only the upper, professional, middle, and better-off artisan classes would be sure of obtaining graves in the new burial-ground. Those further down the social scale would have to be buried in the overcrowded parish burial-grounds as before. This imputation was to prove largely true, as the early history of Kensal Green cemetery shows.

The plan to establish the bogus 'Life, Death, Burial, and Resurrection Company' included provision for entertainment in the form of banquets laid on by the Directors at which copious draughts of *Vin de Grave* and *Lachryma Christi* would wash down the food. A fashionable clientèle would also be diverted by concerts performed by the 'Opera Corps', and respectability was to be conferred on the Company by aristocrats such as 'Lord Graves' and a Board (under the presidency of 'Lord Coffin') consisting of members of the College of Surgeons. The author of the spoof clearly understood how to cast doubt on the whole of Carden's enterprise.

Drawing on the plethora of publications about cemeteries appearing at the time, the spoof turned to the question of the provision of garlands and flowers:

> ... artificial, 'tis true,
> But very like Nature in a general view.

Furthermore, a Committee of Taste would ensure that:

> The inscriptions and epitaphs, elegies, too, would all
> ... be poetical, lively, and new.

The insistence on 'newness' struck a note familiar from the more serious publications.[27] The Committee was to ensure that, in the fictional cemetery, tombstone-designs that featured skulls, bones, or any allusions to Death would have no place, just as they were to be banned from Carden's real proposals. Bodies could also be buried in fancy-dress rather than in shrouds to enhance the determined, even desperate atmosphere of gaiety, and (on payment of a fee, of course) the Company would make arrangements for the revival of corpses, but only if shares rose in value: if they did not, then it had to be accepted that all these claims were based on a '"bubble", like others, of lies'.[28]

Whoever was responsible for the spoof 'Prospectus' certainly had an ear close to the ground, as it were, for the cemetery promotion was portrayed as appealing to fashionable society, and several well-known architects (all of whom would later have dealings with the General Cemetery Company) were actually named. The spoof declared:

[27] And late 20th-century advertising. [28] Richardson (1993), 579.

Our aim is to blend in the Picturesque style
Smirke, Soane, Nash, and Wyatville in one pile.[29]

Although Carden's *Prospectus* made no claims to be supported by The Humane Society (which promoted artificial respiration as a means of reviving the dead), the spoof did just that. However, many of the other topics derided in 'The Life, Death, Burial, and Resurrection Company's' bogus *Prospectus* also appear in Carden's publication which, as we have seen, lauded the 'celebrated' cemetery of Père-Lachaise, its beneficial effects on those who visited it, and stressed the 'mildness' of the 'precepts' of a religion that operated 'not by its terrors', but by soothing associations, and allusions to sleep and peace. The anonymous squib certainly ridiculed Carden's efforts, and cannot have done The General Burial-Grounds Association any good at all. Unfortunately, the spoof's reference to 'bubbles' was borne out in fact: the financial crisis of 1825-6 scuppered Carden's scheme, and the whole project was to be shelved for nearly five years.

The Re-Launch of Carden's Proposals

Undeterred by his failure in 1825 to establish his 'General Burial-Grounds Association', Carden revived the idea by convening a meeting at his Chambers (No. 3 Inner Temple Lane) on Monday, 8 February 1830, 'for the purpose of ascertaining the best mode of improving the System of Burial in the Metropolis', with Andrew Spottiswoode, M.P. in the Chair.[30]

From the beginning, the social standing of Carden's Provisional Committee was eminently respectable,[31] and included Carden himself, the Reverend James Harris, H. L. Smale, T. Wilson, William Rothery,[32] J. Stephens, and Robert William Sievier.[33] It was formed 'for the purpose of making the various arrangements', with power to add to its numbers if necessary.[34]

It was resolved that the 'present condition of the places of interment within the Metropolis' was 'offensive to public decency and injurious to public health', and that the space allotted for the purpose was 'wholly inadequate'. Furthermore, 'the numerous public improvements which from time to time' became necessary, 'afforded *no security*[35] against the frequent removal of the dead'. It was decided that 'some other system of interment should be adopted', and that the 'evils' of the current 'system' could 'only be avoided by constructing Cemeteries out of the Town'. To this end, it had become 'expedient that a Company should be formed for the purpose of forming a Public Cemetery or Cemeteries'.[36] Thus, at this stage, there were subtle changes in terminology, and 'burial-ground' was dropped in favour of 'cemetery'. Carden had used the rather old-fashioned term 'Burial-Ground' in the 1825 *Prospectus*. It was realised that the term had rather vile and vulgar associations, whereas 'Cemetery' suggested an altogether better tone. To those sufficiently cultured to recognise its Classical derivations (from the Greek κοιμητήριον or Latin *coemeterium*), it meant a 'dormitory' or a 'sleeping-place'.

[29] 'Smirke' was Robert Smirke (1780-1867), architect of the British Museum (1823-46) and other important public buildings; 'Soane' was John Soane (1753-1837), architect of the Bank of England (1788-1833) and his own remarkable house at 13 Lincoln's Inn Fields (1812-13); 'Nash' was John Nash (1752-1835), the designer of Regent Street and Regent's Park (with its several terraces and Park Crescent), and architect of numerous country houses; and 'Wyatville' was Jeffry Wyatville (1766-1840), the architect of the remodelling of Windsor Castle, Berkshire (1824-40). Smirke, Soane, and Wyatville were all knighted later. [30] Minutes of the Provisional Committee for the General Cemetery Company in the possession of the Company (8 February 1830), 1. [31] Spottiswoode (1786-1866) was Member of Parliament for Colchester and a partner in the printing firm of Eyre & Spottiswoode which made a fortune out of printing Bibles. [32] William Rothery (1775-1864) was Referee of the Court of Admiralty on Slave Trade matters (1821-60). [33] Robert William Sievier (1794-1865), sculptor, inventor, and engineer. [34] Minutes of the Provisional Committee of the General Cemetery Company (8 February 1830), 2. [35] Editor's italics. [36] Minutes of the Provisional Committee of the General Cemetery Company (8 February 1830), 1.

The Provisional Committee and its Business

Andrew Spottiswoode chaired many of the early meetings, before the Company proper had come into being, and the Provisional Committee included Carden and Sievier right from the start. Early attempts to interest well-known architects in the scheme, surprisingly, were rebuffed, but slowly the Committee got its act together once C. B. Bowman[37] had been appointed Solicitor and Secretary. Members of the Committee had to be holders of five shares each, and with every five shares 'tickets of precedence' would be given 'according to priority of payment'.[38] A deposit of £2 10*s*. was to be paid 'forthwith' on each share, and early deposits from Committee members and their friends were to be 'solely applicable to the expenses actually incurred by the Committee'. Carden was appointed Treasurer in February 1830, and Bowman withdrew from membership of the Committee as this would have been inconsistent with his holding the position of Solicitor and Secretary.[39] At the same meeting it was resolved 'that Mr Wyatt[40] be written to, requesting his attendance', and that he be 'nominated as architect' to the Company.

Then there was the question of the site for the cemetery. It was decided that Wyatt, Spottiswoode, Bowman, Carden, and Rothery should 'view the site proposed'. At the next meeting[41] attended by Carden (in the Chair), Rothery, Spottiswoode, Sievier, and Bowman, it seems that matters had been somewhat rushed, for Wyatt had declined to act as architect, although he recommended 'another Gentleman'. It was agreed that various other persons should join the Committee, including the architect Charles Fowler.[42] There seems to have been difficulty in obtaining members for the Provisional Committee: several names were recommended by existing members, added to the list, and subsequently withdrawn. More than one meeting had to be adjourned because the necessary quorum of three members did not materialise.[43] Approaches were also made to the 'heads of various sects of religion' (the Chief Rabbi, the Roman Catholics, etc.) for support,[44] but reactions were at first lukewarm.

Soon afterwards[45] a letter from Spottiswoode was read, in which he suggested the dropping of the name by which Carden's group had been known (The General Burial-Grounds Association) and the official adoption of the title 'General Cemetery Company'. This proposal was accepted, and it was resolved that the Company should 'henceforth be designated "The General Cemetery Company"'.[46] This innovation was deemed essential since the much-trumpeted success of Père-Lachaise in Paris. The fact that Spottiswoode seems to have been behind it is important in the light of what was to happen later. Carden presented estimates of 'the probable expense of watching and guarding the ground' even before any site had been purchased: it is clear that security was a major preoccupation of the fledgling Company.[47]

The problem of inquorate meetings seems to have caused difficulties, and it was not until 20 April 1830 that Carden, Spottiswoode, and Sievier were able to consider a 'form of Prospectus' drawn up by the Secretary (Bowman). From that time the Provisional Committee was in touch with the Companies in Liverpool responsible for the establishment of the Low Hill Necropolis and St James's cemetery, so it is clear such precedents were important and helpful. Communications were received from Liverpool 'relative to the Companies instituted in that Town for establishing two Cemeteries detached from Churches', and it was noted that 'one of the Companies at Liverpool [St

[37] Of Milk Street, Cheapside. [38] Minutes of the Provisional Committee (15 February 1830), 4. [39] Ibid. [40] This was Benjamin Dean Wyatt (1775-1855), Surveyor of Westminster Abbey (1813-27), and architect of the Theatre Royal, Drury Lane (1811-12); York (later Stafford, and now Lancaster) House, St James's (1825-7); and the Duke of York's column, Carlton Gardens (1831-4). [41] Minutes of the Provisional Committee (18 February 1830), 5. [42] Fowler (1792-1867) resided at that time at No. 1 Gordon Square. [43] Minutes of the Provisional Committee (20 February 1830), 6. [44] Ibid. (18 February 1830), 5, 6. [45] Ibid. (26 February 1830), 7-8. [46] Ibid. [47] Ibid.

2.1 'Monument de la Famille Bouchée' in Père-Lachaise cemetery. The tomb on the right with the primitivist square Doric columns and curious acroteria embellished with faces is clearly the model for the Gordon tomb in Kensal Green cemetery. Drawn by Joseph Nash (1809-78) and engraved by W. Faithorn under the direction of A. C. Pugin. From Pugin and Heath (1829-31) (*ECJSC*).

James's] was formed under the sanction of and consecrated by the present Bishop of London when Bishop of Chester'.[48]

It was resolved that Carden should 'apply to the Bishop of London to ascertain his sentiments respecting the operations of the [General Cemetery] Company'. The Secretary should also apply to the Company in Manchester for information as to the institution, fees, regulations, &c., of that Company, and a Petition should be prepared by Carden to be presented to the House of Commons. On 26 April Carden reported[49] that he had met the Bishop of London who 'approved of the object of the Company and promised to recommend it to the consideration of the Clergy of his Diocese'.[50] The Bishop had also 'seen the Archbishop of Canterbury' and explained to him the nature of the undertaking. His Grace requested that a *Prospectus* might be sent to him as soon as it became available. The draft 1830 *Prospectus* and share receipt were shown to the Provisional Committee under the Chairmanship of Spottiswoode, and it was agreed to print them. Two days later, however, the draft *Prospectus* was again altered,[51] but the Minutes are uninformative about the nature of any changes.

Unfortunately the archives do not tell us about the authorship of the *Prospectus*, but the fact that Spottiswoode chaired so many meetings suggests that he had a major say in its final form. The document appears to have originated with Carden, but it was subjected to several changes by the Provisional Committee before it was finalised. The Minutes give no hint of disagreements at that stage (April 1830), and the many alterations may have been only fine-tuning, but not a few attempts were made at getting the *Prospectus* right, and it seems, in the end, to have been a 'committee-job'.

Some architects, prompted, perhaps, by the work of the French Academies in Paris and Rome, had begun to interest themselves in the problems of designing for death, including Augustus Charles Pugin, who exhibited three proposals for cemeteries at the Royal Academy in 1826-7,[52] one of which was intended for Carden's favoured Primrose Hill site. Pugin also helped to promote Père-Lachaise cemetery, views of which appear in

48 This was Charles James Blomfield (1786-1857), Bishop of Chester (1824-8) and Bishop of London (1828-56).
49 Minutes of the Provisional Committee (16 April 1830), 10-11. 50 Ibid., 11. 51 Ibid. (28 April 1830), 12. 52 For A. C. Pugin (1769-1832) *see* Colvin (1995), 788; *D.N.B.*, **xvi** (1917), 449; *Royal Academy Catalogue* (1827), No. 958.

Paris and its Environs (1829-31), a book he produced with Charles Heath (**2.1**).[53] It seems that, around this time, Pugin became allied in some way with Carden, and so was to be associated with the early history of Kensal Green cemetery, as we shall see. It is likely, however, that the Carden-Pugin link was forged by a mutual enthusiasm for the Gothic style: Pugin's importance in the early history of the Gothic Revival is well known.[54]

Architectural matters appear to have subsided into the doldrums when Fowler resigned 'on account of other engagements', but membership of the Committee was strengthened by Thomas Wilson[55] and Frederick Bull,[56] both Carden nominees. By the end of April 1830, however, another architect, Lewis Nockalls Cottingham,[57] was introduced by Carden to the Provisional Committee. Clearly, Carden was getting through a fair smattering of possible architects for his scheme. It could well be significant that Cottingham was brought in by Carden, for he too was a pioneering Gothic Revivalist, whereas Fowler was a staunch Classicist. Reading between the lines, it would seem that Carden was trying to promote a Gothic style for the proposed cemetery buildings. If so, there were others on the Committee who were opposed to Gothic, a style that, in 1830 (before the publication of A.W.N. Pugin's [1812-52] polemics[58]), had not yet acquired the moral imperatives implicit in its association with Christianity. Gothic was just another architectural style on offer from the available palette.

It is interesting that although the architects Wyatt, Fowler, and Cottingham were proposed for membership of the Provisional Committee, none of them remained long. It is not possible to ascertain why they appear to have taken fright so quickly, pleading pressure of work or simply 'declining' any further association. One might have thought that the opportunity to design a cemetery and its buildings would have been grasped eagerly by any architect, so there must have been something off-putting. It could have been incompatible personalities, the embryonic nature of the proposals, perceptions that the success of the venture was deemed unlikely, or the fact that the Company had not yet been incorporated, nor had it so far acquired a site, that caused potential designers to disassociate themselves. Possibly, too, architects keen to get ecclesiastical work steered clear because a controversy was looming with clergy concerning a feared loss of burial-fees occasioned by the establishment of cemeteries.

However, on 30 April 1830, Spottiswoode introduced the architect John Griffith[59] as a member of the Provisional Committee, an event that was to have momentous consequences. It was Griffith, more than anyone, who was to determine the cool, Grecian, understated character for the architecture of the cemetery as it was eventually realised. It is probably significant that Griffith was brought in by Spottiswoode, who was obviously[60] a far more important personality in the history of the foundation of the cemetery than has hitherto been perceived. Few of Carden's introductions had remained for any significant period. Had Carden been jealously guarding his 'baby'? We do not know, but the records suggest that his nominees saw a problem and bolted. It may well be that Carden was an 'ideas' man, and Spottiswoode provided the business acumen, guiding the Provisional Committee in the direction it eventually took. It certainly looks as thought there was what today we would call a 'power-struggle' going on, that Carden was over-vehement and emotional and favoured decorative Gothic, and that Spottiswoode, being a City man, favoured something more solid and substantial best represented by the Classical style. It should also be remembered that Regency Gothic was

[53] Pugin and Heath (1829-31), *passim*. For Charles Heath (1785-1848) *see D.N.B.*, **ix** (1917), 340-1. [54] Colvin (1995), 788. [55] Of Montague Street, Montague Square. There seems to be some confusion about the identity of Wilson, some sources stating that he was Thomas Willson (born *c*.1780), of whom more anon, but the Wilson of the Provisional Committee does not appear to have been Willson at all. Indeed, Wilson was not an architect. [56] Of Holles Street, Cavendish Square. [57] Cottingham (1787-1847), resided at Bazing Place, 43 Waterloo Bridge Road. *See* Colvin (1995), 271-2 and Myles (1996) *passim*. [58] Pugin (1843, 1853, 1973). [59] John Griffith (1796-1888), of 16 Finsbury Place South, London. [60] From the records of the General Cemetery Company.

associated with frivolous fripperies, with George IV when he was Prince Regent, with the fantastic and the insubstantial: it was altogether lacking in appropriate *gravitas*. Such differences of opinion, or power-struggles, would have been evident to all members of the Provisional Committee, and to all who attended even one or two meetings.

It should also be remembered that the Classical style of architecture, and especially the Neoclassical masterpieces of architects such as Dance[61] and Soane,[62] were associated with security, stability, and inviolability. Therefore a severe Classicism would have had associations with one of the main aims of the Provisional Committee — to provide a secure place of sepulture that would keep out body-snatchers. The Gothic style did not then have associations with security, and it was clear that fanciful Regency Gothick, with its insubstantial materials and unhistorical jokiness, would not create an impression appropriate for the purpose.

Meanwhile, a great deal of lobbying was going on to 'soften up' opinion before Carden's Petition was presented to the House of Commons. Once more the *Prospectus* was read, altered, and ordered to be printed[63] for approval at the following meeting. But it was not finally settled until 6 May 1830, by which time a new clause had been added limiting the responsibilities of the shareholders to the value of their shares. Like the first *Prospectus* of 1825, the new one gave priority to security matters, listing first among the General Cemetery Company's aims the provision of places of interment SECURE FROM VIOLATION.[64] The text assured readers that the ground would 'be laid out and planted, ... surrounded with an ornamental enclosure of sufficient height, and so walled and guarded as to prevent the possibility of the sepulchres being *violated or disturbed*'.[65]

By 3 May 1830 the Provisional Committee had resolved that the capital of the proposed Company should be reduced from £300,000 to £200,000, and Carden saw his ambitious dreams of a splendid national cemetery fading away.[66] Furthermore, although Griffith[67] was probably very tactful and diplomatic, he was not an architectural 'name' in the league of Wyatt, Fowler, or even Cottingham,[68] and, being Spottiswoode's nominee, Carden may have resented him. To strengthen his position, therefore, Carden introduced[69] his brother, Robert Walter Carden,[70] to the Provisional Committee.

It was decided that shares should be fixed at £25 each, and the *Prospectus* was 'settled' at last. It was decided to hold a meeting at *The Freemasons' Tavern* in Great Queen Street 'to ascertain' the mood of the public, with 'Lord Viscount Milton' in the Chair. This was the distinguished title of Charles William Wentworth Fitzwilliam,[71]

[61] George Dance (1741-85), architect of Newgate Gaol (1770-84 – demolished 1902), a building that suggested by its architecture that it was secure. [62] (Sir) John Soane's Bank of England (1788-1833 – rebuilt 1930-40) was a Classical building designed primarily for security to keep the London Mob out. [63] Minutes of the Provisional Committee (30 April 1830), 13. Again, this seems to have been a committee-job. [64] In capital letters in the original. [65] Editor's italics. [66] Minutes of the Provisional Committee (3 May 1830), 14. [67] Not very much is known about Griffith. Colvin (1995), 433, only mentions him *en passant*, even though most of Griffith's works were erected before Colvin's cut-off date of 1840. Felstead, Franklin, and Pinfield (1993), 381, are more informative: he was elected FRIBA in 1842, and his obituary was published in *The Builder*, **iv** (10 November 1888), 345. He died at 6 Hanover Terrace, Regent's Park. [68] Cottingham, as noted above, had been introduced by Carden himself on 28 April 1830, but was removed from the Provisional Committee for non-attendance in June. *See* Minutes of the Provisional Committee (28 April 1830), 12, and entries for June 1830. [69] Minutes of the Provisional Committee (12 May 1830), 16. [70] Robert Walter Carden (1801-88) was later Lord Mayor of London (1857-8), M.P. for Gloucester (1857-9) and Barnstaple (1880-5), and was created 1st Baronet 1887. [71] Viscount Milton (1786-1857) became 3rd Earl Fitzwilliam in 1833. As Viscount Milton he was returned to the House of Commons for Malton, and in 1807 for Yorkshire, which he represented through five successive Parliaments. In 1830 he was elected for Peterborough, in 1831 (with Lord Althorp) for Northamptonshire, and in 1832 for the northern division of the same county. Described as a 'man of chivalrous honour, high moral courage, and perfect independence and disinterestedness', he became a convert to Parliamentary Reform, was an early advocate of the repeal of the Corn Laws (when his own family fortunes depended mainly on the land), and, with his father (William Wentworth, 2nd Earl Fitzwilliam [1748-1833]), openly condemned the conduct of the Manchester magistrates after the 'Peterloo massacre' of 1819. This cost him the Lord-Lieutenancy of the West Riding. He was created a Knight of the Garter in 1851 and Deputy-Lieutenant for Northamptonshire in 1853. In the Upper House he generally supported the Liberals. An intellectual, he co-edited the correspondence of Edmund Burke (1729-97), which was published in 1844 in four volumes. In 1847 he advocated the application of Imperial resources to relieve Ireland. His support for the General Cemetery Company was entirely typical of a high-minded, aristocratic landowner, who sacrificed his own self-interest for the common good. *See D.N.B.*, **vii** (1917), 224-5.

whose presence would undoubtedly add tone to the proceedings, and augment the Company's respectability. Meanwhile, Carden was involved in complicated negotiations with the Eyre estate for a site for the cemetery near Primrose Hill, at St John's Wood. Discussions had resulted in some sort of 'agreement',[72] which would indicate that the site was more than a twinkle in Carden's eye.

In due course Carden's Petition to the House of Commons of May 1830 received plenty of publicity in the newspapers,[73] and was widely reported.[74] Spottiswoode presented the Petition, almost inaudibly, according to some sources,[75] which led to reports that it concerned a new road from Waterloo Bridge to the New Road, and that this road would be of great 'benefit in increasing the health, comfort, and intercourse of the citizens of London'.[76] This unfortunate misinterpretation had to be corrected in the papers, and it was made clear that Spottiswoode had been mumbling about the need for a new cemetery, not a new road at all. Several speakers in the House supported the petition (once they had gathered what Spottiswoode was talking about), some going so far as to argue for the prohibition of all burials in the metropolis. It was ordered that Carden's Petition should be printed.

Among many other things, the Petition stated that the number of interments in the metropolis each year 'was not less than 40,000', and described the 'places of sepulture' as 'offensive to public decency and dangerous to the health of the people'. Carden was supported by a letter in *The Morning Advertiser* from John Claudius Loudon,[77] dated 14 May 1830, Bayswater, who suggested that there 'should be several burial-grounds, all, as far as practicable, equi-distant from each other, and from what may be considered the centre of the metropolis'; that they should be 'regularly laid out and planted with every sort of hardy trees and shrubs; and that in interring the ground be used on a plan similar to that adopted in the burial-ground in Munich, and not left to chance like Pere la Chaise'.[78] He went on to propose that the new cemeteries 'and every other burial-ground in the country' could be made, 'at no expenses whatever', into 'botanic gardens; for, were nurserymen and gardeners invited', he was certain 'they would supply, every one to his own parish, gratis, as many hardy trees and shrubs, and herbaceous plants, as room could be found for. It would be for the clergy and the vestries to be at the expenses of

[72] Minutes of the Provisional Committee. (12 May 1830), 16. [73] *The Morning Herald* (14 May 1830), *The Times* (14 May 1830), *The Morning Chronicle* (14 May 1830), and others. [74] *The* Herald (14 May 1830. [75] *Morning Advertiser* (14 & 15 May 1830), in which Carden is referred to as 'J. F. Carding'. [76] *Public Ledger* (14 & 15 May 1830). [77] J. C. Loudon (1783-1843) was a distinguished Scots agriculturalist, encyclopaedist, landscape-gardener, horticulturist, inventor, editor of journals, architect, and critic. His immensely successful *Encyclopaedia of Gardening* (1822) was influential, as was his *Encyclopaedia of Cottage, Farm, and Villa Architecture* (1833). His *The Architectural Magazine* (1834-8) was the first British periodical solely devoted to architecture. He laid out the Botanic Gardens in Birmingham and designed the Derby Arboretum (1839-41). His works on plantations and on the theory and practice of landscape-gardening were important, and his publications dealing with improvements in hothouses (1805) and country residences (1806) contained many innovations and ideas. He invented an iron glazing-bar that made curved glazing of hothouses possible: the principles of his inventions were the bases of the more famous works by Joseph Paxton (1801-65) at Chatsworth and (ultimately) at the Crystal Palace of the 1851 Great Exhibition. He designed a 'double detached villa' for himself at 3 and 5 Porchester Terrace, London (1823-4), an advanced and convenient building erected with the profits of *The Encyclopaedia of Gardening*, and where he edited *The Gardener's Magazine* from 1826, which had a profound effect on taste and expertise. In that journal he published numerous pieces on cemeteries, and in 1843 brought out *On the Laying Out, Planting, and Managing of Cemeteries; and on the Improvement of Churchyards*, probably the most exhaustive book ever written on the subject, which included detailed ideas for the landscaping of cemeteries. He produced designs for three cemeteries: Histon Road, Cambridge; the Bath Abbey cemetery; and Southampton cemetery (all 1842-3). He married the remarkable Jane Webb (1807-58), author of a futuristic novel (1827) about an England in the 21st century, complete with universal air-travel, world-wide instant communications, intolerable burdens of taxation, endemic inflation, and fatuous politicians. J. C. Loudon and his wife are buried in Kensal Green cemetery. His grave [4547/74/PS] is marked by a chaste granite urn set on a plain pedestal (**5.9**). For Loudon *see* Gloag (1970) and Simo (1988). [78] By 'left to chance' Loudon meant that unless a rigid system of numbering of plots and geometric layouts was adopted for cemeteries, locating graves would always be unnecessarily difficult. He advocated laying out grounds in 'double beds with green paths between', and other measures rather than placing reliance on 'imaginary squares or parallelograms': in short, he proposed a clear geometrical layout in which it would be unnecessary to walk over any grave to get to another, and that each plot would be clearly identifiable within a precise arrangement of paths and burial-spaces. *See* Loudon (1843, 1981), 17-31.

rearing these trees if they chose ... if they' got them 'for nothing'. Moreover, Loudon insisted that the 'burial-places for the metropolis ought to be made sufficiently large to serve at the same time as breathing places', and that most churchyards in the country were 'too small for the increased population'.[79] Loudon himself was soon to write and publish his series of articles on laying out and planning cemeteries in *The Gardener's Magazine*, which were later collected and published as a book,[80] in which he emphasised that the grave should rightfully remain inviolate from body-snatchers or from any other agents, and proposed various means to ensure this.

Spottiswoode[81] now introduced the banker John Dean Paul of Rodburgh, Bart.,[82] to the Committee, and proposed that Messrs Snow, Paul, & Paul (of which Paul was a partner) should become bankers to the Company. This was a most important introduction. Sir John's son, John Dean Paul, was later to serve on the Board of the General Cemetery Company. Father and son were to become closely involved in both the affairs of Kensal Green cemetery and the Society for Improving the Condition of the Labouring Classes[83] with which the Prince Consort, Queen Victoria, Lord Shaftesbury, and the architect Henry Roberts[84] were to become intimately involved.

All that, however, was in the future. It is important, nevertheless, to recognise that the Paul family was solidly connected with the aristocracy and landed gentry. In this respect they[85] were typical of the founders of Kensal Green cemetery, in that they were all apparently eminently respectable, either with sound pedigrees, or, like Sievier, had risen by talent to make names for themselves. Sievier made his reputation as a sculptor, but subsequently abandoned art for developing new technologies, and became a Fellow of the Royal Society. In short, the leading members of the General Cemetery Company were well-connected men of substance. Paul and Viscount Milton became Provisional Trustees of the General Cemetery Company, and their names were listed in the 1830 *Prospectus* alongside those of Spottiswoode and Carden. Backing for the project was also obtained from the Earl of Cardigan.[86]

Copies of the new *Prospectus* were sent to the 'Ministers of Dissenting Congregations, Architects, Surveyors, Sculptors, Bankers, the Clergy of the Established Church, and Assurance Offices'.[87] Both Houses of Parliament were canvassed, much lobbying among the clergy and persons of quality was done, and the coming Public Meeting (set for 9 June 1830) was advertised in various newspapers.

It is worth considering how this new *Prospectus* compared with the abortive 1825 one, and the spoof. Once again the precedent of Père-Lachaise was mentioned, and it was stressed that the proposed General Cemetery was to be based 'on the plan' of the Parisian exemplar. Security from violation by body-snatchers was once again a paramount consideration.[88] The *Prospectus* (and those associated with the venture) made it clear that these proposals were above reproach in terms of respectability, which marked an important step in making commercial cemeteries acceptable. The *Prospectus* not only appealed to the public by the novelty, exclusiveness, tastefulness, profitability, and social status overt in the scheme, but above all by its offer of security. The new General Cemetery, with its Picturesque landscaping, was to be as unlike the unsavoury

[79] Loudon's letter and extracts from newspaper reports of the presentation of the Petition are preserved in the Minutes of the Provisional Committee of the General Cemetery Company, 17-19. [80] Loudon (1981), *passim*. *See* footnote 77. [81] Minutes of the Provisional Committee (17 May 1830), 19. [82] Sir John (1775-1852) had been created 1st Baronet on 3 September 1821. [83] Sir John Dean Paul, 1st Baronet, was a Vice-President of the Society. His son (1802-68) became 2nd Baronet. [84] On Roberts (1803-76) *see* Curl (1983c), *passim*. [85] The 1st Baronet's wife (and mother of the 2nd Baronet), Frances Eleanor (d. 1833), was the grand-daughter (maternally) of Thomas, 8th Earl of Strathmore (baptised 1704, died 1753). [86] Robert Brudenell (1760-1837), 6th Earl of Cardigan, father of James Thomas Brudenell (1797-1868), 7th Earl, who commanded the Light Brigade in the famous Charge during the Crimean War. The 6th Earl was closely associated with Lord Milton. [87] Minutes of the Provisional Committee (3 and 7 June 1830), 23-4. [88] It should be remembered that two more years were to pass before legislation put the 'resurrection-men' out of business, and at this stage legislation did not seem all that likely to succeed.

old burial-grounds as possible, not only secure, but beautiful and fashionable too, even a place of resort.

The Nascent Company

The momentous meeting took place on 9 June 1830 at *The Freemasons' Tavern*, Great Queen Street, with the inaudible Spottiswoode in the Chair. More names were proposed for the Provisional Committee including Lords Lansdowne,[89] Milton,[90] and Radstock,[91] another of Paul's sons, Benjamin Dean Wyatt,[92] and J. T. B. Beaumont.[93] At an unspecified point during the meeting Lord Milton took over the Chair from Spottiswoode. It was resolved that no shares of the Company should be transferable until three-fifths of the amount were paid up, and there was much discussion about the Deed of Trust, the running of the Company, and so on. On the architectural front, Lord Milton reported he had received 'a communication from Mr Goodwin, relative to the consideration of his design for a Public Cemetery', and the Chairman and Secretary also produced 'communications' from 'Mr Willson respecting his plan of a Pyramid'.

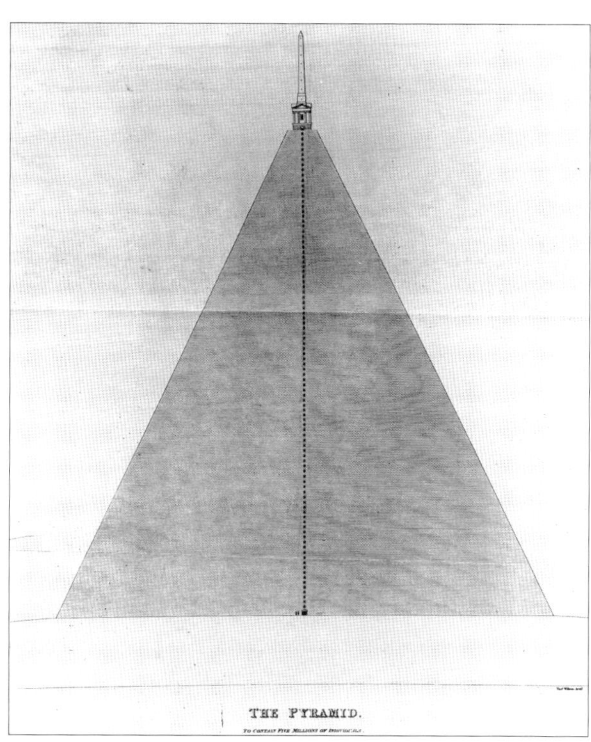

2.2 'Pyramid' to contain Five Million of Individuals designed for the Centre of the General Cemetry [*sic*] of the Metropolis, designed by Thomas Willson (*GLCL*).

These 'communications' are of considerable interest. 'Mr Willson' was Thomas Willson (*c*.1780-), whose vast pyramidal cemetery (in fact a huge multi-storey set of vaulted burial-chambers) was to have a base covering 18 acres, the whole structure being the equivalent of '1,000 acres' of land. Willson later (1831) exhibited his design for a 'Pyramid Cemetery for the Metropolis', an engraved version of which is in the Royal Library at Windsor Castle; another exists in Guildhall Library, City of London (**2.2**).[94] 'Mr Goodwin' was Francis Goodwin (1784-1835), who prepared and published a stunning Classical design for a 'Grand National Cemetery' to be laid out at Primrose Hill, 'intended for the prevention of the Danger and Inconvenience of Burying the Dead within the Metropolis: Proposed to be erected by a Capital of 400,000 l. in 16,000 shares

89 Henry, 3rd Marquess of Lansdowne, and 4th Earl of Kerry (1780-1863). 90 See footnote 71 above. 91 George Granville Waldegrave (1786-1857), 2nd Baron Radstock, who had served in the Royal Navy during the Napoleonic Wars. He was active in the administration of several charities, and was a naval historian. 92 *See* footnote 40 above. 93 John Thomas Barber Beaumont (1774-1841), usually called 'Barber Beaumont', was the founder of insurance offices, and was a talented painter. He created the County Fire and Provident Life offices, and designed the offices (1819) in Regent Street with Robert Abraham (1774-1850). He also established (1806) the Provident Institution and Savings Bank in Covent Garden and (1840) the New Philosophical Institute in Beaumont Square, Stepney, where he had an estate. He was the author of several essays on Life Assurance, Provident and Parish Banks, and Criminal Jurisprudence, some under the pseudonym 'Philanthropos' (which sums up his attitude to life). He resisted fraudulent claims on his Company, exposed the crooked West Middlesex insurance office, and in 1825 fought the Board of Stamps over a false claim by the Inland Revenue. His probity was beyond question. 94 Willson (*c*.1830 or 1831). *See* Colvin (1995), 1062.

2.3 'View of the proposed GRAND NATIONAL CEMETERY' designed by Francis Goodwin for a site at Primrose Hill, London (*GLCL*).

at 25 l. each' (2.3). It appears that this scheme had been exhibited in premises in Parliament Street two months earlier, in April 1830, conveniently close to the House of Commons. The exhibition seems to have been prompted by Carden, and was probably intended to influence Members of Parliament before Spottiswoode presented Carden's *Petition* to the House.[95]

Goodwin's proposed cemetery was to consist of an outer area 'disposed somewhat after the manner of Père la Chaise at Paris', and an inner enclosure containing temples and mausolea that were to be 'facsimiles of some of the most celebrated remains of Greek and Roman architecture': thus it would have had two systems of defence against intruders. At each corner of the enclosure was to be a version of the Tower of the Winds in Athens (which appear to have been intended as watch-towers for security), and there were replicas of the Choragic Monument of Lysicrates, various Greek Doric temples, Roman triumphal arches, and a splendid Propylaeum. Had it been realised, Goodwin's scheme would have been the grandest necropolis ever built, and architecturally the most distinguished.

However, the enormous amount of construction required by both schemes would have used up vast sums of money, and the Provisional Committee saw the problem, so refused to entertain either Goodwin's or Willson's proposals. The colossal costs[96] terrified the Provisional Committee, which had already decided to reduce the Company's capital to £200,000, so these two exercises in the Sublime fell on stony ground.

The Committee passed various resolutions, including one to the effect that interment within the Metropolis was 'highly objectionable' and 'offensive to decency'. It was also resolved that spacious cemeteries should be established 'without the limits of the Town ... rendered in a high degree ornamental to the Metropolis'. Other resolutions were intended to ensure that the cost of interments would be kept as low as possible, to approve the principles upon which the General Cemetery Company had been founded,

95 *The Gentleman's Magazine*, c (1830), 351. 96 Willson's scheme would have cost £2,583,552, would contain freehold vaults selling at between £100 and £500 each, holding in all five million bodies, and would bring in a profit of £10,764,800. *See* Curl (1993*a*), 212-5.

and to recommend the proposals to all who felt 'an interest in the public Welfare and in the improvement of public taste'.[97]

The Provisional Committee in July 1830 consisted of Milton, Paul, Sir Henry Pynn, Spottiswoode, the Reverend James Harris, Carden, Rothery, Sievier, Wilson, J. S. Clarke, Griffith, John Fairlie, R. W. Carden, G. R. Paul, J. T. Barber Beaumont, and Benjamin Wyatt. Griffith was not a member, it seems, although he had been 'requested to make inquiries respecting Land on the North Side of the Town' on 22 June, the day on which Augustus Pugin's name is noted as among those 'summoned' to a meeting. It was Wyatt, however, who undertook to 'look at Col. Eyre's ground', and who proposed that 'some preparatory steps should be taken respecting Primrose Hill'.[98]

A certain unwillingness to allow names to be published either as shareholders or as members of the Provisional Committee had been apparent by June 1830, and several persons wrote to ask for their names to be removed. Clearly something was amiss. Election of Directors was postponed, and the Provisional Committee was reappointed at the General Meeting (again at *The Freemasons' Tavern*) on 5 July.[99] However, two Marquesses, three Earls, and Viscount Milton were appointed Vice-Presidents, Carden was re-appointed Treasurer, and Charles Broughton Bowman re-appointed Secretary and Solicitor. At the meeting of the Provisional Committee of 13 July, Griffith reported on his inspection of 'land in the neighbourhood of London', and was asked to 'pursue his inquiries on the north side of the Town and also between the Edgware and Harrow Roads and Notting Hill'.[100] This seems to be the first indication that possible sites other than Primrose Hill were being considered.

There had been some discussions about the propriety of holding meetings immediately after the death of King George IV (25 June 1830), but it was resolved to go ahead.[101] The short reign of King William IV (1830-7)[102] began well for the Company: letters of support for the venture began to arrive from the House of Commons, and, even more important, it was reported that 'His Majesty approved of the Plan' of the 'Company beyond any other for a similar purchase hitherto published'. This was an *Imprimatur* indeed, and one of the first indications that the new King was not averse to innovation.[103]

In Autumn 1830 it was decided to submit a new Parliamentary Petition, for leave to bring in a Bill in the 'ensuing Session' to incorporate the Company.[104] Around this time several inquorate meetings were adjourned, and very little seems to have happened from December 1830 until June 1831: the only attenders of meetings from 24 November 1830 until 14 June 1831 having been the two Cardens, Spottiswoode (only once), Sievier, and (once) 'The Hon. Mr Grey'. The enterprise seems to have run out of momentum, and the fact that the Cardens turned up for meetings on more than one occasion, but that nobody else did, may mean trouble was brewing. In fact a letter had to be sent to all members of the Provisional Committee drawing attention to poor attendance, and urging action to remedy this.[105]

Acquisition of Land at Kensal Green

Paul (in the Chair of the meeting of 30 June 1831) reported that 'a Spot of Ground at Kelsall [*sic*] Green on the Harrow Road three miles from Tyburn Turnpike containing about 53 acres divided by the Paddington Canal could be purchased at the rate of £200

[97] Minutes of the Provisional Committee (10 June 1830), 29. [98] Ibid. (29 June 1830), 35. [99] Ibid. (13 July 1830), 39. [100] At the time Notting Hill was undeveloped, and, like Primrose Hill, was high ground, so there were desirable aspects about both sites. [101] The late king was not held in great esteem, to put it mildly. [102] Often unjustly dismissed as a buffoon, he and his Consort, Amelia Adelaide Louise Theresa Caroline of Saxe Meiningen (1792-1849), did much to stabilise the Monarchy after the rocky reign of George IV, and left it secure for the young Queen Victoria, William's niece. [103] Minutes of the Provisional Committee (13 July 1830), 41. [104] Ibid. (18 October 1830), 44. [105] Ibid. (27 June 1831), 48.

pr. Acre and that the Vendor would if required allow half the purchase money to remain on Mortgage'. This information, presumably, was the result of Griffith's researches. Paul proposed that if the ground 'should appear eligible for the purposes of the Company' a 'contract should be immediately entered into'.[106] It was decided to inspect the lands.

At the meeting of 4 July 1831 Paul 'produced a Plan of the Ground and proposed it should be purchased forthwith'. He was authorised to 'bid £9,100 for the Kelsall Estate' with £5,000 to be 'paid down', the remainder to remain on Mortgage. Although the Committee did not feel 'sufficiently authorised' to make such a purchase, members agreed 'to take the purchase on themselves in case the Society[107] [*sic*] should not authorise the purchase'. The two Pauls, Sir Robert Price, Spottiswoode, Grey, Money, Walpole, Lord Milton, and Griffith agreed to become responsible for £500 each, and it was decided to maintain secrecy about the proposal. Although they attended the meeting, Pynn, Carden, and Pugin did not agree to become responsible for monies.[108] What appears to have happened was that Paul put up the purchase-money, and that members of the Provisional Committee indemnified him against loss by each agreeing to cover £500 in case of difficulties.

Paul then signed a contract for the purchase of land for £9,500, and the Provisional Committee reported to a General Meeting, held at Exeter Hall on 12 July 1831, that it had endeavoured to promote the interests of the Company despite the 'unfavourable circumstances of the times'.[109] The 'returns of the population'[110] had proved 'its great increase and the consequent necessity of providing places of Sepulture on a scale of much greater magnitude than those heretofore established'. Furthermore, 'accounts received from Liverpool and other Towns of the Success of Public Cemeteries where the Population' was 'infinitely less than that of London and Westminster' sufficiently justified 'expectation of a remunerating Profit'. The Committee had felt it was its 'duty to embrace such opportunities as had arisen for the formation of a Cemetery altho' *on a more limited scale than was at first contemplated*'.[111] In other words, the grand scheme envisaged by Carden had become a much more modest affair.

The Committee also reported the great difficulty of obtaining 'a large quantity of unoccupied land situate near London' at a price not 'unreasonable' or 'exorbitant', so it regarded itself as 'fortunate in having succeeded in the purchase of 54 Acres[112] of very eligible freehold land tithe-free & land tax redeemed on the Harrow Road, two miles from the end of the new Road on an elevated spot with great facilities of approach by land & water surrounded by very beautiful scenery with great capabilities of being adapted to the formation of a Cemetery'.[113] This land, it was announced, had been 'purchased for £9,500, a price which those conversant with the subject' pronounced

106 Minutes of the Provisional Committee (30 June 1831), 50. 107 Meaning the Provisional Committee. 108 Minutes of the Provisional Committee (4 July 1831), 52-3. 109 Ibid. (8 July 1831), 54-5. 110 That is, from the recent Census. The Census was established in Great Britain in 1801, and took place every tenth year. 111 Minutes of the Provisional Committee (8 July 1831), 55. Editor's italics. 112 There is considerable confusion about the extent of the cemetery: in fact the total acreage purchased was 46.41 acres (18.782127 hectares) north of the canal, and 7.67 acres (3.104049 hectares) south of the canal, making 54.08 acres (21.886176 hectares) in all. Then two small parcels (*c*.2.0 and *c*.0.1 acres [*c*.0.8094 and *c*.0.04047 hectares]) were also bought from the 'Manor of Abbots in Kensington'. In 1833 two small plots north of the canal (0.5 and 0.375 acres [0.3541125 hectares]) were purchased from the St Quintin estate. In the 1850s the Company added a further 22.54 acres (9.121938 hectares), bringing the total area up to 79.595 acres (32.2120965 hectares). But this figure includes the land south of the canal, which was never used for burial, and which was sold off later, so the final total area of the cemetery was 71.925 acres or 29.1080475 hectares. Thus at least six parcels of land were involved: the largest, in the tenure of Mr Knight; two smallish pieces of land (along the north side close to the Harrow Road) previously owned by the Manor of Abbots of Kensington; two patches of land purchased from the St Quintin estate in 1833; and the Fillingham lands to the west, of which only 22.54 acres (9.121938 hectares) were retained by the General Cemetery Company. The figure of '53 acres, 3 roods, and 38 perches' is cited in the deeds (53.98 acres or 21.845706 hectares) for the two main patches of land bought at the beginning of the venture, in which case the final total figure would be about 71.8 acres or *c*.29 hectares. *See* Appendix 2 and Appendix 3. The Editor is indebted to Dr Freed for his meticulous research regarding the area of the cemetery: these figures are largely based on his work. 113 *Sic*. The breathless lack of punctuation is typical of the scribes who kept the Minute-books.

'moderate'. It was also decided to 'take immediate steps for obtaining an Act of Parliament to incorporate the Company'.[114]

It was also reported that the sums for which 'the subscribers' had 'already set down their names, tho' inadequate to a very large undertaking', nevertheless was 'sufficient to carry into effect the immediate purpose of the Committee'. Coats evidently had to be cut according to the cloth, and Carden's original vision would have to be tailored to match resources. No doubt to the considerable relief of the Committee, the General Meeting (chaired by Lord Milton) approved its actions, and authorised it to complete the purchase of the land at Kensal Green.[115] The Provisional Committee[116] was appointed for 'another year in lieu of Directors ... with the full power of Directors during that period', and requested to 'take the proper measures for obtaining the necessary Act of Parliament'.

Curiously, Willson, who noted the failure of his plan for a pyramidal cemetery, at this stage offered his own house 'for the office of the General Cemetery Company upon being remunerated for his Expenditure of about £1,000'. Sir John Dean Paul sent a polite note to Willson stating it was not the intention of the Committee to 'incur the expense of a regular office in the present state of the Concern', and that he could not 'hold out any hope' that the Committee would 'become purchasers' of Willson's house. The architect was let down lightly by Paul's 'lament' that Willson's 'success' had not 'been equal' to his 'merits'.

Barber Beaumont,[117] through his lawyers, requested the 'return of £50 deposited on his shares, or so much of it as should remain after payment of expenses', and was duly paid off, although the Committee expressed 'surprise' that he 'should have thought it necessary to apply ... thro' the means' of his solicitors. He was also told that he was 'as much mistaken' in his estimate of 'the success of the Cemetery' as he was 'in the manner of dealing with the Gentlemen' of the Committee.[118] Clearly there had been rumours, evidence of disquiet, and some loss of confidence. The loss of Barber Beaumont was quite a blow to the enterprise, and may be indicative of the reasons why the Provisional Committee did not get the immediate financial support it needed, for Beaumont was influential, and could easily have spread unfortunate impressions about the way things were being run.

Indeed, the Provisional Committee found itself in a quandary, as the Minutes of its very long meeting of 19 July 1831 make clear. Several persons who had attended the Exeter Hall public meeting on 12 July, had even questioned if the Company 'should continue its operations or resell the land purchased', which indicated a collapse of support. In order to bolster confidence, Carden and Sievier added their names to the agreement to indemnify Paul against loss from the purchase,[119] and it was decided that the books of the Company would be closed on 1 September, after which no new shares would be issued to the public.

These problems led to attempts to improve the standing of the Provisional Committee even more. On the recommendation of Sir Robert Price, Bart., Viscount Ingestre[120] joined it in 1831, as did Colonel Henry Ansley Purchas on the motion of Colonel Money. Ingestre was certainly a 'catch', and was to become Chairman of the

[114] Minutes of the Provisional Committee (8 July 1831), 55-6. *See also The Times* (13 July 1831). [115] Ibid. (19 July 1831), 59. [116] Carden was re-appointed Treasurer, Bowman re-appointed as Secretary, and William Fryer and Thomas Cornish were re-appointed Auditors. [117] *See* footnote 93 above. [118] Minutes of the Provisional Committee (19 July 1831), 61. [119] Ibid., 63. [120] Henry John Chetwynd Talbot (1803-68), who in 1826, on the death of his brother, Charles Thomas (1802-26), became Viscount Ingestre. In 1849 he became 3rd Earl Talbot of Hensol, and in 1856 succeeded his distant relative, Bertram Arthur Talbot (1832-56), 17th Earl, as 18th Earl of Shrewsbury and Waterford. A naval man, he was also Captain of the Corps of Gentlemen-at-Arms and Hereditary Grand Seneschal of Ireland. The Talbot family had been connected with northern Kensington ever since Charles Henry Talbot of the Inner Temple purchased Portobello farm in 1755. The name is commemorated in Talbot Road, Notting Hill, to this day.

General Cemetery Company from 1832 to 1834, so was at the helm during the establishment of Kensal Green cemetery.

Thus the *Prospectus*, the names of those associated with the venture, and the decorous tone of the meetings began to give the proposals a certain *cachet*, all of which was necessary in a climate where doubters were plentiful. A few more Barber Beaumonts and the enterprise could well have foundered.

In order to advertise the Company a board was erected on the land at Kensal Green informing the public that shares could be purchased from Snow, Paul, & Paul, of 217 Strand, and from Bowman, of 18 Milk Street, until 1 September 1831. It was decided to print a report of the proceedings of the 12 July meeting, and to send copies to all subscribers.

By this time (mid-1831) it was clear that Paul had become the dynamic driving force of the Provisional Committee, the member who 'got things done'. He was clearly acting closely with the quieter Spottiswoode, who seems to have been happy to wield power and pull strings in more subtle ways. The three main allies to have their way were Spottiswoode, Paul, and Griffith (who, as a nominee of Spottiswoode, clearly owed the last a debt: patronage ensured his loyalty).

The land the General Cemetery Company eventually purchased was bisected by the Paddington Canal, an offshoot of the Regent's Canal. Most of it lay to the north of the canal: only 7.67 acres lay to the south, and this area was never enclosed, nor, as noted earlier, was it used for burial. We are not privy to the negotiations with the owners of the estate, so we do not really know why this southern part was purchased at all, whether the vendors declined to separate the plots, or the intention really was to establish a much larger cemetery. All we can say is that in 1831 it was decided that only the northern portion would be fortified against violation, and laid out for use as a cemetery, and that various attempts were made at various times to sell off the land to the south.

In July 1831 Paul wrote to certain 'iron masters at Sheffield with a plan respecting an iron railing to inclose the ground', and also approached 'Messrs Hunt, Builders', for a 'rough estimate of a Brick Wall of a proper height' for the same purpose. Paul reported that it would cost about £15,000 to enclose the ground, and had the figure confirmed by Decimus Burton (1800-81), the distinguished architect.[121] Thus security of the ground had top priority, and moves to implement this were well under way even before the formalities of legal purchase had been completed. Throughout the deliberations of the Provisional Committee, the importance of security is evident.

From the Minutes of the Provisional Committee, it would seem that the canal was perceived as a valuable asset, providing a cheap and easy means of transportation for building-materials, soil, gravel, and other supplies. It was even envisaged that a water-gate would provide access to the cemetery for water-borne funerals: a Venetian-inspired notion that never took off. Nevertheless, from the point of view of security, although the canal was a natural boundary with value as a moat (far better than had the site abutted a field), yet its vulnerability was understood. What could arrive by water could also steal silently away by the same means. It was therefore an equal priority for the Provisional Committee to secure this watery boundary as it was to protect with high walls the boundary to the north, along the High Road to Harrow.

The Provisional Committee also concerned itself with the problem of removing corpses from one parish to another 'without fee to the Clergy of the original parish or to the one to which they were removed' because such fees could have an adverse effect on the economics of the infant Company. This problem also accounted for the hostility

[121] Minutes of the Provisional Committee (5 August 1831), 64.

of many Anglican clergymen to the entire idea of cemeteries, for a considerable part of their incomes derived from burial-fees. This difficulty was resolved in various clauses of the Act of Incorporation of 1832[122] which allowed fees to be paid directly to an incumbent in the case of a parishioner being buried in the cemetery.

It was decided to press ahead with the preparation of the Bill to go through Parliament. At the meeting of the Provisional Committee on 5 September 1831 it was reported[123] that 'upwards of £30,000 had been subscribed' by the closing-date of 1 September. Paul stated that 'provided a call of five pounds were made forthwith he would advance the sum necessary to complete the purchase upon the credit of the sums to be paid into his hands upon the call as Banker'. It was determined that the land should be purchased at once, outright, 'without allowing any part of the money to remain on mortgage'.[124]

It was also resolved that five hundred more shares should be issued at a premium of £1 per share (to be subscribed for on or before 20 October) to increase the funds available to the Company. The architect, John Nash, was approached 'for his opinion as to the General plan of laying out the Ground previously to issuing an advertisement to the Public for Plans and Estimates'.[125] Again, it was Paul who undertook to approach Nash and report back to the Committee, and on 20 September 1831 he 'presented a sketch by Mr Liddell[126] ... drawn under the eye of Mr Nash ... for laying out the grounds'.[127] Lord Ingestre reported that he was 'present at a meeting with Mr Nash and Mr Liddell', that Nash had 'volunteered his assistance' if Liddell was 'deputed to lay out the grounds', and that both men 'would act gratuitously'. It was Griffith, however, who was 'instructed to furnish plans and sections of the Ground to lay before the Committee.[128] Paul strengthened his position by getting his friend Andrew Macklew appointed to the Committee.

Much lobbying had to be done to bring the Church on side, so Paul and Spottiswoode 'waited upon' the Archbishop of Canterbury and the Bishop of London to acquaint them with the 'general objects of the Company'. They were also deputed to 'communicate with the dissenters and other religious bodies'. The Archbishop and Bishop made it clear that no consecration would take place until the grounds had been properly secured and tidied and a chapel erected, so there was an urgent necessity to enclose the land with high walls and railings as soon as possible, get the landscaping under way, and give consideration to the buildings.

Enclosure of the Ground and First Moves towards Planting

By 4 October it was clear that Nash and Liddell were greatly put out because of Griffith's involvement,[129] and Liddell wrote to the Company withdrawing his plan and stating that Nash would only give his assistance 'on the assurance that' Liddell was employed.[130] Nevertheless, at the same meeting Griffith produced his 'plan and sectional drawing with levels'.[131] Ignoring Nash and Liddell, the Committee instructed Griffith to 'furnish a

[122] 2 & 3 Will, IV, c. 110, XXVII-III, XXIX-V. [123] Minutes of the Provisional Committee (5 September 1831), 65. [124] Ibid. 66. Paul was 'allowed interest at the rate of 5 pr. ct. per annum until he should have received sufficient to cover his advance with such interest'. An instalment of £5 per share was to be paid to Messrs Snow, Paul, & Paul, Bankers, before 9 December 1831, another instalment of £5 per share to be paid on 9 March 1832, and a further instalment of £5 per share on 9 June 1832. Discount 'after the rate of £4 per cent per annum' would be 'allowed to any person paying up the amount of such instalments in the mean time'. [125] Minutes of the Provisional Committee (5 September 1831), 67. [126] The Hon. Thomas Liddell (1800-56), second son of Sir Thomas Henry Liddell (1775-1855), 6th Baronet and 1st Baron Ravensworth. *See* Colvin (1995), 616-7. [127] Minutes of the Provisional Committee (20 September 1831), 68. [128] Ibid. [129] And, equally, it seems that Griffith was equally put out by the possibility that the Liddell/Nash partnership would stymie his own ambitions. [130] Minutes of the Provisional Committee (4 October 1831), 69. [131] Griffith worked hard and fast, and this must have impressed the Provisional Committee.

working plan for inclosing the Ground on the North side of the Canal'. With what appears to be an attempt to mollify him, Nash was invited to 'take twenty shares', which presumably meant subscribing, although it could also be taken to mean that Nash was to be presented with 20 shares for his trouble. It was decided not to advertise for plans or estimates until after the next meeting.

Griffith (who seems, like most of his contemporaries, to have been able to produce drawings and specifications very quickly) laid 'working drawings[132] for a boundary wall' before the Provisional Committee towards the end of October 1831. Tenders were invited for its construction[133] to be delivered to Bowman's office at 18 Milk Street, Cheapside, on or before 20 November 1831. By then both the Archbishop and Bishop had agreed to support the scheme provided the Company paid an 'allowance' to the clergy in lieu of burial-fees, and provided the grounds were 'substantially inclosed with a Wall'. This ecclesiastical support was essential, and the fact that it was forthcoming was of considerable benefit to the Committee. Carden then offered to open communications with Dissenters 'upon the subject of taking part of the Ground'. He was told he 'might do so in his own name but not as the official agent of the Company',[134] which suggests that the Provisional Committee did not wish to undermine its understanding with the Church of England by becoming overtly involved with Nonconformist interests.

Meanwhile, it was 'deemed advisable that if possession of the ground could be obtained, the planting should be provided' quickly, in order to make the place look respectable as soon as possible. So Paul was 'authorised to lay out in planting the ground to the extent of £300'.[135] At the same meeting (1 November 1831) it was resolved that a premium of 100 guineas should be offered for the best design for a 'Chapel and Entrance Gate', and this was duly advertised. The saga of the architectural competition and its aftermath will be discussed later.

Tenders were received for building Griffith's boundary-wall ranging from £7,660 0s. 0d. (Thomas Smith) to £9,020 17s. 6d. (H. Biris), but the second lowest (£7,661 7s. 0d. from William Chadwick) was accepted because his 'scale of prices' was the lowest. Griffith was instructed to 'treat' with Chadwick for the construction of the wall, and a contract was ordered to be prepared upon 'Chadwick's giving proper security'.[136] All this took place before the land had legally passed to the Company. At this stage negotiations took place with lawyers acting for Lord Holland[137] to enable the Company to 'take the necessary measures for enfranchising the Copyhold[138] of the Estates', and Griffith was instructed to take all steps necessary for arranging with the Lord of the Manor and with the proprietors of the adjacent lands 'for forming proper lines of boundary for the Site of the Walls'.[139] Paul, as one of the Trustees, was requested to enter into the necessary agreements (on behalf of the subscribers) with the builder for the works to be executed.

It is worth considering the thinking behind the design of the boundary-walls and -railings. The stock-brick wall with stone coping along the Harrow Road is formidable, buttressed at intervals, and given substantial foundations (some 5 feet 6 inches [1.70688 metres] below ground). It is between 10 (3.048 metres) and 12 (3.6576 metres) feet in height (and is even higher in some places), and was intended to give an impression of security to all who passed along the High Road to and from Harrow. The wall also

[132] They survived in the collection of the General Cemetery Company in 2001, but are not very photogenic, so are not reproduced here. [133] Minutes of the Provisional Committee (25 October 1831), 70. [134] Ibid. (1 November 1831), 74. [135] Ibid., 75. [136] Ibid. (25 November), 78. [137] Henry Richard Vassall Fox (1773-1840), 3rd Baron Holland (from 1774). [138] Ancient kind of tenure of lands being parcel of a Manor, founded upon immemorial custom and usage. As Lord Holland was Lord of the Manor, negotiations had to go through his representatives. [139] Minutes of the Provisional Committee (25 November 1831), 79.

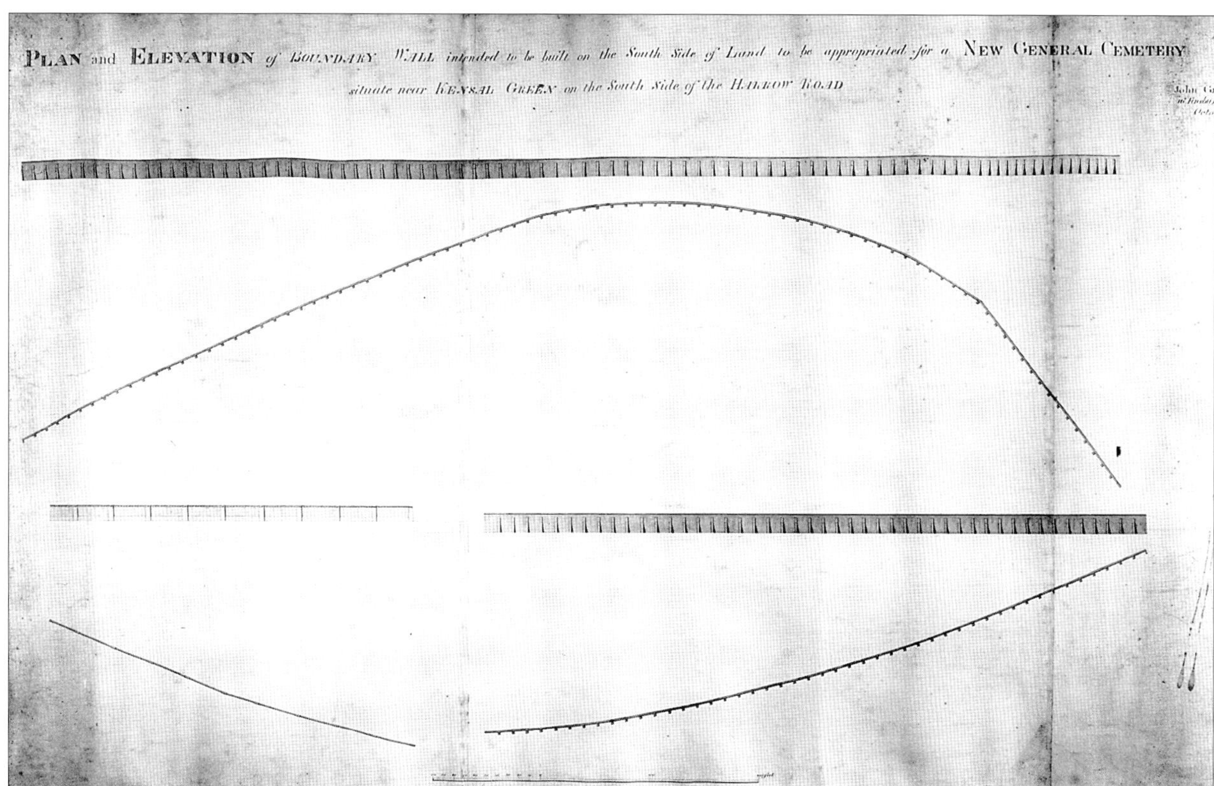

2.4 Griffith's proposals for a boundary-wall of October 1831. Unfortunately the remaining drawings of the walls as realised are very fragile and badly damaged (#27), but the Harrow Road wall was shown as 13 ft. (3.9624 m) high with 5 ft. 6 ins. (1.6764 m) below the ground: it was to be 1 ft. 3 ins. (0.381 m) thick at the top; 1 ft. 6 ins. (0.4572 m) thick at the base; and was to have piers at 13 ft. (3.9624 m) centres. The south wall was to be 15 ft. 6 ins. (4.7244 m) high with 2 ft. 6 ins. (0.762 m) below the ground, and again piers or buttresses at 13 ft. (3.9624 m) centres (*GCC.#37. MC.A230201*).

screened the cemetery as works of landscaping and construction proceeded, and indeed also concealed grave-digging, interments, and other activities. Constructed at the highest point of the land, the wall was therefore a massive physical barrier (**2.4**). However, the land falls away to the south towards the canal, and afforded fine views towards the Surrey hills, so, in order to exploit these, it was decided to erect a cast-iron railing along the southern boundary of the land north of the canal so that visibility outwards was not gravely impeded.

Of course these railings had to be as substantial a barrier to trespassers from the canal-side as the wall along the Harrow Road, and to this end the railings were bedded into a soundly constructed brick wall with stone dressings, and designed as uninterrupted verticals, connected just below the finials by a strong horizontal iron bar. Scaling them would be difficult, not to say hazardous, for any uninvited visitor. The water-gates, too, served as very substantial security grilles. A boundary-wall of brick with stone dressings was also constructed in a curve around the eastern boundary, from the canal to the main entrance and lodges, along what is now Ladbroke Grove.

Unfortunately the records of the Company do not tell us much about which parts of the boundary-walls were tackled first: reports merely refer to progress being made (or work being held up because of lack of bricks or for other reasons), and we do not know much about who made the cast-iron elements of the constructions that defined and protected the cemetery grounds. It seems that, as the need for security was taken as self-evident, there was not much discussion about it, and, as Griffith was fully aware of what was required, he designed solutions to satisfy the Provisional Committee.

Paul emerges from the Company records of 1831-2 as the potential top dog in meeting after meeting. He it was who produced a plan 'prepared by Mr Forrest for planting the ground', and reported that Forrest's friend, 'Mr Ronalds of Brentford' would commence the scheme of planting proposed by Forrest (whose 'time was wholly at the disposal of the

Duke of Northumberland'[140]). However, the Provisional Committee decided to appoint Pugin and Griffith to assist in the matter, and they were asked to meet Forrest at Paul's house in order to 'proceed to the ground for the purpose of making a plan for the partial planting'. Forrest's plan 'not being approved of', Paul was nevertheless authorised to give 'directions for such planting' thought necessary. The appropriately-named 'Mr Forrest' was Richard Forrest,[141] and his colleague was Hugh Ronalds, nurseryman, of Brentford, Middlesex.[142] Thus it appears that Paul, Pugin, and Griffith were responsible for deciding upon the earliest planting (including the cedars that were to line the main avenue for a short time) and the embellishments of the 'circuit of the ground'.

By late 1831, therefore, considerable progress was being made. Now the times became unusually promising for the establishment of the Cemetery Company, for in October 1831 the first outbreaks of Asiatic Cholera (which had been on the way from India since 1821) occurred in England, causing great alarm. The causes of the disease were not understood, but among the theories was one that proposed cholera emanated from the evil 'miasmas' that arose from overcrowded and unsavoury graveyards.

Many poor people, however, believed cholera to be a figment of doctors' imaginations, designed merely to obtain more bodies for dissection. Body-snatching, too, was very much in the public mind in 1831. There were worrying rumours that the famous Edinburgh murders of Burke and Hare (1832) were being replicated in London.[143] 'Burking' was indeed confirmed in London in November, when a pair of seasoned body-snatchers, Bishop and Williams, were caught trying to sell the body of their last victim, an Italian boy, to anatomists at the new King's College medical-school in The Strand. Blood in his mouth revealed unnatural death, and the pair are reputed eventually to have confessed to a further 60 murders for sale to dissectors.[144]

As a result, Parliament reintroduced an Anatomy Bill to requisition (instead of murderers) the corpses of those too poor to pay for their own funerals. Everyone was on high alert for one mortal reason or another. Stories about 'burkophobia' and 'choleraphobia'; the disposal of the dead; and deaths natural, unnatural, and epidemic, peppered every newspaper of the period.[145]

The builder, William Chadwick, had provided, by 12 December 1831, the names of his sureties, and had referred Griffith 'to Mr Soane under whom' Chadwick 'had built the Treasury'. The Secretary wrote to Soane[146] to enquire if Chadwick had carried out the works in a satisfactory manner, and 'Mr Soane'[147] reassured the Committee on this point. Griffith also reported that he had met with Pugin, Paul, Forrest, and Ronalds to discuss the 'plantation', which, it was decided, should be 'confined to the circuit of the

[140] Minutes of the Provisional Committee (25 November 1831), 79. [141] Forrest (*fl.* 1820s-1840s) had been gardener to Robert, Lord Grosvenor (1767-1845), at Eaton Hall, Cheshire, where he helped to lay out the grounds, and he designed the botanic garden at Syon House, Middlesex, for Hugh, 3rd Duke of Northumberland (1785-1847), in 1826. *See* Desmond and Ellwood (1994), 255. Forrest is also mentioned in some of J. C. Loudon's publications. [142] *See* Desmond and Ellwood (1994), 593. Ronalds (1759-1833) is mentioned by Loudon in several of his publications. He was the son of the nurseryman Hugh Ronalds (*c.*1726-88) and the father of Robert Ronalds (*c.*1799-1880), both of whom were known in horticultural circles. [143] William Burke (1792-1829), an Irish vagabond, went to Scotland as a labourer in 1818, and went to live in a lodging-house in Edinburgh run by William Hare (*fl.* 1829), also an Irishman, a native of Londonderry. When an old man died in the lodging-house, Burke and Hare sold the body for £7 10*s.* to the surgeon, Dr Robert Knox (1791-1862), who in 1828-9 had 504 students of anatomy, to whom he gave lectures for three hours each day. Burke and Hare, realising that easy money could be made by keeping Knox well-supplied with fresh corpses, hit upon the idea of plying their victims with drink and then suffocating them before selling the fresh, unmarked bodies on to Knox for prices ranging from £8 to £14 a time. This was much less trouble than digging bodies up from graveyards at night, and became known as 'burking', while to smother became 'to hush up', or suppress quietly. One murder too many in October 1828 aroused the suspicions of neighbours, who knew the victim, and the corpse was found in a box in the cellar of Knox's house. Hare turned King's Evidence, changed his name, and disappeared, but Burke was hanged on 28 January 1829 'amid the execrations of a vast assemblage' (*D.N.B.*, iii [1917], 370-1). Although Knox was attacked in print and his effigy burnt by an Edinburgh Mob, he survived, and died in London aged 71. [144] Bishop (or Bisopp) and Williams were apprehended in November 1831 and hanged in London in December of the same year. [145] Richardson (1987), Ch. 8, *passim.* [146] Minutes of the Provisional Committee (12 and 15 December 1831), 80, 84. [147] He was not knighted until the following year (1832).

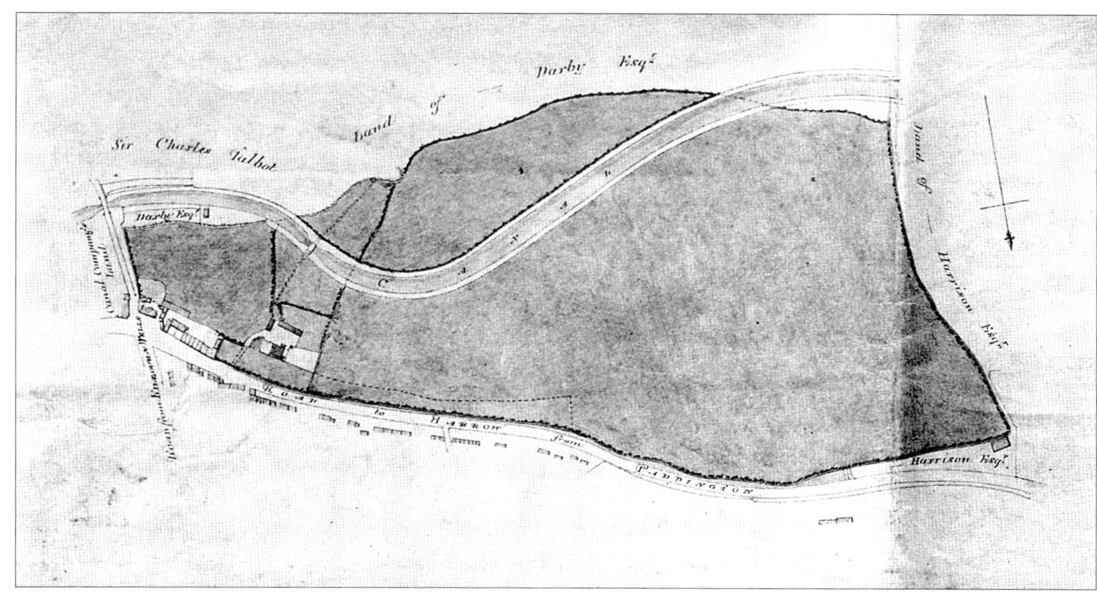

2.5 Land purchased by the General Cemetery Company from Sir John Dean Paul, Bart., on 19 September 1832, showing the larger patch north of the canal and the smaller piece south of the canal adjoining properties of Sir Charles Talbot and William St Quintin (whose father, William Thomas Darby, had assumed the surname St Quintin). The long sliver of land north of the canal, immediately to the west of the 'Road from Kilbourn Wells' and the 'Canal Company's Land', also belonged to 'Darby Esqr.' (i.e. St Quintin). Note also the awkward bubble-shaped piece of land behind the inn at the corner of the 'Road to Harrow from Paddington' and the 'Road from Kilbourn Wells' (*GCC.Indenture.MC.A060201*).

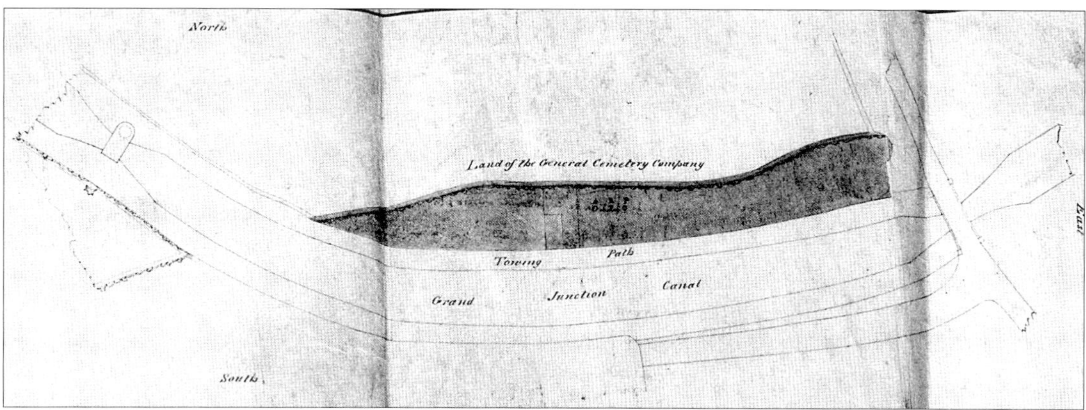

2.6 The narrow, pointed sliver of land immediately to the north of the Grand Junction Canal (see 2.5) purchased by the General Cemetery Company from the St Quintin estate in 1833 for £250 (*GCC.Indenture.MC.B060201*).

ground'.[148] Spottiswoode, Foss,[149] Carden, and Wilson were asked to form a sub-committee to consider all matters relating to the Act of Parliament, and shareholders who had not paid the second instalments due on their shares were reminded of the fact. The Committee was approached by David Ramsay[150] ('supported by several testimonials'), of the Stanhope Nursery, Old Brompton, with proposals for laying out the ground, but was informed that the Company 'had engaged a person to perform the planting'.[151] Ronalds, however, was told that expenditure on planting was limited to £300.

The purchase of the land was completed by 15 December 1831, and the contract with William Chadwick for the building of the boundary-wall was duly signed,[152] even though the question of the Copyhold had not been fully resolved. A cheque for £9,400 was repaid to Paul for 'the sum advanced by him in payment for the Estate'.[153] At the next meeting Wyatt wrote to decline completing his shares, and requesting that his name might be

[148] Minutes of the Provisional Committee (12 December 1831), 82. [149] Edward Foss (1787-1870), solicitor and biographer, was active in founding the Incorporated Law Society, of which he was President in 1842 and 1843. *See D.N.B.*, **vii** (1917), 491-2. [150] David Ramsay (*fl.* 1810s-1850s), nurseryman, of the Stanhope Nursery, Brompton and Fulham, acquired W. Salisbury's (d. 1823 or 1829) nursery in Sloane Street, Chelsea, in 1829, and later worked closely with Stephen Geary (*c.*1797-1854) on the landscaping of Brompton and Highgate cemeteries. His son, David Allan Ramsay, later went into speculative housing developments and went bankrupt. [151] Minutes of the Provisional Committee (12 December 1831), 83. [152] Ibid. (15 December 1831), 84. [153] Ibid., 85.

withdrawn from the list of the Committee. This may be attributable to Wyatt's financial position, for he was declared bankrupt in 1833.

There is evidence that the beautifying of the grounds was being rushed. Griffith had to meet Forrest, the 'agent of Mr Ronalds', on site to discuss matters. Forrest opined that until the wall on the south side of the ground was built it would not be proper to trench the ground and, furthermore, that until 'some general plan for draining the land' and establishing the 'levels and sites of the various buildings' it would not be 'prudent to proceed with either the trenching or planting'.[154] As a result, Ronalds was ordered to suspend further operations until instructed otherwise. Considering that the cemetery grounds lay on London clay (which is particularly heavy and glue-like when wet), it is astonishing that the question of drainage does not appear to have been given much thought.

To sum up, therefore, the land was to be bought by Paul, and then bought back from him once the Company had been properly established. As it happened, Paul and C. B. Bowman completed the purchase of the farm-land in December 1831, and three indentures were involved: one between Paul and the Reverend Frederick William Gray of Castle Carey; one between C. Broughton Bowman and John Hawke; and a third between Paul and John Nicoll of Willesden. On 19 September 1832 the newly incorporated General Cemetery Company legally acquired the lands for £9,400: specific mention was made in the indenture of parcels of ground 'formerly Copyhold holden of the Manor of Abbots Kensington but afterwards enfranchised', which means that the Copyhold problem had been resolved some time in 1832. A plan on the indenture shows the land bought by the Company (**2.5**). It should be noted that a long sliver of land north of the canal and immediately to the west of Ladbroke Grove was not in the original purchase, and that there was an awkward piece of land, like a bite, immediately to the south of the public-house at the corner of the Harrow Road and the 'Road to Kilbourn Wells'. Later, in 1833, William St Quintin sold the sliver of land to the Company for £250, although it was quite a complicated indenture involving several other parties, including Major-General Matthew Chitty Darby Griffith (**2.6**).[155]

Events until early in 1832

Early in 1832 more investors backed off, and the designer of the Pyramid Cemetery, Thomas Willson, joined others in requesting that his shares should be sold. There were also problems with the adjoining St Quintin Estate, for Ronalds appears inadvertently to have committed a trespass when trenching, and the damage had to be made good. Griffith was required to sort this matter out, and investigate the possibility of exchanging small parcels of land with the St Quintin Estate for the benefit of both parties.

Carden revealed he was in communication with the Central Board of Health 'who had applied to him respecting the sale of part of the land for the purpose of burying persons who might die of the Cholera', but was warned about the distinction between private negotiations and communications from the Committee.[156] In fact, the Committee could see no advantage in retaining the land on the south side of the canal, and offered to sell it to the Government provided it would be fenced in a 'manner' corresponding 'in appearance with the Cemetery Ground' then being enclosed. It does not seem to have occurred to the Committee that a burial-ground for cholera victims so close to the cemetery (though on the other side of the canal) might deter custom from using its own property, or that future use of the site might have detrimental effect on the cemetery, as subsequently transpired.

154 Minutes of the Provisional Committee (22 December 1831), 86-7. 155 Indentures held by the General Cemetery Company. *See* Appendix 2 and Appendix 3. 156 Ibid. (5 January 1832), 88-9.

G. F. Carden was appointed Registrar on 5 January 1832, and Wyatt's name was removed from the Committee, to be replaced by Thomas Gaspey.[157] £2,500 in Exchequer Bills was transferred to a new account for the payment of Chadwick, and this 'Wall Account' was placed under the control of Paul. Early in January 1832 Paul had met with George Eden, Earl of Auckland (1784-1849), Chairman of the Central Board of Health and President of the Board of Trade, who informed Paul that the 'Board approved of the undertaking of the Company and recommended that an application should be made to Government for a Charter in lieu of an Act of Parliament'. The Minutes record, laconically, that 'Mr G. F. Carden made a similar report'.[158] As a result, the question of a Charter was raised, and all proceedings in reference to the Bill were stopped. Ramsay (who appears to have been a tenacious soul), in the meantime, through Sievier, offered to supply about 30,000 loads of gravel on 'very moderate terms', and Griffith was asked to follow this up.[159]

While the Committee was awaiting entries for the architectural competition, various problems arose with the London and Birmingham Railway Company, the main line of which was proposed to 'intersect the Ground of the Cemetery'. This must have put the fear of God into the Provisional Committee, for to have express trains rushing through the Field of Repose would have destroyed just about everything the infant Company was hoping for. It is little wonder that shareholders took fright. The surveyors of the cemetery and railway interests were instructed to meet and thrash the matter out, so Griffith[160] met Robert Stephenson (1803-59), surveyor and engineer of the London and Birmingham Railway Company (incorporated by Act of Parliament the year after the General Cemetery Company obtained its Act of Incorporation), and in due course reported back to the Committee.

As far as the proposed Charter was concerned, it became a dead duck as a result of legal opinions obtained,[161] and the Sub-Committee was requested to resume work on the Parliamentary Bill. Negotiations with the Central Board of Health regarding the proposed sale of land to cater for the burial of cholera victims continued, but any decision was postponed pending Griffith's meeting with Stephenson concerning the railway problem. At the Committee meeting on 23 January 1832 Griffith's presented his report to the Provisional Committee, which resolved that 'the Scheme of the London and Birmingham Rail Road as at present proposed would be prejudicial in the highest degree to the new Cemetery, and that the Committee on the part of the Company dissent'.[162] This resolution was communicated to the Railway Company's lawyers.

The Committee also resolved to 'retain at the disposal of His Majesty's Government the plot of ground on the south side of the Paddington Canal for a period of two years for the sum of £70 per annum to commence at Lady day[163] next', and to be 'willing to dispose of it at any time within two years if His Majesty's Government' should require the use of it, for the sum of £2,000. The magnitude of the cholera epidemic was not

[157] Thomas Gaspey (1788-1871) was a novelist and journalist, who became parliamentary reporter on *The Morning Post* for 16 years. In 1826 he became a part-owner of *The Sunday Times*, the tone of which he raised 'as a literary and dramatic organ', as *D.N.B.*, vii (1917), 935, puts it. A member of the council of the Literary Fund, he was said to be genial, witty, kind, and an excellent mimic. His son, Dr Thomas W. Gaspey (d. 1871), was an authority on the Rhine and Heidelberg. [158] Minutes of the Provisional Committee (11 January 1832), 92. [159] Ibid. (5 January 1832), 89. It is not clear what a 'load' actually was: 30,000 *cart*-loads sounds like a lot of gravel, so it must have been a smaller amount. In fact, a 'load' meant a specific amount, though that varied from place to place. In building operations the term implied as much weight as a horse could conveniently draw, which was about a ton. A 'load of gravel' was calculated in the 18th century to mean 18 heaped bushels, where a bushel was about 2,800 cubic inches (or 2219.36 cubic inches if compacted or 'striked'). By the time Kensal Green cemetery was being laid out, 18 heaped bushels were reckoned to form a cubic yard, and were considered a single 'load'. *See* Papworth (*Ed.*) (1852-92), v, 112. [160] Griffith was thus a key man, and was working extremely hard to consolidate his position. Prudently, he had put money into the venture, and although he was being paid as an architect and surveyor for his pains, he clearly had ambitions not only to design the cemetery, but to have some control over its destinies. [161] Minutes of the Provisional Committee (19 January 1832), 94. [162] Ibid. (23 January 1832), 96. [163] i.e. 25 March.

known at that stage, and it is unclear why the Provisional Committee took the actions it did: a possible explanation is the simple desire to rid itself of the problematic 7.67 acres south of the canal, something it did not in fact achieve until several decades later.

There were more difficulties in obtaining second instalments of shares, and letters were sent out reminding all defaulters of their obligations.[164] They were told that unless the second instalments were paid by a specific date, their shares would be forfeited. Paul was requested to ask Lord Milton to present the Petition for the Act of Parliament and to carry the Bill through the House of Commons.[165] Griffith was instructed to prepare schemes for draining the ground, although it soon transpired[166] that the standing orders of the Commissioners of Sewers forbade any sewer through a cemetery. Griffith was therefore instructed to make the drain 'in such direction as the Commissioners of Sewers' would approve.[167]

By 23 February 1832 it was reported that the Petition for leave to bring the Bill had been presented to Parliament and referred to a Committee of the House, and early in March the results of the architectural competition were announced. It will be as well to examine this episode in some detail.

164 Minutes of the Provisional Committee (2 February 1832), 98. 165 Ibid., 99. 166 Ibid. (1 March 1832), 109.
167 Ibid.

CHAPTER III

The Architectural Competition of 1831-2 and its Aftermath

JAMES STEVENS CURL

Announcement of the Competition; The Entries; Kendall's Winning Gothic Scheme; The Rise of Griffith; Controversy and Animosities; The Passing of the Act of Incorporation; Griffith as De Facto *Architect; Conclusion*

> 'To Architects and others' – The General Cemetery Company are desirous of receiving designs for a chapel for the performance of the funeral service and a corresponding Entrance Gate and Lodge and offer a premium of 100 Guâs for the best design.
>
> GENERAL CEMETERY COMPANY (1 November 1831): Minutes of the Provisional Committee of the General Cemetery Company, 75.

Announcement of the Competition

As was mentioned above, it was at a meeting of the Provisional Committee on 1 November 1831 that it was decided to obtain designs for the Anglican chapel and gate-lodges by means of an architectural competition, attempts to get a well-known 'name' as architect having failed. Thus it was resolved that a premium of 'One Hundred Guineas be offered to Architects and others for the best design for a Chapel and Entrance Gate'.[1] An advertisement was prepared and ordered to be inserted in the 'daily and other Papers'. The buildings required were to consist of a 'Chapel with ample Vaults', the building to be used for 'performing the funeral service & for the advantageous display of monuments', the cost of which was not to exceed £10,000, and a 'Principal Entrance Gateway with a lodge or lodges with accommodation of not less than four rooms' to cost not more than £3,000. Drawings were to consist of plans 'of the several Stories, Elevations of the Several Façades', and 'longitudinal and transverse Sections' to a scale of one eighth of an inch to one foot. Perspective views were also to be provided. It was made clear that no designs would be acceptable that did not adhere to the instructions or that could not be built within the cost-limits. Drawings were to be delivered at the office of the Secretary (Bowman), and were to be 'distinguished by a motto, device, or figure', without the names or addresses of the architects. No drawings would be accepted after 26 January 1832.

However, having received a representation from 'Mr Bedford' (Francis Octavius Bedford [1784-1858], the distinguished architect) requesting an extension of time, the Committee decided to move the submission date to 20 February, and an advertisement to this effect was placed in the papers. An error in the printing, substituting 28 February for 20 February, forced the Company to extend the date for submission of designs yet again. A sub-committee of five 'to open and examine the designs for the Chapel &c. delivered at the Office of Secretary' was appointed on 23 February 1832: it consisted of Griffith, Paul, Pugin, Sievier, and Spottiswoode but, at R. W. Carden's request, G. F. Carden's name was added. The fact that he was not on the original list is significant: Paul, Griffith, and Spottiswoode were allies, and Sievier seems to have been on their side, so the only Goth (Pugin) would have been outnumbered, and, in any case, was in Carden's camp. Besides, the driving-force behind the whole idea of founding a cemetery was being excluded from a very important sub-committee, and it would have rankled. Even when Carden's name was added, he and his associates were still in the minority.

The Entries

Any reservations about cemeteries seem to have evaporated, for 48 entries[2] were received, not all of them complete. Fortunately, we can glean some information about these from a few sheets of notes, but, less fortunately, the papers are torn, so some information is missing. It seems that, after the competition had been assessed, some entrants retrieved their drawings, and this fact was duly noted. Regrettably, not all the architects were identified, as their drawings were either collected by third parties (who did not always reveal the names of those for whom they were acting) or not retrieved at all (so the drawings are only identified by the devices, mottoes, etc.). A few sets of designs remain among the papers of the General Cemetery Company, and these vary from the impressive (No. 42 by 'Cambria') to the hamfistedly awful (No. 7). The list of entries may be summarised as follows:

[1] Minutes of the Provisional Committee of the General Cemetery Company (1 November 1831), 75. [2] General Cemetery Company (1832)

Entry No. and General Cemetery Company identification no. (if extant)	**Mark, Motto, or Figure**	**Style**	**Comment**	**Architect or Designer**
1	Shield with three estoiles, two in chief and one below the wavy fess, with motto *Huela* (possibly, or could be *Fula* [which does not appear to mean anything]) *la Muerte* (Here you can sense [or smell] death)	Early English Gothic	None, as drawings were collected	Edward Lushington Blackburne (1803-88)
2	1.M.1	Grecian. No section of gatehouse	None, as drawings were collected	Frederick Wehnert (1801-71)
3	*Modestia* (Temperance)	Roman	None, as drawings were collected	W. M. Williams (see entry No. 46)
4	Possibly *Ingotus* (An unknown person), but could also be *Agrotus* (presumably 'a Surfeit') or *Ogrotus* (which seems to have no meaning at all)	No style noted. Only perspective and section and front elevation of gateway submitted	Incomplete. Drawings do not seem to have survived	Sir John Dean Paul (who was no mean draughtsman)
5	*In hoc signo spes mea* (in or by this sign is my hope)	Early English Gothic. No section of lodge submitted	None, as drawings were collected ? J. McLeslie,	possibly James Leslie (1801-89)
6	Sign torn off, but ends ...*quam Conspici*, so presumably refers to the means by which the entry could be distinguished	Grecian and Gothic. No plan of vaults, no sections of gatehouse, no sections	None	William Bardwell (1795-1890)
7 #16 #33 (3.1)	Patée formée cross	Norman gateway and feeble Gothic chapel	Hamfisted Romanesque and incompetent, unscholarly Gothic	Unidentified
8	Black seal	Roman	Blank	Blank
9 (3.2-10)	Triangle within circle. Could this be entry No. 48?	Roman	Circular body of chapel, with clerestoreyed drum above, over which is Pantheonesque dome. Prostyle tetrastyle Tuscan portico. Arched gate crowned by an open cupola, with a chaste Grecian lodge on either side linked to the entrance by blank walls, enlivened by one niche in each, containing a draped urn	Unidentified. Possibly Thomas Nicholls (*fl.* 1860s). *See* entry no. 48

Entry No. and General Cemetery Company identification no. (if extant)	Mark, Motto, or Figure	Style	Comment	Architect or Designer
10	SF	Gothic Chapel, Grecian Lodge	No sections of gateway	John B. Forbes (*fl.* 1815-35)
11	A.c.B. (W.J.S. crossed out) *Favete linguis* (favour me with your tongue)	Grecian	None, as drawings were collected, but there appear to have been two sets submitted	Received 'for C. Foster'
12	C. Red seal	Grecian	Blank	Blank
13	'by Mistake' (whatever that means)	Gothic	None, as drawings were collected, but no side elevations of lodges	Perhaps by the Hon. Thomas Liddell (1800-56), or perhaps by Thomas Rickman (1776-1841). The annotations on the List are confused, and may mean Liddell collected the drawings on behalf of Rickman. Both men, however, could design in the Gothic style. Entry 13 is further confused because the Catalogue is annotated 'Received for Mr Liddell' and signed 'George Auld'
14	Adelphi	Grecian	None, as drawings were collected	Drawings acknowledged with a mark (X) of William ?Gust or ?Guest
15	Death's Head and Anchor	Blank	Blank	Drawings received by a 'Messenger on prod$^{n.}$ of Device'
16	*Fides Aequitas* (Faith [and] Fairness)	Gothic	Blank	'The Architect as (*sic*) received this Design'.
17	ZZ	Grecian	Incomplete, 'no perspective view'	Illegible initials
18	2	Grecian	Blank	Received (illegible)
19	Leopard's head and Red Seal. Architetto	Roman	None, as drawings were collected	John Ellis, of 22 New Ormond Street, London. This was the Dimond Hotel, although Messrs Ellis & Spaul, Tailors, had premises at 25 New Ormond Street
20	*Numquam non paratus* (Never unprepared)	Grecian	Blank	Blank

Entry No. and General Cemetery Company identification no. (if extant)	Mark, Motto, or Figure	Style	Comment	Architect or Designer
21	Red Seal	Blank	None, as drawings were collected	Edward Jones (*fl.* 1819-35) of 6 Staples Inn, Chancery Lane
22	✠	'Theban'	None, as drawings were collected	'Mr Liddell', who may therefore have entered two designs (13 and 22). The drawings were 'delivered to Mr Liddell thro' Lord Denbigh' (i.e. William Basil Percy [1796-1865], 7th Earl of Denbigh [from 1800]). However, the cryptic remark may mean the design was submitted in a roundabout way by someone else.
23	Hope	Grecian		'Received for Mr Sam.' Breeze' crossed out (presumably Samuel Charles Brees [d. 1865], who exhibited at the Royal Academy between 1833 and 1837). See also 25
24	Lion Rampant *Spero Meliore* (I hope for better things)	Gothic	None, as drawings were collected. The Catalogue comments 'all the drawings'	George Russell French (1803-81)
25	Hope	Egyptian	None, as drawings were collected	James ?Arnet, ?Arnot, ?Amer, for Samuel Charles Brees. This is probably a second entry (see 23)
26	*Non quo sed quomodo* (not by whom but in what manner)	Grecian	None, as drawings were collected	Received by John Tucker
27	None noted	Grecian	None, as drawings were collected	Charles Nathaniel Cumberlege (*c.*1807-59) 'from Burtons'
28	W.J.S.	Greek (*sic*)	None, as drawings were collected	Received 'for Mr Smith', i.e. ?William James Smith (*fl.* 1830s, died 1864)
29	*Excellito*	Grecian	None, as drawings were returned	J. H. Ridley signed for the drawings, but he was not an architect
30	*Palmam qui meruit ferat* (let him bear the palm who has deserved it)	Gothic	None, as drawings were returned. No longitudinal sections noted	Francis Octavius Bedford (1784-1858)

Entry No. and General Cemetery Company identification no. (if extant)	Mark, Motto, or Figure	Style	Comment	Architect or Designer
31	*Nil* (illegible) *labore* (Presumably 'nothing without labour')	Roman	None, as drawings were returned	Edward Powell signed for the drawings, but he does not appear to have been an architect
32	Psalm 90 Verse 17 (i.e. And let the beauty of the Lord our God be upon us: and establish thou the work of our hands upon us; yea, the work of our hand establish thou it)	Gothic	Incomplete. No sections of lodge, and only one of the chapel	Stephen Geary (1797-1854)
33	Iris	Grecian	None, as drawings were returned	Inman. This is noted as 'J. W. & Sons', but was probably William Southcote Inman (1798-1879), who was a regular entrant to architectural competitions
34	Red Seal. 'Lion passant gardant'	Grecian and Gothic	None, as drawings were collected, but no gateway with the Gothic design	Edward Buckton Lamb (1806-69)
35	Sisyphus (mythological character punished by rolling a boulder up a hill, but it kept rolling back and he had to start again – clearly a reference to the frustrations of taking part in architectural competitions)	Grecian	None, as drawings were collected.	?Beaumont, signed X Joseph Wilson, his mark. Could Beaumont have been a son of John Beaumont (*c.*1769-99) ?
36	✡	Grecian	None, as drawings were collected	? S. Gough, but this was probably only the messenger who collected the drawings
37	*Spes* (Hope)	Roman (Grecian crossed out)	None, as drawings were collected	James Harding (*fl.* 1830-41)
38	Illegible	Grecian	None, as drawings were collected	Croshan, Crosham, Croshow, Grosham, Groshem, or Groshew of 7 Fenchurch Buildings (research has revealed nothing)
39	R Q H (or AE)	Roman	None, as drawings were collected	'Mr Park', probably Henry Parke (*c.*1792-1835)
40	Thus	Grecian	Blank	Blank

Entry No. and General Cemetery Company identification no. (if extant)	Mark, Motto, or Figure	Style	Comment	Architect or Designer
41	I P T	Gothic	None, as drawings were collected, but no sections of entrance and no perspectives	'Mr Watson', possibly John Burges Watson (1803-81)
42 #18, #65	Cambria (3.11-18)	Grecian	A powerful Greek Doric peripteral temple on a podium, with a Lodge of impeccable Grecian style	Edward Welch (1808-68), then in partnership with Joseph Aloysius Hansom (1803-82). Drawings 'returned by coach to Messrs Welch & Hansom 14 Sept 1832'
43	*Dum Spiro Spero* (While I breathe, I hope)	Gothic	No sections of Lodge	Henry Edward Kendall (1776-1875)
44	*Dum Spiro Spero* and owl	Grecian	None, as drawings were collected, but a model was submitted	Henry Edward Kendall
45	*Quo sursum volo videre* (I should wish to be able to see from on high, i.e. I wish I could see into the future)	Blank	Blank	Blank
46	ZZZ	Blank	None, as drawings were collected	W. M. Williams (see entry No. 3)
47	Dinocrates (Hellenistic architect [*fl.* mid-4th century BC], supposedly the designer of Alexandria, and co-architect of the great Ionic temple of Artemis at Ephesus [from 356 BC])	Presumably Greek Revival	None, as drawings were collected	Charles Mason (this could be someone collecting for George Mason [1782-1865]
48	[three figures: triangle in circle, triangle in circle, triangle in semicircle]	Blank	None, as the drawings were collected, but clearly three designs were submitted	Thomas Nicholls (*fl.* 1830), of 1 Little Distaff Lane, London. The drawings were collected by D. H. Martin of 28 Michaels Place, Brompton. *See* entry no. 9

Although incomplete, and infuriatingly illegible in parts, this is an interesting list. Some entrants do not appear to have been architects at all, but some were men of distinction. Blackburne (No. 1) was a pupil of John Henry Taylor (*c.* 1792-1867), and became Diocesan Surveyor of Norwich.[3] Wehnert (No. 2) became a partner of John Ashdown (d. 1878) with whom he designed the Lambeth public cemetery.[4]

[3] Felstead, Franklin, and Pinfield (1993), 87. [4] Curl (2000*e*), 152-3.

If 'McLeslie' (No. 5 – of whom nothing seems to be known) was, in fact, James Leslie, the latter was working in Leith and in 1832 was appointed Resident Engineer of the Dundee Harbour Works. Subsequently he had a distinguished career specialising in the design of dock, harbour, and water works.[5] The connection with Kensal Green may be very tenuous, or non-existent.

Bardwell (No. 6) studied in Paris under François Debret (1777-1850), exhibited at the Royal Academy and at the Society of British Artists, and was the author of *Temples, Ancient and Modern, or Notes on Church Architecture* (1837): he is buried in the churchyard of St Edmund, Southwold, Suffolk, where there is a large and very curious monument, in an eclectic style, to his family.[6]

Forbes (No. 10) worked in the office of David Laing (1774-1856) during the building of the Custom House, London (1812-17 – parts of which collapsed thanks to faulty piling), and later designed the Pittville Pump Room (1825-30) and St Paul's church (1829-31), both in Cheltenham. Unfortunately he was convicted of forgery in 1835, having got himself into difficulties over building speculations, and was sent to prison.[7] His entry for the Kensal Green competition was probably a vain attempt to retrieve his situation by diversifying his labours into different channels.

Rickman (No. 13) was a distinguished architect, an important scholar of Gothic, and published his enormously influential *An Attempt to discriminate the Styles of English Architecture from the Conquest to the Reformation* in 1817.[8]

Edward Jones (No. 21) was the author of *Athenian or Grecian Villas, being a series of original designs for Villas or Country Residences* (1835), and was a frequent exhibitor at the Royal Academy.[9] French (No. 24) exhibited at the Royal Academy, became Surveyor to The Ironmongers' Company, was the author of *The Ancestry of Queen Victoria and Prince Albert* (1841), *The Royal Descent of Nelson and Wellington* (1853), *Shakespereana Genealogica* (1869), and other literary works, and designed several Gothic Revival churches.[10]

Cumberlege (No. 27) succeeded to the practice of his uncle, Samuel Ware (1781-1850) in the 1840s.[11] Bedford (No. 30) and John Peter Gandy (1787-1850) were engaged by the Society of Dilettanti to accompany Sir William Gell (1777-1836) as architectural draughtsmen during an expedition to Greece and Asia Minor which resulted in the publication of *The Unedited Antiquities of Attica* (1817) and the third volume of *The Antiquities of Ionia* (1840): subsequently Bedford specialised in the design of churches, including four fine and scholarly essays in the Greek Revival (St George, Wells Street, Camberwell [1822-4], St John, Waterloo Road, Lambeth [1823-4], Holy Trinity, Newington [1823-4], and St Luke, West Norwood [1823-5]).[12]

Geary (No. 32) designed King's Cross, Battle Bridge (1830-6), lampooned by Augustus Welby Northmore Pugin (1812-52) in his *Contrasts*,[13] but was better known for his Gothic and Egyptianising work at the cemetery of St James, Highgate in the late 1830s.[14] W.S. Inman (No. 33) won the competition for the London Orphan Asylum, Clapton (1821-3), with a splendid set of designs in the Greek Doric style (demolished 1977), and subsequently entered (unsuccessfully) numerous other competitions before securing the post of Surveyor of Works and Buildings in the Office of Works and Woods in 1844: he published a report on ventilation, heating, and the transmission of sound in 1836 as well as several papers on aspects of architecture.[15]

Lamb (No. 34) produced numerous drawings for the publications of John Claudius Loudon, wrote many articles for Loudon's *Architectural Magazine*, and designed some

[5] Colvin (1995), 612. [6] Ibid., 99. [7] Ibid., 370. [8] Ibid., 812-17. [9] Ibid., 554. [10] Ibid., 382. [11] Ibid., 284. [12] Ibid., 116-7. [13] Pugin (1973), Contrasted Crosses. [14] Curl (2000*e*), 86-92. [15] Colvin (1995), 526.

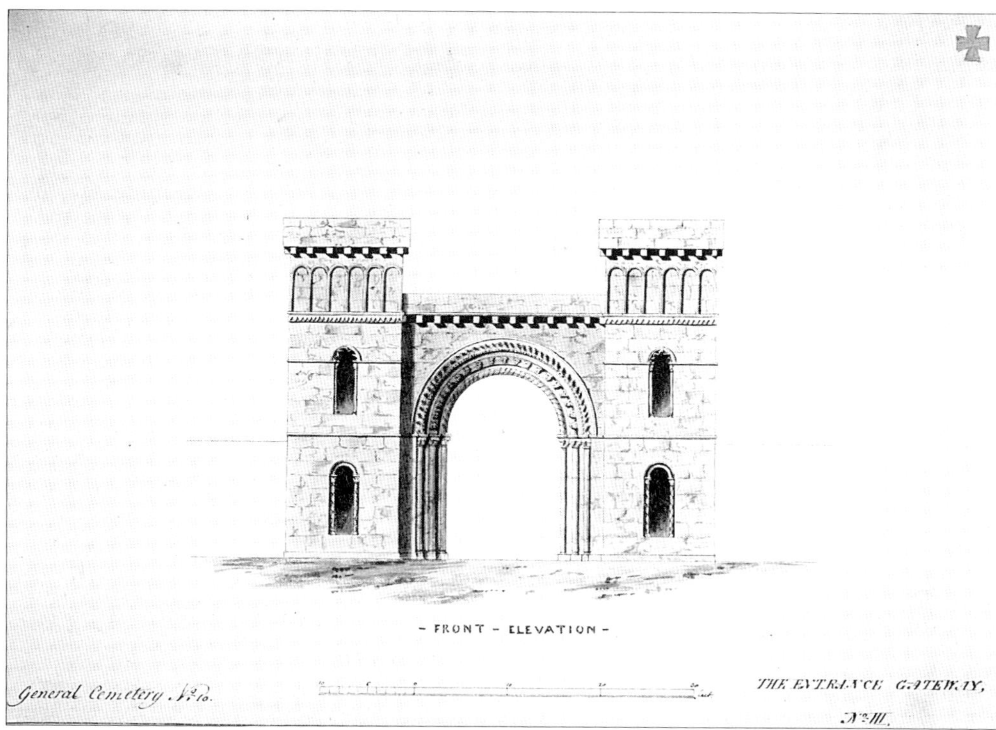

3.1 Anonymous competition entry (No. 7) for a Romanesque entrance-gateway (GCC. #15.MC.AK 140900).

elephantine Gothic churches with frantically busy roofs (e.g. St Margaret, Leiston, Suffolk).[16]

Harding (No. 37) seems to have specialised in ecclesiastical work of no particular merit.[17] Parke (No. 39) was a pupil of Soane and was a distinguished student, later travelling (with Joseph John Scoles [1798-1863] and Joseph Bonomi Jr. [1796-1878]) in Italy, Sicily, Greece, Egypt, and Syria, and published a map of Nubia (1829) indicating the positions of all the temples, tombs, and other monuments in the Nile Valley: he also worked with Frederick Catherwood (1799-1854), Thomas Leverton Donaldson (1795-1885), and others on surveys of ancient monuments in Italy, and exhibited many topographical and architectural drawings at the Royal Academy. He designed the Soane Medallion, awarded annually by the Royal Institute of British Architects.[18] Watson (No. 41) was a landscape-gardener and architect who became Surveyor to the Pentonville Estate, and Master of The Farriers' Company: he was fond of music and had a penchant for blue jokes.[19]

Welch (No. 42), a partner in the firm of Hansom & Welch, architects of Birmingham Town Hall (1830-4 – a similar peripteral temple design to that submitted for the Kensal Green competition, though Birmingham is more Roman than Greek, and uses the Corinthian Order), was a talented architect, although the Kensal Green buildings were to be built of 'Welsh white marble' from Anglesey, the same material used at Birmingham, the transportation of which bankrupted the architects in 1834.[20]

Kendall (Nos. 43 and 44) was a pupil of Thomas Leverton (1743-1824), and, it is alleged, of John Nash. He was one of the founders of the Institute of British Architects, exhibited at the Royal Academy from 1799 to 1843, and was a prolific architect, whose work included churches, town- and country-houses, gaols, and workhouses. Nicholls (Nos. 9 and 48) practised as an architect from various London addresses, and both he and his son, Thomas Nicholls Jr., exhibited at the Royal Academy.[21]

[16] Curl (2000*a*), 370; Felstead, Franklin, and Pinfield (1993), 538. [17] Colvin (1995), 456. [18] Ibid., 734-5. [19] Ibid., 1026-7. [20] Ibid., 1035-7. [21] Ibid., 577-9.

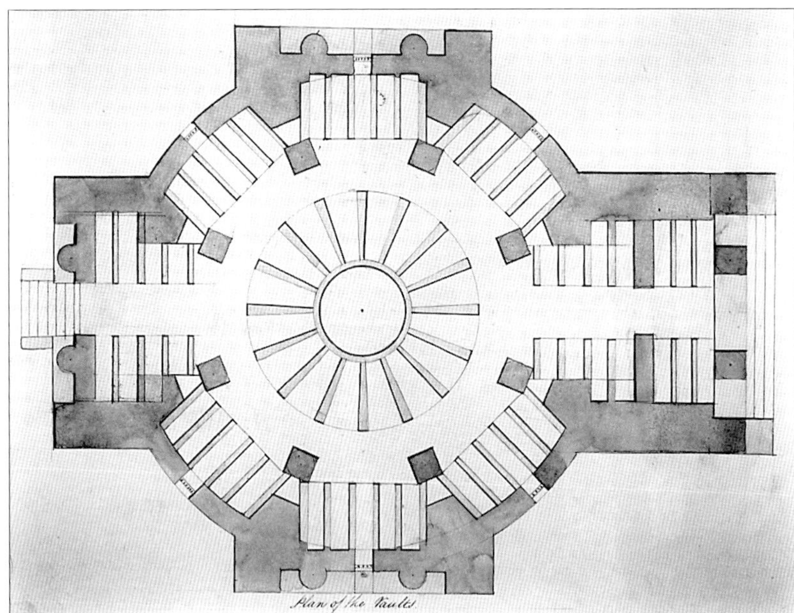

3.2 Plan of vaults, entry No. 9. Note some of the awkward *loculi* into which it would be difficult to place coffins (*GCC. MC.B150900*).

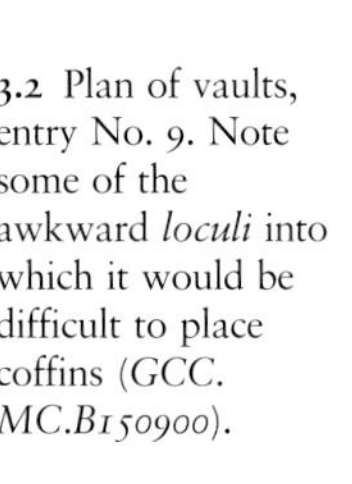

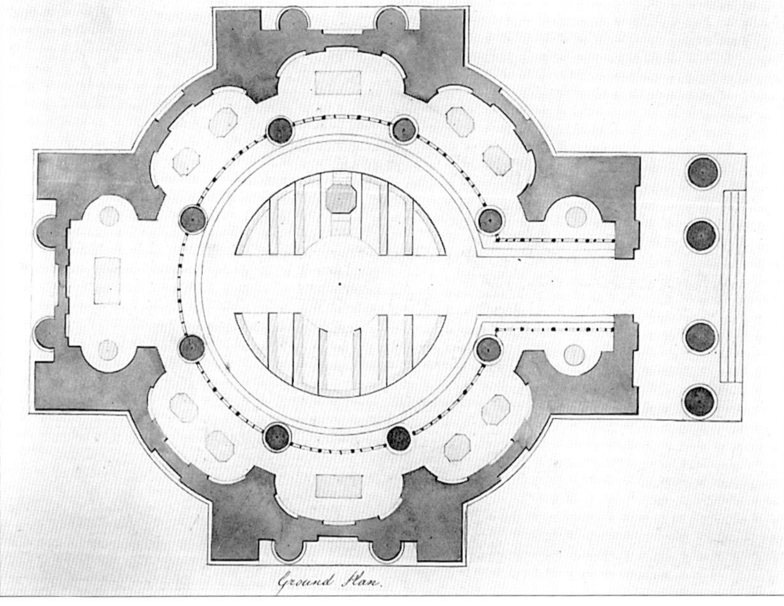

3.3 Floor-plan of chapel, entry No. 9 (*GCC. MC.C150900*).

Nothing appears to be known about W. M. Williams. He could have been the person who collected the drawings on behalf of the architects who had submitted them (and, having failed to win, wished to remain anonymous). It is impossible to establish if Paul's scheme (No. 4) could have been 'ghosted' by someone else (Griffith springs to mind), or if he himself was responsible for the drawings. Both he and his son were gifted draughtsmen, and he exhibited some 20 landscapes at the Royal Academy between 1802 and 1837. He was also the author of several books. The author of No. 7 appears to have been unskilled (to be charitable) in the niceties of the Gothic style, and may not have been an architect at all. Even his lodge, in the Romanesque style, though far more convincing than the Gothic chapel, has very weak blind arcades on the absurd 'towers', and shows little idea of scale (**3.1**). Could 'C. Foster' (No. 11) have been John Foster[22] of Liverpool,

[22] Colvin (1995), 374-5.

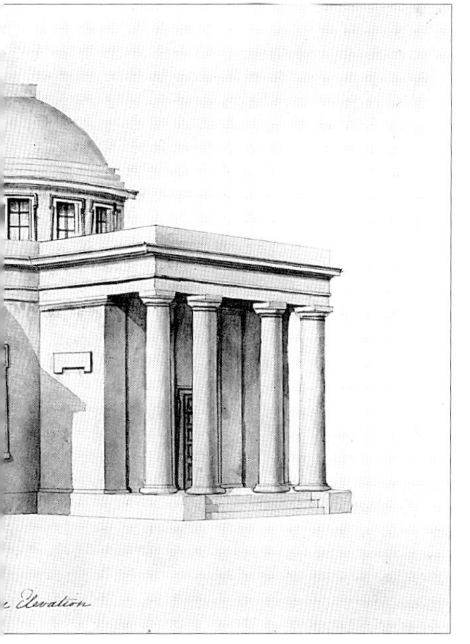

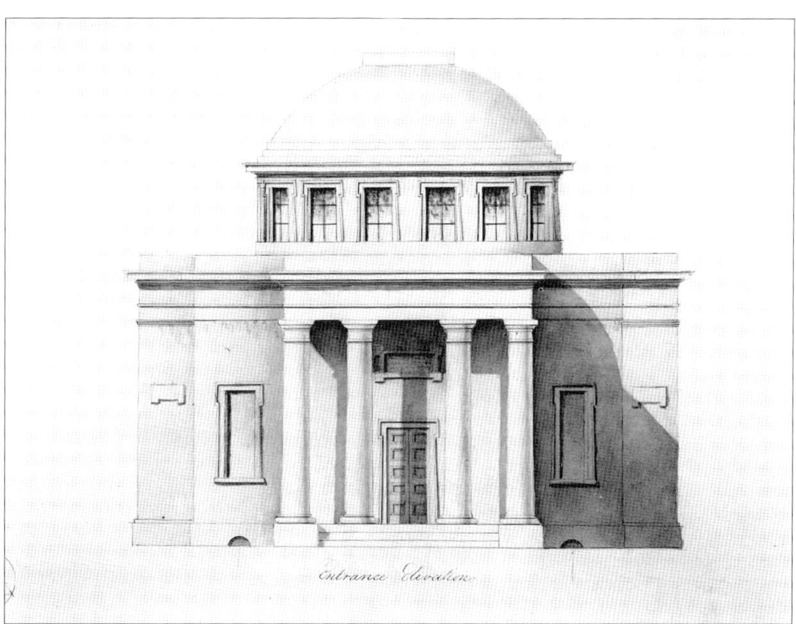

3.4 Perspective of entry No. 9 showing the Tuscan columns, inverted torches, and Pantheonesque dome. The scale of the building is very curious (*GCC. MC.D150900*).

3.5 Entrance elevation of chapel, entry No. 9 (*GCC. MC.E150900*).

3.6 Side elevation of chapel, entry No. 9 (*GCC. MC.F150900*).

who designed St James's cemetery in that city, and was a competent designer in the Greek Revival Style?

Entry No. 9, identified by a triangle within a circle, survives in the General Cemetery Company's archives: it consists of a basement-catacomb (coffins could not have been placed in several of the loculi because of the awkward planning [3.2]), over which is a circular chapel (surrounded by recesses intended to hold memorials) illuminated by windows set in a drum over which is a Pantheon-dome. Entered through a prostyle tetrastyle Tuscan portico, the rest of the exterior of the chapel is unfenestrated and severe, enlivened by three distyle *in antis* arrangements of engaged Tuscan columns (one on each of the three elevations), Vitruvian openings as recesses, and inverted torches (signifying the extinguishing of life). There does not appear to have been much thought given to how coffins were to be got down to the catacombs other than by steps, and the whole

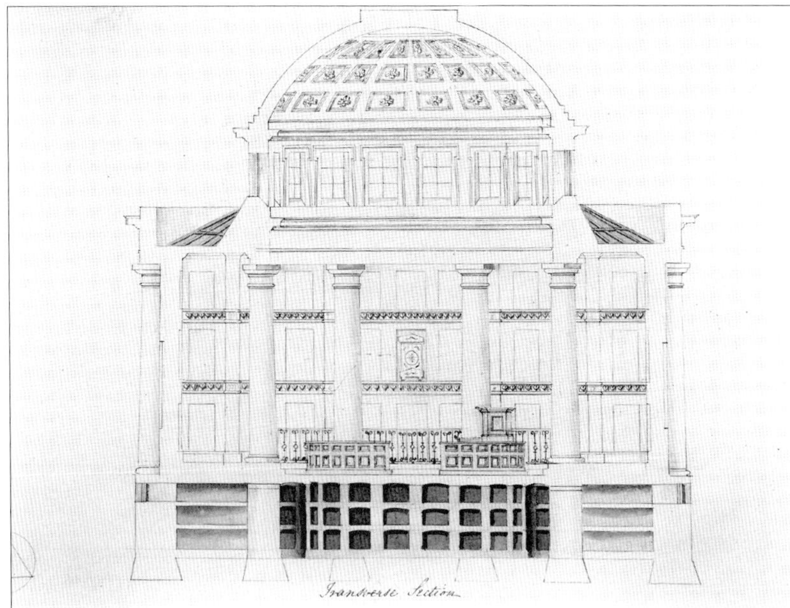

3.7 Transverse section through chapel, entry No. 9, showing the coffered dome and vaults (*GCC. MC.G 150900*).

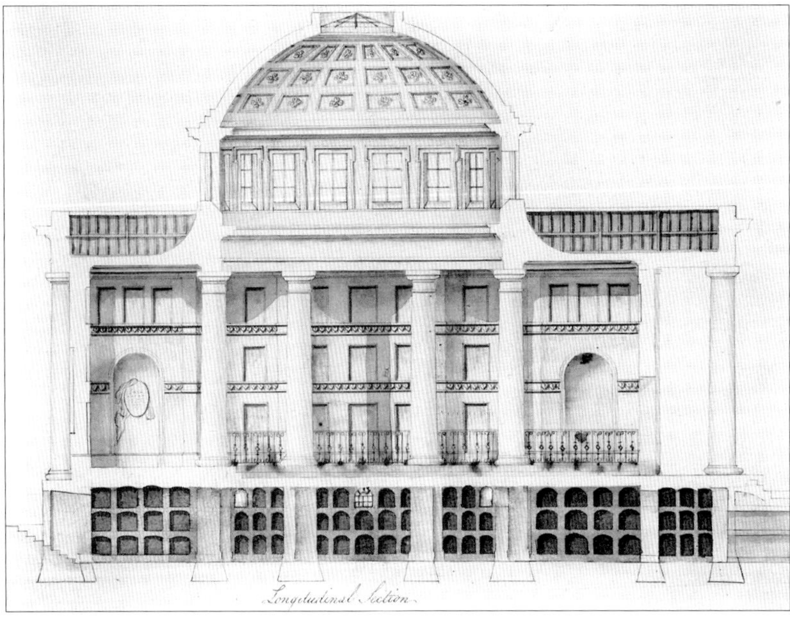

3.8 Longitudinal section through chapel, entry No. 9 (*GCC. MC.H 150900*).

conception is curiously unconvincing and undistinguished (**3.2-3.8**). The gate and the lodges submitted with this design are also nothing special (**3.9-3.10**).

It is a pity so few of the drawings appear to have survived, as it would have been very interesting to see the entries of people such as Forbes (who could be very good), Rickman, Bedford, Geary, Inman, Lamb, Parke, and Watson. By a happy chance, Welch's drawings (No. 42) are extant (though one of the sections is badly torn). His chapel was to consist of a massive, battered, rusticated base, punctuated by a few small openings, which was to contain the vaults, ante-chapel, and vestry, with a corridor surrounding the body of the chapel. On this base was a peripteral Greek Doric octastyle temple with 13 columns along each of the long sides set on a five-stepped crepidoma. The body of the chapel was illuminated by windows at high level, and ceilinged with a

3.9 'Elevation of the Gate and Lodges', entry No. 9 (*GCC. MC.B131200*).

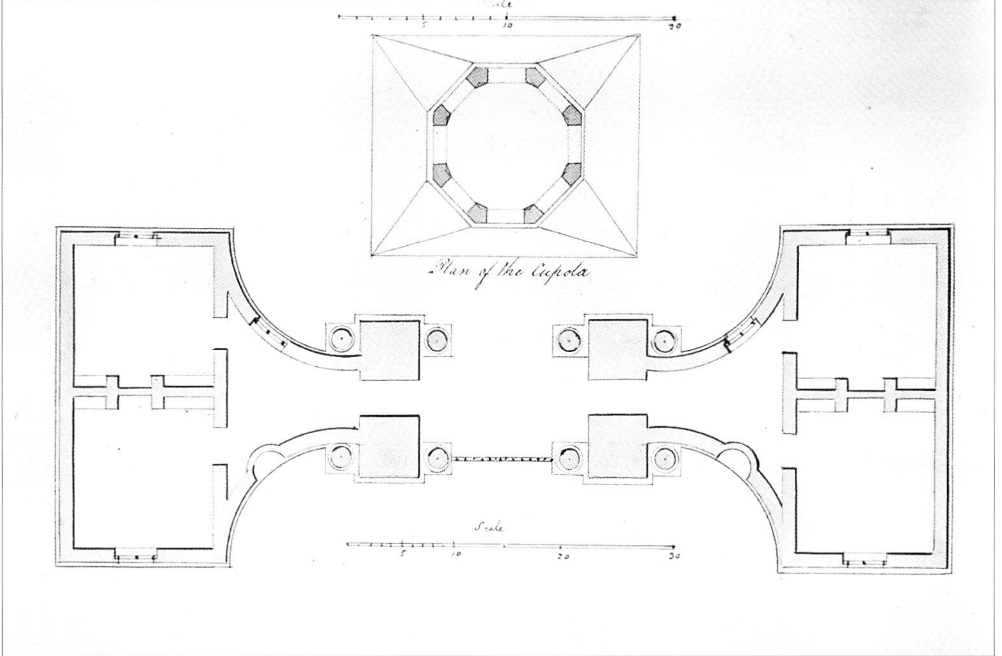

3.10 'Plan of the Gate and Lodges', with 'Plan of the Cupola', entry No. 9 (*GCC. MC.C 131200*).

coffered segmental vault. Interestingly, neither the crepidoma nor the peridrome was to be accessible, and the effect of the chapel interior would have been solemn, dignified, and impressive (**3.11-3.16**). Entry to the chapel was to be through a doorway, set in the battered podium, over which was to be a massive, monolithic, pedimented element resembling a huge sarcophagus-lid, thus emphasising the awe and Sublime Terror of Death. The resemblance to Birmingham Town Hall is immediately apparent.

Welch's 'Sketch of the Proposed Lodges for the General Cemetery' (**3.17-3.18**) shows a handsome Greek Doric *propylaeum* flanked by lower lodges articulated by means of *antae*. This type of formal Neoclassical entrance-gateway owes its origins to the Athenian prototype (fifth century BC), and re-emerged in Western Europe with the Brandenburg Gate, Berlin (1789-94), by Carl Gotthard Langhans (1732-1808), the Propylaeum, Chester

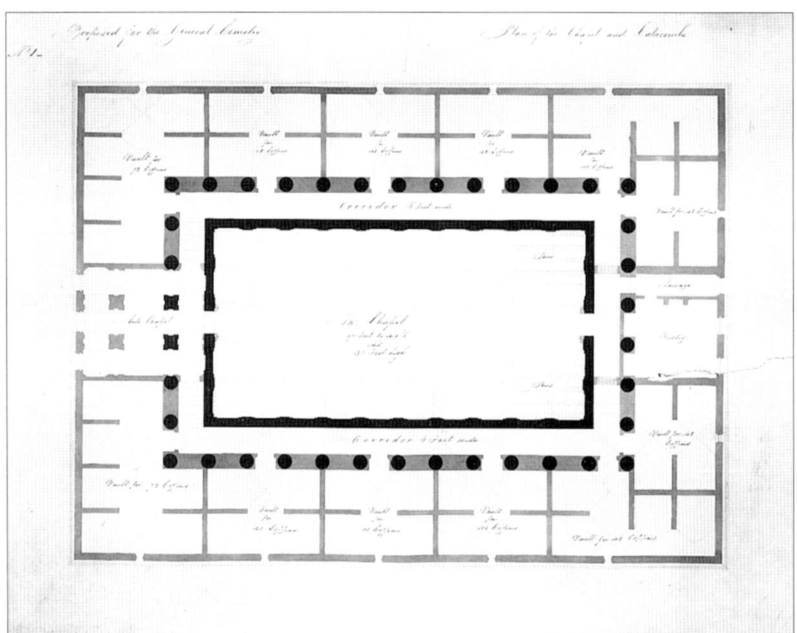

3.11 *(left)* Welch's plan of the chapel (drawing No. 1), entry No. 42. Entry to the chapel was through the massive battered base (which contained the vaults and the chapel that was partially sunk into the base (*GCC.#18/10. MC. Z140900*).

3.12 *(below left)* Drawing No. 2 of Welch's entry, showing the octastyle temple on the massive base, with the entrance under a huge sarcophagus-like block of stone (*GCC.#18/2.MC.Y140900*).

3.13 *(below right)* Side elevation of the proposed chapel (No. 3 of Welch's entry) (*GCC.#18/3 MC.X140900*).

3.14 *(bottom left)* Transverse section through the chapel and vaults. No. 4 of Welch's entry (*GCC.#18/4.MC.W140900*).

3.15 *(bottom right)* Longitudinal section through the chapel and vaults. No. 5 of Welch's entry (*GCC.#18/5.MC.AA140900*).

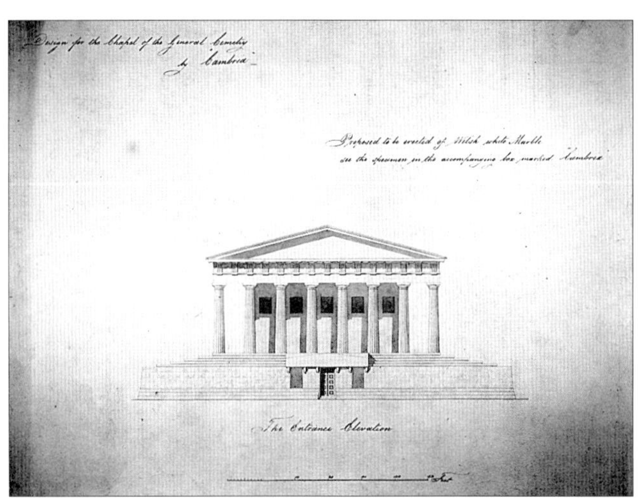

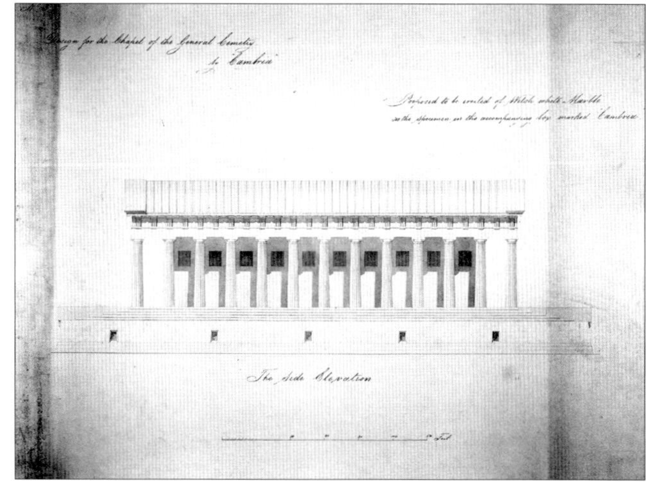

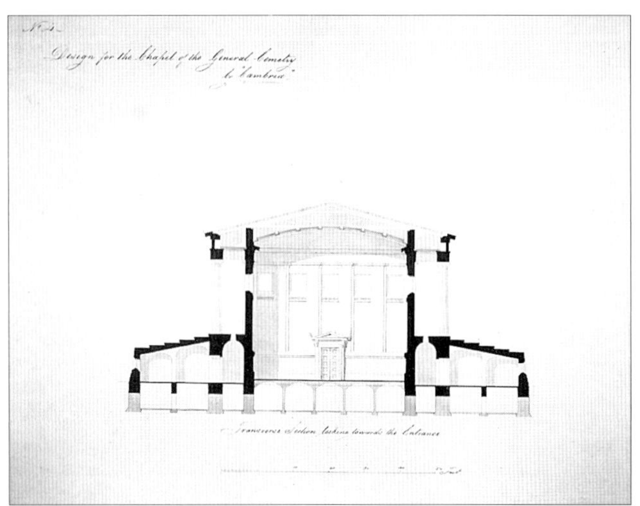

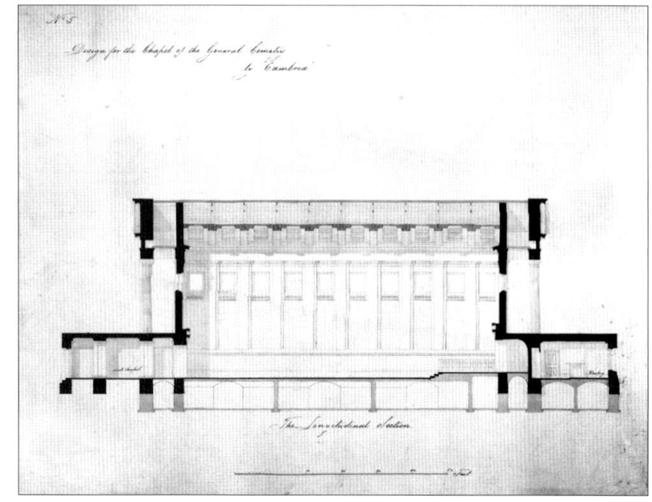

3.16 Perspective of Welch's design for the chapel (GCC.#65.MC.G140900).

3.17 Plan and elevation of Welch's design for the lodges (GCC.#65.MC.R140900).

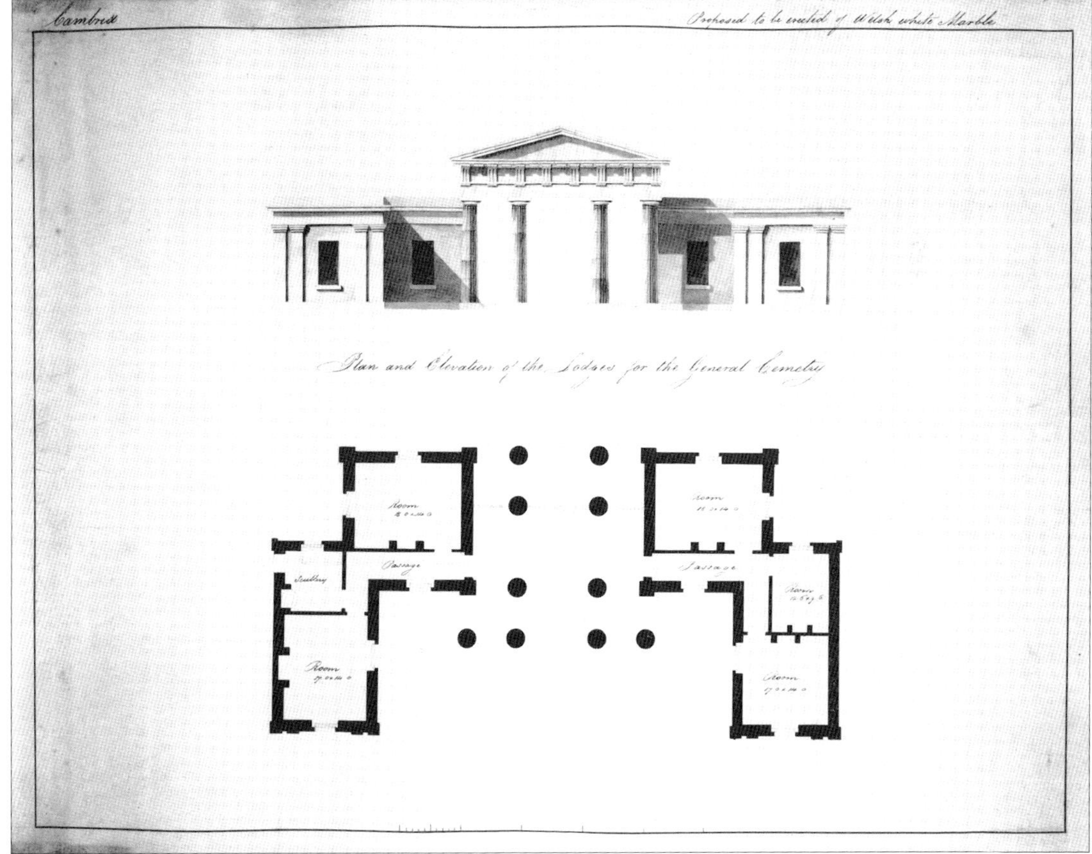

3.18 Welch's 'Sketch of the Proposed Lodges for the General Cemetry' [*sic*] (GCC.#65.MC. S140900C).

(1811-13), by Thomas Harrison (1744-1829),[23] and the unrealised but very fine gateway to Downing College, Cambridge, by William Wilkins (1778-1839).[24]

Kendall's Winning Gothic Scheme

At the Committee meeting of 1 March 1832 it was reported that, the sub-committee having studied the entries for the competition, the premium of one hundred guineas should be awarded to Henry Edward Kendall for his designs in the Gothic style (No. 43) and the Secretary duly wrote to Kendall at his office in 17 Suffolk Street, Pall Mall, informing him of this, and inviting him to apply to the Company's office at 95 Great Russell Street for payment.[25] Curiously, the author of Design No. 4 was invited 'to complete his drawings for the inspection of the Committee' upon the motion of Spottiswoode: as it turns out, the 'author' was none other than Paul, so it seems something rather curious was going on as the conditions of the competition were very clear regarding unfinished submissions.[26]

On 5 March a special meeting was held at which, 'after reading letter from Mr Kendall', 'the design No. 4 which was not clear on account of the incomplete condition of the drawings, be considered, and that the architect thereof be requested to prepare an estimate of the expense of the same and to report thereon'.[27] Soon afterwards the author of the design signed 'Cambria' (No. 42, Edward Welch) wrote to the committee and to Lord Ingestre, but consideration of the letter was postponed. Kendall also wrote to request that he 'attend the Committee for the purpose of giving any explanations or information respecting his design' to which the Company responded by inviting Kendall to do so but that 'the Chairman be instructed to inform him that in calling him in the

[23] Crook (1972), *passim*. [24] Liscombe (1980), *passim*; Watkin (*ed.*) (2000), 5-7. [25] Minutes of the Provisional Committee of the General Cemetery Company (1 March 1832), 108. [26] Ibid. [27] Ibid. (5 March 1832), 110.

Committee' did not 'intend to give him any intimation with respect either to the adoption or rejection of his plan'.[28]

Kendall estimated that his design for the chapel and lodge would cost £12,500 to build, with 'plain facings' to be of white Suffolk brick and the 'ornamental parts of stone', but that if stone were used instead of brick the cost would be increased by £2,000 or £2,500. He was then subjected to questioning about making the chapel wider, and asked to give estimates of the costs off the top of his head, but he was not be drawn, and pointed out that such arbitrary changes would alter the proportions of his design. By 19 March Kendall was able to report that he could widen the chapel by four feet six inches and face it in stone for £13,300. The Committee then compared Kendall's Gothic scheme with those of 'Ogrotus' and 'Cambria' as follows:

	Kendall	'Ogrotus' (as it appears)[29]	Cambria
width	20 feet 6 inches	50 feet	44 feet 6 inches
length	74 feet 6 inches	50 feet	90 feet 6 inches
internal height	31 feet 9 inches	112 feet 'exclusive of cupola'	32 feet
external height	46 feet 0 inches to top of gable	140 feet	57 feet
area	2510 square feet	2500 square feet	3960 square feet
cost	£10,800	£11,000	£11,000
coffins	3030	4000	2500
material	brick and stone	stone	'Mona' marble

Welch was then called in to be questioned about his design, and emphasised that 'the Town Hall at Birmingham' was 'not the same design but of the Corinthian Order'. He also pointed out that his proposals for the chapel were 'not exactly after the Temple of Neptune at Paestum' but that 'the intercolumniations' were the same. There was also talk of what might happen if the 'temple' were to be reduced in size, and various niggling questions of the cheese-paring kind, but in due course it was resolved to 'adopt' Kendall's plan: one member (Foss), however, gave notice of his 'intention to move at the next meeting that the resolution should be rescinded. This was because it was absolutely necessary to defer the selection of a design 'and any further measures for the construction of the same' until Directors had been 'regularly appointed'.[30] Unfortunately, this has been interpreted in the past as indicative of a clash of personalities and different supporters of various styles within the Provisional Committee, but it seems that Foss and those who supported him were concerned that nothing further should be decided until the legalities and proper procedures had been sorted out once the Bill (then progressing through Parliament) had become an Act.

It was around this time, however, that George Frederick Carden and Sir John Dean Paul, Bart., entered into correspondence 'respecting the drawings and designs',[31] the first indication of serious disagreements among members of the Provisional Committee that were to lead later to much acrimony. Meanwhile, Kendall, frustrated, no doubt, by lack of progress, having won the first premium, decided to draw attention to his scheme by publishing his designs.[32] He called in one of the foremost architectural illustrators of the time, Thomas Allom (1804-72), who had been a pupil of Francis Goodwin, as his collaborator, and the result was a slim volume entitled *Sketches of the Approved Designs of a Chapel and Gateway Entrances, intended to be erected at Kensal Green for the General Cemetery Company*, published by J. Williams in 1832 with lithographs by Allom

[28] Ibid. (15 March 1832), 116-7. [29] Ibid. (19 March 1832), 120. [30] Ibid., 123-4. [31] Ibid. (12 April 1832), 135.
[32] Kendall and Allom (1832).

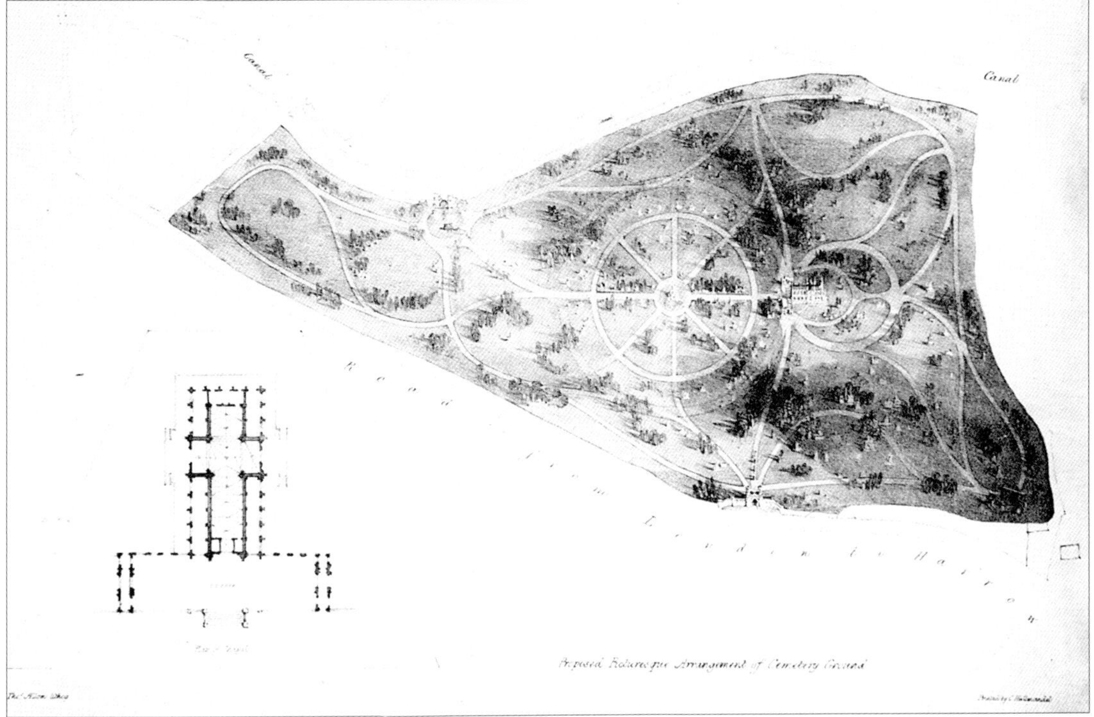

3.19 'Proposed Picturesque Arrangement of Cemetery Ground' showing Kendall's suggestions (probably derived from the Nash/ Liddell scheme) for the siting of the chapel, water-gate, and entrance-gate, lithographed by Allom and printed by Hullmandel. From Kendall and Allom (1832) (*ECJSC*).

printed by Charles Joseph Hullmandel (1789-1850). In this publication Kendall and Allom showed their 'Proposed Picturesque Arrangement of Cemetery Ground' which depicts the entrance-gate sited much further west than in the realised scheme, but the Anglican chapel is shown approximately where the Greek Revival chapel was eventually erected, and there was to be a water-gate through which funerals would proceed from the canal (3.19). The circular arrangement of paths to the east of the chapel, however, may have derived from Liddell and Nash, and was realised in modified form.

The style of Gothic Kendall selected for the buildings was a mixture of 14th-century Second Pointed and late-Gothic Perpendicular of the late 15th and early 16th centuries. This is clearly shown in the plate illustrating 'Entrance Gateway from the Road to the proposed Cemetery, Kensall Green': the effect of the latter was somewhat spoiled by the word CEMETERY carved in a panel set above the pointed water-gate (3.20).

There were two plates of the exterior of the chapel, one the 'North East View of Proposed Cemetery Chapel, Kensall Green', showing a cruciform building with two arcaded wings terminating in arches, the whole ensemble set on a raised platform under which was the catacomb. A

3.20 'Entrance Gateway from the Road to the proposed Cemetery, Kensall [*sic*] Green', and 'Water Gate from the Grounds of the proposed Cemetery Kensall [*sic*] Green' by Kendall, lithographed by Allom and printed by Hullmandel. From Kendall and Allom (1832) (*ECJSC*).

3.21 'North East View of proposed Cemetery Chapel, Kensall [*sic*] Green', by Kendall, lithographed by Allom and printed by Hullmandel. From Kendall and Allom (1832) (*ECJSC*).

3.22 'South West View of proposed Cemetery Chapel, Kensall [*sic*] Green', by Kendall, lithographed by Allom and printed by Hullmandel. From Kendall and Allom (1832) (*ECJSC*).

funeral procession was shown ascending the ramp to the platform, and the grounds were shown with only a few monuments (**3.21**). The other plate, 'South West View of proposed Cemetery Chapel, Kensall Green', shows the entrance-gate on the left, trees planted as though in a spacious parkland, and a few tombs, some Classical, others Gothic (**3.22**).

Inside the chapel the illustration (**3.23**) shows funerary monuments intended to commemorate those buried in the catacomb below, box-pews, and a vaulted ceiling (presumably of plaster, as Kendall intended the interior to be rendered).[33]

The collaboration with Allom, although not unusual in that the latter was in great demand as an architectural draughtsman, may be more significant than has been thought: could the celebrated view of the cemetery (**Frontispiece**) be an impression of Kendall's Grecian entry to the competition (No. 44), or a composite version of some sort?

33 All the above from Kendall and Allom (1832), *passim*.

3.23 Interior of Kendall's proposed chapel, Kensall [*sic*] Green', lithographed by Allom and printed by Hullmandel. From Kendall and Allom (1832) (*ECJSC*).

The Rise of Griffith

Once the result of the competition had been announced, and Kendall had been paid his premium, the impression given in the Minutes is one of indecision, and it is clear the Provisional Committee was unwilling to build anything more until the Act of Incorporation problem had been resolved. Griffith was directed to leave an opening in the wall in a position he deemed 'proper for the Entrance Gateway',[34] however, so there were some signs that further building-works were being contemplated. The Commissioners of Woods and Forests declared their desire to treat with the Company for the purchase of seven acres of the purpose of being used, in case of need, as a burial-place for cholera victims,[35] and the Provisional Committee repeated its earlier offer to sell for £2,000.

To the evident relief of the Provisional Committee, the Bill passed through the Committee-stage of the House, and was ordered to be presented as printed, with only minor modifications. However, the Provisional Committee, together with the Canal Company, were anxiously watching the progress of another Bill, that dealing with the London and Birmingham Railway, as it passed through Parliament, and Price promised to keep his eye on things on behalf of the Committee. It was Price, too, who had a letter proposing a plan for laying out the cemetery ground in terraces in order to save space. Although the Minutes do not reveal the author of the letter, it was probably Loudon, whose views on these matters were well publicised.[36] Griffith managed to get the Canal

34 Minutes of the Provisional Committee (5 March 1832), 111. 35 Ibid. (8 March 1832), 113. 36 Ibid. (19 March 1832), 120.

Company to agree to some modifications of the line of the canal 'by carrying it along the outer boundary of the land at Kensall Green', thus making the erection of a boundary-wall on that side more straightforward.

By 29 March 1832 the Committee had recognised the necessity of postponing any decisions about building the chapel until Directors were 'regularly appointed',[37] so, in spite of all the earlier decisions to award the premium to Kendall, and a resolution (19 March 1832) to adopt his design, the whole question of cemetery buildings was deferred. The matter of selling the land south of the canal was stymied by the Treasury, which was of the opinion that it would be 'inexpedient' (a wonderful word used by bureaucrats, which, if translated, means 'no money is available for this purpose') to 'purchase the ground in question for the purpose specified'.[38] The Provisional Committee was thus left with an awkward patch of land on the opposite side of the canal that would be difficult to connect with the cemetery proper. However, the good news was that the Bill had been read a second time, and would go into Committee very soon.[39]

A sub-committee consisting of Paul, Carden, and Griffith was detailed to negotiate with the Canal and Railway Companies, and the Board of the Canal Company, anxious, no doubt, to make common cause with the Provisional Committee of the Cemetery Company against the railway, collaborated in the re-alignment of the southern boundary of the cemetery ground. The Provisional Committee of the General Cemetery Company paid the Grand Junction Canal Company £1,000 towards 'turning the canal'.

As work on the boundary-wall proceeded, all was not well within the designated cemetery itself, for the trees were 'of a bad description and badly planted', so Ronalds was ordered to propose a solution. The lack of progress led the Committee to resolve that it was 'open to receive any suggestions relating to the Ground or buildings of the Cemetery'.[40] Discussions took place with the Railway Company about the possibilities of running the line through a tunnel, and negotiations proceeded.

Then the Bishop of London, who had been assured by Paul and Spottiswoode that the 'outlines of the Bill should be communicated to him before any measures were taken to obtain the sanction of the legislature', wrote to ask for a copy of the Bill so that he could establish 'in what manner the objects' were provided for 'which he was assured should be carefully attended to in any scheme submitted to Parliament'.[41] This must have caused much fluttering in the columbaria of the Cemetery Company, for, although the Bill passed the Committee of the House of Commons, it was 'stayed on acc[t.] of the Bishop of London's letter' and a clause had been inserted upon the Petition of the Parish of Saint Pancras, preventing the Company from 'purchasing land in that parish for the purposes of the act'.[42]

Controversy and Animosities

By April 1832 disagreements between Carden and Paul had become overt, and Carden copied correspondence between himself and Paul to the Provisional Committee.[43] Paul was obliged to write (as Chairman) to Chadwick to ask him to proceed with the completion of the contract for building the boundary-wall, but not to exceed the sum of £5,000 until further orders. This was probably due to shortage of funds caused by defaulters failing to pay the instalments of their shares, but confidence was badly shaken by the probability that the railway would impinge upon the cemetery grounds. The Provisional Committee instructed its solicitor to procure the insertion of a clause in the 'Birmingham Railroad Act' defining the precise route of the line, and that the 'Rail Road

[37] Ibid. (29 March 1832), 124. [38] Ibid., 125. [39] Ibid., 126. [40] Ibid., 127. [41] Ibid. (12 April 1832), 132. [42] Ibid., 134. [43] Ibid. (12 April 1832), 135.

Company' should 'make a Tunnel as per plan & section'. Furthermore, the Railway Company was to pay 'an adequate compensation' for the land forming the site of the tunnel and for the 'dangers which the Cemetery Company' would suffer.

Matters took a turn for the worse when a letter was received from Manchester respecting an anonymous publication in *The Times*, to which the Company replied that it never noticed anonymous letters published in newspapers. Funds were also disturbingly low, and Paul wrote to the Bishop of London requesting an early communication of his suggestions on and objections to the Bill, as 'it was of great consequence to the Company to have it passed'.[44] Negotiations with the Canal Company were broken off because it was realised a footpath existed through the land on the other side of the canal, and Griffith was instructed to proceed with the erection of the wall on the southern side of the land, 'making proper apertures for iron railing'.[45]

In order to pacify the Bishop of London, Paul, Ingestre, and Spottiswoode went to see him to 'endeavour to enter into a negociation [*sic*] respecting the interests of the Clergy of the several Parishes of the Metropolis as they may be affected by the interment of bodies in the Cemetery'. Funds were running so low that Paul was authorised to 'let the Grass at Kensall Green in such manner' as he thought proper.[46] This was duly let as feed for 200 sheep for the princely sum of £25. Griffith was also instructed to commence work on the drains, and to leave a space 50 feet wide for an 'entrance Gate at the East end of the ground' then 'being enclosed'.

Once the Bishop had been appeased by the undertaking to pay fees to the clergy for interments of corpses deriving from their parishes, the passage of the Bill was eased. This was just as well, because the Bishop had succeeded in stopping the Golden Lane Cemetery Bill, another promotion of the time.[47] The General Cemetery Company's Bill therefore passed through the House of Commons and was 'read a first time in the House of Lords'.[48] It was Paul who 'waited on' Lord Melbourne with a request that he would move for a Select Committee in the Lords, and indeed it seems to have been Paul, with his many connections, who had the clout to deal with Parliament, the clergy, and the Railway and Canal Companies. The passage of the Bill through the Lords was held up because insufficient capital had been subscribed, so Paul offered to lend money to top up the capital for the purposes of the exercise, and this was accepted with thanks by the Committee.[49]

The Railway Company, however, refused to make a tunnel, so the Provisional Committee determined to argue the matter through with Stephenson. The difficulties of the Provisional Committee were compounded by the fact that the Railway Company's Bill was going through Parliament at the same time as that of the General Cemetery Company, so it was important to resolve the tunnel problem if petitioning Parliament against the Railway Bill were to be avoided. However, no agreements could be reached, so the Provisional Committee resolved to prepare a Petition to be presented to the House of Commons against the Railway Bill, and, if necessary, to organise further opposition in the House of Lords.[50]

The General Cemetery Provisional Committee also experienced opposition to its Bill from several clergymen, and it was decided to appease the Rector of St Marylebone by allowing him 2s. 6d. in addition to the 5s. 0d. already allowed him for 'interments' in the cemetery vaults. The parish of St Marylebone then changed tack and declared itself in favour of the Bill. Shortage of funds prompted the Committee to question Griffith's charges of 5 per cent on the costs of the works (including all measuring), and it was

44 Minutes of the Provisional Committee (25 April 1832), 139. 45 Ibid. (10 May 1832), 141. 46 Ibid., 141. 47 Ibid. (24 May 1832), 144. 48 Ibid. (1 June 1832), 145. 49 Ibid. (5 June 1832), 146c (the pages are not numbered at this point in the Minutes). 50 Ibid., 146e and f.

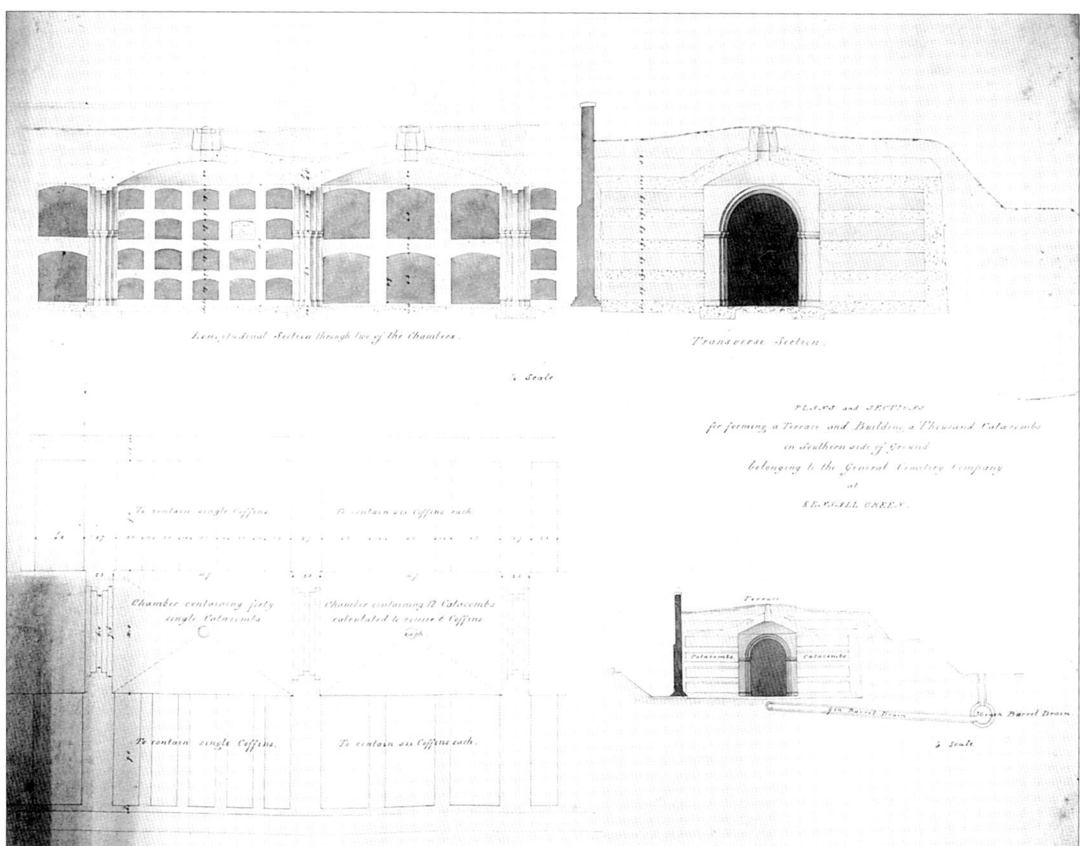

3.24 'Plans and Sections for forming a Terrace and Building a Thousand Catacombs on Southern Side of Ground belonging to the General Cemetery Company at Kensall [*sic*] Green' by William Moseley, 1832 (*GCC #20. MC. AJ140900*).

resolved that he should be satisfied with 3 per cent, otherwise he 'be not enabled to proceed beyond the next Committee day further with the works till this point could be settled and his accounts rendered'.[51] This matter was raised by Pugin, and the Committee resolved to instruct Griffith to abide by its decision, which might indicate friction between Pugin and Griffith. Further evidence of attempts to cut costs is found in Paul's introduction of 'Mr William Moseley of King's Road', who proposed a 'new material for making Catacombs' made of concrete, which would be cheaper than 'the expense of Brickwork at £12 pr rod'.[52] Moseley produced a plan of his design for a catacomb some 100 feet long (**3.24**), and was asked to produce an estimate of its cost. In the event, the project did not get anywhere.

Work on the walls was held up as Chadwick was finding difficulty in obtaining facing-bricks, but a new load was to be barged to the site and he hoped to complete the north and east walls 11 days after delivery, and the rest in three weeks from 28 June. These bricks were made in Ware, in Hertfordshire, and took about a week to reach Kensal Green. However, it should be said that, once Chadwick got his materials, construction-work was remarkably speedy. At the same meeting[53] Paul reported that he, Price, and the Railway Company had agreed terms, but these were 'to be kept secret'. Bowman was to confer with the Railway Company to 'make the best arrangement ... towards the introduction into the Railway Bill of the Clauses necessary to carry the agreement into effect'. Griffith responded to the queries about his charges, stating that 5 per cent on the value was the 'usual allowance', and provided supporting evidence from

[51] Ibid. (19 June 1832), 146h. [52] Ibid. (28 June 1832), 146i. A *rod*, *pole*, or *perch* was 5½ yards or 16½ feet (5.0292 metres), and a rod of brickwork was 272 square feet (25.2688 square metres) of standard thickness of 1½ bricks, or 306 cubic feet (8.66592 cubic metres). [53] Ibid.

'Mr Hardwick',[54] but modestly said he did not 'mean that as between him and the Committee he should claim that percentage, but on the contrary he should be content with whatever compensation the Committee might award'.[55] This disarmed the Committee, Pugin's motion of the previous meeting was rescinded, and Griffith was instructed to proceed with the works.

Thus, although he had been awarded the first premium in the architectural competition for his Gothic designs, and in spite of his handsome publication in collaboration with Allom, Kendall seems to have had little chance that his designs would ever be realised, and this became more obvious as time passed. The reasons for this are possible to ascertain, and one of the problems as far as Kendall was concerned was the presence of Griffith on the Provisional Committee: as time went on, Griffith seems to have consolidated his position, and presumably had the ear of influential members of the inner circle (notably Spottiswoode and Paul) in order to become architect of the buildings himself (after all, he had designed the early layouts of the ground [taking into account ideas from Liddell and Nash], and his boundary-walls were being erected at the time). Griffith (who was a competent architect and no mean draughtsman) doubtless would have found his position untenable if another architect's scheme had been adopted by the Company, and it is clear that, by mid-1832, his services and advice had become of great importance to the Committee, although Pugin had queried Griffith's professional charges, thinking them high,[56] but Pugin's criticisms were swiftly rejected by that Committee. There was also the question of style. Gothic was not yet *de rigueur*, and the fashionable *clientèle* envisaged for the cemetery was used to Classicism, so it was Classicism that eventually won the day for the buildings. Some Committee-members were doubtless correct in taking the view that any decision on the buildings would be premature until the Bill of Incorporation passed through Parliament.

The Passing of the Act of Incorporation

On 11 July 1832 this Act[57] received the Royal Assent, and the Company was duly incorporated under *An Act for establishing a General Cemetery for the Interment of the Dead in the Neighbourhood of the Metropolis*.[58] Named in the Act as Subscribers united into the Company were Lords Milton and Ingestre, Sir Robert Price, Bart., Sir John Dean Paul, Bart., the Hon. William Booth Grey, Sir Henry Pynn, George Neville Adams, John Atkins, George Frederick Carden, John Sherring Clark, Edward Foss, Thomas Gaspey, John Griffith, Andrew Macklew, James Kyrle Money, George Robert Paul, Henry Ansley Purchas, Augustus Pugin, Robert William Sievier, Andrew Spottiswoode, Robert Walpole, and Thomas Wilson.[59] Under the Act the Company was empowered to raise £45,000 (a huge reduction on Carden's original scheme, just short of a seventh part of his ambitious target) in shares of £25 each, purchase up to 80 acres of land, lay out and enclose a cemetery, and build a chapel 'for the Purpose of performing therein the Burial Service according to the Established Form of the United Church of *England* and *Ireland*.[60] In order to soften opposition to the cemetery by the metropolitan clergy (who depended to a large extent on burial-fees for their income), the Act stipulated that for each interment in the new cemetery a fee (ranging from 1s. 6d. to 5s. depending on the type of grave) should be paid to the incumbent of the parish from which each corpse came.[61]

[54] Philip Hardwick (1792-1870), then architect to numerous bodies and estates, including The Goldsmiths' Company (from 1828) and the Westminster Bridge Estate (from 1829). [55] Minutes of the Provisional Committee (28 June 1832), no pagination. [56] Ibid. (19 June 1832), no pagination. [57] 2 & 3 Will. IV, c. 110, local and personal. [58] Printed by George Eyre & Andrew Spottiswoode. [59] 2 & 3 Will. IV., c. 110, I. [60] Ibid., XXII. The Churches of England and Ireland were united as a result of the Act of Union (39 & 40 Geo. III, c. 67, and 40 Geo. III, c. 38) of 1800, effective from 1 January 1801. [61] Act of Parliament (1832), XXVII.

Various other matters probably affected the outcome of the search for suitable designs for the buildings. Carden had exhibited the models and drawings, 'particularly the Gothic Design, for which the Committee awarded to Mr Kendall the premium of 100 guineas', at his offices, Mitre Court Building, Temple, on 6, 7, and 9 April 1832. Carden, in a pamphlet, stated he had 'set apart the days above mentioned … for the purpose of explaining' intentions and 'answering enquiries'. He emphasised that he must naturally feel an interest in the success of his own project, but the Provisional Committee took exception, and resolved that no member of this Committee be permitted to circulate papers relating to the Company without the sanction of the Committee.

The meetings of 5, 12, and 19 July 1832 were the last of the Provisional Committee, and were largely concerned with the Committee's Report to be presented at the General Meeting to be held on 24 July at Exeter Hall, Strand. There was a suggestion that an application should be made to the King (William IV) for His Majesty's Patronage for the undertaking: this was not an unusual step at the time, but Royal Patronage was usually reserved for philanthropic or charitable organisations, such as the Society for Improving the Condition of the Labouring Classes, with which both Queen Victoria and Prince Albert were to be closely involved.[62]

Viscount Ingestre chaired the momentous General Meeting of 24 July at which the clauses of the Act of Incorporation (passed, as previously noted, on 11 July 1832) were read, together with the Report of the Proceedings of the Provisional Committee. Bowman was appointed Clerk to the Company, John Dean Paul Treasurer, George Frederick Carden Registrar, Purchas and Gaspey Scrutineers, Cornish Auditor, and the following Directors of the new General Cemetery Company were elected: Col. Purchas, Lord Ingestre, Sir Robert Price, Bart., M.P., Viscount Milton, J. H. Langston, M.P., Andrew Macklew, Sir John Dean Paul, Bart., Andrew Spottiswoode, The Hon. Thomas Liddell, General William Eden, Captain George Evans, R.N., and James Morison. Gaspey and Col. J. Kyrle Money were appointed Auditors.

The Report dwelled on the difficulties of compensating clergy for loss of burial-fees, and emphasised the fact that the Provisional Committee had been at pains to consult the Bishop of London in order to arrive at suitable agreed rates. The saga of the problems of getting the Bill through Parliament was described, and once more the hideous condition of the crowded metropolitan burial-grounds was cited as the main reason for founding the cemetery. The search for suitable land was outlined, the purchase of the ground at Kensal Green for £9,400 was reported, and the state of the boundary-wall was described as 'very forward', the whole to be completed by 1 August. The Report claimed that the wall gave 'general satisfaction', and the next step, to drain the land, was outlined. A culvert was to be constructed to enable a main drain to pass 'under the Paddington Canal', and the rest of the cemetery was to be properly drained, laid out, and planted. Ruefully, the Report related the negotiations with the Government to buy the patch of land south of the canal for the burial of cholera victims, but, 'when the alarm of the cholera subsided', the Government cried off.

It was reported that a chapel, gateway, and offices would be required to be built, and, to this end, the 'Architectural talent of the Country' had been invited to a consideration of the subject. 'Above 40 designs were accordingly sent in, none of them such as the Committee could recommend for execution.' The first premium was awarded, but the Committee, mindful that 'the period of … its … trust was drawing to a close, resolved it prudent to postpone the decision' of a final design 'until after the appointment of a Director on whom' the task of 'carrying the works into execution' must devolve.[63] Negotiations with the 'Birmingham Railway Company', which had wanted 'leave to pass

[62] Curl (1983*c*), *passim*. [63] Minutes of the Proceedings of the General Meetings (24 July 1832), *passim*.

through the grounds with the "Steam Carriages"' had led to Parliament incorporating certain clauses in the Railway Act that protected the cemetery. Lastly, capital subscribed was £36,725 of which £22,193 17s. 4d. had been paid up.

This demonstrated how sights had had to be lowered. Carden's original scheme envisaged a very grand cemetery, and Goodwin's proposals would have cost £300,000 to realise. The Act of Parliament[64] stated that the Proprietors were given leave to raise capital not exceeding £45,000 'for making and maintaining the Cemetery' divided into 1,800 shares of £25 each. However, the Company had powers[65] to borrow money, not exceeding £15,000, an arrangement that was altered by a subsequent Act[66] which enabled the Company to raise further sums by subscription.

Griffith as De Facto *Architect*

Thus, by the end of July 1832, the General Cemetery Company had been incorporated by Act of Parliament, and Directors had been appointed, so real progress was possible at last. Under Viscount Ingestre (Chairman from 1832 to 1834), considerable strides were made. At the first meeting of the Directors Sir John Dean Paul, Bart., was appointed Deputy Chairman, and Robert W. Carden was requested to act as broker to the Company. The contract entered into by Paul with Chadwick for building the boundary-wall was confirmed and adopted by the Company,[67] and it was resolved that the 'several Works' then in progress and authorised by the Provisional Committee or by Paul should be 'proceeded with'.

Griffith was instructed to 'look out for an eligible piece of land to form a Cemetery for Dissenters', so clearly the Directors were in an expansive frame of mind, although why the patch of ground south of the canal was not set aside for Dissenters is unclear. Griffith was also instructed to arrange for the erection of an iron railing in part of the southern wall of the cemetery.[68]

Sievier was 'requested to furnish a design for a common seal for the Company', the Clerk was instructed to prepare a 'Code of Byelaws' for the consideration of the Board. Other matters included changing the names of various Bank accounts from 'Trustees of the General Cemetery Company' to 'General Cemetery Company', paying the Poor and Highway rate for the land ('due at Christmas last') at once, and collecting arrears from subscribers to shares.

Bowman suggested that his house at 95 Great Russell Street, Bloomsbury, should be taken by the Company on a lease of 21 years at £90 per annum, and that he should continue to reside in the part of the house not required for offices by the Company. This was accepted by the Board.

Griffith 'produced a sketch and plan for a Chapel'[69] and reported that Chadwick would complete the wall in '21 days except as to the iron railing'. Griffith was directed to draw the site of the chapel (on the 'spot now staked out') on plans, and to arrange for the principal entrance to the cemetery to be at the east end of the ground. A 'water entrance' (i.e. gate to the canal) and north entrance were ordered to be 'placed at the distance of about 250 feet to the Eastward side of the Eastern face of the Chapel'. Roads from the entrances to the chapel were ordered to be staked out and commenced and then 'a large circle be formed in front of the site of the Chapel'.[70] Griffith was instructed to meet a sub-committee of the Directors (consisting of Liddell, Lord Ingestre, and Captain Evans) to 'consider the position of the Terraces & Catacombs and other points connected therewith'. He was also ordered to 'enter into contracts for the formation of

[64] VIII. [65] XVI. [66] 2 Vict. c. 5. [67] Minutes of the Proceedings of the Directors of the General Cemetery Company (25 July 1832), 1. [68] Ibid., 2. [69] Ibid. (31 July 1832), 5. [70] Ibid., 6.

Vaults and Terraces ... subject to the final approval of the next ... meeting of the Board'.[71]

Advertisements were inserted in the newspapers stating that the business of the Company would in future be conducted at its office, 95 Great Russell Street, and that the advertisements should contain the names of the Directors and Officers of the Company.

Griffith was authorised to 'treat' for a 'sufficient quantity of land for an approach to the East entrance to the Ground', which meant negotiating with a Mr Weedon, owner of the public-house, *The Plough*, and other land near by (**2.5**). Meanwhile, the buildings sub-committee had 'fixed the site of the Chapel, the position of the Circle, and the line of the principal roads as set out in the plan produced', and recommended that iron railings should be placed between certain points on the south boundary. Griffith was instructed to 'make arrangements for letting the land on the South side of the Canal',[72] as it appears he had found some ground at Peckham suitable for another cemetery at that time. Liddell was 'requested to communicate with Mr Nash relative to laying out the ground, Mr Nash having kindly offered his services in any way they might be useful'.[73]

This is an interesting entry in the Minutes, because it confirms that Liddell, Nash's protégé, was closely involved in the laying out of the essential elements of the ground, that the 'Great Circle' idea, which was very much a Nashean motif, was part of the early plan, and that Liddell was very much a party to that plan. The Board 'approving generally of the design submitted by the Hon.ble Mr Liddell, and coinciding with the expediency of his suggestion that a Model' would be 'requisite for the purpose of forming a correct judgement of any plan for the Chapel', requested that he should 'furnish such model the expense' of preparing which (estimated by Liddell as £50) the Board would be ready to defray. It is quite clear from the Minutes that this model was of a design for the Anglican chapel by Liddell himself, as there is a reference to 'the design proposed by Mr Liddell' to cost about £12,000 if faced in 'Mona marble'.[74] This could have been the genesis of the Anglican chapel design as realised by Griffith, and is possibly the building shown on the bird's-eye perspective (**Frontispiece**), which would confirm the date of that handsome water-colour as 1832.

Sievier, having been unwilling or unable to prepare a design for the Common Seal, seems to have passed the job on to 'Mr Stothard', who 'attended with a design' for the Seal 'which was not approved and he was directed to prepare one after the Mausoleum of Mausolus, also a form of Certificate of shares which was approved'.[75] This 'Mr Stothard' was probably Alfred Joseph Stothard (d. 1864), who was well-known as a medallist: one of the sons of Thomas Stothard (1755-1834 – the celebrated painter, illustrator, and designer of commemorative devices, who by 1832 was very infirm), A. J. Stothard was no mean artist himself. Another design, prepared in a couple of days, was also not approved[76] but the share Certificate met with approbation and was 'ordered to be engraved fools-cap size'.

No. 95 Great Russell Street was duly leased to the Company, and another sub-committee was appointed to 'carry the necessary repairs and alterations ... into effect'. Griffith produced plans of 'roads and plantations as prepared by him and Mr Liddell',[77] which was 'approved of' and would 'be made use of with reference to the disposition of the planting'.[78] The Board also ordered that a specification should be prepared for forming the roads and walks, proposals made for 'executing the same' and that Griffith should be 'empowered to enter into the necessary contracts.[79] It was decided to give instructions that a 'specification of planting' should be made, and proposals obtained from nurserymen for 'furnishing and planting trees and shrubs accordingly, the

[71] Ibid. [72] Ibid. (4 August 1832), 7. [73] Ibid. [74] Ibid. (8 August 1832), 10. The estimate was prepared by J. A. Hansom, architect. [75] Ibid. (4 August 1832), 8. [76] Ibid. (8 August 1832), 9. [77] Ibid., 10. [78] Ibid. [79] Ibid.

Contractor guaranteeing their growth for three years and to replace in case of failure'.[80]

A sub-committee (Paul, Spottiswoode, Purchas, and Eden) was set up to consider bye-laws, regulations, burial-fees, and scales of charges, and Griffith was instructed to prepare a 'ground plan of the Cemetery for the purpose of the sale of Graves, &c.'.[81] The Clerk was requested to take all 'proper steps preparatory to the Consecration of the Ground', and a box was ordered to be 'procured for the Seal with two keys, one to be in the Custody of a Director, and the other of the Clerk'.

3.25 Impression made of the Seal of the General Cemetery Company, designed by Stothard (*GCC.MC. F131200*).

In due course Stothard's design for the Common Seal received the *Imprimatur* of the Board, and Stothard was ordered to execute it. It cost £29 7s. 6d., but was nothing like the Halicarnassus Mausoleum: instead, it depicted the end of a sarcophagus embellished with an annulet, with a curved lid terminating in scrolls supported on aegicranes, with seated gryphons set beneath the aegicranes (3.25). Griffith was requested to proceed with the repairs and alterations at the property in Great Russell Street at a total cost of £455. Tenders for making the roads, walks, and plantations were received, and that of Messrs Ronalds & Son of Brentford was accepted, but 'consideration of the designs for the Chapel & entrance' was postponed until the next meeting. Paul was deputed to apply to the Bishop of London as to the 'early consecration of the ground'. Griffith had employed several people 'to burn Clay for making the roads upon Mr Langston's plan'.[82] Langston, of course, was a Member of Parliament and a Director of the Company, who appears to have had an interest in inventions and who had tried burnt-clay paths before. Nevertheless, Griffith was directed to furnish weekly accounts of 'expenses incurred in burning the clay for the roads', so the Board was keen to control its expenditure by all means possible.

The Bishop of London, as noted above, had refused to consecrate the ground until a chapel was erected, so it was decided to build a temporary chapel 'forthwith', and Paul was empowered to give all necessary instructions. Application was made to the Bishop to fix 1 November 1832 for the Consecration (All Saints' Day). However, it seems that even at that late stage there was still much controversy about the designs of any permanent chapel, for correspondence about this was received from Lords Milton and Ingestre, and from 'Messrs Welch & Co. as to the design marked Cambria' in the architectural competition (described elsewhere). Indeed, Welch attended the Board to explain his design and James Pennethorne (1801-71), another pupil of Nash, was called in to elaborate upon the model of Liddell's proposals, estimating the building would cost £12,000 and would hold 3,000 coffins, the whole to be constructed of red granite. Pennethorne completed Nash's Park Villages, Regent's Park, and from 1832 was employed by the Commissioners of Woods and Forests, but he was probably called in to advise on Kensal Green because he had worked with A. C. Pugin.

Conclusion

The Board seems to have gone to considerable lengths to obtain advice about the Anglican chapel, and Griffith himself 'attended the Board upon his design for the Chapel',[83] estimated to cost £11,000, with space for 5,000 coffins, the facings of the

[80] Minutes of the Proceedings of the Directors of the General Cemetery Company (8 August 1832), 11. [81] Ibid. [82] Ibid. (19 September 1832), 13. [83] Ibid. (10 October 1832), 15.

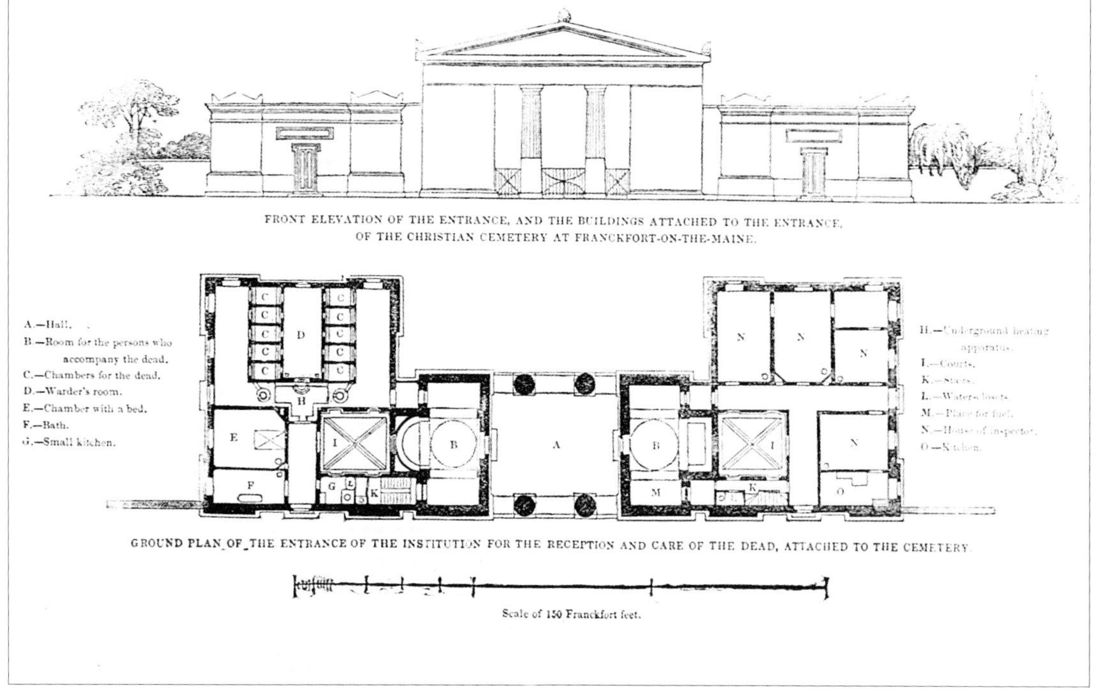

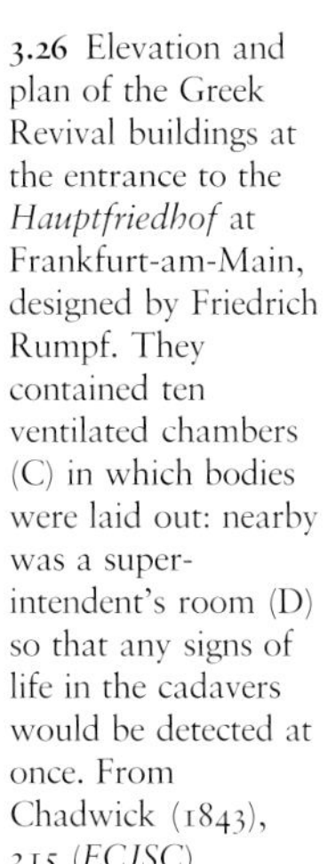

3.26 Elevation and plan of the Greek Revival buildings at the entrance to the *Hauptfriedhof* at Frankfurt-am-Main, designed by Friedrich Rumpf. They contained ten ventilated chambers (C) in which bodies were laid out: nearby was a super-intendent's room (D) so that any signs of life in the cadavers would be detected at once. From Chadwick (1843), 215 (*ECJSC*).

3.27 Section through 'House of Reception and Care of the Dead Previous to Interment' at the *Hauptfriedhof*, Frankfurt-am-Main. Note the drainage channels, ventilators, and connections from the fingers of the corpse to bells in the superintendent's room. From Chadwick (1843), 216 (*ECJSC*).

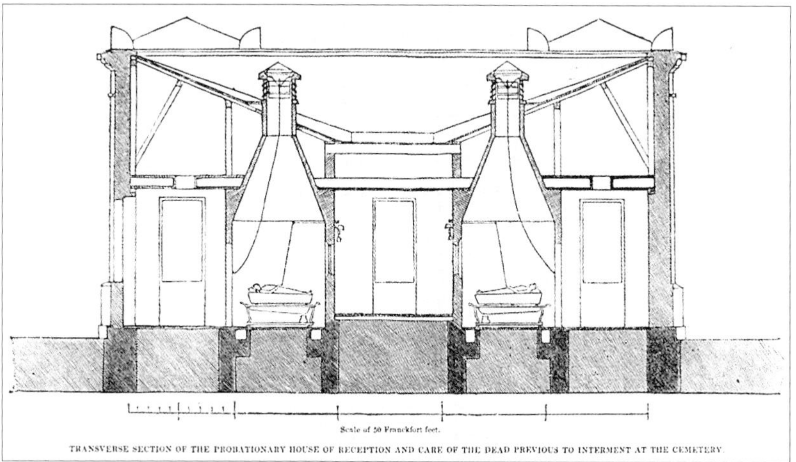

buildings to be of Portland stone. The Directors, clearly unwilling to commit themselves, decided to solicit the opinions of Sir Jeffry Wyatville, Robert Smirke, and Charles Robert Cockerell concerning the rival designs (was the author of the spoof *Prospectus* somebody with inside knowledge, one wonders?), and were requested to attend at the office of the Company.[84]

Towards the end of October the Bishop of London indicated his objections to consecrating the ground 'in its present state', which indicates that things were in a sorry mess, and that the place was extremely untidy: the whole question of Consecration therefore had to be postponed. In the meantime an account of the *Hauptfriedhof* (main cemetery) at Frankfurt-am-Main arrived from Messrs 'Gogel Kort & Co ... accompanied with a Book descriptive of the Cemetery'. The *Hauptfriedhof* was a model

84 Ibid., 16.

of what any modern cemetery should be, and it was greatly admired by many British commentators: the grounds had been laid out (1828) to designs by Sebastian Rinz, and the buildings, including the handsome Grecian entrance-gate and offices were designed by Friedrich Rumpf (1795-1867). Part of the architectural ensemble at Frankfurt contained a 'House of Reception and Care of the Dead Previous to Interment' in which cadavers would lie until it was obvious putrefaction had commenced (to prevent premature interment) (**3.26-27**).[85]

Some adjustments to the cemetery grounds were made when the St Quintin estate agreed to exchange two parcels of land on the north side of the canal for 'an equal quantity on the south side', the Company giving £100 for a cottage on the site and paying all conveyancing expenses.[86] Otherwise things do not appear to have proceeded very smoothly. Paul was sent away by Wyatville with a flea in his ear, for Sir Jeffry 'declined ... to give his opinion on the designs for the Chapel, stating ... he thought ... very few architects would like to interfere in the manner proposed'.[87] The temporary chapel, however, was under construction in October 1832, presumably to Griffith's designs, and Griffith was also instructed to build a 'range of catacombs of 200 feet in length (according to the plan produced by him) on the high ground next the north wall of the cemetery'.[88] Iron gates were placed at the north and south entrances of the ground, and Griffith was also asked to continue his attempts to procure a site for another cemetery for Dissenters on the Surrey side of the Thames.[89] In addition, he was 'directed to make the best arrangement he could for letting' the problematic seven acres of land south of the canal.[90]

Griffith seems to have been involved in many roles other than those of architect and surveyor, but he must have found his position trying at times. The contract for the construction of the catacomb and temporary chapel was again let to Chadwick, who fell behind, and was refused all further advances until he completed the catacomb and fitted out the temporary chapel (which cost £250). Griffith had no luck in finding suitable land south of the river, so it was decided to advertise for 20 acres within two miles from London, Blackfriars, or Waterloo bridges, but this came to nothing. Griffith was instructed to 'prepare a plan for Lodges', and set to work with his customary speed.[91]

Every effort was made to render the grounds fit for the Consecration, but there was a shadow over events. Reference was made several times to letters from G. F. Carden having been read at meetings, but in December 1832 he wrote to propose the Directors of the Company should purchase his shares. Carden was politely thanked, but informed that none of the Directors wished to buy them.[92] It was indicative of a serious rift between the Company and its begetter, and one that was to explode into a very public row.

85 Minutes of the Proceedings of the Directors of the General Cemetery Company (24 October 1832), 17. 86 Ibid. (10 October 1832), 16. This was a narrow sliver of land lying between the Company's boundary and the canal immediately to the west of what is now Ladbroke Grove. As it turned out, the company paid £250 for the land (**2.6**). *See* Appendix No. 3. 87 Ibid. (24 October 1832), 17. 88 Ibid., 18. 89 Ibid., 17. 90 Ibid. (5 December 1832), 20. 91 Ibid., 21. 92 Ibid. (12 December,1832), 22.

CHAPTER IV

The General Cemetery from 1833 to 1842

JAMES STEVENS CURL

The Consecration of the Cemetery and the Open Rift with Carden; Griffith Consolidates his Position; Building Works and Other Developments; The Designs for the Anglican Chapel; The Carden Problem and its Resolution; Other Difficulties; Conclusion

> No sooner was the cemetery opened than the boon was eagerly embraced by the public, and marble obelisks and urns began to rise among the cypresses in all the variety which heathen and classical allusions could suggest.
>
> EDWARD WALFORD (1823-97):
> *Old and New London: a Narrative of Its History, Its People, and Its Places*
> (London: Cassell, Petter, & Galping, *c.*1875), v, 220.

The Consecration of the Cemetery and the Open Rift with Carden

Early in 1833 plans were made for the Consecration of the 'Ground at Kensall Green',[1] and the 'Revd. Edward Johnstone, a Candidate for the office of Chaplain' to the General Cemetery Company, was requested to make himself available on 24 January 'to perform the service at the consecration'.[2] The Petition had been presented to the Bishop of London, and the Consecration was to be advertised if the Bishop approved. By the time of the next meeting on 23 January Johnstone had been 'offered more advantageous preferment', so withdrew his candidacy for the Chaplaincy, but 'consented to perform the services at the consecration and offered his services until he should be otherwise engaged'.[3] In order to lessen hostility among undertakers, Paul and the Clerk 'called upon' all of them to remove the 'impression that it was the intention of the Company to interfere with their trade', and duly won them over. It could have been very awkward if the 'dismal Trade' had boycotted the Company.

The Consecration duly went ahead and was widely reported in the newspapers. The *Morning Chronicle*[4] felt that the 'season of the new year selected for opening the ground' was 'far from favourable, and many years must elapse before the trees and shrubs' would be able to 'attain sufficient growth to entitle it even to comparison with its Continental rival, especially with its exquisite model', Père-Lachaise. The *Morning Chronicle* then went on to describe 'some little differences' that 'existed between certain parties concerned in the management of the Company's affairs', so that the cemetery was 'by no means in so forward a state as the subscribers' were 'entitled to expect'. The paper referred to 'models of some very beautiful designs for Chapels, Mausoleums, &c.', which had been 'made and partly approved of' but about which 'no final decision' had yet 'been arrived at', referring, of course, to the architectural competition.[5] In consequence of the refusal of the Bishop of London to consecrate the ground until a chapel had been put up, a 'temporary Chapel of very small dimensions, and of the Doric Order', had been built, and it was within this structure, 'designated All Souls', that the ceremony of Consecration took place, 'attended by several highly respectable ladies and gentlemen', though it was regretfully reported 'many complaints' were levelled by subscribers 'against the directors for the secrecy which they had endeavoured to preserve' respecting the Consecration. The newspaper also alleged that there were 'some very ill-timed attempts at exclusion' made on the occasion of the Consecration.[6]

The *Morning Chronicle* report is extraordinary, indicating more than mild disagreement, and the Publick Prints clearly picked this up, probably fed by some person or persons (very likely Carden and his associates). The newspaper went on to state that the 'Company... [had]... to contend with much hostility on the part of the Church of England', and fell upon 'an injurious plan to appease it', for 'all the inclosed ground, 42 acres', was consecrated, so 'no Dissenting Clergyman' could perform services therein, and so Dissenters were 'virtually excluded'. However, the paper stated, although the 'Church of England' was in no 'condition to exhibit such symptoms of intolerance', one 'great advantage attendant on' the new cemetery was 'that the last remains of mortality' would be 'consigned to the earth without exorbitant charges, ... and the dust of the departed'... could 'moulder in the tomb without spreading through the abodes of the living that fatal *malaria* which too often' generated disease and death in their 'most awful and terrific forms'.[7]

1 Minutes of the Proceedings of the Directors of the General Cemetery Company (9 January 1833), 25. 2 Ibid. 3 Ibid. (23 January 1833), 26. 4 *Morning Chronicle* (25 January 1833). 5 Ibid. 6 Ibid. The widespread belief that the land on which the cemetery was laid out was purchased from All Souls College, Oxford, must be finally laid to rest: an examination of the indentures makes this clear. However, it will be remembered that the original date for the Consecration was to have been on 1 November 1832, All Souls Eve and the Feast of All Saints. Some recent (and worthless) effusions on the cemetery have declared (a) the land was the property of All Souls College, and (b) the cemetery was consecrated on All Souls Day, which the authors seem to think is 24 January. It is, of course, nothing of the sort. 7 *Morning Chronicle* (25 January 1833).

The prolix newspaper report noted that 'no tombs' had 'yet been built', but vaults [had] been constructed in the upper part' of the burial-ground which would 'be finished in a few days, and which [were] capable of holding 2,500 coffins'. These, of course, are the earliest permanent structures associated with the cemetery (apart from the boundary-wall and -railings), and comprise the north, old, or terrace catacomb, designed by Griffith and built by Chadwick. They consist of underground chambers over which is a handsome colonnade of unfluted Greek Doric columns carrying a plain entablature unembellished with triglyphs. Above the cornice, blocks were capped with pulvins decorated with the anthemion motif, an element reminiscent of Soane's work. This colonnade sheltered a walk, and against the rear wall memorials were erected to those placed in the vaults below. Regrettably, a 20th-century development was permitted on the Harrow Road, with the result that the visual integrity of the terrace catacomb has been much eroded, and vandalism (facilitated by the fact that the roof of the terrace had long been accessible from that development) has taken an appalling toll (**4.1-4.2**). Yet Griffith's colonnade does not lack distinction, and it is derived partly from Antique prototypes, and partly from the Neoclassical search for primitive simplicity that was a feature of much architecture from about 1780 until the 1830s. The direct ancestor of the terrace colonnade is the *Hauptfriedhof* at Frankfurt-am-Main, the powerful exemplar for several early cemeteries.

4.1 The old, north, or terrace catacombs, with modern block behind. Note the one surviving pulvin in 2001 (*JMF*).

4.2 Detail of the unfluted Greek Doric Order of the old, north, or terrace catacombs. Most of the pulvins were pushed off the blocks above the cornice in 1997 (*JSC*).

At the meeting of the Board of Directors following the Consecration, Paul reported that he, Eden, Purchas, Morison, Macklew, and Spottiswoode had been 'perfectly satisfied',[8] and Johnstone was thanked 'for his services' and asked to stay on and

[8] Minutes of the Proceedings of the Directors of the General Cemetery Company (13 February 1833), 29.

perform the duties of Chaplain 'for the present'. In fact, he seems to have had second thoughts about his 'preferment', for on 20 March he was appointed Chaplain to the Company at a salary of £200 per annum and £50 per annum for a house, these amounts to be calculated from the time of 'the Consecration of the Ground'.[9] What is more, the General Cemetery Company acquired its first 'customer' on 31 January 1833, when Margaret Gregory, wife of Barnard Gregory (1796-1852), proprietor and editor of the scurrilous magazine, *The Satirist, or Censor of the Times*, was deposited in the terrace catacomb before later translation to a brick grave [4031/48/RS]. Paul attended a second interment on 9 February.

Various tables of fees and charges for interments were agreed by the Directors. For a private vault holding 12 coffins the charge was £50, for six coffins £36, and for one coffin seven guineas, with a fee of a guinea for opening the vault and five guineas for each interment in a private vault. A common vault for one coffin was four guineas, and one for a child under eight years three guineas, with a fee for each interment of two guineas. Charges for memorial-tablets to be set on the wall behind the colonnade were fixed at a fee calculated on the size of each monument. A vault or brick grave 9 feet (2.7432 metres) long by 6 feet (1.8288 metres) wide cost £21, and one 9 feet long by 4 feet (1.2192 metres) wide 15 guineas. Fees for each interment in these were five guineas, with a charge of two guineas for opening and closing the vault or brick grave. A grave 6 ft. 6 ins. (1.9812 metres) by 2 ft. 6 ins. (0.762 metres), 7 ft. (2.1336 metres) deep cost three guineas, with the 'privilege of placing' flat or head and foot stones over it. A common interment in a grave cost £1 5s. 0d., and the fee for each interment in a purchased grave was two guineas. The removal and replacement of a 'flat stone' was five shillings, and for head and foot stones three shillings. Extra digging of graves beyond seven feet was calculated at 2s. per foot (0.3048 metres) not exceeding ten feet (3.048 metres); beyond 10 feet to 15 feet (4.572 metres) at 2s. 6d. per foot, and from 15 to 20 feet at 3s. 6d. per foot. The 'name of the parish from which the Corpse' was 'intended to be removed' was to be 'given on bespeaking the Ground'.[10] All monuments and vaults were to be kept in repair by the owners.

A 'machine' was ordered to be constructed for lowering coffins into the catacomb, and the Company decided to erect a memorial tablet to Mrs Gregory, and to defray all charges in relation to her funeral, 'in consideration' of 'the first interment'. At the same meeting (13 February 1833) it was reported that 'Mr George Frederick Carden', the Registrar of the Company, 'circulated on the day preceding the consecration of the Ground two printed cards, in one of which, he, being an Officer of the Company, took it upon himself to inculpate the conduct of the present Board of Directors, both cards being calculated to prove injurious to the success of the Company'.[11] As a result, the Directors 'felt themselves under the painful necessity' of resolving difficulties occasioned by Carden's behaviour: Carden was suspended from the office of Registrar, and his duties were taken over by the Clerk *pro tempore*. In one of the printed cards Carden indicated that he intended selling the 30 shares held by him, and had offered them to the Directors 'otherwise ... [he would] direct [his] brother to dispose of them in the market'. He also referred to his having 'added many beautiful models to' his 'former collection', a clear indication he was still arguing against the Directors, presumably in favour of one of the entries to the architectural competition. The Company refused to purchase Carden's shares, and he (Carden) printed C. Broughton Bowman's letter to this effect.

Carden had also announced the Consecration, but noted that in 'a matter so momentous to the well-wishers and supporters of this scheme', it seemed 'a singular

9 Minutes of the Proceedings of the Directors of the General Cemetery Company (20 March 1833), 39. 10 Ibid. (13 February 1833), 30. 11 Ibid., 31-2.

omission of duty that an official Circular was not forwarded to each Member. Several of the subscribers heard of it 'only from' Carden, and he knew it 'only by *accident*, many days after an advertisement had appeared in the public papers', for he 'happened not to see the newspapers of the day in which it was inserted'. He offered to 'make the suitable arrangements' to transport subscribers to the ground if they assembled at his offices in the Temple, and, as a further 'inducement', he stated he had 'several additional models to show' which demonstrated what *could* have been achieved at Kensal Green. When the subscribers got to the cemetery and saw 'what [had] been done', they might 'not perhaps wonder' that they 'were not officially invited' to the Consecration ceremony, for the temporary chapel compared very unfavourably with what various architects had proposed. Specifically, Carden referred to the 'smuggled consecration of a little building' which would have been unnecessary if proper decisions had been made giving the public a chance to have a 'National Cemetery' founded upon 'patriotic and independent principles ... gratifying and honourable to all'. Carden went on to declare his 'constitution' had been 'harassed by seeing so public an object lingering on under a heartless management, when unaided and alone (having command of the Treasury [a dig at his having been removed from that position]), he 'could long since' have brought things to a satisfactory conclusion.[12] This was strong stuff. Carden doubtless felt further isolated by the long illness and death of Pugin (December 1832), so Carden's anti-Griffith and anti-Paul stance was undermined. It all seems to have been rather fraught.

The architectural competition and its aftermath seem to have stirred up all sorts of animosities, for even 'Mr Ramplin of Liverpool' prayed for compensation from the Board for making a 'design for' the Chapel: however, he was referred to the terms of the competition which precluded any such payment. This 'Ramplin' was Clark Rampling (1793-1875), who moved to Liverpool in 1829, and designed numerous buildings in a Greek Revival style. Infuriatingly, it has not been possible to identify his entry to the Kensal Green architectural competition, but it could have been Nos. 11, 12, 14, 15, 17, 18, 20, 26, 29, 38, or 40.[13]

Griffith consolidates his Position

It was at this time (February 1833) that the Company seems to have abandoned its search for land south of the Thames for another cemetery, primarily for Dissenters. As Ronalds was ordered to complete the planting and Griffith was instructed to complete the drain from the catacomb, the completion of the temporary chapel and the interment of the first 'customers' led the Board to look at its newly-enclosed ground with fresh eyes. Griffith made a proposal to 'Mr. Weeden of the Plough Inn, [which stood formerly at the corner of Ladbroke Grove and Harrow Road]... for the surrender of his lease of the piece of the ground at the back of the "Plough" which Mr. Weeden has agreed to in consideration of the rent now due being remitted to him' (**2.5** and **4.3**). This surrender was accepted 'in consideration of the ground having been rendered useless to Mr Weeden during the last Summer'. Griffith was directed to give an estimate for surrounding the ground 'at the back of Mr Weedens house with a Wall & Catacombs & Chapel as a burial ground for Dissenters and also of an Entrance at the East end of the Consecrated ground'. Paul was asked to 'arrange with Lord Holland for the taking in of the Waste on the East side of the piece of ground proposed for Dissenters, which he consented to do': this matter was fully resolved by 27 February 1833. At the same time it was resolved that the cemetery be called All Souls Cemetery.

[12] Ibid., 33, where Carden's printed cards are fixed to the page. [13] Ibid. (13 March 1833), 37.

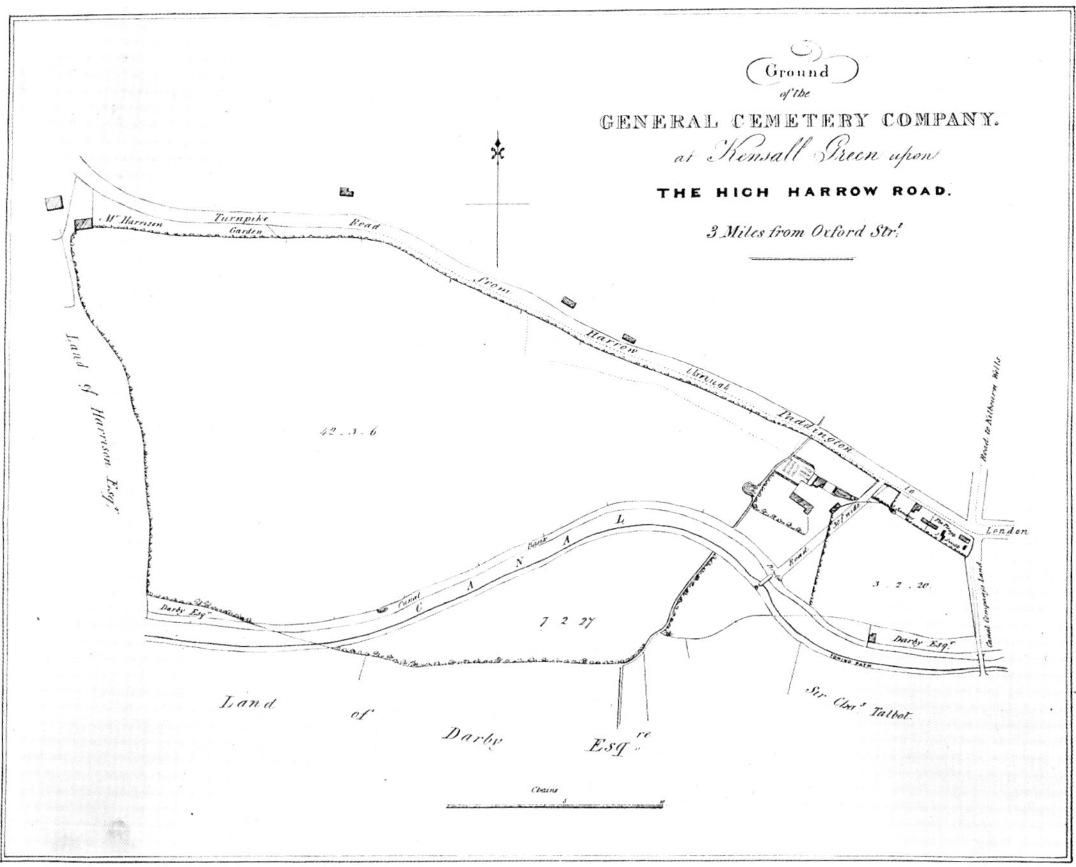

4.3 'Ground of the General Cemetery Company at Kensall [*sic*] Green upon the High Harrow Road', 1832. The main plot of just over 42 acres is shown bounded by the 'Turnpike Road from Harrow through Paddington' on the north, by the canal on the south (although the Cemetery Company land of over seven acres south of the canal is shown), by land owned by Harrison to the west, and by the plot of over three acres south of the Plough public-house. The General Cemetery Company eventually got rid of the plot south of the canal (but not until the 1870s) and acquired all the land to the west, including the old farm buildings, as well as the property to the east at the rear of the *Plough Inn* which is now the unconsecrated part of the cemetery (*GCC. #49.MC. T140900*).

It must have been around this time that Thomas Brown, of the Bedford Nursery, Hampstead Road, prepared a 'Proposed Plan for laying out the General Cemetery Ground'. Brown claimed that the 'Ground' possessed 'great natural advantages and facilities for draining', and proposed a principal drain along the north bank of the canal, with its outlet passing under the canal itself (this was realised by Griffith in 1839-40). Four 'cross drains' running north-south took water to the principal drain. However, Brown's layout of the grounds showed two entrances, each with a lodge, on the Harrow Road, and only meandering carriage-ways. There was no axial path, but he retained the Great Circle idea which seems to have originated with Nash and was introduced by Liddell. Brown's rather unsatisfactory and unimaginative proposals were not accepted by the Board, but it is interesting that the Great Circle survived and was eventually incorporated into the final layout (**4.4**).

Very soon,[14] Griffith's plan for the entrance and division between the consecrated and unconsecrated parts of the cemetery was adopted (**4.5**), and his proposals for the Dissenters' chapel were accepted. The Board resolved that the ground 'at the back of the Plough Public House at Kensal Green' should 'be inclosed and prepared as a Cemetery for Dissenters'.[15] Estimates were ordered to be obtained from Griffith for building a wall around the unconsecrated part of the cemetery, for the entrance-gates, for an 'iron fence between the consecrated and unconsecrated parts', and for 'the Chapel and Catacombs in the latter with the roads planting and draining'. It was also decided to order a 'revolving platform for the reception of the coffins in the Chapel' from 'Mr Smith of Princes Street, Leicester Square', which cost £43 17s. 6d.

14 Minutes of the Proceedings of the Directors of the General Cemetery Company (27 February 1833), 34-6.
15 Ibid., 34.

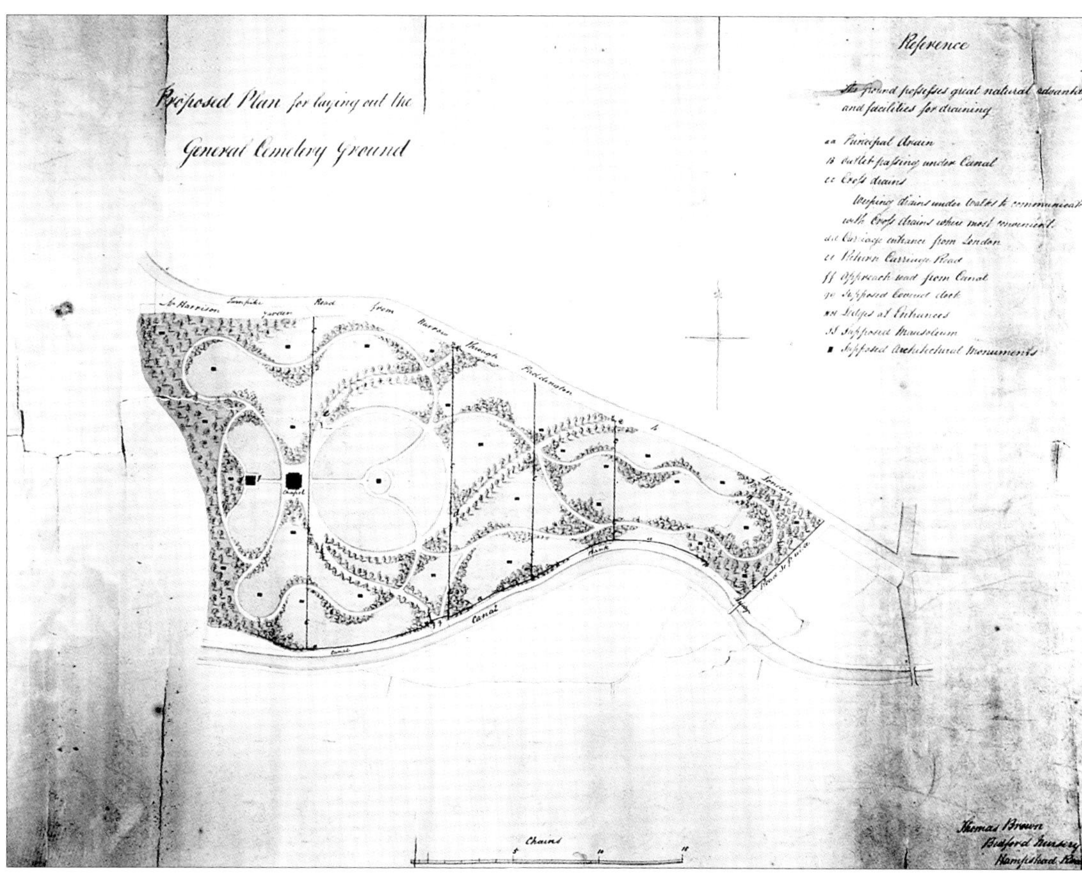

4.4 Thomas Brown's 'Proposed Plan for laying out the General Cemetery Ground'. Four 'Cross drains' were proposed running north-south, connecting with a 'Principal drain' on the north side of the canal. Brown proposed two 'Carriage entrances' on the 'Turnpike Road from Harrow through Paddington to London', each with its own lodge. The Great Circle idea, which appears to have originated from Nash through Liddell's plan, survived in this proposal. Paths are generally meandering, and there is no formal axial avenue, as realised. Behind the 'Chapel' is a 'Supposed Mausoleum', and the other blank rectangles are 'Supposed Architectural Monuments'. It should be noted that the land behind the *Plough* public-house (now the unconsecrated portion) was not included in Brown's plan (*GCC. #42. MC. AF140900*).

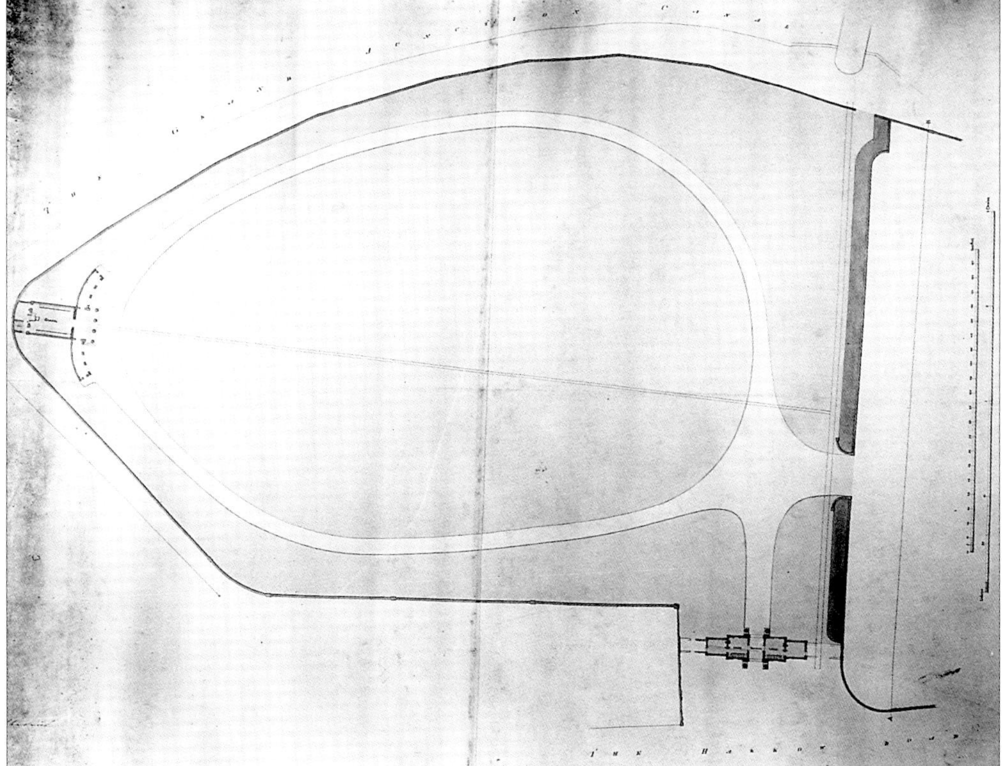

4.5 Griffith's plan (1833) for laying out the ground for Dissenters on land south of the *Plough Inn*. To the *left* (east) is his plan of the Dissenters' chapel; to the *right* (west) is the barrier between the unconsecrated and consecrated parts of the cemetery; at the *top* (south) is the Grand Junction Canal; and at the *bottom* is the Harrow Road with Griffith's proposed entrance-gate and the screen-wall to the left of the gate-lodge (*GCC. #29. MC. AB140900*).

At the next meeting of the Board[16] Griffith produced plans and estimates for the Dissenters' part of the cemetery, including plans for the entrance-gate. By the meeting of 20 March 1833 Griffith was firmly in control of all design matters, even to supervising Ronalds in the matter of planting the cemetery grounds. His plans and estimates for the 'Entrance lodges to unconsecrated Ground' were 'generally adopted', and he was 'instructed to arrange for Contracts with Mr. Chadwick and others for the completion of the work'.[17]

Advertisements were placed in the morning and evening papers to the effect that the cemetery was in business for the interment of both Anglicans and 'those whose friends desire a burial service differing from that of the Church of England', which was pretty all-embracing, and was probably designed to deflect the sort of criticism published in the *Morning Chronicle* and elsewhere. In particular, the Company stressed that All Souls Cemetery was 'laid out as a sepulchral Garden, in the style of the Cemetery of Père La Chaise [*sic*], in the Neighbourhood of Paris', and that it was 'surrounded by a lofty wall & watched by patrols thereby *affording perfect security* against exhumation'.[18]

The Directors were 'confident that the beauty of the situation', 'its security', the 'advantages of registration', and 'the moderate prices of the Catacombs vaults and graves' would 'recommend the General Cemetery to all' who preferred 'decent and reverent interment of deceased friends to the insecure crowded, and, in many cases, disgusting burial places, in London & Westminster'.[19] The Board also emphasised that the 'undertaking' was 'eminently calculated to improve & secure the health' of a 'great & increasing Metropolis'.[20]

Griffith's efficiency and speed had clearly won him the confidence of the Directors, for he was put in charge of all planting, layout, and maintenance of the grounds, as well as being entrusted with the building of permanent structures. His increase of responsibilities would appear to have begun from the time of the death of Pugin and Carden's behaviour at the time of the Consecration. Any pretence that the architectural competition had any further relevance was dropped, and Griffith was able to consolidate his position.

By the time of the Annual General Meeting, held on 13 June 1833 at the Company's Offices, 95 Great Russell Street, Viscount Milton had become 5th Earl Fitzwilliam (from 8 February 1833), which doubtless added lustre to the Company, although he went out of office as a Director (with the Hon. Thomas Liddell and General William Eden) because of the organisation and rules governing the composition of the Board. Lord Ingestre, as Chairman of the Board (1832-4), chaired the AGM, and among those present were Carden, Griffith (Chairman 1864-79), Gaspey, Charles Lushington (Chairman 1852-64), Col. J. Kyrle Money, Langston, Morison, Macklew, Sir Robert Price, Bart., MP, Sir John Dean Paul, Bart., Col. Purchas, A. Spottiswoode, J. Spottiswoode, and W. Strahan (the Banker). New Directors appointed to replace Lord Fitzwilliam, Liddell, and Eden were Thomas Gaspey, Charles Lushington, and Robert William Sievier. The Report of the Directors was read, and stated that the cemetery was 'complete' and 'open to the public', a fact remarkable as the 'great work' had only commenced on 3 February 1832. The temporary chapel costing £250 was in use, and a catacomb for nearly 2,000 coffins had been built with a 'colonnade of simple Greek design' erected for the 'protection of Monuments &c. which' were 'proposed to be affixed to the Wall' and which at a 'very small charge per foot' would repay the 'expense' of the building with a profit. Furthermore, the colonnade was capable of extension 'to any degree' (*see* **Frontispiece**), and was based on the design of the 'Grand new Cemetery at Frankfort'

16 Minutes of the Proceedings of the Directors of the General Cemetery Company (13 March 1833), 37-8.
17 Ibid. (27 March 1833), 40. 18 Ibid., 42-3. Editor's italics. 19 Ibid., 43. 20 Ibid.

which had 'met with the most complete success'. A 'simple and ingenious machine' for lowering coffins and 'placing them in the different parts of the catacomb' had been constructed by 'Mr Smith' at a cost of £134 1s. 0d.

The Report referred to the successful Consecration of the ground by the Bishop of London on 24 January 1833, and then mentioned that an application had been made by 'influential Dissenters' on the subject of land suitable for burial. Stung, no doubt, by criticisms in the newspapers, the Board had decided to 'offer some part' ... 'contiguous to the consecrated Ground' at the 'Eastern Extremity', to build a chapel with catacomb, plantations, etc., for the use of Dissenters. Land had also been obtained between the cemetery and the canal in exchange for an 'equal area lying to the south'. The property in the name of Sir John Dean Paul, Bart., was duly conveyed to the Company in pursuance of the Act of Incorporation. Nearly two miles of roads had been completed in the cemetery, the foundations having been made of burnt clay 'dug on the spot'. Ronalds's tender had been accepted for the planting and other landscape works, and work was proceeding. The principal entrance was formed between the consecrated and unconsecrated lands, and another simpler entrance of cast iron was created in the north wall. A water-gate (again of cast-iron) was put up on the south side for the 'landing and bringing in of Materials and for the admission of Funerals coming by Water'. The Directors had given the name of All Souls to the Cemetery, and the Reverend Edward Johnstone had been appointed Chaplain at a salary of £250 per annum.[21] Most importantly, a Code of Bye-Laws had been drawn up,[22] and the threat from the London and Birmingham Railway was removed because the line avoided the cemetery altogether 'by an alteration' of the route achieved by the Board's negotiations (it was actually placed in a tunnel). However, the Report added (somewhat hopefully, one feels), the railway would 'come near enough to afford a mode of access to the ground'.

The Directors confidently stated that the cemetery presented the public with a place of sepulture of 'unexampled extent and capacity', and noted with satisfaction that the first interments had taken place. Indeed, the very first interment was commemorated with a tablet erected by the Directors to record the event. Chadwick, the contractor, had been paid £12,000 for the 'wall, catacomb, temporary Chapel, &c.'; Ronalds *et al.* £2,041 19s. 10d. for roads and planting; and preparation of clay for the roads and labour expended on levelling the ground and making the roads cost £2,484. Costs incurred to obtain the Act of Parliament came to £817 18s. 6d.; printing and stationery (including the Act) totalled £340 11s. 4d.; and advertising expenditure was £434 7s. 8d.

Griffith reported to the Board that four men at 15s. per week, 2 women at 9s. per week, two watchmen at 17s. 6d. per week, one gatekeeper at 17s. 6d. per week, one boy at 9s. per week, and one extra man at £1 per week would be 'necessarily employed' at the cemetery, but the Board ordered that not more than four labourers should be employed permanently, to act also as watchmen (two dividing each alternate night) at wages not exceeding 15s. per week, with 1s. for each man per night for watching. Additional women and boys could be employed 'to weed &c.' at the discretion of Griffith at wages not exceeding 9s. per week each.

The final break with Carden took place on 26 June 1833 when he was 'removed' from his office, and Bowman was duly appointed Registrar in his place.[23] Thereafter there was no further talk of Gothic buildings: Classicism, and Greek Classicism at that, was to be the style adopted.

21 All the above from the Minutes of Proceedings of General Meetings (13 June 1833), *passim*. 22 Bye-Laws made in Pursuance of the Statute 2° & 3° GUL. IV., c.110, s. 52, 13 June 1833. 23 Minutes of the Proceedings of the Directors of the General Cemetery Company (26 June 1833), 58-9.

Building Works and Other Developments

In spite of the optimistic Report, progress was, in fact, quite slow and, although the Directors had indeed ordered a memorial to be erected to record their first 'customer', the cemetery still had the character of open landscape, capital was in short supply (many shareholders had still not paid the next instalments due on their investments, and several refused to pay any further sums, so forfeited their shares), and income was very small. It was decided to let out parts of the ground for grazing, on condition the farmers provided their own hurdles to ensure the animals did not stray into areas where there were graves, or where burials were taking place. So infrequent were funerals, in fact, that Johnstone did not turn up for one, and the Board demanded an explanation from him. Johnstone's alleged 'preferment', problems with his place of residence (his contract obliged him to live near the cemetery), and other difficulties were to surface later, and he does not appear to have been entirely reliable.

By 31 July 1833 Griffith was able to report that the Dissenters' 'Chapel and screens were in a forward state, and that the Lodges were commenced and would be proceeded with as expeditiously as possible'.[24] His contract-drawings for this little building, in pencil and wash, are exquisite (**4.6-4.13**), and demonstrate a sound knowledge of the language of Greek Revival architecture. The prostyle tetrastyle

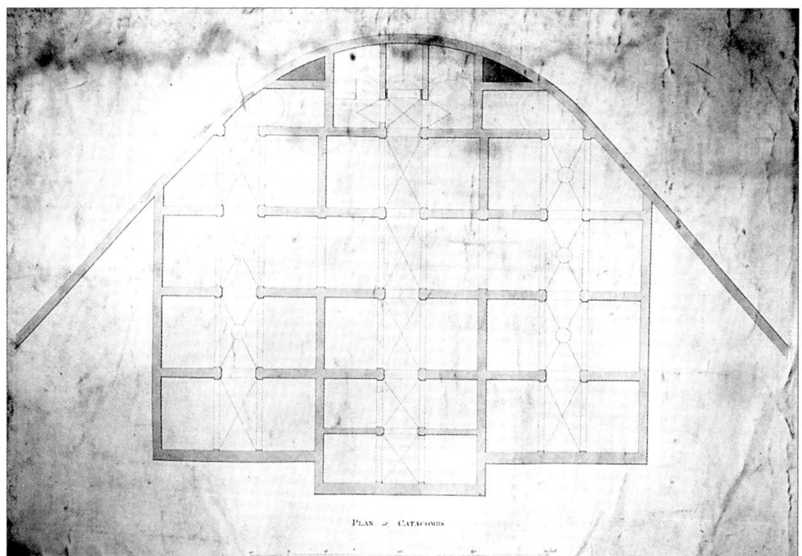

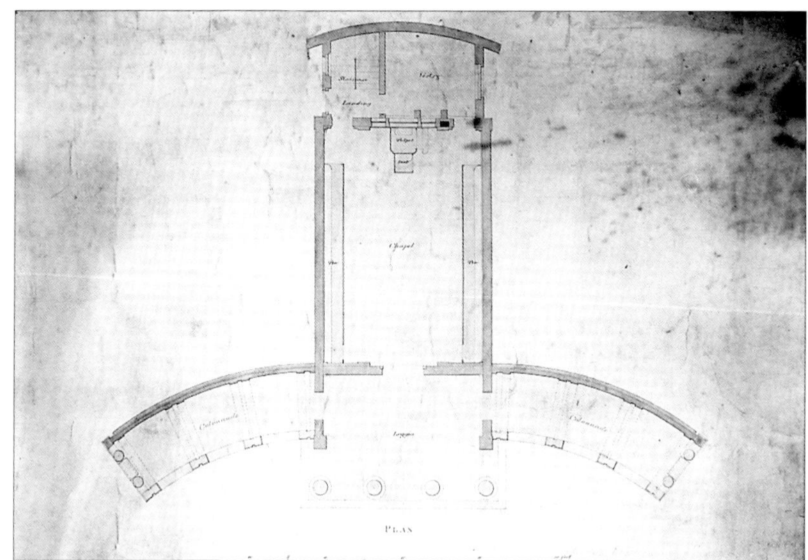

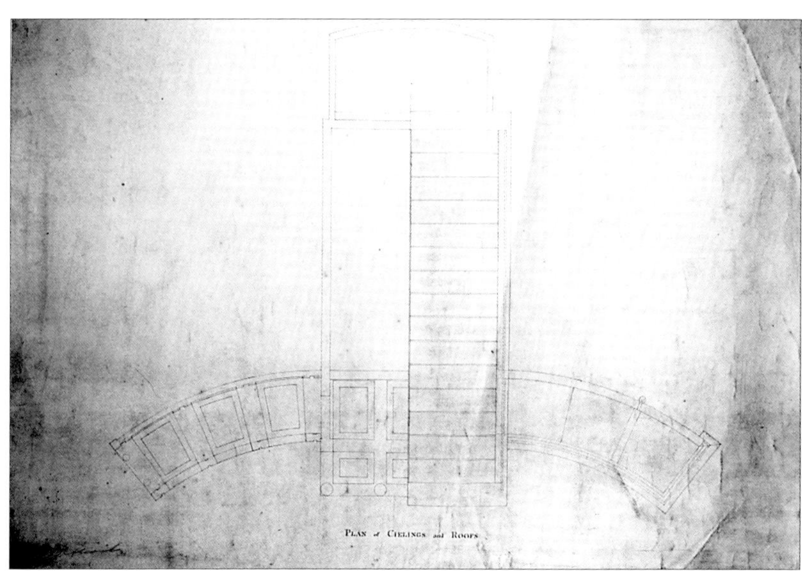

24 Minutes of the Proceedings of the Directors of the General Cemetery Company (31 July 1833), 61.

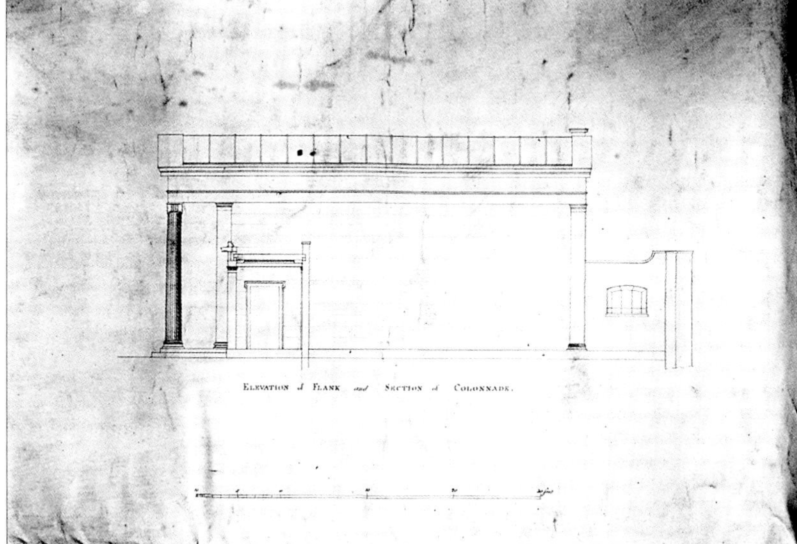

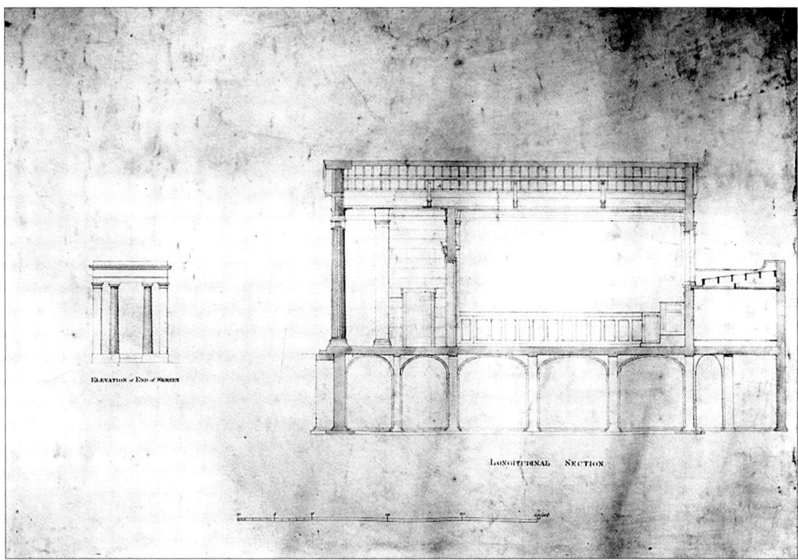

4.6 *(top left)* Griffith's plan of the catacomb under the Dissenters' chapel. Contract drawing of 1833 (*GCC. #68 No. 1. MC. L140900*).

4.7 *(middle left)* Plan of the Dissenters' chapel and colonnade, with 'Loggia' and portico, by Griffith. Contract drawing of 1833 (*GCC. #68 No. 2. MC. J140900*).

4.8 *(bottom left)* Plan of ceilings and roofs, Dissenters' chapel, by Griffith. Contract drawing of 1833 (*GCC. #68 No. 3. MC. K140900*).

4.9 *(top right)* Front elevation of the Dissenters' chapel and flanking colonnades, by Griffith. Contract drawing of 1833 (*GCC. #68 No. 4. MC. H140900*).

4.10 *(middle right)* 'Elevation of Flank and Section of Colonnade' of the Dissenters' chapel, by Griffith. Contract drawing of 1833 (*GCC. #69 No. 5. MC. P140900*).

4.11 *(bottom right)* 'Elevation of End of Screen' (*left*) and Longitudinal Section through the Dissenters' chapel and catacomb, by Griffith. Contract drawing of 1833 (*GCC. #69 No. 6. MC. M140900*).

portico is derived from that of the Temple on the Ilissus, Athens (*c.* 450 BC), a fine example of the Ionic Order that had been widely published (**7.9**) by 1833, notably in Volume I of *The Antiquities of Athens* (1762),[25] and the square columns of the lower colonnade are variations on the Choragic Monument of Thrasyllus, Athens (319-279 BC), published in Volume II of *The Antiquities of Athens* (1789) (**7.11**).

At the end of August the Dissenters' chapel and colonnade were 'covered in', and a tender had been received from Messrs. Jessop & Eley for completing the landscaping and 'ground-work' in the unconsecrated portion of the cemetery[26] for the sum of £529 10s. 0d. There was also much debate about obtaining suitable images depicting views of the cemetery to be engraved and used to illustrate Kensal Green in various journals for publicity purposes. Griffith was asked to prepare some drawings as the bases for engravings to illustrate an account of the cemetery in *Leigh's Picture of London* and Gaspey was detailed to procure an appropriate illustration for use in *The Penny Magazine*.[27]

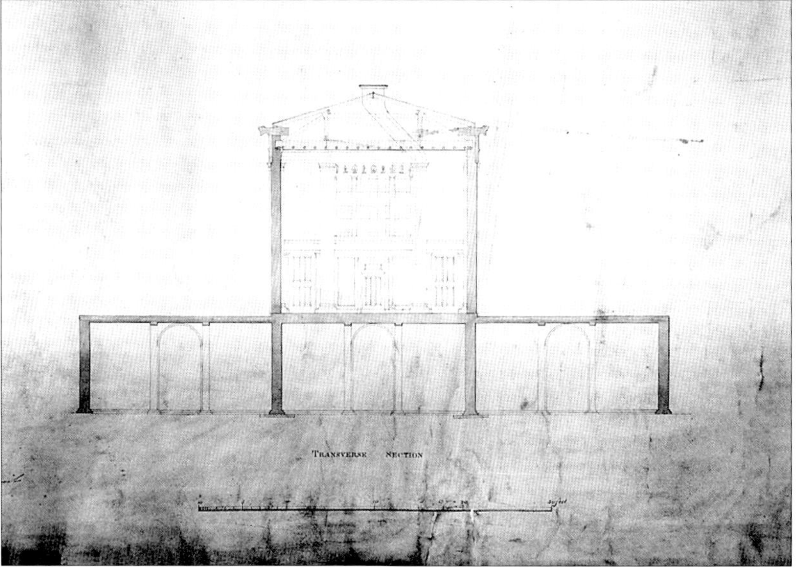

4.12 'Transverse Section' of Dissenters' chapel and catacomb, showing the east window and refined Grecian detailing, by Griffith. Contract drawing of 1833 (*GCC. #69 No. 7. MC. Q140900*).

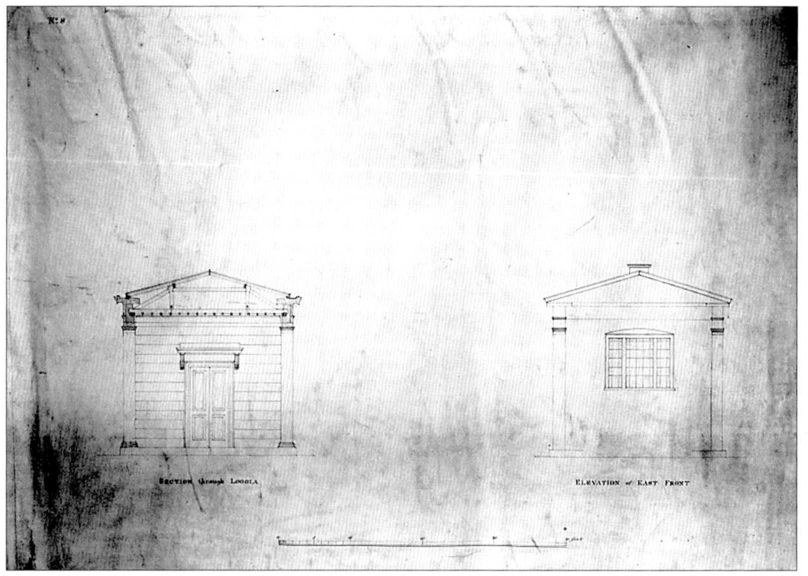

4.13 'Section through Loggia' (*left*) and 'Elevation of East Front' (*right*) of Dissenters' chapel, by Griffith. Contract drawing of 1833 (*GCC. #69 No. 8. MC. N140900*).

Early in 1834 Chadwick was asked for an explanation as to why the works were delayed,[28] to which he replied that the quality of the masonry was such that it would 'in some measure compensate for the delay, as great pains' had been taken to render it some of the best in London. In addition, the architraves were 'the longest ever executed in London' and had 'caused considerable delay'. On the other hand, Ronalds had completed the 'handsome plantation', to Griffith's 'approbation' and duly was paid.

Various items were purchased, including a 'Tarpawling' to 'protect the men while digging Graves', a robe for the Clerk and Sexton, a cloak for the bell-ringer, and, ominously, a 'Blunderbuss for the Watchman'. It seems that there were problems with miscreants invading the cemetery grounds, and various precautions had to be taken to seal and protect the catacombs.[29]

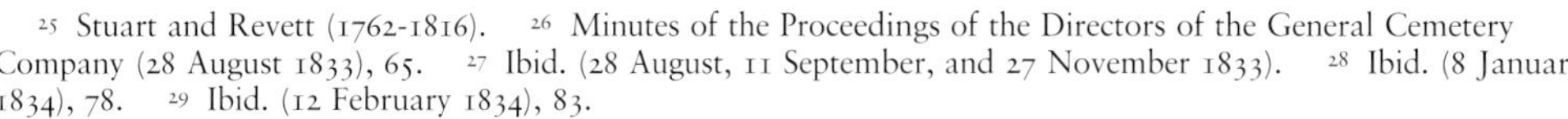
25 Stuart and Revett (1762-1816). 26 Minutes of the Proceedings of the Directors of the General Cemetery Company (28 August 1833), 65. 27 Ibid. (28 August, 11 September, and 27 November 1833). 28 Ibid. (8 January 1834), 78. 29 Ibid. (12 February 1834), 83.

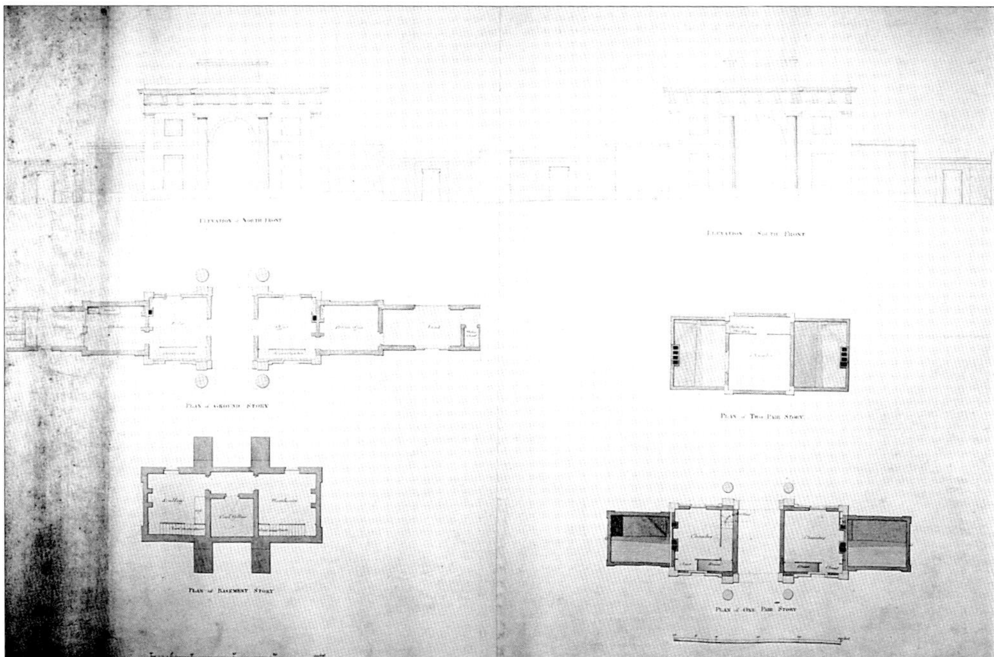

4.14 Plans and north and south elevations of the arched entrance-gate and lodges, by Griffith. Contract drawing of 1833 (*GCC. #12 Nos. 1 and 2. MC. AD140900*).

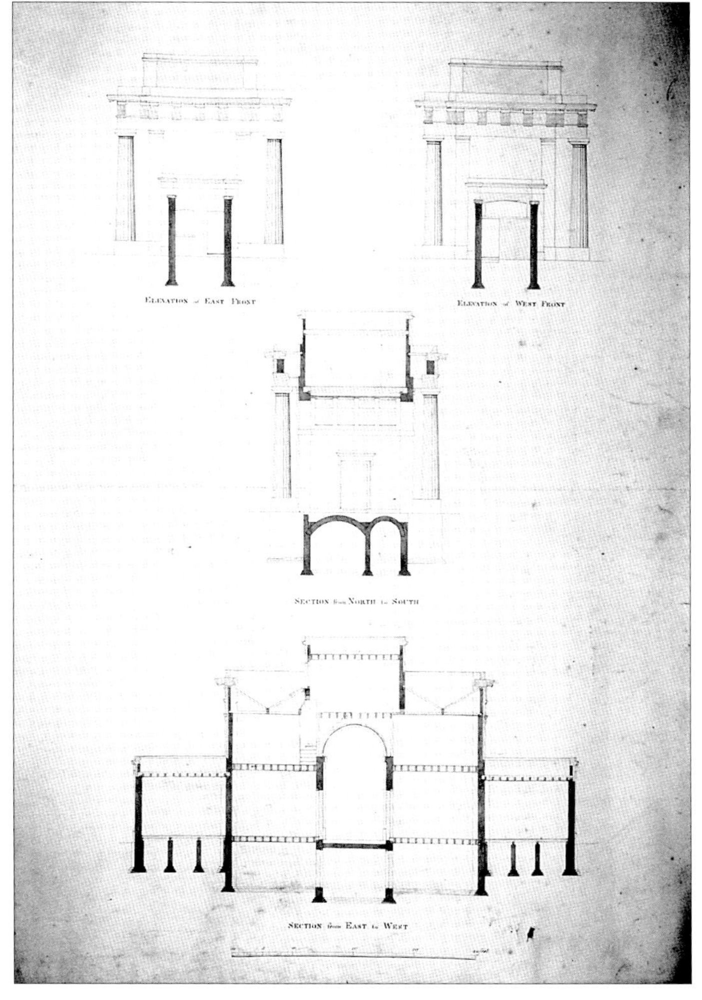

4.15 Elevations of the east and west elevations of the arched entrance-gate, with sections, by Griffith. Contract drawing of 1833 (*GCC. #12 Nos. 3. MC. AE140900*).

By March 1834 building-works on the Dissenters' chapel were completed, and it was decided to hang part of the interior with black cloth 'above the seats', and to colour the rest 'with distemper'. Chadwick reported[30] that all his workmen would be off the site that month, whereupon the Directors hastened to publicise the Dissenters' part of the cemetery in *The Evangelical Magazine*, *The Wesleyan Methodists' Magazine*, and *The Evangelical Register*.[31]

So, by the end of March the Dissenters' chapel and catacomb, boundary-walls and railings, gates, terrace catacomb, temporary Anglican chapel, and entrance-gate and lodges had all been completed by Chadwick to Griffith's designs. Work on the paths, landscaping, and planting had also moved ahead. Buildings were faced with Portland Stone or Roman cement (a type of stucco), and the walls were made of stock-bricks with Portland Stone dressings. Griffith's propylaeum-like entrance-gate ensemble was very handsome, a kind of Grecian triumphal-arch containing the office, a kitchen, stores, a parlour (for living accommodation), and various 'chambers' (**4.14-4.15**). It is clear that

30 Ibid. (12 March 1834), 88. 31 Ibid. (26 March 1834), 89.

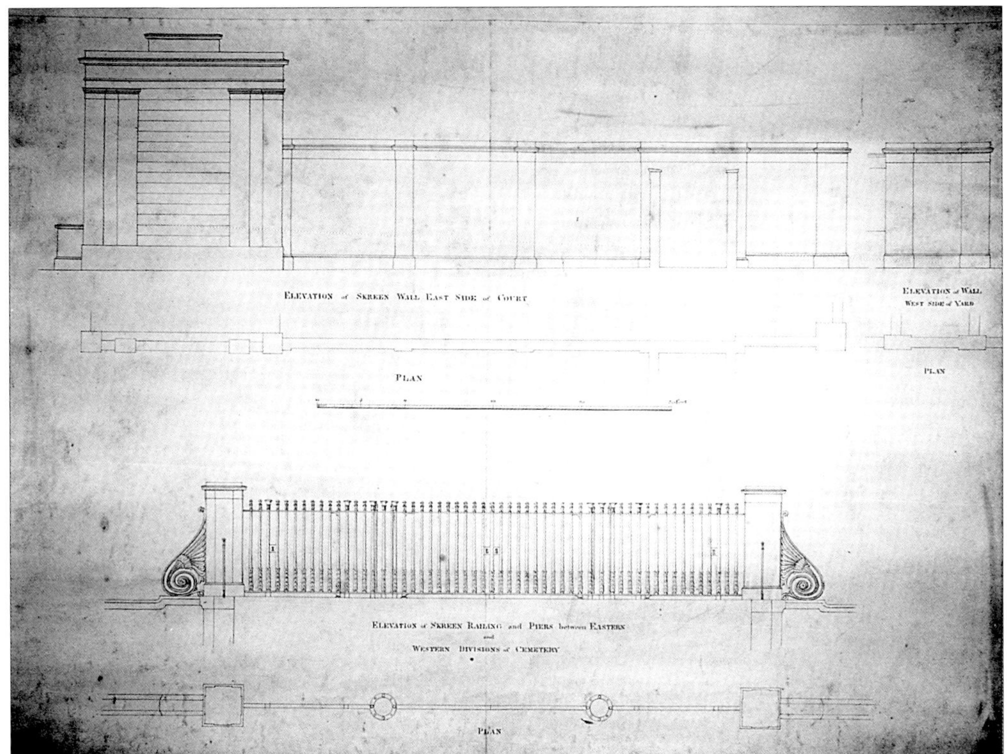

4.16 Elevation of screen-wall east of the entrance-court in front of the arched entrance-gate on the Harrow Road, showing the Grecian treatment of the blank wall and the end of the adjoining terrace, embellished with *antae* and entablature. Below is the 'Skreen Railing and Piers between Eastern and Western Divisions of Cemetery', all by Griffith. Contract drawing of 1833 (*GCC. #29. MC. AC140900*).

4.17 'Kensall [*sic*] Green Cemetry [*sic*] (Entrance Lodge)', showing the stone piers and cast-iron railing dividing the consecrated and unconsecrated parts of the ground. In the background is the twin-towered church of St John the Evangelist (1844) by Henry Edward Kendall Jr. (1805-85) (*RBCK K60/135, neg. no. 4686.614.61.KEN*).

Griffith and the Directors knew the importance of giving the entrance to the cemetery a proper setting, so the gable-end of the houses on the Harrow Road, east of the entrance-court, and the boundary-wall were given an applied stucco Grecian architectural treatment so that the whole court became a handsome unified ensemble (**4.16**). Griffith also designed a very beautiful cast-iron railing between the two parts of the cemetery. This, with its stone piers, is represented in a view of the entrance-lodge, 'Kensall Green Cemetry' (*sic*) (**4.17**).

The next Annual General Meeting was held at 95 Great Russell Street on 5 June 1834, with Sir John Dean Paul, Bart., in the Chair. Ingestre, Evans, and Morison went out of office as Directors, and Kyrle Money as Auditor. They were replaced by Major-General Eden, Robert Maconochie, and the Reverend Henry John Knapp as Directors, and by John Wardell as Auditor. Paul was to remain Chairman of the Company from 1834 until 1852.

It was reported that the Dissenters' ground had been enclosed, and that a 'handsome Chapel', with its 'colonnade and Vaults', was ready for use. The lodge and entrance-gate building were completed, and the Chaplain was in residence 'in the immediate vicinity of the Cemetery'. Farmers in the area had been granted rights of feeding sheep 'on the herbage, thus saving expense' and making a profit.

At the time, several churches in the City of London were closed, and there was much speculation about the possibilities of interring remains from those redundant churches. In spite of a modest profit of £117 6s. 8d., the Directors hoped that the interment of 'several persons of distinction and the purchase of ground by their relatives' would secure 'the countenance of those classes in society whose patronage would place the establishment in the same rank among cemeteries in London as Père-Lachaise had obtained in Paris.

Expenses, though, had been high. The land had cost £9,679 15s. 2d., the walls had cost £8,516 17s. 6d. to build, the temporary chapel £263, the roads and planting (1833-4) £4,310 4s. 5d., wages for levelling, planting, etc., came to £3,105 6s. 5d., tools and materials accounted for £384 13s. 6d., drainage had eaten up £1,557 4s. 1d., the enclosure

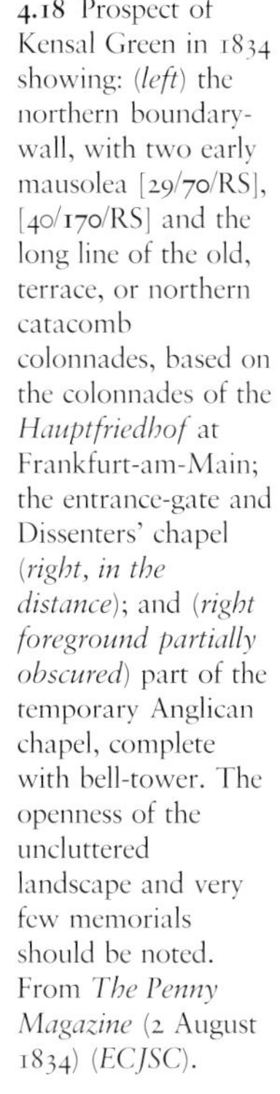

4.18 Prospect of Kensal Green in 1834 showing: (*left*) the northern boundary-wall, with two early mausolea [29/70/RS], [40/170/RS] and the long line of the old, terrace, or northern catacomb colonnades, based on the colonnades of the *Hauptfriedhof* at Frankfurt-am-Main; the entrance-gate and Dissenters' chapel (*right, in the distance*); and (*right foreground partially obscured*) part of the temporary Anglican chapel, complete with bell-tower. The openness of the uncluttered landscape and very few memorials should be noted. From *The Penny Magazine* (2 August 1834) (*ECJSC*).

of the eastern end, chapel, and entrance had cost £5,863 2s. 8d., the catacombs £2,489 19s. 0d., vaults and graves £1,242 17s. 0d., and architect's fees and expenses £2,146 3s. 6d. Expenditure on the office at Great Russell Street had been £1,077 17s. 9d., and 'disbursements' came to £60 2s. 8d. Only £1,601 15s. 4d. had come in from burial-fees.

In order to increase the public appeal of the cemetery, it was proposed[32] to offer a gift of ground in the cemetery to the value of £100 as a site for a memorial to the actor Edmund Kean (1787-1833), but this did not get anywhere, although other proposals for monuments were made from time to time. Then, on 2 August 1834, *The Penny Magazine of the Society for the Diffusion of Useful Knowledge*[33] published the long-awaited prospect of Kensal Green Cemetery, which, though hardly High Art, is interesting

[32] Minutes of the Proceedings of the Directors of the General Cemetery Company (30 July 1834), 99. [33] iii/150 (2 August 1834), 297-300.

because it shows the northern boundary-wall, the colonnaded or terrace catacomb, two severe Neoclassical vaults, the new entrance-gate, the Dissenters' chapel, and part of the temporary Anglican chapel, complete with bell-tower. The grounds were still very much a park, with few memorials placed therein, and planting was sparse (**4.18**). Within the same journal the articles on the cemetery went over the 'evil custom' of interring the dead 'in and near the places devoted to public worship'; familiar horror-stories of foul vaults and burial-grounds were re-told; candles being extinguished in 'vitiated' air were mentioned yet again; there was much talk of 'effluvia' and 'nuisances'; and there was a great deal more, repeated *ad nauseam* from many publications of the period, a sort of grand exercise in re-cycling copy. It was also claimed that 'many tons of human bones' were 'every year sent from London to the north', where they were 'crushed in mills ... and used for manure'.

The Dissenters' chapel was described as 'the finest building that the cemetery at present affords', with 'interior arrangements' that were 'neat' and 'well adapted to the purpose for which' the building was intended. By the time the article appeared, only 193 interments had taken place, most of which were in the 'subterranean catacombs' in which the coffins were 'received upon a sort of platform' (which 'descended slowly during the performance of the funeral ceremony'), and were 'afterwards conveyed by machinery through the subterranean passage to the places where they... [were] ... to be laid'.[34] However, despite all the praise showered on Griffith's buildings, neither the triumphal-arched entrance nor the Dissenters' chapel has columns with entasis (the diminution of diameter with height that results in a subtly convex curved swelling): rather, the slightly battered straight inclination actually formed is archaeologically inaccurate, although entasis is correctly incorporated in the unfluted Doric shafts of the terrace catacomb colonnades.

All shares forfeited at the Annual General Meeting were sold at public auction at a premium of £1 per share.[35] Prompted probably by Loudon's writings, Ronalds was requested to furnish 'an estimate of the expense of removing into clumps some of the trees ... standing in belts', presumably to create a more Picturesque and varied effect. During 1834, however, the cedar avenues required reinstatement where the trees had failed,[36] and early in 1835 David Ramsay, of the Stanhope Nursery, Old Brompton, offered to maintain the grounds, but his approaches were at first rejected, then, after modification of his proposals, accepted.[37] Essentially, he was to keep the whole of the cemetery in order, dig, plant, and complete all graves for a year for £400, after which he was to be paid a 'fair remuneration' for all graves dug beyond the number made in the first year of the contract. He also proposed forming new plantations in the unconsecrated ground, transplanting 'shrubs, &c.', from the consecrated part of the cemetery, and 'upholding' the same for a season for £45 5s. 0d. The contract was to start on 16 February 1835.

Discussions also took place with the Abbé de la Porte, priest 'of a French Roman Catholic chapel in Little George Street, Portman Square', concerning the possibility of enclosing part of the unconsecrated ground for the burial of Roman Catholics, but this idea does not seem to have got very far,[38] although the Company was willing to sell a portion of land for the purpose for £600.

Meanwhile, there were continuing problems with the Chaplain, Johnstone, who seems to have had a propensity for being late to officiate at funerals, so he was instructed to turn up 15 minutes before 'the appointed time'.[39] Another problem, that of beautifying

34 *The Penny Magazine of the Society for the Diffusion of Useful Knowledge*, iii/150 (2 August 1834), 299.
35 Minutes of the Proceedings of the Directors of the General Cemetery Company (12 August 1834), 101. 36 Ibid. (26 November 1834), 108. 37 Ibid. (10 February 1835), 117. 38 Ibid. (26 November 1834), 108. 39 Ibid. (9 June 1835), 127.

the grounds with monuments, also recurred. The Board was approached with numerous suggestions concerning the erection of memorials to various worthies that would, in reality, be cenotaphs: among those proposed for commemoration were Byron, Shakespeare, and, of course, Kean, mentioned above. This was doubtless intended to add tone to a place where 'running, jumping, and otherwise acting in a manner at variance with the solemnity which ought to prevail in a place of sepulture' was all too common, especially on Sundays.[40] As 'no monument of importance' had yet been erected in the cemetery, the Directors decided it would be 'for the advantage of the Company to induce a competent person to erect something of the kind' and offered to Sievier the gift of a 'piece of ground not exceeding eighteen feet square on which a monument to cost at least' £300 would be raised. Sievier accepted.

The Annual General Meeting was held on 11 June 1835, with Paul in the Chair. It was reported that the 'success of the undertaking equalled if not surpassed the most sanguine expectations', attracting the 'higher and middle classes of society', but burial of the 'lower orders' was also taking place, and all classes expressed their utmost satisfaction. Ramsay, who had been employed by the Commissioners of the Woods and Forests to lay out and keep in order St James's Park, had entered into a contract for keeping the grounds and roads in good repair, and the flowers and shrubs planted by him gave 'great satisfaction'. The Directors were particularly gratified to report that shares had advanced in value from par to 12 per cent, and so a small dividend was payable to shareholders.

Discussions with the operators of omnibuses led to a contract with Mr Peirce to 'send an omnibus three times a day, to start from the Red Lion at the corner of the Harrow and Edgware Roads', the General Cemetery Company to pay the mileage and turnpike tolls for three journeys per day, a total of two guineas a week. This fact was advertised in the newspapers to encourage the public to inspect the cemetery.[41] However, Peirce did not adhere to the terms of his contract, so payment of his account was postponed. Eventually, he was paid off with £15.

Another problem was the disposal of 'surplus clay' excavated from graves and the sites of buildings, so a mound was created to be managed by Ramsay who, however, reported a loss on his contract over the previous six months.[42] By February 1836 relations with Ramsay had deteriorated, and the Directors felt that employing him 'had not been a success', so his contract was terminated, although his losses were paid by the Company. There were other difficulties when the Parish of Kensington announced an increase in the rating of the Company for the land at Kensal Green from £289 to £350, and enquiries were made as to whether or not land used as a burial-place was subject to the payment of Poor Rates (it was).

The Designs for the Anglican Chapel

Early in 1836 the subject of replacing the temporary chapel was resurrected, and Paul offered to lend the Company (which by then was financially somewhat stretched) £2,500 'with the view of building a chapel' at the same time as 'new catacombs'.[43] Griffith was instructed to submit plans for a chapel with 'vaults as the foundation'.[44] and this he duly did at a meeting of the Board on 27 April 1836. He was then commanded to 'prepare plans of part of the Catacombs according to the design produced together with a Chapel and the East front Colonnade with an estimate specifying the difference of the expense of constructing the latter of stone or of iron'.[45]

40 Ibid. (30 September 1835), 135. 41 Ibid. (30 June 1835), 132. 42 Ibid. (30 September 1835), 135. 43 Ibid. (30 March 1836), 148. 44 Ibid. 45 Ibid. (27 April 1836). 151.

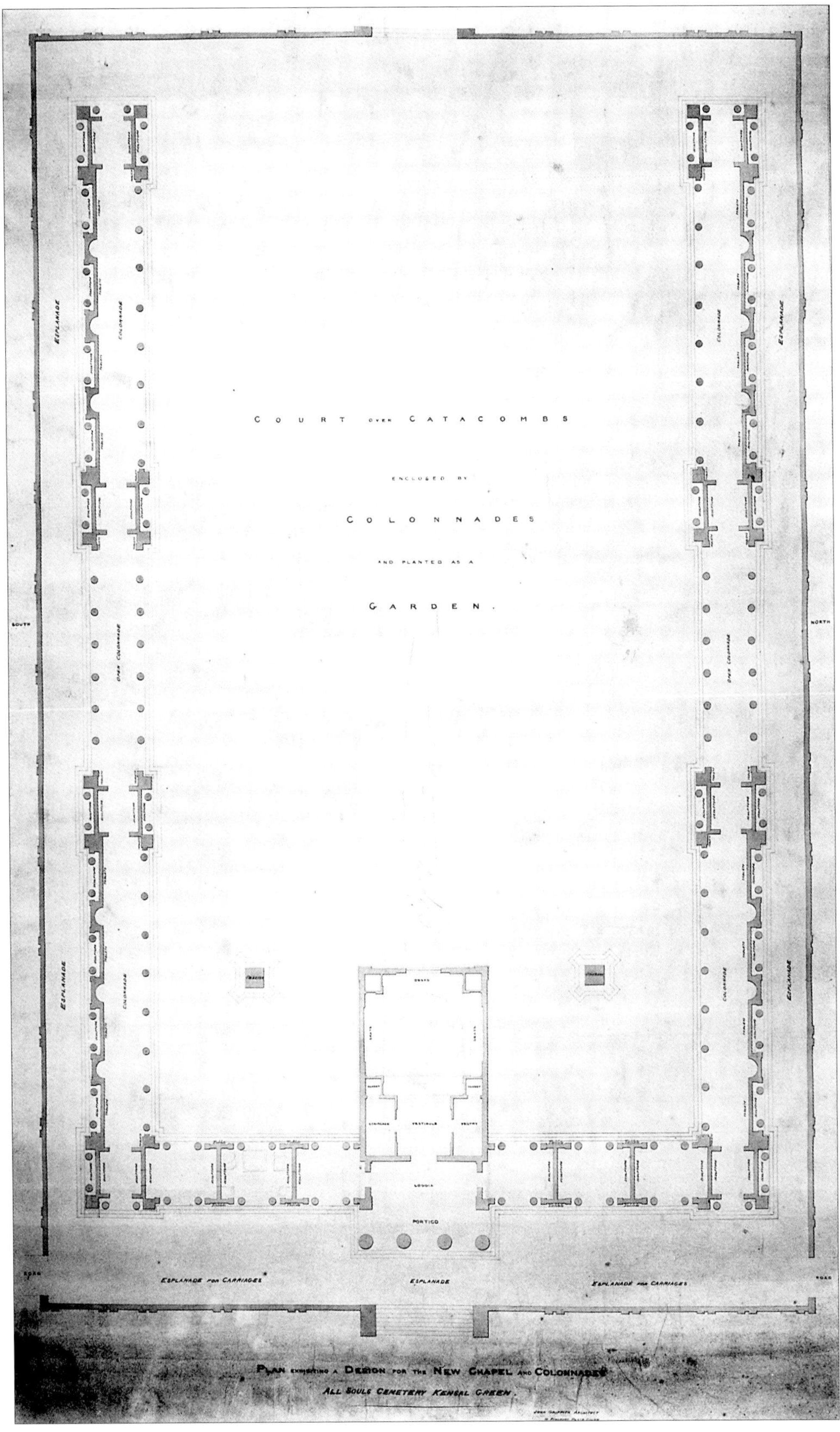

4.19 *(left)* 'Plan exhibiting a Design for the New Chapel and Colonnades' showing the vast ranges of covered cloister-like walks set behind colonnades enclosing a 'Court over Catacombs ... planted as a Garden'. Note the obelisks on either side of the chapel. The entire ensemble, raised above the surrounding ground-level, also included an 'Esplanade' for carriages and contemplative reverie. Drawn in ink with a pale wash in Griffith's office, May 1836 (*GCC. #66. MC. A140900*).

4.20 *(above right)* Front (east) elevation of the Anglican chapel, drawn in ink and water-colour in Griffith's office in May 1836. Note the evergreen trees (presumably cedars) (*GCC. #70. MC.U140900C*).

4.21 *(below right)* 'Design for Catacombs Chapel and Colonnades' showing the north elevation of the colonnades and chapel, with the funerary garden behind, drawn in ink and water-colour in Griffith's office in May 1836. (*GCC. #57.MC.V140900C*).

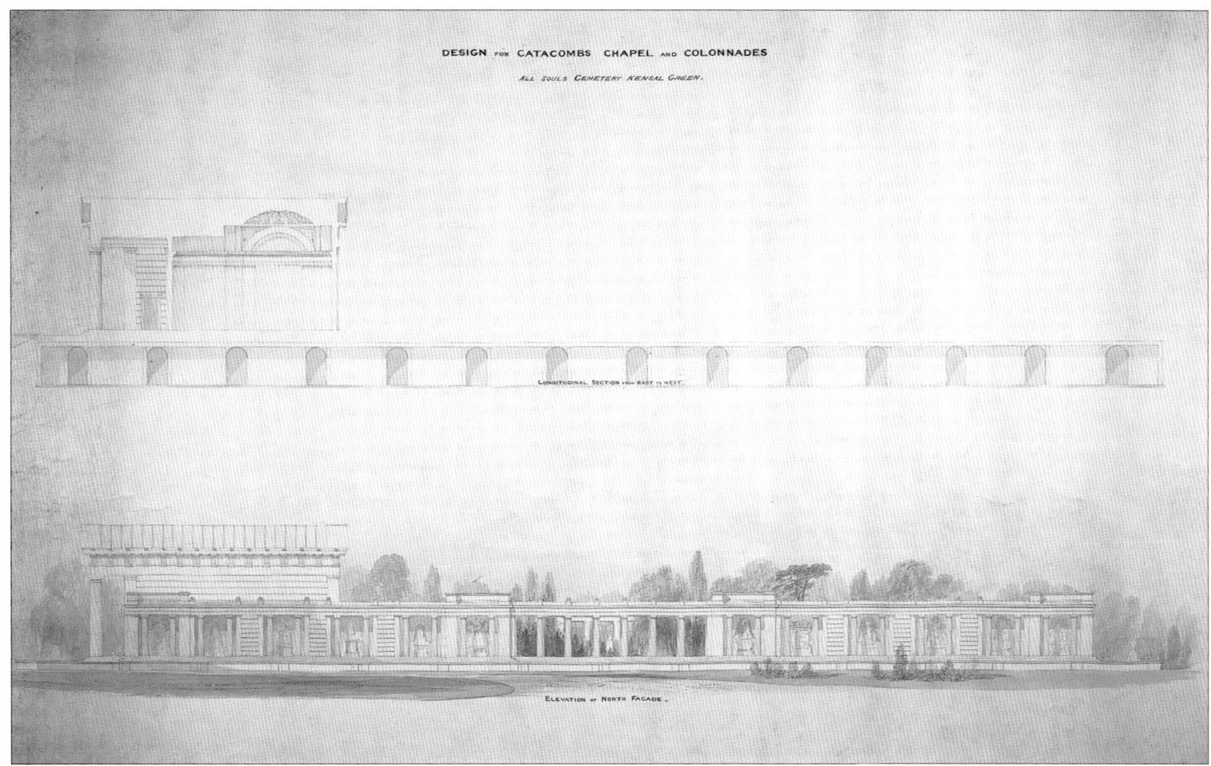
DESIGN FOR CATACOMBS CHAPEL AND COLONNADES
ALL SOULS CEMETERY KENSAL GREEN.
LONGITUDINAL SECTION FROM EAST TO WEST
ELEVATION OF NORTH FACADE.

These drawings appear to have been the very beautiful 'Design for Catacombs, Chapel and Colonnades All Souls Cemetery Kensal Green' (**4.19-4.21**) which consist of a 'Plan exhibiting a Design for the New Chapel and Colonnade: All Souls Cemetery Kensal Green' (signed by John Griffith Architect, of 16 Finsbury Place South, and dated May 1836), a front elevation (i.e. facing east), a section through the chapel and catacombs, and an elevation to the north. The colonnades were arranged in a series of elements with *in antis* Greek Doric columns. There were three rectangular components (open between the *antae* on the east and west façades) on either side of the prostyle tetrastyle Greek Doric chapel, terminating in square pavilions from which long ranges of colonnades were to run east-west consisting of two ranges of seven bays again terminating in pavilions (so effectively each nine bays long), joined by a Doric colonnade of six columns between pavilions. Thus these long east-west colonnades (designed to provide settings for monuments to the persons entombed in the vaults below) were actually to be 25 bays long. The walls on the north and south elevations were solid behind each pair of *in antis* columns, thus providing recesses for the protection of funerary monuments, and between each recess was a solid wall terminated by *antae*. On the other (inner) sides of these solid walls were to be niches for statuary. The entire ensemble of catacomb and garden was almost two-thirds larger than that realised. Griffith's drawings show two obelisks placed on either side of the chapel in an exquisitely planted funerary garden. This scheme was estimated to cost £18,000.

After much discussion it was decided to limit the extent of the catacomb to cut expenses to £15,000, and the Directors decided to raise such a sum by borrowing £7,500, leaving £7,500 still to be acquired. Griffith was then empowered to 'take proposals from Mr Chadwick for the execution of the works connected with the proposed Chapel and Catacombs'.[46] Griffith set to work producing a set of contract-drawings, and these were ready in June 1836. The contract was signed with William Chadwick, of Park Street, Southwark, on 26 July 1836, who was to build the chapel and a much-reduced catacomb and colonnade for £14,451 10s. 7d. These drawings (**4.22-4.26**) are very clear, and finely delineated. If there were any details provided, they do not appear to have survived, but it is interesting that a contract could provide a price on the strength of five drawings and a specification (themselves produced in an amazingly short time).

Chadwick agreed to 'perform all the works' for the proposed chapel and catacomb 'as per drawings &c. for £14,201 4s. 3d.' to which additional costs were to be added for heating, constructing a sewer, and making the catacomb watertight. However, all these long-overdue plans to provide a suitable centrepiece for the cemetery were bedevilled by events described below. Nevertheless, work began on the Anglican chapel and catacomb, the finest architectural ensemble in the cemetery, and Griffith's great building began to take shape over the huge brick-built vaulted catacomb.

The Annual General Meeting of 9 June 1836 heard that prejudices were breaking down, and shares were going up in value. The cemetery was 'fast becoming a very favourite place of Sepulture', and the sale of private vaults in the catacombs had been such as to render it necessary that more accommodation should be provided. It was therefore decided to build a considerable catacomb serving as the 'foundation' (actually a podium) for a 'chapel and ornamental colonnade for monuments' in the centre of the grounds. This chapel would be worthy of the 'increasing celebrity' of the cemetery. The Directors claimed that Kensal Green combined the 'extent and variety' of the cemeteries in Paris and Frankfurt with 'secluded enclosures' of the *Campi Santi* of Bologna and Pisa. Once more, the thought of laying out another cemetery south of the Thames was mentioned, but this, like the other schemes, fizzled out.[47]

4.22 'Plan of Catacombs Concrete Drains &c at All Souls Cemetery Kensall [*sic*] Green'. Contract drawing No. I by John Griffith, dated June 1836, showing the foundations of the Anglican chapel and the arrangement of brick-built and brick-vaulted compartments comprising the catacomb. The semi-circular apsidal arrangements permitted light and air to enter through cast-iron grilles above (*GCC. #67/I. MC.B140900*).

4.23 'Plan of Chapel and Colonnades at All Souls Cemetery Kensall [*sic*] Green'. Contract drawing No. II by John Griffith, dated June 1836. The extent of the catacomb and colonnades was drastically reduced compared with the original design of May 1836 (**4.19**), and the semi-circular niches were replaced by square 'recesses'. The interior arrangement of the chapel has also changed, notably with the two columns *in antis* between the 'vestibule' and the chapel proper (*GCC. #67/II. MC.C 140900*).

46 Minutes of the Proceedings of the Directors of the General Cemetery Company (18 May 1836), 153.

47 Minutes of the Proceedings of General Meetings (9 June 1836), *passim*.

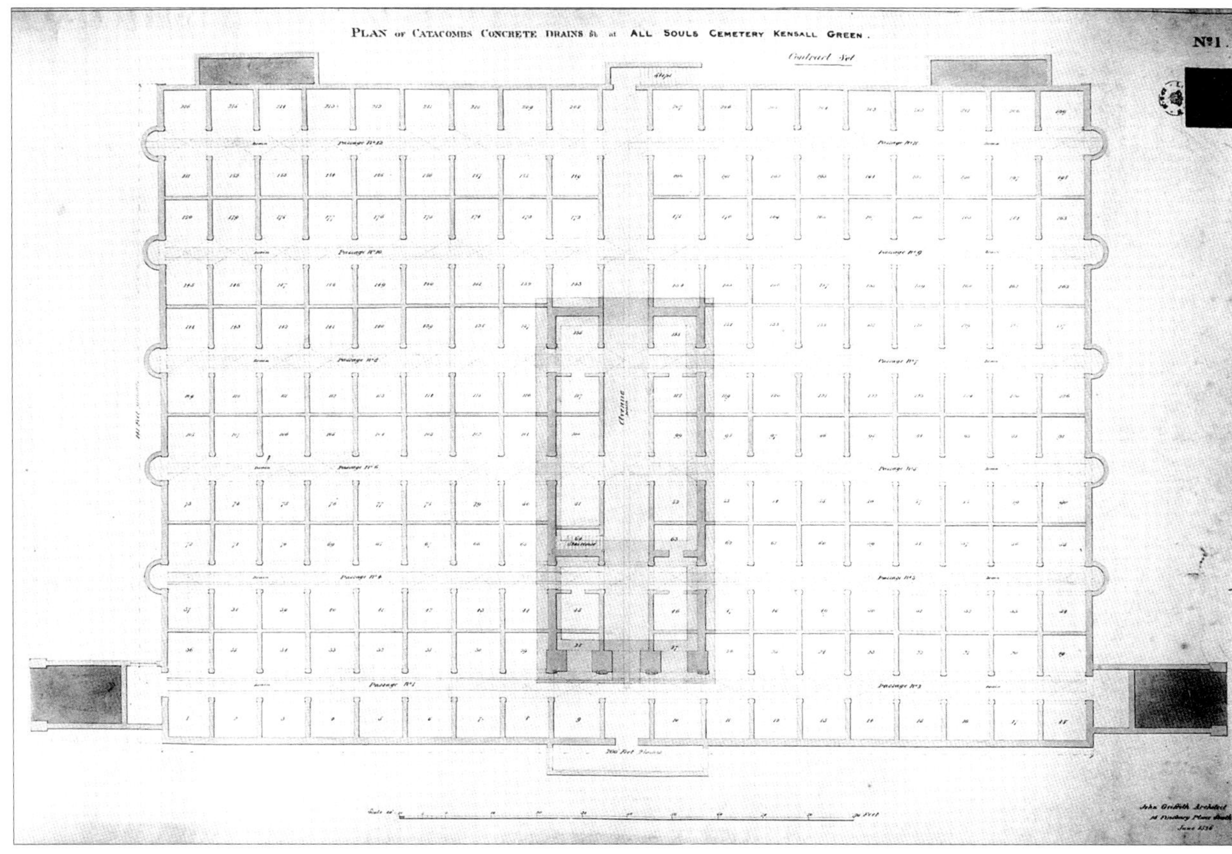
PLAN OF CATACOMBS CONCRETE DRAINS &c at ALL SOULS CEMETERY KENSALL GREEN.
Contract Set
No. I.
Passage No. 1
Passage No. 2
Avenue

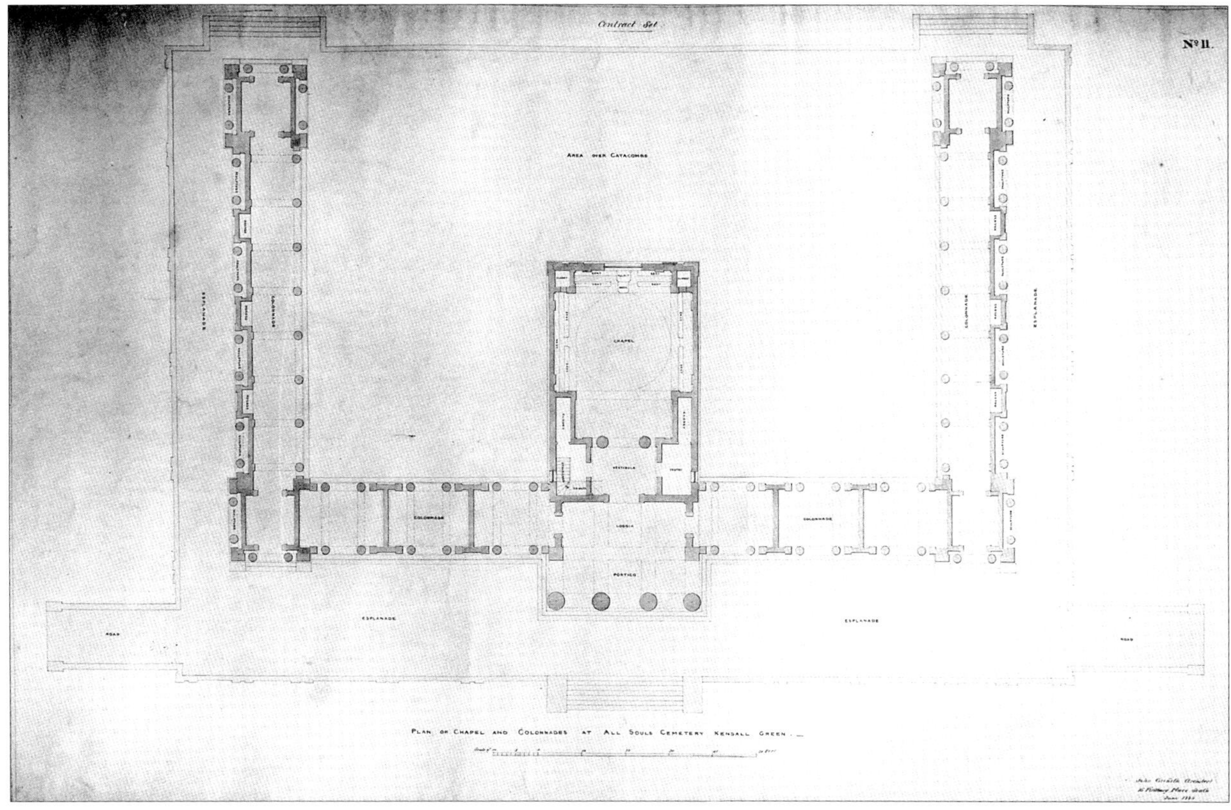
Contract Set
No. II.
AREA OVER CATACOMBS
CHAPEL
COLONNADE
PORTICO
ESPLANADE
PLAN OF CHAPEL AND COLONNADES AT ALL SOULS CEMETERY KENSALL GREEN.

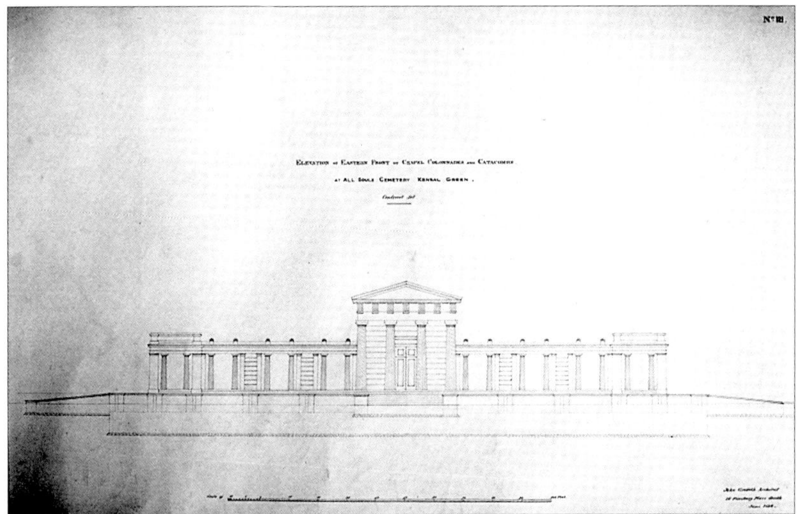

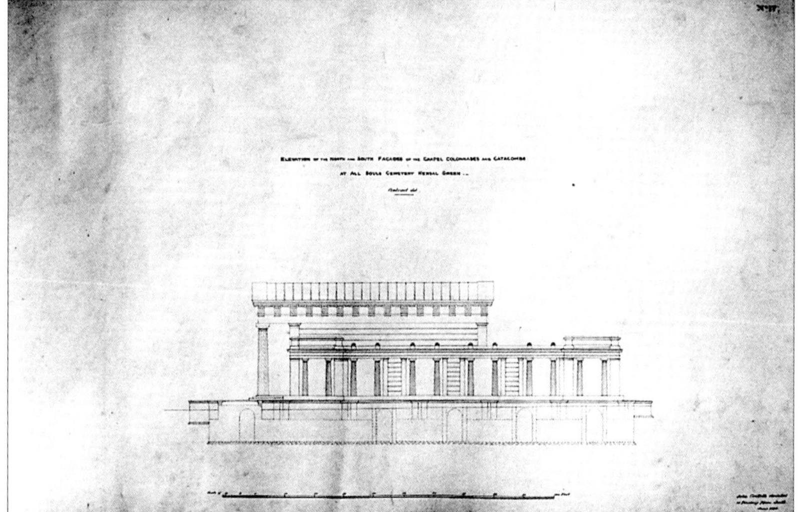

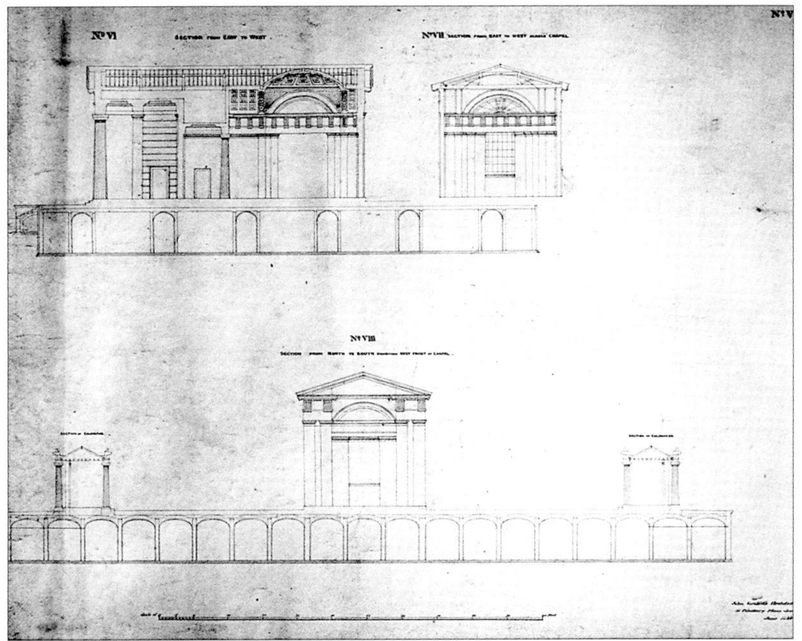

4.24 'Elevation of Eastern Front of Chapel Colonnades and Catacombs at All Souls Cemetery Kensal Green'. Contract drawing No. III by John Griffith, dated June 1836. If compared with the design drawing of May 1836 (**4.20**) it will be seen that the Soanesque pulvins above the entablature are now over the *in antis* columns rather than the *antae*, and, in fact, they were realised over the columns as on the contract drawing (*GCC. #67/III. MC.D140900*).

4.25 'Elevation of the North and South Façades of the Chapel Colonnades and Catacombs at All Souls Cemetery Kensal Green'. Contract drawing No. IV by John Griffith, dated June 1836, showing the colonnades as built in relation to the section through the catacomb below (*GCC. #67/IV. MC.E140900*).

4.26 Contract drawing No. V by John Griffith, dated June 1836, showing: 'Section from East to West' (No. VI) through the Anglican chapel, with the low saucer-dome and the relationships of the triglyphs to the centre-lines of *antae*, which is not the case today, so either the relationship was altered by the contractor or subsequently changed; 'Section from East to West across Chapel' (No VII), where again the triglyphs are placed on the centre-lines of the *antae*; and 'Section from North to South exhibiting West Front of Chapel' (No VIII) with sections through the north and south colonnades and the vaulted catacomb. The draughtsman has avoided showing the eastern range of colonnades. Note that the triglyphs are placed correctly off-centre in relation to the *antae* because in this case the triglyphs *terminate* the entablature (*GCC. #67/V. MC.F140900*).

Very soon, however,[48] more unpleasantness reared its head in the form of Carden, and this business was to cause many difficulties.

The Carden Problem and its Resolution

G. F. Carden (whose behaviour seems to have been odd, to be charitable) had attended a meeting on 12 March 1834 and demanded to know the names of the Directors present when the decision was taken to dismiss him from the office of Registrar, but he was informed that it was an 'Act of the Board and not of Individuals'.[49]

True, in almost all the literature, Carden was credited with the 'exertions' that led to the founding of the General Cemetery Company and the passing of the Act of Parliament by which the Company was incorporated,[50] but his sniping and public rows with the Board over the architectural competition must have been at least very trying. Clearly Carden was opposed to Griffith's designs (which may have been very close to Sir John Dean Paul's intentions), but he certainly made enough noise about it, and he was to remain a thorn in the Board's flesh for some time.

Things came to a head when Griffith's proposals for the Anglican chapel were accepted by the Board. Carden, acting through solicitors, wrote to claim £5,000 'for loss of time and expenses in the formation of the Company',[51] to which the Board replied that the 'Directors, while … always ready to acknowledge that Mr G. F. Carden was the original Promoter of Suburban Cemeteries in Great Britain', could not 'recognize any pecuniary claim whatsoever on his part against the Company'.[52]

The decision to build a design by Griffith rather than any of those submitted for the competition appears to have been the trigger that excited Carden's rage. Very soon, Carden's lawyers were demanding of the Secretary certain copies of documents, but this was refused, but Carden was sent £24 16s. 7d. 'due on his Treasurership accounts'.[53]

Then a Magistrate's summons was served on the Clerk of the Company requiring him to attend 'the Police office in Hatton Garden to answer the Complaint of Mr. G. F. Carden for refusing to permit him to peruse the book containing the list of Proprietors'.[54] Carden, it seems, just would not go away, and produced a pamphlet setting out his case against the Board. However, he offered to 'circulate with his Pamphlet any contradiction the Directors might think proper to make to the contents of the same'.[55] The Board resolved that 'no answer should be sent'.

The next blow[56] was a Writ of Summons from the Court of Common Pleas in the suit of Carden against the General Cemetery Company in an action of Debt for £5,000. This the Directors determined to defend, so Counsel was retained. Carden proceeded with his action by 'delivering a Declaration claiming £6,000 for services and expences from 1820 to the 12th July 1832'.[57] The dispute dragged on, and eventually[58] the Company found itself in some difficulties as the lawyers opined Carden might have something of a case, so the Board decided to buy him off on condition he should give 'unequivocal admission' that he had 'no legal claim against the Company'. The General Cemetery Company recognised that Carden should be compensated for all the time and exertions he had expended, and made a final offer of £1,000 in full settlement. To everyone's relief Carden accepted the offer,[59] and released the Company from all or any further obligations to him as well as undertaking he would not take any more legal actions against the Company.[60]

[48] Minutes of the Proceedings of the Directors of the General Cemetery Company (13 July 1836), 161. [49] Ibid. (12 March 1834), 88. [50] *Penny Magazine* iii/150 (2 August 1834), 297-300. [51] Minutes of the Proceedings of the Directors of the General Cemetery Company (13 July 1836), 161. [52] Ibid. [53] Ibid. (27 July 1836), 162. [54] Ibid., 165. [55] Ibid. (28 September 1836), 168. [56] Ibid. (20 March 1837), 185. [57] Ibid. (26 April 1837), 192. [58] Ibid. (19 January 1839), *passim*. [59] Ibid. (26 June 1839), 266-7. [60] Ibid. (29 September 1839), 276.

Other Difficulties

4.27 Mausoleum designed by Robert Shout and built by William Milligan, erected 1836-8, in 1997 [383/50/RS]. It is very Parisian in style, clearly influenced by some of the grander tombs in Père-Lachaise cemetery, Paris. *See* Chapter VIII, §28 (*JSC*).

Further problems arose to try the patience of the Board. First of all, the mason building the mausoleum of James Morison (1770-1840) was accused of 'improper conduct' towards the Clerk and four of the Directors, and consequently was banned from entering the cemetery at all.[61] Morison had been a member of the Company at the passing of the 1832 Act, and his tomb was designed by Robert Shout (*c*.1763-1843) who, with his brother, Benjamin, kept a mason's yard in Holborn in which they made funerary monuments. The mausoleum (obviously intended as a landmark to beautify the grounds) was constructed by William Milligan (1812-78), the sculptor, who was obliged to grovel to the Directors and write a letter of apology for his 'misconduct'. Having promised to behave, and 'expressed his sorrow', he was permitted access to the cemetery to continue his work (**4.27**).[62]

Secondly, the chaplain, Johnstone, who, reading between the lines, was more than a bit of a prig, complained of the 'Drunkenness of the Boy at the Gate of the Cemetery', and the 'Boy' was 'dismissed from the service of the Company'. Johnstone was also to cause trouble by residing at Cambridge Terrace, Edgware Road, 'in violation of the understanding entered into at the time of his appointment' as Chaplain. In addition, it appears that Johnstone carried out other 'clerical duties', notably for the National Society for Promoting the Education of the Poor, and had to be reminded in no uncertain terms that the 'exclusive services of the Chaplain' were required by the Company, and that he should reside nearer to hand.[63] Johnstone, who seems to have complained about many employees of the Cemetery Company, was himself a poor timekeeper (as noted above), absented himself without leave on several occasions, and broke his contractual obligations to the Board relating to his place of residence (he was obliged to live near the cemetery) and not taking any other employment. He was therefore a troublesome Chaplain, and in due course resigned, to be succeeded by the unfortunately named Joseph Twigger in May 1838.

Thirdly, the Vestry of the Parish of Kensington claimed a right of way through the cemetery grounds and intended to 'exercise it on going the bounds of the Parish on 4 May 1837: the Board decided that 'in the event of such proceeding the gates of the Cemetery' should be 'closed against them'.[64] Worse was to come, for the Portland Cemetery Company proposed laying out a cemetery at Primrose Hill (Carden's old preferred site), and a Bill was about to go through Parliament.[65] Immediately the Board drew up a draft of a Petition against the Bill, for it feared the competition.

Then, on 4 May, as threatened, a mob led by the overseers of the Parish of Kensington arrived at the cemetery gates, broke through, and crossed the unconsecrated ground, breaking through the opposite gates whereupon the determined walkers crossed the canal by means of a barge and subsequently passed through the Company's remaining land on the south side of the canal.[66] The 'right of way' seems to be the path shown on **4.3**. Although the Board considering taking proceedings 'at law against the

[61] Minutes of the Proceedings of the Directors of the General Cemetery Company (27 July 1836), 164. [62] Ibid (31 August 1836), 166. [63] Ibid. (29 March 1837), 186-7 and (12 April 1837), 189. [64] Ibid. (26 April 1837), 192. [65] This eventually did not materialise. [66] Minutes of the Proceedings of the Directors of the General Cemetery Company (5 May 1837), 194-5.

parties asserting an alleged right of footpath through the Cemetery' it did not 'deem it expedient to take any steps ... at present'.[67]

There were also other problems associated with the Parish of Kensington, for the Poor Rate assessed on the cemetery was the enormous sum of £2,000. The Company appealed, and at the Court of Quarter Sessions this was reduced to £444 10s. 0d. All these problems were constant drains on patience and resources, and the Company, finding itself short of money, decided to bring in another Bill in Parliament to increase its capital and enhance the powers of the Board. In due course *An Act for enabling the General Cemetery Company to raise a further Sum of Money; and for amending the Act relating to the said Company* became law on 14 May 1839,[68] by which the Company was authorised to raise a further £15,000.

By Summer 1837 it was clear that the cedar trees would not 'take', and were given up for lost. It was decided to replace some of the 'cedar avenue' planting with 'silver firs' instead.[69] Thus the Company could be said to have had its fair share of difficulties. Throughout the 1830s too there were continuing problems with the Canal and Railway Companies, and the Directors went to considerable trouble to ensure that those modes of transport and their associated construction-workers would interfere as little as possible with the new cemetery. To have trains clattering by, belching smoke, would have harmed the prospects of the cemetery, so everything was done to minimise their impact on the peace and quiet of the grounds, and the Minutes contain many references to meetings with representatives of both Companies. There were problems too with the Clerk and Sexton, one Pasquier, who had been claiming the wages of a man who had not been employed by the Company for some time: Pasquier was 'permitted to resign the Office of Clerk and Sexton upon his refunding the amount retained by him', but was replaced.[70] Unfortunately, the replacement only lasted a few weeks before he, too, was removed from office for unspecified unsatisfactory behaviour. Nevertheless, the Company kept these problems quiet, for to make overt any wrong-doing on the part of its employees would not have helped.

Conclusion

Despite all these trials and tribulations, the Company concerned itself with aesthetics. Much consideration was given to the question of erecting monuments in the cemetery to improve its appearance, something with which Sievier was closely concerned. Indeed, Sievier designed the elegant memorial (**4.28**) to John St John Long (1798-1834), which is one of the finest in the cemetery, and certainly intended to add aesthetic tone, although the dubious quack celebrated by it was scarcely out of the top drawer.

4.28 Memorial to John St John Long (1798-1834), in 1997 [283/**88**/RS], designed by Sievier and erected to add character to the cemetery. *See* Chapter VIII, §55 (*JSC*).

Near the completion of the works at the Anglican chapel, Chadwick, doubtless worn out by the demands made upon him to build well, quickly, and cheaply, announced[71] that he was 'retiring from business' and that he declined to do any further work

[67] Ibid. (24 May 1837), 195-6. [68] 2 Vict. c. 5. *See* the Minutes of the Proceedings of the Directors of the General Cemetery Company (30 January 1839), 250. [69] Minutes of the Proceedings of the Directors of the General Cemetery Company (24 June 1837), 199. [70] Ibid. (29 November 1837), 211-2. [71] Ibid. (28 February 1838), 220.

in the cemetery (apart from what remained to complete his contract for the erection of the chapel). However, he recommended his foreman, 'Mr Lander of Kensall Green' to succeed him, and Lander was duly employed as builder and mason at the cemetery, subsequently establishing his thriving business as a monumental mason. By April 1838 Griffith was able to report that the new chapel was all but finished, bar the painting, 'which would not interfere with' its use, and the installation of 'the machine for lowering the coffins which Mr Smith had promised should be finished forthwith'.[72] Griffith also presented a painted glass window for the new Anglican chapel, drawings for which he had produced as early as 28 June 1837: this act of generosity was well-received by the Board.

By April 1838, therefore, the temporary chapel was no longer required, and Griffith recommended it should be demolished,[73] and the materials sold. It was also decided to plant 'the space within the inclosure of the Colonnade of the new Chapel ... with flowering shrubs &c.', to replace all the dead cedars (i.e. most of them) with silver firs, and to replant 'other avenues'. A severe frost had 'destroyed the greater part of the evergreens and other shrubs at the Cemetery ... and ... herbaceous plants were much wanted'.[74] Griffith also suggested laying a new drain under the 'principal road' to render 'a very valuable part of the ground' occupied by a drain available for burial.

By the end of the decade the General Cemetery had acquired its handsome Greek Revival buildings, finished outside in Portland Stone and stucco, and the Anglican chapel, with its truncated colonnades, was completed. The interior was washed with distemper, and any paintwork was light, in tune with the pre-polychrome phase of Neoclassicism. Woodwork was grained to resemble oak, and dark blue cloth was hung on the walls behind the seats. After many teething troubles the catafalque was operating satisfactorily, and was richly hung with cloth.

Efforts were also made to beautify the new colonnades attached to the Anglican chapel by encouraging the erection of suitable funerary monuments. To this end the Board granted the space necessary for 'the erection of the monument to Mrs Palmer the construction of which cost 1500 guineas ... gratuitously ... to Mr McKinnon in consideration of its being the first monument of such a description and value, and that the site be selected by the party'. This was a reference to William Alexander Mackinnon (1789-1870), Member of Parliament, a tireless fighter against intramural interment, who had married (1802) Emma Mary Palmer (d. 1835), only daughter of Joseph Budworth Palmer (1756-1815), whose wife, Elizabeth, is presumably the person commemorated by the monument.

Thus, after many delays and false starts, the cemetery had been laid out, walled, and planted, and had four distinguished works of architecture designed by Griffith within its grounds. Various mausolea and memorials were erected in the landscaped fields of repose, and London's first great garden-cemetery was in business, and doing well (**4.29**).

It is obvious from the Minutes of both the Provisional Committee and the Board of the General Cemetery Company that much effort was expended on the question of quality buildings, landscaping, enclosing, and securing the ground, and attracting a 'clientèle' capable of spending money on fine tombs and memorials (and filling the considerable numbers of *loculi* in the catacombs). Work on the enclosure of the ground, as has been described above, started almost as soon as the land at Kensal Green was acquired, and that alone was no small matter. The temporary Anglican chapel was necessary because, as has been made clear, the Bishop of London would not consecrate the cemetery without it, but it is curious that the terrace or old catacomb, entrance-gate and lodges, and Dissenters' chapel were erected *before* the permanent Anglican chapel. The reasons for this appear to have been the necessity of providing for the demand for

[72] Minutes of the Proceedings of the Directors of the General Cemetery Company (28 February 1838), 221.
[73] Ibid. (25 April 1838), 227. [74] Ibid. (28 March 1838), 224, and (25 April 1838), 227.

4.29 'The General Cemetery, Kensal Green': a view of 1838 showing the recently completed Anglican chapel (*left*), the long colonnade of the old, north, or terrace catacomb (*right*), the Ducrow mausoleum [820/76/RS] (*foreground*), and the St John Long memorial [283/76/RS] (*right*). Note the surviving evergreen trees before they were replaced with deciduous varieties. From *The Mirror of Literature, Amusement, and Instruction*, 890 (28 April 1838) (*RBKC K.66/514, neg. no. 4683.614.61.KEN*).

'burial' in *loculi* as the vaults under churches were well-filled by then; the desire to cater for Nonconformists in order to stifle criticism of the Company from the massed ranks of Dissenters, always on the look-out for perceived slights; and the obvious need to have offices for the Clerk and Chaplain on site. An imposing entrance-gate would also be an advertisement, would give the appearance of respectability and security, and suggest confidence. Dignified architecture and well-crafted buildings were essential for the standing of what was a completely new venture, unfamiliar to the public, and doubtless regarded with suspicion by many. Furthermore, the grounds had to be prepared, planted, and well-groomed, for nobody would relish interring loved ones in a muddy field, and one of the most important aspects of the cemetery promotion was that it was a place 'of repose' quite unlike the untidy and disgusting urban burial-grounds. Thus expenditure on landscape-gardening, layout of paths, tree-planting, and so on, was a considerable item, and advice was sought from no less a personage than Nash, just as the opinions of leading architects were canvassed regarding the buildings.

The catacombs were designed to appeal to those who desired the security of vault-burial. High perimeter walls, solid gates, railings that could not easily be climbed, and substantial lodges (suggesting the entrance to a great country estate) were key elements in the appeal of the enterprise. The need for an *appearance* of security extended to the architectural *style* chosen for the cemetery's buildings. Although the Kendall design was Gothic, and won the premium in the architectural competition, a Greek Revival style was selected, apparently because it gave a superior impression of solidity, strength, and security, precisely what the promoters of the cemetery wished to transmit to the public.

Almost as soon as the cemetery opened for business, however, the whole question of security of bodies became irrelevant by the passing of the 1832 Anatomy Act and subsequent legislation,[75] which made the bodies of paupers available to the medical

75 The Anatomy Act, 2 & 3 Will. IV, c. 75, and The Poor Law Amendment Act, 4 & 5 Will. IV, c. 76. The impact of these utilitarian pieces of legislation was enormous, and should not be underestimated.

schools. Despite public revulsion and much opposition, the many who died in poverty provided a more certain supply of corpses than did the gallows. Thus the buried remnants of most members of society were rendered safe from the 'resurrectionists', and the relatives of those who lay within the General Cemetery of All Souls at Kensal Green needed no longer to fear nocturnal theft of their loved-ones' cadavers. The body-snatchers were put out of business because bodies were supplied from the Workhouses' morgues.

The infant Company, therefore, was not only mindful of the necessity to adopt 'some better system of interment' in order to remove 'offences to public decency' and 'injuries to public health', but to cater for a desire to treat the dead with tenderness and dignity, reuniting families after death, and permitting proper commemoration. It was also essential to provide a place that would be secure from grave-robbers, outrages, and obscenities, and where *permanent* 'resting-places' could be purchased, in stark contrast to the impermanency of choked, smelly, revolting urban graveyards that had been tolerated for far too long.

It is curious that the building of a permanent Church of England chapel was left so late, because the temporary chapel cannot have attracted a class of well-heeled Anglicans, and the delay in providing a proper and worthy architectural centrepiece to the cemetery alienated Carden[76] and his supporters so much that they carried on a vociferous public campaign of hostility towards the Board. It was not just a question of disagreement over the style of the buildings that caused such delays and recriminations, but a shortage of funds. The Anglican chapel and catacomb could not be erected on a shoestring, and it would not have done if it had turned out a less distinguished pile than the Dissenters' chapel and entrance-gate. Money therefore had to be raised, but it had proved difficult enough to get investment from potential shareholders. Nevertheless, the long delays in building the noble Anglican chapel did not increase confidence in the venture, certainly led to violent arguments and unpleasantness, and contributed to a slow trade in burial-spaces during the 1830s. Furthermore, the passing of the 1832 Anatomy Act led to a gradual fall in demand for catacomb burial, and so, after initial interest in vaults for burial, that soon subsided. Along with the collapse of the body-snatching business, the character of the cemetery at Kensal Green reassured 'clients' that graves would remain inviolate. There were some difficulties with certain members of staff, who failed to pass on complaints from the public, made several serious mistakes, and were responsible for 'unaccountable and discreditable' actions that could only lead to 'serious ruin',[77] including carelessness in recording correct facts in ledgers. These problems had to be resolved at once, and seemed to have been flagged by Twigger, the Chaplain.[78] Eventually, however, although the viability of the cemetery looked dodgy for a time during the 1830s, fortunes were to change with dramatic effect in the 1840s, as we shall see.

[76] Carden's alienation did not prevent his burial in the cemetery (1874) in a plot [24631/113/4] directly in front of the Anglican chapel, and near the tomb of Princess Sophia. His marble headstone has lead lettering proclaiming that he was the founder of the cemetery. [77] Minutes of the Proceedings of the Directors of the General Cemetery Company (24 November 1841), 341. [78] Ibid. (29 September 1841), 330.

CHAPTER V

Kensal Green Cemetery, 1842-52

JAMES STEVENS CURL

Public Health; Burial of the Poor, and Other Matters; The First Royal Burial; The Monumental Chambers; More Problems; A Second Royal Funeral; Further Difficulties and the Company's Responses; Resolution

> Cemeteries, rightly selected and properly arranged, may be made subservient to some of the highest purposes of religion and human duty; they may preach lessons to which none may refuse to listen, and which all must live to hear. [All Souls' Cemetery, Kensal-Green], adorned as it is with beautiful flowers and freshest evergreens, presents a smiling countenance as well amidst the gloomy winter as in the sunny days of summer; and unlike the desolate pent-up burial-grounds of the crowded metropolis, instead of repelling approach, allures us to enter its sacred precincts, both by the floral charms within, and the view afforded thence of the extensive and pleasing scenery without. There is nothing to revolt the feelings – no profane hand scatters the ashes of the dead; no rattling sounds of wheels or the roaring tumult of an onward commerce disturbs the deep serenity; and affection seems to have lavished all its endearing tenderness in hallowing the last mournful recollections of departed excellence.

ANONYMOUS (1849): 'Extra-Mural Interments. All Souls' Cemetery, Kensal-Green', in *Illustrated Historic Times*, 149.

Public Health

Early in 1842 the Board decided that the 'land on either side of the centre road' should be 'reserved for Monuments to be erected at a cost of at least £200 exclusive of the price paid for the ground'.[1] In other words, the Directors were keen to improve the appearance of the cemetery, and especially of the main avenue leading to the Anglican chapel, by ensuring it was embellished with fine funerary monuments and mausolea. Aesthetic considerations, therefore, were regarded as very important, not least because they would have a profound effect on the commercial aspects of the enterprise by attracting a better class of 'customer'.

However, the Directors were also aware that public debate about the provision of burial was by no means over. Asiatic cholera, outrage, and masses of publications had concentrated minds sufficiently to enable Parliament to authorise the establishment of metropolitan commercial cemeteries from 11 July 1832, of which Kensal Green was the first,[2] followed by the South Metropolitan at West Norwood by an Act of 28 July 1836,[3] the cemeteries of the London Cemetery Company (Highgate and Nunhead) by an Act of 17 August 1836,[4] and a further four London cemeteries to 1847.[5] Nevertheless, pressure was growing for more radical changes, and in some instances opposition to burial within churches and churchyards was becoming shrill, even to the extent of closing *and clearing* the vaults at St George's Chapel, Windsor. Imperfect understanding of how infection was transmitted encouraged the 'miasmatists' to greater efforts. The publication of the 1838 Report by Thomas Southwood Smith (1788-1861) on the appalling conditions prevailing in parts of London focused attention on the fact that epidemic fevers were directly related to the conditions in which the poor lived, and that fevers could only be brought under control by improving the physical conditions of the labouring classes. Smith's researches were supported and augmented by the monumental *Report on the Sanitary Conditions of the Labouring Classes in Great Britain* of 1842 by Edwin Chadwick (1800-90). Meanwhile, George Alfred Walker (1807-84), philanthropist, surgeon, and sanitary reformer, had been busy collecting material for his publications, and gave evidence to a Select Committee of the House of Commons in 1840, later published as an appendix to his *Graveyards of London* (1841), after which he was dubbed, unsurprisingly, 'Graveyard' Walker. Walker was indefatigable, and published numerous works on the evils of insanitary interment, of which his *Gatherings from Graveyards* (1839), *Interment and Disinterment* (1843), and *Series of Lectures on the actual conditions of the Metropolitan Graveyards* (1847) are the most celebrated.[6] These debates have been well-aired elsewhere, and would be superfluous to go over them again here: it is sufficient to observe that Walker uncovered a scandalous, disgusting, ghastly, and degrading state of affairs that no civilised society should have tolerated. Full weight was given to his findings by Chadwick's *Supplementary Report on the Results of a Special Inquiry into the Practice of Interment in Towns* (1843) which accepted that gases and liquids from decomposing bodies were dangerous, and that overcrowded burial-grounds were major sources of contamination in proletarian parts of London and elsewhere: 'all interments in towns', the *Report* stated, 'where bodies decompose, contribute to the mass of atmospheric impurity which is injurious to public health'.[7] Chadwick's *Report* subscribed to the 'miasmatic' and 'pythogenic'[8] theories, ultimately

[1] Minutes of the Proceedings of the Directors of the General Cemetery Company (27 April 1842), 8. [2] Act of Parliament (1832), 2 & 3 Will. IV, c. 110. [3] See Curl (2000*e*) 83-108. *See also* Act of Parliament (1838*a*), 6 & 7 Will. IV, c. 129. [4] Act of Parliament (1838*b*), 6 & 7 Will. IV, c. 136. [5] Sheppard (*Ed.*) (1973), 335. [6] These matters are covered in Curl (2000*e*), *passim*. *See also* George Alfred Walker (1839, 1843, 1847), *passim*. [7] Chadwick (1843), 31. [8] 'Miasmatic' = pertaining to or having the nature of infectious or noxious exhalations from putrescent organic matter consisting of poisonous particles or germs floating in and polluting the atmosphere. 'Pythogenic' = generated by or from corruption or filth.

5.1 Intramural Interment. Section through a typical London inner-city churchyard and church showing (A and B) the ground crammed with coffins to a level higher than the church-floor, and only a few centimetres from rooms occupied by families in the dwellings overlooking the unsavoury ground (which includes an open common grave [D] in the paupers' burial-place). Below the church-floor is a crypt (C) with coffins piled on top of each other. The original surface of the churchyard (E) was coincident with the floor-level of the church, which explains why many churchyards are much higher than surrounding land. To sink any new grave in such conditions would inevitably involve disturbing earlier burials, and indeed the destruction of coffins and human remains, often by the most brutal and hideous of means. From *The Lady's Newspaper* (16 September 1849), 145 (*ECJSC*).

found to be untenable, but, although appreciation of the mechanisms of how epidemic and infections were spread was vague, it was realised that dirt and decay were certainly contributing factors (5.1).

Burial of the Poor, and Other Matters

One of the difficulties the Board of the General Cemetery Company came up against was the vociferous campaign (resulting from the work of Walker, Chadwick, and others[9]) against all intramural interment, which was starting to swing public opinion against 'burial' in catacombs or vaults. Considerable expense had been incurred to provide facilities for deposits of lead-lined coffins in the terrace catacomb, the vaults under the Dissenters' chapel, and the very large catacomb beneath the Anglican chapel, partly to cater for those who could no longer acquire spaces in the crypts of churches, and partly to offer security to those who feared the depredations of the 'resurrectionists' (who had been put out of business by the Acts of 1832 and 1834[10]). Now, campaigns were being launched against *all* vaults and catacombs, only nine years after the first range of vaults had been built at Kensal Green.

Thus, when the Company received a letter from William Alexander Mackinnon, MP (1789-1870), 'Chairman of the Committee for the Improvement in the Health of Towns',[11] relating to the prohibition of 'interments' within the 'precincts of towns', there was some

9 *See*, e.g. , Peggs (1840), *passim*. 10 2 & 3 Will. IV, c. 75, and 4 & 5 Will. IV, c. 76. 11 Minutes of the Proceedings of the Directors of the General Cemetery Company (27 April 1842), 9.

consternation, and suitable representations were made to counter such moves. Well over £2,200 had been spent on laying drains to improve the condition of the soil, and to ensure that the catacombs were also properly connected to the drainage system, so the new developments must have caused the Board many problems. As if these were not enough, a letter was received from 'Mr James Carden', presumably a brother of G. F. Carden, but the Board resolved that 'no notice be taken of the letter'.[12] The response to Mackinnon, however, was comprehensive and included a history of why the cemetery had been founded in the first place, together with a factual description of its extent and buildings. Proof that the 'prejudices firmly opposed to suburban burial and the establishment of cemeteries were rapidly subsiding'[13] was provided by the steady rise in interments at Kensal Green: 84 in 1833, 197 in 1834, 360 in 1835, 427 in 1836, 677 in 1837, 787 in 1838, and thereafter 'about 900 in each year', including 'members of nearly 200 noble families in whose vaults' there remained 'room for 1000 more interments'. The Directors argued that it was 'beginning to be known that economy' was one of the chief 'recommendations' of the cemetery, and that a common grave only cost £1 5s. 0d., although the 'proportion of burials' had been 'hitherto in favor of the higher and middle classes of society … shown in the increased costliness and taste displayed in the erection of monuments … which also strongly' evinced that the cemetery was becoming 'a favourite place of sepulture'.

The Directors were 'anxious to meet the views of those' considering 'the propriety of removing' burial of paupers and others from the 'precincts of the Metropolis' by offering 'such accommodation' as would 'satisfy the public demand for many hundred years to come' provided 'an arrangement' could be made with the different parishes.[14] Implicit in this offer was a great reduction in the 'parochial rate', which had been such a bone of contention, involving considerable legal charges and other expenses. The Directors estimated that the following parishes required an annual burial facility for the disposal of the cadavers of paupers: St Marylebone (40), St George, Hanover Square (85), St James, Westminster (85), Paddington (80 – excluding Bayswater, which included its figures in the returns of Kensington, Paddington, and St George, Hanover Square), St Pancras (260), and St Martin-in-the-Fields (130). Those parishes had 'together a population equal to nearly one half of London', and the Directors estimated that a 'space of ground containing 7 acres would be sufficient for the interment of their paupers for ages to come'.[15] Accordingly, the Board offered seven acres of the ground at Kensal Green 'adjoining the cemetery for the burial of the poor under such regulations' as might be thought fit. The Company estimated that the seven acres would accommodate 133,000 graves, with 10 coffins in each grave, so the seven acres would hold 1,330,000 'deceased paupers' at 'an average of 1,000 burials a year', so the ground would 'not be filled for 1330 years'. This was to be high-density burial indeed. Interestingly, the Directors recognised that 'a cemetery always' lowered the value 'of the property around', so they envisaged using the land on the south side of the canal as a neat way of ridding themselves of property that was of no use to them. Such proposals savoured of utilitarian exploitation, however, and the furore they provoked soon led to their abandonment.

A letter on behalf of the Committee of the Greek Community was received[16] in which a piece of ground in the unconsecrated part of the cemetery was sought, and the Board offered land provided the Community erected a suitable fence around it to define its holding. It was also suggested that the Board might be willing to 'let the Committee'

[12] Minutes of the Proceedings of the Directors of the General Cemetery Company (27 April 1842), 10. [13] Ibid., 11. [14] Ibid., 12. [15] Ibid., 13. Loudon was horrified by the proposals, recorded in the *Annual Report of the General Cemetery Company* (9 June 1842), 8, and castigated the 'idea of accumulating such a mass of corruption in such a limited space': he hoped it would 'never be listened to for a moment by the public', who should be put 'on their guard against men who can hazard such statements' (Loudon [1843], 46-7). [16] Minutes of the Proceedings of the Directors of the General Cemetery Company (11 May 1842), 16.

have land 'forty feet square ... at half the price charged for the inclosed land' on the patch south of the canal.[17] However, negotiations with the Greek Community got nowhere, and the Greeks eventually obtained land in the South Metropolitan cemetery, West Norwood. There were difficulties with some of the Company's employees, two of whom were 'uncivil' to one of the Directors, Wardell, who was showing his family around the cemetery. It was also discovered that none of the buildings was insured against fire, so the Board ordered 'that competent insurance on the same' should be 'forthwith effected'.[18] Much was also made of the possibilities of selling grass for fodder, and it was resolved to charge 'not less than £40 ... for the crop of ... this season in the Western Division of the Cemetery', and five guineas for the grass in the 'Eastern' (i.e. unconsecrated) part of the grounds. At the next meeting[19] 'the number of labourers' in the cemetery was 'reduced to 15 men and boys', so the two 'uncivil' labourers were dismissed.

By 1842 something had to be done about the planting on the main avenue, and Ronalds was approached to supply 'ornamental trees of the heights of 8 feet and 10 feet respectively ... at the prices of 75/- and 100/- per hundred', and it was resolved to plant the 'sides of the centre road' with Spanish and Horse Chestnut trees, set 'in alternate order'. These trees are now almost at the ends of their lives, but the documentary evidence shows that much of the character of the cemetery today (2001) derives from the scheme of planting of 1842, although some of the surviving evergreens date from the 1830s.[20] Fifty 'red and white lime trees' were also ordered to be purchased and planted in the cemetery.[21] At the Annual General Meeting on 8 June 1843 it was reported that chestnut and other 'ornamental forest trees' had been planted on each side of the road running through the centre of the grounds.

Under-funding had been a problem from the start of the venture, and, in 1842, 2,600 tenths of shares were created at £2 10s. 0d. per share, making a total of £6,500. Each proprietor of a whole share had the option of taking one such tenth share, and there were other attempts to raise capital from time to time. The demands of the Poor Rate Assessments caused endless problems, and many costs were incurred when appealing against these. In 1836 there had been difficulties raising funds, and cash had to be borrowed at high rates of interest. In 1837 the building of the Anglican chapel and catacomb required capital, and the litigation over the Carden affair not only dragged on, but cost money too. Nevertheless a dividend of 5 per cent was payable in that year, and the Directors expressed confidence in the future of the cemetery. By 1838 the Company had been obliged to borrow money from Sir John Dean Paul, Bart., at 4 per cent interest, and it was decided to apply for a new Act of Parliament in order to increase capital by issuing additional shares. Nevertheless, a dividend of 6 per cent was paid to shareholders, and again in 1839, despite the cost of £15, 711 14s. 3d. incurred for the building of the Anglican chapel and catacomb, and architect's commission of £973 0s. 0d. By 1840 the shares had risen in value to £44 each and the debts of the Company were liquidated, although Carden had to be paid £1,000 in consideration of his 'outlay and personal exertions'. 1841 saw the Company being assessed for £4,000 Poor Rate, which was regarded as excessive, and the Company attempted to get public cemeteries placed on the same footing as parochial burial-grounds, but as pressure mounted to close old burial-grounds the new cemeteries seemed to be in a better position financially in the immediate future. Eventually, the Company was successful in its appeal against the Kensington Poor Rate, which was reduced from £3,700 to £2,100, but even this was a major charge on limited resources.[22]

[17] Ibid., 18. Various attempts were made to sell off this land. [18] Ibid. (24 May 1842), 20. [19] Ibid. (9 June 1842), 24. [20] Ibid. (26 October 1842), 46. [21] Ibid. (30 November 1842), 50. [22] Ibid., 51.

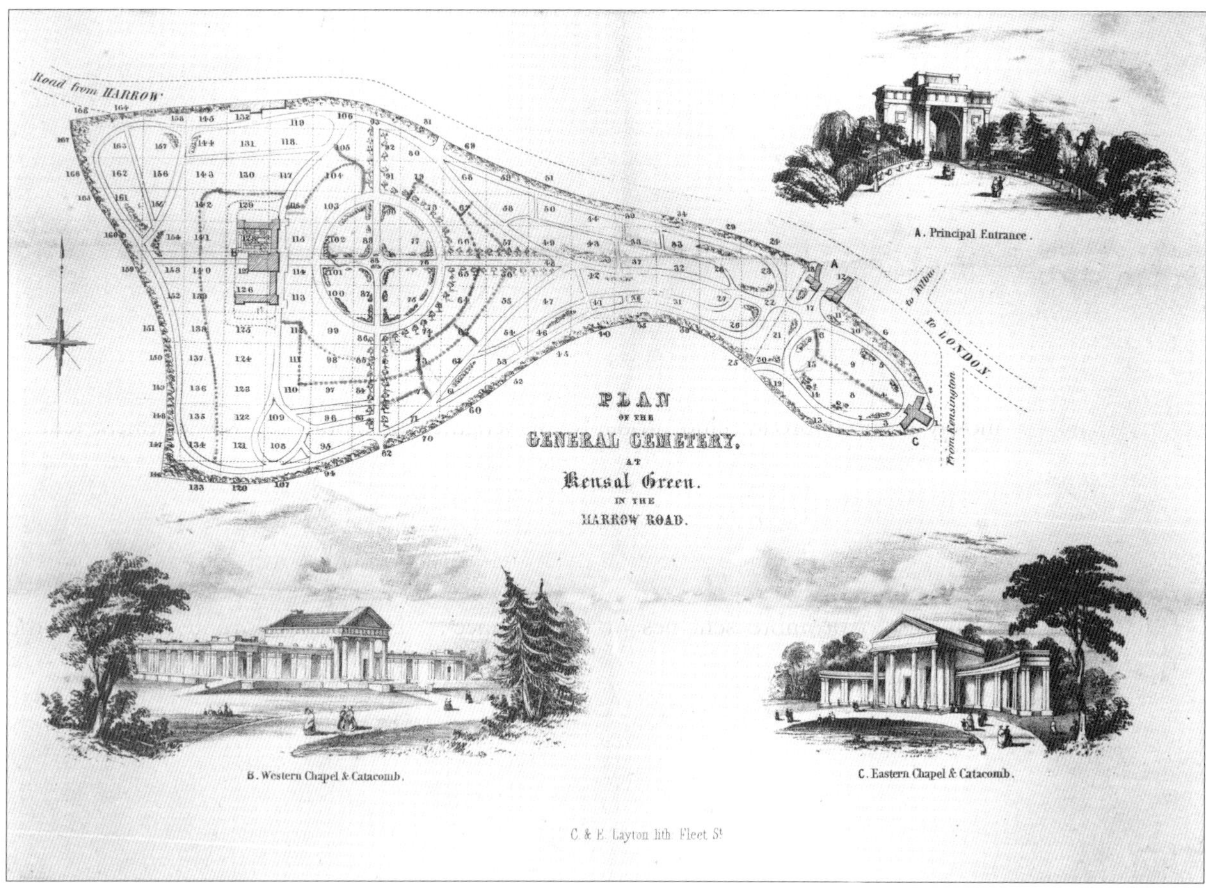

5.2 *Plan of the General Cemetery at Kensal Green in the Harrow Road*, lithographed by C. & E. Layton of Fleet Street. It shows the layout of roads, the newly-planted central avenue, the garden behind the colonnades of the Anglican chapel (*left*, B), the old or terrace catacomb (*top*), the entrance-gate and lodges (*top right*, A), and Dissenters' chapel (*right*, C). The entire boundary of the site was well planted with trees and shrubs. Vignettes showed the 'Principal Entrance', the 'Eastern Chapel & Catacomb', and the 'Western Chapel & Catacomb' (*GCC. MC.D131200*).

This was not the only problem, for the Company was obliged to 'defray the expence' of a funeral 'from the circumstance of the grave having been prepared in the wrong spot at the Cemetery', a difficulty that seems to have recurred. There were also 'serious complaints' about the behaviour of the Superintendent, one Bangs, and these led to his dismissal because of the 'serious injury to the wellbeing of the Company'.[23] Unfortunately, the Minutes are reticent about the nature of Bangs's misdemeanours, but one suspects the Demon Drink may have been at the bottom of it all, and responsible for errors in preparing graves and other matters. He was accused of 'general uncorteous behaviour' (*sic*) over a 'long period', and, as a result, James Samuel Farley was appointed to carry out the duties of Chapel Clerk and Sexton at two guineas per week 'upon his giving security to the amount of £500'. It must have been around 1843 that a *Plan of the General Cemetery at Kensal Green in the Harrow Road* was published: it shows three of the buildings, the layout, and a planted garden behind the colonnades of the Anglican chapel (**5.2**).

The First Royal Burial

However, in April 1843 the fortunes of the Company took a decided turn for the better. The Commissioner of Police, Richard Mayne (1796-1868), required that the Clerk should 'wait upon' Sir James Robert Graham (1792-1861), the Home Secretary, and George John West, 5th Earl De La Warr (1791-1869), who, as Lord Chamberlain, was in charge of arrangements to discuss the funeral of Augustus Frederick, Duke of Sussex, K.G. (1773-1843), sixth son and ninth child of King George III and Queen Charlotte, at Kensal

23 Minutes of the Proceedings of the Directors of the General Cemetery Company (22 February 1843), 63-4.

Green, and explain the 'capabilities' of the cemetery with regard to the due observance of the obsequies 'should the interment of the Duke be permitted to take place therein'. This was a major *coup* for the Company, for to obtain the body of a Prince of the Royal Blood could do nothing but good and raise the tone of the cemetery.[24] The Company was clearly delighted by the prospect, and offered full co-operation. It was decided to cancel all other funerals on the day of the Duke's funeral.

The Duke had married twice, but neither had been recognised under the Royal Marriages Act[25] of 1772: the first (1793) to Lady Augusta Murray (d. 1830), was declared void in 1794, and his second (1831), to Lady Cecilia Letitia (d. 1873), daughter of the 2nd Earl of Arran and widow of Sir George Buggin, survived until long after his death. His second wife was created Duchess of Inverness in 1840. As the *Dictionary of National Biography* noted, from 'the time he entered the university of Göttingen until 1804 he mostly resided abroad', and probably 'his lengthened sojourn on the Continent tended to foster his intellectual tastes ... and ... liberalise his sentiments'.[26] The Duke gave 'energetic support to all the progressive political policy of his time, including the abolition of the slave trade, catholic emancipation, the removal of the civil disabilities of Jews and dissenters, the abolition of the corn laws, and military reform. His interest in the advancement of art and science was also genuine and enlightened, and he readily lent his influence to promote schemes of benevolence'.[27] He became Grand Master of the Freemasons in 1811, President of the Society of Arts in 1816, and President of the Royal Society from 1830 until 1838. He collected books, had a vast library, and was probably the most intelligent of all the children of King George III.

So why was the Royal Duke buried at Kensal Green? First of all, his wife could not be buried in the vaults at St George's Chapel, Windsor, and, secondly, the Duke himself had not been favourably impressed by the funeral of his brother, King William IV, and is supposed to have vetoed any suggestion that he should be buried at Windsor. In accordance with his liberal views, the Duke also seems to have desired that his body should be donated to one of the London hospitals for dissection, but this was something the Establishment could not accept, and Kensal Green (where the Duchess of Inverness's body was eventually to join that of her husband) was regarded as a lesser evil than an anatomist's slab.

It was not only His Royal Highness's corpse being exposed to the vulgar probings of surgeons and their students that seems to have clinched matters, however: there seems to have been some wavering in favour of Windsor, but the possibility of 25,000 Freemasons invading the Castle concentrated minds, so Queen Victoria gave her assent to interment at Kensal Green, and the Lord Chamberlain duly inspected the cemetery and pronounced himself satisfied. The Company decided to place the grounds and the conduct of the whole royal funeral in the hands of the Government, and this was duly arranged. Admission to the cemetery would be by ticket only, and the Directors of the Company were to carry black wands to help the Police to identify them. The portico of the Anglican chapel was to be enclosed with black cloth (5.3-5.4), and the two side rooms (one of which was to be set aside for the Royal Family) were also to be hung with black cloth, all by the Government Undertaker. In the event, however, the Directors arranged for the fitting up of the portico, waiting-rooms, and chapel, and it was agreed the Government Commissioners would pay the bill.[28]

The Duke's funeral took place on 4 May, and a huge cortège, over a mile long, proceeded from Kensington Palace along Kensington High Street, Kensington Church Street, the Uxbridge Road, and the Paddington Canal Bridge to the cemetery, where

24 Ibid. (26 April 1843), 72. 25 12 Geo. III, c. 11. 26 *D.N.B.*, i (1917), 729. 27 Ibid. 28 Minutes of the Proceedings of the Directors of the General Cemetery Company (28 April 1843), 76.

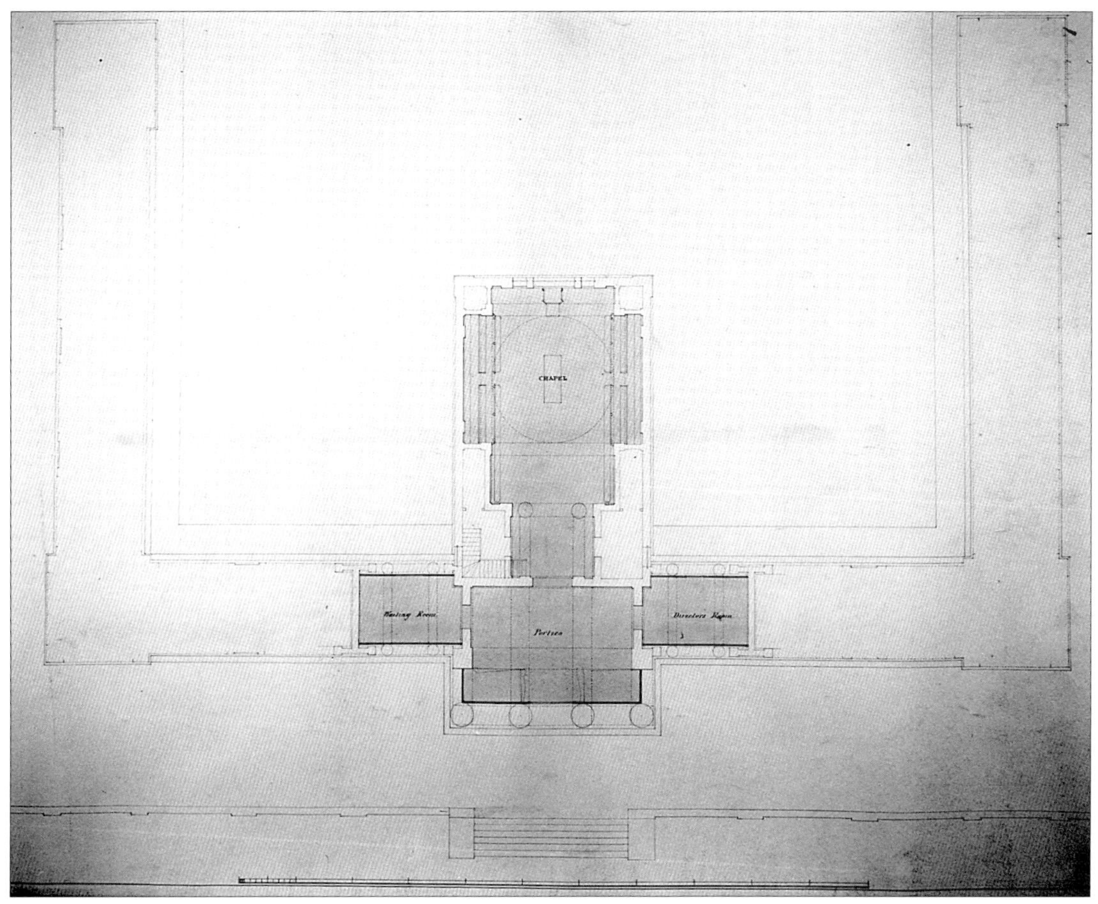

5.3 Plan of the Anglican chapel showing the black hangings for the Duke of Sussex's funeral in 1843. To the left a waiting-room was created, and on the right a Directors' room, with the portico also partly enclosed (*GCC. #10. MC.AH140900*).

5.4 Elevation of the Anglican chapel showing the black hangings for the Duke of Sussex's funeral in 1843 (*GCC. #10. MC.AG140900*).

5.5 Tomb of H.R.H. the Duke of Sussex, of Cornish grey granite, designed by Matthew Wharton Johnson, and completed in 1845 [5268/114/PS]. The miniature unfluted Greek Doric columns were intended as bollards to carry bronze chains (stolen). Photograph of 2001. *See* Chapter VIII, §103 (*MC.B130101*).

25,000 Freemasons had assembled. A catacomb space had been prepared under the Anglican chapel and the 'lowering apparatus' was ordered to be 'immediately put into proper working condition' as the prospect of the Duke's coffin descending noisily or getting stuck on the way down was one the Directors did not wish to countenance.

As it happens, the funeral was a huge affair, and the Great Western Railway placed an engine and carriage at the disposal of the Directors of the General Cemetery Company to leave Paddington at 0900 hrs on 4 May, provided 20-30 tickets of admission were issued to the Directors of the G.W.R. The Bishop of Norwich (who was to officiate at the funeral) asked for 'a few tickets', and got twelve. Each Director of the General Cemetery Company was given 10 tickets, each shareholder six tickets, and each proprietor of a grave two tickets. The Lord Chamberlain's office also authorised the Directors to issue tickets of admission to 'as many decently dressed persons' as they thought fit.[29]

After the funeral (15.1 and 15.2), which was widely reported,[30] the black hangings remained *in situ* for three more weeks 'for the gratification of the public', but trouble was brewing almost at once. The Company incurred costs associated with printing, bricking up the Duke's coffin in its *loculus* in the catacomb, and various other matters, which the Lord Chamberlain refused to pay on the grounds that the Directors were responsible. Banting, the Undertaker, also tried to charge the Company for 'fitting up the Directors Room at the Cemetery'.

It seems that the 'lowering machine' had caused one or two anxious moments at the Duke's funeral, so the Directors visited the South Metropolitan cemetery at West Norwood to inspect the 'Coffin Lowering Machine' there, and also the asphalte covering of the vaults, which were 'perfectly dry'. It was decided to obtain estimates for a new machine (duly supplied by Bramah & Robinson) and for asphalting the catacombs at Kensal Green.[31] The 'improved hydraulic apparatus' was duly installed in the Anglican chapel, and by 1844 was working in 'perfect silence', as it was reported at the Annual General Meeting of 13 June 1844.

[29] Minutes of the Proceedings of the Directors of the General Cemetery Company (3 May 1843), 88, and *passim*.
[30] Bland (1986), 152-6. [31] Minutes of the Proceedings of the Directors of the General Cemetery Company (24 May 1843), 93-5.

In due course a plot was purchased in front of the Anglican chapel for the tomb of the Duke of Sussex: it cost £358, and the expense of erecting the massive Cornish grey-granite burial-place came to £312. Designed by Matthew Wharton Johnson (*fl.* 1820-60), it consists of a raised hipped ledger on a massive podium, with bollards in the form of capped unfluted Greek Doric columns that once supported bronze chains (5.5). The Duke's coffin was moved to its new home [5268/114/PS] on 21 April 1845.[32]

The Monumental Chambers

The acquisition of the Duke of Sussex worked like a charm. Just as Père-Lachaise had acquired Molière and La Fontaine as secular seals of approval (1.11), and medieval churches needed Relics to attract the faithful (even in death), Kensal Green's Royal Duke increased demand from Polite Society for burial-plots, and the cemetery's financial future seemed assured. Indeed, the General Cemetery Company, which had not had a huge commercial success in its first 10 years, was extremely fortunate to obtain the Royal corpse: Dr Litten has likened the event to holding a winning ticket for the National Lottery, and the upswings in demand and revenue were almost instantaneous.

The immediate effects were enquiries about the catacomb (which had started to fall from favour), so Griffith was instructed to prepare plans and estimates for roofing over the entire area at the back of the [Anglican] chapel, and forming corridors beneath suitable for the reception of monuments.[33] His plans were ready the following month, and his estimate of the costs of realising them at £4,500, so the Directors instructed him to amend his plan for 'roofing over the northern half of the area only',[34] that is, the ornamental gardens shown in the plan in 5.2. The Directors sought to make as much wall-surface as possible available for the erection of memorial tablets, even within the main portico, not only to commemorate those placed in the catacomb below, but to maximise income by letting the wall-space at a rate of £1 per square foot. Space for statues was to cost £50 a time, and no statue was to be erected until the design and specification had been approved. Griffith proposed further plans for roofing in the whole area between the colonnades and the rear of the Anglican chapel by which a 'superficial area of wall to the extent of 20,000 feet might be obtained',[35] bringing in an income of 25 shillings per square foot for a capital expense of £5,000.

However, such grandiose plans were set back by the discovery of a serious outbreak of dry rot inside the Anglican chapel, and the internal cornices were found to be 'entirely decayed'. So concerned were the Directors by this that William Cubitt (1791-1863) was called in to advise as 'the most practical builder in the metropolis', and William Tite (1798-1873), 'an architect of great experience', whose work at West Norwood cemetery had been admired by the Directors, was also consulted.[36] Fortunately for Griffith, Cubitt and Tite exonerated him from any blame, and recommended that the cornices should be reinstated quickly. It could well be that it was then that the problems with the incorrect placings of the triglyphs took place, but if this were so it is odd that Griffith did not correct them (5.6). However, the fact that Griffith was prepared to fill in part of the symmetrically disposed court behind the chapel for what were to become known as the 'Monumental Chambers' would indicate that he no longer cared much about the Greek Revival style, and there is no doubt that, although there may have been commercial reasons for erecting the Monumental Chambers, their architectural relationship with the original chapel and colonnades was less than happy.

[32] Minutes of the Proceedings of the Directors of the General Cemetery Company (24 May 1843), *passim*.
[33] Ibid. (30 August 1843), 108. [34] Ibid. (27 September 1843), 114. [35] Ibid. (25 October 1843), 119. [36] Ibid. (29 November 1843), 129.

5.6 Interior, looking west, of the Anglican chapel in 2000, showing the memorial window of 1951 by A. T. N. Achet, the ceiling, the Greek-key patterns, the catafalque, and the positioning of the *antae* on the west wall under the metopes rather than the triglyphs. A comparison with Griffith's contract drawing No. V (**4.26**) proves that Griffith's drawing is correct, but the work as it stands is architecturally incorrect (the bodged corner-details and the relationships of triglyphs to *antae* bear little resemblance to Griffith's original designs) (*MC. A111200*).

During this period also, the question of purchasing more land adjoining the cemetery was coming to the fore, and problems of cash-flow, capital, income and expenditure were tending to push aesthetics to one side. Griffith attended the Board, was instructed to obtain estimates from different builders for roofing over the northern half of the area between the colonnades separately as well as the whole, and to lay the tenders before the Board in due course.

In January 1844 Griffith was elected a Director of the Company,[37] and at the same meeting George Lander's tender of £5,671 for roofing over the area between the colonnades was accepted, but he was instructed to proceed with only the northern half

37 Ibid. (31 January 1844), 138.

'at present'. Such decisions are always dangerous, for it is always more expensive to continue at a later stage, and the appearance of a lopsided extension to a dignified symmetrical composition creates a bad impression. In fact Griffith's plan for roofing in the whole area was never carried out, and what became known as the Monumental Chambers, sited between the chapel and the northern range of colonnades, stood until they were pulled down after being damaged in the 1939-45 war.

What was even odder about this business was that Griffith's designs did not line up with the geometry of the catacomb below, and so he reported that the vaults would have to be strengthened at a cost of £500. As it was, to construct only the northern half of the 'Chambers' would cost £3,000, to which would have to be added a further sum of £500 to 'remove a considerable portion of the mound of clay at the rear of the Chapel' and to provide proper drains.[38] The Monumental Chambers were completed by Autumn 1844 'adjoining the principal chapel' and were 'open for the reception' of marble tablets and monumental sculpture':[39] the final cost was £3,529. It is clear from the Company's records that his work for the Company following his appointment as a Director was carried out in an honorary capacity only, although he was paid £255 2s. 0d. for his work on the Monumental Chambers, as was reported at the Annual General Meeting of 12 June 1845.

It is curious that no drawings for the Monumental Chambers seem to have survived, and if there were ever any photographs of them they have not surfaced. However, they may be seen on aerial photographs taken before 1940 (5.7), which show that they had clearstorey lighting, a point confirmed by a photograph in Mrs Basil Holmes's *The London Burial Grounds* of 1896[40] (5.8).

Most commentators have assumed that these 'Chambers', where the columbarium was erected to designs submitted by Robert Willey (*c.*1837-1918 – architect, of Ludgate Chambers, 66 Ludgate Hill, London), on 28 October 1891, also dated from the 1890s, but the Minutes are quite clear they were erected to Griffith's designs in the 1840s, and the mural tablets erected within them were stylistically of the period *c.*1845 to the 1930s. Willey's columbarium was made of Caen stone, with panelled piers at each angle, and moulded base and cornice: the *antae* between each of the 44 compartments were of polished Siena Marble, and the panels in the piers were filled in with polished Rouge Royale Marble. E. M. Lander constructed this rather gorgeous Renaissance Revival object for £168 10s. 0d., and Willey designed the cinerary urns to be placed in the niches.[41] George Lander is recorded as having repaired the Monumental Chambers, reinstated broken glass, and carried out repainting operations;[42] each Chamber was distinguished by a number;[43] the door at the north-east entrance to the Chambers was repaired;[44] various other repairs were carried out in 1871;[45] a defective rooflight was repaired in 1874;[46] and one of the Chambers had been fitted up as an extra chapel in 1865 to be used during inclement weather.[47] There can be absolutely no doubt, therefore, of the fact that the Monumental Chambers were in existence from 1845.

Much was made of the Monumental Chambers at the Annual General Meetings.[48] It is obvious from the papers in the possession of the General Cemetery Company that it was as a direct result of the interment of the Duke of Sussex that demand for catacomb burial took an upsurge (having been moribund) with consequent need for wall-space for monuments to commemorate those entombed below. Because of the destructive effects of the polluted atmosphere (and rain) on marble (this was clearly visible on monuments

[38] Minutes of the Proceedings of the Directors of the General Cemetery Company (7 February 1844), 141.
[39] Ibid. (30 October 1844), 199. [40] Holmes (1896), 271. [41] *The Daily Graphic* (28 August 1892), 14. [42] Minutes of the Proceedings of the Directors of the General Cemetery Company (29 June 1849). [43] Ibid. (27 July 1853). [44] Ibid. (25 November 1857). [45] Ibid. (30 April 1871). [46] Ibid. (26 August 1874). [47] Ibid. (27 December 1865). [48] AGM (13 June 1844).

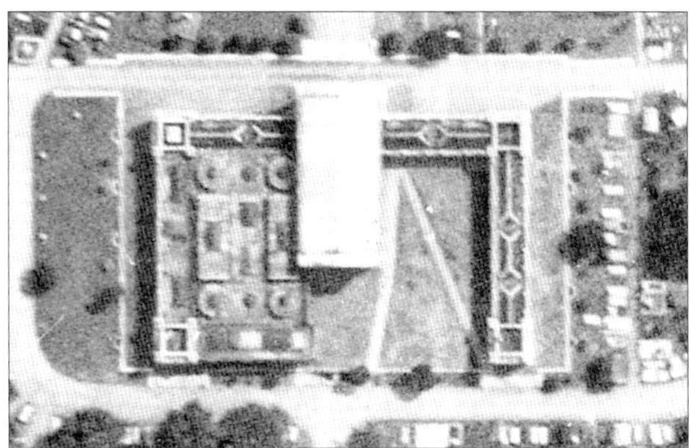

5.7 The Anglican chapel, colonnades, and Monumental Chambers in August or September 1937. The roof-lights and extent of the Chambers are clearly shown. (*Aerofilms Ltd., 5371*).

5.8 Interior of part of the Monumental Chambers, erected to designs by John Griffith in the 1840s: note the clerestorey roof-lights and the mural tablets dating from earlier than the columbarium. The columbarium was built by E. M. Lander to designs by Robert Willey in 1891-2, and its materials were Caen Stone with panels of Rouge Royale Marble in the piers, and polished Siena marble between the compartments holding the urns. From Holmes (1896), 217 (*ECJSC.MC. N130101*).

in the cemetery grounds as well as on the memorials erected behind the colonnades above both the terrace catacomb and the catacomb under the Anglican chapel), the Company determined to provide protection for marble tablets, and to this end it decided to erect the Chambers for that purpose. The Chambers consisted of two handsome corridors, or galleries, extending from east to west, about 80 feet in length, with one corridor running north-south. There were two 'spacious and lofty chambers for monuments and sculpture of the first class, and four handsome chambers of smaller dimensions'.

More Problems

The improvement in demand occasioned by the gratifying acquisition of the remains of a Royal Duke was offset by two problems, one of which was the decline in mortality in 1845-6 which led to a 'slight fall in profits'.[49] The other difficulty was rather more serious and was so menacing it was likely to lower the tone of the area to such an extent that all the kudos gained by the burial of the Duke of Sussex was likely to be dissipated, and indeed further losses were probable. Railways had been bad enough, but in 1845 the Western Gas-Light Company decided to erect a gasometer and form extensive works at Kensal Green in 'close proximity' to the General Cemetery on land purchased from Sir George Talbot, Bart. (1763-1850), who was related to Viscount Ingestre. This was viewed with alarm by the Directors, and reported at the Annual General Meeting when Carden's payment of £1,000 also showed up in the 1846-7 accounts.[50] In the Minutes of the Board of Directors it was noted that the 'Western Gaslight Company' was actively proceeding with the construction of 'extensive gas-works immediately contiguous' to the cemetery, and that this would be a 'serious injury to all property', but chiefly to the cemetery. Attempts were made to stop construction by preventing a licence being issued by the Board of Trade. The threat was so serious that the General Cemetery Company went to law, but the Master of the Rolls, in his judgement, said that the Cemetery Company had

49 AGM (10 June 1846). 50 AGM (9 June 1847).

not made a strong enough case,[51] and the Directors regretfully concluded they could do nothing more. Not only were gasworks large and menacing, but they produced foul smells, which was not helpful to cemeteries and their managers. Furthermore, pollution from gasworks was damaging for stonework, and some of the spectacular failures of stone in the cemetery must have been accelerated by the effluvia emanating from the works.

5.9 Monument over the grave [4547/74/PS] of the cemetery theoretician and gardener, John Claudius Loudon (1783-1843). Photograph of 2000. *See* Chapter VIII, §45 (© *English Heritage [NMR].AA/020141*).

At that time, too, the debate concerning intramural interment and other matters concerning urban hygiene was becoming more vociferous following the publication of Chadwick's *Supplementary Report* in 1843[52] and the sensational findings of G. A. Walker and others. Another influential volume to appear in 1843 was John Claudius Loudon's *On the Laying Out, Planting, and Managing of Cemeteries; and on the Improvement of Churchyards*,[53] which had previously appeared in instalments in Loudon's *Gardener's Magazine*,[54] and is probably the most exhaustive tome ever written on the subject. Loudon envisaged cemeteries as arboreta, as places where sculpture, architecture, and landscape-gardening could be studied, and as places were the public could muse and reflect on life, death, and nature. He also acknowledged that cemeteries might 'improve the moral feelings' and 'manners', 'extend virtuous and generous' sentiments, 'improve taste', and 'serve as *historical records*'.[55] Interestingly, he abhorred 'burials' in vaults or catacombs, perceiving that it was a certain invitation to vandals (as well as being 'unhygienic'); saw that cemeteries, like the smaller churchyards and burial-grounds, would fill up and then should become public parks, 'the gravestones and all architectural or sculptural ornaments being kept in repair'; and prophesied that cremation would one day become universal, a remarkably prescient forecast for 1843. Loudon died in 1843 and is buried in Kensal Green cemetery, where he is commemorated by a severely chaste urn (5.9).

Chadwick's *Report*, however, cast its net wider than did Loudon's work, and his suggestions were revolutionary. The gist of his proposals was that existing burial-grounds should be closed; that intramural interment should be prohibited; that burial as a source of private emolument be abandoned as unseemly; that national cemeteries should be laid out and maintained under the direction of officers qualified in the care of public health; that 'corpse-houses' should be established in every town for the immediate reception (and respectful and appropriate care) of the dead, under superior and responsible officers, to avoid the prolonged retention of the body in rooms occupied by the living, and also to remove 'painful apprehensions of premature interments'; that all requisite materials and services for all classes, but especially for the poor, be made available 'suitable to the station of the deceased, and the condition of the survivors' to provide the means of 'respectable interment, at reduced or moderate prices', for the 'abatement of oppressive charges for funeral materials, decorations, and services'; that 'officers of health qualified by medical education and special knowledge' should be appointed for overseeing arrangements necessary for the protection of public health 'in respect of the practice of interment'; and that no interment be allowed without the

[51] 30 December 1846. [52] Chadwick (1843), *passim*. [53] Loudon (1981), *passim*. [54] Loudon (*Ed.*) (from 1826), *passim*, especially **xviii** (1842) and **xix** (1843). [55] Loudon (1981), 44.

'verification of the fact and cause of death by the officer of health'. Other recommendations were concerned with raising money by means of loans to establish national cemeteries, the use of burial-fees to form a fund to buy out existing interests, and the reduction of the costs associated with funerals.[56]

The passage referring to 'apprehensions of premature interments' is important: several books and papers had appeared dealing with this gruesome subject, including tomes by Count Léopold von Berchtold[57] and Joseph Taylor,[58] the latter a particularly lugubrious (if derivative) compendium of horror-stories. Fear of being buried alive was widespread, and there is evidence to prove this.[59] Several German cities already provided facilities where bodies could be stored until death and corruption were beyond all dispute. Both Loudon and Chadwick referred to the buildings (designed by Friedrich Rumpf [1795-1867]) at the entrance to the cemetery at Frankfurt-am-Main (established in the 1820s), where ventilated rooms were provided in which bodies would lie for several days before inhumation: cords were fixed to the fingers of the deceased, communicating with bells, so that 'the least motion, in case of a person's revival, would be instantly known to an attendant stationed in the apartment adjoining these cells'.[60] Loudon noted that it was 'strictly prohibited to inter any corpse until infallible signs of decomposition had become obvious'.[61] Chadwick published a plan, sections, and an elevation of the building at Frankfurt-am-Main, a handsome Neoclassical composition symmetrically disposed on either side of a Greek Doric propylaeum[62] (**3.26** and **3.27**).

Chadwick's far-reaching proposals rejected joint-stock company cemeteries as too expensive, and he was critical of the new cemeteries established over the previous decade because, although they were a great improvement on small, foul, burial-grounds, they, too, would soon be engulfed in urban development and would therefore become harmful to public health, but on a much larger scale than ever before. However, one of his most damaging criticisms was that joint-stock cemeteries were essentially 'trading associations', and so shareholders would always be reluctant to agree to any improvements that did not 'provide an immediate return for the expense incurred'.[63] Thus Chadwick argued convincingly that private enterprise would not solve the burial crisis (it was nothing less), and he did not believe the parishes of the Established Church could be relied on to provide answers either. He advocated that the proposed 'national cemeteries' should be formed on well-drained soils, preferably on gravel or sand on rising ground so that decomposition would be rapid. One of the problems with the joint-stock London cemeteries was that they were all on London clay, which was difficult to drain, *retained* water, and actually *prevented* dissolution.

Meanwhile, in Parliament, Mackinnon had brought in a Bill to outlaw intramural interment in populous cities and towns which proposed, *inter alia*, that parochial Boards of Health should be set up, run by incumbents and churchwardens, with powers to lay out cemeteries outside the metropolis, and form unions with other parish Boards of Health if necessary. Chadwick did not like this proposal, not only because the Church had failed to solve the problem before, but because Dissenters (already vociferous objectors to having to pay Church rates) would be excluded and become more resentful, and because he saw that costs would probably rise because of multiplication of Boards and effort. What Chadwick really advocated was radical reform by which the State would intervene as part of a nation-wide scheme of sanitary improvement that foreshadowed aspects of public-health enactments leading to the Welfare State in the 1940s.

[56] Chadwick (1843), 198-200. [57] Berchtold (1791), *passim*. [58] Taylor (1816), *passim*. [59] Curl (2000*e*), 122-3; Puckle (1926), 22-5, 27; Hallam (*Ed.*) (1905-8), *passim*. [60] Loudon (1981), 49. [61] Ibid. [62] Chadwick (1843), 215-7. [63] Ibid., and *passim*.

Chadwick proposed national cemeteries, large and sited well away from metropolitan and other urban developments, which would not only be well-planned and -drained, but re-usable, with graves cleared every 10 years, and remaining bones buried in common graves (as was the practice in German cemeteries which, by their superior planning, organisation, and management, were exemplars quoted by both Loudon and Chadwick). Communication with the national cemeteries was essential, so the new necropoleis should be sited near waterways (canals and rivers) by which 'collection points' would be established. Furthermore, as the railway-system expanded, coffins could be transported to the rural cemeteries by train. Loudon specifically mentioned the 'thousands of acres of the poorest gravely soil' over which the London-Southampton railway passed, which would be ideal as a cemetery 'for all the poor of London, and the rich also, for ages to come'.[64] He could 'see no sufficient reason against having permanent, monumental cemeteries, as well as temporary ones which' would 'have no monuments, laid out on poor soils at great distances from London, along the railroads, with cooperative railroad hearses, and other arrangements to lessen expense'.[65]

Loudon also influenced Chadwick in the matter of landscaping and planting cemeteries, not just for show, but because plants were perceived as the best means by which 'mephitic vapours' from decomposition, 'miasmas', and the like, could be absorbed, although it was important that breezes could circulate without hindrance to keep such places sweet. Chadwick also proposed that the national cemeteries might have sections devoted to various crafts, trades, professions, and the like, in which private soldiers might lie near generals, operatives near great engineers and architects, and so on, thus fostering pride, social cohesion, and national honour, commemorated, perhaps, by grand monuments in each section. Chadwick saw the huge advances being made in engineering, transport, building, and the resolution of problems of massive and sudden urbanisation as having been made possible only through the efforts of armies of workers, who were mostly unsung and ignored. His idea of celebrating the industrial 'private soldiers', so to speak, by burying them near the inventors, entrepreneurs, designers, organisers, and leaders (the officers, generals, and field-marshals, as it were), pointed to a kind of social engineering aimed at curing the fragmentation and divisiveness all too clear in early-Victorian British society.

Some of Chadwick's proposals seem to have been triggered by German exemplars (e.g. the *Invalidenfriedhof* in Berlin, and the cemetery in Mainz, in both of which officers were buried with private soldiers).[66] Artisans could derive consolation from 'accommodation within the same precincts as the more public and illustrious dead'.[67] Thus the 'foot-soldiers' of the thrust towards innovation, industrialisation, urbanisation, and the creation of wealth would be honoured in death with the 'officers' who designed, led, imagined, planned, and made possible those huge achievements. This concept owes something to the cemetery of Père-Lachaise too, for there various *savants* associated with Napoleonic studies are buried near each other (1.12), sundry Napoleonic marshals and admirals are commemorated in another section, and Delille and Brongniart lie side by side in the cemetery (1.13).

A Second Royal Funeral

Kensal Green cemetery acquired its second Royal corpse on 6 June 1848, when the body of Her Royal Highness, Princess Sophia (1777-1848), fifth daughter of King George III and Queen Charlotte, was brought and deposited in the catacomb under the Anglican

64 Loudon (1981), 49. 65 Ibid., 49-50. 66 Chadwick (1843), 146. For other Berlin cemeteries *see* Fischer and Schein (*Eds.*) (1987), *passim*. 67 Chadwick (1843), 147.

chapel. The first intimation that this would occur was on 1 June, when an official communication from St James's Palace was received by the Directors. Once again the Anglican chapel was hung with black cloth, but this time the work was done entirely by the Royal Upholsterer to avoid confusion and difficulties over payment of bills. It appears that the Princess herself had expressed a wish to be buried at Kensal Green near her brother's grave, for she seems to have been very attached to the amiable old Duke of Sussex, and shared some of Augustus Frederick's independence of mind. As it happens, the funeral was a very small and discreet affair, and took place at 7 a.m. in the presence of Prince Albert, Adolphus Frederick, 1st Duke of Cambridge (1774-1850 – the dead Princess's brother, seventh son of King George III and Queen Charlotte), and Prince George William Frederick Charles (1819-1904 – later [1850] 2nd Duke of Cambridge). At Queen Victoria's wish, the cemetery was closed to the public until after 'the interment of H.R.H. the Princess Sophia' had taken place, and no 'persons except those belonging to the funeral procession' were admitted to the cemetery unless they carried an 'order of admission under the signature of the Lord Chamberlain'. Only four Directors of the General Cemetery Company were permitted to 'attend at the cemetery' on the day of the funeral, so Lord Ingestre, Sir William Eden, Sievier, and A. J. Valpy[68] were nominated. The Princess's body was placed in catacomb [45] pending the preparation of her permanent tomb [8028/114/PS]. Queen Victoria bought her aunt's plot for £444, and ordered the construction of the vault and monument, designed by the art-advisor to Prince Albert, Professor Ludwig Grüner (1801-82), and paid for by the Royal Family: it is one of the most distinguished works in the cemetery (5.10). The exequies of Princess Sophia were extremely modest compared with those of her brother, the Duke of Sussex, and were, perhaps, partly due to the fact that she had been a recluse for a number of years, and partly due to the circumstances of her having taken a lover, the Court Equerry Thomas Garth (1744-1829), by whom she had a son, Thomas Garth (1800-75), whose existence was concealed from the King. Nevertheless, the Directors expressed pleasure in their new Royal, and the Minutes refer to the 'encouraging circumstances in regard to the increased value of the property of the Coy'.[69]

5.10 Tomb of H.R.H. Princess Sophia, photographed in 1997 [8028/114/PS]. The inscription on the exquisite marble sarcophagus (in the style of the *Quattrocento* of the Italian Renaissance) is simply SOPHIA and her dates. The dignified podium was by Edward Pearce of Euston, and is inscribed, 'Come unto me all ye that labour and are heavy laden and I will give you rest' and 'Her Royal Highness The Princess Sophia, 5th daughter of His Majesty King George III, Born November 3rd 1777, died May 27th 1848'. *See* Chapter VIII, §102 (*JSC*).

[68] Abraham John Valpy (1787-1854), editor and printer, was elected a Director of the Company on 28 September 1836 following the disqualification of the Revd. H. J. Knapp by his ceasing to hold a sufficient number of shares. Previously (10 June 1830) another Valpy (presumably a brother) had been ejected from the Provisional Committee for failing to attend meetings. Their father, Richard (1754-1836), is entombed in a Greek Revival mausoleum in the cemetery designed by Griffith [687/101/RS]. *See D.N.B.*, **xx** (1917), 84-6. [69] Ibid.

Further Difficulties and the Company's Responses

In 1849 an unpleasant incident occurred when a member of the public, a Mr Tudor, wrote a letter to the Company in which he stated he had wished a friend, a clergyman of the Church of England, to officiate at his son's funeral, and had applied to the Chaplain, Joseph Twigger, who 'to the great annoyance of Mr Tudor's feelings sent him' a reply couched in offensive terms demanding that 'fittings' should be given to him (Twigger) otherwise it would be impossible for him 'to permit any precedent to the contrary'.[70] The Directors were obliged to write to Tudor offering apologies for 'feelings of distress' having been 'enhanced', informing him the 'Chaplain received an ample remuneration for his services', and that they 'highly disapproved' that 'an accommodation sought by relatives in the season of affliction' should have been 'conceded only for a pecuniary consideration'. Twigger was given a roasting, in writing, for demanding payment of 'fittings' (an early 19th-century euphemism for 'considerations', or, put bluntly, having his palm greased). Twigger resigned as Chaplain in 1851 and was replaced by the Reverend J. N. Heard.

Also in that year a dividend of 8 per cent 'clear of the Income Tax' was paid to shareholders,[71] which was a very healthy return on capital, and compared favourably with other Victorian speculations such as housing or railways. However, there were anxious times ahead in the light of possible compulsory purchase, and representatives of the Board of Health visited the cemetery, expressing 'unqualified approbation both of the manner in which the Coy. conducted its business and the appearance and state of the cemetery'. Interestingly, those representatives were none other than the Rt. Hon. Lord Ashley[72] and the redoubtable Edwin Chadwick himself: they were shown round the cemetery by Griffith, who obviously did an excellent job persuading the Commissioners of the excellence of the way in which Kensal Green was managed.[73] However, as the records of the Company make clear, the Board of Health pestered the Directors with complicated questionnaires that involved the Company's staff in much work, and the Company in expense: in 1849 bureaucracies were as demanding as they are today, and little heed was taken of the trouble and costs involved in answering interminable questions and in filling in innumerable forms. The Metropolitan Interments Bill was then before Parliament, and there was a distinct likelihood that the Board of Health would acquire Kensal Green cemetery, a threat that was not to be lifted for some time. The trees, shrubs, and some monuments were damaged by a 'severe tempest' around that time,[74] which cannot have helped morale. The proposed enactments also had an unfortunate effect on the business, for the public once again started to show extreme reluctance to take graves and vaults until the effects of the Bill should be known. Despite these difficulties the Company again was able to announce a dividend of 8 per cent 'clear of Income Tax'.

These various uncertainties alarmed the joint-stock Companies, but inertia won the day until cholera struck again in 1849-50, 'chiefly among the poorer classes', so the number of interments in London burial-grounds greatly increased. In 1849 John Simon (1816-1904) presented his devastating report on the dreadful state of affairs that prevailed in the nation's capital. The Government was forced to act at last, and it was proposed to establish a Commission with powers to close all urban burial-grounds and purchase all the existing cemeteries founded by joint-stock Companies, some of which would be

[70] Minutes of the Proceedings of the Directors of the General Cemetery Company (30 May 1849), 72. [71] AGM (14 June 1849). [72] Anthony Ashley Cooper [1801-85], later [1851] 7th Earl of Shaftesbury, who was associated with numerous reforms and philanthropic activities, including the housing of the working classes, conditions in factories, collieries, and mines, education of the poor, missionary efforts, and much else. [73] Minutes of the Proceedings of the Directors of the General Cemetery Company (28 November 1849), 105. [74] AGM (12 June 1850).

closed. Vast new cemeteries were to be created: Kensal Green was to be retained, expanded, and re-named the Great Western cemetery; and a huge Great Eastern cemetery was to be laid out at Abbey Wood, Erith. Furthermore, all funerals were to be rationalised and controlled, so that decent, civilised burial would be available to everyone regardless of means. In 1850 an Act of Parliament was passed to make Better Provision for the Interment of the Dead in and near the Metropolis.[75]

The various debates concerning intramural interment and other matters were discussed at the Annual General Meeting in 1848,[76] and it was decided that the Directors should meet the Boards of the other London cemeteries to consider the implications of the matters referred to above. They were clearly anxious times, and on 12 April 1848 the General Cemetery Company invited deputations from the London Cemetery Company, the West London and Westminster Cemetery Company, and Abney Park Cemetery Company to a meeting, chaired by Sievier, at which it was resolved to instruct the Parliamentary Agents to give the Directors of the General Cemetery Company notice of any Bills that were to be introduced into either House of Parliament on the subject of intramural burials and send them copies of such Bills. The Directors would then share this information with the other cemetery Companies 'with the view of concerting measures for protecting their mutual interests'.[77] Subsequently, Griffith chaired another meeting, attended by representatives of the other London joint-stock Cemetery Companies, at which it was hoped that 'no legal enactment' would be passed which might interfere with the value of the property in the care of the Companies.

The Directors of the General Cemetery Company, as a result of these upheavals, were authorised by the shareholders to take any steps necessary regarding the Metropolitan Interments Bill, but this became an Act on 5 August 1850, and the various London cemeteries seemed set fair to be acquired by compulsion. Indeed, the Company was informed by letter on 5 September 1850 that Robert Rawlinson, one of the Superintending Inspectors of the Board of Health, would be making a valuation of Kensal Green cemetery under the provisions of the Metropolitan Interments Act, and that the General Cemetery Company would be obliged to provide Rawlinson with 'the requisite facilities for obtaining any information' including plans, descriptions, details of drains, and all the facts about the physical condition of the cemetery.[78] However, Rawlinson or no Rawlinson, the Directors made it clear that the 'interests of the General Cemetery Company' were 'suffering injury consequent on the powers contained in the Act', and they 'respectfully' urged the Board of Health to make up its mind quickly if it intended to acquire Kensal Green cemetery.[79] Furthermore, the Company had not received any information from the General Board of Health as to intentions with regard to Kensal Green, and the uncertainty which the Act placed upon property was gravely affecting business. It all seems to have been very unsatisfactory and a lower dividend of 7½ per cent was paid in 1851.[80]

The Act made London a Metropolitan Burial District under the General Board of Health which was empowered to create new cemeteries and to purchase or take over 'all or any' of the existing joint-stock cemeteries. In fact, what was proposed was 'nationalisation' of private-enterprise cemeteries, and both Brompton and Nunhead cemeteries were identified for takeovers. However, the expense of buying out various

[75] 13 & 14 Vict., c. 52. [76] 7 June 1848. [77] Minutes of the Proceedings of the Directors of the General Cemetery Company (12 April 1848), 1-2. [78] This Rawlinson (1810-98) had been appointed one of the Inspectors in 1848, and later became head of the Department, but he is better-known for his work as head of the Commission sent out to the Crimea in 1855 to look into the deplorable sanitary conditions of the troops, for superintending the construction of St George's Hall, Liverpool, from 1841 (completed in 1851), and for his sterling work to improve public health and sanitation. He was knighted in 1883. [79] Minutes of the Proceedings of the Directors of the General Cemetery Company (25 September 1850), 165. [80] AGM (14 June 1851).

interests frightened the Government off, and only one cemetery, Brompton, was actually acquired, but this was because the shareholders of the West London and Westminster cemetery determined to enforce the sale.

However, confidence in joint-stock cemeteries generally had been severely dented, and the Directors of the General Cemetery Company sent a deputation to the Government pointing out the loss and injury suffered because of the uncertainty and doubt regarding the property at Kensal Green. Was it to be acquired or not? Was it to be extended as the Great Western cemetery or not? Or was it to be left alone? In short, clarification was required.

Resolution

It all looked very black for the Company, and the Directors' dissatisfaction is clear from a reading of the Minutes. With culpable tardiness however, the Government, having been saddled with Brompton cemetery, backed down, and gradually relinquished any possible claims upon or threats to the General Cemetery of All Souls. It was a narrow squeak for Kensal Green, and the Directors heaved a collective sigh of relief when it was decided to leave the existing cemeteries alone, although legislation was passed to stop all interments in any burial-ground or place of burial in the metropolis, and a workable system of inexpensive public interment was established between 1852 and 1857 that effectively ended the burial crisis. Even so, Dickens noted

> Too late the wished-for boon has come,
> Too late wiped out the stain –
> No Schedule shall restore to health,
> No Act give life again
> To the thousands whom, in bygone years,
> Our City Graves have slain![81]

From the mid-1850s most cemeteries were established by Burial Boards, and later in the century provision for burial was administered by local authorities.[82] Nevertheless, for some time the General Cemetery Company was still bombarded with yet more bureaucratic questionnaires, demands for information, and much else, which was time-consuming and expensive as an activity. And although the threat of immediate compulsory purchase had receded, it had by no means gone away: a shadow lay over the General Cemetery Company for some time, as will be outlined in the following Chapter. This was not the only difficulty that the Company was to face, however, for the following 10 years almost saw the ruin of all the high hopes and endeavours of more than two decades.

[81] Dickens (1850), 277. [82] *See* 15 & 16 Vict., c. 85, 16 & 17 Vict., c. 134, 18 & 19 Vict., c. 68, 19 & 20 Vict., c. 98, 20 & 21 Vict., c. 81.

CHAPTER VI

The Cemetery and its Fortunes, 1852-2001

JAMES STEVENS CURL

Uncertainty and Change; Acquisition of More Ground; Near Disaster; Summary of the Near Disaster and Other Troubles; Sale of Part of the Surplus Land; The Cemetery from the 1850s to the 1930s; The Building of the Crematorium; The 1939-45 War; Post-War Reconstruction

My friends, we will not go again or ape an ancient rage,
Or stretch the folly of our youth to be the shame of age,
But walk with clearer eyes and ears this path that wandereth,
And see undrugged in evening light the decent inn of death;
For there is good news yet to hear and fine things to be seen,
Before we go to Paradise by way of Kensal Green.

GILBERT KEITH CHESTERTON (1874-1936):
The Rolling English Road (1914), lines 19-24, 204.

Uncertainty and Change

Early in 1852 the Company's Chairman, Sir John Dean Paul, 1st Bart., died (having ceased to be the Chairman through indisposition in 1851), and the Right Honourable Earl Talbot (as he then was, formerly Lord Ingestre) was elected Chairman once more, with Charles Lushington M.P. (1785-1866), as Deputy Chairman. Lushington was another person of substance, and was Member of Parliament for Westminster from 1847 to 1852.

The General Board of Health, it was reported to the Directors, 'had found great practical difficulties in carrying into effect the provisions of the Metropolitan Interments Act', and, consequently, 'the General Board of Health did not intend to take the Cemeteries', so the proprietors of Kensal Green cemetery noted with bemusement 'that the alienation of their property was not required for the public welfare'. In other words, the Government had got cold feet because of the costs involved in buying out interests, but immense damage had been done to the finances of the Companies and to public confidence in joint-stock cemeteries. It was a typical bureaucratic piece of bungling. The General Cemetery Company required assurances in 1852 that moves to 'take the Cemetery had been abandoned'.[1]

For a brief period Lord Edward Adolphus Seymour (1804-85),[2] First Commissioner of the Works, tried to get the Government off the hook by opining that 'if the General Board of Health could be relieved of the contract to purchase the Brompton Cemetery, no other Cemetery would be taken'. At a meeting between the General Cemetery Company and Lord Seymour it appeared to the Directors that His Lordship seemed to be sympathetic to the plight of the Company. It is difficult to avoid coming to the conclusion that Seymour was attempting to get the General Cemetery Company to 'lean on' the Directors of the West London and Westminster Cemetery Company to get them to cease trying to force the Government to buy them out. The London Cemetery Company, on the other hand, agreed not to proceed with the sale of Nunhead cemetery (it had asked for £99,000 but had only been offered £42,000), but Brompton (owned by the West London and Westminster Cemetery Company) had been in financial trouble from the start, and there was little hope of putting things to rights: it had cost £147,685, and, advised by the formidable William Tite, the Directors demanded £168,762,[3] but in due course, after arbitration, a Government offer of £74,921 was made. At a meeting of the West London and Westminster Cemetery Company in January 1852 it was reported that the Board of Health had requested the award should be set aside, and some of the Directors (including the Company's Chairman, Philip Pleydell Bouverie [1788-1872]) proposed that the award should not be accepted, but a majority of the shareholders dissented from this view, and insisted that the Directors should enforce the award. Thus Brompton was the only metropolitan cemetery to be acquired by the Government, and was duly conveyed to the Commissioners of Works and Public Buildings on 5 November 1852.[4] Nevertheless, many of the original shareholders lost more than half of their investments and the dividends had been tiny, so something must have seemed better than nothing.

In this respect it is interesting to note that the Board of Health considered that only the General Cemetery Company's operations at Kensal Green had been anything like a commercial success, and that all the other metropolitan joint-stock Companies had been failures as commercial undertakings. A reading of the Minutes of the Board of the General Cemetery Company is sufficient to demonstrate that the Directors were shrewd,

[1] Minutes of the Proceedings of the Directors of the General Cemetery Company (28 January 1852), 229. [2] Later (1855), 12th Duke of Somerset, who had fought a duel in 1835 with Sir Colquhoun Grant. [3] P.R.O. WORK 6/67, 23, (30 April 1851), 599, 600. [4] Sheppard (*Ed.*) (1983), 246-52.

and played their cards very well: clearly they had the ears of those in high places who mattered.

All these difficulties had not gone on without covert reactions from Directors. Hardly had he been elected Chairman before the Clerk announced that Earl Talbot had got rid of his shares, and so was ineligible to hold a Directorship let alone occupy the Chair, so he was replaced by Charles Lushington, M.P., and Robert Maconochie was elected Deputy Chairman.[5] Captain Charles Wardell and Robert Makin Bates (one of the partners in the Company's bank, Strahan, Paul, & Bates) were also elected Directors. However, it was with some relief that the Directors learned that the Metropolitan Interments Act was to be repealed and a major threat to the Company was thereby removed.[6] Vigilance was urged regarding any future Bills that might surface in Parliament, and Griffith was deputed to keep an eye on developments.

Kensal Green cemetery experienced another hostile attack from the Great Extra-Mural Cemetery Association, a group formed to promote new cemeteries outside London. This Association claimed in advertisements placed in various newspapers, including *The Times*, that Kensal Green cemetery would 'ere long be full', that it was smaller in area than it was in fact, and inaccurate information was given about dividends and values of shares. The Board demanded that the Association should immediately correct these errors which were 'detrimental to the interests of the General Cemetery Company'.[7] The Association was obliged to apologise and publish a new *Prospectus* from which all 'objectionable statements' were excised.

The Board then arranged for notices to be placed in the press announcing that the General Cemetery Company was in good shape, would not be 'interfered' with, and announced that the cemetery was of extensive acreage and capable of 'affording proper places of sepulture' following the closing of so many of London's burial-grounds and crypts as a result of a series of vociferous campaigns and subsequent legislation.

Acquisition of More Ground

Adverse publicity and rumours about Kensal Green cemetery's area and capacity clearly stung the Directors, and in 1852 the first serious moves were made to acquire more land to allow for future developments. Accordingly, Griffith and the Clerk called on the solicitors for the Fillingham estate who 'promised to communicate immediately with the Trustees relative to the sale of that estate, or a portion thereof and to acquaint the Company with the result'. The Board also resolved 'that the Clerk' should 'again call upon the solicitors and urge them to procure an early answer on the subject'.[8] Once more the Company tried to sell the small patch of land south of the canal, and approached the authorities to find out if the Kensington Burial Board would be interested in acquiring it 'for their intended cemetery', but this never seems to have got anywhere. As has been mentioned earlier, the few acres south of the canal had been acquired at the very beginning, but every attempt to sell them failed, and the land was very much a wasting asset, cut off from the rest of the ground. However, the cemetery itself was well supplied with monuments, mausolea, and tombstones, the planting was maturing, and the grounds, though well tended, were of limited extent, the western boundary lying not far from the back of the Anglican chapel and its colonnades, and urgent measures would have to be taken if more acres were to be purchased.

By 1852, then, the General Cemetery of All Souls at Kensal Green had acquired all its major 19th-century buildings, including the new Monumental Chambers somewhat

[5] Minutes of the Proceedings of the Directors of the General Cemetery Company (28 February 1852), 254. [6] Ibid. (26 May 1852), 246. [7] Ibid. (10 June 1852), 249. [8] Ibid . (27 October 1852), 274.

clumsily tacked on to the Anglican chapel and colonnades. The dangers of being compulsorily bought out had receded, and two royal corpses had been deposited in their splendid tombs. However, the gasworks concern was in business, and London was spreading outwards, engulfing the countryside: it became clear that the cemetery would have to be enlarged if it were to survive.

The position was that 49.385 acres (19.984086 hectares) had been acquired for use as a cemetery, but the awkward piece of land south of the canal (7.67 acres or 3.104049 hectares) was still owned (but not enclosed or used) by the Company, and there were small portions of land outside the boundary-wall. The only way the cemetery could expand was westwards, and there was much debate about acquiring the Fillingham estate at £16,000 for about 50 acres. Unfortunately, the General Cemetery Company was restricted by its Act of Parliament to hold a maximum of 80 acres (32.376 hectares), so, if it succeeded in purchasing the Fillingham estate, it would have to sell any surplus land over and above the 80 acres. The Directors calculated that the actual cost to the Company would be £9,000.[9]

The first blow fell later in 1852 when Cardale, Iliffe, & Russell, the solicitors acting for the Fillingham estate, wrote to the Company to decline the proposal made by Griffith on behalf of the 'Kensal Green Cemetery Company' for the purchase of 20 or 30 acres, and could not 'entertain any offer except for the purchase of the entirety'. The Directors realised they had no alternative but to buy all the land on offer, and it was resolved 'that the Company enter into treaty for the purchase of the Fillingham Estate at a price not exceeding £15,000 subject to the consent of the shareholders and subject to an approved title'.[10] However, the Company's solicitor informed the Board at a Special Meeting 'that the Company had no power to purchase any quantity of land [if its] extent ... together with the land at present belonging' to it should exceed 80 acres.[11] It was therefore resolved 'that enquiry be made of Sir John Dean Paul, the Treasurer, whether the bankers of the Company would be willing to purchase the Fillingham Estate and would sell to the Company such quantity as they were empowered to hold according to the provisions of the Act of Parliament under which they were incorporated and would then sell (subject to the direction of the Company) the remnant of the property so as to indemnify themselves from loss'.[12]

Griffith then went to see William Strahan, of the banking firm Strahan, Paul, & Bates, who 'stated that subject to his not incurring expense liability or trouble', and also subject to his being protected from any law expenses he would accept the office of Trustee'. Thomas, the General Cemetery Company's solicitor, also saw Strahan to explain that there was 'a deficiency of £3000 in the fund applicable to the proposed purchase of the Fillingham Estate and to take his advice on this point'.[13] There appears to have been some opposition from certain shareholders to the purchase of more land, and Earl Talbot was not the only Director to get rid of his shares, for Sievier was discovered (in 1852) to have sold his shares, and so he, too, was debarred from a Directorship, although he maintained some connection with the cemetery, for he was buried there in 1865. All this would indicate a loss of confidence in the early 1850s among some early supporters of the Company. This was not surprising, for the Company only applied to renew its lease of the premises in Great Russell Street until 1854 because 'the recent interference of the Legislature with Cemetery Companies and the possibility that this interference' might recur.[14] So the relief when the Act had been repealed began to evaporate as more anti-joint-stock cemetery agitation began to boil up again. Sir William

9 Minutes of General Meetings (29 December 1852). For details of areas *see* Chapter II, footnote 112. 10 Minutes of the Proceedings of the Directors of the General Cemetery Company (24 November 1852), 279-80. 11 Ibid. (6 December 1852), 282, and *passim*. 12 Ibid., 283. 13 Ibid. (8 December 1852), 284, and *passim*. 14 Ibid. (2 February 1853), 298.

Eden, Bart. (1803-73), resigned from the Board in 1853 as he 'lived too far from town', so the two vacancies were filled by the Reverend Edward Johnstone (who had once been Chaplain to the Company, had maintained his connections with the cemetery, and indeed was a shareholder), replacing Sievier, and Colonel George Morton Eden (1806-62), replacing his brother.

The attention of the Board 'having once again' been directed 'to the expediency of obtaining the land lying to the Westward of the Cemetery and having taken into consideration the peculiar circumstances under which the proposed purchase was negotiated by the Special General Meeting of the 29 Decr last objections being made to the magnitude of the sum demanded', it was resolved by the Board that the special Sub-Committee should immediately 'apply to the Trustees of the land referred to offering the sum of £14,000 for the property subject to the same conditions as those on which the former tender was based'.[15] The Fillingham estate, however, would accept 'nothing less than the terms previously agreed upon for the purchase of the property', and warned the Directors that the land was 'becoming daily more valuable'.

Meanwhile, the Company had had numerous enquiries from London parishes about the possibilities of burying the dead (including paupers) in the cemetery as a result of the enactments closing overcrowded burial-grounds and prohibiting intramural interment, so it was clear there was going to be a growing demand for burial-space from the parishes. The problem was cost, and a standard reply was sent out to all enquirers to the effect that the General Cemetery Company had a fixed scale of fees and charges from which it had no intention to deviate.[16] However, the existence of such demand prompted some reconsideration of the matter, and soon the 'question of Fees and Charges for Common Interments' was being 're-considered'.[17]

It was decided to make the Annual General Meeting of 9 June 1853 also a Special Meeting to discuss, as a matter of urgency, the matter of the acquisition of the Fillingham estate,[18] because the lawyers acting for that estate informed the Board that the 'owners' would 'not entertain any Contract until the Directors' had 'obtained authority from the Shareholders', but were willing to sell the 50-odd acres (20.235 hectares) for £15,000.

In June 1853, not before time, the Directors were authorised to proceed with the purchase of the Fillingham estate and to sell the surplus land, so some degree of confidence in the Company must have revived as the shares regained their value after the slump occasioned by the 'changes contemplated to be introduced by the Board of Health'.[19] However, in order to buy the land more capital had to be raised by issuing shares, but there was opposition in 1853-4 to the proposed purchase by the Company's bankers (reported at the 1854 AGM), which is very odd indeed, and indicative that something was going wrong.[20] Tenants on the estate also had to be bought out.

Following the Special Meeting of 1853, the Board requested 'Mr Strahan to purchase the Fillingham Estate for a sum not exceeding £15,000', 'to sell such parts of the Estate as the Board' should thereafter direct, and to 'convey the parts not sold to the Company, so that the quantity of land vested in the Company' should 'not exceed 80 acres in the whole'. In addition, the Company would protect Strahan 'from all loss consequent on the transaction'.[21] Bates, who was at the meeting when this was discussed, was to 'communicate with Mr Strahan', and the Company's solicitor was requested to 'take the opinion of Counsel as to the construction to be put upon the Act with reference to the additional shares authorised to be issued and particularly whether a premium' could be

[15] Ibid. (23 February 1853), 301-2. [16] Ibid. (30 March 1853), 304-8, and *passim*. [17] Ibid. (27 April 1853), 311. [18] Ibid. (18 May 1853), 315. [19] AGM or Special Meeting Minutes (9 June 1853). [20] AGM (8 June 1854). [21] Minutes of the Proceedings of the Directors of the General Cemetery Company (29 June 1853), 323.

taken upon 'such shares by which the actual Capital received' would 'exceed the sum of £90,000 the amount constituted by the Act as the Capital of the Company'.[22]

By July 1853 Strahan had indicated he was willing to purchase the Fillingham estate, and it was agreed that the General Cemetery Company would pay interest at the rate of 5 per cent on all payments made in advance by Strahan. The Company's solicitor was instructed to settle the draft contract, and it was ordered that a survey should be prepared of the land to be bought, with sections and all levels.[23] Unfortunately, Counsel opined that the Board could not legally issue shares that would raise the Company's capital above the sum of £45,000 fixed by the Act of Incorporation, but that it could issue sufficient shares up to that figure. A further complication arose with reference to the title of the Fillingham estate because one of the parties was 'incapacitated',[24] and the Company's solicitor was obliged to procure an order under the Lunacy Regulation Act of 1853 to enable the 'incapacitated party to join in the conveyance to the purchaser'.[25] This involved a Commission of Lunacy which would 'obviate the necessity of an Act of Parliament', and the solicitors for the Fillingham estate were asked to share the expenses because the Commissioners of Lunacy would have to be involved in respect of all 'other property of the lunatic' to be disposed of.[26] By February 1854 Messrs Cardale, Iliffe, & Russell had completed the evidence regarding ownership and had presented the petition, a copy of which would be served on the 'incapacitated' Mrs Osler, who would then have to be examined by 'one of the Masters'.[27]

Meanwhile, numerous complaints had been made concerning the 'manner in which' the funeral services were performed by the Chaplain, Heard. Bates, Griffith, and Langston were deputed to confer with the Bishop of London on this problem. The Board asked Heard 'whether in the course of the ensuing two months' he could not 'suggest some plan by which the Board' would 'be spared the painful necessity of further unavoidable proceedings'. Heard then 'read letters testifying his ability as to performing the service' after which the Board asked him 'to continue', for two more months, but 'unless all cause of complaint' ended, the Board would ask him to resign.[28] The Bishop of London supported Heard, which did not help the Company, because the complaints multiplied: the problem seems to have been that the inappropriately-named Heard was a mumbler, and was inaudible both in the chapel and by the graveside.

The Master's report was laid before the Lords Justices for their confirmation, and 'the usual steps' were taken 'to get the appointment of Committee completed': this was the means by which a special committee was officially and legally appointed to act for a mentally impaired person.[29] That was not the only problem, for at a meeting of the Board on 13 September 1854 the Chairman (Maconochie) reported that Strahan, the Trustee approved to purchase the Fillingham estate, 'had expressed his unwillingness to advance the requisite funds'. A deputation consisting of General Eden, Captain Wardell, and the Company's solicitor was instructed to 'wait upon' Strahan to find out what was going on. On 16 September, this deputation duly met Strahan who 'consented to advance the requisite funds for the purchase of the Fillingham estate in accordance with the Resolution of the Board of 29 June 1853.[30] There is no hint in the Minutes of what transpired at the meeting with Strahan, but a letter of thanks 'for the accommodation' was duly sent to him from the Board.

It was decided to raise funds by issuing more shares not exceeding £10,780 in value, bringing the total to £90,000.[31] In November 1854 Valpy, who had been a Director since 28 September 1836, died, and the Board noted its considerable loss. He was replaced by

[22] Minutes of the Proceedings of the Directors of the General Cemetery Company (29 June 1853), 324. [23] Ibid. (7 July 1853), 326-8. [24] Ibid. [25] Ibid. [26] Ibid. (28 December 1853), 350–2. [27] Ibid. (22 February 1854), 360-1. [28] Ibid. (6 April 1854), 371-2. [29] Ibid. (24 April 1854), 375. [30] Ibid. (27 September 1854), 17. [31] Ibid. (15 November 1854), 25.

Joseph Browne. By December Strahan had paid the purchase-money for the Fillingham estate to the solicitors for the vendors,[32] and the Board referred to a sub-committee the consideration of the best means of disposing of that part of the estate surplus to requirements, that is 'beyond the quantity which the Company' was authorised to hold 'under the provisions of the several Acts of Parliament incorporating the Company' and enlarging its powers. Agreement was reached with Strahan's solicitor on the terms of a 'Deed of Declaration of Trust for the Fillingham Estate' between Strahan and the Company 'arranging as to the liquidation of the purchase money of the same'. Strahan then appointed Sir John Dean Paul, Bart., the Treasurer of the General Cemetery Company, 'to receive' on his account 'all sums of money' to be paid 'to him as such Treasurer on account of the issue of shares (1854) in liquidation' of his 'advance of the purchase money for the Fillingham Estate with the interest thereon'.[33] It will be remembered that Paul, the 2nd Baronet, was also a partner of Strahan in the bank. Early in 1855, Bates, Strahan & Paul's partner, resigned as a Director of the General Cemetery Company,[34] and was replaced by Captain W. C. Caldwell of Audley Square.

Further difficulties arose when the London and North Western Railway Company constructed a 'pickling depot' on land near the Fillingham estate 'for chreosoting timber', and 'a portion of the land was let to persons who had deposited thereon offensive matter in accordance with a contract they had entered into with the authorities of the parish of Paddington for the removal of the refuse from that parish'. In view of the likelihood that both the 'pickling' and the dumping of refuse were 'calculated to become a serious nuisance to occupiers of the Fillingham Estate' (i.e. any tenants for the time being, and the General Cemetery Company at all times), the Company's solicitor was instructed to 'write to the proper parties on the subject'.[35]

Near Disaster

Shortly after these events William Justyne was appointed junior clerk in the offices of the Company at a salary of 10 shillings per week: Justyne was later to write *Guides* to both Kensal Green and Highgate cemeteries.[36] However, this innocuous piece of information is in close proximity to intelligence of trouble ahead: money received from the sale of Bonds and other assets was being deposited by early 1855 with the 'Bloomsbury branch of the London & Westminster Bank' rather than with Strahan, Paul, & Bates.[37] An account was opened with the London & Westminster 'in the names of the members' of the sub-committee, and it was resolved that 'all receipts shall for the present be paid to that Account and that their cheques be honored'.[38] Furthermore, 'Mr. W. Ewings, Manager of the Bloomsbury Branch of the London & West^r Bank ... was appointed Treasurer of the Company on his providing two or more securities who with him' were to 'enter into a Bond for the sum of £2000 – to the Company for the due performance of the Office'.[39]

These bland, even laconic entries mask what was, in fact, a major crisis. Two days before the Annual General Meeting of 1855 the Directors of the General Cemetery Company faced near-disaster when the appalling news broke that the Company's bankers, Strahan, Paul, & Bates, had suspended payment on 11 June 1855. As has been noted above, Sir John Dean Paul, Bart., had also been Treasurer of the General Cemetery Company; his partner, Strahan, had been intimately involved in the purchase of the Fillingham estate; and his other partner, Bates, had been a Director of the General Cemetery Company. At the General Meeting, 'deep regret' was expressed at the

[32] Ibid. (13 December 1854), 36. [33] Ibid. (27 December 1854), 40-41. [34] Ibid. (28 February 1855), 52. [35] Ibid. (28 March 1855), 56. [36] Justyne (*c.*1858 and *c.*1864). [37] Minutes of the Proceedings of the Directors of the General Cemetery Company (28 March 1855), 57. [38] Ibid. (13 June 1855), 69. [39] Ibid.

'misfortunes' of Paul, who, of course, had had to be removed from his position. Something rather like the worst sort of nightmare seemed to be taking shape. Nevertheless, in spite of all the problems and the vast amount of time and energy expended on the acquisition of the Fillingham estate, it was eventually bought, and it was reported that the purchase of the new land had been completed. Moves were also afoot to dispose of the surplus land (including the problematic land south of the canal, which had never been of any use to the Company).[40] In addition, an extra strip of land was bought at the north-west corner of the property to improve access to the ground: this purchase cost £150, and was completed in July 1856.

If a brave front had been put on things at the 1855 General Meeting, it was a different story behind the scenes. The Company's solicitor, Thomas, attended the Board and reported he had made application to the 'solicitor of General Eden on the subject of the failure of the Treasurer and *the loss to the Company consequent thereon*'.[41] Thomas also said 'he had searched and found that no judgement had been recorded against Mr Strahan which would affect him as Trustee of the Fillingham Estate'. Three new Trustees had to be appointed, however, to accept the conveyance of the estate from 'Strahan and all other necessary parties of the Fillingham Estate' and the said Trustees were authorised to borrow the amount 'due to Mr Strahan or his Assignees'. The Chairman and Deputy Chairman of the General Cemetery Company and Langston were duly appointed Trustees. All money deposited with the London & Westminster Bank was transferred to a current account, which indicates that the financial position was dire. The solicitor was required to find out if the sureties provided by the former Treasurer (Paul) were sufficient to cover his 'deficiency'.[42]

Thomas duly reported[43] that the 'Deed of Conveyance of the Fillingham Estate was in his possession and that the earlier Title Deeds were in the possession of Mr Bell the official Assignee'. He had also had several conversations with 'Mr Bloxam the solicitor for General Eden' and that, subject to the approval of the Board, he had arranged to seek the 'opinion of Counsel as to the duties of the Directors in claiming a set off in respect of the amount due by the Company to Mr Strahan'. The General indicated he would raise no difficulty in the matter of paying the amount for which he was liable (Eden had been one of Paul's guarantors). This question of involving Counsel was dropped following General Eden's assurances.[44] The Board instructed Thomas to 'endeavour to complete as quickly as possible the Conveyance of the Fillingham Estate to the new Trustees' and to 'urge the settlement of the Company's claim on the Surety of the late Treasurer'.[45]

There were more problems in 1855, because some monuments had been damaged, 'having been occasioned by the great concourse of people at the funeral of the late Feargus O'Connor', former leader of the Chartists,[46] on 10 September 1855. The Company decided to make good the damage itself, in the interests of peace. Three boat-loads of gravel had to be brought in to repair the roads and paths, and many plants had to be replaced.[47]

Three Directors were authorised to 'draw a cheque for the balance due to the assignees of Strahan, Paul, & Bates subject to the Assignees handing to the Company's

[40] AGM (13 June 1855). [41] Minutes of the Proceedings of the Directors of the General Cemetery Company (27 June 1855), 73. Editor's italics. [42] Ibid. (25 July 1855), 80. [43] Ibid. (29 August 1855), 82-4. [44] Ibid. (11 September 1855), 85. [45] Ibid. (26 September 1855), 88. [46] Feargus O'Connor (1794-1855) had been M.P. for County Cork (1835) and Nottingham (1847), and leader of the Chartist movement: a popular demagogue, 'his powers of attracting huge audiences' were extraordinary, and 'the sight of his person was calculated to inspire the masses with a solemn awe' (*D.N.B.*, **xiv** [1917], 846). His increasingly violent and intemperate behaviour led to his committal to a lunatic asylum in 1852, but he moved to his sister's house in Notting Hill in 1854, and there he died on 30 August 1855. 'He was publicly buried at Kensal Green on 10 Sept. 1855, and fifty thousand persons are said to have been present at his funeral' (*D.N.B.*, **xiv** [1917], 847). 'His intemperance during these years was probably only a symptom of his disease' (Ibid. 847). [47] Minutes of the Proceedings of the Directors of the General Cemetery Company (28 November 1855), 95.

solicitor the Deeds of the Fillingham Estate and to their agreeing to the propositions of the Company's solicitor'.[48] In due course the solicitors of the assignees of Strahan, Paul, & Bates rendered an account of the balance to be paid, and the Order of the Court of Chancery was made for the reconveyance of the Fillingham estate to the new Trustees. At last, in 1856, the solicitor was able to report that the estate 'was legally vested in the names of the new Trustees' and the solicitors for the 'Assignees of the bankrupts Paul Strahan & Co [*sic*]' were paid the sum of £2,850 18s. 7d. 'being the nett balance they claimed after allowing as a set off the amount due by the surety of the late Treasurer as well as the amount standing in the name of the Clerk of the Company'.[49] It was decided to set in motion the sale of that part of the Fillingham estate not required, and to have the remainder vested in the General Cemetery Company 'so as to make up the complement of 80 acres, which the Company are [*sic*] entitled to hold under their Act'.[50] There must have been considerable relief when the Clerk reported that 'he had obtained from the custody of the solicitors of the Assignees of Strahan & Co [*sic*] the Company's Deed Box which had been deposited in the strong room in the Office' and that 'a Schedule of the contents of the box was filed in the Office'.[51] The Deeds of the Fillingham estate were deposited with Thomas, the Company's solicitor.

The Board's sub-committee reported that it had 'inspected' the Fillingham property and 'recommended that measures be adopted for the sale of a portion of the same Viz. the Western portion so that the Eastern portion might at some future date be added to the present Cemetery'. Attempts were also again made to sell off the few acres south of the canal. Advertisements were ordered to be placed in *The Times*, *Daily News*, *The Builder*, *The Morning Advertiser*, 'and other public papers' to let it be known that 30 acres of freehold land were for sale. Griffith was the leading figure in drawing up boundaries and establishing the optimum areas for future use.

Summary of the Near Disaster and Other Troubles

So what had actually occurred to bring about these hair-raising problems? The firm of bankers, formerly Snow, Paul, & Paul, as it was, changed its name after William Snow elected to alter his surname to Strahan in 1831.[52] As noted above, the bank suspended payment in June 1855, and during the bankruptcy proceedings which followed, a list of securities (totalling £113,625 belonging to the bank's clients, but which had been fraudulently sold or deposited by the bankrupts) was voluntarily handed over to the Court, signed by Strahan, Paul, and Bates (all three of whom had been intimately involved, as has been made clear, with the General Cemetery Company). Criminal proceedings ensued, and in October 1855 the three men were indicted at the Old Bailey before Sir Edward Hall Alderson (1787-1857), Baron of the Court of Exchequer, for having illegally converted to their own use certain bonds entrusted to them for safe-keeping by Dr John Griffith, Canon of Rochester.[53] Although Paul was accused by the other two partners of having been solely responsible for the whole affair, all three were found guilty and sentenced to transportation for 14 years. Debts proved against the firm amounted to about three-quarters of a million pounds, and the dividend eventually realised only came to 3s. 2d. in the pound (just over 15p in today's money[54]). The business of Strahan, Paul, & Bates was taken over by the London & Westminster Bank,[55] and a branch office was established in the premises in The Strand formerly occupied by the bankrupt firm.

[48] Ibid. [49] Ibid. (30 January 1856), 103-4. [50] Ibid., 104. In fact, the final total was far short of 80 acres, and was about 71.9 acres plus the 7.67 useless acres south of the canal. [51] Ibid. (27 February 1856), 108. [52] *D.N.B. Missing Persons* (1994), 640. [53] He may, or may not, have been related to John Griffith of Finsbury, architect of the General Cemetery Company. The name is not uncommon. [54] The comparison is not really fair, as a gold sovereign (£1) in 1855 was a lot of money. [55] *D.N.B.*, **xv** (1917), 518-9.

To digress for a moment, there are some views of Paul that are worthwhile to consider in the light of the history with which we are concerned. Another child of Sir John Dean Paul, 1st Baronet, was Anne Frances (d. 1864), who married (in 1828) Francis George Hare, and they were the peculiar parents of that agreeable old gossip, Augustus John Cuthbert Hare (1834-1903), author of many books, including the indispensable (to any visitor to the Italian capital) *Walks in Rome* (1871 and many subsequent editions). A. J. C. Hare was renounced by his parents, and adopted by his Godmother Maria (d. 1870), daughter of Oswald Leycester, Rector of Stoke-upon-Tern, Shropshire, and widow of his uncle, Augustus William Hare (1792-1834). It was Maria Hare who brought him up, and who became, to all intents and purposes, his mother. Hare, in what the *Dictionary of National Biography*[56] calls his 'long, tedious and indiscreet autobiography', *The Story of My Life*,[57] enjoyed some success with his tales of society tittle-tattle, and earlier, he had also published *Memorials of a Quiet Life*,[58] an elegy to his adoptive mother. Hare was to describe Sir John Dean Paul, 2nd Baronet, as 'rather mad. After he had done his best to ruin all his family, and had totally ruined hundreds of other people, he said very complacently, "This is the Lord's doing and it is marvellous in our eyes"'.[59] There resounds the authentic voice of the Evangelical. Paul was released from prison in 1859, and seems to have spent the rest of his days as a wine-merchant. Needless to say, he was 'reputed to be a man of the highest religious principles'.[60]

It is almost unbelievable, but the General Cemetery Company, it was claimed at the General Meeting of 1856, suffered 'no material loss' from the collapse of the bank because, first of all, it had prudently moved most of its funds to the London & Westminster Bank shortly before the calamity, and, secondly, it had claims upon the surety of the 'late Treasurer' regarding the Fillingham estate. It was not until after the trial that a cheque[61] was drawn for the balance due to the assignees of Strahan, Paul, & Bates, bankers, subject to the assignees handing to the General Cemetery Company's solicitor the Deeds of the Fillingham estate. Following the appointment of new Trustees so that the estate could be reconveyed to them (because the Cemetery Company could not acquire the whole of the estate as its area would have put the Company's holdings in excess of the maximum permitted by its Act of Parliament), the property was legally vested in the Trustees by January 1856.[62]

Thus the General Cemetery Company was incredibly fortunate on two counts: it could easily have lost much of its capital; and it could have missed the last chance of purchasing land for future use as Paul and Strahan were closely involved in the convoluted history of the Fillingham estate. The Company acknowledged that there had been 'considerable difficulties' involved in the 'purchase of the Estate' because of the bankrupts' connections with the affair, and it was lucky that there was the safety-net of sureties provided by the likes of the unfortunate General Eden, who seems to have borne things with gentlemanly stoicism.[63] However, the experienced historian does not buy the good-luck story (especially as the Company opened accounts with the London & Westminster Bank shortly before the catastrophe), and can only conclude that the Directors of the General Cemetery Company must have had early warning of the failure of their bankers, and moved their account to another bank in good time. Amazingly, the Deed Box relating to the Company's property was still held by Strahan, Paul, & Bates past the time of the bankruptcy, and was only reported as having been 'removed' from the bank's strong-room as late as 27 February 1856. It should also be remembered that at one point Strahan refused to advance the purchase-money for the Fillingham estate, which might indicate he knew his business was in trouble.

56 *D.N.B.* (1901-11), 212-3. 57 6 volumes (1896-1900). 58 3 volumes (1872-6). 59 Hare (1896), 494.
60 *D.N.B.*, xv (1917), 519. 61 Dated 28 November 1855. 62 AGM (13 June 1856). 63 AGM (8 June 1857).

So who tipped off the Board of the General Cemetery Company that all was not well with Strahan, Paul, & Bates? It could have been any one of the three partners, or someone who had got wind of impending trouble. The Directors were men of some substance, and presumably had their ears close to the ground. Perhaps the disgrace of being associated with two failed Companies (the General Cemetery Company would probably have gone into liquidation if steps had not been taken to avoid disaster) was too much, and a decision was made to ensure that Kensal Green survived the storm by giving early warning. The Minutes are reticent on this matter, but, reading between the lines, something must have prompted the evasive action that saved the Company and its new estate. It was, however, a close-run thing. On balance, it is likely to have been Strahan who warned the Company.

Throughout the 1850s, apart from the major difficulties outlined above, the parish of Kensington was still proving troublesome over the question of a right-of-way through the cemetery grounds, and every year the gates had to be closed against the invading hordes of organised walkers who turned up to demand access. On occasion there was violence, and damage was done to the Company's property. Popular perceptions of the Victorian period are of a sedate, repressed, decorous society, but these are false: special bullet-proof shutters[64] had to be fitted to the Duke of Wellington's London house to protect it and him from the dangerous mob, and, as has been mentioned earlier, the General Cemetery Company had had to provide some of its employees with firearms to protect themselves and the cemetery from felons intent on robbing the dead or stealing other property. Moreover, during 1850 there was a plague of thefts of flowers from graves, and so various 'servants' of the Company had to be sworn in as Constables.[65] As the *Survey of London* wryly noted, 'rustic pursuits and disorders still prevailed' in the 1850s and 1860s at Kensal Green, and gypsies sometimes wintered there.[66]

Kensington proved to be problematical in other ways, for the assessments of the Poor and Parochial Rates were an annual thorn in the corporate flesh of the General Cemetery Company, involving tussles, litigation, and considerable expense. In the early 1840s, for example, the Poor Rate assessment had been reduced from £4,000 to £1,820, an enormous difference, but the following year the assessment was for £3,700 which the Company appealed against at the Court of Quarter Sessions, and got it reduced to £2,100. In 1858 the cost shot up from £2,450 to £3,200, a gigantic sum for the time, and one that, given the limited resources of the Company, was undoubtedly rather more serious than a mere difficulty. At one point (1849) the Sewers Rate rose from 2d. to 6d. in the pound, but, after considerable discussions with the Commissioners for Sewers and various lawyers (which cost money), it was decided nothing could be done about it, and that the Rate would have to be paid.

Captain Wardell died in the summer of 1856, and Mr O'Brien Bellingham Woolsey of 49 Westbourne Terrace, Hyde Park, was elected a Director in his place. Following the entombment of the Duke of Sussex and his sister in the 1840s there had been a steady demand for burial-plots near their monuments, and the Company was careful to ensure that only substantial plots were sold so that the tone of the squares in front of the Anglican chapel was maintained and enhanced. The Company was still being pestered with questionnaires from the Burial Acts Office in 4 Old Palace Yard, mostly dealing with the minutiae of burial, including the amount of earth between coffins in a deep grave, and so on.

64 Loudon (1834) §557. Manufactured by Bramah of Pimlico, these shutters were efficacious. Loudon also praised Smith, of Princes Street, Leicester Square, for his apparatus installed at Kensal Green for raising and lowering the catafalque (Loudon [1981], 24), and for other inventions, such as mechanisms for French windows (Loudon [1834], §2066). 65 Minutes of the Proceedings of the Directors of the General Cemetery Company (3 July 1850), 147.
66 Sheppard (*Ed.*) (1973), 333.

Complaints were received about the 'improper' language of gravediggers at funerals, the fact that the earth was sprinkled on coffins by workmen 'in clayey dress instead of by the Clerk', and the wetness of the ground. It was clear that the chaplain's performance at funerals also left something to be desired, and in March 1847 Heard, the chaplain, resigned. The Reverend Charles Stuart of Rye, Sussex, was appointed to replace him. The superintendent, chapel clerk, and sexton, one John Abbott, had to be dismissed in October 1857 for being absent from his duties without permission, and for not making up his books. He was replaced by Daniel James Johnson in November 1857. Early in 1858 Gates, the head gardener, also had to be discharged for 'improper conduct' and being abusive. There were also problems with members of staff (such as Gates) who seem to have established profitable private businesses by doing deals with members of the public, and who, having been dismissed, then had to be forbidden access to the cemetery because they still attempted to 'trade' despite having no rights to do so. It all seems to have been rather fraught.

Apart from the perennial problems with staff, surly gravediggers, inaudible and incompetent chaplains, and near-disaster over the bank business, passions could be aroused by inscriptions on tombstones. In 1858 the words

Turn thee again, O Lord, at the last;
and be gracious to thy servants here departed

appeared on a memorial, and caused a rumpus.[67] It should be remembered that the Roman Catholics were very much in the public eye, for Pope Pius IX (1846-78)[68] had re-established the Roman Catholic hierarchy in England and Wales in 1850, regarded by Protestants as 'Papal Aggression', which was the catalyst for the Ecclesiastical Titles Act of 1851[69] that prohibited the assumption of territorial titles by Roman Catholic Archbishops, Bishops, and Deans. However, the Act was never enforced, and was repealed in 1871, but it does give some idea of the apprehension with which the Roman Catholic Church was viewed at that time (when anti-'Papist' riots were not uncommon).

The inscription (on a stone in the consecrated part of the cemetery) was deemed to be 'objectionable' by the chaplain, so the Board felt obliged to seek the views of John Sinclair (1797-1875), Archdeacon of Middlesex (from 1844) and Vicar of Kensington (from 1843),[70] as well as of the Bishop of London.[71] The problem was that any hint of prayers for the dead savoured then of 'Popery' and aroused antagonism. Bishop Tait, who was of the Evangelical persuasion, had to deal in 1869 with the disastrous riots at the church of St George-in-the-East occasioned by the High Church Ritualistic innovations of the incumbent, Charles Fuge Lowder (1820-80), which forced Tait to close the church for a couple of months, but when it was re-opened order had to be kept by the police. In these early 21st-century days of (largely) religious indifference, when most people have no idea what an Anglican, a Dissenter, or a Roman Catholic is, the passions of the mid-19th century (only 150 years ago) seem strangely remote and inexplicable. Nevertheless, in 1858, the Board of the General Cemetery Company not only felt it had to refer suspect inscriptions with 'Papist' overtones to the Bishop, but found itself faced with two more dilemmas: a Mr Waldron wrote to request permission to burn a body in the cemetery grounds 'in lieu of its being interred'; and a Mr Shrubsole submitted a

67 Minutes of the Proceedings of the Directors of the General Cemetery Company (28 July 1858), 259-60.
68 Known, almost universally, as 'Pio Nono', he was particularly associated with anti-secularism, and was widely hated by nationalists and liberals. 69 14 & 15 Vict., c. 60, abolished by 34 & 35 Vict., c.53. 70 Who was to be instrumental in building the great Gothic Revival church of St Mary Abbots to designs by George Gilbert Scott (1811-78). 71 At that time Archibald Campbell Tait (1811-82), Bishop of London (1856-69), later Archbishop of Canterbury (1869-82). Tait was responsible for legislation (Burial Laws Amendment Act [43&44 Vict., c. 41]) permitting Nonconformists to be buried in consecrated ground with non-Anglican funeral services in 1880, an enactment that removed many animosities.

drawing for a cruxifix he proposed to erect over a brick-lined grave instead of 'the inscription which was ... deemed objectionable'.[72] Both requests were deemed unacceptable 'under any circumstances', and the required permissions were refused. What with the gasworks, the noxious pickling, the railways, the gypsies, mobs at funerals of demagogues, claims of rights-of-way, excessive rates, abusive employees, dodgy bankers, and other problems, smouldering, malodorous funeral-pyres (not to mention 'Papist' allusions) would have been the last straws, breaking the back of respectability[73] as far as the cemetery was concerned.

Sale of Part of the Surplus Land

Although negotiations with various Burial Boards to sell off a portion of the surplus land bought from the Fillingham estate had been going on in a desultory way for some time, the General Cemetery Company had a stroke of good fortune in 1857. It will be recalled that, much earlier, the Roman Catholics had discussed purchasing a plot *within* the *unconsecrated*[74] ground, but the great increase of Roman Catholics in London (partly because of immigration following the disaster of the Irish Famine of the 1840s) and the enforced closure of burial-crypts and overcrowded burial-grounds as a result of recent enactments prompted the need for cemeteries specifically set aside for the exclusive use of Roman Catholics. The West London and Westminster Cemetery Company had originally considered providing three chapels (one for Anglicans, one for Dissenters, and one for Roman Catholics), all of which appear on a view of the cemetery drawn by G. Hawkins and printed by Day & Haghe published in 1840.[75] Designed by Benjamin Baud (*c*.1807-75), only one (the Anglican chapel) was built, but clearly that Company anticipated custom from various religious persuasions.

In September 1857 the General Cemetery Company received an offer of £10,000 for 30 acres (12.141 hectares) to be used as a cemetery by representatives of the Roman Catholic Church,[76] and early in January 1858 it was decided to erect walls on the west and north side of the newly acquired land (22.54 acres or 9.121938 hectares), the costs of the western wall to be partly met by the new Roman Catholic owners of the excess 30 acres. Shortly afterwards the Trustees of the Fillingham estate executed a Deed of Conveyance to the 'Revd. Canon O'Neale' (*sic*), and the balance of the purchase-money was paid.[77] St Mary's Roman Catholic cemetery (as it became) was opened on 10 May 1858 for burial, but it did not acquire any refinements such as the chapel and lodge until 1860, both to designs by Samuel Joseph Nicholl (1826-1905) and his partner, Thomas John Willson (1824-1903).[78] Nicholl was a former pupil of the Roman Catholic architect Joseph John Scoles (1798-1863) and former assistant to Philip Hardwick (1792-1870): for a brief period he worked with another Roman Catholic architect, George Jonas Wigley (d. 1866), who may have been involved in the works at St Mary's cemetery. The fact that burials began to take place within a few days of the completion of the purchase from the Trustees shows how urgently it was needed (**6.1-6.2**).

That still left the problematic patch south of the canal which had been a difficulty since the very beginning of operations. By 1871 the Gas Company indicated it would rent

[72] Minutes of the Proceedings of the Directors of the General Cemetery Company (25 August 1858), 263-4. [73] The unacceptable 'Papist' inscription is also referred to in a book of Memorabilia (1858) held in the Company's records-room. [74] As Roman Catholics did not conform to the doctrines, beliefs, and practices of the Anglican Church, they, too, were regarded as Nonconformists. [75] It is reproduced in Curl (2000*e*), 96. [76] 30 September 1857, reported in the Company papers. [77] 28 April 1858. [78] Son of the architect Edward James Willson (1787-1854), also a Roman Catholic, of Lincoln, who was a well-known antiquary with an extensive knowledge of medieval English architecture. It is not known if these Willsons were in any way connected with the Thomas Willson (born 1780) who projected the 'Pyramid Cemetery' noted earlier.

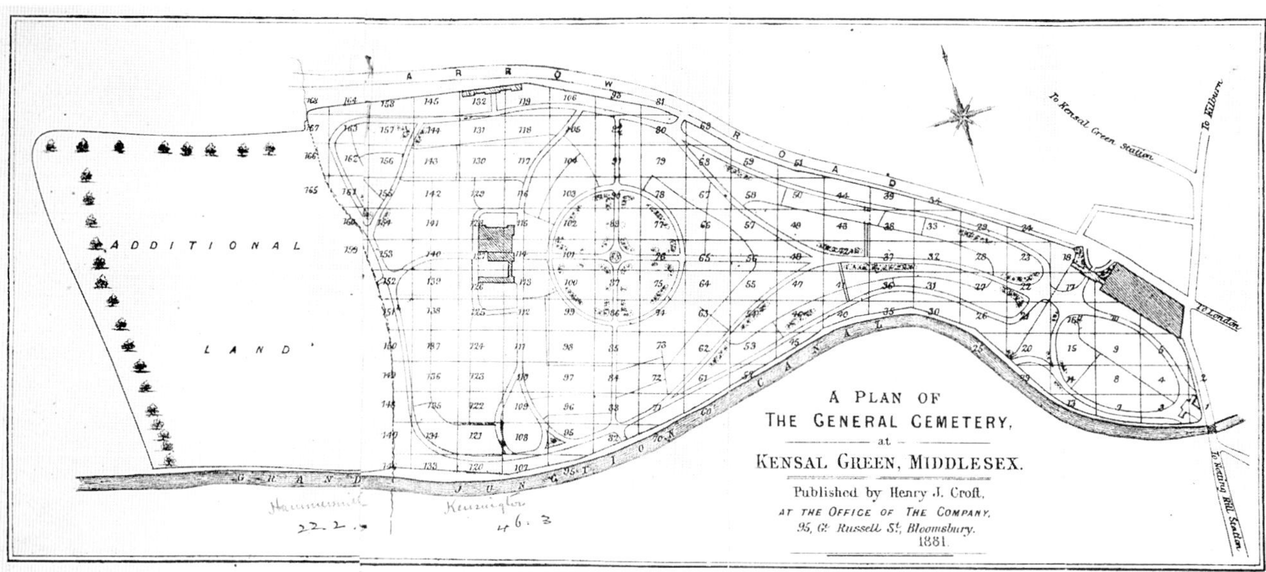

6.1 *A Plan of the General Cemetery at Kensal Green, Middlesex*, produced by Henry J. Croft at the office of the Company, 95 Great Russell Street, Bloomsbury, 1881. This shows the cemetery after the acquisition of the 'additional land' from the Fillingham estate in the 1850s. On the right is what is now Ladbroke Grove, and on the left the new land. The Monumental Chambers may be seen clearly, attached to the Anglican chapel and colonnades (*GCC.MC.E131200*).

some of this land, and was offered the whole 7.67-acre (3.104049 hectares) patch, but, on learning why the land was required, the General Cemetery Company refused to let it. From the 1840s the gasworks had been a nuisance, and certainly did not add tone to the area, but by 1872 the foul smells emanating from the works were being associated with the cemetery, and the evil 'miasmas' legends were revived. Early in 1873, 'owing to the increase in nuisance' caused by smoke and vapour from the gasworks, the General Cemetery Company sought to join with other owners of contiguous properties to act together to improve matters, but this proved a non-starter, as apathy reigned. The final blow came when the Gas, Light, and Coke Company (as it had become) applied to Parliament for powers to acquire the General Cemetery Company's land south of the canal and the Board decided it was pointless to resist and sold the land to the Gas Company, thus consolidating all its property north of the canal, but ensuring that a large, looming, and offensive near-neighbour south of the canal would be able to expand and do more damage.[79]

Griffith was instructed to 'apply to Mr Kemp for a plan for laying out the Company's new ground West of the Cemetery'.[80] This 'Kemp' became 'Kempe' when he inspected the grounds in 1861,[81] but was actually Edward Kemp (1817-91), the landscape-designer, who had worked at Chatsworth under Joseph Paxton (1801-65), laid out Birkenhead Park (1843-7), designed Anfield cemetery, Liverpool (1856-63), and carried out numerous other works.[82] Kemp's plans, submitted in May 1861, were referred to a sub-committee. Difficulties arose over the consecration of the new ground, and in 1861 the Bishop of London intimated that he did not consider he would be justified in consecrating it unless it 'be enclosed with a brick wall similar to that surrounding the existing Cemetery or other substantial fence'.[83] By September 1861 the sub-committee had started to take

79 All the above from the Minutes of the Proceedings of the Directors of the General Cemetery Company, *passim*. 80 Ibid. (29 August 1860), 33. 81 Ibid. (27 February 1861), 344. 82 Desmond and Ellwood (1994), 395. *See also* Elliott (1986), *passim*. 83 Minutes of the Proceedings of the Directors of the General Cemetery Company (31 July 1861), 369-70.

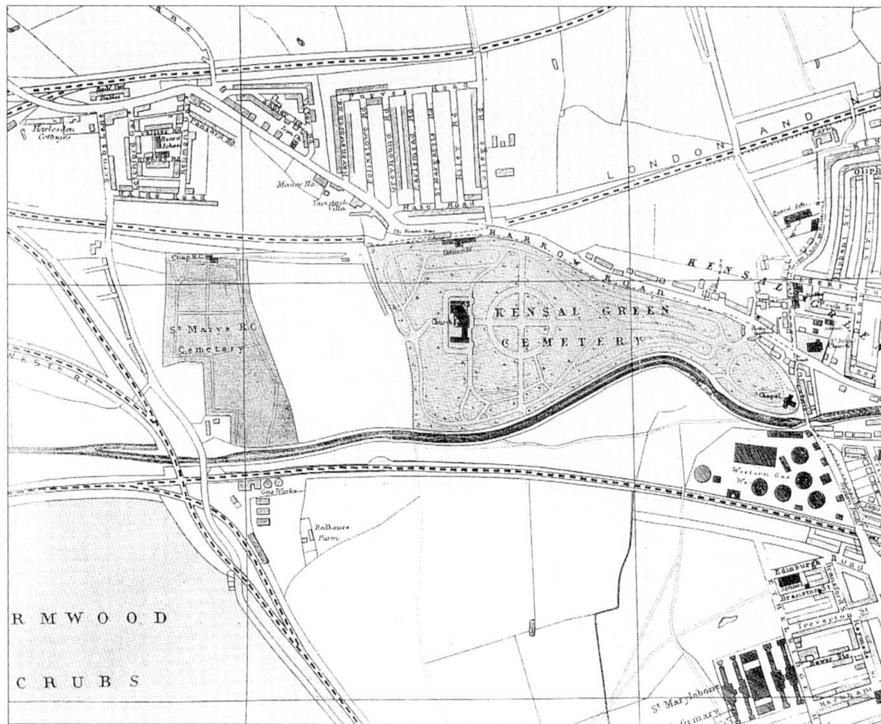

6.2 Plan showing Kensal Green cemetery, with the Monumental Chambers attached to the Anglican chapel and colonnades; the new land purchased from the Fillingham estate; and the part of the Fillingham estate that was sold off in 1857 to become St Mary's Roman Catholic cemetery. The lines of the railways are shown: what was the London and Birmingham Railway (touching the north-eastern boundary of the cemetery) became the London and North Western Railway, and the Great Western Railway runs south of the canal. Note the 'Western Gas Works' which were to expand over the patch of ground between the canal and the Great Western Railway. Note that the London and North Western Railway runs in a tunnel under *The Mason's Arms*. This map must date from around 1881, or perhaps the late 1870s (*GCC.MC.A1312000*).

measures to drain the land, and a contract was entered into with the builder, one Hollins, for the construction of the boundary-wall, the design of which was essentially a continuation of Griffith's original work of the 1830s.

The Cemetery from the 1850s to the 1930s

From the period following the calamity of the collapse of their bankers, the Minutes of the Board of Directors are relatively dull, and are mostly concerned with accounts, dividends, and other mundane matters, with very little in the way of controversy, scandal, or major problems, all of which must have been a considerable relief to the Board. Robert Maconochie, though, died in 1858, and the Board minuted its 'high sense' of the 'valuable services' he had 'rendered to the Company during the time he was a Director'.[84]

The next quarter of a century passed uneventfully under the Chairmanship of Lushington, Griffith, Bengough, and Morison, although several long-serving Directors died, including Thomas Barnardiston Wrightson (d. 1861). It really was a time of consolidation, and in 1884 the *Bayswater Chronicle*[85] reported that the cemetery had 'recently' been 'improved'. The 'ornamental beds on either side of the main gravel walk ... revealed quite a new departure in the floral management of the cemetery'. This transformation must have occurred under Bengough and Morison, for there was a distinct air of conservatism under Griffith's long tenure of the Chair (1864-79). The late 1870s and 1880s, therefore, saw splashes of colour that must have startled those more used to the sombre hues of the landscape. Reports in the 1880s refer to 'leafy and umbrageous screens', and to two 'fine specimens of the manna tree or flowering ash'[86] at the entrance to the main walks having 'again borne masses of their greenish-white flowers'.

84 Ibid. (2 June 1858), 250. 85 26 July 1884. 86 *Fraxinus Ornus*, or manna-ash, found mainly in Calabria and Sicily.

Earlier, it had been noted that the cemetery was 'planted and laid out in walks, parterres, and borders of flowers, and other styles of landscape-gardening'.[87] However, by the 1880s some opinion was beginning to swing against the great cemeteries established in the 1830s, and some writers began to advocate cremation, notably the Ulsterman William Robinson (1838-1935), whose *God's Acre Beautiful or The Cemeteries of the Future*[88] first appeared in 1880. Robinson's successful book was essentially a manifesto for what we would call garden-cemeteries, and also promoted arguments in favour of cremation. His work has been described in detail elsewhere.[89] Mrs Basil Holmes[90] was one of a number who wished to turn all cemeteries and burial-grounds into public parks, expunging all references to death: in fact, she, like many, deplored the 'waste of money' expended on memorials and monuments. 'There is a special interest attached to Kensal Green Cemetery', she wrote, 'from its having been the first, but I think it is also the worst.' She quoted another Ulsterman, William John Loftie (1839-1911), the author of *Kensington Picturesque and Historical* (1888), as having written that the General Cemetery of All Souls was 'the bleakest, dampest, most melancholy of all the burial-grounds of London'.[91] Mrs Holmes found large cemeteries 'sad sights', with tombstones 'no use to the departed' and 'grievous burdens laid on the shoulders of succeeding generations'. She was appalled to 'think of the amount of money' spent on monuments, and wondered how many churches might have been built or restored, missionaries 'sent to foreign lands', 'hospital beds ... endowed', or 'open spaces ... secured and laid out for the people'. Drinking-fountains, schools or secular institutions, and many other worthy objects and causes might have been built or supported with the cash expended on tombstones.

The arguments are familiar ones, for Mrs Holmes's utilitarian beliefs reflect not only the climate of pro-cremationist opinion in her own time, but have come to dominate our own (though her enthusiasm for sending missionaries to foreign parts would occasion sharp intakes of breath in certain circles today). There are three pernicious ideas in Mrs Holmes's book that have done immense damage: first, she could see no merit in Victorian funerary art and architecture; second, she favoured clearing burial-grounds and cemeteries so that they could be converted into recreation-grounds; and, third, she felt the poor should not be allowed to commemorate their dead because they had to deny themselves material goods to pay for the privilege. The nanny-knows-best attitude is still profoundly offensive to some.[92] Mrs Holmes and her associates saw the erection of monuments as a hindrance to 'giving the people grass', which was thought, for some time, to be beneficial. The wholesale clearance brigade is still going strong, and has destroyed many cemeteries (Hull's Spring Bank is one major casualty at the hands of latter-day disciples of the prejudiced and destructive attitudes of the graveyard destroyers of the 1880s and 1890s). The bleak, bald wastelands that are supposed to be grassed areas are a familiar sight in many wretched towns and cities, and have not been conspicuously successful in improving behaviour, social conditions, or urban aesthetics.[93]

The Building of the Crematorium

The Board of the General Cemetery Company was aware of the advent of cremation, and, as early as 1891, resolved to erect a columbarium in the Monumental Chambers, which Lander built to designs by Willey (as mentioned above) (5.8). However, by the 1930s it became obvious that demand for cremation was on the increase, and the Directors decided to build a crematorium in the cemetery grounds. Even by that time the

87 Timbs (1867), 81. 88 Robinson (1883), *passim*. 89 Curl (2000*e*), 186-90. 90 Holmes (1896), 255.
91 Ibid. 92 Including the Editor of this book. 93 For a critique of Holmes *see* Curl (2000*e*), 176-9 and *passim*.

'new ground' laid out to designs by Kemp was only sparsely filled with graves, as is clear from aerial photographs (**6.6**). However, in order to build a crematorium, a special Act of Parliament would be needed, and designs would have to be prepared.[94]

At the same time it was decided to build new offices to adjoin the entrance-gate and lodges, and plans, developed early in 1937, were approved in March.[95] The architect of the new offices was 'Mr Green', and the building was to cost £1,687, the tender of T. M. Mansfield having been accepted. This need for new offices seems to have been prompted by a growing conviction that the Company should abandon its offices in Bloomsbury (it had moved from its old offices to No. 21 Bloomsbury Square some time earlier) because telephones and modern transport were rendering the Bloomsbury connection superfluous. However, connections with Bloomsbury could not be ended until the lease had expired.

The crematorium was to cost around £25,000, but first a new Bill had to be steered through Parliament, and on 7 May 1937 the Company obtained the Royal Assent for its new Act.[96] Essentially this amended 2 & 3 Will. IV, c. 110, and 2 Vict., c. 5, by enabling the Company to erect a crematorium and to raise additional capital not exceeding the whole of its existing capital by borrowing money and issuing new shares. It was made clear that cremations would have to be carried out under the provisions of the Cremation Act of 1902,[97] and the designs for the crematorium and its apparatus were to be subject to the approval of the Minister of Health. Fees were to be paid to the incumbents of parishes from which corpses originated as under section XXVII of the earlier enactment, so ashes were to be treated as bodies.

Ladbroke Grove was widened in 1937, and the Company received £1,032 7s. 4d. in compensation, because not only did the wall have to be taken down and rebuilt from a position behind the Dissenters' chapel, but bodies had to be exhumed and reburied. This required much shoring-up and buttressing, and was quite an operation. It was also decided to move the strong-room from the Bloomsbury office to Kensal Green, and instructions were given to the architect to allow for the building of a new strong-room within the new offices.[98]

Having taken advice, the Board decided to go to Gerald Berkeley Wills, F.R.I.B.A. (1882-1979),[99] of 7 Stone Buildings, Lincolns Inn, for designs for the proposed crematorium. Wills had built the crematorium at Reading (having won the commission in an architectural competition): soon he had produced sketch-designs which he presented to the Board in November 1937,[100] and was duly appointed architect. Plans were drawn up by February 1938, and allowed for two chapels, although the Board decided only one should be fitted up for use 'as it would be many years' before a second chapel 'would be required'.[101] Wills's plans were approved in March 1938 (**6.3**).[102]

Tenders were invited, and that of Walter Lawrence & Son for £17,957 was accepted. It was decided that a 'curved glass roof' should be placed over the 'fountain court', and to substitute a curved ceiling for a flat one in the chapel. This 'fountain court' was the space in the middle of the building on either side of which was to be a chapel: it was to be open and approached through a distyle *in antis* arrangement of Ionic columns, a concept of some dignity (**6.4-6.5** and **7.37-7.39**). These variations and some other requirements pushed the costs up, and the contract with Lawrence for £18,438 was sealed and signed.[103] Approvals were quickly given and work began almost immediately. Building was mostly funded by borrowing money from the bank.

94 Minutes of the Proceedings of the Directors of the General Cemetery Company (25 December 1936). 95 Ibid. (30 December 1936, 27 January 1937, 24 February 1937, and 31 March 1937). 96 1 Edw. VIII & 1 Geo. VI, c. 23. It was called the General Cemetery Act, 1937. 97 2 Edw. VII, c. 8. 98 Minutes of the Proceedings of the Directors of the General Cemetery Company (September 1937), *passim*. 99 Sheppard (*Ed.*) (1973), 337, does not mention Wills, and only remarks that a 'crematorium was built here in 1938', and Cherry and Pevsner (1991), 468, give the date as 1939 and call the architect 'Willis'. 100 Minutes of the Proceedings of the Directors of the General Cemetery Company (24 November 1937). 101 Ibid. (4 February 1938). 102 Ibid. (15 March 1938). 103 Ibid. (8 June 1938).

6.3 'Kensal Green Crematorium. View of South End of Chapel'. Presentation drawing by Gerald Berkeley Wills, exhibited at the Royal Academy in 1938 (*R.I.B.A. Library Drawings Collection, RAN 34/I/22 18*).

6.4 Main front of the crematorium, showing the original open court in the centre. Photograph of 1939 (*R.I.B.A. Library Drawings Collection, RAN 34/I/22 1-20*).

6.5 Garden-front of the crematorium showing the arcaded wings protecting the memorial tablets, and the Ionic open centrepiece. Photograph of 1939 (*R.I.B.A. Library Drawings Collection, RAN 34/I/22 1-20*).

Meanwhile part of 21 Bloomsbury Square was let, and it was decided to call in a landscape-architect to design the area around the new crematorium. On the recommendation of the Royal Horticultural Society, Edward White (*c.*1873-1952), of Milner, Son, & White, Architects, 7 Victoria Street, Westminster, was appointed. White was responsible for the crematorium garden and setting. All this is very interesting, because it shows that the Board members, more than a century after the founding of the cemetery, were still anxious to get good advice and go for quality. Wills, having won a competition for another crematorium, was seen as the man of the moment with regard to the design of this building-type; White had been President of the Institute of Landscape Architects (1931-2), and was highly thought of as a designer.[104]

Wills designed 'cloisters' for the crematorium, but although his proposals were approved, the Board decided not to proceed with the work for the time being. Late in 1938 Wills was instructed to improve the north-west entrance to the cemetery (shared with St Mary's Roman Catholic cemetery since the 1850s), but these plans were not realised. A tender of £1,028 from Burley & Sons for the crematorium garden, designed by White, was accepted, and another tender for walls around the garden and 'part of the walls for future cloisters' for £1,092 6s. 8d. from Lawrence was also accepted.[105]

In 1939 the new crematorium was opened by Lord Horder,[106] and a Service of Dedication was conducted by the Bishop of Kensington, assisted by the Reverend B. C. H. Andrews, chaplain to the General Cemetery Company, and the Reverend

104 Desmond and Ellwood (1994), 733. *See also Who was Who, 1951-1960*, 1158. 105 Minutes of the Proceedings of the Directors of the General Cemetery Company (30 December 1938). 106 The Rt. Hon. Thomas Jeeves Horder (1871-1955), 1st Baron Horder, Chairman of the Council of the Cremation Society.

A. J. Burgoyne, representing the Nonconformists. How times had changed since the 1830s! A vote of thanks was proposed by the Mayor of Hammersmith.[107]

Some things had not changed, however, because the Company's superintendent had to be dismissed for 'many misdemeanours', including selling plants to a nursery, soliciting money from the Company's customers, selling metalwork from grave-surrounds, and so on. These problems seem to have been endless, and the Minutes of the Victorian period of the cemetery's history are full of references to dishonest behaviour, insubordination, absenteeism, sloppiness, and other problems caused by employees.

War was declared on 3 September 1939, and Hammersmith Borough Council offered the loan of 'mechanical excavators and operatives for trench burials' in the event of heavy civilian casualties. It is forgotten today how terrified the Government was of huge numbers of deaths in the event of bombing and gassing, and there are plenty of documents of the time that attest to the amount of effort expended on planning for the disposal of bodies in such an event. The immediate effect on the Company was not a sudden need to dig *fosses communales*, but the need to economise by dismissing several members of staff. Some of the Company's land was requisitioned by the War Office, and anti-aircraft defences were constructed in the north-west portion of the grounds.[108]

Signs of a rift between the Company and Wills, the architect, were evident early in 1940, and the Board noted he should not have issued a final certificate for the crematorium as there were many defects still obvious and in need of being made good. The electric wiring was very faulty, even dangerous; the electric pump for the fountain had broken down; and there were sundry problems with the woodwork. Wills was written to in very strong terms.[109] Members of the Company's staff had received electric shocks from the most unexpected quarters, and it was clear much of the workmanship was sub-standard. Things were put to rights as far as possible, however, and the new building undoubtedly enhanced the grounds and the business.

The 1939-45 War

Holborn Borough Council requisitioned the basement of 21 Bloomsbury Square for Air-Raid Precautions (ARP) use, and the Company made it clear that any damage should be made good. The Bedford estate was also approached concerning a reduction of rent. Then the first serious damage occurred when incendiary bombs landed on the roof of the Monumental Chambers, and a bomb fell on the 'circular roadway' opposite the crematorium, forming a large crater, but fortunately there was no damage to the new building. Bombs also fell in squares [105, 124, and 137], damaging memorials and disturbing coffins. So bad was the bombing in the area that the catacombs were used as air-raid shelters by cemetery employees and their families.[110]

It might seem a peculiar use of the destructive potential of the *Luftwaffe* to bomb a London cemetery, but it should be remembered that 'precision-bombing' was largely a myth,[111] and accuracy was more a matter of luck than anything else. A glance at maps or aerial photographs of the area, however, is sufficient to show there were main railway-lines (the Great Western and the London, Midland, and Scottish[112] Railways) immediately to the south and north of Kensal Green cemetery, a large gas-works to the south, and an armaments factory to the north, all good reasons for bombs to fall in the vicinity. On the nights of 15/16 November and 27 November 1940 more bombs were dropped, damaging many memorials and disturbing human remains. During 19/20 April

[107] Minutes of the Proceedings of the Directors of the General Cemetery Company (6 July 1939). The boundary between Kensington and Hammersmith runs through the cemetery. [108] Ibid. (25 October 1939). [109] Ibid. (28 February 1940 and June meetings, 1940). [110] Ibid. (30 December 1940). [111] Then and now. [112] Formerly the London and North Western Railway.

Monumental Chambers altogether. By the end of 1949 the War Damage Commission had accepted Harriss's proposals.[119]

The Board gave its backing and Harriss drew up finalised plans. Tenders were invited, and when received varied from £15,923 to £16,785.[120] In 1952 the War Damage Commission agreed to pay £14,900 towards the costs,[121] but a few months later a Building Licence was refused.[122] Harriss then recommended tidying the buildings up, moving the monumental tablets from the Chambers and colonnades to the catacombs, and simply reducing the complex to the bare bones of Griffith's pared-down scheme. At the end of 1952 the Ministry of Works (Ancient Buildings Section) recommended an application for a Licence for £7,400, and further applications were made in 1953.[123] Building Licences totalling £10,000 were granted, and Harriss negotiated with 'Messrs Greenwood Ltd' to carry out the work. All the delays, bureaucratic interference, and so on, cost money, and the cheeseparing solution proved to be a disaster for the survival of the memorials.

A contract was signed in 1953, but the manner in which the works were carried out proved to be very destructive. During the dismantling of the mural monuments, about 30 per cent of them were damaged. 566 tablets from the colonnades and Chambers had been removed, of which 360 had been stacked, but 123 were broken or 'not accounted for'. This looks very like poor supervision and lack of expertise, for one would expect a very large proportion of monuments to have survived. It is clear that many ended up in a skip through carelessness and inappropriate handling.[124]

More Building Licences were applied for in December 1953, and a total expenditure of £14,064 was allowed. It was proposed to commemorate the names of all those buried in the cemetery whose graves and memorials had been destroyed, but this does not seem to have materialised. Harriss's rather drastic works of restoration were completed in 1954, and he also carried out works at the lodge, the contractor there being Green. In the event, Harriss did not manage to obtain the last War Damage Commission cheque (for £749 18s. 7d.) until November 1958.

The monuments that survived (but were often damaged) were stored in the catacombs, and simply left to gather dust and dirt, and there many of them, in 2001, remain. As for the old or terrace catacomb, it continued to suffer from vandalism, which got worse during the 1950s and thereafter, so today it is in a sorry state. The damaged Dissenters' chapel was used as a store and let out to various users, including Kenyon, the funeral directors, until by early 1970 its condition was giving cause for concern, and a Building Preservation Order was issued in 1971 to give some protection to it. This, despite the intervention of the Historic Buildings Division of the Greater London Council, was insufficient to prevent the colonnaded wings from being demolished, and by 1992 the charming little building, abandoned, partially demolished, and badly vandalised, was in great danger. However, as Lady Freeman will outline in Chapter VII, the Friends of Kensal Green Cemetery, working with other bodies, stepped in, and the chapel was fully restored (with its colonnades rebuilt) and opened in 1997 (**7.13-7.17**).

Future restoration-schemes involving the other buildings in the cemetery are essential if they are to survive, but the difficulties are many, not least those associated with finance, protection, and long-term conservation. Nevertheless, this great 19th-century Valhalla deserves urgent attention and care, for the entire ensemble, including many monuments, mausolea, the boundary-walls and -railings, and the landscape, comprises a rich artefact, a monument not only to those who lie there and who created it, but to aspects of urban reform that are not usually given the attention they deserve.

119 Minutes of the Proceedings of the Directors of the General Cemetery Company (8 December 1949). 120 Ibid. (29 May 1951). 121 Ibid. (31 March 1952). 122 Ibid. (10 June 1952). 123 Ibid. (15 December 1952). 124 Ibid. (27 May 1953).

CHAPTER VII

The Cemetery Buildings

JENNIFER M. FREEMAN

Brief History; The Greek Revival Style; The Boundary Wall, Railings, and Main Entrance; The Arch and Lodges; The Dissenters' Chapel; The North Terrace Colonnade and Catacomb; The Anglican Chapel; The Catafalque; The Catacomb beneath the Anglican Chapel; Monumental Chambers; The Crematorium; Afterword

> After a pleasant walk of between two and three miles along the Harrow road, the handsome, substantial-looking Doric gateway meets the eye on the left, standing a little back; we pass through, and the grounds of Kensal Green Cemetery are before us. These are extensive, comprising about fifty acres, and are surrounded with a lofty wall on either side of the gateway, now almost covered by a wide belt of young forest-trees, evergreens, and shrubs; whilst the opposite boundary is left partially open to the eye, so as to admit of fine prospects, from different parts, over the country round Shepherd's Bush, Hammersmith, Notting Hill, and Bayswater. In the interior the grounds are divided by broad winding and straight walks, the rest being laid out in grassy lawns, relieved by parterres of flowers, clumps of trees and shrubs, and, above all, by the glitteringly white monuments of every possible outline, style, and size, from the simple flat stone, up to places large enough for their owners to reside in whilst living. The chief buildings are the two chapels and the colonnade. The chapel for the Dissenters on the left, in the unconsecrated ground, (divided from the consecrated by a clearly marked boundary), is, with the exception of its front, ... markedly plain; the chapel for ... the Church of England, on the right, is, on the contrary, both noble and handsome, and the interior, with its solemn gloom, ... rich though simple.
>
> CHARLES KNIGHT (*Ed.*) (1791-1873):
> *London*, iv (London: J. S. Virtue & Co. Ltd., 1841-4,
> revised and corrected by EDWARD WALFORD [1823-97], *c*.1870), 170-1.

Brief History

Once the decision had been reached (confirmed in July 1831)[1] to develop the General Cemetery on 46.41 acres (18.78 hectares)[2] of land at Kensal Green, several architects presented themselves to design the buildings but none was commissioned. Nevertheless, the elaborate, even grandiose, proposals of 1830 for a *Grand National Cemetery* (2.3) by Francis Goodwin (for the site previously considered by Carden and his associates at Primrose Hill) perhaps had some influence on the architecture as realised over the next few years at Kensal Green,[3] not least in terms of architectural style.

In November 1831, as has been described above,[4] it was decided to hold the architectural competition for designs for a chapel (with underground burial-vaults) and a separate entrance-gate with lodges. One of the judges, it will be recalled, was the Company's surveyor, John Griffith,[5] himself to become a shareholder of, and, in 1864, Chairman of, the General Cemetery Company. It seems to have been Griffith's influence that was the deciding factor in many of the decisions taken later, supported by his allies, the most important of whom were Spottiswoode and Paul.[6]

Indeed, before the competition, Griffith had already been active on behalf of what was to become the General Cemetery Company. In September 1831 he had been asked to prepare a ground-plan dividing the cemetery into numbered squares for subdivision into burial-plots. A month later, Griffith produced working-drawings for a boundary-wall, and tenders for its construction were invited.[7] During 1832 Griffith represented the Board of the Cemetery Company at meetings with Robert Stephenson, the engineer of the London and Birmingham Railway, over the design of the line proposed to run immediately north-west of the cemetery, and eventually, after a great deal of difficulty and considerable lobbying by the influential members of the Provisional Committee, Stephenson and the Railway Company agreed to construct a tunnel, as the effects of the original proposals for the railway would have been very damaging to the future success of the cemetery. On that occasion, and subsequently, Griffith proved to be a skilled negotiator. It is probable that around this time the General Cemetery Company's intention of building the main entrance to the grounds further west along the Harrow Road[8] was abandoned because of the site's closeness to the railway.[9]

In March 1832 Griffith was instructed to proceed with the construction of the boundary-wall, work on which was in hand early in that year.[10] The contractor, Chadwick, was a builder with experience of working for Sir John Soane, and, apparently, of railway construction. Soane, as has been noted above, provided a

1 *See* Chapter II: *Acquisition of Land at Kensal Green. See also* Chapter XIV and Appendices II and III. 2 As described earlier, 7.67 acres (3.1 hectares) lay to the south of the canal. But see Chapter II, footnote 112 for details. 3 The scheme included an Anglican church in the form an octastyle Greek temple modelled on the Athenian Parthenon, with long ranges of terraces constructed over catacombs; vast colonnades to allow for the erection of memorial-tablets; an impressive propylaeum based on the Athenian original; four pavilions derived from the Tower of the Winds in Athens; two structures modelled on the Erechtheion; two circular temples; two hexastyle temple-like buildings derived from the Theseion; two elements reproducing the design of the Choragic monument of Lysicrates; two Roman triumphal arches; and two small temples based on the temple on the Ilissus. *See* Curl (1984*b*), 228, and Curl (2000*e*), 49. 4 In Chapter III. 5 Little is known of John Griffith except that he lived and practised at 16 Finsbury Place South, was a member of the Architectural Society, was elected a Fellow of the Institute of British Architects (the Institute was not authorised to add 'Royal' to its title until 1866) in 1842, and was Chairman of the General Cemetery Company from 1864 to 1879. He built several houses in Coleman Street in the City of London. A single design by him for an unidentified house is held in the Drawings Collection of the Royal Institute of British Architects (RIBA Nomination Papers F v1, 166, fiche 73/E6, and *The Builder*, **lv** [10 November 1888], 345). He is buried [233/157/RS] with his brother and father in the cemetery (*see* item 121, Chapter VIII). 6 *See* earlier Chapters for this, especially Chapters II and III. 7 The contract with William Chadwick of Southwark for the building of the wall was reported as having been signed early in December 1831. 8 The position is shown on the plan published in Kendall and Allom (1832), *see* **3.19**. It was to be approximately where the upper gates are now. 9 The second site chosen for the main entrance was also slightly awkward because of the existing buildings on its eastern flank. These were masked by means of a stuccoed screen, featuring Grecian *antae* and other elements, designed by Griffith, applied to the blank walls (*see* **4.16**). 10 It was to be completed by 1 August.

testimonial on Chadwick's[11] behalf for the General Cemetery Company. The wall, constructed of London stock bricks, strengthened at intervals by piers with simple capstones, was dignified and severe, without any sort of ornament (**2.4**).

The competition duly went ahead,[12] and from among 48 entries the Gothic designs of H. E. Kendall were chosen (**3.19-3.23**).[13] If Griffith, as one of the judges, dissented from what may have been a majority decision, the surviving papers of the General Cemetery Company are silent on the matter. But it was a tricky period for Gothicists, when the romantic, Regency style of Gothic was gradually giving way to a more scholarly seriousness which blossomed as the Victorian Gothic Revival. An article in *The Gentleman's Magazine*, which reviewed Kendall's designs, describes a reaction to his proposal:

> we cannot help arriving at the conclusion that the architecture of Henry the Third's time, or even an earlier period, would have suited the nature and destination of the intended chapel, better than a design formed in imitation of a period when the simplicity of the early works had given way to a luxuriant and elaborate display of embellishment.[14]

However, there was an even more important reason why Gothic would not have met with the approval of the Committee: much Regency or late-Georgian Gothic was light, frivolous, and insubstantial; it most certainly did not suggest solidity and security, unlike Soane's Bank of England, Dance's Newgate Gaol, and other Neoclassical buildings in London. It will be remembered that, in 1831-2, security from violation was one of the nascent Company's prime aims.[15]

Although Kendall had received support from G. F. Carden and others (especially A. C. Pugin) the scheme did not please Sir John Dean Paul, Bart., and some other members of the Provisional Committee, who felt, with some justification, that fancy Gothic would not only be expensive to maintain, but would not necessarily attract custom from a potential clientele used to a Classicism associated with security, modernity, and firmly-based establishments. Furthermore, Paul, like most of his contemporaries, to some extent would have associated medieval architecture and its revival with 'Popery' and with ancient superstition. Eventually it was decided that the Provisional Committee would take the final decision on the appointment of an architect only after the Bill incorporating the Company had passed through Parliament. Even the Act seems to have envisaged the adoption of a Classical style of architecture for the buildings.[16] The postponement of the matter may have been partly an attempt to defuse controversy, but the fact that there was no Company as such at the time does seem to have given the Provisional Committee a sound reason to delay decisions.

The comments and opinions of leading architects of the day were sought on design matters relating to the cemetery, and, although we lack information about their detailed

[11] Chadwick was active as a builder on the Ladbroke estate, and he was still involved there well into the 1840s. He also described himself as an architect. [12] *See* Chapter III for details. [13] Kendall's son, Henry Edward Kendall, Junior (1805-85), designed the church of St John the Evangelist of 1844, a tough, gritty Neo-Romanesque composition of stock brick and flint sited at the corner of Kilburn Lane and Harrow Road, and described in Cherry and Pevsner (1991), 675, perhaps unkindly, as 'atrocious' (**4.17**). [14] 'Sketches of the approved Design of a Chapel and Gateway entrance ...'. *The Gentleman's Magazine*, cii/2 (September 1832), 246. Elaborate Gothic fripperies, at the time, had associations with decadence, corruption, and 'Romanist superstitions', so would have aroused some opposition. By Henry III the critic meant 13th-century First Pointed (otherwise known as Early English Gothic): the perception that the Second Pointed (or Decorated) and Perpendicular Gothic styles were somehow over-elaborate and even decadent is difficult to defend today. [15] *See* Chapter II for a full discussion of this. [16] Act of Parliament (11 July 1832). 2 & 3 Will. IV, c. 110. Clause XXII refers to covered porches or colonnades, and colonnades do not occur in Gothic architecture.

contents, they were undoubtedly influential. Those consulted were C. R. Cockerell,[17] one of the architects (with W. H. Playfair [1790-1857]) of the unfinished National Monument (1824-9) at Calton Hill, Edinburgh; James Pennethorne,[18] primarily an urban planner and landscape-architect who had worked for John Nash and A. C. Pugin; Robert Smirke,[19] already enjoying fame for public buildings in the Greek Revival style (including the British Museum [1823-46]); and Sir Jeffry Wyatville,[20] architect to Kings George IV and William IV at Windsor Castle (1824-37). Kendall meanwhile published his winning designs,[21] but support for Gothic seems to have weakened after Carden's rather public quarrel with the embryonic Company and his subsequent removal from influential positions on the Provisional Committee, and after the death in December 1832 of A. C. Pugin, a leading shareholder and Gothicist.[22] Interestingly, Kendall was also an accomplished Classical architect in the 1820s, having designed No. 24 Belgrave Square in London (1827-33), various houses in Brighton, Sussex, including Nos. 19-20 Sussex Square (1829-31) and, significantly, the Greek Revival Spilsby Sessions House (now Spilsby Theatre) and House of Correction in Lincolnshire (1824-6) (**7.1**). As was described earlier, he also submitted a Classical scheme for Kensal Green which does not appear to have survived. In the event, John Griffith's plans for the various buildings, the general designs of which he seems, with some percipience, to have prepared earlier than they were called for, were eventually adopted.

As has been described earlier, Consecration by the Bishop of London of the General Cemetery of All Souls, Kensal Green, took place on 24 January 1833, by which time a small temporary chapel (demolished in 1838) had been erected for Anglican use, and the boundary-wall was complete. By March 1834 the Dissenters' chapel (**4.5-4.13**) and main entrance (**4.14-4.15**) were finished, also to Griffith's designs. In July 1836 Griffith was instructed to proceed with the Anglican chapel and catacomb, and a contract was drawn up with Chadwick again acting as builder (**4.22-4.26**).

Although Kendall did not have direct responsibility for the buildings, nevertheless important elements of his proposals lived on into Griffith's scheme, including the excellent choice of site for the Anglican chapel, where his Gothic cloisters were reinterpreted by Griffith as Greek Revival colonnades. Unfortunately, we do not know what Kendall's Greek Revival entry to the competition was like, but it may have had a more direct influence on Griffith's scheme than has been suspected. Quite clearly the general disposition of elements realised at the Anglican chapel was already on the cards when the bird's-eye perspective of the cemetery was prepared (**Frontispiece**), and it may well be that the built fabric derives from a composite of ideas from Kendall, Liddell, and Griffith. Kendall's design for the façade (**7.1**) of Spilsby Sessions House reappears at Kensal Green in the prostyle tetrastyle portico of the Anglican chapel (**7.2**): indeed, the two porticoes are almost identical, even to the point of not having any entasis on the

[17] Cockerell had worked in Asia Minor, Italy, and Greece from 1809-16, examining antiquities and carrying out excavations at what was then known as the Temple of Zeus Panhellenius (actually the Temple of Aphaia [*c.*490 BC]) on the Island of Aegina (with Karl Christoph Joachim Haller, Freiherr von Hallerstein [1774-1817], John Foster [*c.*1787-1846] of Liverpool [who was later to design both the Necropolis (1823-4) and St James's cemetery (1827-9) in that city], and the Swabian painter Jacob Linckh [1786-1841]), where the celebrated Aegina marbles (now in the Glyptothek, Munich) were discovered, and at the Temple of Apollo Epicurius at Bassae in Arcadia (*c.*420 BC), where the same team discovered the Phigaleian Marbles, now in the British Museum. Cockerell later designed the tomb of Lady Pulteney (1849) at Kensal Green cemetery (*See* Hakewill [1851], pl. 23). *See also* Colvin (1995), 256-9, Crook (1972), 56-9, and Watkin (1974), *passim*. [18] He designed the Public Records Office, Chancery Lane, London (1851) and completed Park Villages, Regent's Park, London. [19] One of Smirke's pupils was C. R. Cockerell. [20] Colvin (1995), 1128-33. [21] Kendall and Allom (1832), *passim*. [22] The architect Auguste (or Augustus) Charles Pugin (1769-1832) had been a member of the General Committee set up to plan Kensal Green cemetery in 1830. Pugin's *Specimens of Gothic Architecture* (London: 1821-3) and *Examples of Gothic Architecture* (London: 1828-34) included letterpress prepared by Edward James Willson (1787-1854), the architect and antiquary who compiled (*c.*1820) a pioneering glossary of medieval architectural terms. A. C. Pugin, therefore, was very much in the pro-Gothic camp.

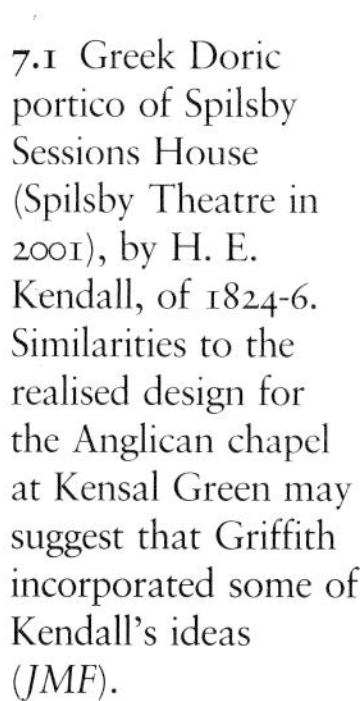

7.1 Greek Doric portico of Spilsby Sessions House (Spilsby Theatre in 2001), by H. E. Kendall, of 1824-6. Similarities to the realised design for the Anglican chapel at Kensal Green may suggest that Griffith incorporated some of Kendall's ideas (*JMF*).

7.2 Portico of the Anglican chapel at Kensal Green in 1990 (*JSC*).

columns.[23] Something of Kendall's arrangement of paths and walks was perpetuated, especially the circular path (**3.19**) directly east of the Anglican chapel (although this design may have originated with Liddell's plans, mentioned earlier). It was Kendall's scheme, too, which graphically suggested the possibility of waterborne funerals entering the cemetery through elaborate iron gates from the bank of the Grand Union Canal. Just what was the professional relationship between the two men? No light has yet been shed, but it may have been friendly and collaborative. Kendall's body is interred [2397/48/RS] beneath a hefty, muscular-Gothic memorial (designed, it seems, by himself) located between Central Avenue and South Branch Avenue, facing east, so he may have harboured no grudges against the Company (**8.8**).

The Greek Revival Style

The Company's decision to adopt Greek Revival as the style for its buildings was hardly surprising given contemporary preferences. It had become widely accepted in the early years of the 19th century and was at the height of its fashionable appeal by the end of the 1820s. Untainted by the Baroque of Absolutism, or other associations after the long years of war with France,[24] it was used in several countries at the time precisely because its only associations were with Antiquity, with Greek learning, and with Classicism freed from Roman impurities.[25] The Gothic Revival, on the other hand, was only to achieve

[23] Entasis, the subtle diminution with height of Classical column-shafts, involves slight curvature of the shafts rather than straightforward battered profiles. It was said to have been discovered by Thomas Allason (1790-1852) in *c.*1814, and was subsequently confirmed by Cockerell and Haller von Hallerstein. Allason (who designed Mulready's studio in Linden Grove, Bayswater [1827], and who made designs for many houses on the Ladbroke estate, Kensington, from 1823) published a paper on entasis in 1823. Subsequently, Pennethorne published work on optical corrections in Greek architecture (1844), and Francis Cranmer Penrose (1817-1903) published his definitive studies on the matter in 1851. [24] Curiously, France never adopted the Greek Revival style to any great extent, although there were isolated examples in that country: it certainly never had the widespread acceptance it enjoyed in England, Scotland, the United States of America, Prussia, Bavaria, and elsewhere. [25] Examples include the works of Karl Friedrich Schinkel (1781-1841) in Prussia; of Leo von Klenze (1784-1864) in Bavaria; of Thomas Hamilton (1784-1858) and others in Scotland; of William Wilkins (1778-1839) and others in England; and, of course, of numerous architects in the United States of America, especially William Strickland (1788-1854).

wide acceptance somewhat later, and became intimately associated with Christian worship, with morality, and proselytisation.

It was during the latter part of the 18th century that the Greek Revival had been given a tremendous boost by the publication in London of *The Antiquities of Athens* by James 'Athenian' Stuart (1713-88) and Nicholas Revett (1720-1804) which appeared in four volumes in 1762, 1789, 1795, and 1816.[26] Their archaeological researches in Athens and elsewhere were illustrated by a series of carefully measured drawings of which those engraved and published in the second volume became immensely influential.

Stuart and Revett's own architectural activities soon provided examples of the style in England for public buildings, churches, gateways, and garden buildings. The first Greek Doric temple portico in England was James Stuart's own Temple of Theseus in the grounds of Hagley Hall, Worcestershire, constructed in 1758. Other leading architects, such as Cockerell, Smirke, Soane, and William Wilkins followed Stuart and Revett's lead, reinforcing the ascendancy of the Greek Revival,[27] and many budding architects travelled to Greece and Asia Minor to study the remains of Antique buildings.

The new knowledge of Greek architecture was popularised among surveyors and builders by means of somewhat derivative manuals and pattern-books such as Stephen Riou's (1720-80) *Grecian Orders of Architecture delineated and explained from the Antiquities of Athens* (1768), Peter Nicholson's (1765-1844) *The Student's Instructor* (1804), Edmund Aikin's (1780-1820) *Essay on the Doric Order* (1810), and John Billington's *The Architectural Director* (1829 and 1834), which gave directions for composing the Orders in the Greek manner and for establishing the measurements involved. Chadwick is likely to have been familiar with these. Even so, as Professor Crook[28] has noted in his book on the subject, the Greek Revival was never wholly Greek. In addition, elements of Egyptian Revival,[29] Neoclassicism, and Palladianism in the works of its leading exponents are also apparent in Griffith's work.[30] Other factors that weighed with the Board of the General Cemetery Company were the celebrated successes of Père-Lachaise cemetery in Paris (which was predominantly Classical in style) and of the two new cemeteries in Liverpool (the Necropolis [1825] and St James's cemetery [1829])[31] which contained Greek Revival buildings, and, perhaps even more significantly, at the time were paying handsome financial dividends to their shareholders. The dramatic and handsome Glasgow Necropolis (opened 1832) was laid out on hilly ground: it received considerable favourable publicity[32] and was yet another important precedent.

The Boundary Wall, Railings, and Main Entrance

The first requirement of the newly established cemetery for a 'boundary wall to give privacy and protection to the property',[33] and to prevent vandalism, had been met in 1832. Griffith's wall is a dominant feature on the Harrow Road, where it is over half a mile in length and varies between ten feet (3.048 metres) and thirteen feet (3.9624 metres) in height. In 1861 part of the wall close to the Dissenters' chapel was taken down and rebuilt to plans by Henry Dawson (1827-1915), an architect who worked with

[26] Though others, including William Newton (1735-90), Willey Reveley (1760-90), and Joseph Woods (1776-1864), were involved in the preparation of Volumes II-IV. [27] It is worth noting that C. R. Cockerell's research into the Greek architecture of Syracuse was published in London as *Antiquities of Athens and other Places of Greece, Sicily, etc.*, the supplementary volume to *The Antiquities of Athens* (1830), and in a German translation (1829). [28] Crook (1972), 77. [29] Curl (1994*b*), *passim*. [30] Griffith, along with many contemporaries, was equally 'impure' in his handling of structure, incorporating windows into his walls and roofing his buildings in lead rather than in the archaeologically correct stone. [31] The architect of the Liverpool Necropolis and St James's cemetery, as has been mentioned above (footnote 17), was John Foster Jnr., who was himself a highly accomplished architect, well versed in the Greek Revival style. [32] Curl (2000*e*), *passim*. [33] 'London and its Vicinity' in *The Gentleman's Magazine* cii/1 (August 1832), 171. The main purpose of the wall was to reassure the public that the dead were safe from the 'resurrectionists', or body-snatchers.

7.3 Iron gates and gate-piers on the canal-side of the cemetery in 2001. Note the tops of 'piers' in the form of Classical horned cinerarium-lids (*MC.D300301*).

7.4 Gates and railings on the Harrow Road (north) side of the cemetery in 2001. Note the cast-iron tops of the iron 'piers' in the form of horned cinerarium-lids (*MC.F300301*).

7.5 Detail of ironwork on the upper gate on the Harrow Road in 2001. Note the elegant braces and cast-iron tops of the 'piers' (*MC.A300301*).

Griffith,[34] so this stretch now follows the line of Ladbroke Grove (which was widened at the time, necessitating the rebuilding works and a number of exhumations). Today the wall remains otherwise as completed, although one part is much lower in height at the western end of Harrow Road.

A desire to form attractive views into and from the cemetery was an important aspect of its planning, as a contemporary writer in the *Penny Magazine* of the Society for the Diffusion of Useful Knowledge observed:

> from this spot, which extends between the road and the Paddington canal for about a quarter of a mile, a very delightful view, bounded by the Surrey hills, is commanded over the western environs of the metropolis. That this view may not be excluded, the high wall which incloses the cemetery is in some parts broken by an iron railing of equal height. The ground thus inclosed is laid out in gravelled roads of sufficient width for carriages, and planted with forest trees, evergreens, and other shrubs and flowers.[35]

The cast-iron railings bordering the canal are about eight feet (*c.* 2.4384 metres) high, and consist of uprights of circular section, 1¼ in. (31.75 mm) in diameter, with spear-head finials about 9¼ in. (234.95 mm) high. These uprights, or spears, are set closely together and fixed into stone copings on low brick walls: the only horizontal element is the iron bar, immediately under the finials, that separates the uprights and holds them in place at the top. Thus they formed a handsome and functional barrier that was difficult to climb.

Two pairs of cast-iron gates offered access from the canal, one pair to the eastern Dissenters' section, the other identical pair giving on to the Anglican, consecrated, ground. The taller gate-'piers' are also of iron, displaying an attractive interlacing diamond-pattern, with rosettes at the intersections, set between the main vertical elements (which are hefty pieces of cast iron of square section bevelled at the corners, 1⅜ in. [about 35mm] square). These open-work 'piers' are capped with cast-iron ornament in the form of cinerarium-lids with horns (much broken) (7.3).

Along the Harrow Road the wall is breached again, roughly half-way along its length, by a more richly elaborated set of iron gates and railings (7.4-7.5). The gate-'piers'

34 Henry Dawson took over Griffith's architectural practice, and continued to work from 16 Finsbury Place South, eventually moving to 6 Finsbury Circus. He was Architect and Surveyor to The Salters' Company, and father of Walter Cecil Dawson (1866-1950 – also an architect and surveyor) and Bertrand Henry Dawson (1864-1945), later (1936) Viscount Dawson of Penn, the physician. 35 'Report of the first meeting of shareholders after incorporation' in *The Penny Magazine for the Diffusion of Useful Knowledge*, iii/150 (2 August 1834), 299.

7.6 Gates and piers giving access to the western part of the cemetery, photographed in 2001 (*MC.E300301*).

also have lattice-work set in lozenge patterns, and Grecian horned cast-iron tops in the form of cinerarium-lids, but the main upright members are 1⅝ in. (about 40 mm) square, again with bevelled corners. Between the iron gate-'piers' and the Portland Stone piers that terminate the brick wall are lengths of spear-headed railings set on low plinths, and this time there are low subsidiary miniature spear-headed railings between each pair of full-height spears, and about a third of their height. Under both the main spear-heads and the subsidiaries are two horizontal bars to keep the uprights apart and stiffen the whole construction: between the pairs of bars are iron crosses set diagonally as saltires, and between the pairs of bars below the lower spear-heads are lozenge-shaped elements of iron; thus the subsidiary railings stop at the lower bar, and the spear-heads are fixed to the uppermost of the lower pair of bars. The gates themselves are further stiffened by iron bars rising from the top of the lower pair of bars in a quarter-circle and terminating under the lower of the upper pair of bars where the gates join together. Instead of the lozenges and saltires, the 'piers' are ornamented with iron eyelets with semicircular tops and bottoms. Further stiffening is given to the lengths of railings by means of elegant cast-iron braces featuring a motif derived from the anthemion device. These gates are known as the upper gates,[36] through which are good views of the cemetery (**7.4**).

The wall on its stone-topped plinth here is an impressive 12 feet (3.6576 m) high, with dignified stone piers standing at about 14 feet (4.2672 m). This entrance may have been built out of a desire to shorten the journey to the Anglican chapel, but it is equally possible that mourners wished to avoid the main entrance which led directly to the unconsecrated sector of the cemetery,[37] and so would have been shunned by many Anglicans, all too aware of the schismatic tendencies in Nonconformity, as well as of certain nuances concerned with class consciousness.

A third set of gates, again set between stone piers derived from Griffith's designs, gives access to the western part of the cemetery, but these were not part of the original scheme, as the land there was not acquired until the 1850s (**7.6**).

It is hard to appreciate today the sensitivities attached to the distinction between consecrated (for Anglicans) and unconsecrated (for Dissenters) ground, but the difference was very important in the 19th century, and often aroused controversies, resentments, and even vitriolic abuse. Dissenters objected to being buried in consecrated ground, and, perhaps even more important, disliked any payment to the Anglican Church and its clergy in respect of burial-fees. Anglicans, on their side, resented what they regarded as the 'betrayal' by Nonconformists, and insisted that burial-grounds for Dissenters should be clearly demarcated and set aside from consecrated land. At Kensal Green the boundary was originally defined by a 'sunk fence' following a straight course from the west side of the main entrance south to the canal-bank. Today, only the piers of the gates

[36] The upper gates are often incorrectly referred to as the 'Royal Gates', on the misunderstanding that they were erected to enable Queen Victoria's carriage to enter the grounds. As with other myths about the cemetery, including frequent and incorrect attributions in reference-books to the wrong architects, this should be discounted, together with spurious guess-work regarding the extent of the cemetery. [37] At the time, unconsecrated land and any associations with Dissenters would have had social implications.

which gave entry to the Centre Avenue of the Anglican grounds survive, with vestigial remains of the footings of the fence on either side. Some of the elaborate iron fencing once set beside the gate piers (**4.16** and **4.17**) is in storage.

The cemetery was also furnished with a number of simple cast-iron seats for visitors, of which two survive, now positioned behind the crematorium. There are several square-shaped cast-iron signposts, modestly ornamented and bearing the names of the paths in the cemetery.

The Arch and Lodges

The probable first designs for the main entrance and Anglican chapel appear in a watercolour of the early 1830s (**Frontispiece**), possibly by Thomas Allom or by Griffith himself, now in the Museum of London, and entitled *A Prospect of Kensal Green Cemetery*.[38] It shows a boldly pedimented composition supported on four closely-spaced fluted Doric columns placed two on either side of a coffered, barrel-vaulted arch.[39] This tall element (the main entrance) is flanked by single-storey wings each having three bays. A Greek (perhaps Doric but possibly Ionic) portico flanked by lower colonnades is indicated for the chapel. This design for the main entrance was abandoned in favour of

7.7 Propylaeum of 1810-22 at Chester Castle, designed by Thomas Harrison (Photograph by Eric de Maré © *Crown copyright. NMR. AA98/04512*).

7.8 Entrance propylaeum at Kensal Green before the re-ordering (*JSC*).

the present arrangement with an attic storey instead of a pediment, which may have been prompted by Thomas Harrison's widely proclaimed Propylaeum (**7.7**) at Chester Castle (1810-22), although the barrel-vault is retained from the earlier proposals at Kensal Green.

Another possible source of influence on the design of the main entrance was the cemetery of Frankfurt-am-Main in Germany, the *Hauptfriedhof* of 1829, which is also thought to have provided inspiration for the arrangement of the colonnade of the north terrace catacomb (described below). In Frankfurt, the cemetery was entered through a

38 It is usually attributed to Thomas Allom but Professor Curl has suggested it could well be by Griffith, who was a talented draughtsman. Either way, it would appear that the buildings shown are Griffith's, although they may owe something to Kendall's Classical entry to the architectural competition, and to designs by Liddell. The fact that Allom collaborated with Kendall to produce the published volume of Gothic designs might point to a strong link with Kendall. The likely date of the drawing is 1832. Could it even show Kendall's proposals? If, in fact, it does, it is probably indeed by Allom. 39 An arch was not strictly a Greek feature but one that Thomas Harrison (1744-1829), for example, had shown in unexecuted proposals for the entrance to Chester Castle of *c*.1793.

pedimented Doric *in antis* Propylaeum (entirely trabeated without an arch) with single-storey wings on either side (3.26). In one wing was the residence of the overseer. At Kensal Green, the superintendent's accommodation mainly occupied the east wing, with additional chambers over the arch and in the west wing. According to the original drawings it was planned to provide a scullery, coal-cellar, and wash-house in the basement, a kitchen and parlour at ground level, and other rooms, presumably bedrooms, above (4.14-4.15). The interiors still retain much original joinery, fireplaces and other features of interest. Completed in 1833, the main entrance forms a signally austere and impressive entrance to the cemetery, and it is unquestionably a building of considerable architectural distinction (7.8).

During the late 1930s the present boardroom,[40] offices, and some single-storey extensions to the lodgings were erected in a sympathetic Graeco-Egyptian manner.[41] The forecourt and bollards were redesigned in 1988 with grant-aid from the Royal Borough of Kensington & Chelsea.

The Dissenters' Chapel

The Dissenters' chapel, completed in 1834, is in the south-eastern corner of the cemetery well away from and off-axis with the Anglican chapel: its roof is just visible from Ladbroke Grove over the boundary-wall. The building is rectangular on plan with a pedimented tetraprostyle Ionic portico, the design of which can be directly traced to an illustration of the Order from the temple on the Ilissus in Volume I of *The Antiquities of Athens*[42] (7.9) and later repeated in *The Antiquities of Ionia*.[43] This Order 'became the Ionic norm of the Greek Revival'.[44] On either side of the portico are low covered colonnades, gently curved to follow the original alignment of the boundary wall and path in front. They were a great innovation marked by paired *antae* derived from the baseless *antae* of the Choragic monument of Thrasyllus in Athens. The ends of each of the wings contained a distyle *in antis* arrangement of Doric columns set between the fine Thrasyllus *antae* (7.10).

It is interesting to note that the Thrasyllus Order was also published by Stuart and Revett in *The Antiquities of Athens* (7.11).[45] C. R. Cockerell employed a similar arrangement in the ends of the wings shown in his competition designs of 1830 for the University Library at Cambridge. His design model for Langton House (1827-33, demolished 1949), at Blandford Forum, Dorset,[46] of *c*.1823 also shows similar *antae* used in a straight colonnade, but Kensal Green many well be a unique example where Thrasyllus *antae* were used as columns, paired, and set on a curved Palladian plan. Whatever his inspiration Griffith here demonstrates great deftness in welding elements of Greek architecture and Palladian devices into a consistent whole, aptly scaled for the site.

The façade and important features of the Dissenters' chapel are constructed of Portland Stone while the main body of the building is built of brick rendered with Roman cement, discreetly lined to resemble ashlar. Original roof-coverings were of lead, but are now been replaced with Steelex. The colonnades were of Portland Stone with inner walls of brick, rendered with Roman cement and intended for the display of tablets to commemorate those entombed below. In the event there were few of these as the catacomb proved less popular than anticipated. A vestry and a stair that leads down to

40 Some of the furniture in the present boardroom (including the sideboard with attractive Egyptianising heads) appears to date from the inception of the General Cemetery Company and may have been brought from its former headquarters in Bloomsbury. 41 The plans, by 'Mr Green, Architect', were approved in March 1937, and built by T. M. Mansfield Ltd., whose tender for £1,687 was accepted on 28 April. 42 The fluted Ionic columns and pediment were almost certainly copied from the published illustrations save for the substitution of Attic for Asiatic bases. Robert Smirke was especially influenced by the design of the Temple on the Illissus and there are other Smirkeian features in this building. 43 Revett (1769-97), *passim*. 44 Wiebenson (1969), 66. 45 Stuart and Revett (1789) ii, Ch. 4, Pl. 3. 46 The model is now in the possession of the Royal Institute of British Architects.

7.9 *(above)* Portico of the temple on the Ilissus, Athens, showing the Ionic Order with Asiatic base and angle-capitals at the corners, in which the volutes are splayed outwards at 45° (or 135° to the planes of the front and side elevations). From Stuart and Revett, i (1762), Ch. II, Pl. III *(R.I.B.A. Library Photographs Collection).*

7.10 *(above right)* The Dissenters' chapel in 1965, before the curved colonnades were demolished. The Ionic portico differs from that of the temple on the Ilissus (**7.9**) in that there are no angle-capitals, the bases are of the Attic rather than Asiatic type, and the shafts appear to be more slender *(London Metropolitan Archives. The photograph was taken by the Greater London Council Photographic Unit, Department of Architecture and Civic Design, Serial No 65/ 06174).*

7.11 *(right)* The Choragic monument of Thrasyllus, Athens, from Stuart and Revett, ii (1762-1816), Ch IV, Pl. III. This important monument (now destroyed) was the model for many Greek Revival details, including the colonnades of the Dissenters' chapel. Note the continuous row of guttae under the taenia, and the wreaths on the frieze *(R.I.B.A. Library Photographs Collection).*

the catacomb are located at the east of the building. Below the chapel and colonnades the catacomb extends in a series of brick-lined vaults. Three approximately equal-spaced corridors run down and across the length of the catacomb and across the lines of the barrel-vaults: the intersections result in a series of groined vaults above each corridor (**4.6**). The chapel floor has a central opening through which coffins were lowered, though the aperture is not shown on Griffith's drawings. Coffins rest on iron racks placed in the bays. Drainage and ventilation were also provided.

Inside the chapel Griffith introduced reticent architectural features that were appropriate to the Greek Revival style. They included timber panelling, pews, and a decorative scheme in fawn colours with the pilasters finished to resemble polished marble or stone. *The Penny Magazine*[47] reported that 'only three interments have as yet taken place there ... but the finest building that the cemetery at present affords has been erected on it. This is the chapel for the performance of burial rites. It occupies the centre of a colonnade, and the front presents a pediment supported by four columns of the Ionic order. The interior arrangements are neat,[48] but perfectly simple, and well adapted to the purpose'.

Two rows of pews (one each side of the chapel) are shown facing the centre on Griffith's drawings (**4.7, 4.11**). At the east end he designed a pulpit with a reading-desk in

47 *The Penny Magazine*, iii/150 (2 August 1834), 299. 48 A favourite word of the period, it meant, in architectural terms, 'economical', eschewing unnecessary show or expense, and had approving connotations.

front, and behind this, on either side, doors led to the vestry on the right and to the catacomb on the left. The interior is lit by a variation on a Wyatt window[49] above the pulpit (4.12), and this window has a shallow segmental arch over the exterior elevation (4.13). An *oculus* in the pediment above lights the roof-space. Decorative enrichment inside is confined to a frieze of anthemia and palmettes above the window and pilasters mentioned before. A flue for the chimney is concealed behind the south-east pilaster leading from the fireplace in the vestry. The ceiling-rose, cornice, and four implied pilasters in the corners of the chapel (a feature which Griffith made peculiarly his own at Kensal Green) survive almost intact. The lower parts of the walls were originally panelled in timber. A stencilled pattern of palmettes forming a dado is a later addition. The Minutes of the General Cemetery Company indicate that in 1834 the chapel was hung with black cloth above the seats.

7.12 The Dissenters' chapel in 1992, showing the distressed condition of the building after the colonnades had been demolished in the 1970s (*JMF*).

7.13 Dissenters' chapel in 1997, showing the restored colonnades (*JSC*).

By 1992 the chapel presented a sorry sight, for the curved colonnades had been demolished (7.12) on the grounds that they were dangerous, and the catacomb and chapel had been systematically vandalised. The Friends of Kensal Green Cemetery determined to initiate its repair as part of a wide-ranging programme of conservation and restoration and set up a Fabric Committee to get this started. In 1996-7 the chapel was the subject of a major scheme grant-aided by North Kensington City Challenge, English Heritage, and the Heritage Lottery Fund (with other smaller donations). The main body of the chapel was repaired and the lost fittings reinstated to Griffith's designs. The colonnades were in part rebuilt and in part restored largely using masonry found buried or lying on the site (7.13). The catacomb was overhauled. A spacious new exhibition-gallery and meeting-room was built on the site of the former maintenance yard behind the northern colonnade, and the ruined vestry was reconstructed as an office for the Friends of Kensal Green Cemetery (7.14). The Historic Chapels Trust has taken a long lease of the chapel from the General Cemetery Company and, in turn, the Friends of Kensal Green Cemetery are licensed to use it as their headquarters (7.15). The chapel was re-opened in May 1997 by Sir Jocelyn Stevens, then Chairman of English Heritage. The present revived scheme of painted decoration dates

49 Tripartite window resembling a serliana, but with the arch over the central opening omitted, and the entablature carried over the whole window.

KEY TO PLAN
1 Chapel
2 Vestry
3 Stairs to catacomb
4 Loggia
5 Colonnades
6 Meeting-room/exhibitions
7 Kitchen
8 WC
9 Store
10 Yard to new facilities
11 New entrance from Ladbroke Grove
12 Extent of catacomb (shown dashed)

7.14 Plan showing the extensions to the Dissenters' chapel, completed in 1997 (© *English Heritage*).

7.15 Office for the Friends of Kensal Green Cemetery attached to the Dissenters' chapel, opened in 1997, and used for meetings and exhibitions (© *Crown copyright. NMR.BB97/1592*).

7.16 Interior of the Dissenters' chapel in 2001 showing the pulpit and reading-desk reinstated to Griffith's designs, with the 1860s scheme of painted decorations partly conserved. The commemorative plaque is by Michael Rust. The window and frieze are part of Griffith's original design (*JMF*).

from the 1860s with the original 1830s scheme (which could not be satisfactorily retrieved) retained underneath (**7.16-7.17**). The project won a Europa Nostra Award (1998) and the Royal Borough of Kensington and Chelsea's Environment Award (1997).

7.17 Details of the 1860s decorations in the Dissenters' chapel (north wall), showing the anthemion and palmette motifs in 1997 (© *Crown copyright*. *NMR.BB97/1596*).

The North Terrace Colonnade and Catacomb

The colonnade and its catacomb are constructed against the north wall of the cemetery on its highest ground (**4.1-4.2**). There are spectacular views towards the hills to the south. The Portland Stone unfluted Greek Doric colonnade (with entasis) is constructed on a terrace of York Stone below which is a brick-built catacomb, the oldest in the cemetery. Below ground is a long corridor parallel to the boundary wall with recesses for coffins on either side. This catacomb served the Anglican community before the permanent Anglican chapel and catacomb were completed. Access was obtained through openings in the terrace. The wall behind the colonnade itself was intended for the display of memorial-tablets, and was rendered in Roman cement.

It is clear from the Minutes that the design of the colonnade and catacomb was Griffith's own, that originally it was to be of much greater extent (*see* **Frontispiece**), and that the whole structure dates from 1832-3. The central group of six columns and four at each end project forward and are contained within *antae*: the arrangement comprises a projecting tetrastyle *in antis* portico, an octastyle colonnade set back from the porticoes, a central projecting hexastyle *in antis* portico, another octastyle colonnade set back from the porticoes, and a second projecting tetrastyle *in antis* portico, giving a handsome symmetrical composition (**4.1**). There is a simple entablature with prominent Soanesque pulvins or capping-blocks, though most of these are now missing. The inner wall with its memorial tablets is now much deteriorated and many of the monuments have been broken or removed. The main inspiration for the arrangement of the terrace and colonnade may have been the cemeteries of Frankfurt-am-Main and Munich, where colonnaded and arcaded vaults were formed along one wall of a rectangular plot. In the case of Munich the colonnade was in front of a semicircular building containing the *Leichenhaus*, where the dead were placed until signs of decomposition had begun.[50]

The catacomb proved attractive, and the spaces for 'two thousand coffins' were in great demand.[51] 'The remains of the Duchess of Argyll, Marchioness of Headfort, Ladies Fitzroy and Stanley, and Sir W. and Lady Douglas and Generals Bell, Orr, Broughton, and other distinguished persons are deposited in this receptacle', reported an admiring writer in *The Mirror of Literature, Amusement, and Instruction*.[52] A writer in *The Penny Magazine* describes how the lifting mechanism for the coffins worked:

> the coffins intended to be deposited in the catacombs are received upon a sort of platform, which descends slowly during the performance of the funeral ceremony; and they are afterwards conveyed by machinery through the subterranean passage to the place where they are to be laid.[53]

[50] Loudon (1981), 49. [51] It is described by Charles Dickens as having 'long been filled' in an article on Kensal Green cemetery in *All The Year Round*, **x** (19 September 1863), 93-96. The number of coffins is greatly exaggerated. [52] *The Mirror of Literature, Amusement and Instruction*, **xxxi** (28 April 1838), 273-5. [53] *The Penny Magazine*, **iii**/150 (2 August 1834), 229.

7.18 The Anglican chapel and colonnades in 1963, with the Duke of Sussex's tomb on the right (*London Metropolitan Archives. The photograph was taken by the Greater London Council Photographic Unit, Department of Architecture and Civic Design, Serial No 63/1258*).

7.19 Anglican chapel and colonnades from the south-east in 1997 (© *Crown copyright. NMR.BB97/1163*).

The openings into which the coffins were lowered can still be seen but the mechanical equipment has long disappeared and the whole structure is in a poor state of repair, despite its undoubted architectural and historical importance.

The Anglican Chapel

The Anglican chapel stands on rising ground flattened into a terrace (or 'esplanade' as Griffith styled it), near what was then the western boundary of the cemetery.[54] The catacomb was formed below the terrace, which was once entirely paved with York Stone flags and granite setts, the latter intended to carry carriages. A short flight of steps leads up to the chapel's prostyle tetrastyle Greek Doric entrance-portico which faces east towards the Centre Avenue. On either side of the building are double covered colonnades

54 That is, before the new lands were bought in the 1850s.

with pavilions at each corner where they turn to the west. From all viewpoints the chapel composition is the dominant feature of this part of the cemetery (**7.18-7.19**).

As at the Dissenters' chapel the columns are of Portland Stone, the body of the chapel being of brick rendered in pigmented Roman cement with Portland Stone dressings: 'joints' in the rendering are scribed and coloured to resemble ashlar, the horizontal joints being deeply scribed, the verticals expressed by fainter V-grooves. The west façade of the chapel is relatively plain, with paired *antae* supporting the interrupted entablature. Between the *antae* is a simple arrangement of recessed *antae*-like strips carrying a rudimentary entablature over which is a lunette, and framed by the two strips and entablature is the west window (**7.20**). Griffith's contract-drawings date from 1836 when he intended to build the whole chapel ensemble for £14,201 4s. 3d. (**4.22-4.26**).

Variations of the final design had appeared in illustrations long before its construction, including *The Prospect of Kensal Green Cemetery* (**Frontispiece**). Kendall's Spilsby Sessions House (**7.1**), as noted above, had been completed in 1826, and may have provided an exemplar for the portico and other elements of the frontage. Smirke's British Museum was an Ionic variant of the portico with flanking colonnades and projecting wings that had been exploited by Sir Edward Lovett Pearce (*c.*1699-1733) at the Parliament buildings in Dublin of 1729.[55] Smirke's church and mausoleum at Milton, West Markham, Nottinghamshire (1831-2),[56] also had a fluted Doric portico at the entrance to the mausoleum-end of the building that bears comparison with Kensal Green.[57] Similarly, Nicholas Revett's important church at Ayot St Lawrence, Hertfordshire (1778-9),[58] was designed with single colonnades that flank the church and terminate in mausoleum-like cenotaph pavilions, but, despite its Greek detail, is a Palladian composition (**7.21-7.22**), and is an obvious precedent for the chapels at Kensal Green.[59] The Doric lodge[60] in the garden at Wentworth Woodhouse in South Yorkshire of 1830 may have been known to Griffith and provided ideas.[61]

7.20 Anglican chapel from the south-west, showing the west elevations of the chapel and colonnades in 1997 (*JSC*).

Whilst a variety of buildings and people clearly influenced the design of the Anglican chapel, it is the grouping of the component parts and the perfection of their scale in relation to the setting that command attention at Kensal Green.[62] However, neither chapel has entasis on the columns, although entasis is employed at the colonnade of the north terrace catacomb, the columns of which are unfluted, so perhaps entasis on fluted

55 Pointed out in Curl (1992), 142. 56 The mausoleum is the tomb of Georgiana Elizabeth, Duchess of Newcastle (d. 1822). 57 Illustrated in Crook (1972), Pl. 36. It was intended to replace the parish church of All Saints, Markham Clinton. 58 One of the earliest churches with a Greek Revival front (the Order is derived from that of the temple of Apollo at Delos, with plain shafts, the flutes only appearing at the tops and bottoms of the shafts). The Delos temple is illustrated in Stuart and Revett, iii (1794), Ch. 10, Pl.1. 59 Illustrated in Curl (1993*b*), 81. 60 Designed by Charles Watson (*c.*1770-1836) and his partner James Pigott Pritchett (1789-1868). Interestingly, James Stuart also worked on the great house itself. 61 Lord Milton's family had close connections with Wentworth Woodhouse.

62 Griffith was not as skilful in managing his contractors for there are several errors in the aligning of the different parts of the building and in the detailed arrangement of the Classical detail, especially the relationship of triglyphs to pilasters inside the building. These relationships are correctly shown on his drawings, but the arrangements existing today are not as designed, and may date from repairs carried out in the 1840s (or, perhaps, in the 1950s).

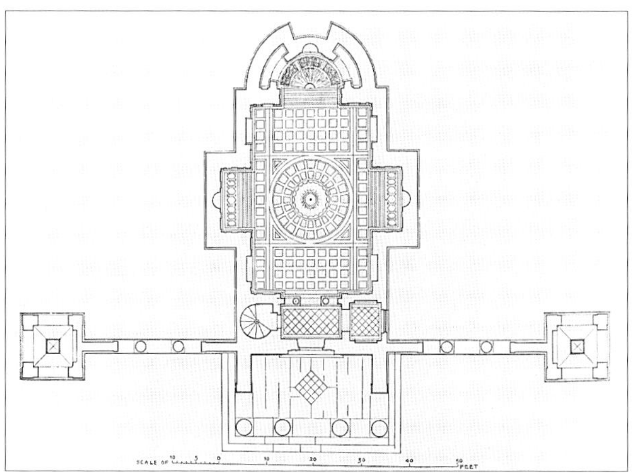

7.21 Plan of Ayot St Lawrence church, Hertfordshire, of 1778-9, by Nicholas Revett (*BTB/SH*).

7.22 Ayot St Lawrence church, Hertfordshire, of 1778-9, by Nicholas Revett, showing the Order from the temple of Apollo at Delos and the colonnades linking the church to the cenotaph-pavilions, in 1990 (*JSC*).

columns had proved too much for Griffith's office to detail, or too much for Chadwick's team to carve.[63]

The colonnades on either side of the Anglican chapel terminate on the north and south sides in single-storey pavilions (the comparison with Ayot St Lawrence is apposite) to form a courtyard open to the west (**7.23**). They were originally intended to be twice as long (**4.19-4.21**), but now extend for seven bays terminating in a second pair of pavilions housing important funerary sculpture: on the south side is a powerful life-sized family monument sculpted by Robert Sievier (1794-1865), one of the Directors of the General Cemetery Company (**9.19**). The outward sides of the colonnades are partly filled with walling which was rendered for the erection of memorial-tablets. More recently the range facing east was partly filled in to form additional utility-rooms. The blocking-course over the cornice is ornamented with Greek pulvin-blocks. The roofs were originally of lead but during the 1980s the chapel received a new roof of stainless steel.

It is remarkable that much of 'Old Humphrey's' (George Mogridge) rapturous appreciation of the cemetery can be recaptured today by visitors standing on the terrace outside the chapel entrance:

> from the colossal pillars of the portico of the chapel, the view of the cemetery is a sweet one, and quite in character. There is no affected sentimentality; no littleness, nor gewgaws to catch the eye. No child's play of making gardens, as in many parts of "pere la Chaise" – all is vast, sober, chaste, field-like, beautiful; rather sweet than romantic; and the prospect to the south is extensive. A cemetery should soothe sorrow, as well as call forth profitable reflection. Judging by my present feelings, this place is calculated to do both.[64]

A handsome pair of doors gives access to the interior, first into a vestibule, then the chapel proper. Smaller doors on each side of the vestibule lead to a former vestry on the right and to the catacomb on the left. Blank panels, intended for memorials, occupy the wall-spaces above these doors. A pair of Doric columns marks the entrance to the ceremonial area (**7.24**).

63 Entasis was certainly known at the time, but, to be fair to Griffith and Chadwick, they were by no means alone at the time in failing to provide it. 64 Mogridge (1846), 308-13.

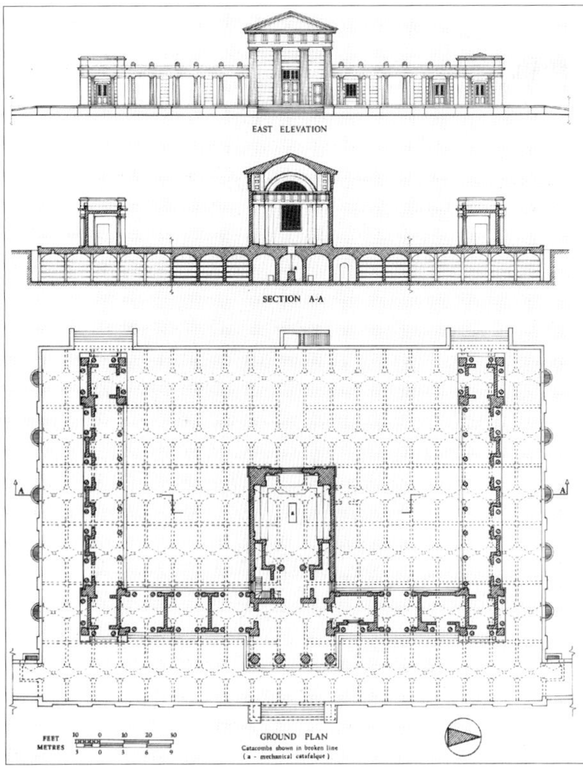

7.23 Anglican chapel, colonnades, and catacomb. East elevation (*top*), Section A-A (*middle*), and plan (*bottom*) showing the relationship of the chapel and colonnades to the catacomb structure beneath. Measured drawing of 1972 by Mr John J. Sambrook, reproduced in Sheppard (*Ed.*) (1973), 338, Fig. 89. Print kindly provided by the General Editor, Survey of London (Survey of London *drawing © English Heritage [NMR]. 96/04633. The photograph was taken by the Greater London Council Photographic Unit, Department of Architecture and Civic Design, Serial No 74/4716*).

7.24 Interior of the Anglican chapel in 1997, showing the restored catafalque and two Doric columns leading to the vestibule and entrance-doors. Note the incorrect positioning of triglyphs in relation to the columns (© *Crown copyright. NMR.BB97/1612*).

Some of the original furnishings and fittings survive, including the York Stone paving, timber flooring,[65] and two short iron railings which link the columns to the wall. Originally there were also iron gates. All the ironwork was painted a patinated bronze colour and the doors were grained to resemble oak. Walls were plastered and distempered with the ornamentation highlighted in colour. The pulpit occupied the west (ritual east) end where the altar now stands,[66] and pews were aligned to face the centre.[67]

Even without most of its original furniture, the interior of the chapel is memorable. In plan it is not unlike Ayot St Lawrence church (minus the apse), but also, more obviously, it resembles Sir John Soane's long-demolished Princes Street vestibule for the Bank of England in the City of London (1804-5) (7.25). The layout is cruciform, with coffered barrel-vaults and simplified Greek-key decoration over each arm of the cross. Piers and pilasters carry a deep entablature which is enriched with triglyphs and mutules. Over the main body of the chapel the ceiling, raised on pendentives (embellished with rosettes), forms a canopy-like vault, its shallow plasterwork ribbed and scalloped. At the

65 Griffith's plan shows a floor of Portland Stone with small black marble squares but this was apparently not executed. 66 A drawing and article on the funeral of HRH Augustus Frederick, Duke of Sussex (1773-1843), in the Anglican chapel, describes how the walls, reading desk, chairs etc. were entirely covered in black cloth for the occasion. *See* 'The Late Duke of Sussex' in *Illustrated London News*, ii/53 (1843), 300-307. 67 Professor Curl has discovered from the minutes of the Company's meetings that the seating was covered with deep blue cloth.

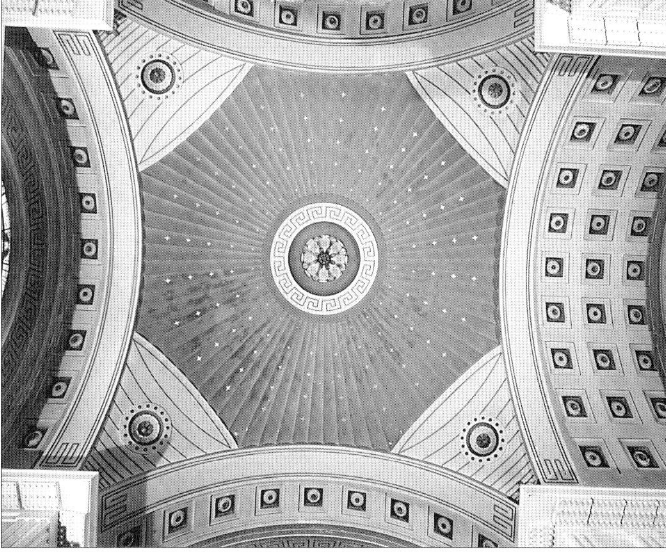

7.25 Entrance-hall (Princes Street vestibule), Bank of England, designed by Soane. The treatment of the pendentives and domed ceiling, together with lunettes, and use of the Greek Doric Order, are clear precedents for the Anglican chapel interior at Kensal Green (*SJSM*).

7.26 Ceiling and lunette of the Anglican chapel in 2001 (*JMF*).

7.27 Ceiling of the Anglican chapel in 1997. Compare with 7.25 (© *Crown copyright. NMR.BB97/1174*).

apex is a rose of acanthus-leaves surrounded by a Greek-key pattern on a circlet (**7.26-7.27**). Investigation by Dr Bristow has shown that the colour-scheme was originally of cool fawns and beiges. The interior is lit by a lunette over the entablature and by a single window at the (liturgical) east end. The latter is now filled with coloured glass designed by A. T. N. Achet (who worked for Wainwright & Waring, church-window designers), and dates from 1951. Achet's design replaced a painted window[68] that was presented to the chapel by Griffith in 1837, but destroyed in the 1939-45 war (**7.28**).

At first sight it may appear odd that Griffith looked for inspiration to part of a large secular building completed in 1805, but it should be remembered that the Directors of the Company (notably Paul) may well have been anxious to replicate Soane's success, and Griffith had already shown himself adept at reworking ideas by others. Soane's designs for funerary monuments and mausolea were well-publicised, including his sepulchral chapel of 1800 at Tyringham House, Buckinghamshire.[69] C. R. Cockerell had succeeded Soane in his appointment at the Bank in 1833 and could have drawn attention to Soane's work there, and of course there was the Soane-Chadwick connection that may have played an important part in the genesis of the building at Kensal Green.

[68] A plain one would have been more suited to the Greek Revival manner, perhaps with amber glass set in the margin-panes. [69] *See* Summerson (1978), 147-55.

Whilst a comparison of the Anglican chapel and surviving illustrations of the Bank vestibule indicates that the placing of columns and entablatures, the shallowly domed ceiling, and the detail of the enrichment were clearly borrowed from Soane, Griffith's ingenuity in reworking Soane's ideas[70] has given the chapel undeniable presence. The sureness of its proportions, the convincing rhythms of its architecture, and the confident handling of spaces are a tribute to Griffith's personal abilities, and there is no doubt that the chapel and its associated colonnades are among England's most distinguished examples of Greek Revival architecture.

7.28 Restored catafalque, lunettes, and west window (by A. T. N. Achet) in the Anglican chapel, in 1997 (© *Crown copyright. NMR.BB97/1608*).

The Catafalque

A sumptuous catafalque can be raised from the vaults through an opening in the centre of the floor of the Anglican chapel (7.29). Hinged doors cover the opening that was once protected by iron railings, the bases of which may still be seen in the paving. The operating mechanisms for the doors are concealed within the chapel floor beneath iron plates. This catafalque is a precious survival, unique in its virtually unaltered state and retaining its 1840s hydraulic pumping equipment intact (7.30). Originally the lifting-equipment was operated wholly by hand and installed about 1837, soon after the chapel was completed. It appears to have given a great deal of trouble, was always having to be repaired, and was very noisy in operation.

J. C. Loudon, in his book *On The Laying Out, Planting And Managing of Cemeteries*, describes the mechanics of the manually operated system he saw in some detail and his remarks are worth quoting in full:[71]

> in the chapels of some of the new London cemeteries, instead of biers for the coffins, there is a table, the top of which has one or two spaces, each of the width of a coffin, filled in with rollers, and the entire top of the table turns on a pivot. The coffin or coffins, when brought in, are put on the table, by sliding them on the rollers; and, after the service has been performed, the table is turned round on its pivot, when the coffins being thus placed in the right position for going out are carried away by the bearers. The rollers facilitate the sliding on and drawing off of the coffins, and the turning of the table, by means of the pivot, saves the most difficult and awkward portion of the labour performed by the bearers, who, when not much accustomed to it, are apt to stumble, and create alarm in the mourners lest the coffin should fall. When a bier-table of this kind is used, the area left for it

70 Possibly with some assistance from Chadwick, who, after all, described himself as an 'architect and builder'.
71 Although the manual system Loudon viewed was converted to an hydraulic one in 1843-4.

7.29 Catafalque in lowered position in central vault of catacomb in 2000 (*MC.J111200*).

7.30 Hydraulic pump equipment for the catafalque in 2000 (*MC. H111200*).

need not exceed 8 ft. in diameter, which will thus save 4 ft. in the entire length, and the same in the breadth, of the chapel.

A very convenient apparatus of this kind has been put up at the Kensal Green Cemetery. In the body of the chapel is a bier, in the form of an altar, about 8 ft. long, 4 ft. broad, and 4 ft. high, hung round with black velvet. The upper surface of this altar-like structure consists of a top for holding one or two coffins; and, to facilitate the putting on and taking off of these, this plate or top is furnished with rollers. After the desk service has been read, the top containing the coffin or coffins can be turned slowly round by machinery, operated by a small movable winch handle on one side, which is done after the service has been read, when the interment is to take place in the open ground, or in the catacombs at a distance from the chapel;[72] but, when the coffin is to be removed to the vaults under the chapel, there is machinery below, worked by a man there on a signal being given by ringing a small bell, by which the entire bier, and the coffin or coffins which may be on it, are slowly lowered into a central area in the vault beneath. The mourners having descended by a staircase *much too small for a chapel so magnificent in other respects*,[73] the coffins are carried from this area to the vaults, which radiate from it in four directions, and occupy nearly an acre of ground. The machinery by which the bier is lowered consists of two vertical male screws, worked by two female screws or nuts, which are moved by means of two bevelled wheels set in motion by a man turning a windlass handle. This machine, while it lowers the bier through the floor, moves at the same time two horizontal shutters, which gradually close the opening in the floor as the coffin descends from the view of the spectators in the chapel; while, by the time they have arrived in the area below, the bier is already at

72 That is, the old, or north terrace catacomb. 73 Editor's italics. It is curious that the stair is indeed so mean and inadequate. It was intended for use by coffin-bearers only, but it appears that, from an early date, it was also used by mourners for gaining access to the catacomb rather than the wide, shallow, flight of steps to the west of the platform over the catacomb.

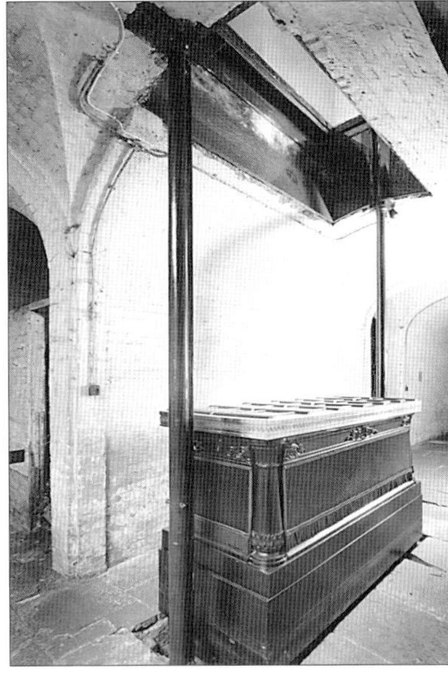

7.31 View in catacomb in 2000 showing the underside of the catafalque in its raised position, the ram that supports it, and the cast columns that provide housing for the guide-wheels and -pins (*MC.F111200*).

7.32 View in catacomb in 2000 showing the catafalque in its lowered position, with the trap-doors giving access open to the chapel above (*MC.G111200*).

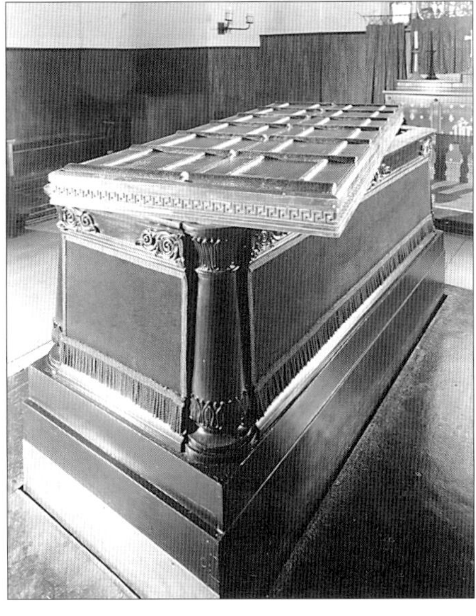

7.33 Restored catafalque in position in the Anglican chapel in 2000 (*MC.B111200*).

7.34 Restored catafalque showing swivelling top in 2000 (*MC.C111200*).

> the bottom, with the coffin on it, ready to be removed to the vault. The great advantage of using the screw mechanism for the descent of the bier is, that the motion can never be otherwise than slow and solemn, and that it cannot run down in case of the handle being set at liberty. This admirable contrivance was invented and executed by Mr. Smith, Engineer, Princes Street, Leicester Square, the patentee of an excellent window shutter, and of several other inventions noticed in our *Encylop. Of Cott. Architecture*.[74] The cost was about 400 l.[75]

In 1843-4 this somewhat troublesome apparatus[76] was replaced by a new hydraulic system, mercifully quieter than its forerunner. The work was completed in 1844 by Bramah & Robinson. The hydraulic lifting-equipment is held in a beautifully engineered 14 ft. deep brick pit below the floor of the catacomb, from which rises a cylinder encasing

74 Loudon (1834), 2066. 75 *See* Loudon (1981), 23-4. 76 It had been a source of worry during the funeral of the Duke of Sussex, which seems to have been the catalyst that prompted its replacement.

the bronze ram (7.31). A manually operated dual pump works the hydraulic engine that allows the catafalque to be raised and lowered as necessary. Two cast-iron columns each side of the pit provide tracing for the guide-wheels and -pins which are fitted to the main bearer-beam. The top of the ram locks into a socket in this main beam, and the ram assembly is supported at the top by iron girders that span the pit (7.29-7.32).

The catafalque or bier itself has a timber frame, with wooden panel-boards reinforced with iron straps and ties: upon this structure are decorative carvings in fruit-wood, and fittings of brass in a Greek-key design. Hangings of black velvet, closely patterned on the original, have been recently (1997) reinstated. The top of the catafalque rotates so that coffins can slide in various directions. It is a remarkable piece of early industrial engineering as well as an item of great opulence, and must have provided a memorable spectacle for mourners as it slowly glided down to the catacomb below. Within the constraints of good conservation practice the whole apparatus and bier have now been returned to full working order[77] (7.33-7.34).

7.35 Typical north-south brick groin-vaulted passage of the catacomb (in 2000) showing the iron grilles protecting the coffins in their *loculi* (*MC.K111200*).

7.36 Bay in the catacomb (in 2000) showing coffins on their shelves protected by cast-iron grilles. Note that the *loculi* on the right have been sealed in (*MC.L111200*).

The Catacomb beneath the Anglican Chapel

The catacomb occupies huge brick-lined vaults in a rectangular space created beneath the chapel's terrace. There are two staircases, one in the middle of the west side of the terrace and the narrow staircase leading from the chapel vestibule. In his *The Victorian Celebration of Death* Professor Curl thus vividly describes the catacomb-vaults as

> ... awesome. In the dark vaults ... coffins ... lie in serried rows. ... Some of the wood has rotted; and the lead lining may be seen. Today, [the catacomb is] an extraordinary reminder of the heroic age of cemetery design.[78]

[77] This was restored by Dorothea Restorations Ltd. and completed in May 1997, the project being commissioned by the Friends of Kensal Green Cemetery, grant-aided by English Heritage and other sponsors. For a recent discussion of the catafalque and its mechanism *see* Pepper (2000), 7-10. [78] Curl (1972), 68-69. I am grateful to Professor Curl for his comments on this Chapter and for some of the annotations.

The catacomb-vaults are symmetrically arranged along straight barrel-vaulted passageways which run north/south (7.35) and east/west (7.29) under the chapel and colonnades. Provision was made for about a thousand coffins and these are laid in bays on stone racks in numbered *loculi*, some with elaborate iron grilles covering the ends, some without (7.36). Several of the *loculi* are sealed with stone tablets and a few with glass windows. Numerous ventilation shafts give a subdued natural light. A drainage system along the passageways is connected to the extensive complex serving the whole of the cemetery. Cast-iron gates were placed at intervals along the corridors.

Monumental Chambers

In 1844 the Monumental Chambers were constructed to Griffith's designs, abutting the north colonnade of the Anglican chapel. They were intended to provide wall-space for inscription-panels and memorials to commemorate those entombed below in the catacomb, and so were illuminated by roof-lights (5.7). Many memorials were erected during the ensuing decades, and in the 1890s the Board decided to build a columbarium within the Chambers. This was created in 1891-2 for urns containing cremated remains, cremation having been declared not an offence provided no nuisance was caused thereby to others, as a result of the *R.* v. *Price* case at Cardiff Assizes in 1884. In his well-known judgement, Sir James Stephen (1829-94) thereby acquitted the eccentric Dr William Price (1800-93) from the supposed crime of having tried to burn the body of his dead son, named, somewhat curiously, Jesus Christ. The Kensal Green columbarium was built by E. M. Lander of Kensal Green to designs by Robert Willey (*c*.1837-1918), architect (5.8).[79] The Chambers and columbarium were badly damaged in World War II and their remains were demolished in 1953. Restoration of other bomb-damaged parts of the Anglican chapel, as recorded on a plaque in the south colonnade, were carried out at this time under the direction of Edward Richard Bingham Harriss (1899-1980).

The Crematorium

This stands in the newer, western end of the cemetery on land bought from the Fillingham estate in the 1850s, and was built in 1938-9 to designs by Gerald Berkeley Wills (1882-1979). It is constructed in a pinkish brick with stone dressings, and consists of a tall central entrance-hall with a distyle *in antis* arrangement of Ionic columns, and chapels on either side. To the rear are two arcaded elements and a sunken landscaped garden. Over the main entrance is the Latin inscription *Mors Janua Vitae*[80] incised in the frieze (6.4, 7.37).

The penetration of natural light and sky through the building was clearly a preoccupation of its designer: the vault linking the two halves of the building is glazed with small square lights flooding the paved courtyard below with daylight (7.38). This courtyard is extended into a terrace on the south side of the building: here are two open loggias (6.5, 7.39) facing a rose-garden centred on a small pool with a fountain. Much

79 *The Daily Graphic* (28 August 1892), 14, describes it: 'In view of the probable great advancement of the practice of cremation in England, the General Cemetery Company has erected a Columbarium for the reception of Cinerary Urns at their cemetery at Kensal Green. The structure, which is placed in the Monumental Chambers, forms a prominent object in the centre of *a hall of some magnitude* (Editor's italics), and contains accommodation for some forty-two urns. There are three tiers of compartments on each of the four sides, and each one is enclosed by a metal-framed, lever-locked door filled with plate glass. The fronts are in fine Caen stone, with panelled pilasters at each angle, and moulded base and cornice. The shafts between the compartments are of polished Sienna Marble, and the panels in the pilasters are filled with polished Rouge Royale. The columbarium, probably unique in London, has been built by Mr E. M. Lander, of Kensal Green, from the designs of the architect, Mr Robert Willey, of Ludgate Hill.'

80 Death the Gateway of Life.

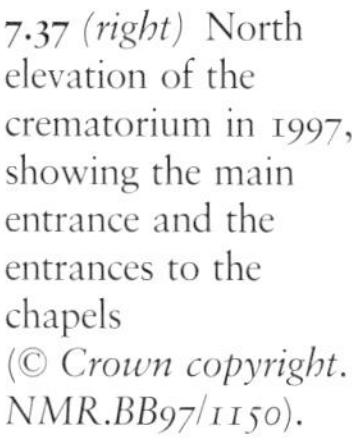

7.37 *(right)* North elevation of the crematorium in 1997, showing the main entrance and the entrances to the chapels (© *Crown copyright. NMR.BB97/1150*).

7.38 *(below)* Interior of the central volume of the crematorium in 1997, showing the segmental ceiling (© *Crown copyright. NMR.BB97/1160*).

7.39 *(below)* Loggias facing the rose-garden behind the crematorium in 1997 (© *Crown copyright. NMR.BB97/1161*).

of the wall-space is given over to simple memorial tablets of a uniform rectangular design. The chapel east of the central hall is enriched inside with oak panelling and a marble bier (**6.3**, **7.40**). It was always intended there should be a second chapel on the western side of the arch and this was eventually fitted out in 1996. To the south side of the crematorium garden is a further secluded garden and war-cemetery (**7.41**).

7.40 Interior of the original (east) crematorium chapel in 1997 (© *Crown copyright. NMR.BB97/1157*).

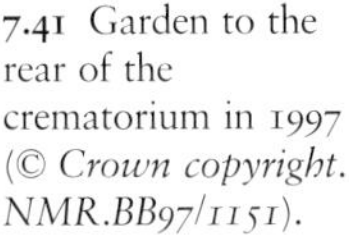

7.41 Garden to the rear of the crematorium in 1997 (© *Crown copyright. NMR.BB97/1151*).

Afterword

The General Cemetery of All Souls contains four outstandingly handsome buildings in the Greek Revival style, all built in the 1830s, and all designed by Griffith. They (the two chapels with catacombs, the north terrace colonnade and catacomb, and the entrance-gate with lodges) comprise a distinguished ensemble of funerary architecture, and deserve to be better known. Griffith's boundary-wall, iron railings, and gates are also very fine. The crematorium added in the 1930s is also a building of considerable dignity, continuing the Classical theme of the cemetery buildings. Although the Dissenters' chapel has been restored and extended, much still needs to be done, especially to the fabric of the Anglican chapel and catacomb, and to the north terrace colonnade and catacomb: the last is in a derelict state at the time of writing.

CHAPTER VIII

Introduction to and Gazetteer of the Monuments in Kensal Green Cemetery

ROGER BOWDLER

Preamble; Gazetteer of the Monuments; Postscript

Tombs are the clothes of the dead;
a grave is but a plain suit,
and a rich monument is one embroidered.

THOMAS FULLER (1608-61):
The Holy State and the Profane State (1642), *Of Tombs.*

Preamble

Most scholars of 19th-century urban and social history, architecture, art, and landscape-design are agreed that the General Cemetery of All Souls, Kensal Green, is a place of exceptional importance. It is an extremely complex historical landscape, densely packed with masonry and statuary, but, curiously, its legion tombs of note are only beginning to receive the notice they deserve. A national lack of interest in commemorative art is beginning to be replaced with a growing concern for its significance and survival.

During the mid-1990s a survey was undertaken of Kensal Green cemetery's myriad monuments in order to revise the listing[1] coverage of the cemetery. Selecting the finest monuments for inclusion in the list proved to be a challenging, if rewarding, activity given the sheer number and quality of tombs there. The purpose of the listing is to highlight a building or structure of particular note, to which particular attention needs to be paid in future debates. For a monument to be listed by the Department of Culture, Media, and Sport, it has to have a solid claim to *national* interest on historical, architectural, or sculptural grounds. It is not lightly undertaken, as it has consequences for the future upkeep and preservation of a tomb. This designation can be used during discussions concerning priorities for conservation: it can be used to help promote a cemetery's interest; it affects eligibility for grant aid; or it can have a real influence if monument clearance is under consideration.

It is a measure of the cemetery's significance that it now possesses far and away more listed monuments than any other English cemetery: West Norwood and Highgate cemeteries, the next most intensively listed, each has around half the number. Cemeteries are infinitely greater than the sums of their parts, however, and it should be stressed that there is no question of a competition taking place here between the great metropolitan necropoleis. In addition, such intangibles as formal planning, planting, compositional juxtapositions, and atmosphere all have their rôles to play. Compared with America and Continental Europe,[2] British cemeteries are, thus far, little studied. It is hoped that a better understanding of our nation's sepulchral inheritance will be encouraged as a result of this introduction to Kensal Green cemetery's unsurpassed collection of memorials, and that greater attention will be given to their appreciation and protection in the future.

What follows here is a gazetteer of the present author's personal selection of the cemetery's finest monuments. They have been chosen for a variety of reasons, as the following entries make clear. Various criteria lie behind the decision to list them: these include sculptural or architectural qualities; historic interest (perhaps associated with the person or persons commemorated, the designer of the monument, or other allusions that will be referred to in the specific entries); unusual materials used in their construction; symbolism; or other curious aspects. Selectivity is inevitable, and, as knowledge increases, further additions will no doubt be made. It should be remembered, however, that monuments remain the legal responsibility of heirs-at-law of the grave-owners, and it is not up to the General Cemetery Company to maintain individual tombs (unless, of course, an agreement to keep a structure in good repair in perpetuity is still in force). Yet it is all too true that many of Kensal Green's many monuments do not undergo any sort of regular maintenance at all.

There remains much work still to be done in the field of coemeterial studies, a discipline still in its infancy. Outdoor monuments exposed to England's ever-changing climate continue to decay, and, increasingly, attempts are being made across the nation

[1] A 'listed' building or other man-made structure is one officially listed as being of special architectural or historic interest, which cannot be demolished or altered without official consent. [2] *See*, for example, Andalucía (1993), *passim*; Diéquez Patao and Giménez (*Eds.*) (2000), *passim*; Etlin (1984*a*), *passim*; Fischer and Schein (*Eds.*) (1987), *passim*; and Hunt and Schuyler (*Eds*). (1984), *passim*; among many other studies listed in the Select Bibliography.

to re-use burial-space and clear older graves and memorials. Cemetery monuments face an uncertain future in some cases, and listing designations will assume considerable practical importance in these discussions.

Henry Vivian-Neal's pioneering *Paths of Glory* offers a far more detailed historical survey of the inhabitants of Kensal Green cemetery than this gazetteer, and readers in pursuit of such information are directed towards his work.[3] Where early references or depictions of the monuments have been found, these are cited. This gazetteer is arranged sequentially, by square-number,[4] and starts at the east end, in the unconsecrated (or Dissenters') section, and continues westward. Those tombs previously listed are noted as such by means of an asterisk. The condition assessments are included as a guide to future conservation strategies and are based on initial, rather than detailed, inspection.

Gazetteer of the Monuments

1 JAMES POOLE (*c.*1778-1843)

[3899/10/RS]. A chest-tomb of Welsh Slate, with two panels per side, one per end, each containing cusped ogive arches, set between clustered shafts. A very unusual monumental use of this material, more commonly used for headstones.[5] Condition: poor. West side becoming detached, slate beginning to laminate (**12.4**).

*2 ROBERT OWEN MEMORIAL (1879)

[26655/14/PS]. A pink and grey-granite obelisk on sandstone base with bronze portrait-relief on east face. Erected by public subscription to the philanthropist Robert Owen (1771-185), who is buried in Wales. A rare instance of a non-funerary monument in a private cemetery, erected in memory of the pioneering socialist and founder of the New Lanark experiment in benign employment, a manifestation of the mid-Victorian Nonconformist awareness of its own heritage: compare with the Martyrs' Memorial at the cemetery of All Saints, Nunhead. Condition: good, restored in 1997 (**8.1**).

3 THE REFORMERS' MEMORIAL (1885)

[29691/14/PS]. A grey-granite square pillar on a sandstone base, signed by *J. S. Farley*, masons. Erected by Joseph W. Corfield in 1885 'to the memory of men and women who have generously given their time and means to improve the conditions and enlarge the happiness of all classes of society'. Lists of names of reformers and radicals on north and east sides (together with further names added in 1907 by Emma Corfield): an interesting glimpse into the composition of the Radical Parnassus. The monument echoes the Robert Owen memorial, and is a second instance of a non-funerary memorial in the cemetery's Nonconformist section. Condition: good, restored in 1997 (**8.1**).

4 JOHN MCDOUALL STUART (1815-66)

[19834/9-15/PS]. A grey-granite pedestal with hipped ledger-slab, signed *Carey and Co.* of Kensal Green. The epitaph describes Stuart as 'South Australian explorer, the first who crossed the continent from the Southern to the Indian Ocean'. Stuart was the first man to cross the centre of the Continent, and the tomb was erected by his sisters. Listed for colonial/geographical interest: the calmness of the grave is a far cry from his epic journeys. Condition: fair. The pedestal and ledger-slab are in good condition, but the obelisk is missing, having fallen at some time during the 20th century.[6]

[3] Vivian-Neal (1999), a guide that will be subjected to further revisions and updating in the future. All the locations in the Gazetteer have been checked and corrected by Mr Robert Moulder, and it is to him and to the Editor that the present writer records his grateful thanks for the many alterations and additions that have helped to bring this Chapter to its present form. [4] See the Editor's *Explanatory Note on the Layout of the Cemetery* at the beginning of the book. [5] Poole was in trade as a cooper in Great Titchfield Street. The grave also contains the body of his son-in-law, James Meyrick, auctioneer, surveyor, and estate agent (d. 1861), formerly of Bruin Llewellyn, Ffestiniog, Merioneth, which may explain the use of Welsh Slate for the monument. [6] A photograph of the monument, complete with obelisk, was published in *The Magazine of The Friends of Kensal Green Cemetery*, **xxvii** (December 2000), opposite page 5.

8.1 Memorial to Robert Owen (*left*—[26655/14/PS]) and the Reformers' Memorial (*right* – [29691/14/PS]). Both are of granite, of contrasting colour. Photograph of 2001. *See* Chapter VIII, §2 (*MC.P080101*).

8.2 Headstone [3174/21/RS] of Edward Scriven in 2001. *See* Chapter VIII, §8 (*MC.A7*).

5 GEORGE and MARY WAUGH (*c*.1802-73 and 1805-86)

[1995/**15**/IR]. A statuary marble figure of a seated woman mourning over an urn and holding a bowl, over the inscription 'I am the Resurrection and the Life'. Tall rectangular plinth with inscription in lead letters. Epitaph on south side commemorates Fanny Waugh, first wife of the Pre-Raphaelite painter William Holman Hunt (1827-1910), who died in Florence in 1866. Visually above average, the historical interest of the inscription makes it of particular note.[7] Condition: poor; the marble has begun to sugar, and some lead letters are missing.

6 DABODA DEWAJEE (d. 1861)[8]

[16848/**16**/2]. Grave-marker of red sandstone (from the Delhi area of North India) on a weathered base of British red sandstone: this formerly bore an inscription which has all but perished, and the tomb is only identifiable from the General Cemetery Company's records. Dewajee was an Indian judge: this is an apparently unique example of an Indian monument, derived from Mughal examples, deliberately imported to England. English marble monuments were despatched in their hundreds to India, but this shows that the trade occasionally ran the other way. Condition: poor; upper (Indian) part generally sound but with some detached fragments, but the lower part is very weathered and the whole is beginning to lean over.

7 REV. RIDLEY HAIM HERSCHELL (1807-64)

[18459/**16**/RS]. A two-stage monument by *E. J. Physick*. The statuary marble sarcophagus stands on a raised chest of Portland Stone with paired angle colonnettes of granite. Herschell was a prominent German-Jewish convert to Christianity, whose epitaph commences 'A Hebrew by birth, educated in the Jewish faith, converted in early youth to belief in Christ, and evermore devoted to the service of his master'. A prominently placed tomb to a prominent Nonconformist divine, and a powerful composition too.[9] Condition: fair.

8 EDWARD SCRIVEN (1775-1841)

[3174/**21**/RS]. A Portland Stone headstone by *Charles Harriott Smith* (1792-1864), a sculptor and authority on building-stones, with a profile portrait-medallion surmounted by a garland of bay-leaves. Scriven, described here as 'an eminent engraver', founded the Artists' Benevolent Fund in 1810.[10] Condition: much overall weathering; the epitaph is barely legible (**8.2** and **9.21**).

9 ELIZABETH (d. 1893) and CHARLES BROUGHTON BOWMAN

[192/**22**/3]. A Portland Stone Ionic column set on a square plinth, surmounted with a capital and urn of artificial stone (as is the base) of *c*.1835. Among the first generation of monuments in the

7 Waugh, Chemist to the Queen, was also father-in-law of the sculptor, Thomas Woolner (1825-92). 8 The General Cemetery Company Records spell the name 'Dawajee', but other sources (e.g. the Bishop's Transcripts) give it as Dewajee. 9 *See* Croft (1867), 73. 10 Hakewill (1851), Plate 27.

8.3 Gothic monument [12687/27/3] over the grave of Feargus O'Connor (1794-1855) in 2001. *See* Chapter VIII, §12 (*MC.D030101*).

8.4 Gothic canopied tomb [14166/31/PS] of Viscount Strangford, by Edward James Physick (1829-1906), in 2001. *See* Chapter VIII, §13 (MC.C030101).

cemetery, and a fine example of a canonical Neoclassical monument type. Visually it forms a focal point at the entrance to the Anglican section. Bowman was the Cemetery Company's first Solicitor and Secretary, and is buried in the old cemetery, Windsor, Nova Scotia; his wife died in 1893 and was also buried with C. B. Bowman at Windsor, N.S.[11] Condition: fair; some losses to urn and overall weathering of the shaft (**12.10**).

10 WYNDHAM LEWIS (1779-1838)

[1489/**26**/IR]. Steeply pointed pyramid of Portland Stone on a raised base: it has projecting panels on each face with armorial or lotus-flower reliefs. A heavy sandstone slab lies over the vault entrance. Lewis was a Tory MP whose widow married Disraeli.[12] Condition: fair (**9.26**).

11 WILLIAM PRICE LEWIS (1783-1848)

[7277/**27**/IR]. A squat Portland Stone obelisk with battered sides and anthemion finials; the central stage sports shallow segmental pediments containing armorial or anthemion reliefs, flanked by angle acroteria. A heavy sandstone slab marks the entrance to the vault. A particularly rich example of first generation Neoclassical cemetery monuments, and one which, with its pyramidal neighbour, forms a fine pair epitomising tendencies in Neoclassical funerary architecture at the end of the Georgian period.[13] Condition: fair; some weathering and cracking at corners of lower section.

*12 FEARGUS O'CONNOR (1794-1855)

[12687/**27**/3]. A hexagonal spirelet of Portland Stone on a sandstone base, with an inset marble inscription panel. The epitaph commences: 'this monument erected by subscription chiefly from the working classes ... while philanthropy is a virtue and patriotism not a crime, will the name of O'CONNOR be admired and this monument respected'. O'Connor, a Radical MP and proprietor of the *Northern Star*, formed the very pinnacle of the Chartist movement in 1848 but died insane. Radicals tended towards the Classical style: this tomb is notably Gothic. Condition: fair (**8.3**).

13 GEORGE AUGUSTUS FREDERICK PERCY SYDNEY SMYTHE, 7th VISCOUNT STRANGFORD and 2nd BARON PENSHURST (1818-57)

[14166/**31**/PS]. A sandstone ledger within a Gothic canopy of Portland Stone, guarded by Carrara Marble angels by *Edward Physick*. The canopy has two cusped arches per side, carried on sandstone colonnettes, with drip-moulds above. Angle-set crocketed finials prop the corners. On the north side is an inscription to Percy Ellen Frederick William Smythe, 8th and last Viscount

[11] The grave in Kensal Green contains three bodies: two Bowmans, probably infant daughters (d. 1834 and 1841) and a Miss Mary Flexney (d. 1852). [12] Hakewill (1851), Plate 4. [13] The Revd. William Price Lewis of New House, Glamorgan, was the brother of Wyndham Lewis (*see* §10).

Strangford (1825-69). A Tory MP, the 7th Viscount as a prominent member of the Young England movement and is believed to be the model for the hero of Disraeli's 1844 novel, *Coningsby, or The New Generation* (1844). He fought in what was said to be the last duel to take place in England, in 1852. The soot-besmirched angels possess great grace: this is as close as one gets to Pre-Raphaelite monumental sculpture. A rock, symbolising Christian steadfastness, is placed on the ledger-slab. Condition: poor; the canopy weathered but sound; the blackened angels within need closer investigation (**8.4** and **9.13**).

14 PHILIP HARDWICK (1792-1870)

[11638/31/PS]. A humble pair of sandstone slabs with Gothic lead lettering, marble cross with instrument of the Passion. These commemorate the Hardwick dynasty of architects: Thomas (1752-1829 – buried at Brentford), Philip (1792-1870 – designer of the Euston Arch [wantonly destroyed in 1962]), and Philip Charles (1822-92 – responsible for the exquisite Beauchamp Almshouses and chapel, Newland, Worcestershire [1862-4]). They clearly intended their buildings to speak rather more eloquently on their behalf than their monument. Condition: very dirty.

15 JOSEPH RICHARDSON (*c.* 1790-1855)

[27918/32/RS]. Monolithic obelisk of pink Peterhead Granite on a square pedestal above a stepped base. Richardson, of Cumberland, is here described as 'Inventor of the Instruments of the Rock, Bell, and Steel Band'. The largest obelisk in the cemetery, and a powerful display of the massy potential of machine-polished granite.[14] Condition: good (**12.6**).

16 MARY SCOTT HOGARTH (1819-37)

[997/33/RS].[15]

17 WILLIAM MAKEPEACE THACKERAY (1811-63)

[18177/36/1]. A thick marble slab, monogrammed on the south end, over a grey-granite base upon a red-brick plinth, standing within cast-iron dwarf rails. Thackeray, author of *Vanity Fair* (1847-8), *Barry Lyndon* (1844), *Pendennis* (1848-50), and much else, is a colossal figure in terms of the Victorian novel. This reticent memorial is paired with a near-identical one to his friend from childhood, John Leech (1817-64), the outstanding illustrator of his day: in death they are divided only by an interrupting tomb. Compare the monuments of Wilkie Collins and Trollope for other instances of highly restrained memorials to outstanding writers. Condition: cleaned in 1998, but weathered.

18 GUSTAV E. (*c.*1858-1901) and NINON (*c.* 1864-95) MICHAELIS

[37384/37/RS]. A tall, curved panel of Carrara Marble, inscribed at top NINON: in front is an elegantly draped figure of a grieving Grecian woman bestowing a garland on a tomb. An exceptional example of late-Victorian commercial statuary, prominently located on the main avenue. This monument would not be out of place in any cemetery in the Christian world.[16] Condition: dirty, otherwise sound (**9.1** and **10.12**).

19 JOHN ROBINSON McCLEAN (1813-73)

[23912/37/RS]. Massive Carrara Marble Roman altar, on tall granite base, designed by *Edward Adams* and carved by *George Sinclair*, inspired by the monument of Naevoleia Tyche at

14 This grave contains only the body of one of Joseph Richardson's sons (Samuel [d. 1888]). Joseph is buried under a humble headstone [12373/47/6]. 15 A Portland Stone headstone with acroteria. The modern tablet within the kerb explains her connection with Charles Dickens: she was his sister-in-law and died aged seventeen. Dickens, a devoted admirer, composed her epitaph. The literary interest greatly outweighs the visual. Owing to the numbering system used throughout this book, mention of the headstone has had to be retained in the Gazetteer, but the monument will *not* appear on any official list for the present. It is mentioned here only for its connection with Dickens, and its inclusion does not imply official listing. Condition: much-weathered; the renewed inscription is, however, generally legible. 16 This monument is twelve feet (*c.*3.66 metres) tall, and weighs between five and six tons (*c.*5,000-6,000 kilograms). The grave-owner was Sir Maximilian Michaelis, who died in Zürich in 1932. Sir Max, of German descent, was a South African diamond millionaire, and left his collection of Dutch paintings to the South African Government: it formed the nucleus of the National Gallery in Cape Town. He bequeathed £20,000 to the University of Cape Town to found the Michaelis School of Fine Art. *See* Rosenthal (1966).

8.5 Fine Neoclassical tomb [23912/37/RS] of John Robinson McClean in 1997. *See* Chapter VIII, §19 (*JSC*).

8.6 Tombstone [8590/41/PS] of Sir Marc Isambard Brunel (1769-1849); his wife, Sophie (1775-1855); their son, Isambard Kingdom Brunel (1806-59); I. K. Brunel's wife, Mary Elizabeth (1831-81); *their* sons, Isambard (1837-1902) and Henry Marc (1842-1903); and other members of the Brunel family. Photograph of 1997. *See* Chapter VIII, §20 (© *Crown copyright. NMR.AA 97/1176*).

8.7 Monument [20242/47/RS] designed by William Burges to Captain Charles Spencer Ricketts, R. N. (1788-1867), in 2001. It was built in 1867-8. The chest and elaborately carved canopy are of Portland Stone. Supporting columns are of polished Peterhead Granite, contrasting strongly with the deeply corroded colonnettes of green Cornish Serpentinite [20242/47/RS]. *See* Chapter VIII, §21 (*MC.G030101*).

Pompeii.[17] The inscription-panel is set in a border of rinceaux. McClean was an MP, FRS, and President of the Institute of Chartered Engineers: among his works were the Plymouth Breakwater and Barrow docks. The monument also commemorates Francis (Frank) William McClean (1837-1904), the astronomer, son of J. R. McClean.[18] Condition: fair (**8.5**).

*20 SIR MARC (1769-1849) and ISAMBARD KINGDOM BRUNEL (1806-59)

[8590/**41**/PS]. A rectangular block of Carrara Marble with raised lead letters, grey granite kerb, designed by *Sir Marc Brunel*. This austere monument to two of the greatest of all engineers belongs to a tradition of plain, austere memorials to men of science: compare mathematician Charles Babbage's (1791-1871) monument [23003/**84**/PS], or the fellow railway engineer Joseph Locke's (1805-60) memorial [6865/**99**/PS].[19] Condition: sound (**8.6**).

*21 CAPTAIN CHARLES SPENCER RICKETTS (1788-1867)

[20242/**47**/RS]. 1867-8 by *William Burges* (1827-1881). An exuberantly gabled Portland Stone canopy, densely crocketed, on eight ringed shafts of Peterhead Granite. On each side are three trefoil-headed openings: each crocketed gable has a tympanum enriched with a relief of a green man, and terminates with a robust crocketed finial. Gargoyle waterspouts animate the corners,

[17] Gell and Gandy (1852), Plates III, IV, V, VI, VII, VIII, and *passim*. [18] *The Builder*, **xxxiv**/1718 (8 January 1876), 36. *See also D.N.B. 1901-1911* (1920), 505-6. [19] Brunel's successor at the Great Western Railway, Michael Lane (*c*.1803-68), is commemorated by a similar monument [20809/**115**/PS], sited just north-east of the Anglican chapel.

and beast-heads guard the gabled sides. The chest at the heart of the tomb apes a medieval bier, the sides of which are embellished with Achievements of Arms and the Union Flag and enriched with mastic-filled inlay: it is carried on eight colonnettes of Serpentinite. Ricketts was a naval officer and later a Buckinghamshire squire: the tomb was erected by his daughter and son-in-law.[20] Condition: despite recent cleaning, poor. The Serpentinite colonnettes are perishing and wilful damage has snapped off stonework (**8.7**).

22 OWEN JONES (1809-74)

[24334/47/RS]. A chaste Athenian *stele* of Carrara Marble with eared anthemion terminal, standing over a plain coped ledger slab. Jones, a key figure in High Victorian design, responsible for overseeing the 1851 Great Exhibition and author of *The Grammar of Ornament*, surely selected this design himself. Condition: fair.

23 HENRY EDWARD KENDALL (1776-1875)

[2397/48/RS]. A large Gothic monument of Portland Stone, enriched with Minton tiles, erected in 1853 by the architect *H. E. Kendall* as his family tomb. It consists of an elephantine Gothic grave-marker, with a cross set within a lobed surround, in front of which is a seated angel, arms crossed over the breast, watching over the hipped and enriched slab. Flanking the angel are trefoil reliefs with Freemasonic emblems. As outlined in Chapter III above, Kendall was the winner of the competition to design the cemetery in 1832, but his Gothic scheme was never built; the prominent position of this plot was perhaps by way of a consolation prize. Condition: fair. However, many of the tiles are loose or missing: they inject a vital note of polychromy into the sepulchral sea of stones (**8.8**).

24 MARGARET GREGORY (d. 1832), her husband, BARNARD GREGORY (1796-1852), and Margaret Gregory's uncle, JOHN THOMPSON (1756-1843)

[4031/48/RS]. A Portland Stone and Carrara Marble structure prominently positioned at the head of the avenue, made up of twin projecting aedicules on quoined bases, linked by a central bay with the eroded marble inscription panel. Each aedicule, with its odd Egyptianising bell-capitals, contains a niche with plinths, the western one inscribed TEMPUS FUGIT and the eastern one MEMENTO MORI: the statues or urns that once filled them have long since vanished. An unusually architectural, late Neoclassical memorial that almost attains mausoleum status.[21] Condition: poor (**8.9**).

[20] *See* Crook (1981), 227-8. [21] Margaret Gregory, the second wife of Barnard Gregory, was the first person to be buried in the cemetery (31 January 1833, only a week after the Consecration), and her husband was owner and editor of *The Satirist, or Censor of the Times*, who prospered by extorting money from persons who did not wish to be the subjects of damaging articles. Thompson, who made a fortune as a brewers' surveyor and valuer, was originally buried in [3993], but was subsequently re-interred here. During his lifetime he presented his collection of antique furniture (including the ebony bedstead and pontifical chair of Cardinal Wolsey) to Queen Victoria on the occasion of the birth of the Prince of Wales (later King Edward VII) in 1841. He built Frognall Priory, Hampstead, to his own designs. *See Gentleman's Magazine*, **xx** (July 1843), 102.

8.8 Muscular Gothic monument [2397/48/RS] of Henry Edward Kendall, designed by him. Photograph of 2001. *See* Chapter VIII, §23 (*MC.H060101*).

8.9 Monument [4031/48/RS] of Barnard and Margaret Gregory and John Thompson in 1972. Thompson was originally buried in 3993. *See* Chapter VIII, §24 (*London Metropolitan Archives. The photograph was taken by the Greater London Council Photographic Unit, Department of Architecture and Civic Design, Serial No 72/753*).

8.10 O'Brien/Perry mausoleum [10833/48/RS], showing the extensive water-damage to the Mansfield Red Sandstone of the side walls, the deep rotting of the green Pennant Sandstone of the front face promoted by the insets of pale Jurassic limestone. The carved Achievements at the top of the tympanum of the gable are of Carrara Marble. Photograph of 2001. *See* Chapter VIII, §26 (*MC.J060101*).

25 JAMES COMBE, M.I.C.E. (*c.* 1806-67)

[9901/48/RS]. A prominently sited mausoleum of pink Peterhead and Grey Granite signed by *A. MacDonald* of Aberdeen and dated 1852. The grey cell, surmounted with an arca with a cross on top, has a framed granite door beneath an HIS-emblazoned lozenge on the east side; the plinth, the angle-set corner buttresses with acroterion finials, and the superstructure are all of contrasting pink granite. An early and flamboyant example of machine-polished Scottish granite, erected in memory of Combe's wife.[22] Condition: good. (**9.28**).

26 LIEUTENANT-GENERAL JAMES PERRY (*c.*1791-1863) and SIR PATRICK O'BRIEN, BART. (1823-95)

[10833/48/RS]. A large, disintegrating Gothic mausoleum of divers sandstones with Portland Stone dressings and decorations, erected in *c.*1868 and embellished by Ida Sophia, Lady O'Brien (d. 1910 – who was Perry's widow), in *c.*1895 when widowed for the second time. A gabled single-cell structure with finials on each end, the south elevation has a blocked arched door, and a tympanum of Carrara Marble depicting the Deposition set within voussoirs of orange sandstone below an heraldic relief. Single arched windows (blocked) to east and west sides. The north side has triple lancets and quatrefoil openings. A formerly splendid polychrome pile. Condition: very bad (**8.10**).

27 MARYAN or MARION ROSS (*c.*1835-68)

[21157/48-56/2]. A Gothic mausoleum of Bath Stone with Portland Stone statuettes and Serpentine shafts. The south elevation has a blocked arched door below a cinquefoil panel containing an armorial Achievement in mosaic (itself unusual) with the motto THINK ON. The three-bay side walls are lined with paired (and blocked) lancet-windows flanked by shafts of Serpentine supporting finials in the form of angels (some missing); below are inscription-panels of green granite set below a depressed arch. Peering through the damaged north window, the interior can be seen. This was formerly stencilled: the exceptional richness of the Ross mausoleum was not confined to the exterior.[23] Condition: very bad, having been damaged by a bomb on 19 April 1941.

28 JAMES MORISON (1770-1840)

[383/50/RS]. A powerful Portland Stone mausoleum (of 1836-7) with battered walls of massive (almost cyclopean) ashlar blocks and a cast-iron door, designed by *Robert Shout* (*c.*1763-1843), mason.[24] The northern pediment contains an armorial relief; prominent acroteria define the corners. Below the frieze of wreaths and fillets are suspended garlands. One of the largest and most impressive of the earliest memorials, strongly influenced by Parisian exemplars. Morison, a proprietor of patent medicines called Morison's Pills, was popularly known as 'the Hygeist', and was an early promoter of the cemetery. The original design is in the Victoria and Albert Museum. Condition: poor (**4.27**).

29 CHARLES (1775-1854) and FRANCES ANNE ('FANNY') KEMBLE (1809-93)

[11981/55/RS]. A ledger-slab of inscribed Portland Stone with a segmental top, on a York Stone base. Its plainness belies the interest of its occupants. Charles, younger brother of the thespian, John Philip Kemble (1757-1823), was one of the great actors of Regency London, renowned for playing romantic and comic parts. Fanny Kemble, his daughter, was also a celebrated Shakespearian actress with a great reputation on both sides of the Atlantic. An instance of historic interest greatly outweighing visual impressiveness: a shrine need not be ornate. Condition: fair but weathered.

*30 SIR RICHARD MAYNE (1796-1868)

[21708/56/RS]. A pink Peterhead Granite obelisk (the second tallest in the cemetery), perched on an inscribed podium, standing on a two-stage base of grey granite. An Irish barrister, Mayne was the first Joint Commissioner of the Metropolitan Police, an office he held for over forty years; this monument was erected by the Police. Condition: good.

22 *See The Builder*, **xii**/604 (2 September 1854), 460. 23 Mrs Ross was the wife of Captain George Ernest Augustus Ross, FRGS, FGS (d. 1900), whose body is not within. 24 Shout is entombed in [4238/**CAT. B**/Pub. Vault 25].

8.11 Cenotaph of Major-General The Honourable Sir William Casement (1780-1844), of Portland Stone and artificial stone [5400/**56**/RS], in 2001. *See* Chapter VIII, §31 (*MC.K060101*).

8.12 Granite Molesworth mausoleum [12766/**56**/RS] in 2001. *See* Chapter VIII, §33 (*MC.E130101*).

8.13 Monument [23601/**56**/RS] of Mary Eleanor Gibson in 1972. *See* Chapter VIII, §34 (*London Metropolitan Archives. The photograph was taken by the Greater London Council Photographic Unit, Department of Architecture and Civic Design, Serial No 72/742*).

*31 GENERAL SIR WILLIAM CASEMENT (1780-1844)

[5400/**56**/RS]. An artificial stone and Portland Stone canopied monument by *E. M. Lander*, Kensal Green's resident statuary. On a tall Portland Stone base stands a coffin, draped with Casement's cloak, and topped with his bicorne and sword. The canopy, with its Egyptianising cavetto cornice enriched with lotus-leaf decoration, is borne by four telamones in the form of Indian bearers, each wearing a turban and with his arms crossed. The cast-iron railings consist of cannon-barrels. Casement, for long a senior figure in the government of Bengal, died on the eve of his return to Britain. This is a cenotaph: Casement lies under a similar (but figureless) monument in the New Burial-Ground, South Circular Road, Calcutta, with an almost identical inscription.[25] As a tribute to a Soldier of the Empire this is among the greatest of all Victorian cemetery monuments. Condition: poor (**8.11** and **12.9**).

32 LUDWIG ALEXANDER BLUMBERG (*c*.1803-57).

[13881/**56**/RS]. A large Classical mausoleum of Carrara Marble with grey granite Corinthian columns, bronze capitals, and a bronze door (partly bricked up). Within the shallow pediments on each face are ventilation openings. One of the largest (and probably one of the costliest) mausolea in the cemetery, prominently positioned on the Centre Avenue.[26] Condition: poor, having been bomb-damaged on 19 April 1941.

33 SIR WILLIAM MOLESWORTH, BART. (1810-55)

[12766/**56**/RS]. A grey granite mausoleum with shallow pyramidal roof, by the mason-sculptor *John Thomas* (1813-62). Steps lead down to the now-blocked entrance of this severely monumental depository for the dead. Molesworth was a Whig MP, a reforming Colonial Secretary under Palmerston, and an associate of John Stuart Mill (1806-73); the epitaph reads 'A firm adherence to convictions the result of deep thought won for him the title of an honest statesman'. His widow, Lady Andalusia (1809-88), a leading Victorian singer and hostess, known as 'Lady Moley', is buried here too. Condition: fair, save for the door (**8.12**).

*34 MARY ELEANOR GIBSON (1854-72)

[23601/**56**/RS]. An open canopied tomb of Carrara Marble, by *J. S. Farley*, mason. The coped coffin, with its frieze of lilies, stands within a peristyle of 12 Corinthian columns, three per corner, with a frieze (again of lilies) running around the entablature. From this rises a baldacchino of four angels; their outstretched left arms once supported a crown or wreath. This fusion of architectural

[25] *The Bengal Obituary* (1848), 273. [26] Blumberg was a partner in the firm of Berens, Blumberg, & Co., of 33 St Paul's Churchyard, London, and 60 Rue de Bondy, Paris, importers and dealers in French, German, and British fancy goods. In his Will, Blumberg directed that he was to be buried in the South Metropolitan Cemetery, West Norwood, and that no more than £300 was to be spent on his memorial. His estate was valued at £60,000, a considerable sum then.

8.14 Monument [17933/56/PS] to William Mulready, R. A. (1786-1863), in 2001, designed by Godfrey Sykes (1824-66), and made by James Pulham & Son. *See* Chapter VIII, §35 (*MC.L060101*).

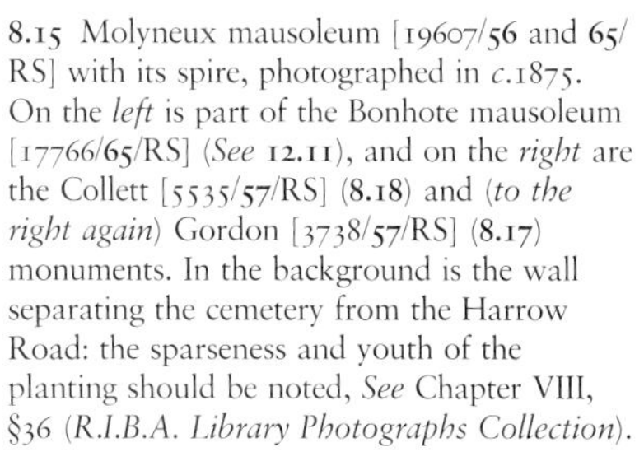

8.15 Molyneux mausoleum [19607/56 and 65/RS] with its spire, photographed in *c.*1875. On the *left* is part of the Bonhote mausoleum [17766/65/RS] (*See* **12.11**), and on the *right* are the Collett [5535/57/RS] (**8.18**) and (*to the right again*) Gordon [3738/57/RS] (**8.17**) monuments. In the background is the wall separating the cemetery from the Harrow Road: the sparseness and youth of the planting should be noted, *See* Chapter VIII, §36 (*R.I.B.A. Library Photographs Collection*).

masonry and figure-sculpture constitutes one of the most flamboyant of all Victorian cemetery monuments, and demonstrates that commercial statuary firms were capable of extravagant flights of fancy. Condition poor: the marble is beginning to sugar, and the underlying structural stability of the monument is causing increasing concern (**8.13** and **10.4**).

*35 WILLIAM MULREADY (1786-1863)

[17933/56/PS]. A recumbent effigy within a canopy of artificial stone, designed by *Godfrey Sykes* and made by *James Pulham and Son*, a firm better known for 'Pulhamite', or artificial rocks for garden embellishment. Mulready wears the gown of a member of the Legion d'Honneur, a mildly mischievous smile, and lies on a rolled mat, as befits a Tudorbethan tomb. The symbolism celebrates Mulready the artist: on the sides of the stepped base are incised versions of his best-known paintings; on the projecting plinths of the six Portland Stone columns which carry the canopy are reliefs of palettes, brushes, and scrolls; and the frieze is decorated with wreaths and garlands. The Irish-born Mulready was one of the most popular early Victorian painters, specialising in *genre* scenes, and, like his tomb's designer and modeller, he was closely connected with the South Kensington School of Art.[27] This monument was exhibited at the 1867 Paris Exposition Universelle, where it won a prize. It is among the finest outdoor tombs ever erected in memory of a British artist.[28] Condition: fair (**8.14** and **12.8**).

*36 EDMUND MOLYNEUX (1798-1864)

[19607/56&65/RS]. A large octagonal Gothic mausoleum by the architect *John Gibson* (1817-92), executed by *John Underwood*, mason. It is a mixture of pink Peterhead Granite and Carrara Marble on a base of grey Rubislaw Granite, with a panelled door of bronze. Each side sports a crocketed gable with finial, under which are arched panels with shields set in the tympana, over rectangular panels of granite: above the door is a cusped trefoil-headed opening. Each panel is

[27] Mulready also designed the short-lived 'Mulready Envelope' for the penny postage system, introduced by (Sir) Rowland Hill (1795-1879) in 1840, but quickly superseded by the adhesive postage-stamp. [28] It was renovated in April 1938 at the expense of the Royal Society of Arts at a cost of £9 12s. 6d.

8.16 High Victorian Gothic mausoleum of the Molyneux family, designed by John Gibson. Photograph of 1997. *See* Chapter VIII, §36 (*JSC*).

8.17 Monument of John Gordon [3738/57/RS]. The urn beneath the canopy has been stolen since the photograph was taken in 1997. *See* Chapter VIII, §37. On the *right* is part of the Collett memorial (*see* **8.18**) (© *Crown copyright. NMR.AA97/1160*).

flanked by clusters of triple granite shafts with foliate capitals, supporting praying angels and crocketed pinnacles. The upper stage of the mausoleum, with its frieze of trefoils and ball-flower decoration, originally supported a short spire (**8.15**). The door on the south side is embellished with eight panels with a six-pointed star in each and the family name MOLYNEUX inscribed along the stile. The whole is set within cast-iron Gothic railings, and is among the most opulent of High Victorian Gothic mausolea in any cemetery. Its inscription reads:

> Edmund Molyneux / Son of William Molyneux / Of Sandfield Liverpool / Born 6th September 1781 / Died 19th November 1864 / Eliza Harriet / Widow of the above / Born 30th November 1809 / Died 1st July 1872.

Around the monument is another Gothic inscription which reads:

> The Family Vault of Edmund Molyneux Esq H.B.M. Consul for the State of Georgia died in Paris on the 19. Nov 1864. This edifice over his remains was erected to his memory by his sorrowing widow and children.

Condition: fair, having been conserved in 1996, but seedlings were growing from the upper parts in 2001, and the mausoleum suffered from further vandalism in the same year (**8.16**).

37 JOHN GORDON (1802-40)[29]

[3738/57/RS]. A Greek Revival aedicule of Portland Stone upon a York Stone base. The four tapering square columns support a heavy pedimented canopy with horns in the form of Egyptianising heads; within the frontal pediment is a relief of a butterfly and a tail-biting snake, emblematic of resurrection and eternity. Below this is the rather more secular armorial Achievement. The canopy stands on a two-stage base and formerly sheltered an urn; this has been missing since 1997. The monument, closely based on Parisian exemplars such as the tomb of Molière and other monuments in Père-Lachaise cemetery (**1.11** and **2.1**), is among the finest Greek Revival outdoor memorials of its day.[30] Condition: fair (**8.17**).

*38 JOHN COLLETT (1798-1866)

[5535/57/RS]. A Portland Stone Greek Doric aedicule on a tall base, erected in *c.*1846 in memory of Collett's first wife Emma (d. 1845). Within the aedicule, which is capped with a full entablature and pedimental roof, is a large, unadorned, and severe block. The outer rail and posts are also of Portland Stone. A distinguished late Neoclassical monument, showing the influence of French exemplars such as General Foy's monument in Père-Lachaise cemetery, Paris, of 1825, designed

29 A West Indian proprietor. 30 Hakewill (1851), Plate 13. *See also* Pugin and Heath (1829-31), illustration entitled 'Monument de la Famille Bouchée' in Père-Lachaise cemetery, drawn by Joseph Nash (1809-78) (**2.1**).

8.18 Greek Revival Portland Stone monument over the family vault of John Collett, Liberal MP for Athlone from 1843 [5535/57/RS]. Photograph of 2001. *See* Chapter VIII, §38 (*MC.D060101*).

8.19 Monument [33942/64-65/PS] to John Gibson, architect (1817-92), in 2001, designed by himself in the Italian Gothic style. The 'structural polychromy' of Red Mansfield Sandstone and Portland Stone has been problematic, with spectacular failure of the sandstone because of the incompatibility of the materials. The deterioration of the Mansfield Red Sandstone has been caused by the contrasts in moisture absorption alongside the white Portland Stone. *See* Chapter VIII, §40 (*MC.S060101*).

by Debray. Collett was a Whig/Liberal MP who shot himself in 1866. Condition: fair, but railings collapsed at rear (**8.18**).

39 SIR CARL WILLIAM SIEMENS (1823-83)[31]

[28127/63/2]. A Celtic cross and slab of pink Peterhead Granite, with portrait-medallion of Carrara Marble set within a granite wreath. Siemens was one of the brothers responsible for founding the great engineering firm, and was responsible for designing, amongst other things, the earliest successful commercial crematorium furnace. Condition: fair.

*40 JOHN GIBSON (1817-92)

[33942/64-65/PS]. A Lombardic Gothic shrine designed by *John Gibson* himself. Made of banded Portland Stone with Red Mansfield Sandstone over a pink granite base, each face consists of an arched opening with moulded contrasting voussoirs; within each main arch is a pair of open arches with sandstone shafts at the corners and flanking the openings. Above the moulded corbel-table is a steeply-pitched truncated pyramidal roof. Within one face of the battered base is an inscription-tablet. Gibson was a highly successful commercial architect best known for his buildings for the National Provincial Bank and is described here as 'Grand Superintendent of Works 1878-82'. Condition: poor, owing to erosion of sandstone and unfortunate combination of incompatible stones (**8.19**).

41 JOHN CAM HOBHOUSE, BARON BROUGHTON DE GYFFORD (1786-1869)

[21596/65/RS]. A heavy sarcophagus of Carrara Marble, signed *Lander & Co.*, masons. The eared, pediment-lidded sarcophagus stands on four squat square colonnettes above a triple-stepped base: the design is based on Greek prototypes. Hobhouse, a close friend of Byron in his youth, became a writer, Whig MP, and minister. Inscribed 'He was eminent alike in political and literary life and after a public career of success and honour found unbroken happiness in domestic repose'. Condition: fair (**9.25**).

42 THOMAS DANIELL RA (1749-1840)

[2422/65/RS]. A Portland Stone tomb-chest with paired pilasters at each corner and fielded panels to the sides and end. A conventional late-Georgian monument, but of particular historic interest: Daniell was an outstanding topographic artist remembered for his Indian scenes. The inscription reads in part:

> He was distinguished in art by the natural beauty and graceful representation of
> his oriental scenes which realised to the imagination the splendour of British India.

31 He had a brother called Carl, so never used his first name, but was always known as Wilhelm, or, in England, William.

He worked in conjunction with his nephew, William Daniell (1769-1837), who is also buried in Kensal Green.[32] Condition: fair, but the inscription is very worn.

43 FREDERICK ALBERT WINSOR (1763-1830)

[24394/65/RS]. An obelisk on a Roman altar-base of mixed sandstones, Carrara Marble, and granite, erected by the Gas Light and Coke Company. The obelisk, edged with inverted torches and decorated with a filleted wreath, bears a tripod finial in the form of a flaming bowl with lion-mask and paw enrichment. Below is an eared, pedimented altar made from a large block of marble. The upper part is based on 16th-century French heart monuments. This is a memorial to F. A. Winsor and not his tomb:[33] Winsor (buried in Père-Lachaise cemetery in Paris beneath an almost identical monument '*exécuté, sur les dessins d'un architecte anglais, par M. Levasseur, marbrier*') was a pioneer of gas-lighting of streets, hence the biblical inscriptions 'in the evening time it shall be light' and 'I am come, a light into the world'. Condition: poor, owing to erosion of sandstone, algae staining, and dirt.

44 MICHAEL WILLIAM BALFE (1808-70)

[22407/74/2]. A conventional small pink Peterhead Granite obelisk on a stepped base, above a York Stone slab. Of historical interest: inscribed 'Balfe the Composer', it commemorates a celebrated mid-Victorian Irish baritone and operatic composer with a gift for melody,[34] best remembered for *The Bohemian Girl* (1843) and the parlour song *Come into the garden, Maud*. Condition: good.

45 JOHN CLAUDIUS LOUDON (1783-1843)

[4547/74/PS]. A plain Portland Stone pedestal with a weathered inscription surmounted by an urn of grey Aberdeen Granite. Of particular historical interest: Loudon was the outstanding writer and theorist of garden design in the late-Georgian and early-Victorian period, and the author of the important book on cemetery design.[35] Condition: fair but inscription very weathered (**5.9**).

46 THOMAS HOOD (1799-1845)

[5449/74/PS]. A once-impressive pedestal with bust by the sculptor *Matthew Noble* (1818-76), of 1854. The pedestal of pink Peterhead Granite, over a stepped grey granite base, formerly sported oval reliefs on each side, and carried a bronze bust: bust and reliefs have been stolen. Hood was an immensely popular poet and humorist: his best known work, *The Song of the Shirt*, is referred to on the pedestal. Despite the losses, still of interest.[36] Condition: very bad (**8.20**).

47 JOSEPH DURHAM (1814-77)

[26191/75/IR]. A Portland Stone and Carrara Marble tomb-chest, possibly by *Durham* himself. An inscribed marble block with trefoil inset reliefs depicting sculptor's tools on each end, over a moulded base and under a pitched hipped lid. Durham was a leading mid-Victorian sculptor specialising in architectural decoration and ideal compositions. Condition: fair.

48 SARAH ELIZABETH SMITH (*c.* 1813-35)

[448/75/IR]. A Carrara Marble and Portland Stone column by *Joseph Browne* (*fl.* 1815-48), mason. The fluted shaft with lotus-leaf capital stands on a square pedestal; above the abacus is a tapering finial. One of the earliest memorials in the cemetery, and representative of the more exotic tendencies in late Neoclassicism.[37] Condition: fair.

[32] [1090/134/RS] [33] *See* Marty, Lassalle, and Rousseau (n.d.), for Winsor tomb description and plate. However, the Kensal Green monument stands partly over an adjacent plot, the grave of his son, Frederick Albert Winsor (1796/7-1874), barrister, who took out a patent for the production of light in 1843. *See D.N.B.*, **xxi** (1917), 675-7. [34] Some critics have described this as a 'gift for facile melody'. *See* Blom (*Ed.*) (1996), **i**, 370-1. [35] Loudon (1843), and other items in the Select Bibliography. [36] *See The Builder*, **xii**/604 (2 September 1854), 460, and *The Illustrated London* News, **xxv**/692 (15 July 1854), 36. The plots contiguous to Hood's [10467, 10468] were granted to Murdo Young (1790-1870 – newspaper editor and author) and to the poet, Eliza Cook, who initiated the subscription to erect a monument to Hood. These plots were never used, and were given up in 1854. Murdo Young was buried in [153/74/PS], contiguous to [10467]. [37] Miss Smith was the only daughter of the Revd. Edward Langdale Smith, of Folkingham, Lincolnshire: she died of consumption in Southampton.

8.20 Remains of Noble's monument [5449/74/PS] to Thomas Hood (1798-1845) in 2001. *See* Chapter VIII, §46 (*MC.B080101*).

8.21 The severe Neoclassical Freeling monument by Robert Johnson [680/75/IR], commemorating Sir Francis Freeling (1764-1836) and other members of his family. Photograph of 2000. *See* Chapter VIII, §49 (© *English Heritage [NMR]. AA 020143*).

8.22 Mausoleum of Sir George Farrant [4795/65 and 76/RS] in 1997. *See* Chapter VIII, §52 (© *Crown copyright. NMR.AA97/1169*).

49 SIR FRANCIS FREELING (1764-1836)

[680/75/IR]. A severe column of Carrara Marble on a cubic sandstone base, signed by *Robert Johnson* (d. 1845),[38] mason, of Westminster. The lower section, on a three-stepped base, consists of a huge block of grey sandstone with an inscription on each face; above, on a base, stands the demi-column or (properly) elongated circular pedestal, with moulded necking. One of the earliest monuments in the cemetery, and characteristic of the more severe tendencies in late-Neoclassical monumental design.[39] Condition: fair (**8.21**).

50 JOHN MURRAY (1778-1843)

[4236/75/IR]. A grey Aberdeen Granite cross on square inscribed base, above a matching ledger-slab, with Gothic lettering and ornament, signed by MacDonald & Leslie. Of considerable historical interest: Murray, one of the founders of the *Quarterly Review*, was the publisher of Byron and the *Edinburgh Review* as well as of *Murray's Handbooks for Travellers*. Condition: fair.

51 ALFRED COOKE (1822-54)

[11719/76/PS]. A limestone chest surmounted with a sculptural group of a horse with a seated boy by *Thomas Milnes* (1813-88).[40] The badly damaged carving (1854) alludes to Cooke's career as a prominent performer on, and breeder of, circus horses. The monument echoes that of another great equestrian showman, Andrew Ducrow [820/76/RS], who is buried close by (§53). Condition: very bad.

*52 SIR GEORGE FARRANT (*c.*1770-1844)

[4795/76/RS]. A Portland Stone Egyptianising mausoleum with battered walls and a reeded cavetto cornice. The blocked, pylon-shaped doorcase is crowned with a winged disc; other Egyptian motifs are the hieroglyphs and stylised head in the cornice. The more conventional pylon-shaped inscription-panel on the south side is flanked by inverted torches. Stone railings in a matching idiom have largely toppled. An early mausoleum in the Egyptian style. Condition: poor (**8.22**).

*53 ANDREW DUCROW (1793-1842)

[820/76/RS]. A flamboyant Graeco-Egyptian mausoleum of rendered brick, with extensive Carrara Marble and artificial-stone enrichments, set within cast-iron railings. It was designed by the theatrical scene-painter, *George Danson* (1799-1881), and built by *John Cusworth* (1795-1856 – of Stoke Newington), mason. The inner cell, with Egyptianising reeded columns and lotus and palm bell-capitals at the angles supporting a cavetto cornice (enriched with curious pseudo-triglyphs and

[38] Johnson is buried in [5445/110/RS]. [39] Freeling, as Secretary to the General Post Office, was responsible for reforming the mail-coach and postal systems. [40] Milnes is buried in [25207/43/4].

8.23 Mausoleum [820/76/RS] of Andrew Ducrow (1793-1842), drawn in 1972 by the late Frank A. Evans at the request of the Editor of the present volume and reproduced in Sheppard (*Ed.*) (1973), Plate 31*a*. Permission to print this image has been cleared by the current General Editor of the *Survey of London*. It should be noted that the original door was still visible in 1972. *See* Chapter VIII, §53 (Survey of London *drawing* © *English Heritage [NMR]*. *96/10663*).

8.24 Ducrow mausoleum in 1997. Erected at a cost of £3,000 in 1837 in a Graeco-Egyptianising style (the sphinxes, for example, were copied from Roman work in the Egyptian Taste). The poor-quality artificial stone (originally painted) has deteriorated to reveal the grainy interior once the smooth surface was breached. The photograph shows a new grave in the path. *See* Chapter VIII, §53. To the left of the mausoleum is the Freeling monument [680/75/IR] (8.21) (*JSC*).

guttae), has a blocked doorcase on the north-east face with a reeded surround surmounted by a cavetto cornice (ornamented with a winged disc) over which is an eared pediment (essentially representing the end of a Neoclassical sarcophagus-lid). Above, the open-topped pediment contains a rectangular marble relief of Pegasus and a mourning genius beside an urn, amid clouds. The other pediments are triangular, with horns embellished with incised anthemion ornament at the extremities, and bee-hives in the tympana, and are set over battered sides sporting reliefs of angels holding wreaths over marble inscription-panels (broken on the north-west face). At two of the angles are diagonally-set plinths with sphinxes. The upper section consists of an urn decorated with horses' heads and garlands placed on a tapering pedestal incised with inverted palmettes: this, in turn, rests on a battered plinth with reliefs of winged horses on each side. Standing within the enclosure surrounding the mausoleum are two free-standing broken columns: that on the north-west supports a wide-brimmed hat and gauntlets; that to the south-east is hung with garlands. The cast-iron railings are decorated with wreaths, swags, and inverted torches. Ducrow was a celebrated equestrian circus performer and proprietor of Astley's Amphitheatre. The mausoleum was erected during his own lifetime for his wife at a cost of £3,000, and subsequently much embellished for his own interment. The epitaph describes it as ERECTED BY GENIUS FOR THE RECEPTION OF ITS OWN REMAINS. Among the outstanding funerary monuments of the first half of the 19th century in England, it is the acme of self-promoting, highly demonstrative, stylistically hybrid, and wholly secular tombs. When built, it was painted. Condition: poor (**8.23**, **8.24**, and **10.11**).

54 CAPTAIN GEORGE ROBERTSON AIKMAN (1760-1844)

[4627/76/RS]. A Portland Stone temple-tomb (1844) by *John Griffith* (1796-1888), architect of the cemetery buildings, who here again used elements derived from the Choragic Monument of Thrasyllus (7.7) that he had employed in the designs of the Dissenters' chapel (the square straight *antae* without entasis, and the fluted Greek Doric columns set *in antis*). The pedimented front has

8.25 The Aikman mausoleum [4627/**76**/RS] by John Griffith, in 2000. This design was repeated for several other mausolea in the cemetery. *See* Chapter VIII, §54 (*© English Heritage [NMR].AA 020145*).

8.26 St John Long monument [283/**76**/RS] by Robert William Sievier, in 2001. *See* Chapter VIII, §55 (*MC.A080101*).

8.27 Birkbeck mausoleum [19470/**76**/RS] in 1997. *See* Chapter VIII, §56 (*JSC*).

a stone-sealed door with an inscription, set between the columns, and, continuing the Thrasyllus theme, there are wreaths on the frieze above the *antae*. Over the side entablatures are rows of antefixa. It also commemorates Col. Frederick Aikman VC (1828-88), hero of the Indian Mutiny.[41] One of several mausolea of this design in the cemetery: compare the Dean Paul (§67) [10065/**86**/RS] and the Valpy (§87) [687/**101**/PS] mausolea, also by Griffith. Condition: fair (**8.25**).

*55 JOHN ST JOHN LONG (1798-1834)

[283/**76**/RS]. A Portland Stone and Carrara Marble open *tholos* standing on a square base, by *Robert William Sievier*, sculptor (1794-1865). The lower section, on a stepped base, has four projecting framed panels, topped by segmental pediments the tympana of which contain wreaths or snakes at a bowl on each face: these projecting inscription-panels are flanked either by quills or by snake-entwined staffs of Aesculapius. At each corner, between the segmental pediments, are elegant Grecian scrolls and anthemion ornaments. The upper section contains a marble statue of Hygeia, the Greek goddess of health, holding a cup, placed within a canopy carried on columns based on those of the Choragic Monument of Lysicrates, with an entablature enriched by a frieze of anthemion and palmettes, bed-mouldings of egg-and-dart, and a cornice crowned by antefixa. Over the entablature is a dome-shaped roof ornamented with a rope-moulding and leaf-and-dart enrichment, and at the very top is a tripod. Having trained as an artist, Long set up as a medical practitioner, and ran a lucrative practice treating ailments via friction and other quack methods; he was twice tried for the manslaughter of unsuccessfully treated patients; the extravagant inscription on the south side appeals to the passer-by not to condemn him. One of the earliest and most celebrated monuments in the cemetery. Condition: poor (**4.28**, **8.26**).

*56 DR GEORGE BIRKBECK (1776-1841)

[19470/**76**/RS]. A Portland Stone mausoleum, consisting of a rectangular cell with pedimented roof, angle-pilasters (or *antae*), and a (blocked) doorcase on the south end. Birbeck is remembered as the founder of Mechanics' Institutions and of University College London; he gave his name to Birkbeck College. Condition: fair, having been conserved in 1997 (**8.27**).

57 GEORGE CRUIKSHANK (1792-1878)

[29171/**76**/RS]. A pedestal of pink Peterhead Granite, formerly supporting a bronze bust (now missing) by *William Behnes* (1795-1864). The inscription describes him as an 'artist, designer, etcher, painter ... for 30 years a total abstainer and ardent pioneer and champion by pencil, word, and pen of UNIVERSAL ABSTINENCE from INTOXICATING DRINKS'. There is a marble version of the bust in the Dickens House Museum. Cruikshank, after Rowlandson, was the

[41] As well as George Aikman (1817-79), Hugh Henry Aikman (1820-82), William Aikman (1822-1903), Col. T.S.G.H. Robertson Aikman (1860-1948 – captain of the British Olympic Curling Team which won the Gold Medal at Chamonix in 1924), and Duncan Forbes Aikman (1867-1920).

outstanding cartoonist and illustrator of the 19th century.[42] Condition: very bad, on account of the stolen bust, but, like the Hood monument, still of historic interest.

58 GEORGE, 8th EARL OF GALLOWAY (1768-1834)

[98/77/IR]. A giant Portland Stone sarcophagus, 1838, by the Neoclassical architect, *John Buonarotti Papworth* (1775-1847). The massive chest has squat, tapering angle-piers surmounted with scrolled consoles, and flanking armorial reliefs on each end. An egg-and-dart bed-moulding runs below the deeply-projecting cornice. The tomb retains extensive remains of protective layers of paint. One of the finest and largest of Neoclassical monuments in the cemetery, and an early instance of an outdoor aristocratic tomb in a public cemetery. Condition: fair (**9.4**).

59 BARON JOHN FREDERICK ANDREW HUTH (1777-1864)

[2735/77/IC]. A massive mausoleum of Portland Stone. Above the tall base, with its torus moulding, each face has a central panel with an inscription or an armorial achievement, set between urns in relief. The frieze contains inscriptions in Latin on each side (The Lord gave, and the Lord hath taken away; blessed be the name of the Lord [*Job*, i, 21]); the stepped pyramidal roof has pierced openings for ventilation. This exceptionally large and severe mausoleum over a vault is said to have room for 40 coffins within, and to have cost £1,500.[43] Huth was a merchant banker, whose family came from Hanover. Condition: fair (**8.28**).

60 GEORGE PRICE BOYCE (1826-97)

[11012/77/IC]. A Portland Stone chest-tomb on a large slab of York Stone, a subtle and unusual design in a Free Gothic idiom. The shallow hipped lid is carried on a corbel-table, and there is a roll-moulding to the base. The inscription is in Gothic script. Boyce was a noted Pre-Raphaelite watercolourist, best-known for his views of the Thames Valley, and an associate of the architect Philip Speakman Webb (1831-1915). Condition: fair.

61 MAJOR-GENERAL ARCHIBALD ROBERTSON (*c.*1783-1847)

[6887/77/RS]. An eared sarcophagus of Carrara Marble, standing on Portland Stone base by *William Theed the Younger* (1804-91), sculptor (buried in [12140/79/12]). The sunken inscription-panels are flanked by Roman swords entwined with branches of laurel. Robertson rose to become a Director of the East India Company. Condition: poor, on account of staining.

62 FREDERICK THOMAS YATES (*c.*1835-39)

[2241/77/IR]. A Portland Stone sarcophagus, in the form of a massive block with raised panels on each side flanked by inverted torches, with a Carrara Marble effigy of a sleeping infant with cushion on the top. The effigy was removed for safe-keeping in 1998. A striking fusion of severe Neoclassical masonry and late-Romantic sentiment.[44] Condition: fair, but for the loss of the figure.

63 WILLIAM CHAPPELL (1809-88)

[8197/77/PS]. A Gothic block of grey Cornish Granite (1849), designed by *Owen Jones* (1809-1874): it is a far cry from Jones's other, more exuberant, productions. The rectangular block, with chamfered sides, stands on a moulded base: each face terminates in a pointed arched head containing an incised cross. Chappell was a musical publisher and historian.[45] Condition: fair (**9.27**).

64 LADY MARGARET PULTENEY (*c.* 1786-1849)

[8521/78/PS]. A tall Carrara Marble grave-marker by the distinguished architect *Charles Robert Cockerell* (1788-1863). The tall shaft, on a moulded plinth, has an arched terminal containing an armorial hatchment set against a field of acanthus decoration.[46] Condition: fair.

[42] Cruikshank's body was never buried in the plot: before it was entombed in St Paul's Cathedral it was buried in [26329/78/3], so [29171/76/RS] is the grave of Cruikshank's wife. [43] According to Blanchard (n.d.), 9. [44] The child was the son of Frederick Yates, solicitor, of Great George Street, Westminster. [45] Hakewill (1851), Plate 25.
[46] Ibid., Plate 23. Lady Pulteney was the daughter of Sir William Stirling of Ardoch, Bart. She married, first, Andrew Stuart , the lawyer (d. 1801), and second, Sir William Johnson Pulteney, 5th Baronet, of Wester Hall. Her executors were Henry Horne Drummond, MP, and C. R. Cockerell.

8.28 Mausoleum of the banker, Baron Huth [2735/77/IC] in 2000. It is one of the largest mausolea in the cemetery, with room for 48 coffins within its capacious vault. *See* Chapter VIII, §59 (© *English Heritage [NMR]. AA 020146*).

8.29 Monument [3714/80/RS] of Alexis Benoît Soyer (1809-58), the chef, and his wife, Elizabeth Emma (1813-42), the painter, called 'The English Murillo', by Puyenbroeck, in 2001. It also commemorates François Simonau, Madame Soyer's stepfather, who taught her drawing and painting. *See* Chapter VIII, §65 (*MC.A060101*).

*65 ELIZABETH EMMA (1813-42) and ALEXIS BENOÎT SOYER (1809-58)

[3714/80/RS]. An elaborate Portland Stone and marble monument conceived by *Alexis Soyer*, and carved by *Pierre Puyenbroeck* of Brussels, 1844. The plain base bears raised capital letters reading TO HER. The central section consists of a marble portrait relief of Madame Soyer *à la Van Dyck*, set within a surround of a tail-biting snake from which hangs an easel and brushes; billowing clouds gather below, while cherubs, gathering up a drape, are seated above. On the rear of the middle section is an oval recess, now empty but formerly glazed, which originally contained her easel, set against a wreath presented by Mlle Cerito, the Milanese dancer. The upper section consists of a standing female draped figure of Faith: her right arm (now missing) was raised upwards, and she held a large cross (now missing) in her left hand. The figure was originally illuminated by a jet of gas-light: a bronze nozzle is still *in situ* below her feet. The ensemble retains extensive remains of original paint. Bespoke rustic rails in cast iron, designed by *William Rogers*, were removed in the mid-20th century (a drawing for them survives in the V&A). Elizabeth Soyer was a popular painter known as the 'English Murillo', who miscarried and died, aged 29; her husband, Alexis Soyer, was the leading chef and dietician of the mid-19th century, responsible also for reforming army catering in the Crimea. The tomb also commemorates Madame Soyer's step-father, François Simonau (1783-1859), the 'Flemish Murillo'.[47] Condition: poor (**8.29**).

66 CHARLES BABBAGE (1791-1871)

[23003/**84**/RS]. A hipped slab of grey Rubislaw Granite, on a base of York Stone, signed *Lander*, mason. Babbage was an outstanding mathematician whose 'calculating engines' heralded the principles of the computer without ever quite getting there. A monument of considerable historic, rather than visual, interest. Condition: good.

67 WENTWORTH FRANCIS DEAN PAUL (1870-93)

[10065/**86**/RS]. A Neoclassical mausoleum of Portland Stone by *John Griffith* (1796-1888), architect of the cemetery's buildings. The (blocked) door is flanked by two fluted Doric columns *in antis*: the frieze above is inscribed THE TOMB OF THE PAUL FAMILY, and above is a pediment with a tympanum containing an heraldic shield with acanthus decoration. The sides are articulated with *antae*.[48] Compare the Aikman (§54) [4627/**76**/RS] and the Valpy (§87) [687/**101**/

47 *The Illustrated London News*, v/123 (7 September 1844), 160. The monument was renovated in 1923, at a cost of £24 10s., by Lady Elise Isabelle Watts (d. 1930), daughter of Chevalier Gustave Simoneau de St-Omer of Brussels and wife of Sir Philip Watts (1846-1926), naval architect: he designed many of the warships that were present at the Battle of Jutland. Lady Elise is buried in the vault. 'F. Simonau' is as given on the grave, and Lady Watts is also referred to as '*née* Simonau'. It is also 'Simonau' in the Bishop's Transcripts, in the General Cemetery Company archives, and in other sources: Turner (*Ed.*)(1996) confirms 'Simonau'. 48 Sir John Dean Paul, Bart. (1775-1852), the Banker, was one of the principal backers of the General Cemetery Company, and was much involved in the creation and design of Kensal Green cemetery. Paul was one of those who insisted on the Neoclassical style for the buildings, and his mausoleum (in reality his cenotaph, because his body is deposited in **Catacomb B/**Vault 82, next to that of his son, the 2nd Baronet, also Sir John Dean Paul [1802-68]) is in keeping with this decree.

RS] mausolea for near-identical designs, also by Griffith. Condition: poor, on account of the blocked door.

68 JAMES DUNLOP (1769-1841)

[3258/86/RS]. A large Portland Stone mausoleum. The entrance (now blocked, formerly with a bronze door, judging by the copper staining) is under a shouldered pedimental lintel, and is flanked by urn-capped pedestals; over the rusticted base rise walls of channelled ashlar with inscription-panels on the sides. The roof possesses a shallow pediment. One of the most impressive of the early Neoclassical mausolea in the cemetery, and an elegant display of masonry construction. Dunlop was a tobacco-merchant who died at the Treasury.[49] Condition: poor, on account of the loss of the door.

69 ALEXANDER BRUCE (*c.*1755-1827)

[5769/86/IR]. A two-stage monument of Carrara Marble. The plain rectangular pedestal stands upon a heavy tomb-chest with a relief of mourning women beside a huge urn in a tropical landscape. The weathered inscription refers to Bruce as 'late of India', hence the flavour of the relief.[50] Condition: fair.

70 LADY ANNE ISABELLA NOEL BYRON (1792-1860)

[15958/87/IR]. An inscribed slab of Kemnay Granite with an urn at its head, surrounded by squat posts with cast-iron rails. Anne Milbanke was Lord Byron's unfortunate wife and the mother of the computer pioneer Augusta Ada, Countess of Lovelace (1815-52); she devoted herself to reforming causes. Of historical interest by association, rather than a fine example of the mason's art. Condition: fair.

71 JOSEPH HUDSON (*c.* 1776-1854)

[1578/87/RS]. A large mausoleum of Portland Stone. The (blocked) pylon-shaped doorway is surrounded with a border decorated with poppies, emblematic of the sleep of death; the flanking pilasters are decorated with reliefs of sunflowers. On the front, beneath the moulded cavetto cornice, the frieze is decorated with a meander pattern. The eared pediment has anthemion ears and antefixa, and the front pediment contains acanthus scrolls and a triangle within the tympanum. The plainer sides have inset panels. One of the most opulent of Classical mausolea in the cemetery.[51] Condition: fair.

72 FREDERICK TILLSON (*c.*1823-70)

[22047/88/RS]. A Gothic canopied tomb of Portland Stone, sandstone and marble colonnettes, with a wrought-iron screen. The panelled chest stands on a raised, moulded base with applied Lombardic lead letters on its southern end; above the angle-colonnettes of red sandstone is a foliate frieze. The upper canopy is carried on eight colonnettes of green Serpentine Marble, between which is a screen of scrolled wrought iron; above is a gabled roof. An exceptionally elaborate Gothic Revival outdoor monument, based on medieval shrine-tombs. Condition: poor (**9.17**).

73 JOSEPH ALLMOND CROPPER (*c.*1782-1862)[52]

[17407/88/RS]. A Gothic, Portland Stone, two-stage monument with pink Peterhead Granite shafts. The lower section consists of a tall square pedestal with blind, cusped arched openings on each side below a corbel table; those on the east and west sides, between granite shafts to angles, sport relief sculptures of acts of mercy inscribed 'I was sick and ye visited me' and 'A stranger and ye took me in'. The upper section consists of a statue of Christ within a tall pyramidal canopy carried on four

[49] Dunlop owned tobacco plantations in Chesterfield, Virginia. His executors were Joshua Bates (1788-1864 – buried in [214/86/PS]) and Robert Leslie of Petersburg, Virginia, possibly a relative of Charles Robert Leslie, RA (1794-1859 – buried in [15036/55/2], whose work was supported by Dunlop. [50] Bruce was originally buried in St George's church, Bloomsbury, and was re-interred at Kensal Green in 1845 during the intramural interment controversy. His daughter, Sarah, was also buried in the grave (1878). [51] Hudson was Tobacconist to the Royal Family, and had premises at 132 Oxford Street. The inscription records that as a young man he served as a midshipman under Admiral Lord Howe (1726-99) at the battle of 1 June 1794 when the French fleet was defeated. [52] Banker and philanthropist, he left property to St George's, Middlesex, and Westminster hospitals, hence the inscription.

8.30 The enduring quality of granite: the monument [533/90/RS] of Captain The Hon. Sir Henry Duncan (1786-1835) in 2000. He was originally buried in 428. *See* Chapter VIII, §77 (*©English Heritage [NMR]. AA 020148*).

8.31 Tuscan temple-tomb of Joanna and Charles Stevenson [2821/90/RS] in 1997. Note the pulvinated frieze. *See* Chapter VIII, §78 (*JSC*).

colonnettes of pink granite, with a trefoil-headed opening on each face. An exceptionally opulent Gothic memorial, loosely based on medieval North Italian exemplars. Condition: fair.

74 AMELIA JANE RICHMAN (1821-37)

[794/88/RS]. A Portland Stone urn on a pedestal, signed *Hemmens, Regent Street*, mason, within cast-iron spear-headed railings. The square pedestal on a base, with sunken panels to each side, supports a partially draped, gadrooned urn above. Extensive remains of original whitewash are still evident. An exceptionally well-preserved example of this conventional Neoclassical type.[53] Condition: good.

75 DAVID EDWARD MORRIS (1770-1842)[54]

[2627/89/RS]. A large, rectangular chest of artificial stone, described as 'mausoleum' in inscription, with angle-pilasters and fielded inscription-panels on each side, and anthemion acroteria at the corners; the sloping roof sports antefixa, and the upper stage terminates with a gadrooned flaming urn on a stepped base. The cast-iron railings are decorated with an inverted torch motif. A late example of a Neoclassical artificial-stone monument in the Coade-stone tradition. Condition: fair.

76 CHARLES HAWLEY (*c.*1793-1842)

[3645/90/RS]. A massive pedimented block of Portland Stone with the seated figure of an angel in front, over a relief of poppies (emblematic of the sleep of death) on the curved base below. The angel is well-sculpted, and is among the earliest of such figures to appear in the cemetery.[55] Condition: fair.

77 CAPTAIN the HON. SIR HENRY DUNCAN RN, CB, KCH (1786-1835)

[533/90/RS]. Duncan's huge grey granite sarcophagus shows the potential of the new techniques of granite-cutting. With battered sides on a stepped base, the immaculately legible inscription on the front below the cavetto cornice is in sunken block capitals; the upper stage is enriched with a martial relief of a gun-barrel, sword, and the Union Flag.[56] Condition: fair (**8.30**).

78 CHARLES (*c.*1799-1863) and JOANNA (*c.*1809-40) STEVENSON

[2821/90/RS]. An elegant Portland Stone miniature temple on a square plinth, with peripteral Roman Doric colonnettes and square columns at the corners supporting a pedimented cover.[57] Condition: fair (**8.31**).

53 This is the family grave of Francis Richman (*c.*1779-1848), builder. 54 Proprietor of the Haymarket theatre, 1817-37. Most of the leading actors the day worked under him. 55 Hakewill (1851), Plate 15. Charles Hawley was Goldsmith and Watchmaker to the King, and had premises in Coventry Street. Also buried in the plot is John Hawley (*c.*1775-1842), who was originally deposited in St James's church, Piccadilly, and translated to Kensal Green in 1842. 56 The youngest son of Admiral Viscount Duncan, KB (1731-1804), Sir Henry was sometime Principal Storekeeper at the Board of Ordnance, in charge of military supplies. 57 Stevenson was a builder and surveyor.

8.32 Sarcophagus [4257/90/PS] of Colonel Robert Ellison (d. 1843), a veteran of Waterloo, photographed in 1997. *See* Chapter VIII, §79 (*JSC*).

8.33 The family tomb of Robert Kirby, 1839 [2215/92/RS], in 1997. *See* Chapter VIII, §82 (*JSC*).

79 COLONEL ROBERT ELLISON (*c.*1789-1843)

[4257/90/PS]. Sarcophagus of Carrara Marble with a pedimented, eared lid, on a stepped base, with Roman swords and wreaths on the sides, and a relief of palm, sword, sash, and wreath on the north end. An exceptional example of the Neoclassical military tomb, of Attic simplicity and power.[58] Condition: fair, apart from weathered inscription on the south end (**8.32**).

80 JAMES WARD R.A. (1769-1859)

[15560/90/3]. A shattered Carrara Marble relief by the Irish sculptor, *John Henry Foley* R.A. (1818-74), best-known for the statue of Prince Albert within the Albert Memorial. The tall, broken, arched surround contains a high-relief figure of the Muse of Painting, a draped and laurel-crowned female figure holding a palette. Ward was an outstanding late-Romantic painter of landscapes and animals, best known for his epic landscape of 1814, *Gordale Scar* (Tate Gallery). The inscription states he was 'distinguished as an engraver and afterwards as an animal painter. His works in the National Gallery and the British Museum prove his great and varied powers in each pursuit'. Perhaps the most forlorn monument in the entire cemetery.[59] Condition: very bad.

81 JULIA SLATER (*c.*1834-58)

[3960/91/RS]. A triangular, altar-like monument of Portland Stone on a circular plinth. On each face is a relief of an allegorical seated female: Hope is on the south-west face with her anchor; Charity is on the north face with her infants; and Faith is hidden by overgrowth. Worn palm-trees articulate each corner.[60] Condition: very bad.

82 ROBERT KIRBY (*c.*1776-1844)

[2215/92/RS]. A pair of grey granite Classical sarcophagi joined together (dated 1839), and topped with a tripartite cover consisting of a pair of shallow pyramids with horns decorated with anthemion, flanking a squat obelisk form with the robustly-cut inscription and the Kirby crest: an elephant's head.[61] One of the very earliest monuments employing polished granite on a large scale, and still in remarkably good condition (**8.33**).

83 JOHN BALSIR CHATTERTON (1804-71)

[22733/93/3]. A Carrara Marble headstone (with curved ledger-slab in front), enriched with inlaid

[58] The inscription states that the tomb was erected by the Duke of Wellington and officers of the Grenadier Guards, with whom Ellison had served at Waterloo, defending Hougoumont farm. [59] *The Builder*, **xxi**/1083 (7 November 1863), 789. [60] Mrs Slater was the wife of Captain Mortimer John Slater. The plot is the family grave of John Pannett Bull (1802-72), woollen-draper. [61] Kirby was a partner in the firm of Kirby, Beard, & Kirby, of 46 Cannon Street, Pin and Needle Manufacturers to the Queen.

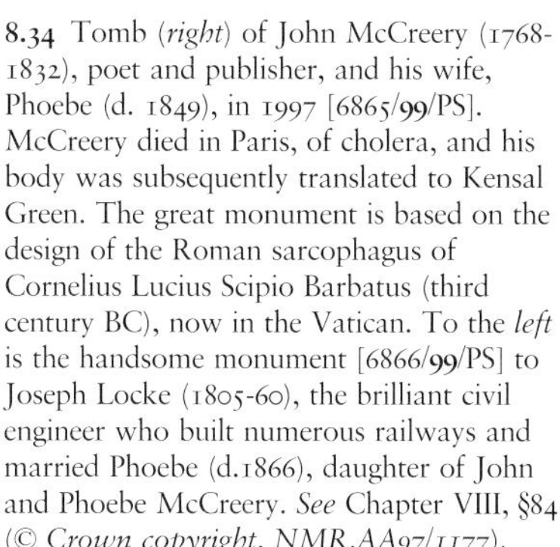

8.34 Tomb (*right*) of John McCreery (1768-1832), poet and publisher, and his wife, Phoebe (d. 1849), in 1997 [6865/99/PS]. McCreery died in Paris, of cholera, and his body was subsequently translated to Kensal Green. The great monument is based on the design of the Roman sarcophagus of Cornelius Lucius Scipio Barbatus (third century BC), now in the Vatican. To the *left* is the handsome monument [6866/99/PS] to Joseph Locke (1805-60), the brilliant civil engineer who built numerous railways and married Phoebe (d.1866), daughter of John and Phoebe McCreery. *See* Chapter VIII, §84 (© *Crown copyright. NMR.AA97/1177*).

honeysuckle and meander-pattern ornament, and a relief of a lyre and wreath. The inscription describes Chatterton as 'Harpist to Her Majesty'. Condition: fair.

84 JOHN McCREERY (1768-1832) and JOSEPH LOCKE (1805-60)

[6865 and 6866/99/PS]. A pair of sarcophagi set on a huge grey granite base with posts. The left-hand sarcophagus is of pink Peterhead Granite, with pointed inscription-panel and battered sides, and was erected in 1862 to Locke, the outstanding Victorian-railway engineer, by his former pupils. It contains, on the left-hand side, two signatures: *T. Gaffin* of 63 Regent Street, and *A. MacDonald*, of Aberdeen. The right-hand sarcophagus, of Carrara Marble, based on that of Scipio Barbatus, is to John and Phoebe McCreery, and is signed, on the right-hand side, *A. MacDonald Field & Co Aberdeen*. They stand side by side on a raised base with a paved surround, edged by posts, and all of grey granite, inscribed ENLARGED AND RESTORED 1870 BY SARAH McCREERY. This ensemble is as imposing as any mausoleum. Condition: fair (**8.34**).

85 WILLIAM HOLLAND (1779-1856)

[7219/100/PS]. An exuberant Portland Stone sarcophagus, carried on four pairs of addorsed winged couchant mythical beasts, part-gryphon, part-wyvern. The chest is in the style of the French *Empire* architects, Charles Percier (1764-1838) and Pierre-François-Léonard Fontaine (1762-1853), with three roundels on each long side and one at each end: between the three roundels are inverted arches, and beneath all of them are festoons. At the corners are figures of angels reminiscent of the style of John Flaxman (1755-1826). The pedimented eared cover is enriched with feigned roof-tiles. This is an exceptionally rich instance of High Victorian eclectic Classicism, well befitting its occupant: Holland, with his partner Thomas Dowbiggin (d. 1854), was a leading furniture-manufacturer and undertaker, who supplied much furniture to the Royal Family. Condition: poor (**8.35**).

86 THOMAS SIMPSON COOKE (1782-1848)

[7420/100/PS]. A chaste Portland Stone headstone by *Edward William Wyon* (1811-85), sculptor and member of the celebrated dynasty of medallists. The central arched headstone is flanked by relief figures of addorsed mourning women, one with a lyre, one with a scroll. Cooke was a prominent opera-singer, composer, and teacher.[62] Condition: poor.

87 DR RICHARD VALPY (1754-1836)

[687/101/RS]. A Portland Stone mausoleum designed by *John Griffith* (1786-1888), architect of the cemetery's buildings. It is signed *Adron* of New Road, i.e. *William and Charles Adron*, statuaries

[62] Hakewill (1851), Plate 27.

8.35 Holland tomb [7219/100/PS] in 1997. *See* Chapter VIII, §85 (*JSC*).

8.36 Rendel tomb [13511/101/RS] in 1997. *See* Chapter VIII, §90 (*JSC*).

and masons. William (*c*.1780-1867) and his brother,[63] Charles (*c*.1787-1865), are buried in [6863/**68**/RS]. Greek Doric columns *in antis* flank an inscription panel with Achievement of Arms, in place of a door, and the sides are articulated with *antae*. Above is a frieze with wreaths placed over the *antae*, and a pediment with the crest of an oak tree within the tympanum, and the roof sports antefixa. Valpy was for 50 years Headmaster of Reading School. Compare the Aikman (§54) [4627/**76**/RS] and Paul (§67) [10065/**86**/RS] mausolea for near identical designs, also by Griffith.[64] Condition: fair (**9.2**).

88 ISABEL ALEXANDER HANKEY (1835-7)

[1051/**101**/RS]. A Portland Stone aedicule (1838) by the architect *George Basevi* (1794-1845). A tall plinth with an armorial relief carries the pedimented aedicule, within which is a relief of a grieving woman weeping over an urn. The York Stone slab, flanked by six rusticated posts, was formerly within railings.[65] Condition: fair.

89 WILLIAM STAVELEY (*c*. 1784-1837)

[978/**101**/RS]. Staveley's mighty Portland Stone obelisk and giant urn (with incised capital-letter initials) was designed by *Charles Harriott Smith* (1792-1864), an architecturally-trained sculptor and an authority on building-stones. Its heavy mouldings speak of a tomb intended to last; it has done so.[66] Condition: fair.

90 JAMES MEADOWS RENDEL (1799-1856)

[13511/**101**/RS]. A pink Peterhead Granite sarcophagus with pitched lid and a pediment at each end, designed by *Sir Matthew Digby Wyatt* (1820-77 – the design was exhibited at the Royal Academy – in 1862). The rectangular chest on a moulded base is enriched with Byzantinesque decorations, including crosses within the pedimental ends of the gabled cover. As the epitaph relates, Rendel was an outstanding marine-engineer, responsible for many dock and railway projects, including the harbours at Holyhead and Portland, mentioned in the inscription. Condition: good (**8.36**).

91 HOWE PETER BROWNE, 2nd MARQUESS OF SLIGO (1788-1845)

[4867/**101**/3]. A severe and chaste Neoclassical sarcophagus standing on two supports, above a two-stepped base; the sides have a sunken inscription panel flanked by slender lachrymal vases in

63 Gunnis (1968), 14-15, states that William was Charles's father, but this cannot be the case. There must have been another William Adron, probably the father of William and Charles, who flourished, as Gunnis says, from *c*.1792 to 1838. 64 Like the Aikman (§54) and Paul (§67) mausolea, it was intended as a *fabrique* in the garden-cemetery, partly as an ornament, and partly to add tone. 65 Ibid., Plate 2. The original deposit was in **CAT. A**/988. The child was the infant daughter of John Alexander Hankey, Banker. 66 Hakewill (1851), Plate 19. *See also* the Scriven monument (listed No. 8 in the Gazetteer).

relief. Sligo was an associate of the Prince Regent and of Lord Byron; the excavator of the Treasury of Atreus at Mycenae; and sometime Governor of Jamaica who oversaw the implementation of the emancipation of slaves.[67] Condition: good.

92 REAR-ADMIRAL THOMAS TUDOR TUCKER CB (1775-1852) and MAJOR-GENERAL SIR WILLIAM HILL (1805-86)

[10346/102/2] and [14195/102/2]. An exceptional pair of complementary military monuments, each consisting of a Portland Stone pedestal with an arched inscription panel on the front, supporting trophies, with York Stone slabs in front. The southern monument commemorates Rear-Admiral Thomas Tudor Tucker: on the base is a relief of a sword and wreath, and above is a naval trophy of an anchor, flag, cable, and cannon-barrel. The northern tomb commemorates Major-General Sir William Hill, brother-in-law of T. T. Tucker: below is a relief of a scroll, quill, wreath, and scales; above is a hussar's trophy with a busby, sabretache,[68] sabre, cartridge-box, and ensign. Associated with this pair of monuments is an obelisk [7528/102/PS] commemorating Henry St George Tucker (1771-1851), eldest brother of Thomas Tudor Tucker.[69] Condition: poor, owing to weathering and loss of inscription (**9.9**).

93 PETER BURROWES (1753-1841)

[3256/103/PS]. A Carrara Marble pedestal supporting a draped urn, with a relief portrait-medallion on the tall base by *Timothy Butler* (b. 1806-*c*.1878), sculptor. Burrowes was an Irish MP and lawyer, active in championing the rights of Irish Roman Catholics. Condition: fair, despite the erosion of the marble's surface. Inscription restored *c*.1993.

94 THOMAS HANCOCK (1786-1865)

[19066/104/RS]. A conventional enough Corinthian column of Carrara Marble on a rectangular plinth with an interesting inscription which describes Hancock as 'the inventor and founder of the India Rubber manufacture'. Hancock also helped to perfect weatherproof clothing, but it is the name of his partner, Charles Macintosh (1766-1843), that has been immortalised in this respect. Condition: fair.

95 ROBERT SMIRKE RA (1752-1845)

[5224/105/RS]. A Carrara Marble headstone with a sunken circular niche, containing a frontal bust within a wreath surround, and with a coped ledger in front. This Smirke (father of the architects Sir Robert [1781-1867] and Sydney [1798-1877], of the lawyer and antiquary, Sir Edward [1795-1875 – also buried in the cemetery (5224/105/RS)], and of Richard Smirke [1778-1815], the antiquarian and draughtsman) was a prominent Royal Academician and painter of religious and literary scenes. Condition: very bad, owing to the rather grotesque weathering of the bust.

96 ADMIRAL SIR JOHN ROSS (1777-1856)

[13388/111/4]. A Carrara Marble cross, entwined with anchor and chain, set upon a cairn, placed on a stepped pedestal. Ross, described here as THE ARCTIC EXPLORER, left his retirement at the age of 73 to search the Arctic for his friend, Sir John Franklin (1786-1847) in 1850-1; this symbol of the anchor and cross on cairn, emblematic of Christian hope and fortitude, became a commonplace of later Victorian funerary sculpture.[70] Condition: poor, owing to settlement and damage to anchor and chain.

97 ROBERT WILLIAM KENNARD (1800-70)

[22600/113/RS]. This intricate and exuberant Portland Stone mausoleum, stylistically indebted to the Byzantine Revival, stands on a base of grey granite. The three-panelled bronze door is set within a shouldered frame, the lintel of which is inscribed FAMILY MAUSOLEUM OF ROBERT

[67] Hakewill (1851), Plates 6-7. [68] Flat bag slung from a cavalry-officer's sword-belt. [69] Henry St George Tucker served as Captain in a cavalry corps and as commandant of the militia in Bengal. He wrote on financial matters, was a Director of the East India Company in 1834, and Chairman again in 1847. While in India he was imprisoned for six months and fined for attempted rape in 1806. *See D.N.B.*, **xix** (1917), 1207-9. [70] His nephew, Sir James Clark Ross (1800-62), was an even more noted Arctic explorer.

WILLIAM KENNARD. Above is a segmental pediment with scrolled border, containing the sacred monogram amid vine decoration, with a finial of a pelican on top. The sides of channelled ashlar above a rusticated granite base support a continuous frieze inscribed I WILL ARISE AND GO TO MY FATHER; the pediment at the rear (west) end carries a relief of a rising sun above waves. The ridged roof is embellished with cresting of flaming torches. Kennard was an ironmaster, railway developer, and MP. Condition: poor, owing to settlement and consequent cracking (**9.16**).

98 LIEUTENANT-COLONEL CHARLES SETON GUTHRIE (1805-74),[71] SOPHIA GUTHRIE (d. 1866), and FLORENCE INGLISS (d. 1874)

[20022/113/3] A large, prominently sited Egyptian-style mausoleum of pink and grey granite. The (blocked) door on the west side is flanked by tapering columns with bulbous capitals supporting a cavetto lintel with winged solar disc; the battered side-walls carry the cavetto cornice above pylon-shaped inscription-panels on each side: the rear (east) has a blind pylonic doorcase with Egyptian-influenced bronze ventilation-grilles above. Condition: fair, apart from the blocked door.

99 GENERAL SIR WARREN MARMADUKE PEACOCKE (1766-1849)

[8354/100-13/PS]. A large, austere, grey-granite obelisk on a plinth, with a slab in front. Its interest is substantially enhanced by its prominent position among the most visually prominent group of monuments in the cemetery, just in front of the Anglican chapel. Condition: fair.

100 HARRIET MANGIN BROWNE, VISCOUNTESS D'ALTE (*c.*1802-62)

[17442/113/PS]. A Carrara Marble sarcophagus standing on a tall grey granite plinth. The curved sarcophagus stands on lions'-paw feet, and has heraldic Achievements on each side and a relief of a flaming heart within a wreath at each end. On top is a coronet on a cushion. Lady d'Alte was the wife of the Portuguese Minister at Rome; her monument was closely based on that of Princess Sophia near by, and is among the more obviously emulatory tombs in the cemetery.[72] To the north is the needle-obelisk of Isabella Hedgeland [9839/109-113/PS]. Condition: good (**8.37**).

101 ISABELLA HEDGELAND, also known as KELLY (1762-1857)

[9839/109-113/PS]. An acute pointed needle-obelisk (actually an acutely-pointed pyramid) on a pedestal, all of Carrara Marble, above a four-stepped base, to the north of Viscountess d'Alte's tomb. The pedestal's cavetto cornice is enriched with palmettes, flowers, and wreaths. Another memorial that contributes signally to the visually most prominent group of monuments in the cemetery.[73] Condition: fair (**8.37**).

*102 H.R.H. PRINCESS SOPHIA (1777-1848)

[8028/114/PS]. One of the prominently-positioned pair of tombs to children of King George III, located in front of the Anglican chapel. This consists of a sarcophagus on a tall plinth, all of Carrara Marble, above a base of grey Cornish Granite. The sarcophagus was designed by *Professor Ludwig Grüner* of Dresden (1801-82), Prince Albert's artistic adviser, and carved by *Signor Bardi*. The rest of the monument was erected by the London mason *Edward Pearce*. The crown-topped sarcophagus in the *Quattrocento* manner stands on lions'-paw feet, with winged lion-heads to the angles; the body is decorated with rinceaux, and the upper sides are embellished with floral garlands, fillets, and the Princess's cipher; on each end are the royal Arms. A tall plinth, on a two-stage base, has an inscription on the east end. It, in turn, stands on a rectangular base of granite blocks. Princess Sophia was the 5th daughter and 8th child of George III, and had a child by a courtier in 1800: thereafter she led a withdrawn existence; she opted for burial near her favourite brother (*see below*).[74] Condition: good (**5.10** and **8.38**).

[71] Boase (1965), col. 1264. Guthrie, of the Bengal Engineers, made the largest collection of Eastern coins ever assembled. [72] Harriet Browne died in Civitavecchia, the sea-port, in September 1862 and was deposited at Kensal Green the following November. [73] It commemorates a remarkable political novelist, the mother of Sir Fitzroy Kelly (1796-1880). [74] *The Illustrated London News*, **xvii**/442 (17 August 1850), 164.

8.37 Sarcophagus-monument [17442/113/PS] of Viscountess d'Alte (*left*, on high podium surmounted by a coronet), with (*right*) needle-spire [9839/109-113/PS] of Isabella Hedgeland, a.k.a. Kelly, and (*centre*) monument [13152/113/2] of Admiral James Ryder Burton, K.H. (*c.*1793-1876 – of 15 Park Square, Regent's Park), with female figure atop a pedestal. To the *right* of Admiral Ryder Burton's monument can be seen the Egyptianesque memorial [47236/114/RS] to Sir Ernest Joseph Cassel, P.C., G.C.M.G., G.C.V.O. (1852-1921), philanthropist, financier, and friend of King Edward VII: his grand-daughter, Edwina Cynthia Annette Ashley (1901-60), married in 1922 Lord Louis Mountbatten (1900-79), later 1st Earl Mountbatten of Burma. These memorials are all to the east of the Anglican chapel (part of the colonnades and portico of which can be seen [*background*]). Photograph of 2001. *See* Chapter VIII, §§ 100, 101 (*MC.B250401*).

8.38 Monument [8028/114/PS] of H.R.H. Princess Sophia, designed by Ludwig Grüner, carved by Signor Bardi, and supported on a massive, but elegant, podium by Edward Pearce. The portico of the Anglican chapel is behind. Photograph of 2001. *See* Chapter VIII, §102 (*MC.E080101*).

103 H.R.H. AUGUSTUS FREDERICK, DUKE OF SUSSEX, KG (1773-1843)

[5268/114/PS]. The male counterpart of his sister's elegantly Florentine memorial, this pioneering royal monument consists of a massive hipped ledger-slab on a heavy rectangular base, ringed by 14 posts (actually miniature unfluted Greek Doric columns), all of grey Aberdeen Granite, by *M. W. Johnson*, mason (*fl.* 1820-60). The ledger-slab bears an inscription in sunk block-capitals; the 14 tapering cylindrical posts with round caps which surround it were originally linked by bronze chains. Sussex was the 6th son of King George III. Noted for his liberal sympathies, his horror of entering the royal vault at Windsor (glimpsed at William IV's funeral in 1837), together with his desire to rest with his morganatic wife (Cecilia Letitia, Duchess of Inverness [d. 1873]), made him the first member of the Royal Family to be buried outdoors in a public cemetery. His arrival at Kensal Green ensured the cemetery's social success. This tomb is remarkable for its massiveness and severity.[75] Condition: fair, but the chains are missing from the posts (5.5 and 7.18).

104 JOSEPH HUME (1777-1855)

[12212/115/2]. A reduced version of the Duke of Sussex's monument, and located close to it, Hume's tomb is a massive slab with hipped cover of unpolished grey Cornish Granite, placed on a two-stage base with 10 perimeter posts, and covered with an inscription in block-capital letters. Hume was a prominent Radical MP and one of the founders of University College London.[76] Condition: fair, but the chains are missing from the posts.

105 JAMES HENRY LEIGH HUNT (1784-1859)

[13650/121/3]. A sadly depleted Carrara Marble pedestal on a raised base, the east face of which has a relief of a garlanded urn over the inscription 'write me as one that loved his fellow men'. This was formerly surmounted with an *all'antica* bust of Leigh Hunt by *Joseph Durham* (1814-77 – buried in [26191/75/IR] which has been stolen; a cast of it exists in the Keats House Museum,

[75] Ibid., **vi**/156 (26 April 1845), 272. [76] Ibid., **xxix**/829 (8 November 1856), 474.

Hampstead. This monument, erected by public subscription, commemorates an outstanding man of letters of the early 19th century, who, through his journal, *The Examiner*, championed Keats and Shelley (at whose cremation he was present).[77] Condition: very bad, on account of loss of bust.

106 WALTER PEART (d. 1898)

[37102/123/10]. A renewed Carrara Marble headstone, with an inset relief plaque (replaced) of a train, set over branches of bay and within a moulded hood. Over the ledger-slab are feigned railway-tracks.[78] Condition: good.

107 SIR CHARLES LOCK EASTLAKE (1793-1865)

[19540/125/PS]. An austere Carrara Marble gabled headstone with colonnettes at the sides carrying the pedimental top; the inscription consists of inset lead lettering placed below a cross; below is an incised wreath enclosing Eastlake's monogram.[79] Condition: poor, owing to the perishing of the lead letters.

108 SIR CHARLES THOMAS NEWTON (1816-94)

[19525/125/PS]. A badly damaged, but historically intriguing, slender marble headstone (now fallen and broken) with an anthemion terminal and an inset relief of a seated woman (possibly a re-used antique piece), in imitation of an Attic *stela* of the fourth century BC.[80] Condition: very bad.

109 ADMIRAL HENRY COLINS DEACON (1788-1869)

[19697/125/PS]. In a cemetery containing many naval and military memorials, this is outstanding. The Portland Stone pedestal supports a naval trophy of Carrara Marble, comprising a pile of cannon balls, an anchor, an ensign, and carronade-barrel.[81] Condition: poor (**8.39**).

110 WILLIAM JOHN CAVENDISH-BENTINCK-SCOTT, 5th DUKE OF PORTLAND (1800-79)

[23032/**112, 113, 125, 126**/RS]. A strange, impressive, and yet reticent memorial to a strange and reticent aristocrat. The Portland plot, dotted with yews, is by far the largest in the cemetery, and is strategically positioned to the south of the Anglican chapel. It is bounded by kerbs and posts of grey granite (formerly linked with bronze railings and chains). Within are several family tombs, the grandest of which is the Duke's: a pink Peterhead Granite slab signed by *MacDonald, Field & Co*, masons, of Aberdeen. His two-stage slab with coped upper surfaces rests on a base of York Stone.[82] Condition: fair, apart from the theft of the bronze fittings.[83]

111 GENERAL FORSTER WALKER (*c.* 1808-66)

[18863/**129**/RS]. A once-elaborate (and now extremely forlorn) Gothic tomb-chest of granite, marble, and Portland Stone, designed by the eminent architect *Edward Blore* (1787-1879), and carved by the eminent sculptor *James Forsyth*. Over the pink Peterhead Granite plinth is a moulded base, from which rises an arcade of alternating cusped arches and lancets, divided by

[77] *The Illustrated London News*, lv/1563 (23 October 1869), 413. [78] The original was erected by the Amalgamated Society of Railway Servants in memory of a heroic train-driver and his fireman, Henry J. L. Dean (d. 1898), who both died trying to save passengers on the Paddington-Windsor Express when the boiler of the steam-engine exploded. The monument was restored and the plaque renewed by Dean}s family in 1994. [79] Eastlake, a painter of literary and Italian scenes, was President of the Royal Academy in 1850-65 and sometime Director of the National Gallery, and a major figure in the development of Victorian taste. [80] Newton was an outstanding Classical archaeologist and Keeper of Greek and Roman Antiquities at the British Museum, best remembered as the discoverer (1856) of the fourth-century BC Hellenistic Ionic tomb of King Mausolos at Halicarnassus, one of the Seven Wonders of the Ancient World. Only Newton's wife's name is recorded as having been buried in the grave, although his name appears in the burial register. [81] The long inscription recounts Deacon's 62-year naval career which included service under Nelson and the incurring of 23 wounds. [82] Portland, known as the 'Mole Duke', was a vastly wealthy landowner who devoted his later years to pushing the architecture of privacy to new extremes, including elaborate underground complexes at his seat of Welbeck Abbey. [83] The monument was damaged by a bomb in the 1939-45 war. The railings were stolen in three separate raids between 1951 and 1952.

8.39 Monument by J. S. Farley [19697/125/PS] of Admiral Henry Colins Deacon (1788-1869), who joined the Royal Navy in 1800, served under Nelson, and was wounded 23 times on the service of his country. Photograph of 1997. *See* Chapter VIII, §109 (© *Crown copyright. NMR.AA97/1186*).

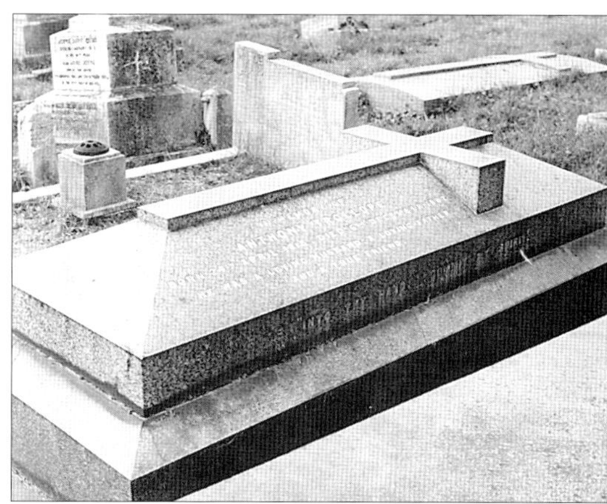

8.40 Visual interest and historical significance do not always combine in one monument: the grave of Trollope [28529/138/PS] in 2000. *See* Chapter VIII, §114 (© *English Heritage [NMR]. AA 020153*).

Sicilian marble shafts; the canopies over the projecting, finial-topped, angles once contained statuettes of Faith, Hope, Charity, and Patience.[84] Condition: very poor.

112 JOHN PERCY, FRS (1817-89), and his wife, GRACE (d. 1880)

[27446/129/3]. This immaculately preserved memorial, consisting of an arched headstone and coped ledger on a moulded base of flecked grey granite, is signed by *T. Woolner* (1825-92), a founder-member of the Pre-Raphaelite Brotherhood and one of the leading High Victorian sculptors. This is an apparently unique instance of his commercial memorial output, and is therefore important. Condition: good.

113 REV. SYDNEY SMITH (1771-1845)

[5680/131/5]. Another reticent memorial to a major figure in the late-Georgian cultural firmament, this conventional Portland Stone sarcophagus with plain angle-piers and a segmental lid covers the mortal remains of an outstanding wit, Whig, and man of letters; one of the founders of the *Edinburgh Review*, Smith was a leading advocate of Catholic emancipation. Buried with him is his daughter, Saba, Lady Holland (1802-66). Condition: fair.

114 ANTHONY TROLLOPE (1815-82)

[28529/138/PS]. A conventional pink granite hipped ledger with cross on top, on a coped base of grey granite, marking the resting-place of the outstanding novelist and author of the 'Barsetshire' series, which opened in 1855 with *The Warden*, and the 'Palliser' novels. Trollope was also the civil servant responsible for introducing the pillar-box. Condition: fair (**8.40**).

115 ÉMILE BLONDIN (1824-97)

[31398/140/RS]. A pink Peterhead Granite and Carrara Marble monument, signed *MacDonald & Leslie*, masons. The gabled, granite headstone, with shafts and base of grey granite and matching kerb and posts, sports an IHS monogram set in a star; beneath, within bronze surrounds, and formerly glazed, are two inset marble portrait-reliefs facing each other of Blondin and his wife, Charlotte. Above stands a statue of Hope. Blondin (a.k.a. Jean-François Gravelet) was the celebrated showman and tightrope-walker, renowned for his crossings of Niagara Falls; as the epitaph relates, he retired to Niagara House, Ealing. Condition: fair (**8.41**).

84 *The Builder*, **xxiv**/1212 (28 April 1866), 305-6. The long description of the monument in *The Builder* refers to it as the 'monument to General Forster Walker': Isabella Forster Walker did indeed commission Blore to design this 'tribute of affection to the memory of her parents', but the General's body was not entombed beneath it. The tomb contains only the body of Lydia S. F. Walker (d. 1864), possibly the wife of the General.

8.41 Monument [31398/140/RS] to Jean-François Gravelet (known as Émile Blondin) (1824-97) and his wife, Charlotte Gravelet Blondin (d. 1888), and daughter, Katherine Gravelet Blondin (d. 1901), in 2001. The French-born Blondin is celebrated for crossing the Niagara Gorge, N.Y., on a tightrope, first in 1859, then following the feat with different thematic variations: blindfolded; in a sack; pushing a wheelbarrow; carrying a man on his back; and sitting down half-way while he made and consumed an omelette. He appeared in the Crystal Palace at Sydenham in 1861, where, on a tight-rope 170 feet from the ground, he turned somersaults on stilts. His last performance was given in Belfast in 1896, and he died the following year at 'Niagara House', Ealing, his residence. *See* Chapter VIII, §115 (*MC.130101*).

116 GENERAL SIR JOHN AITCHISON (1789-1875)

[22621/140/RS]. A large Portland Stone mausoleum, with a blocked entrance below an enriched lintel between consoles; the eared pediment above is crowned with a crucifix-finial. Walls and entrance have pronounced batters. The eastern side-wall carries a lengthy encomium in lead letters, outlining Aitchison's military career. Condition: poor, owing to bricked-up door.

117 WILLIAM WILKIE COLLINS (1824-89)

[31754/141/PS]. The plainest of memorials, consisting of an utterly conventional Carrara Marble cross on a stepped base within a marble kerb, marking the final resting-place of the outstanding novelist.[85] Condition: fair (**8.42**).

118 H.R.H. GEORGE WILLIAM FREDERICK CHARLES, 2nd DUKE OF CAMBRIDGE (1819-1904)

[28623/153/RS]. An exceptional pink-and-grey granite mausoleum (the designer has not been identified), impeccably maintained, which houses the remains of the cemetery's third royal interment. The arched doorway on the south face, set below a cavetto cornice, is set within battered side-walls (with roll-mouldings to corners) that support a stepped roof with a curved finial. Marble posts with chains border the irregular plot.[86] Condition: good (**8.43**).

119 JOHN LUCAS (1807-74)

[24348/153/RS]. A slender obelisk of grey Cornish Granite (with a portrait-relief and inscription-

[85] He is best remembered for *The Woman in White* (1860) and *The Moonstone* (1868). [86] A grandson of King George III, Cambridge served as Commander-in-Chief of the British Army for 39 years (1856-95) at the height of Britain's imperial power; he is remembered more for his hostility to reform than for any prowess as a commander. Like the Duke of Sussex he elected for burial here in order to be at rest with his morganatic wife, Sarah Louisa Fairbrother (1816-90), an actress who specialised in 'trouser-rôles', subsequently known as Mrs FitzGeorge.

8.42 Grave [31754/141/PS] of Wilkie Collins and his mistress, Caroline Graves (*c*.1831-95) – on whom the character of Anne in *The Woman in White* is based, in 1997. *See* Chapter VIII, §117 (© *Crown copyright. NMR. AA97/1158*).

8.43 Mausoleum [28623/153/RS] of H.R.H. The Duke of Cambridge, K.G., and his family, in 2000. *See* Chapter VIII, §118 (*MC.C090101*).

plaques of Carrara Marble on a square pedestal) in memory of this once-prominent portrayer of Victorian beauties, who exhibited at the Royal Academy between 1828 and 1874. Condition: fair.

120 DECIMUS BURTON (1806-81)

[4791/155/3]. An acutely downward-tapering sarcophagus of grey Cornish Granite with a shallow pyramidal cover, perched on a stepped base. As with the Hardwicks in square [31], so with Burton: a visually minor memorial to one of the great architects of his day. He designed the Athenaeum Club in Waterloo Place (1827-30), the palm-house at Kew Gardens (1845-8), the Arch and Screen at Hyde Park Corner (1824-5), much of Tunbridge Wells and St Leonard's-on-Sea, Sussex, and a great deal besides. Condition: poor, owing to settlement.

121 SAMUEL GRIFFITH (*c*.1766-1833)

[233/157 or possibly 144/RS]. A richly Roman Portland Stone altar-tomb (*c*.1833) on a stepped grey granite base, probably by *John Griffith* (1796-1888), architect of the cemetery's buildings.[87] The fielded panels to each face are flanked by inverted torches; the fluted frieze boasts cherub heads at the corners, and is surmounted with a scrolled segmental pedimental cover. This would have been one of the very earliest monuments in the cemetery. Condition: poor.

122 LADY MARY MONTGOMERIE (*c*.1787-1848)

[7614/157/IR]. This is an unusually colossal sarcophagus of Carrara Marble on a base of grey granite; the frieze of alternating paterae and fleurs-de-lys runs below the crisp dentil cornice; above is a shallow pedimental cover, cracked, with acroteria.[88] Condition: poor.

123 WILLIAM HENRY KENT MRCVS (*c*.1822-74)

[24555/157/2]. A conventional draped urn-topped pedestal of Carrara Marble. The base and inscription are more special. The former contains a canine relief and the latter explains that Kent (a vet), was 'the friend of the friend of man: THE DOG'. Condition: poor.

124 MARY ANN THURSTON (1810-96)

[36163/157/2]. This weathered Carrara Marble stylised Celtic cross, on a stepped base and slab, contains a Raphaelesque circular relief of the Madonna and Child. Inspection of the base reveals the lead signature of no less a sculptor than *H.R.H. Princess Louise Caroline Alberta, Duchess of*

[87] Samuel Griffith's two sons, Richard Clewin Griffith, MRCS (1791-1881 – who helped to establish Regent's Park Zoological Gardens in 1827), and John Griffth, FRIBA (architect of the cemetery buildings and one-time Chairman of the General Cemetery Company), are also buried in this grave. [88] The romantically-tinged aristocratic assertiveness accords perfectly with the fact that Lady Mary was the daughter of Archibald, 11th Earl of Eglintoun (1726-96 – the title only became 'Eglinton' in the 19th century). She married, first, Archibald, Lord Montgomerie (1773-1814), and then Sir Charles Lamb, Bart. (d. 1860).

8.44 The poignant monument [47220/160/PS] of Winston Churchill's infant daughter, Marigold, by Eric Gill, in 2001. The cross is a recent replacement for the stolen relief of the Crucifixion. *See* Chapter VIII, § 126 (*MC.M130101*).

8.45 Faithful unto death [40226/165/RS]: the effigy of the tragic Alexandrina Allingham (d. 1904) with her lap-dog. Photograph of 2000. *See* Chapter VIII, §127 (© *English Heritage [NMR]. AA020157*).

Argyll (1848-1939), so is a unique instance of a cemetery memorial carved by a member of the Royal Family.[89] Condition: fair.

125 EDWARD ADOLPHUS SEYMOUR, 11th DUKE OF SOMERSET

[4501/**157**/4]. Portland Stone Neoclassical mausoleum, with battered sides. Battered doorway (door missing) below shallow pediment with coronet in tympanum; angle-pilasters with battered sides; stone roof with antefixa over the longer sides; stepped element on roof supporting draped urn on stepped base; marble inscription-reliefs inside. Condition: poor.

126 MARIGOLD FRANCES CHURCHILL (1918-21)

[47220/**160**/PS]. Hopton Wood headstone by *Eric Gill* (1882-1940), with his characteristic lettering, in memory of the infant daughter of Winston Leonard Spencer-Churchill (1874-1965) and his wife, Clementine Ogilvy (1885-1977). The inscribed pedestal, on its hammered base, was formerly surmounted by an octagonal shaft with a relief of the Crucifixion: having been stolen it was replaced in *c.*1992 with the present plain Cross.[90] Condition: fair, save for the loss of the upper section (**8.44**).

127 HERBERT WILLIAM ALLINGHAM (1862-1904) and his wife, ALEXANDRINA (d. 1904)

[40226/**165**/RS]. Elaborate Carrara Marble monument, an exceptional example of commercial Edwardian cemetery sculpture. The recumbent effigy of a woman with her lap-dog reclines within the lower recess; above, entwining a demi-column and decorating an urn with a wreath, is the powerfully sorrowful figure of a grieving angel: perhaps here the Angel of Death is intended. The circumstances behind the tomb's erection were bleak indeed: Allingham, a prominent surgeon and authority on diseases of the rectum, took his own life, having accidentally infected his wife with syphilis while pursuing a cure for the disease. Condition: fair (**8.45** and **9.15**).

128 COLONEL GIDEON GORREQUER (1777-1841)

[3119/**168**/2]. An elaborate military memorial of Portland Stone, consisting of a square pedestal on a rusticated base, with a weathered Carrara Marble inscription-panel. Above the entablature, with its bed-mouldings of dentils, is a cushion supporting a military still-life composed of a shako, sword, sash, and medals. Dwarf cast-iron railings defend the grave-slab. One of the best of the early military monuments in the cemetery, this commemorates the sometime ADC to Sir Hudson Lowe (1769-1844), Governor of St Helena (1815-21) during Napoleon's final exile there: Gorrequer kept a journal of this period (published 1969) which chronicled the two men's squabbles, and portrayed Lowe as an eccentric to the point of insanity, while Lady Lowe was depicted as a grotesque Dickensian character. Condition: poor, owing to settlement, weathering, and partial loss of railings (**8.46**).

89 The monument was erected at the expense of Queen Victoria and her children in memory of their former nurse.
90 *See* Peace (1994), 103.

8.46 Napoleon's keeper: the monument [3119/168/2] of Colonel Gideon Gorrequer. Photograph of 2000. *See* Chapter VIII, §128 (© *English Heritage[NMR]*. AA 020159).

8.47 The collapsing monument [284/170/RS] of Thomas Fenwick (*c*.1834), in 2000. Bath Stone has not proved to be a sound choice of material for outdoor monuments. *See* Chapter VIII, §131 (© *English Heritage [NMR]. AA/020161*).

129 FREDERICK ORLANDO TOMPSON DELMAR (d. 1895) and his wife, MONA (d. 1859)

[1487/**168**/3]. A large Portland Stone sarcophagus, signed *Browne*, mason, erected in *c*.1838. The neat chest has projecting pilasters at the corners supporting a Doric frieze; on each end are palm-flanked hatchments, and the scrolled pedimental cover is enriched with acanthus ornament. One of the best of the earliest generation of Neoclassical sarcophagi in the cemetery.[91] Condition: fair.

130 JOHN TERNOUTH (*c*.1796-1848)

[7891/**168**/6-7]. A Carrara Marble *stela* with a Classical relief of a grieving draped woman embracing an urn-topped pedestal set within a recess (compare James Ward's [15560/**90**/3] memorial [§80]). This may be one of his own works.[92] Condition: poor.

***131 THOMAS FENWICK (*c*.1774-1837)**

[284/**170**/RS]. A collapsing mausoleum of Bath Stone, among the very earliest mausolea in the cemetery, with battered sides, a primitive door-architrave, an iron door, and a simple moulded cornice; the upper pedimented section sports the Fenwick arms and the inscription THE FAMILY TOMB OF THOMAS FENWICK ESQ.[93] Condition: very bad (**8.47**).

***132 RICHARD GREGORY, FRS (*c*.1760-1839) and his two wives, ISABELLA (*c*.1810-33) and CHRISTIAN (d.1836)**

[40/**170**/RS]. A second collapsing mausoleum of Bath Stone, forming part of the very earliest group of memorials within the cemetery. Its battered sides and primitive door-architrave, this time blocked, support a moulded cornice and an upper pedimented section. The railings set into the stone kerb around the plot have gone.[94] Condition: very bad (**4.18**).

133 HALL FAMILY (*c*. 1834)

[29/**170**/RS]. A near-identical mausoleum to the above two items, forming the third constituent part of the earliest group of memorials within the cemetery.[95] Condition: as deplorable as the previous two (**4.18**).

[91] Delmar was a stockbroker. The early date of the monument probably indicates either prudent provision or burial of an infant. The grave was originally owned by Henry Philip Hope (1774-1839), collector of pictures and diamonds, and brother of Thomas Hope (1769-1831), the great protagonist of English Neoclassicism. The grave was transferred to Maria Tompson (or Thompson) in 1838 for five shillings. She took the name Delmar in 1840.
[92] Ternouth, the sculptor, is best-remembered for modelling one of the reliefs on the plinth of Nelson's Column in Trafalgar Square. [93] Fenwick was formerly called Thomas Lambert, but took the name Fenwick on inheriting Burrow Hall, near the Westmorland border, North Lancashire, in 1801 from a distant cousin. [94] Gregory, of Coole Park, Galway, founded the Gregory Scholarship and endowed the library at Harrow School in memory of his first wife (*née* Nimmo). He was the elder brother of William Gregory (1762-1840), Under-Secretary at Dublin Castle (1812-30), an efficient administrator and strong opponent of 'Catholic Emancipation'. William's grandson married Augusta, Lady Gregory (1852-1932), an important figure in the Irish Literary Revival (*c*.1890-*c*.1914). Richard Gregory's second wife (*née* Steer) is also deposited in the vault. *See Burke's Irish Family Records* (1976), 511. [95] This was the family mausoleum of Edward Hall, of Beaulieu Lodge, Winchmore Hill (d. 1861). His coffin was opened by licence in 1893, and certain papers were removed. Also entombed within is his son, John Edward Hall (1837-86), barrister and reporter. The mausoleum was vandalised in 1980, after which the entrance was bricked up.

134 MARIA TUSTIN (*c*.1859-1914)

[44123/**174**/3]. An unusual memorial in terms of style, date, and quality. It consists of a Carrara Marble statue of a seated woman in medieval dress, perched on a base of red granite with angles decorated with torches of pressed metal. This figure (which owes something to Sir Richard Westmacott's [1775-1856] monument, known as 'The Distressed Mother' in Westminster Abbey to Mrs Warren [d. 1816]) shows the sculptural quality of which monumental masons were capable at that time.[96] Condition: fair, but badly discoloured with algae (**8.48**).

8.48 Late Romanticism: the monument [44123/**174**/3] of Maria Tustin (d. 1914), photographed in 2000. *See* Chapter VIII, §134 (© *English Heritage [NMR]*. *AA/020163*).

Postscript

The monuments listed in the above gazetteer are but a personal skim[97] of the 70,000-odd tombs in Kensal Green cemetery. What conclusions can be drawn from them?

For one, Kensal Green needs to be thought of as a late-Georgian phenomenon and not just a Victorian one. Most of its early tombs drew inspiration from the established Neoclassical sculptural tradition that was to be found in churchyards across the country, and the story is one of continuity rather than change. The exceptions to this were the swagger tombs such as those of Ducrow, St John Long, or Soyer: for them, the restraints of graveyard decorum were done away with, and attention-craving exuberance could flourish as never before. The exemplary and the egregious stand side by side.

Sculpture, in England, and even at Kensal Green, has never played the rôle it did in the grand Continental cemeteries; that Thomas Woolner is represented here with an austere architectural design seems strangely fitting. Qualities of mass and material assume great importance for the tombs here, and the primacy of granite, slate, and artificial stone over all other stones in terms of endurance and legibility are immediately apparent. Monuments are messages to posterity; pleasing decay no longer pleases when the original meaning is lost.

Sadly, an overall decline in standards of monument design is immediately apparent. This decline commenced around 1880, and steepened sharply in the 20th century. There are modern tombs (such as those of the German poet Erich Fried[98] and of Joshua Compston[99]) that, one day, perhaps, may be listed too, but in general, even in elegant Kensal Green, most modern memorials are of interest to immediate mourners alone. The visual splendours of much older tombs put present-day practices to shame. If we are to continue to admire them, we shall have to continue to pay for their upkeep and repair; this survey was carried out because we shall need to know which ones on which to concentrate. Old memorials do more than bring pleasure to generation after generation of visitor: the consolations they afforded their builders remain relevant also to the newly bereaved, and they go on providing food for thought and refreshment for the spirit. Kensal Green cemetery is a place of death but it never oppresses.[100]

[96] Maria Tustin was the wife of Walter Tustin, builder. [97] Personal they are, but the present writer owes a very considerable debt to the Editor for fleshing out the entries. Professor Curl's penetrating insights and wide-ranging scholarship have greatly improved the original drafts. [98] [62909/**113**/PS]. [99] [65657/**57**/PS]. [100] The Editor acknowledges, with many thanks, the contribution of Mr Moulder in checking, providing, and correcting many locations, and for answering innumerable questions about the G.C.C. records. Mr Moulder has also provided biographical notes, and some information in footnotes in this Chapter is derived from material he provided. His and Mr Vivian-Neal's assistance has been of the greatest help.

CHAPTER IX

The Monuments of the General Cemetery of All Souls, Kensal Green: Meaning and Style

CHRISTOPHER BROOKS

Introduction; The Monuments; Afterword

> ... both the sculptors and their patrons must get rid of the ideas which have placed so many melancholy mistakes in these same grounds. They must not think that largeness of structure is synonymous with grandeur, or that a style of architecture unlike anything the world ever saw, necessarily meets our view of originality, or that a really good idea cannot be sufficiently repeated without endless repetitions of it.
>
> CHARLES KNIGHT (*Ed.*) (1791-1873):
> *London*, iv, revised and corrected by EDWARD WALFORD (1823-97)
> (London: Virtue & Co. Ltd., *c.*1870), 172.

Introduction

The commemoration of the dead held a key position in the Victorian imagination. It was intimately associated with status in an age of rapid social change and shifting class identities; with notions of the individual in a period wedded to the values of *laissez-faire* self-help; with religious faith in a culture that was becoming increasingly secular; and with the whole affective complex that gave shape to the idea of the family. Funerary monuments were the most permanent product of this commemorative passion. Designed – like cemeteries themselves – for the benefit of the living rather than the dead, they were public statements, texts to be read and interpreted (both individually and as components of the larger text established by the whole cemetery), and the languages they used were social and cultural, stylistic, and iconographic.

By the 1830s, the growing importance of trade, commerce, and industry, the expansion of the professions, and the emergence of new managerial and entrepreneurial élites, had brought increased social standing for those people who formed what the 18th century called 'the middling sort'. Newly empowered, this social group commissioned memorials that affirmed and celebrated family coherence in a way only available previously to the gentry and aristocracy. Since the Middle Ages, in parish churches throughout Britain, burial-vaults had been appropriated to aristocratic families whose grand monuments and lengthy epitaphs were assertions of social and political power handed down through the generations. This dynastic function was translated into middle-class terms in 19th-century British cemeteries, where – following the lead of Père-Lachaise cemetery in Paris – the burial-plots offered for sale could be purchased in perpetuity. Exclusive possession of property in the cemetery could thus both extend and confirm the property-ownership that was the basis of class status. A mausoleum or a large plot that could contain a dozen or more coffins (and that was marked by an imposing memorial) assumed and symbolised family continuity, an inheritable identity, and social prestige. Thus, at Kensal Green, the family-tombs of bankers, financiers, tradesmen, men of letters, and – above all – the solid representatives of the professional and commercial classes, stand out on the prestigious principal avenues and at the focal points of the cemetery's layout. Alongside them, however, indeed vying with them, are memorials to a sizeable proportion of the British aristocracy, for the family celebration of the newly rich and influential was matched with dynastic reassertion by the traditional governing classes. The General Cemetery of All Souls at Kensal Green was fashionable even before its reputation was assured by the royal interments of the Duke of Sussex (**5.5**), the brother of King William IV, and of Princess Sophia (**5.10**, **8.38**), the last surviving daughter of King George III: their monuments stand in pride of place before the Anglican chapel.[1] In the year of Sussex's death, Clark's *Hand-book for Visitors to the Kensal Green Cemetery* already claimed 'members of more than two hundred of the first families in the kingdom'[2] among the cemetery's dead. And for social aspirants of 'the middling sort' the possibility of buying into a piece of ground also occupied by royalty and the *haut ton* was not the least of Kensal Green's many attractions.

The Monuments

The General Cemetery and its monuments were created by the dynamics of late 18th- and early 19th-century capitalism, the force that had revolutionised Britain's agricultural and industrial economy, and, as a result, the whole of British society. Nineteenth-century capitalism found its classic ideological expression in the principles of *laissez-faire* – the

1 [5268/114/PS] and [8028/114/PS] respectively. 2 Clark (1843), 85.

doctrine of economic individualism. Although the promotion of aggressive self-interest was uncomfortable both for middle-class domestic pieties and for aristocratic claims to an enlightened paternalism, *laissez-faire* was inseparable from the economic success of barons and bourgeoisie alike. However morally problematic, the entrepreneurial thruster needed a place in the mythology of Victorian Britain: somewhat unsettling as a Carlylean Captain of Industry,[3] he became more manageable as one of Samuel Smiles's (1812-1904) diligent self-helpers.[4] And, as Kensal Green cemetery demonstrates, he earned his place there as well. The self-made man is at his most assimilable in the great railway engineer Joseph Locke (1805-60) (**8.34**),[5] or in the writer and horticulturalist John Claudius Loudon (1783-1843) (**5.9**),[6] who actually won himself a whole page of praise in the canonical *Self-Help*.[7] Less obvious as acolytes of the work-ethic are popular entertainers such as the tightrope artiste Émile Blondin (1824-97) (**8.41**),[8] and the equestrian Andrew Ducrow (1793-1842), who was the proprietor of Astley's Circus[9] and whose mausoleum, reputed to have cost £3,000, stands in prime position at the junction of the Circle and Centre Avenue (**8.23-8.24**).[10] It is an unblushing piece of posthumous self-advertisement, 'erected by genius', says the epitaph, 'for the reception of its own remains'; 'ponderous coxcombry' said *The Builder*.[11] We move from the not-quite-respectable to the downright fraudulent with the quack doctor John St John Long (1798-1834), whose monument,[12] facing Ducrow's across Centre Avenue, boasts a statue of Hygieia (Ὑγίεια), the Greek goddess of health (**4.28, 8.26**). Long's career scarcely merited her presence as he was found guilty of manslaughter in 1830 after his peculiar ministrations killed a patient: his memorial was raised – to quote the reproachful inscription – 'by those who knew his worth, and the benefits derived from his remedial discovery'. A fitting companion for Long and Hygieia is James Morison (1770-1840), self-styled 'the Hygeist', the inventor of 'Morison's Pills' and the most successful patent-medicine entrepreneur of the century. He was also one of the original members of the Board of the General Cemetery Company, which helps to explain the prominence and quality of his mausoleum, a fine Neoclassical design (profoundly influenced by French exemplars) by the mason-architect Robert Shout (*c*.1763-1843)[13] that is the principal tomb[14] on Northern Avenue (**4.27**). So ubiquitous was Morison's 'Pill' that Carlyle, diagnosing early Victorian Britain's ills in *Past and Present*, adopted it as a metaphor for the nation's fevered attempts to find a quick-fix cure for social unrest.[15]

The masculine world of *laissez-faire* enterprise found its complement – and its conscience – in the feminine world of hearth and home. For the middle-classes (who were the principal clients of Kensal Green, as indeed of most other 19th-century cemeteries), the rôles of men and women were fixed in separate spheres, each defined by the other. A public economy driven forward, often ruthlessly, by Carlylean Captains of Industry, necessitated a private economy presided over by the idealised figure that the poet Coventry Patmore (1823-96) famously called the 'Angel in the House'.[16] In every sense, she was the heart of what social historians have come to call 'the affectionate family' – the close family-unit created by the values of 'the middling sort' in the 18th century and

[3] Thomas Carlyle coined the phrase 'Captains of Industry' as the title of Chapter IV of the fourth book of *Past and Present* (1843), claiming in the chapter that 'The Leaders of Industry ... are virtually the Captains of the World': Carlyle, **xiii** (1882), 335. [4] Smiles (1905). First published in 1859, *Self-Help* went through four editions in a month and was reprinted 47 times before the Popular Edition; it was also translated into almost every European language, into Arabic, Turkish, and Japanese, and into the major languages of India. [5] [6866/**99**/PS]. [6] [4547/**74**/PS]. [7] Smiles (1905), 129-30. [8] [31398/**140**/RS]. [9] For Ducrow's extraordinary career *see* Saxon (1978), *passim*. [10] [820/**76**/RS]. [11] 'Tombs at Kensall-Green', in *The Builder*, **xiv**/725 (27 December 1856), 700. [12] [283/**76**/RS]. [13] Vivian-Neal (1999), 73. I am greatly indebted to this compilation for many of the details of individual memorials discussed in this Chapter, and also to the Editor for his many suggestions and corrections. For Shout *see* Colvin (1995), 867. Shout is entombed in [4238/**CAT. B**/Pub. V/25]. [14] [383/**50**/RS]. [15] Carlyle, **xiii** (1882), 29; 'Morrison's Pill' – thus mis-spelt in the title of Chapter IV in Book I. [16] 'The Angel in the House' is a long poem originally published in four parts between 1854 and 1862. *See* Patmore (1909), 1-145.

reinforced by the ideals of Romanticism, its members tied to one another by mutual feeling. Within the affectionate family,[17] with its emphasis on personal sensibility and domestic virtues, death and bereavement took on new meanings which, in turn, became part of the cemetery's commemorative language. The 19th century ushered in 'the Age of the Beautiful Death'[18] in which individual affection aspired to transcend mortality itself. But the ethos of the Beautiful Death also made loss irreparable, tolerable only through cherished memories or equally cherished fantasies of future reunion. This found definitive expression for the Victorians through Alfred Tennyson (1809-92) in his great poem *In Memoriam* (begun 1833, published 1850), its grief for the loss of the poet's friend Arthur Henry Hallam (1811-33) only just offset by a consolation that comes more from reiterated emotional intensity than from conventional religious faith.

Dear heavenly friend that canst not die,
Mine, mine, for ever, ever mine[19]

wrote Tennyson, perhaps trying to convince himself of a continuing togetherness.

Kensal Green cemetery has its monuments of the Beautiful Death: three, from the early, middle, and late years of Victoria's reign will indicate something of their expressive range. On Northern Avenue, opposite the gate leading to the Harrow Road, the chef Alexis Soyer (1809-58) erected a memorial (**8.29**)[20] to his young wife, the artist Elizabeth Emma Jones (1813-42), who, terrified by a thunderstorm, died of a miscarriage after only five years of marriage. The monument, sculpted by Pierre Puyenbroeck and costing £500, consists of a figure of Hope standing on a tall pedestal which is carved with putti mournfully hovering above a draped medallion portrait of Emma, below which are representations of her palette and a cornucopia. The whole assemblage rises from a base bearing the words 'TO HER', as if any further identification were redundant, and the back of the pedestal originally incorporated Emma's actual palette, talismanically enshrined behind glass (like much else in the cemetery, stolen). The monument is discussed in more detail in the following Chapter.

On Centre Avenue, surrounded by some of the grandest monuments in the cemetery,[21] the grave of Mary Eleanor Gibson (1854-72), an only child who died at the age of 18, is marked by a miniature Corinthian peristyle surmounted by four angels, reaching heavenward and at one time holding a ceramic funerary wreath aloft above the tomb (**8.13** and **10.4**). Further along Centre Avenue, towards the main gate, stands the exquisitely lovely monument[22] to Ninon Michaelis (d. 1895) (**9.1** and **10.12**), its strikingly expressive female mourner, slightly larger than life-size, breaking down and weeping, as she tries to deck the tomb's tapering pedestal, which carries the single word 'Ninon'. Such memorials are moving because the commemorative act they embody, elaborately and expensively, tries so hard to deliver a comfort that cannot quite be managed or quite believed.

The meanings expressed by Kensal Green's monuments are particularly clear because the policy of the General Cemetery Company allowed complete freedom of design. Liberty was channelled, however, through a range of historicist styles. The first of these was Neo-Greek[23] – smart and aristocratic, dominant in late-Georgian polite architecture, and the style adopted for the cemetery's own buildings. The great majority of the tombs erected before the 1850s are in a Greek Revival style, and several can be traced to prototypes in Père-Lachaise cemetery, that Elysian inspiration of the British cemetery movement. Two examples are the Doric canopy of *c.*1840 that forms the family tomb[24]

[17] For a discussion of death and the affectionate family *see* Brooks (1989), 4 ff. [18] *See* Ariès (1983), 409 ff.
[19] Tennyson (1850), CXXIX. The inscription on the Momerie monument [38386/177/PS] clearly owes a debt to Tennyson's *In Memoriam*. [20] [3714/80/RS]. [21] [23601/56/RS]. [22] [37384/37/RS]. [23] For the history of the style *see* Crook (1972), *passim*. [24] [5535/57/RS].

9.1 *Stele* in the *Jugendstil* of Central Europe [37384/**37**/RS], in memory of Ninon Michaelis (d. 1895). Photograph of 2001. *See* Chapter VIII, §18 (*MC. A030101*).

9.2 Portland Stone mausoleum of Dr Richard Valpy [687/**101**/RS]. A handsome distyle *in antis* temple-tomb in the Greek Revival style, it combines Doric columns with *antae* and a frieze derived from the Choragic monument of Thrasyllus, Athens [*see* **7.11**], and was designed by John Griffith of Finsbury, the architect of the cemetery buildings. Photograph of 2001. *See* Chapter VIII, §101 (*CB*).

of John Collett (1798-1866) (**8.18**), and the tall plinth with crowning sarcophagus which commemorates John Brine (1774-1847).[25] The style offered a wide expressive range, from the primitive to the refined, and an extensive, if largely standardised, funerary iconography. Greek is at its most formidable in some of the early mausolea, their designs, largely stripped of historicist detail, exploiting the style's capacity for primitivism. Good examples are the mortuary blockhouses of James Dunlop (1769-1841),[26] and Sir William Molesworth, Bart. (1810-55)[27] – the grey-granite austerity of the latter wholly appropriate to a man sympathetic with the sterner precepts of Utilitarianism (**8.12**). For the really heavyweight, however, nothing at Kensal Green surpasses the mausoleum of the merchant banker Baron John Frederick Andrew Huth (1777-1864).[28] Forcefully detailed, with an emphatic cornice (over a frieze carrying a Latin inscription) and shallow-pitched stone roof, its massiveness is emphasised rather than relieved by the lachrymal vases in niches that decorate the exterior: costing £1,500 and built over a catacomb capable of taking 48 coffins, the Huth mausoleum is probably the largest tomb in the cemetery, and certainly one of the most insistently dynastic (**8.28**). Neo-Greek mausolea with columnar porticoes are less overbearing. Two good early examples are those of Dr Richard Valpy (1754-1836)[29] (**9.2**), and of George Robertson Aikman (d.1844)[30] (**8.25**). Both built of Portland Stone and conceived on similar lines, they were designed by the architect of Kensal Green's Greek Revival buildings, John Griffith: each has Doric columns *in antis* with a decorated frieze below a moulded pediment, and is raised on a plinth with inset steps up to the entrance from the roadway. A good late example, and a telling instance

[25] [10824/**42**/RS]. Brine, a sculptor, executed chimney-pieces for the Royal Pavilion, Brighton, and the Quadrant, Regent Street, London. He exhibited chimney-pieces at the Great Exhibition of 1851. In 1826 he made statues for Lady de Grey's garden at Wrest Park, Bedfordshire. Among monuments by him may be mentioned those to John Elmslie in Windsor parish-church (1829); the Dick family, St Mary's church, Chilham, Kent (1837); John Rogers, Streatham parish-church (1840); and Lady Preston, Beeston St Lawrence, Norfolk (1846). *See* Gunnis (1968), 61. [26] [3258/**86**/RS]. [27] [12766/**56**/RS]. [28] [2735/**77**/IC]. [29] [687/**101**/RS]. The Valpy mausoleum is signed Adron of New Road. *See* Chapter VIII, §87 (*Editor's note*). [30] [4627/**76**/RS].

9.3 Greek Doric-temple mausoleum [47543/32/RS] erected by Imre Kiralfy (1845-1919) for the 'interment' of his 'children and grandchildren', photographed in 1997 (© *Crown copyright. NMR.AA 97/1172*).

9.4 Classical tomb-chest above the vault [98/77/IR] of the Stewart family of Galloway, designed by John Buonarotti Papworth (1775-1847); among those interred in the vault are George Stewart, 8th Earl of Galloway (1768-1834), and his brother, the Rt. Rev. the Hon. Charles James Stewart (1775-1839), Bishop of Québec. Photograph of 2001. *See* Chapter VIII, §58 (*CB*).

of the style's longevity, is the Kiralfy mausoleum[31] of 1919, again Doric but with prostylar columns and all in grey granite (**9.3**). Among smaller tombs there is considerable formal inventiveness, as shown by the memorials ranged along the northern half of Junction Avenue: the box-tomb – half mausoleum, half sarcophagus[32] – of David Edward Morris (1770-1842), with acroteria, antefixa, and funerary urn; the delightful miniature temple, perched on its pedestal like a scale model, commemorating Charles (*c*.1799-1863) and Joanna (*c*.1809-1840) Stevenson (**8.31**);[33] and a tall, tapering pedestal carrying a ritual brazier on lion's claw feet, the inscription now illegible.[34]

More complex tombs combine Classical architectural elements with figure sculpture. Mary Gibson's monument,[35] with its clustered Corinthian columns and bevy of angels has already been mentioned (**8.13** and **10.4**); produced by the local statuary James Samuel Farley (1811-66), whose workshop stood (and stands) opposite the cemetery entrance, it gives striking proof of the high level of craftsmanship achieved by the commercial firms of Victorian monumental masons. On John St John Long's memorial,[36] also already mentioned (**4.28** and **8.26**), Hygieia stands within a rotunda of columns below an ornately detailed circular canopy, the frieze ornamented with lotus-leaf and palmette motifs linked by scrolls, anthemion-form antefixa running continuously above the cornice, and a finial in the form of a tripod and vase topping off the domed roof. The whole tomb is a distant echo of the Choragic Monument of Lysicrates in Athens (334 BC). The statue was the work of Robert William Sievier, well established as a fashionable sculptor by the 1820s, and one of the original Board-members of the General Cemetery Company. Set at a key point in the cemetery, the St John Long memorial was a species of advertisement both for Sievier's work and for what Kensal Green could offer its intended clientele; the Valpy mausoleum, designed by Griffith and sited in a similarly prominent position westward along Centre Avenue, functioned in a similar way.

The aesthetic appeal of Kensal Green's monuments, crucial to its commercial success, was enhanced by the involvement of leading architects, several of them notable practitioners of Neo-Greek. The tomb of Isabel Alexander Hankey (1835-7),[37] its carved relief framed by pedimented columns, was designed by George Basevi (1794-1845), a pupil of Soane and the architect of aristocratic developments in Belgravia and South

31 [47543/**32**/RS]. 32 [2627/**89**/RS]. 33 [2821/**90**/RS]. 34 [3141/**92**/RS]. This is the grave of Edward James Andrews (*c*.1810-41), of Upper Bedford Place, Bloomsbury. 35 [23601/**56**/RS]. 36 [283/**76**/RS]. 37 [1051/**101**/RS]. There was an earlier deposit in [988/**CAT. A**].

9.5 Classical tomb-chest [1279/101/RS] with life-size female mourner, to the memory of Alexander Nesbitt Shaw (1804-74) of the Bombay Civil Service. Photograph of 2001 (*CB*).

9.6 Pedimented, pink-granite tomb-chest [10114/100/IR] of Carl Joachim, 1st Baron Hambro (1807-77), founder of the London branch of Hambros Bank Ltd.; he was created Baron in 1851 by King Frederick VII of Denmark (reigned 1848-63). Photograph of 2001 (*CB*).

Kensington.[38] Rather more architectonic is the fine tomb-chest above the family vault of The Rt. Rev. The Hon. Charles James Stewart (1775-1839), Bishop of Québec[39] (**9.4**), its diagonally-set corner-pilasters decorated with modillions and framing, at one end, an elaborate Achievement of Arms. The designer was John Buonarotti Papworth (1775-1847), a prolific architect and architectural writer, with an extensive country-house practice, who, in 1836, was appointed Director of the Government School of Design.

The Hankey relief shows a mourning woman embracing a draped funerary urn. This icon occurs on Classicising tombs throughout the cemetery, and was particularly suited to the gender rôles that dominant middle-class ideology assigned to the Victorian family: grief belongs with things of the heart, and its overt expression was identified with the feminine. 'For men must work', as Charles Kingsley (1819-75) put it, 'and women must weep'.[40] The popularity of the trope was productive of considerable variety: kneeling on a tall podium and sculpted in the round, the woman wraps both arms round the urn of Henry Briant (d. 1847);[41] with the urn propped on her knee, she sits holding an eternal flame on the tomb of George and Mary Waugh (d. 1873 and 1886);[42] a floral spray and a butterfly, symbol of the soul taking wing, amplify the icon on the memorial to John Cooper (*c*.1793-1870).[43] Most dramatic – and dramatically positioned where Centre Avenue crosses the Circle in front of the chapel – is the life-sized mourner who attends the tomb of Alexander Nesbit Shaw (1802-72)[44] (**9.5**) dressed in a Victorian gown, her hair coiffured into a matronly bun: the contemporary and the conventional fuse to create a surprising emotional intensity.

The solitary funerary urn, unattended by any mourning figure, was the commonest commemorative icon in the mortuary repertoire of Classicism, whether its stylistic base was Greek or Roman – or indeed an indeterminate fusion of both. The urn offered an objectified symbol for death, dignified and aloof, with a hint of agreeably aristocratic stoicism. Draped or undraped, variously shaped, sometimes garlanded, there are hundreds of examples: representative early groups stand south of the eastern end of Centre Avenue,[45] along the Circle in front of the Anglican chapel,[46] and in the north-west

[38] The Hankey monument was illustrated in Hakewill (1851), Plate 2. [39] [98/77/IR]. [40] Kingsley (1889), 255. The poem was written in 1851. [41] [6790/40/RS]. The grave of Henry Briant, publican and wine-merchant. He was landlord of *The Artichoke*, 20 Clare Street, Clare Market; of *The Drummond Arms*, Drummond Street, Somerstown; and of *The Chequers*, 11 Abingdon Street, Westminster. [42] Dissenters' section [1995/15/IR]. [43] [3448/92/RS]. John Cooper was an actor. *See D.N.B.*, iv (1917), 1070. [44] [1279/101/RS]. A Bombay civil servant. The grave also contains Isabella Forbes Shaw (1800-77), daughter of Major-General John Shaw. The inscription reads: 'she being dead yet speaketh'. [45] [28] and [32]. [46] [101].

9.7 Classical tomb-chest surmounted by a sarcophagus [5009/**56**/PS], in Carrara Marble, to the memory of the Rev. Arthur Robins (1834-99), Chaplain in Ordinary to Queen Victoria and Rector of Holy Trinity, Windsor. Photograph of 2001 (*CB*).

9.8 Classical altar-tomb [168/**90**/IC] of the Peninsular War veteran, General Christopher Tilson Chowne (*c*.1771-1834), made by Joseph Browne. The handsome draped urn on its tall pedestal behind the Chowne tomb-chest commemorates Mary Ann Stephens (*c*.1798-1843). Photograph of 2001 (*CB*).

quadrant. Vying with the urn in popularity, often indeed combined with it, was the Classical tomb-chest or – to give it its Greek name – sarcophagus.[47] Again there are numerous examples, and the formal variation is considerable: in Portland Stone, with plainly panelled sides and ends for the tea magnate Richard Twining (1772-1857);[48] in pink granite, with corner-pilasters, moulded cornice, and a pedimented lid for the monument to the banker Carl Joachim, 1st Baron Hambro (1807-77)[49] (**9.6**); rusticated corners and a segmentally pedimented lid, all in white marble, on the grave of Major-General George de Lacy Evans (1787-1870);[50] in pale grey Cornish granite, with sharply raked sides and a hipped lid, all set on a stepped and moulded base, for the architect Decimus Burton (1800-81).[51] The more elaborate conceptions include the monument to the miniature-painter François-Théodore Rochard (*c*.1804-57),[52] where the elegantly raked and cross-pedimented chest sits on ball feet upon a rectangular plinth, and the memorial to the Revd. Arthur Robins (1834-99)[53] (**9.7**), which has a miniature sarcophagus set on top of a large and elaborately decorated tomb-chest. A variant on the tomb-chest was the Roman altar-tomb, with a scrolled top and a Doric frieze below the cornice. The form was based on the third-century BC tomb of Cornelius Lucius Scipio Barbatus, found by the side of the Via Appia outside Rome, excavated in 1780-2 and subsequently adopted as a model for cemetery monuments throughout Europe and America.[54] There are several examples, variously reinterpreted, at Kensal Green (**8.34**). One of the finest is also, probably, the earliest, and is particularly close to the original – the monument to the Peninsular War veteran, General Christopher Tilson Chowne (*c*.1771-1834) (**9.8**),[55] the work of the carver Joseph Browne (*fl.* 1815-48), who was the principal marble contractor for London's Marble Arch in 1827. A variation on this type,

47 From the Greek *σαρκοφαγος* (from *σαρκο-*, *σαρξ* = flesh + *φαγος* = eating), meaning a stone coffin in which the flesh of a dead body within it was consumed. 48 [1920/**157**/IR]. 49 [10114/**100**/IR]. 50 [7355/**100-113**/PS]. 51 [4791/**155**/3]. 52 [14122/**48**/RS]. 53 [5009/**56**/PS]. Chaplain in Ordinary to the Queen. He was the son of George Henry Robins (1778-1847), auctioneer (also buried in the grave), who specialised in selling the properties and treasures of the rich and famous, including Horace Walpole's collections at Strawberry Hill; Shakespeare's house; and the Colosseum, Regent's Park. Famed for his grandiloquence and repartee, his catch-phrase, 'a work of supererogation', was echoed in the literature of the period. *See D.N.B*, **xvi** (1917), 1322-3. 54 *See* Colvin (1991), 61. *See also* Curl (2000*e*), 77, Pl.34. It is now in the Vatican Museum. 55 [168/90/IC]. Chowne was a friend of Henry, the brother of Jane Austen (1775-1817). He took part in amateur theatricals with the Austen family: his performance as 'Frederic' in *Lovers' Vows* (by Mrs Elizabeth Inchbald [1753-1821]) was mimicked by 'Mr Crawford' in *Mansfield Park* (1814).

9.9 Paired *stele* monuments [10346 and 14195/**103**/2] of *c.*1840 to members of the Tucker family, the one surmounted by a naval trophy to commemorate a naval officer, the other by a military trophy to commemorate a cavalry officer. Photograph of 1995. *See* Chapter VIII, §92 (*CB*).

9.10 Classical, Carrara Marble altar-tomb [15282/**57**/IR] of General Sir James Law Lushington (1779-1859) of the Madras Army; the design, like that of the Tilson Chowne monument [*see* **9.9**], derives from the Scipio tomb, but is surmounted by military insignia in the form of a cocked hat and sword, and carries the Coat of Arms of the East India Company, of which Lushington was Chairman in 1838-9. Photograph of 2000 (*MC.E060101*).

but actually derived from the monument of Naevoleia Tyche at Pompeii,[56] is the later and particularly impressive marble and granite tomb of John Robinson McClean (1813-73),[57] which stands at Centre Avenue surrounded by its own privet hedge (**8.5**).

Among other Classically-derived forms and motifs, perhaps the most striking architecturally is the broken column, often symbolising the death of the head of the family, the patriarchal pillar (see **10.11**). A good example is the garlanded column to Lewis Jones (*c.*1784-1862).[58] Elsewhere are inverted torches, signifying the extinction of life; butterflies – as on the previously mentioned tomb of John Cooper[59] symbolising both the brevity of life and the soul's departure; the serpent biting its tail, a symbol of eternity – one element in the commemorative medley that makes up Emma Soyer's monument (**8.29**);[60] and funerary garlands or festoons – laurels for fame, palms for peace, poppies for sleep, willow for mourning. Military iconography is also particularly associated with the cemetery's Classicising monuments, usually taking the form of a trophy – a sculpted composition of arms, accoutrements, banners, and other emblems of war. The paired *stele* monuments of *c.*1840 to members of the Tucker family (**9.9**)[61] carry their trophies on top, one for a naval officer, the other for a cavalryman. Alternatively, a trophy could be piled in the centre of a chest, as with the cocked hat and sword on top of the Scipio-derived altar-tomb of Sir James Law Lushington (1779-1859) (**9.10**),[62] and the cannon-barrels atop the mighty sarcophagus of Captain the Honourable Sir Henry Duncan (1786-1835),[63] 'sometime principal storekeeper of the ordnance' (**8.30**), his tomb making the most of its position at the crossing of the Circle and Junction Avenue.

Contemporary with the Greek Revival was the Egyptian, its funerary associations deemed particularly appropriate for the architecture of death.[64] The style appears, tempered by Greek, in the tomb of John Gordon (1802-40),[65] its design (**8.17**) derived

56 Gell and Gandy (1852), Plates III, IV, V, VI, and VIII, and *The Builder*, **xxxiv**/1718 (8 January 1876), 36.
57 [23912/**37**/RS]. 58 [17244/**90**/PS]. Jones was a tailor, of 47 Conduit Street. His epitaph reads: 'Here sleepeth one who while he lived on earth / Possessed a character of priceless worth, / Patient and truthful, virtuous in mind, / Sincere in friendship, generous and kind. / Free from reproach his course through life he ran, / The noblest work of God "An honest Man".' The grave is also that of Donald Nicoll (1820-91), Civil Engineer, who was a pioneer of telegraphy using underground cables. Sheriff of London and Middlesex from 1849 to 1850, he was MP for Frome from 1857 to 1859. From 1843 until 1869 he was a cloth manufacturer and tailor. 59 [3448/**92**/RS]. 60 [3714/**80**/RS]. 61 [10346 and 14195/**103**/2]. 62 [15282/**57**/IR]. 63 [533/**90**/RS]. 64 For the Egyptian Revival *see* Carrott (1978), Curl (1982*a* and 1994*b*), and Curl (2000*c* and *d*). 65 [3738/**57**/RS].

from a model provided by a prototype in Père-Lachaise (**2.1**).[66] The neighbouring Collett tomb (**8.18**) is also influenced by Parisian exemplars. In style Graeco-Egyptian, but without the mediation of Père-Lachaise, is the cenotaph of Major-General The Honourable Sir William Casement (1780-1843) (**8.11** and **12.9**)[67] – a mortuary pile that Dr Coones rightly describes as 'awe-inspiring'.[68] Standing high above the path, the canopy over the sarcophagus is supported by four life-sized telamones in the form of turbaned Indians muffled in long cloaks – their nationality a reference to Casement's membership of the Supreme Council of India. As original as it is powerful, the whole tomb was the work of the local monumental mason E. M. Lander, whose workshop was – and still is – a few yards from the cemetery entrance. The sombreness of unmodified Egyptian was particularly suitable for mausolea, and there are numbers of these in Kensal Green. Yet 'sombre' is hardly an appropriate epithet for the most famous of them, the mausoleum of Andrew Ducrow,[69] already mentioned as one of the cemetery's key statements in the ideology of individualism (**8.23**, **8.24**, and **10.11**). Designed by George Danson, who was one of Ducrow's stage designers,[70] and carved by John Cusworth of Stoke Newington,[71] its iconographic scheme has an eclecticism that comes close to riot. Egypt provides the ground-base: a pair of guardian sphinxes, reeded corner-columns with lotus-capitals, a hollow cornice, and a medley of hieroglyphs. The rest of the carving joins in with merry abandon. On the mausoleum itself, angels support the inscription-panels, a relief over the door shows a translated Ducrow greeting winged horses amidst the clouds, beehives[72] nestle in the hollow pediments, and a tapering pedestal bearing an urn with horse-head handles sits on the roof. The hat and gloves of Ducrow the ring-master lie on a broken column, and the railings are made up of wreaths, swags, and inverted torches.[73] Ducrow's self-celebration is certainly immodest, but it is also carried off with an exuberance that defeats the solemnity of funerary Egypt, and comes close to outfronting death itself. After this, Kensal Green's other Egyptianising mausolea – indeed, virtually all the other tombs – look reticent. Just across from Ducrow's, the family mausoleum of Sir George Farrant (*c.*1770-1844) (**8.22**)[74] is a carefully detailed early example; later Egyptian mausolea tend to greater severity, emphasised by their polished granite construction. Characteristic are those of the Guthrie family (1869)[75] and the Ashbury family (n.d.),[76] while the mausoleum of the Duke of Cambridge (1819-1904),[77] one of Kensal Green's royal tombs, is striking in its formal simplification and remarkable for using an Egyptianising style at such a late date (**8.43**).[78]

The stylistic tardiness of Cambridge's tomb is surprising because of the profound impact that had been made by the third of the cemetery's great historicist styles – Gothic. Styles approximating more or less to those of the Middle Ages had been in the repertoire of Georgian architects from the mid-18th century, and had been increasingly widely used during the Romantic period. But the adoption of Gothic for the new Palace of Westminster in 1834, and, even more, the publication in 1836 of *Contrasts* by the young Augustus Welby

66 The Gordon tomb is illustrated in Hakewill (1851), Plate 14. For its Parisian prototype *see* Curl (1982*a*), 155-8. 67 [5400/**56**/RS]. 68 Coones (1987), 59. 69 [820/**76**/RS]. 70 Danson's career was much involved in the creation of visual spectacle, for he painted panoramas as well as working on Ducrow's sensational productions. He is also buried at Kensal Green, below a plain coped ledger stone, west of the Anglican chapel [27682/**141**/PS]. 71 Gunnis (1968), 119. 72 On tomb sculpture, bees leaving the hive symbolised the soul leaving its earthly abode for the afterlife. 73 Much of this iconographic scheme was devised by Ducrow himself. The final wording of his epitaph was decided by his wife, who based it on a version composed – at Ducrow's request – by C. A. Somerset, who penned dialogue, songs, and choruses for various of Ducrow's productions. *See* Saxon (1978), 370-5. 74 [4795/**76**/RS]. 75 [20022/**113**/3]. 76 Centre Avenue [19999/**65**/RS]. John Ashbury was a railway engineer: he founded the works at Openshaw, Manchester, for building railway-carriages and -wagons. He constructed a railway-wagon in 13 hours for the 1862 International Exhibition. His son, James Lloyd Ashbury (1834-95), was a civil engineer. He constructed the Riga-Dünaburg railway (1859-61), was MP for Brighton (1874-80), and a keen yachtsman. In 1871 his yacht *Livonia* defeated the American yacht *Columbia*, the first race ever won by a challenger for the America's Cup. 77 [28623/**153**/RS]. 78 The mausoleum probably dates from 1890 – still late – when Cambridge's wife by a morganatic marriage, the actress Sarah Louisa Fairbrother (1816-90), died.

Northmore Pugin (1812-52), changed the whole cultural context of medievalist style.[79] Pugin made the most uncompromising claims for the style's high religious seriousness, not only identifying it exclusively with Christianity itself, but also lambasting all styles drawn from the ancient non-Christian world as irretrievably pagan. The strength of Pugin's onslaught derived from its ideological nature: stylistic choice was no longer a mere matter of taste; it was an article of religious faith. What did it mean for a Christian nation to build like Greece or Rome? And what kind of belief was to be read in the 'shameful inconsistency' of funerary monuments covered with the iconography of paganism?

> The inverted torch, the club of Hercules, the owl of Minerva, and the cinerary urn, are carved, in lieu of saints and angels, on the tombs of popes, bishops, kings, ecclesiastics, statesmen, and warriors, frequently accompanied by Pagan divinities, in Pagan nudity; the pious supplication for a prayer for the soul of the deceased, is changed into a long and pompous inscription detailing his virtues and exploits.[80]

As Pugin asked in his equally influential book, *True Principles*, 'what have we, as *Christians*, to do with all those things illustrative *only of former error*?'.[81] To the range of meanings that made up the commemorative text of the Victorian monument was added the need to demonstrate Christian belief, and Gothic 'articulated much of the growing religious consciousness, and self-consciousness, of the early Victorian middling sort'.[82]

The number of tombs at Kensal Green wholly in the Gothic style is relatively limited, but includes some of the most elaborate and aesthetically ambitious monuments, often employing the polychromatic construction so distinctive of High Victorian design. The Molyneux mausoleum (**8.15** and **8.16**),[83] designed in 1866 by John Gibson (1817-92) and built by J. Underwood of Camden Town, is a dynastic tomb in the very grandest manner. Octagonal on plan, built from Carrara Marble and polished granites from Peterhead and Rubislaw, it has clustered columns surmounted by demi-angels and pinnacles at each angle, the crocketed and finialed gables to each face filled with tracery, shields, and foliage. Originally it was even larger, for the whole edifice was surmounted by an octagonal spire (**8.15**). On a similar scale, and only a few yards to the west, is Gibson's (1817-92) own monument, which he designed himself:[84] an Italianate polychrome Gothic canopy tomb with vigorously striped red-and-white masonry and a short truncated spire set behind a parapet carried on machicolations (**8.19**). When built on a rectangular ground plan, the cemetery's Gothic mausolea take on the appearance of small chapels, daintily scaled for the tomb of Erle Elton (d. 1899) (**12.6**),[85] robustly structural in the Bayley (1878) (**9.11**) and Martin (n.d.) mausolea, which confront the Anglican chapel's pagan Doric from each end of the terrace,[86] granite down to their

9.11 Gothic mausoleum of the Bayley family [25601/115/IR], erected 1876, a tough and architecturally expressive structure all in grey granite. In the foreground is a fine Celtic cross [43718/115/IR] to the memory of Henry Ulick Browne, 5th Marques of Sligo (1831-1913), and his wife Catherine (d. 1914). Photograph of 1995 (*CB*).

79 Pugin (1836). An enlarged second edition appeared five years later: Pugin (1841). 80 Pugin (1841), 12. 81 Pugin (1841), 46. 82 Brooks (1989), 22. 83 [19607/56 and 65/RS]. 84 [33942/64-65/PS]. 85 [37929/32/RS]. Captain Erle Elton, Royal Highlanders (Black Watch), was killed in the Boer War on 11 December 1899. The tomb also commemorates Colonel Frederick Coulthurst Elton, CB, RA (1836-1920), who served in the Crimean War, and was awarded the *Légion d'Honneur* by the French. 86 [25601/115/IR] and [22591/113/6]. Edmond Kelly Bayley (1847-98), barrister [25601/115/IR], Sheriff of London and Middlesex (1879-80) and Sheriff of Roscommon (1883). He was an Officer of the Greek Order of the Redeemer, and Chevalier of the Belgian Order of Léopold (1888). The architect of his mausoleum was Alfred Blackburne Frend (*fl.*1868-1900), and it was made by A. MacDonald, Field, & Co. Eustace Meredyth Martin (1816-92), barrister [22591/113/6] was the author of *A Tour through India in Lord Canning's Time* (1881), *A Visit to the Holy Land, Syria, and Constantinople* (1882), and *Round the World* (1883).

very doors. In the French Gothic mausoleum of Lieutenant-General Perry (d. 1868) and Sir Patrick O'Brien (1823-95)[87] the character of a church-in-miniature was emphasised by including stained glass windows (**8.10**) – a feature that assumed regular family visits to the mausoleum, giving it something of the function of a private mortuary-chapel.[88]

Kensal Green's smaller Gothic monuments usually take the form of tomb-chests, arcaded canopies, or pinnacles, frequently with representational carving. The tomb-chest of the novelist, Catherine Grace Frances Gore (1799-1861),[89] has plain arcaded sides and ends, its coped lid bearing a cross carved in relief; that of John Gilchrist (d. 1866),[90] has sides made up of traceried panels with naturalistic foliage in the spandrels; that of Sir Archibald Galloway (*c*.1780-1850) (**9.12**),[91] has corner buttresses with simple traceried panels, but is topped off with a splendid trophy made up of medieval arms and armour – a neat Gothicising of a Classical concept. The substantial two-bay canopy (**8.4**) over the tomb of the 7th Viscount Strangford (1818-57)[92] shelters, on the rear wall, a pair of elegant guardian angels carved in relief (**9.13**) by the successful academic sculptor Edward James Physick (1829-1906); more medieval in feeling are the excellent little reliefs of Corporal Works of Mercy that decorate the sides of a two-tier pinnacle at the centre of the Circle.[93] But the outstanding tomb from this group is the monument to Commander Charles Ricketts (1788-1867) (**8.7**),[94] designed by that quirkiest of High Victorian Goths, William Burges (1827-81). The Portland Stone sarcophagus, its surfaces covered with

[87] [10833/48/RS]. [88] Many of the house-tombs at Père-Lachaise contain a *prie-dieu*, a provision for family piety that allows a neat conflation of dynasty and deity. I have seen a *prie-dieu* in several Victorian mausolea in English cemeteries, so its presence was not confined to Roman Catholic France; to date, I know of none in Kensal Green.
[89] [16402/58/3]. [90] [20089/91/RS]. John Gilchrist was a Scots-born Australian shipping-merchant, and resided in Australia from 1828 to 1854. He traded as Gilchrist, Alexander, & Co., Gilchrist, Watt, & Co., and Gilchrist, Watt, & Sanderson, Ltd. He was one of the most prominent businessmen of his day, and Director of many Companies, including the Union Bank of Australia and the Bank of Australia. He was a founder and member of the first Board of Directors of the Royal Exchange (1851). [91] [8828/117/RS]. [92] [14166/31/PS]. [93] [4184/87/RS]. The monument of Ann Wissett (d. 1843), widow of Robert Wissett of Forest Hill, Kent, writer on trade, agriculture, and politics.
[94] [20242/47/RS].

9.12 Gothic tomb-chest in white marble and granite [8828/117/RS], for Major-General Sir Archibald Galloway, K.C.B. (*c*.1780-1850) of the Bengal Army, an expert on siege warfare in India who became Chairman of the East India Company in 1849. The chest is surmounted by a medievalising trophy of arms and armour, and the whole ensemble is sinking. Photograph of 1995 (*CB*).

9.13 Guardian angels in Carrara Marble carved by Edward James Physick (*fl.* 1850-70), from the Gothic canopy tomb [14166/31/PS] of George Augustus Frederick Percy Sydney Smythe, 7th Viscount Strangford (1818-57), who, in 1852, fought what is believed to be the last duel in England, and died of the cumulative effects of drink and dissipation. Photograph of 2001. *See* Chapter VIII, §13 (*MC.A5 detail*).

shields and diaper patterning that incorporates Union flags, stands on stubby French Gothic colonnettes with shafts of veined green Cornish Serpentinite; surrounding the sarcophagus, and tightly banded to it, outer columns with Peterhead Red Granite shafts support a stone-vaulted canopy, its multiple gables sprouting finials, crockets, and little gaping gargoyles. In its ingeniously contrived plasticity, its sculptural richness, and density, the Ricketts tomb has no equal in Kensal Green or any other of London's remarkable cemeteries.

Although the perceived signification of Victorian Gothic was predominantly Christian, especially in a commemorative context, the style's semantics had another dimension, inherited from an earlier period. In the 17th and 18th centuries, the term 'Gothic' labelled an influential cluster of political beliefs that traced the tradition of English constitutional liberty, and particularly the sovereignty of Parliament, back to the politics of the Germanic – thus 'Gothic' – tribes who settled in England after the Roman withdrawal. Of key importance in bolstering the cause of Parliament in its 17th-century struggles with the Crown, Gothic history and Gothic political theory had informed the style's adoption for many garden-buildings erected in the parks of 18th-century country houses. Perhaps the best known example is the Temple of Liberty designed by James Gibbs (1682-1754) and built in the grounds of Stowe in 1741.[95] Although the identification of Gothic and political liberty gradually weakened in the course of the 19th century, it was still sufficiently strong to influence the decision to build the new Palace of Westminster – the Houses of Parliament – in Gothic after the old Palace had burnt down in 1834. It is the style's political significance that explains its adoption for the monument to Feargus O'Connor (1794-1855) – a slender octagonal structure with traceried sides below tall gables (8.3).[96] In the 1840s, O'Connor, much feared by supporters of the *status quo*, had led the so-called 'physical force' party within Chartism in its great campaign to secure the vote and parliamentary representation for the working-classes – the first proletarian mass-movement in modern British political history. The style of his memorial effectively recruits him to the Gothic history of English liberty, a narrative that, in the early Victorian period, still retained its place in the consciousness of popular radicalism. And the memorial, appropriately, was itself a popular creation, as the inscription informs us. Now weathered almost to illegibility, it is worth quoting in full:

> To the memory of Feargus O'Connor elected MP for the County of Cork in 1833 also for the Borough of Nottingham in 1847. Born July 18th 1794 Died August 30th 1855 Aged 61. Whose funeral was defrayed and this monument erected by subscription chiefly from the Working Classes. Reader Pause, Thou lookest [?] on the grave of a patriot. While philanthropy is a virtue and patriotism not a crime will the name of O'Connor be admired and this monument respected.

Pugin would have deplored the use of Gothic to signal the historical pedigree of a radical firebrand.[97] But then, for all Pugin's passionate insistence and that of his successors, Gothic's meanings were too richly diverse to be subject to a religious monopoly. Nor was its stylistic rule over funerary design anything like absolute. After all, bourgeois individualism insisted on a free market in worship and aesthetics as well as in trade.

Nevertheless, the semiotic imperative at the heart of Pugin's campaign was heeded: the tombs of Christian people should signify Christian faith. At Kensal Green the impact of this development in consciousness is most obvious in the enormous number of crosses

95 For an account of Gothic history and political theory and their influence on the Gothic Revival, *see* Brooks (1999), particularly Chapters 2, 3, 6, 7, and 8. 96 [12687/27/3]. 97 *D.N.B.*, **xiv** (1917), 847, suggests that O'Connor's intemperate behaviour 'was probably only a symptom of his disease'. He is reckoned to have died insane.

used as memorials after the 1850s. They are of all shapes and varieties: of plain calvary form for the novelist William Wilkie Collins (1824-89) (**8.42**);[98] decorated with symbolic flowers, like the Annunciation lilies that sweep across the memorial to Alfred Sutherland Sutton (*c.*1845-88);[99] set horizontally above a coped ledger-stone, as on the tomb of Henry James Dunnell (1810-76);[100] and incorporating the circle of eternity to form a Celtic cross, as for Sir William MacCormac, Bart. (1836-1901).[101] Amidst this multiplicity of crosses, the tomb of the architect Henry Edward Kendall (1776-1875) (**8.8**)[102] is uniquely powerful – 'muscular' would have been the Victorian term. The cross is set within a massive multi-cusped headstone, at the foot of which rests an angel, gazing down on the coped ledger that covers the grave itself. As well as musing on eternity, she could be contemplating the fact that Kendall's Gothic designs for Kensal Green had won first place in the competition for the cemetery's buildings, only to be set aside in favour of Griffith's Neo-Greek. In the key position it occupies, at the junction of Centre Avenue with the North and South Branch Avenues, Kendall's tomb, uncompromisingly Gothic and almost ostentatiously Christian, has a look of rebuke.

Kendall's angel is but one member of a host, for, in the later Victorian cemetery, angels joined crosses – often literally – as the commonest means of signifying Christian belief. Their predecessors were the allegorical figures that Victorian commemoration inherited from 18th-century funerary iconography. Of these the most popular, and the most long-lived, was Hope. She poses with her anchor on top of the monument to Madame Soyer (**8.29**);[103] perches on an obelisk to commemorate Ruth Boyer (d. 1862);[104] and, in an adjacent plot, stands on a pedestal over the grave of Grace Macaulay (1857-1921).[105] Allegory had a good Low Church pedigree: in the Protestant mind, angels were long tainted with Popery, and their adoption as funerary icons is one indication of the growing High Churchmanship of later Victorian Anglicanism. Hosts, even choirs, of angels arrived in the cemetery in force from *c.*1870, many of them Italian imports, made from statuary marble in the great monumental-masons' workshops of Genoa and Milan. For the more elaborate effects they could be disposed in groups, as with the three angels kneeling in prayer on the grave of Joseph Hill (1812-82).[106] More usually they are solitary, and appear in a wide permutation of poses. Frequently they embrace a cross, like the soulful example on the tomb of the last Marques of Hastings (1842-68) (**9.14**).[107] Hastings had need of angelic support: a descendant of the Plantagenets, he earned the title 'The King of the Plungers', ruined himself on the Turf, and died at the age of twenty-six. Other angels stand at prayer, their feet on the rock of faith, as on the grave of Ellen Fleming (1868-86);[108] or carry the trumpet of the Resurrection, as on the adjacent monument to Grace Bishop (d. 1919) (**10.7**);[109] or sit on top of a sarcophagus, pointing skyward, as on the tomb of John Crook (d. 1902).[110] Although these angelic figures can become routine, the quality of the carving is often high and individual monuments can obtain to a genuine drama. One such is the tomb of Herbert William Allingham (1862-1904) and his wife, Alexandrina (**9.15**).[111] Anguished, though still elegant, an angel sinuously embraces a broken column, a funeral wreath hanging listlessly form one hand;

98 [31754/**141**/PS]. 99 [31339/**64**/PS]. Sutton was a journalist. The inscription on his monument records that he was 'The Man About Town', i.e. a society columnist. 100 [16942/**42**/RS]. This is a family grave, and contains Dunnell's infant daughter, Mabel (d. 1861). 101 [35862/**37**/RS]. 102 [2397/**48**/RS]. 103 [3714/**80**/RS]. 104 [17523/**103**/PS]. This is the family grave of Thomas Duck Hopper (*c.*1803-72), shipowner, of 25 Eastcheap. Ruth Boyer, probably Hopper's daughter, was the wife of George Philip Boyer (d. 1893). 105 [47503/**90-103**/2]. Wife of John Laing Macaulay (*c.*1833-97), buried in [19867/**90-91**/RS]. Curiously, she was originally buried with her husband, but was removed to her present site in 1922. 106 [28570/**126**/PS]. Hill lived at Barrah, Chumparun, Bengal. Two of the angels have been removed. 107 [21195/**77**/IR]. 108 [30382/**64**/PS]. She died in Brunswick. The grave was owned by Louis Remi Fleming, JP, MRCS, LRCP (1869-1944), house surgeon, Westminster Hospital, and house physician, Bethlem Royal Hospital, probably Ellen Fleming's brother or husband. He is not buried in the grave. 109 [46535/**64**/PS]. Grace Bishop was the wife of Lieutenant-Colonel Alfred Conway Bishop (*c.*1880-1923). 110 [38615/**141**/PS]. 111 [40226/**165**/RS].

9.14 Carrara Marble angel and cross over the grave [21195/**77**/IR] of Henry Wreysford Charles Plantagenet Rawdon-Hastings, 4th and last Marques of Hastings (1842-68), who ruined himself by gambling. Photograph of 1995 (*CB*).

9.15 Classical monument with mourning angel, in Carrara Marble [40226/**165**/RS], to Herbert William Allingham, F.R.C.S. (1862-1904), and his wife, Alexandrina (1868-1904), whose miniature recumbent effigy occupies the niche. Photograph of 1995. *See* Chapter VIII, §127 (*CB*).

inset below lies a miniature effigy of Alexandrina, her pet dog stretched disconsolately in the crook of her limp arm (**8.45** and **9.15**).

Alongside the dominant tones of Greek, Egyptian, and Gothic, and amidst the crosses and angels, are other historicist styles. Most frequent are those that draw upon the Renaissance. Fashionably genteel after Charles Barry (1795-1860) introduced the palazzo style into London's Clubland, Renaissance design received the royal assent at Kensal Green in the sarcophagus that Professor Ludwig Grüner (1801-82) – who was to be the architect of royal mausolea at Frogmore – designed for the tomb of Princess Sophia (1777-1848).[112] Raised high on its pedestal, the elegantly profiled tomb-chest, surmounted by a crown, is richly encrusted with decorative carving by Signor Bardi (**8.38**). A dozen metres south, the memorial to Harriet Browne, Viscountess D'Alte (d. 1862), appears to have been conceived in a spirit of obsequious emulation (**8.37**).[113] A few steps further on, and deferring to nobody, the Portland Stone tomb-chest[114] that marks the family vault of William Holland (1779-1856) (**8.35**) affords the most extravagant sculptural display of any of Kensal Green's Renaissance-inspired monuments. Resting on the wings of eight couchant mythical beasts, part-gryphon, part-wyvern, the pedimented chest, its top carved to imitate roof tiles, has angels standing at the corners with circular inscription panels, bulging swags, and inverted torches filling the sides and ends. Holland prospered both as a cabinet-maker and an undertaker: in the first capacity he supplied showpiece furniture for the very rich; in the second he staged showpiece funerals for the same clientele. The design of his tomb, something between a presentation sideboard and a papal sarcophagus, manages to suggest both aspects of his career. Other Renaissance tombs include the pretty little mausoleum of Robert William Kennard (1800-70),[115] its segmentally arched stone roof decorated with a phoenix and a row of eternal flames (**9.16**); the giant urn that commemorates Andrew

[112] [8028/**114**/PS]. [113] [17442/**113**/PS]. [114] [7219/**100**/PS]. [115] [22600/**113**/RS].

9.16 Renaissance-style mausoleum [22600/113/RS] of Robert Kennard (d. 1870), crested by a phoenix, symbolising the Resurrection, and by eternal flames, and still retaining its fine bronze door. Photograph of 1995. *See* Chapter VIII, §97 (*CB*).

9.17 Rococo sarcophagus [6827/**88**/RS] of Amelia Ramsey Cowell (d. 1847), wife of William Cowell of the Bengal Civil Service; beyond it, and making a striking stylistic contrast, is the elaborately detailed French Gothic canopy-tomb [22047/**88**/RS] (*See* Chapter VIII, §72) of Frederick Tillson (d. 1870). Photograph of 1995 (*CB*).

9.18 Romanesque canopy-tomb (*left*) [36582/**178**/RS] of Anna Steedman (d. 1907), and, to the *right*, the intricately carved Gothic enclosure surrounding the Shaw family vault, apparently dating from 1897. Photograph of 2001 (*MC.E.090101*).

Macklew (d. 1847);[116] and the Pattison family's lantern cross,[117] its earliest memorial date 1849. Baroque is used in the design of several tomb-chests, typically with giant consoles set upright for the corners – as with the monument of Elizabeth Weston (d. 1850).[118] The curvaceous lines and curling foliage of the sarcophagus of Amelia Cowell (d. 1847) are naughtily Rococo (**9.17**).[119] Anna Steedman (d.1907) is commemorated by a heavyweight Romanesque arch (**9.18**),[120] and south of the Anglican chapel, Byzantine makes an appearance in an eight-poster canopy tomb, now sadly despoiled of its inscription and much of its delicate metalwork.[121]

Two types of monument in Kensal Green cross the boundaries of the historicist styles: commemorative figure-sculpture and geometric tombs. The outstanding example of the former is Robert Sievier's[122] memorial to his parents (*c*.1840) in the Anglican chapel's south colonnade (**9.19** and **10.1**), probably dating from the 1830s. John Sievier lies on a Grecian chaise-longue while his wife kneels, her arm reaching across him in a gesture of embrace. They gaze intently at each other as he caresses her hair with one hand, with the other holding open a Bible at Chapter 22 of the Gospel according to St Luke – the account of the Last Supper. Here, indeed, is 'the Beautiful Death': piety, conjugal affection, and patriarchy, frozen into the iconic moment in which domesticity

[116] [4/**86**/IR]. [117] [8270/**102**/IR]. James Pattison (1786-1849), merchant; Director of the East India Company; MP for the City of London 1835, 1837, and 1843-9; and Governor of the Bank of England, 1834-7. [118] [4472/**92**/RS]. This is the family tomb of John Weston (*c*.1779-1863) of 97 High Holborn, possibly a relative of Edward Weston of Weston's Music Hall, 242 High Holborn. Also interred in this grave is the body of James Weston (*c*.1808-60), who committed suicide by taking poison (Inquest 11 July 1860, St Pancras). [119] [6827/**88**/RS]. The grave also contains the bodies of William Cowell (*c*.1775-1852 – of the Bengal Civil Service and Gloucester Square), Lady Eliza R. Elliott (d. 1876), and Shadwell S. Boulderson (d. 1911). [120] [36582/**178**/RS]. [121] [22218/**125**/2]. This is the grave of Harriet Johnson, *née* Walls (d. 1870). The owner of the grave was William Russell, 8th Duke of Bedford (1809-72), who never married. The splendour of the tomb suggests that its occupant was held in high regard by its builder. [122] He is buried in [19149/**90**/2].

9.19 Monument in the colonnades of the Anglican chapel (photographed in 1997) to John and Frances Sievier and their son (William Robert Sievier) and daughter-in-law, sculpted by R. W. Sievier, F.R.S. (1794-1865). Photograph of 1997 (© *Crown copyright. NMR.AA97/1170*).

9.20 Recumbent effigy and tomb-chest (in the colonnades of the Anglican chapel) of Georgiana Clementson (d. 1868), sculpted by John Graham Lough (1798-1876), who was her father. Photograph of 2001. *See also* 10.2 (*MC.G080101*).

is transfigured into the divine. Opposite the Sievier monument is another almost equally imbued with the ideology of the affectionate family, the sculptor John Graham Lough's memorial to his daughter, Georgina Clementson (d. 1868): she lies in her last sleep upon a tomb chest decorated with kneeling angels on either side of a triple-portrait medallion (**9.20** and **10.2**). Individualist celebration in figure sculpture is most fully realised in the fine Renaissance monument[123] to the painter William Mulready (1786-1863),[124] designed by Godfrey Sykes (1824-66) and made by James Pulham & Son. Arrayed in his Academician's robes, Mulready lies on a draped bier below a six-poster canopy, the base of the tomb decorated with incised cartoons of his best known paintings (**8.14** and **10.3**). The cartoons not only testify to the popularity of Mulready's *genre* pieces, but also imply an audience that would find cultural confirmation in the act of recognising their favourite pictures. A less literal-minded, but also less original, celebration of a man and his work was the monument to another painter, James Ward (1769-1859):[125] a single figure in relief representing the muse of painting, carved by John Henry Foley (1818-74) – perhaps the most consistently impressive High Victorian sculptor – once decorated the stone, now lying flat, broken in two pieces. For those of less celebrity, commemorative figure sculpture could take the form of a portrait head carved in relief. Good examples are those of Edward Scriven (1775-1841) (**8.2** and **9.21**)[126] and Peter Burrowes (1753-1841)[127] both in Classical profile: the latter is signed 'Butler Sculptor Gower Place London', presumably Timothy Butler (1806-*c*.1880), well-known for his portrait-busts. Later portraits, such as the characterful head of William Frederick Meredith (*c*.1828-82),[128] tend towards greater naturalism (**9.22**). Meredith's tomb carries the signature of A. L. Hine of Highgate, though the inset medallion with the head was surely the work of a professional sculptor.

Kensal Green cemetery's sculptors and their work are discussed more fully in the following Chapter, but some mention may be made here of the number of portrait-busts the cemetery once contained, for they were an important part of its complement of figural sculpture. The bust was an indicator of social esteem during the 18th and 19th centuries, and was thus widely used to represent the famous, and to commemorate them

123 [17933/**56**/PS]. 124 The whole monument is of artificial stone. Sykes was an expert in working with such materials and at the time the Mulready tomb was being produced he was employed on the ceramic decorations of the South Kensington museum. *See* Physick (1982), *passim*. 125 [15560/**90**/3]. 126 [3174/**21**/RS]. 127 [3256/**103**/PS]. 128 [28203/**65**/RS]. Meredith was a steam biscuit manufacturer.

9.21 Headstone with portrait-medallion [3174/**21**/RS] of the engraver Edward Scriven (1775-1841), who was centrally concerned in the establishment of the Artists' Benevolent Fund, which erected the memorial. Photograph of 2001. *See* Chapter VIII, §8 (*MC.A6*).

9.22 Headstone in red granite with inset white marble portrait-medallion [28203/**65**/RS] of William Frederick Meredith (d. 1882); the naturalism of the portrait should be compared with the Classicising profile of Scriven (*see* **8.2** and **9.21**). Photograph of 2001 (*MC.Co80101*).

after death: there are many examples in churches and cathedrals throughout Britain. In the open setting of a cemetery, however, busts have been easy targets for modern vandalism and theft. So it has proved at Kensal Green, where the tombs of some of the cemetery's most celebrated dead have been despoiled of the very feature that signalled their celebrity. Joseph Durham (1814-77), whose work included the memorial to the Great Exhibition that stands south of the Albert Hall, sculpted the portrait-bust that formerly completed the memorial to James Henry Leigh Hunt (1784-1859),[129] the essayist and critic who championed the work of Keats and Shelley. The pedestal that marks the original resting-place of the illustrator and caricaturist George Cruikshank (1792-1878),[130] whose body was re-interred in St Paul's Cathedral, once carried a bust by William Behnes (1795-1864), who specialised in this form of portraiture. Both Behnes and Durham are buried in Kensal Green, and both, somewhat ironically, have tomb-chests that rely aesthetically upon formal qualities rather than sculptural display: that of Behnes[131] was carved by his pupil Morton Edwards; that of Durham,[132] which features a relief carving of his tools, was probably his own work.

Standing a few feet in front of Durham's monument is perhaps the saddest example of sculptural loss in the cemetery – the tomb of Thomas Hood (1798-1845) (**8.20**).[133] Hood was an outstandingly versatile comic writer who also had great sympathy for the plight of the marginalised and the dispossessed: his poems 'The Song of the Shirt', about the exploitation of seamstresses, and 'The Bridge of Sighs', about the suicide of a prostitute,[134] particularly touched the social conscience of the early Victorians. Hood, impoverished and overworked, died prematurely. A few years later, the popular poet, Eliza Cook (1818-89), found his grave unmarked and was moved to write 'Poor Hood' in protest.

129 [13560/**121**/3]. 130 [29171/**76**/RS]. 131 [18202/**74**/PS]. 132 [26191/**75**/IR]. 133 [5449/**74**/PS]. 134 Hood (1869-73), **ix**, 27-30 and 204-8. 'The Song of the Shirt' was first published in 1843, the 'Bridge of Sighs' in the following year.

Give him the dust beneath his head,
Give him a grave – a grave alone –
In Life he dearly won his bread; —
In Death, he was not worth a stone.

Her distress at such anonymity, eloquent in itself on the importance commemoration held for the Victorians, was sharpened into indignation by the ostentatious presence, a few yards away, of the tombs of Andrew Ducrow (**8.23** and **8.24**) and John St John Long (**8.26**):

Let the Horse-tamer's bed be known
By the rich mausoleum-shrine;
Give the bold Quack his charnel throne –
Their works were worthier far than thine.[135]

Cook's poem resulted in a public subscription that funded a fine monument by the sculptor Matthew Noble (1817-76) – a substantial pedestal of polished Peterhead granite surmounted by a bronze portrait bust and inset with relief medallions, also in bronze, illustrating two of Hood's most famous poems. Neither the humanity of Hood's poems nor the grateful respect of the Victorian public have served to save his tomb: the bust has gone and the medallions have been ripped from the granite. 'Poor Hood' indeed.

Among the more recent monuments erected in the cemetery, two deserve especial mention. The first is that commemorating Joshua Richard Compston (1970-96) and his brother Harry (born and died 1969),[136] sited not far from the celebrated Mulready tomb. Sculpted by Zebedee Helm (born 1970) in Portland Stone, it is in the form of a dinghy (Compston, a leading light in the art world of Shoreditch in the 1990s, was fond of exploring the tidal River Thames in his dinghy with oars and outboard motor), and has the legends:

THE DIVISION BETWEEN LIFE AND DEATH IS MERELY PERIPHERAL[137]

and

WHO WOULD TRUE VALOUR SEE LET HIM COME HITHER[138]

carved in relief around the gunwale. On the stern BON VOYAGE is inscribed. Also carved on the side of the 'boat' is the logo FN, standing for Compston's Company, Factual Nonsense.[139] Lying on the top of the 'boat' is a stylised effigy of Compston, with a representation of his pet dog at his feet. The allusions are to medieval tombs, the Arthurian and knightly legends, to passing, and to the journey over the River of Death (**9.23**).

The second modern monument of note is the dignified chest-tomb[140] of Michael Ronald (called Charles) Channon (1936-92), Guardian of the Holy House at Walsingham, Norfolk, inscribed

CHRISTIANUS FIDELIS AMICUS STUDIOSUS
SCRIPTOR ADMIRANDUS
'DOMINUS ILLUMINATIO MEA ET SALUS MEA'[141]

It is a fine and noble work, signed J. S. Farley (**9.24**).

Aesthetically, emotionally, and – in the end – ideologically, the antithesis of commemorative figure sculpture is the Geometric tomb. Simon Jervis[142] has identified the

[135] Cook (1870), 576-8. Despite Cook's irritation at the proximity, Hood himself would probably not have minded being close to the 'Horse-trainer': among the London pleasures jauntily evoked in his poem 'A Nocturnal Sketch' is 'to see Ducrow with wide stride ride/ Four horses as no other man can span'; Hood (1869-73), **i**, 50. [136] [65657/**57**/PS]. *See* Cooper (2000), *passim*. [137] Supplied by Compston's sister and mother, whose assistance is acknowledged. [138] John Bunyan (1628-88), *The Pilgrim's Progress* (1684), Pt. 2, 247. [139] Information provided by Mr Zebedee Helm. [140] [64165/**76**/2]. [141] A faithful Christian, diligent friend, admirable writer. 'The Lord is my Light and my Salvation'. [142] Jervis (1983), Chapter 8.

9.23 Monument of Joshua Compston (1970-96) by Zebedee Helm [65657/**57**/PS], erected in 2000. Photograph of 2001 (*MC.C300301*).

9.24 Chest-tomb of Michael Ronald Channon (1936-92), signed by J. S. Farley [64165/**76**/2], photographed in 1997 (*JSC*).

Geometric style as a distinctive Victorian design mode, typified by the abstraction of geometric forms initially derived from a historically-based vocabulary. Funerary design first goes Geometric with Neo-Greek. As early as 1836, the tomb of Sir Francis Freeling (1764-1836)[143] reinterprets the conventional broken column as a cylinder set on a cube (**8.21**). Similar geometric simplification is evidently in many of the more austere Classical designs, and subtler handling can produce the abstract sculptural massing of a tomb[144] like that of Baron Broughton de Gyfford (1786-1869) (**9.25**). Egyptian funerary forms like the pyramid and the obelisk obviously suited a taste for abstraction. At Kensal Green cemetery the slender, acutely pointed, Portland Stone pyramid that marks the tomb of Wyndham Lewis (1779-1838)[145] manages to combine elegance with visual drama (**9.26**). And obelisks abound – indeed, the Victorian versions outdo the originals. With their sheer surfaces unrelieved by ornament or hieroglyphs, their mirror-like finishes, and their impeccably sharp edges, great granite obelisks like those to Sir Richard Mayne (1796-1868)[146] or to Joseph (*c.*1790-1855) and Samuel (d. 1888) Richardson[147] seem to reach beyond inherited geometry and strive for the realm of pure form (**12.6**). Even Gothic was capable of a new abstract identity: small-scale in the subtly shaped cross and coped stone that marks the vault of John Owen Smith (1804-71);[148] massive in the square granite pillar that commemorates William (1809-88) and Margaret (d. 1860) Chappell (**9.27**),[149] its design only conceding to historicism in the incised cross decoration and the arcuate form given to the head of the stone. The Chappell monument was the work of the design theorist and reformer Owen Jones (1809-74), who was responsible for the colour-scheme of the Crystal Palace housing the 1851 Great Exhibition, and whose book, *The Grammar of Ornament*,[150] marks a major shift in Victorian attitudes to decoration. Very similar to the Chappell monument is that to the printer Thomas De La Rue (1793-1866):[151] as he was a keen proponent of improved commercial design and chaired one of the exhibit classes at the Great Exhibition it seems likely that he knew Owen Jones and that his tomb is another example of Jones's work.

Among Kensal Green cemetery's dead, one group seems particularly associated with these Geometric tombs: the engineers. Despite its vestigial Greek details, the grey and pink

143 [680/**75**/IR]. 144 [21596/**65**/RS]. 145 [1489/**26**/IR]. 146 [21708/**56**/RS]. 147 [27918/**32**/RS]. 148 [22920/**42**/RS]. John Owen Smith, Cape of Good Hope. The vault also contains the body of Rowland Stephenson (1847-1901), son of Sir Rowland M. Stephenson (1808-95), the railway engineer and author [21131/**80**/2]. 149 [8197/**77**/PS]. 150 Jones (1856). 151 [14755/**86**/south-east quadrant].

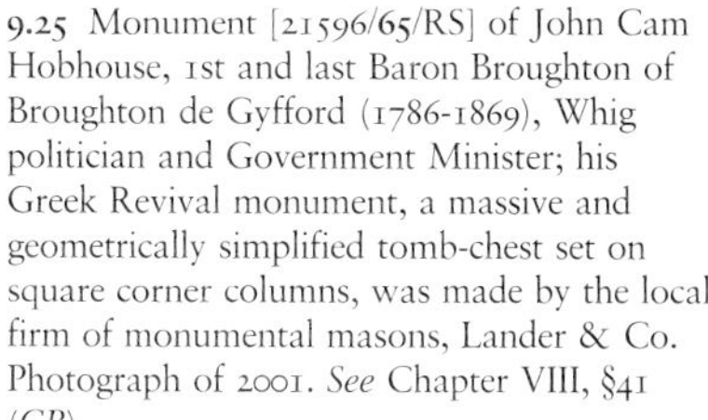

9.25 Monument [21596/65/RS] of John Cam Hobhouse, 1st and last Baron Broughton of Broughton de Gyfford (1786-1869), Whig politician and Government Minister; his Greek Revival monument, a massive and geometrically simplified tomb-chest set on square corner columns, was made by the local firm of monumental masons, Lander & Co. Photograph of 2001. *See* Chapter VIII, §41 (*CB*).

9.26 Monument [1489/26/IR] of the Tory politician Wyndham Lewis (1779-1838), a steeply pitched pyramid of Portland Stone on a stripped Classical base. Photograph of 1995. *See* Chapter VIII, §10 (*CB*).

9.27 Monument [8197/77/PS] of Margaret (d. 1860) and William Chappell, F.S.A. (1809-88), the music publisher and antiquary. It is constructed of grey granite, designed in a radically abstracted Gothic style by the architect and design reformer Owen Jones (1809-74), author of *The Grammar of Ornament* (1856). Photograph of 1995. *See* Chapter VIII, §63 (*CB*).

9.28 Mausoleum [9901/48/RS] of James Combe (*c.*1806-72): of pink and grey granite, it was designed by Combe, a civil engineer, for his wife, and erected in 1852 by A. MacDonald of Aberdeen, founder of the firm of granite specialists MacDonald & Leslie, of Aberdeen and London, many of whose monuments are to be found in Kensal Green. Photograph of 1995. *See* Chapter VIII, §25 (*CB*).

9.29 Monument [10309/48/RS] of Sir James Nichol McAdam (1786-1852) and his son James (*c.*1818-53), both of whom served as Surveyor-General of Roads; in pink and grey granite, this is one of the most powerful of the cemetery's Geometric tombs, and is signed H. Bisson, Guernsey. Photograph of 2001 (*CB*).

granite mausoleum of the civil engineer James Combe (*c.*1806-67),[152] erected in 1852 at the junction of Centre Avenue with the North and South Branch Avenues, is an abstract composition of horizontals and verticals. It was designed by Combe himself and made by the Aberdeen firm of MacDonald & Leslie, whose products appear in Victorian cemeteries throughout Britain, and whose machine-polished granite ideally complemented formal severity (**9.28**). The tomb of the surveyor and road engineer Sir James Nicholl McAdam

[152] [9901/48/RS].

(1786-1852) and his son, James (*c*.1818-53),[153] is also pink and grey granite, but more simple in conception – an austere panelled plinth topped by a composition of rectangular and bevelled blocks (**9.29**). Similar in aesthetic feeling, but plainer in its economy of form, is the low pyramid and Portland Stone pedestal that commemorates John Shae Perring (1813-69),[154] a water and railway engineer. Geometry is at its most minimal for the most famous of all Victorian engineers: a single-stepped, shallowly coped, white marble block to mark the grave of the Brunels (**8.6**),[155] where lies Marc Isambard Brunel (1769-1849), his son, Isambard Kingdom (1806-59), and other members of the family. As if in homage, a precisely similar but slightly smaller block commemorates a later chief engineer of the Great Western Railway, Michael Lane (*c*.1803-68).[156]

Afterword

Whatever abstractions may signify in other monuments, the tombs of the engineers exemplify the mathematical geometry that was the basis of the new technological culture they both created and served. Engineers, often from working-class origins, had a special place in Samuel Smiles' pantheon of self-helpers,[157] and he doubtless would have approved their preference for the reticence of geometry over the surrounding cemetery's voluble rhetoric of sculpture and ornament and historicist style, with all its personal and dynastic promotion. But such a contrast is deceptive. Precisely because the cemetery is so rich and so extraordinary in its celebration of individuals and families, the engineers' very preference for an abstract commemorative aesthetic marks them out, and for all its ostensible impersonality conveys its own sense of a distinct, and distinctly self-conscious, claim to fame. For all its differences, the tomb of a man like Michael Lane bids for posterity's recognition alongside those of Ducrow or Princess Sophia, just as surely as the Brunels' plot affirms a family identity and continuity to match, indeed to rival, the dynastic assertions of aristocratic mausolea. The language employed for the tombs of the engineers is not an exception but an alternative, one of the many through which the 19th century's great culture of commemoration is expressed in Kensal Green.[158]

153 [10309/**48**/RS]. Sometimes given as 'Macadam', but *D.N.B.*, **xii** (1917), 395-6, gives it as 'McAdam'.
154 [21350/**85**/RS]. 155 [8590/**41**/PS]. 156 [20809/**115**/PS]. 157 *See* Smiles (1862). The work was subsequently enlarged and reissued in five volumes in 1874. 158 Nearly all the locations of graves in this Chapter have been checked and corrected by Mr Moulder (*Editor's note*).

CHAPTER X

Sculptors and Sculpture: A Supplement

JOHN PHYSICK

Introduction; The Monuments; Epilogue

The sculptured dead, on each side, seem to freeze,
Emprisoned in black, purgatorial rails.

JOHN KEATS (1795-1821):
'The Eve of St Agnes' (1820), st. 2.

A sculptor wields
The chisel, and the stricken marble grows
To beauty.

WILLIAM CULLEN BRYANT (1794-1878):
The Flood of Years, l.42.

Introduction

The range of sculpture displayed in the thousands of gravestones, monuments, and mausolea reflects both the stylistic variety of the 19th century, as discussed in the previous Chapter, and the broad shift in taste from 'pagan' allusions to the Christian symbolism of angels and crosses.[1] The materials changed as well: marble and Portland Stone were joined by granite from Scotland and Cornwall, some sandstones, slates, and artificial stone; and embellishments were added in the form of ceramic tiles, mosaics, bronze, and, occasionally, terracotta and other artificial stones. Outdoor sculpture does not survive long without suffering from the effects of England's weather, so it is only the extremely hard granite memorials[2] that show few signs of deterioration today. During the 19th century, therefore, elaborate and expensive sculpture was often considered a waste of money, especially if a stained-glass memorial-window could be placed in a church. For example, Isambard Kingdom Brunel (1806-59) is buried, together with his father and mother, beneath a simple stone block[3] in Kensal Green (**8.6**), but he is commemorated much more splendidly by a stained-glass window of 1868, in Westminster Abbey, designed by the architect Richard Norman Shaw, R.A. (1831-1912). Nonetheless, works by some of the leading sculptors of the century are to be found in the cemetery, although most are now somewhat careworn, and some, which survived the ravages of the 1939-45 war, have succumbed to the onslaughts of vandals and thieves during recent times.

From the earliest days of the cemetery, comments about its display of monuments have not been without criticism. The influential architectural periodical, *The Builder*, in 1856,[4] commented that on entering the grounds the visitor was confronted by several hundreds of memorials, some of which were to the worthies of the age. How few of them, the writer complained, spoke flatteringly of 19th-century taste in art: he felt that there was plenty of room for improvement. *The Builder*'s verdict was far too sweeping, for Kensal Green has many tombs that rise far above mediocrity, and possesses some that are outstanding. Moreover, as the following pages will indicate, there is much to reward the modern visitor in search of sculptural merit, as well as much that is entertaining, eccentric, quirky, and worthy of attention from numerous points of view.

The Monuments

Beneath the colonnades west of the Anglican chapel is the memorial[5] to his wife, parents, and himself by the sculptor Robert William Sievier, F.R.S. (1794-1865), among whose works is the statue (1825) of Dr Edward Jenner (1749-1823) in Gloucester Cathedral. The group (**9.19** and **10.1**), earlier than the building of the colonnades, is discussed in the previous Chapter, and shows a man (probably a portrait of one of the Sievier clan) reclining upon a Classical death-bed comforting a young woman who kneels beside him: regrettably, her right arm has been broken off. Funerary monuments such as this, and of this quality, are more usually seen in our cathedrals and parish churches. In the arcade opposite is another typical church-memorial (which, like the Sievier sculpture, was once protected under a long-gone roof) to Georgiana Clementson Lough (1834-68),[6] by her father, the sculptor John Graham Lough (1798-1876). The

[1] *See* Burgess (1963), *passim*. [2] Kerney (1987-8), *passim*. [3] [8590/**41**/PS]. [4] *The Builder*, 725/**xiv** (27 December 1856), 700, and *passim*. The index in *The Builder* during the 1840s, 1850s, and 1860s has many entries for cemeteries, including facts about their foundation and opinions regarding their artistic worth. [5] [19149/**90**/2], which is not the location of the memorial. In any case his parents are buried separately in [1109/**90**]. Another surviving work in the cemetery is the memorial tablet in the colonnade of [**Catacomb A**] to Alexander Boswell, senior member of the Madras Medical Board, who died in 1835 and was entombed in the vaults of St Marylebone parish-church. [6] Wife of Major-General Sir George Bourchier (1821-98). Neither she nor her husband is buried in Kensal Green cemetery.

10.1 Monument (photographed in 2001) to John and Frances Sievier and their son (Robert William Sievier) and daughter-in-law, sculpted by R. W. Sievier, F.R.S. (1794-1865). The almost illegible inscription records that 'in the grounds of the cemetery are deposited the remains of John Sievier and his wife ...'. Apparently added below were the names of R. W. Sievier and Ann, his wife: there were no dates. *See also* **9.19** (*MC.No80101*).

10.2 Details of effigy and altar-tomb of Georgina Clementson by J. G. Lough (1798-1876). Photograph of 2001. *See also* **9.20** (*MC.Go80101*).

artist has gone back to the Middle Ages for his inspiration, although the undated monument could not be mistaken for any other but the Victorian period. Lough shows his daughter as a recumbent figure on a tomb-chest on which are portrait-reliefs flanked by angels (**9.20** and **10.2**). Although Lough received a large number of important commissions during the middle years of the 19th century, and his 'extraordinary genius', capable of producing works of 'perfectly miraculous power', was absurdly over-praised in some quarters, he was also unkindly criticised, and his sculpture denounced for 'maudlin sentimentality rarely outdone by the most drivelling essays'. One of his commissions subjected to savage abuse was his statue of Queen Victoria (1845) for the Royal Exchange in London, the 'gross vulgarity' of which was stated to exceed 'that of the worst production that has ever been publicly exhibited'.[7]

Sievier's monument to the Irish *médecin à la mode*, John St John Long (1798-1834)[8] is certainly one of Kensal Green's most elegant and refined, particularly in contrast to its extraordinarily idiosyncratic neighbour, the mausoleum of Andrew Ducrow (1793-1842)[9] (**8.23** and **8.24**). Both monuments are discussed at length in the previous two Chapters. Sievier modelled Long's tomb on the Choragic Monument of Lysicrates, its high, domed *tholos* acting as a protective canopy for an allegorical female figure representing Hygeia. The conscious use of Classical precedent gives scholarly dignity to the whole conception and the overall quality is an indication of Long's status at the time – despite his chequered career.[10] In its key position on the main avenue, it was also erected as an aesthetically pleasing *fabrique* in the garden-cemetery, *pour encourager les autres* (**8.26**).

The fashion for public cemeteries created a demand for the work of monumental mason-sculptors: some of these set up in London in the neighbourhood of the New (now Marylebone) Road, where both their materials and finished works could be transported by canal. One of the entrepreneurs who took advantage of the canal alongside the cemetery established the local firm of Lander, and many works by what became

7 Gunnis (1968), 243. Gunnis may be consulted, with benefit, about nearly all the sculptors mentioned in this paper. For architects *see* Colvin (1995), *passim*. 8 [283/**76**/RS]. 9 [820/**76**/RS]. For the Egyptian style *see* Curl (1994*b*), *passim*, Curl (2000*c* and *d*), *passim*, and Curl (2000*e*), 65-6. 10 *D.N.B.*, xii (1917), 106-7.

E. M. Lander may be found at Kensal Green.[11] There is one that is particularly worthy of note: not far away from the Ducrow mausoleum is the monument (1844-5) [12] by Lander to Major-General The Hon. Sir William Casement (1780-1844), of the Bengal Army, and Member of the Supreme Council of India. Elements are quite conventional: on a base, surrounded by upright cannons as bollards, is the coffin upon which are placed the general's cloak and plumed hat, but above these is a large flat canopy, with Egyptianising coved cornice,[13] supported on the heads of four draped and turbaned *telamones*[14] (**8.11** and **12.9**).

The Casement monument has a certain charm, but it cannot compare for quality with that, not far away,[15] to the Irish-born painter William Mulready, R. A. (1786-1863). This very elegant Renaissance Revival design is reminiscent of many surviving Elizabethan and Jacobean monuments that may be found in parish churches and cathedrals. It depicts Mulready, modelled in artificial stone, lying on a woven rush mattress, beneath a canopy held up by six curiously primitive, vaguely Tuscan columns – a six-poster bed, in fact (**8.14**, **10.3**, and **12.8**). Around the base are incised representations of Mulready's paintings and drawings.[16] This outstanding work, one of the most distinguished memorials in the cemetery, is by Godfrey Sykes (1824-66), the designer of most of the terracotta decoration of the South Kensington (now the Victoria and Albert) Museum's buildings. Sykes had been a pupil in Sheffield of the one really great British designer-sculptor of the middle years of the 19th century, Alfred Stevens (1817-75), and the influence of the master shows. The refinement of the Mulready monument contrasts sharply with its neighbour (**8.12**), the severe, powerful, blocky, Cornish Granite mausoleum[17] of Sir William Molesworth, Bart. (1810-55), First Commissioner of the Board of Works (1853) and Colonial Secretary (1855), and his wife, Lady Andalusia, *née* Grant (1809-88). It was Molesworth who first proposed a national monument to Arthur Wellesley (1769-1852), 1st Duke (from 1814) of Wellington, which controversially resulted in Alfred Stevens's masterpiece (1857-1912) in St Paul's Cathedral.

10.3 Mulready tomb, designed by Godfrey Sykes, in 1997 [17933/**56**/PS]. *See* Chapter VIII, §35 (© *Crown copyright. NMR.AA97/1162*).

One of the more prolific sculptors of the century was Matthew Noble (1818-76), whose memorial statues of the Prince Consort were erected at Salford, Leeds, Manchester (all 1865), and Bombay (1870), and who created several monuments that stand in Westminster Abbey, St Paul's Cathedral, York Minster, and other churches. At least two

[11] The firm's establishment is still (in 2001) outside the gates of the cemetery. Several of the Lander family of mason-sculptors are buried in the cemetery, notably George Lander (*c.*1799-1861) [31215/**29**/RS]: his monument records that he was 'employed by the General Cemetery Company as mason from the commencement of their operations'. Edward Manuel Lander (1836-1910) is buried in [30858/**140**/PS]: he was responsible for many of the cemetery's monuments. There appear to have been two E. M. Landers, for some of the monuments are too early to be the work of the above-named Edward Manuel Lander (e.g. the Soyer monument, signed 'E. M. Lander, mason to the cemetery'). The massive Huth mausoleum is also by the elder E. M. Lander. What is surprising is the scarcity of monuments signed by George Lander. The Landers originally hailed from Dorset. Edward Manuel Lander (according to the 1881 Census) was born in West Lulworth. [12] [5400/**56**/RS]. [13] Parts of which have fallen. [14] These are often inaccurately called caryatid(e)s, which are female figures, and should not be confused with the male *telamon* (pl. *telamones*), a straight, unbowed male whole figure acting as a column supporting an entablature on its head. *See* Curl (2000*a*), *passim*. [15] [17933/**56**/PS]. It is described in the burial register as a 'terra cotta canopy tomb'. [16] Mr Moulder has identified the paintings represented on Mulready's tomb as: *Dog in Two Minds* (1830); *The Careless Messenger Detected* (1821); *The Wolf and the Lamb* (1820); *Sophia and Burchell Haymaking* (1847); *The Last In* (1835); *Brother and Sister*, a.k.a. *The Younger Brother* (1837); *The Seven Ages* (1838); *Giving a Bite* (1836); *Choosing the Wedding Gown* (1846); *The Sonnet* (1839); *The Travelling Druggist* (1825); *Boy Firing a Cannon* (1827); *The Butt – Shooting a Cherry* (1848); and *Male and Female Nudes* (1857). [17] [12766/**56**/RS].

monuments by him were erected in Kensal Green cemetery, both of which were well thought-of at the time. One of them, to Lieut-General Thomas Fiddes[18] and Lieutenant George Pauli,[19] had three medallion heads, although the upper portion in the form of an elongated finial was thought to be unpleasing. It is not certain if this monument is still identifiable, and may have been a casualty of the 1939-45 war. The same critic considered there was a greatness, which reflected credit upon Noble, in his memorial[20] to the poet Thomas Hood (1799-1845) which, as the preceding Chapter describes, was erected by public subscription in 1854.[21] This, a granite pedestal, had a bronze bust and two books on top: on either side were bronze reliefs illustrating 'Eugene Aram' and 'The Bridge of Sighs', while in front, at the base, were a bronze mask and lyre. Unfortunately we shall never know the quality of these, as the bust and all the other bronze decorations have been stolen (**8.21**).

South of the main path, standing beneath a Gothic canopy is the monument[22] to George Augustus Frederick Percy Sydney Smythe, the Viscount Strangford (1818-57), with two rather blackened 'life-sized' angels. Lord Strangford fought what is thought to be the last duel in England, in 1852, and was one of Benjamin Disraeli's 'Young England' party. The monument (**8.4** and **9.13**) is by Edward James Physick (1829-1906). Others by him, his brother Robert, and his father Edward Gustavus Physick (1802-75), are to General Sir James Kempt (1764-1854) of 1854[23] (formerly in the Monumental Chambers), Vice-Admiral Percy Grace (*c.*1789-1859),[24] and Lieutenant-General John Tulloch (1789-1862).[25] Three of this family of sculptors, including the first, Edward William Physick (*c.*1774-1862), are buried in the cemetery.[26] Edward James Physick, who, like his father, exhibited sculpture at the Great Exhibition of 1851, is credited, *c.*1853, with the innovation of infilling lettering on monuments and gravestones with lead, thus providing supposedly imperishable inscriptions. The lettering of the Strangford memorial is a good example, although elsewhere there has been a tendency for the lead to fall out.

A short walk away from this monument is the now pathetic remains of the group on the memorial[27] to Alfred Cooke (1822-54), of 1854, sculpted by Thomas Milnes (1813-88).[28] This, most unfortunately, has been the target of repeated vandalism, and is now in an advanced state of decay.[29] A horse, today minus a leg or two, stands over a small seated boy (recently decapitated). A strange work, the precise significance is undoubtedly related to the fact that Cooke was a breeder of horses for circuses. Milnes was highly paid (700 guineas) in 1844 for his statue of Lord Nelson at Norwich, and he was commissioned to sculpt the lions for the base of Nelson's Column, Trafalgar Square, which, as they were rejected, are now at the Mechanics' Institute in Saltaire in Yorkshire.

[18] Mr Humpage located Fiddes's tomb in 2000 [17791/**77**/PS]: it had collapsed and is covered with ivy. The grave contains only the bodies of Fiddes and a female, probably his wife. [19] This is probably an error on the part of Gunnis: there is no mention of Pauli in the Company's records. [20] [5449/**74**/PS]. [21] *See The Builder*, **xxi**/1083 (7 November 1863), 789-90, and **xxiv**/1212 (28 April 1866), 305-6, for contemporary opinions. *See also* Gunnis (1968), 274-5. [22] [14166/**31**/PS]. Also the grave of Percy Ellen Frederick William Smythe, 8th Viscount (1826-69), and his wife, Emily Anne (d. 1887). *See D.N.B.*, **xviii** (1917), 605-6. [23] [12065/**CAT. B**/Vault 57/Comp. 10]. Kempt has an entry in *D.N.B.*, **x** (1917), 1284-5. [24] [15242/**CAT. B**/Vault 67/8]. Percy Grace was the brother of Sir William Grace of Grace Castle, County Kilkenny, and of Sheffield Grace, F.S.A. (*c.*1785-1850). He fought at Copenhagen, was shipwrecked in 1808, and was held prisoner for eight months in Batavia. He was badly wounded during the capture of a flotilla of Malay pirates in 1809. He was among the first to begin destroying the barracoons or slave depots on the coast of Africa in 1822-3. [25] Tulloch, of the Bengal Native Infantry, is commemorated by a chest-tomb with military accoutrements [17126/**77**/PS]. Gunnis (1968), 302, calls him 'Sir John Tullock'. [26] [86/**158**/RS]. There are four Physick graves in the cemetery as follows: Edward William Physick (1774-1862) [17495/**158**/RS]; Edward Gustavus Physick (1802-75) [86/**158**/RS]; Edward James Physick (1829-1906) [14998/**158**/RS]; and Walter F. Physick (d. 1907) [41196/**158**/2]. The only surviving monument is that to Edward James. [27] [11719/**76**/PS]. The memorial actually covers two graves [11719 and 11720]. The latter is the grave of Thomas Taplin Cooke (1782-1866) and William Cooke (d. 1886), the father and brother, respectively, of Alfred. The Cookes were circus owners and performers (*See* Vivian-Neal [1999], 41-2). William was a celebrated trainer of horses, and, in the manner of Ducrow, composed a piece of self-adulatory doggerel: 'Bucephalus was once by Alexander tamed; At least the fact is in some History named: But William Cooke, why he had done much more; Alec tamed one Bucephalus, and Cooke a score.' [28] Buried in [25707/**43**/4]. [29] Thus no illustration of it appears here.

The bronze lions in the Square, of course, are by Sir Edwin Landseer (1802-73), unveiled in 1867.

The cemetery contains several mausolea and tombs designed by architects. One of the most notable and outstanding is the monument (1867-8) of Captain Charles Spencer Ricketts (1788-1867),[30] designed by William Burges A.R.A. (1827-81), the creator of Cardiff Castle and Castell Coch for John Patrick Crichton-Stuart (1847-1900), 3rd Marquess (from 1848) of Bute. Ricketts had joined the Royal Navy at the age of seven[31] and served under Thomas Cochrane, 10th Earl of Dundonald,[32] called by Napoleon 'the Sea-Wolf', so was really a relic from the time of Nelson. His daughter, Julia Anne, married a lawyer named George Bonnor (1822-93), who had artistic tendencies, and it was Bonnor who commissioned Burges to design his father-in-law's funerary monument. It is, in Professor Crook's memorable words, 'bristling with gargoyles, and groaning with a surfeit of crockets ... Hunched like a porcupine, fattened to the point of obesity, its reptilian silhouette is almost a parody of Early French ... [All] the hallmarks of its architect's Gothic style are there to see: the ringed colonnettes, the studded trefoils, the muscular soffits, the mastic-filled inlay, the foliate masks, the compassed proportions, [and] the overscaled sculpture'.[33] Nikolaus Pevsner[34] said of the Ricketts tomb in 1952 that it was 'atrociously rich',[35] a serious misjudgement, perhaps, that became a 'gorgeously rich Gothic shrine'[36] in 1991. It is certainly that, and more (**8.7**).

At about the same time, Edward Blore F.R.S.,[37] the retired Surveyor of the Fabric of Westminster Abbey,[38] and architect of the east wing facing The Mall at Buckingham Palace,[39] designed the monument (1866) to General Forster Walker.[40] This, one of Blore's last recorded works, was based on 13th-century tombs, but unlike them was a mixture of granite, Portland Stone, and various marbles, with angels beneath canopies, and at the angles the figures of Faith, Hope, Charity, and Patience: the sculptor was James Forsyth. As discussed in the previous Chapter, other architects whose work may be found in the cemetery include George Basevi (1794-1845) and John Buonarotti Papworth (1775-1847).

Notable sculptors who are represented at Kensal Green include Musgrave Lewthwaite Watson,[41] who was responsible for the monument[42] to Allan Cunningham,[43] and the Irishman, John Henry Foley, R.A.,[44] who provided the tomb of Lieut-General John Williams Morris (*c.*1760-1848).[45] Foley was also the sculptor of the monument[46] to James Ward, R.A. (1769-1859), the painter and engraver, on which stood the figure of the Muse of Painting, brushes and palette in her right hand and a laurel wreath in her left (the stone now lies flat, and is broken in places). William Behnes (1795-1864), Sculptor-in-Ordinary to Queen Victoria, was responsible for the (now-missing) bust of 1859 on the pedestal-monument to George Cruikshank (1792-1878).[47] Behnes himself died impoverished in the Middlesex Hospital, having been found lying in the gutter, and Cruikshank became the secretary of an appeal to collect money for a monument to him[48] in Kensal Green. Sufficient sums could not be raised, however, and his modest Portland Stone Classical sarcophagus-tomb was made by Behnes's last pupil,

30 [20242/**47**/RS]. 31 Crook (1981), 228 and notes 13-16. 32 Born 1775, died 1860. 33 Crook (1981), 228. 34 Born 1902, died 1983. 35 In *The Buildings of England, London*, ii (Harmondsworth: Penguin, 1952), 303. 36 Cherry and Pevsner (1991), 469. This judgement appears to have been made after the authorship of the monument became known. 37 Born 1787, died 1879. 38 From 1827 to 1849. 39 1847-50 – refronted by Sir Aston Webb (1849-1930) in 1912-13. 40 [18863/**129**/RS]. *The Builder*, **xxiv**/1212 (28 April 1866), 305-6. *See also* Blore (1826), which demonstrates he had a long-standing interest in medieval funerary monuments. There is only body in the grave, that of Lydia Walker (d. 1864): the tomb nevertheless commemorates several of General Walker's children. 41 1804-47 – a one-time assistant of Sir Francis Leggatt Chantrey, R.A. (1781-1841). 42 [3804/**169**/4]. The grave adjoins [22310/**169**/4], which contains other members of the Cunningham family. 43 1784-1842 – the biographer of British painters, sculptors, and architects. 44 1818-74 – the sculptor of the statue of the Prince on the Albert Memorial in Kensington Gardens (1874). 45 [4875/**90**/IR]. 46 [15560/**90**/3]. 47 [29171/**76**/RS]. The illustrator Cruikshank's body was translated to the crypt of St Paul's Cathedral in 1878, and the grave in Kensal Green cemetery is occupied by the remains of his widow, Eliza (1807-90). 48 [18202/**74**/PS].

10.4 Marble entablature, column-tops, and angels above the grave [23601/**56**/RS] of Mary Gibson, showing the deterioration of marble due to acid rain, in 2001. *See* Chapter VIII, §34 (*MC.Q060101*).

Morton Edwards.[49] William Theed (the Younger)[50] created the tomb of Louisa Eliza Bright of Civitavecchia (*c.*1827-57),[51] and Thomas Woolner, R.A.[52] designed the monument to Hepworth Dixon (1881), in Highgate cemetery.[53] Woolner, who emigrated for a while to Australia, is portrayed with his wife by Ford Madox Brown (1821-93) in his well-known painting of the couple gazing from the ship at 'The Last of England' (1855).[54] A lost bust on the monument[55] to James Henry Leigh Hunt (1784-1859) was by Joseph Durham A.R.A.[56] Peter Hollins (1800-86) was a sculptor of monuments and statues all over the country: he executed the memorial (1855)[57] to the painter, his cousin John Hollins, A.R.A.[58] Trained by his father, William (1763-1843), he later worked under Sir Francis Chantrey, with whose work his own has been favourably compared. The ubiquitous firm of Thomas and Edward Gaffin, of Regent Street, responsible for large numbers of mainly simple mural tablets of black and white marbles, is represented at Kensal Green, among others, by the handsome monument[59] to the Reverend James Fleming (1830-1908): it is a raised hipped marble ledger, carved with passion-flowers.

One of the earliest monuments in the cemetery is that to Jean Miller (d. 1831), in the colonnade of the old or terrace catacomb, the work of John Ternouth (1795-1849), who is perhaps best known for the bronze relief panel of 'The Battle of Copenhagen' on the base of Nelson's Column in Trafalgar Square. Unfortunately, nearly all the monumental tablets in the colonnade over [**Catacomb A**] have been destroyed, but one of the few survivors, the tablet depicting a finely carved figure of a woman kneeling before a draped urn, might possibly be the work in question. Regrettably, the inscription that was once attached to the memorial has disappeared, so it is unlikely we will be able to identify the carving with certainty. Other significant memorials in the cemetery include that[60] to John McCreery (1768-1832) of County Tyrone (**8.34**): it is one of several in Kensal Green cemetery the design of which is based on the celebrated Roman sarcophagus of Cornelius Lucius Scipio Barbatus, as discussed in the previous Chapter.[61] John Edward Carew (*c.*1785-1868),[62] who came to London from Ireland in about 1809, and became an assistant to Sir Richard Westmacott, R.A. (1775-1856), created the monument[63] of 1846

49 *See* Grant (1953) and Graves (1905) for Morton Edwards, who exhibited five works at the Royal Academy in 1864-70, including busts of: the Prince of Wales (1864) for the Corporation and City of Toronto; the Bishop of London (Archibald Campbell Tait – 1867); and Dr Propert (1869 – who is buried in Kensal Green cemetery).
50 1804-91 – sculptor of the monument (1864) to Queen Victoria's mother, the Duchess of Kent (1786-1861), in her mausoleum at Frogmore. Theed is buried in [12140/**79**/12]. 51 [13987/**77**/IR]. The wife of Joseph Bright, and only child of George Bateman, M. D. (*c.*1788-1857), of Leamington, Warwickshire. The grave also contains the body of Bateman. The red granite monument is signed by MacDonald of Aberdeen. 52 1825-92 – the sculptor-member of the Pre-Raphaelite Brotherhood. 53 Gunnis (1968), 445, states the monument of William Hepworth Dixon (1821-79) is in Kensal Green, but *D.N.B.*, v (1917), 1033-5, gives his place of burial as Highgate cemetery. There is no record of Dixon's burial at Kensal Green, which shows the perils of relying on secondary sources. 54 Now in the City Art Gallery, Birmingham. 55 [13650/**121**/3]. 56 1814-77 – among whose works is the memorial to the Great Exhibition, with its standing figure of the Prince Consort, to the south of the Royal Albert Hall. 57 Formerly in the Monumental Chambers, but in 2000 in Vault 139. 58 1798-1855 [**CAT. B**/Vault 57/Comp. 14, grave number 12291]. 59 [39082/**128**/PS]. Entry in *D.N.B.* 60 [6865/**99**/PS]. 61 Curl (2000*e*), 77. The original is now in the Vatican Museum. 62 Buried in [10374/**14**/BC]. 63 [5343/**38**/PS]. A plain headstone with an unrecognisable portrait-medallion.

10.5 *(above left)* Monument [20030/152-153/RS]of Edward Lewis in 2001 (*MC.F090101*).

10.6 *(above centre)* Monument [35709/153/3] of Caroline Liardet in 2001 (*MC.J130101*).

10.7 *(above right)* Angel and cross over the grave [46535/64/PS] of Conway and Grace Bishop in 2001 (*MC.J090101*).

10.8 *(right)* Detail of the marble angel on the Bishop memorial [46535/64/PS] in 2001 (*MC.K090101*).

to the Irish writer, drama-critic, and poet, Michael Nugent (1780-1845), and was also responsible for the bronze relief at the base of Nelson's Column in Trafalgar Square, 'The Death of Nelson', exhibited at the Great Exhibition. He is buried in the cemetery in a now unmarked grave.

Prominent among other sculptural memorials (as mentioned in previous Chapters) is the 12-Corinthian-columned marble peristyle[64] by James Samuel Farley[65] to Mary Eleanor Gibson,[66] on top of which four angels swirl around a long-departed ceramic wreath: the monument is now in poor condition, as the marble has deteriorated as a result of pollution (8.13 and 10.4). Everywhere there are rustic (or rugged) crosses of

[64] [23601/56/RS]. [65] 1811-66. Buried in [17669/92/8]. [66] 1854-72. Formerly of Redland, Bristol, she died in the Great Western Hotel, Paddington.

10.9 Memorial [40750/**166**/PS] to Charles Locke Eastlake in 2001 (*MC.D090101*).

10.10 Bagnold memorial [14194/**62**/RS] in 2001 (*MC.H090101*).

10.11 Ducrow mausoleum [820/**76**/RS], showing the broken column, in 2001. *See* Chapter VIII, §53 (*MC.T060101*).

various dates: examples include those of Edward Lewis (*c.*1801-66 – with ivy twining around it, the sculptural ensemble set on a rocky base, and the whole supported on a granite plinth [**10.5**]);[67] Caroline Sophia Evelyn Liardet (1824-95 – with an angel hanging decorations on it [**10.6**]);[68] and Lieutenant-Colonel Conway Bishop (*c.*1880-1923) and his wife, Grace (d. 1919 – with an angel standing in front of it [**10.7** and **10.8**]).[69] It seems it was during the late 18th century, and particularly during the 19th century, that sculptured angels ceased to be masculine, or, at best, androgynous, and became female.[70]

Towards the end of the 19th century, influenced by a revival of interest in the antiquities of Scotland and Ireland, arrays of Celtic crosses began to become manifest in the cemetery. A good example is the handsome monument to Charles Locke Eastlake (1836-1906), Secretary to the Royal Institute of British Architects (1866-77), Keeper and Secretary of the National Gallery (1878-98), and author of *A History of the Gothic Revival* (1872) (**10.9**).[71] This fine cross also commemorates Eastlake's wife, Eliza (d. 1911).

Sarcophagi and plinths abound, with swords, cloaks, and other military insignia commemorating soldiers and sailors, as, for example, on the monuments of Major-General Frederick Macdonald Birch (*c.*1837-1901),[72] Major-General Michael Edward Bagnold (1787-1857), of the Bombay Army, and his wife, Eliza Larkins (1817-73) (**10.10**),[73] General Sir James Law Lushington (1779-1859) (**9.10**);[74] and Admiral Henry Colins Deacon (1788-1869) (**8.39**),[75] the last located almost opposite the grave[76] of Sir Charles Lock Eastlake, P.R.A. (1793-1865).

Scattered throughout the cemetery are broken columns, signifying life ended, or cut off; an example may be found associated with the Ducrow mausoleum (**8.23, 8.24** and **10.11**),[77] and another over the grave of Sir George Rendlesham Prescott, Bart. (1846-1894).[78] There are also plenty of urns, draped and undraped: a good example is the

[67] [20030/**152-153**/RS]. Lewis, a solicitor, of 25 Upper Harley Street, died at the *Star and Garter Hotel*, Richmond. [68] [35709/**153**/3], immediately behind the Duke of Cambridge's mausoleum. She was the wife of John Evelyn Liardet (1828-1902), who is also buried in the grave. Liardet was the son of Wilbraham Frederick Evelyn Liardet (1799-1878), who emigrated with his family to Australia in 1839, and became a successful hotel-keeper and watercolourist. His son was sent to London to study law, but is listed in the *Kelly's Post Office Directory* of 1888 as a marine engineer, of 16 Condon Street. [69] [46535/**64**/PS]. [70] For example, the monuments to Henry, 3rd Earl of Effingham (1837-98) [37007/**140**/RS], and Eli Josiah Brand (1830-1914) [39358/**42**/RS]. [71] [40750/**166**/PS]. [72] [15167/**68**/RS]. Birch was one of the old garrison at Lucknow, and A.D.C. to Sir John Inglis during the siege. [73] [14194/**62**/RS]. This monument was damaged during the 1939-45 war. [74] [15282/**57**/IR]. Lushington's monument is signed by Edward Richardson, Melbury Terrace, Harewood Street, 1860. [75] [19697/**125**/PS]. [76] [19540/**125**/PS], the uncle of Charles Locke Eastlake, referred to above. [77] [820/**76**/RS]. [78] [34906/**166**/PS]. Prescott was Sheriff of Sussex, 1882-3.

memorial to Mary Lambton Horn (1824-81).[79] A few pinnacles in various shapes and sizes may also be found, including a tall one with an abundance of crockets commemorating Alice Helena Colyer (*c.*1847-70).[80]

A sculptural monument of considerable prominence and interest is that (**8.29**) to Elizabeth Emma (d. 1842), artist wife of the cook Alexis Benoît Soyer (1809-58), famous for the eponymous stove that he introduced to the army during the Crimean War.[81] The memorial's ideological significance has already been considered in the previous Chapter, and it was sufficiently remarkable at the time of its erection to attract the attention of the *Illustrated London News*.[82] The journal's account of the monument, which was accompanied by an engraved view, is worth quoting at length:

> [the] original design was by M. Soyer himself, who, as is generally known, fills the office of *chef-de-cuisine* at the Reform Club-house. The pedestal is rather more than twelve feet in height, and on top of this stands the heroic figure of Faith ... This figure has the attributes of her office, and is in some degree after the manner of Raphael['s] religious or sculptural figures. She points with her right hand [now broken off] to Heaven, whilst, in her left, she holds the cross [also now missing], symbolic of Christianity. The countenance of the figure is calm and composed, full of character and very finely cut. The drapery is magnificent. On the upper portion of the pedestal are two cherubs, which float freely in the air, and are very happily designed and executed. One holds a crown over the head of an effigy of M[me]. Soyer, represented as large as life, on a medallion of white statuary marble, whilst the other holds a branch of palm, emblematic of peace. The medallion is surrounded by a serpent, the emblem of eternity. Beneath the medallion are suspended a palette and the implement of the delightful art in which Madame Soyer excelled, surrounded with laurels. This noble monument was executed by M. Puyenbroach,[[83]] of Brussels, one of the principal sculptors to his Belgian Majesty. At the back of the pedestal a space is left for the crown of laurels or funeral wreath presented at the inauguration by the admirable *artiste* Mdlle. Cerito, and made from the celebrated wreath presented to Cerito, at La Scala, Milan.
>
> The wreath together with the palette of the artiste, will be placed in a glass case, and fixed at the back of the pedestal. The inscription on the pedestal will be simply the words 'To Her', without any addition whatever.

Needless to say, both the 'palette of the artiste' and the wreath have been stolen. The Soyer memorial and the Ducrow mausoleum were both singled out (as noted previously) by *The Builder* as displaying 'ponderous coxcombry',[84] though these days we might regard them as robust pieces of showy eclecticism, and none the worse for that. Also surmounted by a standing allegorical woman (in this case Hope) is the red-granite memorial (**8.41**) by Messrs MacDonald & Leslie, to the tight-rope walker Émile Blondin (1824-97),[85] with white marble relief portraits of himself and his wife.[86]

The Scottish granite trade began to flourish at about the same time as the opening of the cemetery, so it is not surprising that this hard stone, which is able to shrug off the worst that the weather can do, found a ready market in churchyards and cemeteries. The stone is exceedingly hard to sculpt, and an example of how a mason overcame the problem is seen in the memorial[87] to William Frederick Meredith (*c.*1828-92). The urn

79 [13478/58/RS]. Wife of Richard Horn (1818-83), solicitor, of 46 Stanhope Gardens and Gun Lodge, Stevenage, Herts. He is also buried in this grave. 80 [21990/116/2]. The wife of Captain Harrel and daughter of Thomas Colyer of Wombwell Hall, Northfleet, Kent. Her husband, James Wharton Harrel (*c.*1836-1909), served in the 2nd Queens and 89th Princess Victoria Regiments. 81 [3714/80/RS]. 82 *The Illustrated London News*, v/123 (7 September 1844), 160. 83 *Sic.* His name was actually Puyenbroeck, indicating a cavalier attitude to foreign names even then. 84 *The Builder*, **xiv**/725 (27 December 1856), 700. 85 His real name was Jean-François Gravelet. 86 [31398/140/RS]. 87 [28203/65/RS]. Meredith was a 'Steam Biscuit Manufacturer'.

10.12 Detail of the Ninon Michaelis monument [37384/37/RS] in 2001. *See* Chapter VIII, §18 (*MC.G060101*).

that once crowned it is now missing, but, for ease of sculpting, the portrait relief is of marble, and this nestles within a roundel gouged out from the granite background (**9.22**). Similarly, the pink Peterhead granite obelisk erected to commemorate the socialist and philanthropist, Robert Owen (1771-1858) – who is actually buried in his native Newtown, Montgomeryshire – has a small relief portrait set into one face (**8.1**).[88]

An even finer example of a carved granite tomb is the large pinkish-grey tomb-chest with a pitched roof and pediments at either end,[89] erected to the memory of James Meadows Rendel, F.R.S. (1799-1856), the distinguished engineer, who designed and reported on numerous harbours and docks (including those at Genoa and Rio de Janeiro), and planned railways in England, India, and Spain. He also advised the Prussian Government on naval installations, and the Hamburg Senate on the Elbe from Hamburg to Cuxhaven.[90] The handsome monument was designed by Sir Matthew Digby Wyatt (1820-77), and the drawings for it were exhibited at the Royal Academy in 1862 (**8.36**).

Two other sculptural monuments, very different from one another, but each memorable in its own way, are decades apart. The first, on the Centre Avenue, is a charming *Jugendstil stele*, curved on plan, against which a beautiful Classically-draped female figure, in an attitude of despair, clasps her head in her left hand and holds a garland in her right: this is the memorial[91] to Ninon Michaelis of 1895, and is by a sculptor who has not been identified, but was probably Continental (**9.1** and **10.12**). The second[92] is a small simple cross on a plain lettered base, of Hoptonwood stone (**8.44**), by Eric Gill, A.R.A. (1882-1940), in memory of Marigold Frances (1918-21), daughter of Sir Winston (1874-1965) and Lady (1885-1977) Churchill; Gill's lettering of 1922 had to be recut *c.*1992.[93] Originally the monument consisted of an octagonal pillar, with a crucifix and a group of figures. Other monuments carved by Gill included those to William Smith Williams (1800-75 – journalist who corresponded with Charlotte Brontë [1816-55]) and Elizabeth Williams, his wife (1909), which also commemorated Williams's son-in-law, the artist Lowes (Cato) Dickinson (1819-1908);[94] the gravestone to the poet Alice Christiana Gertrude Meynell (1874-1922); and the hogback stone (1930) in memory of Anthony Polimeni (1844-1928),[95] but, again, the weather has caused unfortunate deterioriation of the lettering (for which Gill was once so famous).[96]

[88] [26655/**14**/PS]. [89] [13511/**101**/RS]. [90] *D.N.B.*, **xvi** (1917), 896-8. [91] [37384/**37**/RS]. [92] [47220/**160**/PS]. [93] Peace (1994). In his catalogue Peace does not state who renovated the Churchill memorial. [94] [18770/**111**/6]. Dickinson is buried in an adjoining grave [25738/**111**/6]. [95] Polimeni was a wholesale perfumer, of 12 Mark Lane, City of London (1888). [96] Peace (1994) lists these and others in the adjoining Roman Catholic cemetery, including Gill's altar-tomb of the poet Francis Thompson (1859-1907), of 1911 (Peace [1994], No. 219, 69).

When one comes to consider the monuments to sculptors themselves, these are usually of the simplest kind, and, one could say, are often unremarkable or modest. As we saw earlier, William Behnes has a very plain sarcophagus, but Joseph Durham, as Dr Brooks has noted, fares somewhat better, his Portland Stone and Carrara Marble tomb-chest decorated with sculptor's tools.[97] If Thomas Campbell (1790-1858), one of whose better works is the monument (1827) to the Duchess of Buccleuch at Warkton parish church, Northamptonshire, had a monument over his grave,[98] it has now disappeared, as has that to John Edward Carew. The sculptor of the statue of Shakespeare in Leicester Square, London, Giovanni Giuseppe Fontana (1821-93), now has a broken headstone,[99] whilst Humphrey Hopper (1767-1844) lies under a raised, much eroded, gabled ledger.[100] The sculpture historian, Rupert Gunnis (1899-1965), considered Hopper 'a competent, occasionally a very good, sculptor, but he was at his very worst when given a commission for a large national monument. The responsibility seems to have paralysed his invention, as the lamentable mass of marble commissioned by the House of Commons to commemorate General Hay (1814) in St Paul's Cathedral only too clearly shows'.[101] An unexceptional tomb-chest[102] commemorates Samuel Joseph (1791-1850), whose masterpiece is the seated statue (1838) of William Wilberforce (1759-1833) in Westminster Abbey.

John Graham Lough[103] rests in the catacomb of the Anglican chapel as do George Rennie (1802-60)[104] and Robert Shout (1763-1843).[105] An album of designs by the Shout family is in the Victoria and Albert Museum and includes the large Portland Stone mausoleum[106] to James Morison (1770-1840), the patent-medicine entrepreneur whose career is considered in the previous Chapter. The mausoleum, erected by William Milligan (1812-78),[107] has steeply battered sides, a frieze from which hang swags, and a pitched roof with pediments at each end with anthemion-decorated acroteria-blocks at the corners (**4.27**): it is influenced by French designs, many of which had been published during the 1820s and early 1830s, and dozens of extant examples survive in Père-Lachaise and in other Parisian cemeteries. Another inhabitant of the catacomb is Joseph Theakston (1772-1842),[108] assistant to John Flaxman, R.A. (1726-95), Edward Hodges Baily, R.A. (1788-1867), and Sir Francis Chantrey, R.A. Charles Raymond Smith (1798-1888), sculptor of the recumbent effigy (1844) of Grace Horsley Darling (1815-42 – now in the north aisle of the parish-church of St Aidan, Northumberland), is only commemorated at Kensal Green by a worn ledger-stone.[109] Another simple ledger and low headstone[110] commemorate Edward Bowring Stephens (1815-82), elected an associate of the Royal Academy in 1864, it was thought, because he was confused with the gifted Alfred Stevens, at the time almost equally unknown.[111] Even so, there are several more than competent statues by Stephens in his native Exeter, including one of the Prince Consort (1864).

John Ternouth, mentioned earlier, has the dubious distinction of being reported dead in his lifetime: he wrote to the journals in 1846 to put them right, whereupon *The Athenaeum*[112] published a notice to the effect that Ternouth had written to say he was not dead, and the paper gave 'him the benefit of the assertion', a double-edged swipe at

97 [26191/**75**/IR]. *See* Vivian-Neal (1999), 59. 98 [14337/**74**/PS]. 99 [34436/**66**/3]. 100 [1670/**6**/RS].
101 Gunnis (1968), 209. 102 [3377/**44**/2]. 103 [**CAT. B**/Vault 198/6-7]. 104 [15826/**CAT. B**/Vault 121/2].
105 [4238/**CAT. B**/Public Vault/25]. 106 [383/**50**/RS]. 107 William Milligan is buried in [12041/**91**/12]: the General Cemetery Company registers incorrectly give the 'square' number as [**96**]. Mr Moulder has located the grave, which has the grave-number inscribed on the memorial. 108 [52/**CAT. A**/Vault 46/2-3]. A memorial-tablet in the colonnade commemorating Theakston's wife, Elizabeth (d. 1833), and Theakston himself is signed by the artist.
109 [23865/**48**/2]. 110 [10087/**49**/2]. Incorrectly entered in the G.C.C. records as [10007]. 111 Gunnis (1968), 372.
112 14 November 1846. *See* Gunnis (1968), 384.

the poor man's fading reputation.[113] His memorial[114] is rather more distinguished than most, with a marble headstone, on which is sculpted a relief of a mourning woman leaning on a cylindrical pedestal supporting an urn. A broken tomb-chest,[115] however, is all that now reminds one of John Thomas (1813-62), who produced much sculpture for the new Palace of Westminster. Henry Weekes, R. A. (1807-77), who had a very large practice as a monumental sculptor, and was responsible for the 'Manufactures' group on the Albert Memorial, has a simple red-granite hipped ledger-stone.[116] The 'Agriculture' group on the Albert Memorial was produced by another sculptor buried at Kensal Green, William Calder Marshall, R. A. (1813-94), who lies beneath a slab of inscribed red granite, raised upon a grey granite base.[117] Another who received commissions with royal connections was the ambidextrous William Pitts (1790-1840), who carried out decorations at Buckingham Palace. His marble ledger[118] now has an illegible inscription.

Epilogue

Kensal Green cemetery is a repository of the bodies of thousands of the great and good and the unknown, with many interesting memorials and inscriptions to be sought out. Although the artistic worth of some of its monuments perhaps does not rise to the quality of the great sculptural displays found in Continental cemeteries such as Père-Lachaise in Paris, the Staglieno in Genoa, or the Cimitero Monumentale in Milan, it does contain several fine mausolea and monuments, some of which rise to a distinction that can be favourably compared with the best of Continental work.

Even among the more ordinary memorials there are many that catch the eye and deserve closer inspection. The tall pedestal with diagonal buttress-bases and a surmounting urn, for example, though not of great artistic value, has some presence: it commemorates John Wilson (1800-49),[119] the Scots tenor, who, though an opera singer, made his name as a singer of 'Scottish Table Entertainments' which appear to have consisted of sentimental ballads with pronounced Jacobite sympathies. Wilson died in Québec, of cholera, and the monument (by Lawrie & Ferguson of Edinburgh) stands over the burial-place of his family (**10.13**).

Among the humbler gravestones is a robust Gothic headstone of the 1860s with colonnettes, dogtooth ornament, foils, crockets, and a finial, in memory of Flora Anne Dew (*c*.1862-4), Charles Dew (*c*.1826-85), and Margaret Ellen Dew (*c*.1826-1915) (**10.14**).[120] More Classical, with a kneeling female figure by a cartouche within a roundel,

[113] Mark Twain (Samuel Langhorne Clemens [1835-1910]) is probably the best-known victim of the premature obituary, but two notables buried in Kensal Green cemetery were subjected to the same indignity. The song-writer, Henry Russell (1812-1900 – buried in [38384/**176**/2]) was reported in *The Illustrated London News* (29 August 1874) as 'having been spoken of as dead', but that he had written to 'state that to the best of his belief, and as far as one can judge of his own identity', he was 'still in the flesh, hale and hearty'. Russell was best-known for his ballad entertainments, such as *The Maniac*, *The Ship on Fire*, and *Cheer, Boys, Cheer*, now profoundly unfashionable and rarely heard. The Austrian-born Ignatius Pollaky (*c*.1828-1918 – buried in [17308/**68**/2]) was famous in his day for his private detective agency at Paddington Green. Gilbert and Sullivan refer to the 'keen penetration of Paddington Pollaky' in the *Colonel of Dragoons*' song in the first act of *Patience* (1881). Pollaky's name often appeared in the 'agony' columns of *The Times*, but in the edition of 6 March 1882 he inserted an announcement to the effect that the rumour he was dead was not true. Doubtless he had enemies enough to wish it had been. [114] [7891/**168**/6-7], according to the G.C.C. records. It is a double plot, hence the inscriptions on both sides of the headstone. [115] [8677/**36** and **37**/2]. Thomas was the sculptor favoured by Prince Albert, for whom he did much work at Windsor Castle, Buckingham Palace, and Balmoral. Sir Charles Barry (1795-1860) described him as 'an unassuming self-taught genius in his way'. He sculpted the colossal lions at the end of the Britannia bridge over the Menai Straits (1848). The difficulties he experienced in getting his enormous Shakespeare monument admitted to the International Exhibition of 1862 hastened his demise. *See* Gunnis (1968), 388-390. [116] [6369/**155**/PS]. [117] [9328/**111**/RS]. [118] [2475/**95**/RS]. He died from an overdose of laudanum. [119] [4274/**74**/PS]. [120] [18690/**68**/2]. Dew was a stonemason and marble cutter, of 17 Omega Place, Alph Road, and is listed as such in the *Kelly's Post Office Directory*.

is the gravestone of the newspaper proprietor and art-collector, John Edward Taylor (1830-1905), and his wife, Martha Elizabeth (d. 1912) (**10.15**).[121]

A Neoclassical pedestal with pediments and anthemion-decorated ears is unusual in several respects: on its die is a serpent eating its tail, an hourglass, a wreath, and wings; above, it supports a kneeling female figure by a Classical altar decorated with inverted torches, so the symbolism of death is driven home (**10.16**).[122] It commemorates Henrietta Howe (d. 1864), Emma Hart (d. 1866), and Joseph Howe (d. 1892) of 1 Beaufoy Terrace, Maida Vale.[123] Elsewhere, a few busts survived in 2001 (including that of Emidio Recchioni [d. 1934]), though badly scarred by atmospheric pollution (**10.17**).[124]

10.13 Monument [4274/**74**/PS] of John Wilson, vocalist, and his family (*c.*1850) in 2001 (*MC.D080101*).

10.14 Robust Gothic headstone [18690/**68**/2] of the Dew family in 2001 (*MC.B060101*).

10.15 Roundel on the tombstone [40618/**161**/RS] of J. E. Taylor and his wife in 2001 (*MC.A4*).

Appreciation and taste change as time passes by, but now, after more than a century, and at the beginning of a new millennium in 2001, one reads the effusions of the

121 [40618/**161**/RS]. He was sole proprietor of *The Manchester Guardian* from 1848, and from 1855 published it as a daily paper. He resided at 20 Kensington Palace Gardens, and died at Eastbourne. *See D.N.B. 1901-1911* (1920), 486-7. 122 [18724/**48**/RS]. 123 Joseph Howe & Son were wholesale and retail bootmakers, of 10 Mansion House Street, 44 Poultry, 7 and 8 Gracechurch Street, and 126 Newgate Street. Howe retired to his native Northamptonshire, and died at Long Buckby. 124 [49845/**152**/2]. Its neighbour, another Italian, was stolen some years ago. Recchioni's lengthy epitaph gives the impression that he had many fine qualities when alive: it refers to 'only a handful of earth and ashes, but impregnated with the spirit of a man who lived, suffered, and deserved well of mankind. He knew no fatherland but the world, no family but the human race, no religion but love, no tomb can prison his soul – from such rare spirits must spring the roots of a society worthy of memory in which Life will be worth living'. An importer of foreign produce, and a provision agent, he was established at 37 Old Compton Street, Soho, from *c.*1913 until *c.*1930. As with many Italian freethinkers, Recchioni was cremated, and his ashes were deposited in the urn over the grave. That urn is now lidless and without contents.

10.16 Neoclassical symbols of death and eternity [18724/**48**/RS]: the inverted torch, the hour-glass, the serpent eating its tail, the winged wreath, and the hooded kneeling mourner, in 2001 (*MC.130101*).

10.17 Marble bust [49845/**152**/2] of Emidio Recchioni in 2001 (*MC.H080101*).

jaundiced writer in *The Builder* in 1854[125] with wry amusement and even surprise. He declared that it was a '*rendezvous* of dreamy inanities', and that there were:

> not half a dozen of the 'monuments' there that you would care to look at twice: you may wander for an hour and not find a piece of art to give you pleasure or a thought; while the great mass of them are repulsively ugly. Some show excellent work and lavish expenditure which, under good direction, should have produced a 'joy for ever', but here all are wasted. Look, for example, at the large red polished red and grey granite monument in memory of the wife of Mr. Combe:[126] one could scarcely fear to find a more elaborate piece of ugliness, and yet how excellent the work is.[127]

It could certainly be argued that these acidic views are misguided, for although there are plenty of uninteresting and artistically indefensible monuments, there are enough buildings and memorials of superb quality to render the General Cemetery of All Souls at Kensal Green a national treasure.

Although this paper has been devoted, in the main, to monuments by and to sculptors, the cemetery houses the remains of many famous artists, among them William Powell Frith, R.A. (1819-1909),[128] George Vicat Cole, R.A. (1833-93),[129] Charles Robert Leslie, R. A. (1794-1859),[130] John Calcott ('Clothes') Horsley, R.A. (1817-1903),[131] and

[125] *The Builder* **xii**/605 (2 September 1854), 460. [126] [9901/**48**/RS]. *See* **9.28**. [127] True, the work is 'excellent', but it is doubtful if all that many would find it 'ugly' today. [128] [20344/**55**/PS]. His works include *Derby Day* (1858 – now in the Tate Gallery, London), and *The Railway Station* (1862 – at Royal Holloway and Bedford New College, Egham). [129] [33985/**138**/PS]. His *The Pool of London* (1888) is now in the Tate Gallery. [130] [15036/**55**/2]. His works include *The Queen receiving the Sacrament at her Coronation* (1838), and *The Christening of the Princess Royal* (1841), both painted at Windsor. [131] [10524/**91-92**/10]. One of Horsley's sisters, Mary Elizabeth (1813-81), married Isambard Kingdom Brunel, and is buried in the Brunel grave [8590/**41**/PS] (**8.6**). Horsley himself was a close friend of Jacob Felix Ludwig Mendelssohn-Bartholdy (1809-47), the distinguished German composer, and of John Leech (1817-64), the illustrator (who is also buried at Kensal Green [18788/**36**/RS – but due to later interments this grave is now in the second row], beneath a blackened marble ledger on a granite plinth). He was called 'Clothes' Horsley because he objected to artistic portrayals of the nude, and favoured domestic scenes influenced by Dutch artists such as Pieter de Hooch (1629-84) and Gerard Terborch the Younger (1617-81). He designed the first Christmas-card for his friend, the influential Sir Henry Cole (1808-82). He was one of the first clients of the Scots architect, Richard Norman Shaw (1831-1912), who designed extensions and alterations to the artist's home at Cranbrook, Kent (1858). His father, William Horsley (1774-1858), the organist, composer of glees, and one of the founders of the Philharmonic Society, is buried beside him [10525/**91-92**/10] beneath a plain marble ledger with a fading inscription. 'Clothes' (sometimes called 'Old Clothes') Horsley lies under a segmental-topped ledger.

John William Waterhouse, R.A. (1849-1917).[132] But one of the most influential designers of the 19th century is Owen Jones (1809-1874), who was Superintendent of the Works of the Great Exhibition of 1851, and Joint Director of Decoration for the Crystal Palace at Sydenham (1852 – where he was involved in the creation of the 'Courts' illustrating various architectural styles as part of the permanent exhibition there). He was a leading figure in the preparation of the 1862 Exhibition and the design of the Oriental Courts of the South Kensington Museum.[133] His headstone, a refined Greek Revival marble *stele* with pitched ledger, was designed by Jones himself.[134]

Only very few memorials of the vast gathering of well-known people (among them soldiers, sailors, writers, politicians, and others) who are buried in the cemetery have been mentioned in this paper: enthusiastic hunters of these monuments and others are urged to consult Henry Vivian-Neal's[135] *Paths of Glory*.[136]

[132] [45456/187/2]. His *The Lady of Shalott* (1888 – now in the Tate Gallery) and *Hylas and the Nymphs* (1896 – now in the City Art Gallery, Manchester) are perhaps his best-known works. *The Lady of Shalott* is a portrait of his sister, Mary, later the daughter-in-law of Edward James Physick (*see* p.235 above) and grandmother of the present writer. [133] *See,* e.g. Sheppard (*Ed.*) (1975), 77-9, 87, 89, 91, 100, 106, 110, 126n., 144, 147, 147n., 260, for details of the work at South Kensington. Jones's *Grammar of Ornament* (1856) became a source-book of international importance, and popularised non-European, particularly Islamic, schemes of decoration. He was very influential in the evolution of polychromatic ornament. [134] [24334/47/RS]. [135] Vivian-Neal (1999), *passim*. [136] *Editor's note*: the footnotes for this Chapter have been mostly compiled by the Editor with extensive contributions by Mr Moulder, who provided all the location-numbers of graves as well as many biographical and factual details. Mr Moulder's assistance has been both invaluable and generous, and his considerable contribution is warmly acknowledged.

CHAPTER XI

The Inscriptions

ROBERT MOULDER

Introduction; Causes of Death; Merits and Eulogies; Careers Military and Naval; Inventors, Politicians, and Explorers; Servants and Others; Epitaphs and Verses; Conclusion

> The writer of an epitaph should not be considered as saying nothing but what is strictly true. Allowance must be made for some degree of exaggerated praise. In lapidary inscriptions a man is not upon oath.
>
> JAMES BOSWELL (1740-95):
> *The Life of Samuel Johnson*, ii (1775)
> (London: Privately printed for The Navarre Society, 1924), Vol. ii, 211.

Introduction

The compiler of an early guide-book to Kensal Green cemetery, Benjamin Clark,[1] was greatly intrigued in his perambulations about the cemetery to discover a 'raised flat stone' in the unconsecrated section bearing the solitary inscription 'Fanny'. This, he informed his readers,[2] was the first instance of this 'inexplicable character' he had seen in the Dissenters' ground. Who was this creature? What was the story behind a name rendered mysterious by its very isolation? Visitors, he felt certain, would ponder this, and reflect on the questions posed.[3]

Earlier, he had been no less curious about a slate headstone he noted in the South Avenue, inscribed only with the name 'Mary Plaw':

> there is an amusing ambiguity here, which awakens an anxiety to know who the deceased was; and which desire, if gratified, might not lead us to seek additional information.[4]

Such a prolix remark was typical of Clark's literary style. As it happens, Mary Plaw (d. 1839) was the wife of Thomas Plaw, landlord of the *Buffalo's Head Tavern* in Greenwich, but if the lady, in life, had been in any way remarkable, neither her monument [2051/31/RS] nor Clark is forthcoming on the subject.

Clark's imagination, it seems, was easily stimulated: today, the sight of the rather unfashionable name, 'Fanny', on a tombstone would be unlikely to kindle the same interest.[5] The point, however, is that an inscription in the form of a name and nothing more can be quite as thought-provoking as a full-blown epitaph. Who, for instance, would not wonder at unusual names like Enid Loverseed Piggin,[6] Thomas Barnabus Daft,[7] or Sophia Panrucker?[8] And what of the slightly improbable, if delicious, piscatorial congruity of Theophilus Haddock,[9] Rowland Herring,[10] and James Bass[11] (all buried within feet of one another off the South Terrace Avenue)? They are there, and did not spring from the imagination of a Lewis Carroll (1832-98) or anyone else.

Causes of Death

Mere dates, too, always aweful in their prime significance, have the potential to open doors in the imagination: sometimes they are the very real and dismal tokens of Fate at her most cruel and ironic. Clark did not fail to notice in the South Avenue the family grave (the 'brief but deeply affecting memorial'[12] is still intact) of George Brooks, MD, where are commemorated the doctor's three children, aged five, three, and 16 months, all of whom died within days of one another in March 1840. It is a sad enough story on which to reflect, necessitating, one would have thought, no further comment. And yet, as if to wring the very last ounce of pity from the reader, the inscription concludes with the mournful remark:

Three buried in one day!

The use of the exclamation-mark (intended, no doubt, to emphasise the grief of the parent) is perhaps one bathetic gesture too far. However, infant mortality in the early-Victorian period was appalling by today's standards, and there are many cemeteries and burial-grounds that provide ample evidence of the devastating effects of infectious diseases on young families.

[1] Clark (1843), *passim*. [2] Ibid., 78. [3] Ibid. [4] Ibid., 50. [5] Clark recorded another 'Fanny', daughter of A. Sweeting and his wife Sarah, who died aged three in 1833 (ibid., 69). [6] Died 1926, aged 29. [7] Daft (1816-78), was a civil engineer and ironfounder [17857/158/RS]. [8] Died 1866, aged 75. [9] Chemist and druggist, died 1842 aged 68. [10] Coffee-house keeper, died 1859 aged 86. [11] Chemist and druggist, died 1882 aged 79. [12] Clark (1843), 51. Brooks's grave is located at [2399/61/RS].

Clark also recorded the deaths of Edward, Charles, and Henry Hollier, who died on the same day in 1838, aged three days. Their passing was commemorated by the lines:

Enshrined within this narrow spot of earth
Three beauteous babes rest, who, at one birth,
Entered this lower world, but short their stay,
Celestial beings hastened them away
To yonder glorious throne, where they now sing
Seraphic strains to heaven's almighty King.
Forbade to sorrow in a world like this,
They breathed, shrank back, and entered into bliss.

Clark noted that 'here, all no sooner came upon the stage of time, than they fled to bloom in a region untouched by the pestiferous gales of our polluted clime'.[13]

Several people are recorded as having died on their birthdays, notably the African explorer Frank Linsly James (1851-90)[14] who, on his 39th anniversary, while hunting for big game at San Benito on the west coast of Africa, was trampled to death by an elephant. His body was removed to West Dean cemetery, Sussex, in 1917.

Of more recent date Willie McCormack died during 'the Silence'[15] on 11 November 1932: this melancholy event evokes, perhaps, a father remembering with his last thought a son who died in Flanders, bringing to mind reflections on a European catastrophe and its subsequent sense of loss, unbearable (almost unbelievably poignant) grief, and individual responses to a national and international tragedy.

The eloquence of dates is reaffirmed in the memorial to the Buller family.[16] The Rt. Hon. Charles Buller, MP (1806-48),[17] described by his teacher and friend Thomas Carlyle (1795-1881) as 'a most manageable, intelligent, cheery, and altogether welcome ... phenomenon; quite a bit of sunshine', and as 'the genialist radical' he had 'ever met',[18] died in his 40s, only six months after his father, also Charles (d. 1848). William Makepeace Thackeray (1811-63),[19] deploring his death, commented at the time:

> Good God! Think about the poor mother surviving, and what an anguish that must be! If I were to die I cannot bear to think of my mother living beyond me as I daresay she will.[20]

Buller's mother died broken-hearted four months after her son, on 13 March 1849, and Thackeray's own mother survived him less than a year.[21]

As dates follow names, so occasionally do causes and circumstances of death follow dates. It is not always easy to understand why some felt the need to commemorate the loss of a loved one in this manner, particularly if the death had been occasioned by violent or unnatural means: perhaps the Victorians were less squeamish in these matters than is the case today. An example of this is found in the inscription:

to the memory of Douglas Hamilton Turner
who was instantaneously killed in a lift accident
on Christmas Eve 1918 aged 8 years and 10 months.

Young Turner was the son of William Turner, FRCS (1870-1944).[22] Other memorials bring home the agony and horror of sudden death in the three words 'perished by fire':

[13] Clarke (1843), 79. [14] [32088/152/RS]. [15] That is, the national mark of remembrance of the Armistice in 1918. McCormack's grave is located at [49602/203/5]. [16] [7563/22/3]. [17] Buller's body was subsequently removed to his family grave [7715/22-3/3]. [18] *D.N.B.*, iii (1917), 246-8. *See also* Thomas Carlyle (1848): *The Examiner* (2 December), 771. [19] Who is also buried in Kensal Green cemetery [18177/36/1]. [20] Brookfield (1905), 771. [21] It might interest, and perhaps astonish, lovers of Thackeray's work to learn that the date of his death as recorded on his tomb in Kensal Green (21 December) anticipates his actual death by three days. [22] The grave is situated at [46234/161/2].

this was not an unusual tragedy in the days when coal-fires, gas-light, and smoking were ubiquitous. Among the victims of fire recorded in the cemetery[23] are John Rufus Reeves and his four young children (d. 1859) who died in a fire at their lodging-house in Lisson Grove (Mrs Reeves survived). The horrors of sudden death encapsulated in tombstone inscriptions reverberate though time and can still evoke feelings of shock and pity today.

Other, no less tragic, ends move us by their poignancy. The actress sisters, Ada (Lester) and Alice Akhurst, *en route* to fulfil an engagement in India, were drowned, along with their father, 11 members of their theatrical troupe, and nearly thirty others, when the *SS Clan Macduff* foundered in the Irish Sea on the night of 20 October 1881. The headstone[24] does not, however, relate the circumstances of their deaths. Cast adrift in a lifeboat, the girls survived the night in the stormy seas, only to die the next morning when the boat capsized in the surf when approaching the shore and safety.[25] The laconic words

the bodies of Ada and Alice were recovered
and are here interred

record the event. More poignant still is the story of Ella, daughter of (Sir) Thomas Edward Mitchell Turton (1790-1854), Chief Judge of the Supreme Register Court of Calcutta, who 'drowned in the wreck of the Conqueror', 13 January 1843.[26] The ship, an East Indiaman on its homeward journey, was wrecked during a hurricane off the Brittany coast, with the loss of 63 passengers and crew, a cabin-boy being the only survivor. This sole witness testified to Ella's heroism during the ordeal. *The Times* carried an account of the disaster:

> as the ship began to founder she [Ella Turton] went from sad group to sad group, sustaining the courage of all, and holding out prospects of succour and safety, ministering life and pure spirit, consolation, hope, and dependence on that Providence who orders all for the best.[27]

Ella's body was naked when it was found on the beach, although she had been fully dressed at the time of the wreck: it was supposed she had been found by some 'inhuman wretches',[28] stripped of everything, and then thrown back into the sea. She was still alive when discovered, but died almost immediately. The pathos of the story is further heightened when we learn that the day of the catastrophe coincided with Ella's 18th birthday.

Some tragic and sudden ends were less the results of natural disasters and more of human wickedness. The inscription on the tomb[29] of George Canning Backhouse (*c.*1819-56) records that he 'died at the Havana by the hand of an assassin, 30 August 1856'. A Commissionary Judge, Backhouse had been stabbed to death after disturbing robbers at his home in Havana, Cuba. His body was brought back to England for burial.

A monument made to resemble a small Gothic chapel situated in the south-west quadrant of the Circle,[30] commemorates Henry Howarden Gillibrand Fazakerley, who was killed by 'an explosion of fire down a coal-mine in Lancashire' on 21 July 1851. Fazakerley, then aged only 20, was the son of a Lancashire landed proprietor, and was on a visit to the mine (at Chorley) with a friend when the accident occurred: his friend and two others were also killed. It was a double tragedy for the Fazakerley family for H.H.G.'s father had died only three weeks earlier.[31] Elsewhere in the cemetery a simple headstone[32] commemorates a victim of an even more catastrophic mine explosion.

23 [15093/93/2]. 24 [28095/29/2]. 25 *The Times* (24 October 1881), 6e; and (2 November 1881), 10c.
26 Located at [3936/75/PS]. 27 *The Times* (20 January 1843), 3e. 28 Ibid. (25 January 1843), 6a. 29 North Terrace Avenue [5810/117/RS]. 30 [9642/101/IR]. 31 *The Times* (25 July 1851), 5e, and (28 July 1851), 8e.
32 [43509/84/5].

George Young died along with 86 others at Denaby and Cadeby Colliery, Conisbrough, Yorkshire, on 9 July 1912. The King and Queen (George V and Queen Mary) had been visiting the village only the day before.

Two families singularly unfortunate in the premature deaths of their sons were those of Major Walter Clopton Wingfield (1833-1912), the inventor of 'Sphairistike' (the forerunner of the modern game of lawn-tennis) and Major-General William Battine, of the Royal (Bengal) Artillery (who died at Langre on 21 July 1851, aged 65, while in command of the Punjab Division of the Bengal Army). The tragedies began in the Wingfield household when Harold Wingfield, RN, aged 17, was 'drowned at sea while gallantly trying to save a shipmate' on 13 December 1874: they continued with the death of Roland Penrhyn Wingfield, aged 20, on 16 January 1882; and culminated in the violent end of Walter Clopton Wingfield (called 'Tic'), aged 15, who was 'shot in Paris on the 11th and died 14th December 1886' – ten years and a day after the death of his eldest brother. The pathetic epitaph:

> and with the morn those angel faces smile,
> which I have loved long since and lost awhile

completes the unhappy story.[33]

Major-General Battine's adventurous sons (like those of Major Wingfield) paid the ultimate price for their intrepidity. The Battine memorial[34] commemorates George and James Battine

> who were drowned in the Medway 15 December 1855 aged 20 and 18 respectively,

and also Lieutenant Charles Battine of the 14th Bengal Native Infantry, who was

> killed at Cawnpore during the Indian Mutiny, 30 June 1857 aged 26, and was buried in the memorial well at Cawnpore.

Battine, one of the defenders of Cawnpore, was taken prisoner when the town fell to the rebels, and was subsequently among the two hundred and more persons, mostly women and children, who were slaughtered and whose bodies were thrown into the town well. The episode remains one of the blackest in British Colonial history.[35]

The inscription on the fine obelisk[36] near the centre of the Circle is worn and not easy to read, but in oblique sunlight the following lines may be discerned:

> In memory of
> the beautiful, the excellent and beloved
> Mrs Tremaine
> who lies within this hallowed tomb.
> She died in the bloom of life and health
> endeared to all who knew her
> on the 21st April 1836
> from injuries received by her dress accidentally
> taking fire three days previously.

The beautiful, the excellent and the beloved Mrs Tremaine, like so many of her sex in the 19th century, quite literally became a 'victim' of fashion. On a mission of mercy to a bed-ridden neighbour, her bustle dress took flame as she stood near an unguarded fire. The helpless invalid called on her to roll upon the floor to extinguish the flames, but Mrs Tremaine panicked and rushed from the room: the draught caused by the opening of the

33 [28150/98/PS]. The grave is contiguous to that of their father. 34 [33782/203/4]. 35 It is often discussed, and the monument illustrated, in *Chowkidar* (from 1977). 36 [569/89/RS].

door turning her into a fireball. By the time she reached the street she was entirely engulfed in flames. Several passers-by came to the assistance of the stricken woman, and, at the cost of quite serious burns to themselves, eventually succeeded in putting the fire out. This horrifying and painful occurrence was bad enough, but was rendered more distasteful when it was discovered that during the commotion one of the rescuers and a bystander had had their pockets picked.[37] The inscription ends with the quatrain:

> bereft affection sheds the burning tear,
> but faith consoles the grieving breast.
> Thy soul dear Charlotte being fled from here
> 'Tis hoped, 'tis prayed, may be for ever blest.

To conclude this section dealing with causes and circumstances of death, we could do worse than to rejoin Benjamin Clark on his 1843 tour of the cemetery. His keen eye had spotted the headstone (now replaced by a granite ledger)[38] of Henry James Mayer, surgeon, who died

> in consequence of accidentally pricking his finger during a post mortem examination, December 17th 1837, aged 28 years.

As usual he brings his reservoir of commonplace remarks to bear upon the subject:

> the axiom that 'little things are sometimes of great consequence' is, alas! in this case, but too clearly demonstrated: and not less is the proof here furnished of the uncertainty of human life, as well as in the way of duty and in paths which bring culpability upon all who walk therein.[39]

A newspaper report[40] of a similar case involving another burial in Kensal Green cemetery, John Phillips Potter, FRCS (1818-47),[41] the anatomist, makes rather gruesome reading, recounting as it does how the five doctors attendant upon Potter, in the course of their efforts to save him (he had contracted pyaemia[42] from a wound received while dissecting a pelvis), removed three pints of pus from his sacral region and two pints from his chest. The writer concluded his report by commenting on the folly of hurrying straight to the dissecting-room without taking any breakfast; an empty stomach being commonly believed to assist in the absorption of noxious matter.[43]

Merits and Eulogies

Whilst it may not have been the expressed aim of 19th-century eulogists to sanctify sinners, it is certainly true that small account was taken of a man's imperfections in the desire to emphasise his merits on memorials. Kensal Green cemetery, as might be expected, contains many examples of the work of skilled fashioners of epitaphs. Sir Thomas Noon Talfourd (1795-1854), judge and author,[44] was a former pupil of Dr Richard Valpy (1754-1836), Classical scholar, poet, and teacher, and it is to Talfourd's pen we owe the tribute which is to be found on the doorway of Dr Valpy's appropriately Greek Revival mausoleum (**9.2**):[45]

[37] *The Times* (25 April 1836), 6b. [38] [1228/**36**/RS]. [39] Clark (1843), 50-51. [40] *The Times* (1 June 1847), 8f. [41] *D.N.B.*, **xvi** (1917), 218. The grave is located at [6846/**168**/3]. [42] Virulent infection of the blood with bacteria from a septic focus, creating abscesses in different parts of the body. [43] *See also The Lancet*, **i** (1847), 576, and *The Gentleman's Magazine*, **ii** (1847), 100, which give sobering reports of his death. *See D.N.B.*, **xvi** (1917), 218. [44] *D.N.B.*, **xix** (1917), 343-6. Talfourd dedicated his *Ion, a Tragedy in Five Acts* (1836) to Valpy. [45] [687/**101**/RS].

Sacred
To the memory of
Richard Valpy, D.D., F.A.S.,[46]
Rector of Stradishall, Suffolk,
and for fifty years Master of Reading School;
in whom unwearied industry,
profound knowledge, and exquisite taste,
combined to produce works which will long survive
to render easy the paths of the scholar;
whose solemn and gentle eloquence
sunk into the hearts of his hearers,
and won them to imitate his example;
whose noble generosity of spirit
diffused happiness on all who came within
the large sphere of its influence;
and who, by the happy adaptation of
his powers and his virtues
to the nurture of the youthful mind
succeeded in training successive generations
in sound learning and Christian piety,
by whom, living and dying,
his name will ever be revered.[47]

Dr Valpy, one feels sure, would have approved, commending his former charge for the soundness of his rhetoric and the sureness of his style. The mausoleum was erected by 11 surviving children 'in deepest gratitude to their father and benefactor, and in the humble hope of being re-united with him in the kingdom of their Saviour and their God.[48] Little should be read into the fact that Talfourd neglected to record that his old master 'had the reputation of being one of the hardest floggers of his day',[49] for the world in which both men lived accepted corporal punishment as normal. However, Valpy's enthusiasm for this form of instruction was deemed worthy of special notice in the *Dictionary of National Biography*, no less, so he must have been particularly severe.

Talfourd's homage, although, perhaps, excessive to modern tastes, appears to have been sincere, and it was probably his championing of the personality and merits of Valpy to his friend Charles Dickens (1812-70), which gave the novelist the idea for his character 'Dr Strong', the amiable old schoolmaster in *David Copperfield* (1849-50). 'Strong' was Master of the school in Canterbury to which the young Copperfield was sent, and was described by the novelist as someone who 'looked almost as rusty... as the tall iron rails and gates outside the house, and almost as stiff and heavy as the great stone urns that flanked them'.[50] His chief work of scholarship was the compilation of a Classical dictionary which by the computations of one of his brighter mathematical pupils would at his current rate of industry have taken him 1,649 years to complete.[51]

[46] *D.N.B.*, **xx** (1917), 85-6. He was a Fellow of the Society of Antiquaries of London, according to *D.N.B.*, something usually designated by the letters F.S.A. [47] Clark (1843), 35. [48] Ibid. [49] *D.N.B*, **xx** (1917), 85.
[50] Dickens (1850*a*), Chapter XVI: 'I am a new boy in more ways than one'. Talfourd's dedication to Valpy in *Ion* (1836) 'is almost a blueprint for Dr Strong' (*See* P. F. Skottowe (1969): 'Thomas Talfourd and David Copperfield' in *The Dickensian*, **lxv** (January), 30. [51] Valpy's youngest son, Francis Edward Jackson Valpy (1797-1882), was the author of etymological dictionaries of Greek and Latin, and his second son, Abraham John Valpy (1787-1854 – also entombed in the mausoleum), brought out (with E. H. Barker) the *Thesaurus Graecae Linguae* of Henry Stephens the Younger between 1816 and 1828, which enterprise suffered from a crushing review by Charles James Blomfield (later Bishop of London, who consecrated Kensal Green cemetery in 1833) in the *Quarterly Review*, **xxii** (1820), 302-48. A. J. Valpy became a Director of the General Cemetery Company in September 1836.

With characteristic immodesty the celebrated equestrian performer Andrew Ducrow (1793-1842) collaborated in the writing of his own epitaph on his showy Graeco-Egyptian[52] mausoleum (**8.23, 8.24**):

Within this tomb erected by Genius
for the reception of its own remains
are deposited those of Andrew Ducrow,
many years lessee of the Royal Amphitheatre London;
whose death deprived the arts and sciences
of an eminent professor and liberal patron,
his family of an affectionate husband and father,
and the world of an upright man.
He was born in London 10 October 1793 and died 27 January 1842.
And to commemorate such virtues
his afflicted widow has erected this tribute.
Beyond expression's power or pencil's skill,
Let this plain record eloquently tell
That deepest grief with which we have to strive,
When those we love are dead and we survive.[53]

Genius is obviously not a word to be used lightly, and in fairness to Ducrow the three other notable instances of its use in Kensal Green: Alfred Cooke (1822-54 – another equestrian),[54] Elizabeth Emma Soyer (1813-42 – painter-wife of the celebrated chef Alexis Soyer[55] [**8.29**]), and Joseph Manton (1766-1835 – gunmaker),[56] show perhaps an even greater degree of presumption. In his lifetime, however, there were many people who would not have demurred in the view that Ducrow's spellbinding feats of horsemanship were indeed the manifestations of genius. One of the most colourful and popular figures of his day, his admirers included Dickens, Sir Walter Scott (1771-1832), the actor Edmund Kean (1789-1833), and the young Queen Victoria (reigned 1837-1901). His few detractors included the tragedian William Charles Macready (1793-1873),[57] who was jealous of Ducrow's success and deplored what he saw as the philistinism of the spectacles presented at Astley's Amphitheatre. In his Diary on the day of Ducrow's funeral – the most splendid, it was said, in the capital for fifty years – Macready wrote: 'rejoiced in my absence from Mr Ducrow's funeral which was attended by a fearful set'.[58] Ducrow's mausoleum, erected in his lifetime, was criticised in *The Builder* for its 'ponderous coxcombry',[59] but by the 1850s, when this judgement was published, the Egyptian Revival style[60] had suffered from the younger Pugin's ridicule,[61] and was seen as not quite respectable.[62]

Directly facing Ducrow's mausoleum on the opposite side of the Main Avenue stands the elegant, chastely Classical monument[63] to John St John Long (1798-1834), quack doctor *par excellence* (**4.28, 8.26**). Long, of humble Irish parentage, trained as an artist

52 Clark (1843), 32, describes it as 'splendid'. [820/**76**/RS]. 53 By 1864 Clark was describing 'this plain record' as 'a large and curious mausoleum'. *See* Clark (1864), 25. This reflects the change of taste partly prompted by the younger Pugin. *See* Pugin (1836, 1841*a*, 1841*b*, and 1843). 54 [11719/**76**/PS]. 55 [3714/**80**/RS]. 56 [189/**145**/RS]. 57 Macready was buried in [**CAT. B**/Vault 96/Comp. 6]. 58 *See* Macready (1875), **ii**, 194. The funeral, on 5 February 1842, was 'attended by vast crowds of people' (*D.N.B.*, **vi** [1917], 96-7). 59 *The Builder*, **xiv/**725 (27 December 1856), 700. 60 Curl (1994*b*), *passim*. 61 Pugin (1843), 12 and Plate IV. 62 Reflected in the changes of Clark's judgements of 1843 and 1864. 63 [283/**76**/RS].

– the Tate Gallery possesses one of his pictures[64] – before turning to medicine. Having devised a method of treating consumption – by the application of 'corrosive liniments and friction'[65] – he established himself at No. 41, Harley Street, and soon acquired a very lucrative and fashionable practice. Fame, however, turned to notoriety when two of his patients died under his treatment. The ensuing court-cases resulted in a conviction and a £250 fine, and an acquittal. His wealthy patrons[66] continued to support him, crowding the courtroom on both occasions, but the journals of the day were less indulgent: a cartoon entitled 'More Don-keys! It is well known that asses are particularly fond of having their backs rubbed'[67] shows Long massaging with vitriol the backs of bonneted donkeys; he is seen again in the background being pursued by a police officer, while a notice in a cemetery announces that the place of burial, 'being nearly full', the 'prices' would therefore 'be raised'.[68]

Long's career came to a premature end when he contracted the very disease he had made his name and fortune in 'curing'. He is said to have refused to treat himself by his own method. He left his 'secret', which he valued at £10,000, to his brother, William, and a Titian with a price-tag of £20 to a certain Mrs Oughton of Elm Grove,[69] Roehampton. The obscurity of the brother tends to suggest that Mrs Oughton had the better of the deal. The inscription on his monument is a curiosity:

it is the fate of most men
to have many enemies, and few friends.
This monumental pile
is not intended to mark the career
but to shew
how much its inhabitant was respected
by those who knew his worth
and the benefits
derived from his remedial discovery.
He is now at rest
and far beyond the praises or censures
of this world.

[64] Long was employed at one time by Sir Thomas Lawrence (1769-1830), the eminent painter, as a colour-grinder and general assistant. He also found work making coloured anatomical drawings in schools of anatomy, which brought him into contact with medicine and surgery and gave him some knowledge of these subjects. Long himself exhibited three paintings at the Society of British Artists in Suffolk Street in 1825 and an enormous canvas entitled *An Allegorical Scene in Ireland* at the British Institution in the same year. He was awarded a silver medal by the Society of Arts for a landscape, also in 1825. In the following year at the Royal Academy he exhibited *The Baptism of Christ* (*See* Thompson [1928], Ch. 22, 301). His picture in the Tate Gallery (T04169) is *The Temptation in the Wilderness* (1824), which owes a clear debt to his teacher, the apocalyptic painter John Martin (1789-1854). He was also for a time the assistant, as an engraver, to William Young Ottley (1771-1836), the writer on art, amateur artist, and collector of drawings and prints. Long may have regarded himself as a genuine visionary, and claimed to have acquired his knowledge by perusing the Scriptures, as well as, *en passant*, an understanding of the nature of Original Sin, which he stated had similar properties to those of acid. His 'cure' involved attracting the acidic, sinful infusion to the surface, to alienate it from the system. It is revealing that among his friends and executors was Lord Ingestre (Will dated 7 March 1833 [PRO Prob. 11.1836, 521]). *See Tate Gallery* (1996), 45-6. Long appears to have arrived in London in 1822, and had become one of only two pupils of Martin by 1823. He must have had the gift of the gab and considerable charm to have ingratiated himself so quickly with so many members of London society. His forays into medicine (from 1827) gained him many adherents, but in 1831 he was denounced in *The Lancet* as 'one of the vilest and most scandalous jugglers that ever disgraced society' (*The Lancet* [26 February 1831], 76). It should be pointed out that Long treated other complaints as well as consumption: indeed most of his wealthy patients were not consumptives. [65] *D.N.B.*, **xii** (1917), 106-7. [66] These included, as previously noted, Viscount Ingestre himself (which probably explains the sumptuous and prominent monument), as well as the Marchioness of Ormonde, Howe Peter Browne (1788-1845), 2nd Marquess of Sligo (buried in [4867/**101**/3]), and the Countess of Buckinghamshire. The last was Anne Glover, daughter of Sir Arthur Pigot, who, in 1819, married George Robert Hobart, 5th Earl of Buckinghamshire (d. 1849), and, in 1854, married secondly David Wilson of Brook Street. She died in 1878 aged 77, and is also buried in Kensal Green cemetery [19090/**115**/PS]. [67] Cartoon by H. Heath published by S. W. Fares, 41 Piccadilly (1830). [68] *See also* the *Gentleman's Magazine*, **ii**, (1830), 461, and **ii**, (1834) 656; *Tate's Observations upon the System of Mr John St John Long*, published in Cheltenham (1831); and *A Defence of John St John Long, Esq.*, published in London (1831). [69] Long himself died at Elm Grove. For his Will *see* footnote 64.

Stranger, as you respect the receptacle for the dead
(as one of the many that will rest here)
read the name of
JOHN SAINT JOHN LONG
without comment.

As an attempt to disarm the 'stranger', it is probably more successful today than it was in the years immediately after his death. The monument itself, designed by Sievier,[70] was erected as an ornament to the cemetery, an exemplar of the sort of thing the Company was trying to promote: the fact that Long was selected as the personality to be so honoured is indicative of his standing with Ingestre and, presumably, other members of the Board.

The inscription on the fallen monument[71] to Ephraim Bond (1803-39) is not a particularly noteworthy example of the panegyrist's art:

He was a man and nothing that
related to a man was foreign
to his feelings.
Of talents rare, of sentiments refined,
and with a heart benevolent and kind;
he might have filled high honour's palmy seat,
when haply rank and genius joy to meet.

But when one considers the character of the man thus eulogised, the writer must be given full marks for ingenuity. 'Effie' Bond, *aka* Cohen, a 'low-life' acquaintance of Benjamin Disraeli (1804-81 – the novelist and future Prime Minister), was simply one of the most infamous personalities of his day. A money-lender, property speculator, and bookmaker, he was also joint-proprietor, with his brothers Robert (d. 1838) and Joseph, of the 'Athenaeum', one of the most notorious of the many 'hells' or gambling-clubs which flourished in London's Mayfair in the early decades of the 19th century. The brothers were rarely out of the police-courts or the newspapers, either in connection with the club, or through some act of violence or intimidation. On one occasion in 1831 they visited the Fleet Street offices of the scurrilous weekly newspaper, *The Satirist or The Censor of the Times*, edited by another disreputable Kensal Green resident, Barnard Gregory (1796-1852) (**8.9**),[72] and beat up two members of the staff, leaving one with serious injuries. It appears that Gregory had published a libel against the Bonds' father, claiming that he had defrauded the Bank of England and been hanged for the offence, and also stating that their mother had married, two weeks later, the chief witness for the prosecution. The brothers were charged with attempted murder, but in this, as in other cases, they escaped with fines, the influence of high-placed patrons apparently saving them from prison sentences.[73]

London society, including the young Disraeli (who was frequently in debt to the brothers), may well have breathed a collective sigh of relief when first Robert and then 'Effie' Bond died at the relatively early ages of 40 and 36 respectively. Joseph (d. 1886) who long outlived his brothers and the notoriety associated with the family name, continued to prosper, and died at Brighton leaving estate valued at £50,000. All three brothers are buried in the family vault.

[70] Buried in [19149/**90**/2]. [71] [1722/**134**/RS]. [72] *The Times* (4 November 1831), 3f, 4a, 4b. [73] Buried in [4031/**48**/RS], Centre Avenue. Barnard specialised in printing libels which were sent in manuscript form to the persons concerned, threatening publication unless a price was paid for suppression. As *D.N.B.* put it, the 'weak yielded and were plundered' and the 'strong resisted and were libelled' (*D.N.B.*, viii [1917], 535). Described as 'a trafficker in character', he was engaged in litigation for some 18 years.

Many epitaphs confine themselves to acknowledging the moral qualities of the deceased. One of the earliest surviving French inscriptions – that on the headstone of Joseph John de Jonville (1755-1837)[74] – is touching in its simplicity and obvious sincerity:

par un frère et un ami à l'homme de bien.

It is ironic that a life and career which might have exerted the talents of the finest obituarists should have been distilled into a single sentiment. De Jonville, who fled to England at the time of the French Revolution, earned, as he records in his will, 'a small fortune ... in the service of the King of England'.[75] One may speculate upon what exactly this service might have entailed, but in wishing to be remembered to friends such as the Duke of Norfolk and other members of the nobility in both England and France, there seem to be reasonable grounds for believing it to have been of the 'secret' variety.

Of all the epitaphs that might have graced the grave[76] of the publisher George Stiff (1807-74) that chosen to illuminate his character was:

Behold the upright man,

which may or may not have been intended as a pun on his name. More precise qualities were called upon to describe the wife of the bookseller and art-collector Francis Harvey (1830-99),[77] who was said to have possessed

The Reason firm; the Temperate Will;
Endurance, Foresight, Strength and Skill.

The family of the publican, Benjamin Williams (d. January 1841),[78] entertained rather more pious sentiments towards their dearly departed:

Beneath reposes all that Heaven could send,
A tender husband, a father and a friend:
In sickness patient, and to death resigned,
He left the world a pattern to mankind.

Benjamin Clark was outraged by these lines and observed that defective poetry may well be forgiven when it is made the vehicle of good sense. But the

> assertion, that even the best man that ever appeared upon earth was '*all* that Heaven could send', would be, at once, a sad depreciation of human guilt and need, and an acknowledgement that the Gift unspeakable, sent to cancel our guilt and render us holy and happy, was redundant. It is to be feared, that the author of the foregoing stanza, at the time it was penned, forgot, at least, the universal ruin of mankind, through sin – and that, to meet our direful circumstances with an all-sufficient remedy, 'God so loved the world that he *gave* his only-begotten Son, that whosoever believeth in him should not perish, but have everlasting life.[79]

There were plenty of 19th-century commentators eager to sniff out sacrilege, and Clark was no exception. His priggish comments are scattered throughout his book, and are found again in respect of another Williams, this time a William Williams,[80]

an only and *idolized* child, born the 14th August 1838;
died the 11th July 1840, to the inexpressible sorrow of his unhappy parents.

74 [868/40/RS]. 75 PCC. PROB 11 (1874) 165. 76 [24626/123/PS]. 77 [28409/47/7]. 78 [2826/109/RS].
79 Clark (1843), 56-7. 80 [2595/95/RS].

Clark informs us that the

> Being, who formed and sustains us, and therefore justly requires us to love him with all our heart, soul, and mind, cannot behold with indifference the affection, which is chiefly due to himself, engrossed by the fairest created object. Such misplaced, *inordinate* attachment almost solicits the rod of correction, and, unknowingly, asks the deprivation of the *idol*. A mind, rightly influenced, will enjoy God in all things, and all things in God![81]

Clark's unctuous preaching was by no means atypical of the period, but he goes on and on in similar vein, finding fault, criticising, seeking out blasphemies, and adopting a spurious high moral tone. His grumblings did not cease with the unfortunate Williams families.

Careers Military and Naval

The detailing of careers on memorials, often of mind-numbing comprehensiveness, was frequently divorced from any account of moral character. Nothing should be inferred from the omission, save that eventful histories have to be compressed to fit on a stone monument. Careers most likely to be of an eventful nature are predominantly naval and military. The following inscription on the monument[82] of Admiral Henry Colins Deacon (1788-1869) is an unusually concise naval biography (**8.39**):

> Entered Royal Navy 1800.
> Served under Nelson
> in the West Indies 1805
> and under Lt Gen Whitelocke
> at Buenos Ayres in 1807;
> at the Isle of France 1810;
> in the capture of Guadaloupe 1815;
> and in other engagements,
> during which he received 23 wounds
> in the service of his country.

Deacon continued to be involved in hostilities long after his death: his monument, surmounted by anchor, flag, cannon, and cannon-shot, was damaged by a bomb in the 1939-45 war. His impressive collection of wounds was mostly accumulated while serving under Captain (later Rear-Admiral Sir) Nesbit Josiah Willoughby (1777-1849) – known among sailors of the day as 'The Immortal'.[83] One of the most reckless characters in British naval history – he was four times court-martialled – Willoughby's own tally of injuries was catalogued by the Annual Register in its notice of his death:

> he was eleven times wounded with balls, three times with splinters, and cut in every part of his body with sabres and tomahawks: his face was disfigured by explosions of gunpowder, and he lost an eye and had part of his neck and jaw shot away… and at Leipzig had his right arm shattered by cannon shot.

Sir Nesbit, who lies buried in Kensal Green's [**Catacomb B**] under the Anglican chapel,[84] had the unusual distinction of being knighted twice, in 1827 and 1832. On the

[81] Clark (1843), 55. [82] [19697/**125/**PS]. [83] *See* 'Appendix to Chronicle' in *Annual Register*, **91** (19 May 1849), 239. [84] [8184/**CAT. B**/vault 125/7].

second occasion he was invested with the insignia of a K.C.H.,[85] a curious blunder on the part of King William IV.[86]

General Anthony Bacon (1796-1864), regarded by Lord Anglesey[87] as the finest cavalry officer he had ever known, enjoyed a highly successful military career. He served in the Iberian Peninsula, at the battle of Waterloo (where 'he had two horses shot under him'), and later in Portugal where he had the command of the cavalry of Maria da Glória (Queen Maria II [1833-53]), and was 'promoted to the rank of General Officer upon the field of Loures in 1833 by the Emperor Don Pedro[88] in person'. What the inscription on his headstone[89] does not relate is that Bacon had once been committed to the King's Bench Prison for debt (he and his wife Lady Charlotte Mary Harley [1801-80], daughter of the 5th Earl of Oxford, were notorious for their extravagance), that he had fled to Portugal to escape his creditors, and that on the death of Dom Pedro (1833) he had lost his command for looting and selling horses.[90] Lady Charlotte's own claim to fame resides in the fact that she was Lord Byron's[91] 'Ianthe', the dedicatee of *Childe Harold*:[92] Byron, indeed, was Lady Oxford's lover, and Lady Charlotte herself may have proved something of a temptation to the libidinous poet.[93]

The impressive granite tomb[94] of Sir Belford Hinton Wilson (1804-58) informs us that he was:

> Chief Aide-de-Camp[95] of the 'Liberator', General Bolivar, who died in his arms, and in whose will, 1830, his zeal, conduct, and fidelity, are gratefully recorded.

In his own will Wilson made a bequest of a sword which had been given to him by Bolivar.[96]

The no less imposing granite obelisk[97] of George Kmety ('Ismail Pasha' – 1813-69) records:

> Lieutenant General in the Armies of the Emperor of the Ottomans. Defender of Kars, Chief of the Forces in Syria. In whom Hungary mourns a brave commander in her National War of 1848-49

and concludes with the inscription to the effect that the monument covering his mortal remains was

> erected by command of The Sultan.

Continuing the military theme, there are several memorials in Kensal Green cemetery to soldiers who were killed overseas and whose bodies, unusually, were returned to England. Among them is that[98] to the Hon. Edmund Verney Wyatt-Edgell, Captain in the 17th Lancers, who was

> killed at the head of his troop in the victory near Ulundi, Zululand, South Africa, July 4 1879 aged 33.

85 Knight Commander of the Hanoverian Order. It should be remembered that until 1837 the King of Great Britain and Ireland was also King of Hanover. 86 *See D.N.B.*, **xxi** (1917), 508-11. The Minutes of his Courts Martial are in the Public Record Office. 87 Henry William Paget (1768-1854), 1st Marquess of Anglesey. 88 Emperor of Brasil (1822-31), King of Portugal 1826 when he resigned his Crown to his infant daughter Maria de Glória. He should be referred to as *Dom* Pedro, not *Don*. 89 [12759/**22**/3]. 90 *See Australian Dictionary of Biography*, **i** (1966), 46-7. 91 George Gordon, 6th Baron Byron (1788-1824). 92 The first two cantos of which were published in 1812, the third in 1816, and the fourth in 1818. 93 It seems that Byron became obsessed with Lady Charlotte, his mistress's 11-year-old daughter. He showered her with gifts, including the keepsakes Lady Caroline Lamb (1785-1828) had given him: these presents seem to have been intended as a prelude to seduction. While at Eywood, the poet later confessed to his wife, Lady Oxford had discovered him in the act of sexually forcing himself on her child. Lady Byron recalled that her husband had told her Lady Oxford 'was enraged with him to the greatest degree' because she had 'detected him one day in an attempt upon her daughter, then a child of thirteen' (*sic*) and that this had occurred 'at the time of his connection with Lady Oxford'. *See* Eisler (1999), Ch. 21, 384: Eisler gives as her source *Lovelace Byron Papers: Box 131, folio 89*. 94 [14950/**64**/4]. It is the work of Edward William Wyon (1811-85). 95 1823-30. 96 Simon Bolivar (1783-1830), leader of the revolutions against Spain that resulted in the independence of what are now Venezuela, Colombia, Ecuador, Panamá, Peru, and Bolivia. 97 [19144/**128**/RS]. 98 [20087/**126**/2].

Col. George Carpenter,[99] who

> having distinguished himself at the Alma and the sorties before Sebastopol, fell mortally wounded at the head of his regiment at the glorious battle of Inkermann 5 November 1854 in the 56th year of his age:

his remains were originally buried in the Crimea 'near the scenes of his bravery', but were brought back to England for interment in Kensal Green cemetery in November 1861. The monument to Charles Milne Cholmeley Dowling,[100] Major in the Grenadier Guards, records that he was

> assassinated in Dublin while serving his King and Country 21 November 1920.

In what became known as 'Bloody Sunday', 14 suspected British secret service agents were shot dead in their Dublin homes on that day by Irish Republican Army murder squads on the orders of Michael Collins (1890-1922). Funerals for nine of the dead were held at Westminster Abbey and Westminster Cathedral.[101]

The inscription on the granite tomb of the Trevor family,[102] whose members included Major-General William Spottiswoode Trevor, VC (1831-1907), captures something of the horror and heroism of Colonial warfare. After commemorating Trevor's father, Captain Robert Salusbury Trevor (d. 23 December 1841):

> one of the victims of the treacherous massacre of the British Envoy
> by Akbar Khan at Kabul, Afghanistan,

tribute is paid to Mary, the Captain's widow (d. 11 October 1889), who 'accompanied her husband to Kabul with her eight children' and was 'among the few survivors of the disastrous retreat of the British Army in 1842.'

Inventors, Politicians, and Explorers

The tomb[103] of Joseph Manton, inventor and gunmaker (1766-1835), is in the form of a handsome Neoclassical sarcophagus. Manton was the owner of a famous shooting-gallery in Davies Street, Berkeley Square, much frequented by Lord Byron and his friends. Rees Howell Gronow (1794-1865)[104] recalled that, on one occasion, delighted by his marksmanship, Byron boasted to Manton that he considered himself to be the best shot in London. Manton disagreed, and observed:

> no my Lord, not the best, but your shooting today was respectable.

'Whereupon Byron waxed wroth and left the shop in a violent passion'.[105] The inscription on Manton's monument was composed by his friend, Peter Hawker (1786-1853),[106] an authority on firearms and all aspects of shooting.[107] It reads:

> In Memory of
> Mr Joseph Manton who died universally regretted
> on the 29th day of June 1835 aged 69 years.
> This humble tablet is placed here by his afflicted family

[99] [16576/101/RS]. [100] [30046/141/PS]. [101] *The Times* (22 November 1920), 12a; (23 November 1920), 12б; (24 November 1920), 12b; (27 November 1920), 10c. A further six were badly injured, and most, but not all, were British intelligence agents. On the same day, two IRA leaders were killed, and the Auxiliary Division of the Royal Irish Constabulary opened fire at a Gaelic football-match (possibly after themselves coming under attack), killing 12 people. [102] [31775/179/PS]. [103] [189/145/RS]. [104] Gronow was an army officer, and his memoirs are usually referred to as Captain Gronow's *Memoirs/Reminiscences/Recollections*. [105] *See* Gronow (1862), **i**, 210. Gronow is useful for much on Byron and other personalities of the time. [106] Hawker is also entombed in Kensal Green cemetery [10956/**CAT. B**/Vault 200/15-16]. [107] *D.N.B.*, **xii** (1917), 985-6.

merely to mark where are deposited his mortal remains.
But an everlasting monument to his unrivalled genius
is already established in every quarter of the globe,
by his celebrity as the greatest artist in fire arms that ever
the world produced, as the founder and the father
of the modern gun trade, and as a most scientific inventor
in other departments, not only for the benefit
of his friends and the sporting world,
but for the good of his king and country.

'Joe' Manton's monument was restored in 1993 to the memory of Peter Wenman – 'a fine gunmaker'.

Political epitaphs in Kensal Green are few, and, with one notable exception, surprisingly moderate in tone and language. There is no mystery about this: politicians then, as now, were only too sensible of the fact that the world of cold reality, inured to the economies of their truths, would no more have put its trust in a eulogy to a dead politician than it would in the words of a living one. Silence sometimes can be kinder to memories and reputations.

The inscription on the tomb[108] of John Cam Hobhouse (1786-1869 – elevated to the peerage as Baron Broughton de Gyfford in 1851), modestly asserted that:

he was eminent alike in political and literary life,
and after a public career of success and honour
found unbroken happiness in domestic repose
which he adorned
by his rare gifts of scholarship and eloquence.

There is little ammunition here for the scoffers. Hobhouse,[109] in any case, had the good fortune to long outlive the days of his youthful indiscretions in the company of his friend Lord Byron, and few would have known of the time they spent together in dissipations of one sort or another (**9.25**).

Perhaps it was because Thomas Barnes (1785-1841) was a 'politician' without a parliamentary seat – he was Editor of *The Times*, and in that capacity was once described by Lord Lyndhurst[110] as 'the most powerful man in the country'[111] – that his friends chose to proclaim his worth[112] in the following far from understated fashion:

> he was a man of eminent service to his country; and his death to a numerous circle of friends was a personal misfortune. As a politician he conducted public opinion with great moral courage, inflexible integrity and genuine patriotism, while he was distinguished by fine talents and a graceful elocution. Learning in him was united with facility, criticism with taste, and elegance with ease. The nation found in him a mind familiar with our native manners and institutions and acquainted, through every grade, with the vast fabric of our social system. He was noble by being beneficial to others and disinterested in himself. In magnanimity above the vicissitudes of the world, he was a generous spirit – amiable in his domestic relations, and in his social qualities without an equal.

On the whole one is inclined to agree with the anonymous poet who remarked on a similarly fulsome panegyric:

[108] [21596/**65**/RS]. [109] *D.N.B.*, **ix** (1917), 941-4. [110] John Singleton Copley the Younger (1772-1863), American-born Lord Chancellor. [111] *D.N.B.*, **i** (1917), 1177-8. *See also* Greville (1875), **iii**, 156. [112] [1376/**29**/RS].

Friend in your epitaphs I'm grieved
So very much is said:
One-half will never be believed,
The other never read.[113]

Before we leave the world of politics one further name merits attention: that of Charles Pelham Villiers (1802-98), whose granite headstone carries a simple statement of fact.[114] It records that he

represented the Borough of Wolverhampton in Parliament
for an unbroken period of 63 years, Jan 1835-Jan 1898.

Nevertheless it is a fact which bestows upon him a unique distinction. Villiers – a lifelong radical and leading campaigner for the repeal of the Corn Laws – is recognised by the *Guinness Book of Records*[115] as having been the MP with the longest continuous service in British political history.

Explorers are well-represented in Kensal Green cemetery, among them Admiral Sir Robert John Le Mesurier McClure (1807-73), who:

as Captain of *HMS Investigator* AD 1850-4 he discovered
and accomplished the North-West Passage.[116]

His monument[117] also records the words

thus we launch into this formidable frozen sea.

Sherard Osborn (1822-75) described McClure as 'stern, cool and bold in all perils, severe as a disciplinarian, self-reliant, yet modest as became an officer. With a granite-like view of duty to his country and profession, he would in war have been a great leader'.[118]

John McDouall Stuart (1815-66), the first to cross the Australian continent 'from the Southern to the Indian Ocean', is commemorated by a grey-granite pedestal and hipped ledger,[119] by Carey & Co. of Kensal Green.[120] John (1807-39) and Richard (1809-34) Lander, the explorers of parts of Africa, are commemorated by a chest in the form of a Neoclassical sarcophagus.[121] John

was the companion of his brother Richard on his second African expedition;
and compiled the narrative of their travels.

Richard Lemon Lander was the first Gold Medallist of the Royal Geographical Society and sole survivor of the expedition led by Captain Hugh Clapperton (1788-1827) to attempt to discover the source of the River Niger.[122] The Landers are credited with having traced the Niger not to its source but to its debouchment into the Bay of Biafra. Richard was wounded by 'the Brass River natives' on a third expedition and died at Fernando Po, where he is buried in the Clarence cemetery.

Servants and Others

The great majority of Kensal Green's famous dead (the scientists, engineers, architects, writers, surgeons, administrators, etc., who helped shape and give meaning to the world

113 *On Too-Wordy Epitaphs*. This has been attributed, on flimsy authority, to Alexander Pope (1688-1744).
114 [36848/140/PS]. 115 McWhirter and McWhirter (*Eds.*) (1972), 193. Winston Churchill was an M.P. for slightly longer than Villiers, but his was not an unbroken period. 116 Credit for discovering the North-West Passage is today usually given to Sir John Franklin (1786-1847). 117 [24045/143/5]. 118 *D.N.B.*, **xii** (1917), 448-9, quoting Sherard Osborn's *Discovery of a North-West Passage by Captain McClure* (1865). 119 [19834/9-15/PS]. 120 *D.N.B.*, **xix** (1917), 103-4. The pedestal once supported an obelisk. 121 [2246/36/2]. 122 *D.N.B.*, **iv** (1917), 372-4; and **xi** (1917), 490-2.

in which they lived) lie in graves the memorials over which (if they survive at all) bear no inscription other than names and dates. Lord Byron's impassioned plea on the subject of his own memorial was evidently widely shared:

Oh may my shade behold no sculptured urns
To mark the spot where earth to earth returns!
No lengthen'd scroll, no praise-encumbered stone;
My epitaph shall be my name alone.[123]

If there are few panegyrics to the most able servants of the age and state, there are fewer still commemorating the servants of those servants. And yet impressive examples of tributes by grateful masters/mistresses to their servants are occasionally found. A good example is the delicately sculptured marble cross over the grave[124] of Mary Ann Thurston (1810-96) which bears the inscription:

> In grateful and loving memory of Mary Ann Thurston by V.R.I. and her children Victoria, Albert Edward, Alfred, Helena, Louise, Arthur, Beatrice. 1810-1896. In the Queen's service as nurse to her children from 1845 to 1867.

'Much grieved', wrote Queen Victoria in her diary, 'to hear of the death of dear old Mrs Thurston': the monument was designed and executed by her daughter, Princess Louise,[125] and paid for by the Queen.

A more humble headstone pays tribute to the delightfully named Regine Lichtwerk, a native of Riga, who died 2 July 1872,[126] and

> was for 34 years a zealous and devoted servant of the family of John Todd esq of Northwick Terrace, where her name will long be treasured up as a familiar household word recalling her many acts of tender and self-sacrificing care.

A servant who, it was claimed, came virtually to rule over her masters was Ann Birch Cockings (*c.*1766-1844), Housekeeper to the Royal Society of Arts.[127] Her epitaph, inscribed in duplicate on either face of a stately roadside monument, attests her worth:

Here
rest the remains of
Ann Birch Cockings
upwards of forty-two years
Housekeeper
to the Society for the
Encouragement of Arts
Manufactures and Commerce.

This Monument
was erected by the
Members of the Society
as a tribute of respect
to the memory of her
whose life
was zealously devoted
to their interests.

[123] Byron (1967), 3. 'A Fragment' from 'Hours of Idleness'. [124] [36163/157/2]. [125] Princess Louise Caroline Alberta (1848-1939), was a gifted sculptress, the pupil of the sculptress, Mary Thornycroft (1814-95), and intimate friend of Sir Joseph Edgar Boehm, Bart. (1834-90), the sculptor. [126] [23395/79/10]. [127] [4680/110/RS].

Died on the
Twentieth day of February
MDCCCXLIV
Aged seventy-eight years.

Ann Birch Cockings was the daughter of George Cockings (d. 1802), who had himself been connected with the Society for 37 years, chiefly in the capacity of Registrar. Cockings was an autodidact, and as a poet and dramatist was sufficiently noteworthy[128] to be accorded a paragraph in the *Dictionary of National Biography*.[129] As a child, Ann became the favoured companion of the Irish painter James Barry (1741-1806), while that eccentric artist toiled away at his self-elected, six-year labour of decorating the Great Room of the Society in John Adam Street[130] with a scheme of large paintings on *The Progress of Human Culture* (1777-83). Ann's portrait finds a place amongst that vast panoply of figures, the most ambitious essay in history-painting in the Grand Manner by any artist of the British School. It was said that Ann, in her childish innocence, was the only person who ever felt love for the irascible, truculent, troubled painter.[131]

Epitaphs and Verses

Of all the persons buried in Kensal Green the solicitor William Shaw (*c*.1776-1852) is possibly unique in that the long and fulsome epitaph on his mausoleum is not actually about him, although an inscription on the side of his tomb[132] begins promisingly enough:

to the memory of William Shaw Esq of Hyde Park Terrace,
died 8 May 1852 aged 76,

but that, as far as his career and talents are concerned, is all. The bulk of the information concerns John Shaw, his father:

late of Calcutta but native of Derbyshire.
A man of great natural abilities;
his acquirements in arithmatick and astronomy
were second only to the immortal Newton.[133]
He went out to India where he quickly gained a fortune
of the greater part of which he was plundered by the Arabs
in concert with Ibrahim Bey who promised the most ample
protection in crossing the desert of Arabia in the year 1779.
The consequent anxiety and fatigue of which event
occasioned by the treachery of the Bey
terminated his life in the year 1785.

The inscription goes on to mention Samuel Shaw, brother of William, who

suffered shipwreck and was murdered by savages
on the south coast of Ghadalcave near Batavia in 1816.

It is almost as though William Shaw's memory had been overwhelmed by intelligence concerning his father and brother.

[128] *See* Wood (1913), 341-2. [129] *D.N.B.*, iv (1917), 657. [130] Ibid., i, (1917), 1241-4. [131] Barry had a vast opinion of his own merit, but *The Progress of Human Culture* is unimpressively drawn, and its rhetoric is feeble, which suggests, perhaps, that the artist's ambitions exceeded his talent. For Ann Birch Cockings *see also* A. Leaf (1847): 'A Leaf on the Grave of a Friend' in *The Builder*, v/209 (6 February 1847), 59. The Royal Society of Arts also possesses a painting of her by Miss E. A. Drummond. *See* Wood (1913), Ch. 8, 174, and Appendix III. [132] [1576/89/IR]. [133] For one referred to in such terms and compared with Newton, it is curious that little biographical information about Shaw seems to exist.

Verse might be said to be the staple of epitaphs: at its best it is pithy and epigrammatic; at its worst it is pattern-book insipidity and mawkish doggerel. In relation to other cemeteries Kensal Green can by no means claim to be an oasis in a desert of banality and bad taste, but it does contain its fair share of what might be called 'original' verse. The following productions, whatever their merits as poetry, have a certain touching charm:

Maria Green though short your life
A wife the duties to fulfil
Three weeks one day and then cut off,
It was your heavenly father's will[134]

suggests resignation; and sudden death by bombing in the 1939-45 war inspired

Two brave souls have marched to glory,
Two kind hearts have ceased to beat;
Faithful, true and free they lived,
Undivided, twain they died;
Storm of conflict closed their story;
Memory lives till we three meet,[135]

which conjures up a world very different from that more than sixty years later. Another quatrain caused something of a stir when it appeared in 1868:

A loving husband and a faithful friend,
Ever the first a helping hand to lend;
Farewell, good-natured, honest-hearted Sam,
Until we meet before the great I AM.[136]

The phrase, 'Rest in peace, good chimney sweep',[137] has been given as his epitaph. The *Illustrated London News* commented that there was

> not a clergyman in England who would not have prevented the inscription which has just been placed on the tomb of a music hall singer, and in which the slang name for a mountebank is made to rhyme with the most solemn and mysterious title which the Scripture records as having been given to Himself by the Deity.[138]

More interesting poetically is the verse commemorating Fanny, daughter of William Turner, who died 6 May 1849, aged 17:[139]

I hoped I saw from birth to womanhood all was fair;
Alas an unexpected hour snatched hope from this world of care.
I hoped I saw her motherhood, and often brought her here;
Alas both snatched by early death, grieved by many a tear.
Hope, alas hope, though often blighted,
Hope the world without could not be requited.

134 Maria Green (d. 27 November 1840, aged 22) [2774/131/2]. 135 Dolly and Charlie Carter, killed by German bombs, Wednesday 16 October 1940 [44264/97/2]. 136 Samuel Collins (1825-65), whose real name was Samuel Vagg, made his name as a music-hall singer and dancer, specialising in stage-Irish rôles. He bought a public-house in Islington which became the celebrated Collins's Music Hall. The marble pedestal over his grave is surmounted by a much-eroded carving of his billycock hat and shillelagh [16492/80/RS]. 137 *See* Haddon (1935), *passim*, for further information. Reference kindly provided by Miss Sarah Ash, of Guildhall Library, Corporation of London. Collins had been a chimney-sweep before he achieved success on the boards, and the phrase, 'Rest in peace, good chimney sweep', is quoted in Haddon (1935) as Haddon's own comment: it never appeared on the tombstone. 138 *The Illustrated London News*, liii (1 August 1868), 111. 139 [8149/96/PS].

For all its lack of sophistication the verse gives evidence of poetic sensibility, and it is perhaps surprising to learn that the author was the girl's father – his initials are appended to the last line – a brass-worker and gas-fitter.

A more finished, if conventional tribute (recorded by Clark[140] but no longer extant) is paid to the scholar and writer George Dyer (1755-1841):[141]

Above the scholar's fame, the poet's bays,
Thus Dyer on the tomb we write thy praise:
A lip of truth, a heart from guile as free,
In manhood and in age, as infancy;
And brotherly affection, unconfined
By partial creeds, and open to mankind,
E'en here did Heaven, to recompense thee, send
Long life uncensured, and a tranquil end.

Dyer,[142] the 'G.D.' of Charles Lamb's (1775-1834) *Essays of Elia*, was noted as much for his amiable eccentricity as his scholarly achievements (he contributed 'all that was original' to Valpy's edition of the Classics [1809-31], which probably affected his eyesight). He was so short-sighted and absent-minded he once accidentally walked into the New River at Islington and had to be saved from drowning by Lamb who exclaimed on the occasion: 'I protest George you shall not venture out again – no, not by daylight – without a sufficient pair of spectacles – in your musing moods especially... Fie man, to turn dipper at your years, after your many tracts in favour of sprinkling only'[143] – an allusion to Dyer's strong Unitarian beliefs.[144] Late in life he married, much to the consternation of his friends, Mrs Mather, a widow who had already buried three previous husbands, but the marriage proved a happy one, and although Mrs Dyer did live to bury a fourth husband, she received only praise from those who saw how completely she had transformed the self-negligent old scholar's life. If there was any temptation to marry for a fifth time she resisted it, dying 20 years after Dyer at the age of 101; her body was deposited with his.

The consolatory nature of the poetical epitaph is a predominant feature of most cemeteries, and Kensal Green is no exception. Religious texts, adapted for the purpose, abound; favourite poets also find a place: all four verses of Henry Wadsworth Longfellow's (1807-82) poem *The Reaper and the Flowers* (1839) are inscribed on the obelisk[145] erected in memory of the 10-year-old Victoria Paget (1848-59), god-daughter of Queen Victoria.

The virtually unknown Irish-American poet John Luckey McCreery (1835-1906) struck the right note with his poem *There is no Death* which first appeared in *Arthur's Home Magazine* in July 1863, and was once wrongly ascribed to Edward George Earle Bulwer-Lytton (1803-73).

There is no death! the stars go down
To rise upon some other shore,
And bright in Heaven's jewelled crown
They shine forevermore.

There is no death! an angel form
Walks o'er the earth with silent tread

140 Clark (1843), 84. The monument was in the unconsecrated section. 141 [2930/14/RS]. 142 *D.N.B.*, vi (1917), 284-5. 143 Lamb (1852), ii, 230-1. 'Amicus Redivivus'. 144 For Dyer and Lamb *see* Lucas (1905), *passim*. 145 [15029/77/IR].

And bears our best loved things away;
And then we call them dead.[146]

Despite the leaden last line, the poem's appeal is obvious, and it appears on the memorial[147] of Robert Priestley (d. 28 November 1878).

A rather Kiplingesque verse by another minor poet, Charles Carey-Barnard (d. 28 November 1905)[148] dutifully serves the memory of its creator:

Out of the ranks they all rise up
For the muster roll of that far off shore,
Where each shall be known, as each shall be judged
By the standard of truth for ever more.

The novelist and poet Charles Francis Keary (1848-1917)[149] was also responsible for his own epitaph:

Here have I made my bed, and o'er my head
Watch one by one the stars that rise and set.
But not in this home, nor 'neath all that dome
Seek me: it is my bed, but I lie not in it.[150]

Keary, whose novels were supposedly influenced by the great Russian writers, collaborated with Frederick Delius (1862-1934) on his opera *Koanga* (1895-7),[151] the plot of which was drawn from the novel *The Grandissimes* (1880) by George Washington Cable (1844-1925), and based the character 'Septus Jonsen' in his novel *The Journalist* on the composer.[152]

One or two more epitaphs of a literary character may be mentioned before some specimens of rarer non-consolatory verses are quoted. Shakespeare was called upon to furnish the epitaph of the celebrated actress Isabella Dallas Glyn (1823-89):[153] appropriately, the lines are from two plays in which she achieved notable successes in the leading female rôles. They are:

Age cannot wither her, nor custom stale
Her infinite variety;[154]

and

After life's fitful fever she[155] sleeps well;
... nothing,
Can touch her[156] further.[157]

The inscription on the grave[158] of James Henry Leigh Hunt (1784-1859), poet, critic and (famously) the original of 'Harold Skimpole' in Dickens's *Bleak House* (1852-3), is a line taken from his own poem *Abou Ben Adhem* (1838):

Write me as one that loves his fellow-men[159]

[146] The poem is published in Felleman (1936), 86-8, and consists of 16 verses. McCreery's name appears in O'Donoghue (1912), 272. The second verse is not printed in the anthology in Felleman: it seems to have been adapted, or rather turned on its head, from the stanza which runs: 'Although with bowed and breaking heart, With sable garb and silent tread, We bear the senseless dust to rest, And say that they are "dead",' which might explain the ineptitude of 'And then we call them dead'. On the monument there is no exclamation-mark after 'death' and 'fairer' has been substituted for 'other'. [147] [26690/**83**/RS]. [148] [40674/**162**/2]. [149] [45713/**187**/2]. [150] From *An Epitaph: Astra Castra Numen Lumen* (the stars are my camp, the Deity is my light). *See* Keary (1923), *passim*. [151] First given at the Municipal Theatre, Elberfeld, 30 March 1904. The subsequent neglect of the opera is partly due to the dreary libretto: his dreadful epitaph is rather typical of the banality of his writing. [152] *See* Keary (1898), *passim*. [153] [31609/**55**/4]. [154] *Antony and Cleopatra* (1606-7), Act 2, Sc. 2, lines 243-4. [155] Originally 'he'. [156] Originally 'him'. [157] *Macbeth* (1606), Act 3, Scene 2, lines 23, 25-6. [158] [13650/**121**/3]. [159] Hunt (1844), 124. 'Abou Ben Adhem and the Angel'.

An exhortation to the angel in the poem who records in a golden book the names of those who love the Lord.

The poet Thomas Hood (1798-1845),[160] already suffering from the disease[161] (tuberculosis) that was to kill him, suggested as his own epitaph:

Here lies one who spat more blood
and made more puns than any living man.

His friends would have appreciated the black humour, but Victorian sensibilities had to be considered, so the realised inscription reads:

He sang the Song of the Shirt

a reference to one of his best-known poems (**8.21**).[162]

The dramatist James Albery (1838-89),[163] whose name is perpetuated in the West End's Albery Theatre, was commemorated by a couplet taken from his own 'fairy' play, *Oriana* (1873):

Truth is near but men forsake it;
And the world is what we make it.[164]

It is not as striking as the facetiously self-mocking lines he would have preferred:

He revelled 'neath the moon,
He slumbered 'neath the sun;
He lived a life of going to do,
And died with nothing done.[165]

The literary inscription on the unusual monument (in the form of an armchair)[166] to the composer and songwriter Henry Russell (1812-1900) [167] reads:

His songs like his acts encouraged the Poor and inspired the Rich

and the rest, a couplet, declares

I love it, I love it, and who shall dare
To chide me for loving this old armchair.[168]

At the height of summer when parts of Kensal Green cemetery run riot with tall grasses and wild flowers, the inscription on the grave[169] of the writer of boys' adventures, Thomas Mayne Reid (1818-83), seems singularly appropriate:

This is the weed prairie – It is misnamed;
It is the Garden of God.

The quotation[170] is from one of Reid's most successful books, *The Scalp-Hunters* (1851).[171]

A literary epitaph of a slightly different kind is that[172] commemorating Mary Scott Hogarth (1819-37): the literary interest lies not so much in the words themselves but in

160 [5449/**74**/PS]. 161 It is now generally believed that Hood suffered from rheumatic heart disease rather than tuberculosis. 162 Hood did not intend his suggested epitaph should be taken seriously: in fact he himself requested that *He sang the Song of the Shirt* should be inscribed on his memorial. 163 [31717/**74**/2]. 164 Albery (1939), 436, 'The Song of the Spirits'. The original reads: 'Oh! the world is well enough, But men tread with cruel feet, Till the pleasant ways are rough, And there's bitter in the sweet. Truth is near but you forsake it, And the world is what you make it.' 165 Hibbert (1916), 13. 166 [38384/**176**/2] 167 A pupil of Rossini, his works include *A Life on the Ocean Wave*, *Cheer, Boys, Cheer*, and *Woodman, Spare that Tree*. Many of his songs (numbering more than 800) were immensely popular in their day. 168 Eliza Cook: *The Old Armchair*, first published in the *Weekly Dispatch* (May 1836), was her most popular poem (set to music by Russell). The original has 'that' in the second line instead of 'this'. *See D.N.B.*, **xxii** (1917), 478-9. 169 [28963/**153**/3]. 170 Reid (1852), Ch. I, 8. 171 *See D.N.B.*, **xvi** (1917), 875-6. 172 [977/**33**/RS].

the author, who was no less a figure than Charles Dickens. The sudden death of his beloved sister-in-law[173] was probably the most devastating event in Dickens's life (its effect on him has never been satisfactorily explained). Intending to be buried in the same grave, he composed the following inscription:

Young, Beautiful and Good;
God in his Mercy
Numbered her with the angels
At the early age of seventeen.

The inscription continues more prosaically:

This is also the grave of her brother George Hogarth
who departed this life Oct 24 1841 aged 20.
Like her he was taken ill and died in one night.

Mary died at home after an evening out with Dickens and her sister, and the cause of her death may have had little in common with that of her brother, who, it appears, died during an evening out at the *Horseshoe* in the Borough.[174] The father of George and Mary Hogarth, George Hogarth (1783-1870), who was also Dickens's father-in-law and a celebrated music-critic, is also buried in the plot.[175]

Epitaphs that offer little in the way of solace are rare, and would seem to give evidence either of a lack of religious conviction on the part of the bereaved or, in certain cases of death by misadventure, perhaps of a determination to remain inconsolable: indeed, the two may very well go hand-in-hand. The lines on the grave[176] of Mary Letitia Burt (d. 12 May 1859, aged 2 years 7 weeks) speak for themselves:

Words may not paint our grief for thee;
Sighs are but bubbles on the sea
Of our unfathomed agony.

Mention has been made above of 'idolatory' in respect of the Williams inscription. On the matter of inordinate attachment it might be worth digressing for a moment to take a look at the sentiments expressed by Ada Louisa, widow of the philosophical writer, the Reverend Alfred William Momerie (1848-1900) on his monument:[177]

O Afriti,[178] Human, Divine, Sweet human hands and lips and eye,
My husband love that cannot die.
Mine, mine, forever mine;[179]
Soul of my soul in Vehaisheim.[180]
You delivered the Lord's message.
You battled for the true, the just.
You were in fellowship with God.
You had the strength, the daring, the courage of a hero.
You will rise again in the hearts and memories of men.
You will see the travail of your soul and be satisfied.

[173] She died in Dickens's own house. [174] Transcripts of the General Cemetery Company's Burial Records give 'Horseshoe' Borough as his place of death, and his home address as Hamilton Place, Kennington. *See Diocese of London Bishop's Transcripts*: DL/T/41/9, 44. [175] *D.N.B.*, **ix**, (1917), 976-7. [176] [3660/**106**/3]. [177] [38386/**177**/PS]. [178] Probably Mrs Momerie's pet-name for her husband. [179] A quotation from Tennyson's *In Memoriam*, CXXIX, second verse. [180] Momerie was Morning Preacher at the Foundling's Hospital in London from 1883, and his sermons given in the chapel there were published in 1890. It is not clear what 'Vehaisheim' means, but it may be a reference to the *Waisenhaus* (German for orphanage) or *Waisenheim* (orphans' home). There is no word 'Vehaisheim' in German, but *Weh* means grief, woe, a pain, or an ache, and the reference may be to some personal imagined place. It could equally be a place-name, possibly in Alsace, but if so, it has eluded discovery.

For such a public display of devotion, Clark, one could easily imagine, might (if he had had the chance) have rigorously denounced Mrs Momerie, for there is certainly not another epitaph in the whole cemetery that displays anything like the sentiments of this, perhaps eccentric, effusion.

On occasion, the horror, terror, finality, and bleakness of death are evoked in memory of a loved one. The following extraordinary epitaph from the pen of the short-lived consumptive minor poet Henry Kirke White (1785-1806), conjures up the devastating and ghastly course of the killer-disease, tuberculosis:

In the dismal night-air dressed,
I will creep into her breast,
Flush her cheek, and bleach her skin,
And feed on the vital fire within.
Lover, do not trust her eyes,
When they sparkle most she dies;
Mother, do not trust her breath,
Comfort she will breathe in death;
Father, do not strive to save her,
She is mine, and I must have her.
The coffin must be her bridal bed,
The winding-sheet must wrap her head,
The whispering winds must o'er her sigh,
For soon in the grave the maid must lie:
The worm it will riot
On heavenly diet,
When death has deflowered her eye.[181]

This strange verse adorns the family grave[182] of John Wakelin (d.1887), and commemorates Louisa Mary Ann Wakelin (d. 18 November 1840, aged 17). Had the poem been morally instructive, its selection might have been easier to understand: however, it achieves no more than the reaction intended – to make the flesh creep and the spirit quail. What, therefore, did Wakelin intend by having the verse inscribed on his daughter's memorial? It clearly describes the effects of 'consumption', for victims' eyes 'sparkled most' when the disease (which also killed the poet) was rioting. However, to view the poem as cold and unfeeling would be a mistake: tuberculosis was all-too-familiar, was a killer, and took many young lives. The voice of the poet is that of Death and Disease: the theme is one of loss, of Death as the insistent lover, and the grave as the marriage-bed. Such sentiments were not out of place in the times, although they rarely found expression in commemorative verse, and Clark clearly disapproved, for he showed no restraint in declaring he was 'backward' to express his

unqualified admiration of the taste

demonstrated. He felt it furnished a 'narrative calculated to create emotions of dread or horror rather than those of a more suitable kind'.[183] However, one shudders to think what Miss Wakelin's epitaph might have been had she died of, say, leprosy or plague.

Didacticism, on the other hand, is certainly in evidence in the inscription on the headstone[184] of James Bell (d. 24 February 1840 aged 77). The style of the verse suggests the influence of the 17th-century religious poet Francis Quarles (1592-1644):

181 White (1850), 136. 'Fragment of an Eccentric Drama: The Dance of the Consumptives'. 182 [2759/108/RS].
183 Clark (1843), 58. 184 [2377/108/RS].

Lord what was I? A worm, dust, vapour, nothing:
What was my life? A dream, a daily dying:
What was my flesh? My soul's uneasy clothing:
What was my time? A minute ever flying.
My time, my flesh, my life, and I,
What were we lord but vanity?[185]

Bell, formerly a Norwich miller, was clearly something of a self-deprecator.

The verse-epitaph[186] to Edward Hewson, landlord of the *Bull's Head* in Windmill Street (d. October 1836 aged 40), points out its moral in sprightlier fashion:

Thy life is but a Winter's day;
Some only breakfast and away;
Others to dine and are well fed;
The oldest man but sups and goes to bed.
Larger his debts who lingers out the day;
Who goes the soonest has the least to pay.[187]

As has been demonstrated, Benjamin Clark was never tardy in expressing his purse-lipped opinions when reflecting upon the epitaphs and inscriptions he found in Kensal Green cemetery: but, in turning his attention to examples of unorthodoxy, he seems to have preferred to allow the illustrations to speak for themselves, without additional comment. Among examples he gave was:

In Adam her head she acknowledged she fell,
But in Jesus the Lord she lov'd much to dwell.
Thus living she felt there was no condemnation,
And dying rejoiced there was no separation,

a Dissenter's[188] ready confession of her sin.[189]

Elizabeth, wife of Daniel Curtis, Dissenting Minister,[190] was commemorated thus:

her love to and zeal in the cause of Zion were exemplary: she was a pattern of good works; and, though her faith was weak, it triumphed over the gates of hell on the very threshold of death; and she began the hallelujahs of heaven before she left the earth on the 28th of June, 1839 in the 42nd year of her age[191]

and Ann Heron (d. 22 August 1834, aged 35) had a stone[192] inscribed:

and when thou thus
shall stand impleaded at the high tribunal
of hoodwinked justice, who shall tell thy audit?[193]

a quotation that was too much for Clark. 'What could prompt the writer to imagine, that at "the high tribunal" justice would be found "*hoodwinked*"? To say the least, the expression is unguarded. If taken in its plain, legitimate acceptation, it is as contrary to commonsense as to Scripture: for who, that thinks as he ought, can be brought to conclude, that, at a tribunal utterly incapable of the slightest departure from the strictest rectitude, justice will be deceived, or hoodwinked? We would charitably hope', Clark concluded 'that the writer attaches a meaning to the words which they do not imply'.[194]

185 Clark (1843), 57. 186 [722/93/RS]. 187 This is derived from 'One doth but breakfast here, another dines, he that liveth longest doth but sup; we must all go to bed in another world', by Joseph Henshaw (1603-79), Bishop of Peterborough from 1663. 188 Elizabeth Harrison (d. 28 December 1841, aged 74) [3323/7/RS]. 189 The verse is a reference to *The Epistle of Paul the Apostle to the Romans*, viii, 1, and to the concluding verses of the Chapter. 190 [2101/7/RS]. 191 Clark (1843), 83. 192 [165/5/RS]. 193 Clark (1843), 80. 194 Clark (1843), 80-81.

It is no small step from distrust in the justice of Divine Mercy to:

Religion! Providence! An after-state!
Here is firm footing: all is sea besides.
Erected by Nathaniel Fenn 1836,

inscribed on the base of Fenn's (1780-1844) massive obelisk[195] eight years before his death. The inscription can only be taken to read that Religion, Providence, and an Afterlife were all on firm foundations, whereas anything else was without any footings.

At the beginning of the 21st century those unfamiliar with literature might have something flippant to say about the inscription found on the headstone of Catherine Finney:[196]

What are these which are arrayed in white robes?
and whence came they?

but it actually comes from the Bible,[197] just before the opening of the Seventh Seal.

More recent epitaphs rarely amuse, arouse interest, or appeal to any sensibilities: they tend to be commonplace of the 'a light from our household is gone', 'we were not there to say goodbye', and 'gone but not forgotten' variety: they do little to stimulate the imagination or refresh the eye. The following inscriptions are among a handful which might be said to be in any way notable:

poems that are much frailer than stone
will perhaps outlast my house of stone[198]

and the more thought-provoking

destiny enshrines paradoxes: in my lifetime I said nay to this soil
where I now rest in peace.[199]

The unoriginal

he burned the candle at both ends:
but oh what a lovely light[200]

might, however, arouse mild speculation about what excesses were enjoyed. Elsewhere may be found:

only your courage and loyalty were greater than your fears,[201]

and the perhaps puzzling

made in Scotland fer girders.[202]

Bicycles, maybe, are suggested by

Re-united with his beloved wife Faith
on their tandem in heaven,[203]

195 [633/22/3]. 196 [47434/96-97/PS]. 197 *Revelation*, **vii**, 13. 198 Erich Fried (1921-88), Austrian poet and social activist [62909/113/PS]. 199 A native of Ethiopia (d. 1976), Tsehafe T'Izaz Wolde-Giyorgis Wolde-Yohannes [59871/31/RS]. 200 *See* Edna St Vincent Millay (1892-1950): *A Few Figs from Thistles* (1920), 'First Fig'. Others have dealt with the same theme. The Kensal Green quote is on the grave [61814/100/2] of Kerry Richard Deering (1953-84). 201 Catherine Susan Verebes (1918-70) [57735/230C/3]. 202 Michael Ian Stewart (1965-97) [65945/175/3]. This is a reference, it seems, to a popular soft drink called Irn-Bru. 203 Frank Williams (1893-1977). Plaque in Garden of Remembrance.

a declaration of faith is enshrined in

O Mercy! O Compassion! Had I not been a sinner
I would never have known thee,[204]

and pious hopes are revealed in the words

may the little beggar man play on.[205]

Something of early 19th-century whimsicality is occasionally hinted at:

beneath this tree there lies a man
who planned his work and worked his plan[206]

and even traces of 18th-century cynicism survive as

how soon he was done for.
We wonder what he was begun for.[207]

An unusual epitaph which has only just appeared (in the early 2000s) deserves inclusion:

my son, my daughters,
you have amazed me with your minds.
You will have no limits to what you
want from life. Whenever you want help
I will be there. By the way,
Enjoy food, it's wonderful![208]

The last utterance, his epitaph discloses,[209] of Thomas Dakin Knight, appears to have been:

fear not for I have redeemed thee. Thou art mine, Hallelujah![210]

In conclusion, the following is worth quoting:

not till the looms are silent
and the shuttles cease to fly,
will God unfold the pattern
and explain the reason why.[211]

Conclusion

Friedrich Nietzsche (1844-1900) observed that 'Wit is the epitaph of an emotion',[212] a remark that is as memorable for its veracity as for its brevity. A consideration of the many inscriptions that adorn the monuments in Kensal Green cemetery will reveal little wit, much bathos, occasional grandeur, and, infrequently, some humour. All in all, though, the place contains what Richard Brinsley Sheridan (1751-1816) called 'a nice derangement of epitaphs'.[213]

It is instructive to read the claims of excellence and virtue made for so many whose remains lie in London's first great necropolis. One is reminded of the advice given to the Emperor of China by 'Wang Pen', who suggested that, having read the inscriptions upon

[204] Igor Miedzianik (1926-71) [58192/180/PS]. [205] Patrick O'Brien (1909-94) [57724/230C/6]. [206] Sir Delbert James Blenman (1911-90) [63477/270/4]. [207] Jason Pillay-Bowen (b. 8.22 p.m., 3 April 1972. Taken from us tragically 20 August 1986 aged 14). [62367/220/3]. [208] Mark Richard Foster (1963-2000) [66819/76/2]. [209] [34410/190/4]. [210] Died 1893, aged 18. [211] Evelyn Bonello (d. 1959, aged 50) [54577/163/RS]. [212] *Der Witz ist das Epigramm auf den Tod eines Gefühls* (*Menschliches, Allzumenschliches* [1867-80]), ii, Sect. 1, No. 202. [213] In *The Rivals* (1775), Act 3, Scene 3.

the tombstones of the cemeteries, the only possible means of improving the people of the Empire was to kill all the living and resurrect the dead.[214]

To paraphrase Sir Thomas Browne (1605-82),[215] time antiquates Antiquities and can 'make dust of all things', yet has spared many of the monuments in the General Cemetery of All Souls at Kensal Green. Nevertheless, vandalism, pollution, war, and other agencies have caused much damage, which, if it cannot be made good, should at least be prevented from increasing. Pyramids, arches, and obelisks, Sir Thomas observed,[216] 'were but the irregularities of vain-glory, and wilde enormities of ancient magnanimity'. Furthermore, to 'subsist in lasting Monuments, to live in their productions, to exist in their names, and praedicament of *Chymera*'s was large satisfaction unto old expectations, and made one part of ...*Elyziums*'.[217] 'Tis all one', he wrote, 'to lye in St *Innocents* Church-yard,[218] as in the Sands of Ægypt: Ready to be any thing, in the extasie of being ever, and as content with six foot as the Moles of *Adrianus*'.[219]

[214] Paul Elridge (b. 1888), American educator and writer. [215] Browne (1893), 71. [216] Ibid., 83. [217] Ibid., 84-5. [218] That is, the cemetery of the Innocents, in Paris, mentioned in Chapter I. [219] Hadrian's mausoleum in Rome, now the castle of Sant' Angelo.

CHAPTER XII

A Geology of Kensal Green Cemetery

ERIC ROBINSON

Introduction; Conditions Underground; Contributions by Man; The Memorials and Tombs; Epilogue

> Grave-stones tell truth scarce fourty years: Generations passe while some trees stand, and old Families last not three Oaks.
>
> SIR THOMAS BROWNE (1605-82): *Hydriotaphia* (1685), v (1893 edition), 76.

Introduction

In the General Cemetery of All Souls, Kensal Green, geology expresses itself in several different ways: first, there is the obvious aspect – the nature of the ground and the subsurface; then there is the human contribution evident in the materials of the buildings, and, more especially, in the stones of the monuments and gravestones. Both the nature of the ground and the stone introduced have been essential to the ecology of the plants and wildlife which are so important in the appreciation of this remarkable 71.9-acre (29.1-hectare) open space in northern Kensington and Kensal Rise.

Conditions Underground

The geology of the area first acquired by the General Cemetery Company is entirely an outcrop of London Clay free from any serious overburden of younger sands or gravels that would be found south of the Grand Union Canal. Grey or blue when freshly exposed, the clay rapidly changes into the tenacious and sticky yellow clay seen in freshly-dug graves. The change is a chemical one, as fine grained iron pyrites, exposed to air and moisture, oxidises to iron minerals with characteristic yellow or brown colour-tones. This process of weathering is accompanied by the generation of heat which has the effect of continuing the process, and causes the clay to swell and flow plastically down the slightest of slopes. In the cemetery, therefore, the excavation of graves by hand is both hard and heavy work, and such excavations are equally difficult to stabilise in wet-weather periods.

With clay of this nature, it is almost impossible to see surface waters drain away as it would in sands or sandy clays: consequently the ground is frequently waterlogged in the wetter winter months, and in hot, dry, summers it visibly cracks and tears apart through shrinkage. However the situation is reviewed, it could be argued that the local geology can present problems for the normal functions of a burial-ground, a view endorsed by most grave-diggers. The history of the cemetery demonstrates that adequate drainage was a perpetual problem and, although several attempts were made to remedy matters (always at considerable expense), no satisfactory solution was ever found, which is not surprising given the properties of the soil.

Against this, the undulating surface of the London Clay offered low mounds and slopes which the first landscape-gardeners and architects were able to utilise in the layout and landscaping of the pathways and the main avenue rising to the site of the Anglican chapel. An awareness of the character and chemistry of the clay should have had considerable influence upon the planting of the trees and shrubs best suited to the ground in order to produce the landscape effects which are so important .for this pioneering model for the London urban cemetery, but the choice of cedars and then firs (**4.29**, **4.20** and **Frontispiece**) created problems, and they had to be replaced during the 1840s by deciduous trees more suited to the physical conditions. Those trees have caused some problems for some of the memorials beneath them, as will be described below.

Contributions by Man

Most of the designs submitted in the architectural competition for the cemetery involved proposals to use natural stone for the buildings required, and, in the event, the structures realised to the designs of Griffith (not, as previously discussed, any part of the competition) were faced in Portland Stone, the best of British building-stones, much favoured by Wren for many new buildings in the City of London after the Fire of 1666.

The choice of Portland Stone was partly because it is ideally suited for Classical architectural detailing (notably porticoes and mouldings), and partly because it added *gravitas* to buildings intended to impress and attract custom. In the cemetery, the material is seen to good advantage in the entrance-arch on the Harrow Road towards the eastern limits of the ground. There, the Portland Stone (actually a white limestone) has light staining with grime, revealing the fact that it is composed of tiny rounded grains of lime referred to as oölite.[1] Generally uniform in its texture, shells of fossil oysters may, in time, break the surface and project from the dressed face. As the shells are tougher and more resistant than the background matrix to the stone, they become prominent when the elements (especially acid rain) attack the limestone, and their projection may be a measure of this effect: a smooth-surfaced ashlar finish of 1832 may lose as much as 5-6 mm. (almost a quarter of an inch) of stone in 160 years. As for the source of such deep weathering, one has only to remember that, only some thirty years ago, the gasometers that are such a dominant landmark south of the canal were linked to a gas-producing plant burning the fossil fuels which generated corrosive clouds twice each day. All the limestones of the cemetery demonstrate the damage done by acid rain to an unrivalled degree.

Iron-shod wheels of hearses and carriages passing into the cemetery through the arch ran upon broad lengths of Cornish Granite, polishing the silver-grey stone to perfection to display the mineral elements characteristic of the granites from South-West England. White laths of the mineral feldspar[2] are the diagnostic features of granites.[3]

To complete the introduction to the principal rock-types of the earth's crust, in the narrow pavings under the arch, and in the approach paths from the road, are the familiar York Stone, Coal Measure sandstone flags quarried in west Yorkshire and shipped south to the Thames to become the preferred paving-stones for London streets at about the same time as the cemetery opened.

The Memorials and Tombs

A simple survey of the gravestones of the cemetery reveals clear trends in the design of commemorative stones, the materials chosen, the most frequently used sources, and measurable rates of decay under the prevailing conditions of wind, rain, and frost attack. In all of these respects, the General Cemetery of All Souls at Kensal Green sets standards against which other urban cemeteries can be compared.

The earliest gravestones were relatively simple and consisted of upright slabs eight to ten cms. thick, roughly one to one-and-a-half metres (3.281 – just under five feet) in height, with a further one-third of a metre (just over a foot) below ground. The tops may be taken to an apex, or rounded and only later elaborated with scrolls and wings at the corners. From a distance, they fall into two clear categories of colour: dark and light.

The dark stones are Coal Measure sandstones from the coalfields of Yorkshire, Staffordshire, or Warwickshire. The first were brought as 'ballast' for the colliers plying from the Humber ports, while the Midland stones came by way of the Grand Union Canal directly to the yards of Lander's or Farley's[4] from the Kensal Dock Basin off Ladbroke Grove. Originally buff or yellow in colour, the stones darkened with age as the iron minerals bonding the sand-grains weathered, and the form of the iron oxides

[1] A concretionary limestone composed of small rounded granules of lime, producing a texture resembling cod's roe. [2] A group of minerals, usually white or fleshy red in colour, a main component of granitic rocks. [3] A crystalline rock, consisting essentially of quartz, feldspar, and mica, and varying in colour, light-grey predominating, although other varieties are white and light red or pink. [4] Monumental masons established near the entrance to the cemetery, very soon after it was established.

changed: black tones in the material are not necessarily due to pollution, but to chemical transformations.

The paler slabs are of Portland Stone sawn into thin cuts from the massive blocks of Whitbed[5] or Basebed[6] units (seen in the entrance and the chapels). Sometimes the blocks were cut across the natural bedding of the stone, and subsequent weathering has picked out the harder and softer bands (actually a trace of the Jurassic[7] sea bed) across the face of the stone to the detriment of the tombstone inscriptions. Upright slabs cut 'with the bed' remain more uniform but are exposed to the problem of layers becoming detached and flaking off when water penetrates the slab and freezes during frosty conditions. Weathering patterns can be very different in the two stones, and indeed are a sure means of identification. The limestones are prone to chemical solvent attack of 'acid rain' which reduces the stone by several centimetres from its original outline: loss of depth in inscriptions can make them illegible, and, in extreme cases, a total loss. An idea of actual loss can be gained by measuring the prominence of fossil-shells upon the general surface. Shell material, although itself lime, as noted above, is tougher and more resistant to weathering than the lime-matrix of the stone. On the assumption that the stone was rubbed smooth prior to the carving of the inscription, the loss in millimetres can be measured against the prominent shells with a standard tyre-gauge. With time, inscriptions cut into Portland Stone slabs become less and less easy to read until the whole is illegible, with only faint lines tracking across the surface (**12.1**).

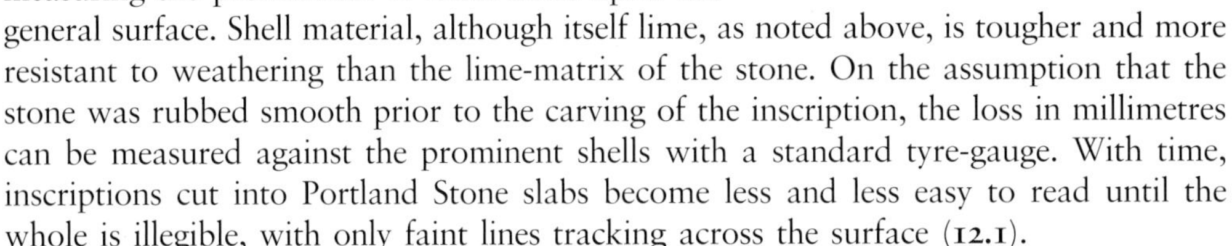

12.1 Two headstones of Portland Stone, showing the effects of weathering: that on the *right* [21095/69/3] (of Peter Ives [d.1883]) has lost several millimetres of its surface, and consequently the inscription is almost illegible; that on the *left* [46287/69/3] (of George Sheperdson [*c*.1863-1919] of 281 Cromwell Road) shows the shell material projecting slightly from the surface. Photograph of 2001 (*MC. C060101*).

Corrosive effects of 'acid rain' have no significance where sandstones are concerned. Problems are usually the consequences of rising dampness and the physical disruption caused by frost: sandstones are porous and so draw up ground-water into the spaces between the sand grains. When that water freezes and expands, the thin laminae of sand grains are pushed apart and detached in sheets from the ground upwards, eventually destroying the inscriptions and other detail which previously had been crisp and sharp (**12.2**). Contrast can often occur between the two faces of a sandstone slab. If one side is regularly sun-warmed, and dries out after wetting, it remains sound, but the other side, saturated for longer periods, may be weakened by the growth of moss and lichen in addition to severe damage caused by frost. Such weakened surfaces can suffer further breakdown form currents of wind swirling behind the stone carrying sand-grains that act as an abrasive to that same surface. There are countless examples of weathering-patterns on limestone and sandstone memorials in the early gravestones of Kensal Green cemetery, many of which provide object-lessons in survival or otherwise of the materials used.

In the history of the cemetery, a significant change occurred about 1850 with the introduction of monuments fashioned from Carrara Marble from the mountain quarries

[5] One of the best beds, or seams, producing the best stone for high-class building-work. [6] The slightly whiter and very finely even-grained stone, easily carved, and therefore used for internal work and for monuments, when fine detail is required. [7] Of or pertaining to the Jura mountains of France. Essentially rock-successions, mainly of clays and limestones lying below the Chalk, providing building-stones of Bath, Oxfordshire, and Portland. The time-period is between 150 million and 200 million years before the present, i.e. the age of the ammonites and dinosaurs.

12.2 Sandstone memorial of James Blomer (*c.*1793-1862 – coachman, of 57 Park Crescent Mews, Marylebone Road), his wife, and daughter [17551/27/2]. Rising damp and frost-action have detached the original prepared surface. Photograph of 2001 (*MC. E030101*).

above Massa in Italy. As a stone for monuments it clearly appealed to the Victorians, in part because of its pure whiteness when new, and equally for the possibilities of fashioning it into elaborate sculpture, as was seen on the Continent by countless travellers visiting Southern Europe. To the monumental mason, the stone was soft enough to carve into three-dimensional sculptured forms, thus enabling more elaborate monuments to be made in place of the simple upright slabs favoured hitherto. Little or no carving work was done by English masons during this new phase, most of the works being carried out in Italy, then the parts imported, to be assembled and inscribed by the Farleys or Landers at the workshops on the Harrow Road. The simpler Carrara slabs were decorated with fronds of ivy leaves, drapes of willow, or palm as frames to the inscriptions which invariably were composed by pinning lead letters into the face of the stone rather than by cutting in the traditional fashion. Soon, the sculptural opportunities of the marble were exploited with the production of three-dimensional anchors of Hope, rugged crosses, and, very often, fully winged angels and weeping figures.

Two main problems have arisen with Carrara Marble monuments after the passage of years. First, the limestone is a true marble (as geologists use the term). This means that it is a stone which has been profoundly altered by heat and pressure when the rock was involved in the crustal processes of mountain-building (in this case, the elevation of the Apennines): thus the limestone is effectively recrystallised, made plastic, and deformed often into tight fold contortions. Marble remains a limestone, despite those transformations, and as such is prone to acid-rain attack which has the effect of etching the contorted patterns within the stone. As a result, monuments which are impressively smooth and polished when new soon become rough-surfaced and even gnarled with time. Surfaces become pimpled by harder knots projecting from the surface of the stone, and can shed crystals of calcite when stroked by the hand, because these basic elements of the stone are released by the loss of surface-skin (**12.3**). Carrara Marble can retain internal stresses throughout the preparation of the monument, only for these stresses to be released subsequently, with unfortunate (if geologically interesting) results. Upright slabs can bend under their own unsupported weight, and continue to flex until total collapse occurs. Similarly, table-tombs supported at four corners by stone upright members can bend as much as 10 cms. from the horizontal, demonstrating an unexpected flexibility in solid stone contrary to popular perceptions.

The second difficulty with Carrara Marble is its marked tendency to darken with age to the extent of inky blackness. Such changes are never seen in the extremes of Mediterranean climate, but are all too readily a response to our weather (also associated with our urban and industrial polluted air). Loss of surface is often measurable from the projection of the lead letters of the inscriptions that were once flush with the polished surface. Down-wash from the letters has the effect of inhibiting lichen and algal growth, as well as the dark crusts mentioned above, the total result being white streaking running downwards across the surfaces.

12.3 An originally smooth-surfaced obelisk of Carrara Marble that has been deeply etched by acid rain to reveal the internal stress-fabric of the altered limestone [14923/112/2], the grave of Charlotte Norman (d. 1858): the grave was owned by Sir Thomas Hare of Stow Hall, Downham Market, Norfolk. Names and dates have been lost completely, in contrast to the crisp detail of the battered granite pedestal behind it. Photograph of 2001 (*MC. L080101*).

12.4 Gothic monument of Welsh slate, commemorating James Poole (who 'entered his rest' in 1843) and Hannah, his wife ('whose warfare ended' in 1840) [3899/10/RS]. The deeply-cut, crisp, sharp lettering and tracery ornament of the tomb-chest should be noted. Photograph of 2001. *See* Chapter VIII, §1 (*MC. H130101*).

12.5 Monolithic block of Lake District Green Slate commemorating the poet, Erich Fried [62909/113/PS]. The rough lower surface reveals the internal cleavage of the slate, rubbed smooth in the upper half of the stone to take the inscription. Photograph of 2001 (*MC. K080101*).

If Carrara Marble has proved to be susceptible to the prevailing weather of urban London and the Harrow Road, this could not be said of slate, probably the stone best suited to specialist letter-cutting and design and guaranteed to stand up to the harshest regimes of physical and chemical attack. There are, however, surprisingly few examples of slate tablets or monuments occurring in the older parts of the cemetery. One or two simple upright slabs stand out for their grey or purple colour identifying them as representing the stone from quarries in North Wales. A neat pedestal, once surmounted by a bowl-shaped urn, is the monument to Rupert Brindley (*c.*1791-1847), 'Slate merchant of Dockhead, Surrey',[8] who shipped slate from the ports on the Menai Straits to the wharves of the Surrey docks. One of the finest examples of work in slate in the cemetery must be the large Gothic tomb-chest, decorated with delicate tracery, in purple Welsh slate, in memory of James Poole (d. 1843), located[9] north of the path leading from the entrance-arch to the Dissenters' chapel (**12.4**). The lettering on this monument is particularly robust. It seems, however, that whatever the appeal of fine lettering and lasting qualities, slate of the finest kind was not the choice of the bereaved of West London.

In very recent times preferences have changed, partly for the opportunities slate offers for fine lettering and designs by members of the registered charity, *Memorials by Artists*,

[8] [6715/49/PS]. Any connection with the firm founded by William Farmer (1823-79) and William Brindley (1832-1919) has eluded discovery. [9] [3899/10/RS].

co-ordinated by Harriet Frazer of Snape, and partly because of the durability of the material. Several examples can now be found in the cemetery, usually involving blue or grey Welsh slate from Penrhyn or Dinorwic in Caernarfonshire. Green and grey-green slates represent the volcanic ashes of the Lake District core-area of Borrowdale and Coniston, soft sediment which became deformed and converted into slate when the Cumbrian mountains were created. Rubbed smooth to take the inscription, these rocks reveal their volcanic origin in the pellets of lava which occur sporadically through the stone which we need to think of as repeated ash-fall. Green Lake District Slate headstones are usually slabs with jagged outlines with the slate fracture surfaces rubbed smooth to take the inscription, but one notable example has a very different form. At the southern end of the terrace in front of the Anglican chapel, the monument[10] to the Austrian poet Erich Fried (1921-88) has a style more often seen on the Continent, especially in Germany. A solid block about one metre above the ground surface has a rounded top surface which has been hammer-dressed (**12.5**). The two smooth-finished upright faces bear the optimistic hope that his verses may last as long as the stone itself. Geological evidence of at least five distinct ash-falls from eruptions as violent as those which occurred in Martinique in 1998 is borne by the stone. This handsome monument contains veins which will deepen with time, but not part, for Lake District Slate is among the toughest of rock types.

The most durable of all stones in the cemetery are members of the granite family of rocks. Historically, granites became available as a choice roughly about the same time as Carrara Marble made its appearance in 1850. By that date, the machinery to cut, shape, and polish this hardest of crustal[11] rocks had been invented and perfected, and was in use in the stone-yards of Aberdeen. In earlier times, granite had been used in rough-hewn slabs and natural joint-blocks taken from hill slopes. At a still later date, lathes were adapted to allow granite to be turned for columns, colonnettes, and urns, while machinery was made to cut mouldings and prepare large slabs of the material. As these technical advances were made, the railway networks connecting London with the east coast of Scotland and with the Welsh ports facilitated the transport of granite to the masons' yards of Euston Road and Kensal Green. Obelisks, broken columns (signifying Death), and handsome tombs, all of granite (**12.6** and **12.7**), soon crowded the main avenues of the cemetery, and, eventually, figured prominently in the larger mausolea along with Portland Stone. The granites included pink Peterhead Granite and the sombre grey foliate-textured Rubislaw Granite from Aberdeen. From County Down in Ireland via Fishguard and the Great Western Railway came the silver-grey Mourne Granite, with its faint purple tinge, as well as the black granite with prominent white crystals known as Bessbrook from Newry. The oldest trade in granite into London, long before the railways, was the seaborne traffic from Cornwall and south Devon bringing the silver-grey granites flecked with white tablets of feldspar from Dartmoor, Bodmin Moor, and Falmouth to provide kerbstones and setts for the streets. Cut with the new machinery, granites from South-West England were introduced to the cemeteries as ledgers, columns, obelisks, and kits of parts for mausolea with the rest. This influx of very prominent granite largely owes its presence to the improved means of transport of bulky freight by rail. Modern methods of carrying heavy materials continue to expand the range of stones available, and many varieties of rock-types are imported from distant parts of the world as cut slabs to be finished in workshops throughout the country.

Mention has been made above of the evolution of techniques in the working of granite. The machinery and tools behind such change were largely perfected in the stone-yard of the Scots firm of Alexander MacDonald from 1830. Throughout Kensal Green

[10] [62909/113/PS]. [11] Pertaining to the earth's crust.

12.6 Tall obelisk commemorating the showman, Joseph Richardson of Keswick (*c.*1790-1855), and his son, Samuel (d. 1888). It is one of the longest unbroken lengths of Peterhead Granite known [27918/32/RS]. *See* Chapter VIII, §15. The Elton mausoleum [37929/32/RS] on the *left* is of Carrara Marble, and the Greek Doric mausoleum [47543/32/RS], erected by Imre Kiralfy (1845-1919) for his children and grandchildren, is made of a fine-grained granodiorite of unknown provenance. Photograph of 2001 (*MC. B030101*).

12.7 Sarcophagus-cenotaph of George Bellas Greenough (1778-1855), first President of the Geological Society of London, and a founder of University College London [12449/42/PS]. It is also the memorial of Francis Smedley (d. 1859), High Bailiff of Westminster, Greenough's heir. Greenhough's body is in [**CAT. B**/Vault 50/Comp.3]: Smedley's was removed to Great Marlow in 1869. The cenotaph is made of Peterhead Granite, and is the work of 'A. MacDonald of New Road'. Photograph of 2001 (*MC. F060101*).

cemetery, many of the larger granite monuments carry the name of MacDonald, or MacDonald and Leslie, carved into the lower part of the stone, perhaps with the addition of their Euston Road address (acquired when their trade justified a London base). An identification can be easier, however, by simply looking for one of their more accomplished offerings, a draped urn surmounting a tall pedestal or chest. The urn will be polished while the overlapping drape remains unpolished. This demonstrates their ability to turn and polish the hardest granite as if it were wood, while controlling the extent of such contrasts of surface-finish at will. Today, with the availability of a wide range of high-speed cutting- and polishing-discs, fine drills, and other tools, modern stone-working has surmounted most of the technical problems confronting artisans in the early 19th century. Kensal Green cemetery, with over fifty examples of different solutions to those problems, stands as a museum to the steam-driven industry and fine workmanship of the MacDonald years.

Whilst quality and variety of natural stone are found in plenty within the cemetery grounds, monuments made wholly or in part of artificial stones of many types could be regarded as a geological highlight of any visit, if only that patent manufactured materials (which were made throughout the 19th and early 20th centuries) have often failed to be preserved in geological museums and have tended to be undervalued by conservationists. Most artificial stones were attempts to provide substitutes for Portland Stone in both their appearance and colour-tone, and had two more major advantages in their favour. First of all, artificial stone could be moulded into elaborate shapes and then reproduced many times, so elements could be turned out in countless repetitions by means of cheap castings instead of by the costly process of carving. Secondly, it had the virtue of resistance to almost all forms of weathering attack. Its cheapness and hard-wearing qualities (it only needed a washing-down every so often to keep it fresh) appealed to the Victorians and Edwardians, an approval which can be judged by the number of exhibits

12.8 Detail of the Mulready monument [17933/56/PS], designed by Godfrey Sykes, fashioned in terracotta by James Pulham of Broxbourne. Photograph of 2001. *See* Chapter VIII, §35 (*MC. No60101*).

12.9 Monument of Major-General The Honourable Sir William Casement (1780-1844), of Portland Stone and artificial stone [5400/56/RS], by the local firm of Lander. *See* Chapter VIII, §31. Photograph of 2000 (© *Crown copyright. NMR. AA97/1167*).

submitted to the Trade Fairs and the Great Exhibitions of 1851 and 1862. A fine example of such a monument made of artificial stone is the canopied tomb to William Mulready (1786-1863), the artist and designer of the first pre-paid (but short lived) postal envelope.[12] This elaborate composition was produced by James Pulham & Son, of Broxbourne, a firm specialising in artificial stone that simulated sandstone, and was used in grottoes and Alpine gardens. For the Mulready tomb (designed by Godfrey Sykes [1824-1866]), Pulham used a fine paste which, when finished, resembled Portland Stone: the paste, once moulded, was fired in a kiln to produce a smooth, hard surface-finish, and the material resembles a type of pale terracotta. The completed Mulready monument was shown at the Paris Exposition of 1867 and it has survived very well, demonstrating all that was expected of artificial stone in monuments[13] (**8.14** and **12.8**). A short distance away, on the main avenue leading to the Anglican chapel, the more frequently admired Casement monument,[14] with all its symbols of Indian service including the sepoy telamones, is another example of the flexibility of artificial stone, although the quality is let down by surface damage and failure of the fixings which reveals the internal composition (**8.11**, **12.9**). As much can be said of the equally famous Graeco-Egyptian Ducrow mausoleum,[15] where only the clouds and the winged-horse motif are of Carrara Marble, the rest being of stucco and artificial stone (**8.23** and **8.24**). Probably the best-known artificial stone is that made by the Lambeth factory of Eleanor Coade (1733-1821), a clay paste with added crushed feldspar which, when fired, produced an effect closest to marble. Examples of this stone are often details added to natural stone structures. There are one or two Coade urns capping fluted columns of Portland Stone or Carrara Marble, the combination clearly revealed by the weathered character of the one against the pristine freshness of the other (**12.10**).

[12] [17933/56/PS]. [13] The effigy has had one of its feet broken off, probably as the result of vandalism, and has no reflections on the qualities of Pulham's material, which has otherwise stood up well to the rigours of the weather and atmosphere. [14] [5600/56/RS]. [15] [820/76/RS].

Any review of the monuments in the cemetery will rightly focus upon the composite structures verging upon architecture, including family mausolea. Many monuments which have been listed by English Heritage are of this category and figure in architectural histories. An example could be the Ricketts monument by William Burges (1827-81)[16] in which that noted exponent of High Victorian Gothic exploited the freestone character of Portland Stone to load the masonry with crockets and finials at all corners (**8.7**). Exploring at the same time contrasts of texture and colour, artificial stone, two types of granite, and Cornish Serpentinite[17] ('Billy Burges was having fun!', as it has been summarised by J. Mordaunt Crook [1981]),[18] the architect, in fact, was setting in train a common weakness in buildings, a consequence of the incompatibility of different stones. Placed alongside one another, stones which have varying capacities to absorb and give off moisture suffer frost damage when they are in contact. Quite simply, limestone set against sandstone, or either stone placed against granite, will, in time, fail. The dramatic consequence of these juxtapositions can be seen in the large mausoleum of Patrick, 2nd Baron O'Brien (1823-95):[19] it is constructed of soft New Red Sandstone set alongside grey muddy Pennant Sandstone from South Wales, with Bath Stone quoins, a combination that has spectacularly failed, for all the stones are disintegrating, not only because of their proximity, but because collapse has been accelerated by the loss of the roof, guttering, and downpipes (**8.10**).

12.10 Fluted column set on a pedestal, with an angular or Scamozzi capital, of the Ionic Order, commemorating Charles Broughton Bowman, the General Cemetery Company's first Solicitor and Secretary, and his wife, Elizabeth (d. 1893), both buried in the old cemetery, Windsor, Nova Scotia, Canada. The grave [192/22/3] also contains two infant daughters (d. 1834 and 1841) and a Miss Mary Flexney (d. 1852). The monument is of Portland Stone, apart from the capital and urn, which are of Coade Stone, the most famous and successful of 19th-century artificial stones. The contrast in weathering is striking. Photograph of 2001. *See* Chapter VIII, §9 (*MC. F130101*).

The monuments which remain sound are those which are entirely of Portland Stone or granite such as the mausolea of merchant-banker Baron John Frederick Andrew Huth (1777-1864)[20] (**8.28**), the East India merchant John Lewis Bonhote (*c.*1805-67)[21] (**12.11**), or the politician Sir William Molesworth, Bart. (1810-55)[22] (**8.12**). Saddest of all monuments could be that[23] to the architect John Gibson (1817-92), who worked with Charles Barry (1795-1860) on the drawings for the Palace of Westminster: the combination of white Portland Stone with soft New Red Sandstone from Mansfield has resulted in the red sandstone becoming distressed and friable to the touch (**8.19**).

Whilst many of the larger monuments were constructed of solid blocks and thick slabs of natural stone, many were more economically designed as kits, with stone elements keyed to receive panels and forming basic chests or pedestals: these kits were delivered to the local masons' yards after which they were erected and completed by journeyman masons. When monuments collapse by ground movements or the breakdown of the brickwork of the grave, the opportunity arises to study the methods used in their construction: metal cramps, sometimes bedded in lead, link adjacent stones,

16 [20242/47/RS]. 17 Serpentinite is a rock of complex history, found in the deep roots of mountains. Alteration of the original mineral results in the prevailing green colour. When fresh, the stone has a lustre suggestive of snake-skin, hence the name, Serpentinite. 18 Crook (1981), 228. 19 [10833/48/RS]. O'Brien was an Irish M.P., and opponent of Parnell. 20 [2735/77/IC]. 21 [17766/65/RS]. 22 [12766/56/RS]. 23 [33942/64-65/PS].

12.11 Mausoleum of John Lewis Bonhote (*c*.1805-67), constructed of massive slabs of Cornish Granite [17766/65/RS]. Although the surfaces are not polished, the white tablets of the mineral feldspar are clearly seen: this is a texture characteristic of granites from South-West England. The door is a violet-coloured Welsh slate. Photograph of 1997 (*JSC*).

and, in other designs, stout pegs of slate are used to fix adjoining elements. At times, chests are supported internally by brickwork cores which are simply clad in natural stone, a form of assembly revealed through weathering, decay, or vandalism. This historic cemetery, with its measure of dereliction, has more to teach the would-be geologist than a well-kept urban cemetery regularly cleared of damaged and weathered stone.

To retain the cemetery as an unrivalled source of geological experience in West London requires understanding on the part of other interested groups, and may involve toleration of decay and breakage rather than wholesale clearance in the interests of tidiness and order. Then there is the need to keep Nature at bay. Invasive shrubs and self-seeding trees could soon overwhelm the monuments and disrupt composite tombs with their roots, unless their vigour is carefully and expertly controlled. The rich canopy of the mature trees (not original, as mentioned above, but planted in the 1840s) of the main avenue is responsible for deep staining of the limestones and marbles beneath, especially when sap and honeydew nurture mosses and lichen crusts. As with the clearance of ivy and bramble, compromise is always achieved through discussions with London Wildlife who ask in turn for a recognition of the value of vegetation cover for small mammals and insects as well as the birds who feed upon them. In this approach to management, Kensal Green once again can serve as a model for other urban cemeteries facing similar problems.

Epilogue

For their own convenience, historians set limits to their studies and rest content within their periods. Geologists have no such options: as a science, it is one that has 'no vestige of a beginning; no prospect of an end'.[24] So it is with the geology of Kensal Green and its monuments. Anyone entering the cemetery and setting out to take in the history of commemorative stones (and changes in popular taste) will recognise most of the categories mentioned so far, but for the post-1970 period will come upon many stones that are difficult to identify at first glance. This is particularly so in the area close to the north wall of the Dissenters' sector of the cemetery extending almost to the Dissenters' chapel, an area where many new burials are concentrated. Here we can find all the monuments which currently would be debarred from churchyards in all the Dioceses of the Church of England on the grounds that they would be out of sympathy with the fabric of the church and the harmony of the older gravestones. Included in this ban are black or red polished granites, with gilded lettering for the inscriptions, and the starkly white new Carrara Marble. The ban also extends to objects such as teddy-bears (a popular choice) and representations of favourite objects such as classic cars. No such restraints apply in urban cemeteries, as is clear from recent memorials in Kensal Green.

Many gravestones are of what the trade would call 'black granite', a term which geologists have to qualify and correct. 'Black granite' is usually a stone which, like

[24] Hutton (1795), i, 200.

granite, originated from a hot melt within the earth's crust which crystallised as it cooled. Being deficient in silica, however, the resulting rock lacks the mineral quartz which would lighten the overall colour to grey or silver tones. This darker rock would be termed 'gabbro'[25] and, in its pure form, is seen in several gravestones as a dark-grey stone flecked with black minerals. The Afrikaans name Rustenburg in the stone catalogues tells that one of the most popular gabbros comes from quarries close to Pretoria in the heart of South Africa. In other parts of the world, however, it has been the fate of gabbro-type rocks to become mineralised by metals such as iron, manganese, chromium, and platinum to such an extent that the rock is totally altered to the dense blackness of typical 'black granite'. The mineralised character of this rock is a feature which is evident to the naked eye, thanks to the high surface polish given to the stone by monumental masons. If the top surface of such a stone is viewed in oblique light, the metals will appear to glisten as a silver filigree through the surface. Such mineralisation is in part the consequence of the age of the rock. Most 'black granite' is from the Precambrian period of geological time and from the core areas of Africa, South America, and India with ages in excess of 1,000 million years. This greatly increases the likelihood of the physical changes referred to as metamorphism and the mineralisation which often accompanies such changes. True granites which have undergone similar changes have banded and contorted textures to a marked degree, and, because of their striking colours, have become popular choices for recent gravestone-tablets. Of much longer favour has been the iridescent blue stone from Larvik[26] in Norway in which the exceptionally large crystals of feldspar crowded with inclusions of black grains of magnetite disperse light as countless mirrors. Larvikite is the stone of the one-metre-high lighthouse monument to the Reverend John Frederick Blake (1839-1906), the evangelical clergyman and geologist, found to the north-east of the Anglican chapel.[27] The base of this realistic model of the Eddystone lighthouse is of Carrara Marble carved into rugged rock formations (and rapidly eroding) (**12.12**). Few modern monuments are treated in this sculptural fashion, decoration today often depending upon air-abrasive stencils or enamel portrait-plaques after the fashion of European countries (especially France).

12.12 Lighthouse-memorial to the geologist, John Frederick Blake (1839-1906) [35437/115/PS]. The slender tower is fashioned in grey-blue Larvikite, a rock from Southern Norway, and the rocky base is of Carrara Marble into which the letters of the inscription are pinned. Photograph of 2001 (*MC. J080101*).

To a great extent, the diversity and extravagance of newer gravestones and monuments owe much to the local peoples of Kensal Green and North Kensington. West Indians and Eastern Europeans, on the whole, seem to prefer traditional interment to cremation, and the former combine their grief with colourful ways of expression (including the placing of toys and trinkets on the grave-plot). Exotic and impressive stonework accords with such feelings and sees a return to the choice of white Carrara Marble (although not on the scale of former years), with three-dimensional winged angels or weeping figures. To many, the character and impact of modern monuments can be a shock, but, to geologists, they add considerably to an already rich display.[28]

[25] Gabbro is, like granite, of molten origin, but, lacking the mineral quartz, is invariably dark if not black in colour. [26] Larvikite is another rock of molten origin, distinguished from granite or gabbro by the size and frequency of the feldspar crystals. [27] [35437/115/PS]. [28] Nearly all the locations of graves in this Chapter have been provided by Mr Moulder, and the footnotes were compiled by the Editor, who thanks Mr Moulder for his invaluable assistance.

CHAPTER XIII

The Landscape of Kensal Green Cemetery

BRENT ELLIOTT

Introduction; Precedents; The Landscaping of the Cemetery; Conclusion

> The planting of all the [London] cemeteries is ... highly objectionable ... It is too much in the style of a common pleasure-ground, both in regard to the disposition of trees and shrubs, and the kinds planted. Belts and clumps can never be required in a cemetery either for shelter or shade; because nothing is so desirable as to have a free current of air, and admit the drying influence of the sun; and because it is impracticable to form graves in clumps and belts. By scattering the trees and shrubs singly, graves may be everywhere formed among them; and, by placing trees continuously along the roads and walks, shade is afforded to those who are on them, and a foreground is established to the scenery beyond. But the plantations in most of the London cemeteries appear to have been made without the guidance of any leading principle. In one we have a thick belt round the margin, occupying one of the finest situations which any cemetery affords for border graves ...; in another trees have been planted which it might have been foreseen would never thrive.

JOHN CLAUDIUS LOUDON(1783-1843):
On the Laying Out, Planting, and Managing of Cemeteries; and on the Improvement of Churchyards (London: printed for the author; and sold by Longman, Brown, Green, & Longmans, 1843), 69.

Introduction

Once the land for the cemetery had been purchased, the Provisional Committee began to cast around for suitable persons to lay out the grounds, but there were several major problems, not least a shortage of funds because of paucity of subscriptions coupled with the huge costs of erecting walls and railings to make the future cemetery secure.[1] There was also the difficulty of finding a suitable precedent, for not everyone had seen Père-Lachaise in Paris[2] (though that necropolis had received widespread publicity), and so several architects, nurserymen, and gardeners were approached for advice.

Thus there was no existing tradition of cemetery-design in England on which the Committee could draw. English churchyards, and the commercial burying-grounds which rivalled them, tended to be roughly rectangular plots of ground (depending on the pattern of surrounding streets), and graves usually were arranged in simple rows, facing the liturgical east, though in the late 18th century that orientation was sometimes abandoned. There were no large-scale coemeterial landscapes in England to offer models for an enterprise on the scale of that proposed for Kensal Green (both Liverpudlian examples were quite small, and Glasgow was unfinished at the time). However, there was a century-old tradition that offered one precedent, exemplified by many private estates and by the Royal Parks: the English landscape park. This was claimed during its 18th-century heyday as an imitation of Nature, and therefore 'superior' to the artificial, regular, geometrical works that had preceded it; its elements were gently undulating ground, a heavy emphasis on open lawn, with clumps and belts of trees for points of emphasis and as bounds for the scene, serpentine areas of water, and considerable ingenuity to keep utilitarian architecture out of sight. If the dwellings of the labouring classes or even whole villages impinged on the view, they would have to be moved. Uniform rows of gravestones within the rectilinear English churchyard did not lend themselves to such an ideal.

Precedents

Precedents for large-scale burial-landscapes did exist on the Continent,[3] but were not generally followed by the pioneers of English cemeteries in the 1820s and 1830s, despite claims to the contrary. Early extramural cemeteries of Vienna, Italy, and Spain were too formally laid out for a taste that had been evolved to appreciate the landscape park.[4] The cemetery of Père-Lachaise in Paris, opened in 1804,[5] was proclaimed in the English press as a model for the establishment of extramural cemeteries but, although it possessed a system of paths, part of which could be said to have a degree of Picturesque[6] diversity, its design was not actually copied: one wonders how many of the British campaigners who cited its example had ever actually visited it. However, Père-Lachaise was the subject of many articles; illustrations of it were widely disseminated; and several major publications made its tombs, mausolea, and memorials familiar to those with access to books.[7]

The result was an initial period of eclecticism. The pioneering cemeteries of the 1820s and 1830s used a variety of design options, all drawn from precedents in private gardens.

[1] Discussed at length by Richardson and Curl in Chapter II, by Curl in Chapter III, and by Freeman in Chapter VII above. [2] *See* Curl (2000*e*), *passim*; Etlin (1984*a*), *passim*; Fisk (1838), *passim*; Marty, Lassalle, and Rousseau (n.d.), *passim*; Normand Fils (1832), *passim*; and Saint-A (1816), *passim*. [3] Etlin (1984*a*), *passim*. [4] Andalucía (1993), *passim*. [5] Curl (2000*a*), *passim*; Etlin (1984*a*), *passim*; Fischer and Schein (*Eds.*) (1987), *passim*.

[6] Eighteenth-century aesthetic category, a standard of taste, largely concerned with composition of landscapes to resemble those in the paintings of masters such as Claude, Salvator Rosa, and the two Poussins, but also involving emotional responses to associations evocative of passions, feelings, personalities, or events. [7] *See* for example, Marty, Lassalle, and Rousseau (*n.d.*), *passim*, and Normand Fils (1832), *passim*, but especially Pugin (1829-31), *passim*.

The extreme case was the South Metropolitan Cemetery, Norwood (1837),[8] laid out as an informal landscaped garden; while at St James's cemetery, Liverpool (1825-9),[9] and the Glasgow Necropolis (1831-2)[10] the development of a disused quarry[11] and of a prominent hillside respectively took cemetery design towards the Sublime.[12] During this period gardening literature was increasingly pressing for a return to formal styles; John Claudius Loudon in particular attempted to revise English aesthetics and substitute Art for Nature as the predominant value in garden design.[13] But however many experiments in geometric layout were made on private estates, public landscaping projects tended to be conservative in the tastes they exemplified. It was not until the beginning of the 1840s that a completely formal design was attempted (on which more below). Nonetheless, a gradual trend towards the integration of formal features into the familiar landscape park was beginning, and the General Cemetery of All Souls at Kensal Green, the first of the great London cemeteries, drew on this mixed model.

The most recent major work of public landscaping in London which could be looked to was the Regent's Park, which, though complete, was not open to the public (it was eventually so opened in 1841). The design of this park was curious, and needs to be explained by its history. When it was first planned, it was to be the setting for the Prince Regent's house, which was to be reached by a carriage-drive from the east, circling round it. As well as the carriage-drive, there was to be a broad walk (laid out at right angles to the carriage-drive) flanked by an avenue of trees. This was to be embellished by a canal and beautified with fountains. By the time practical works were undertaken on the site, however, the Prince Regent had become King George IV, in 1820, and turned his attention to Buckingham House as his new residence. The design of the park was accordingly simplified, though without removing any of its major features. As a result, the grand carriage-drive terminated in a circle around an empty parcel of land; indeed, the problem of what to do with the 'Inner Circle' remained until the ground was leased by the Royal Botanic Society in 1840. The broad walk was laid out, without the canal and fountains, so the place as it would have been seen in 1830 was basically an informal landscape park, with some formal features (avenue, and circular road) that lacked any focus (architectural or otherwise), or indeed any very obvious reason for their existence at all. But this very lack of focus helped to make Regent's Park more acceptable than Nash's full formal scheme would have been. Avenues of trees had been rejected by the later 18th century, and as late as the 1840s it was common to find them condemned as in bad taste: however, the circular road had a precedent in English town-planning as the grand circus, and curvature had been such a principle in the planning of roads and paths in the landscaped garden – justified by William Hogarth's (1697-1764) 'line of beauty' – that circular forms were the most easily assimilated of formal patterns.[14] As a cautious integration of formal and informal design, Regent's Park was able for a brief period to satisfy the demands of both the old and new aesthetics.

The Landscaping of the Cemetery

Just as Regent's Park featured a broad avenue and a circular carriage drive, so the General Cemetery at Kensal Green came to possess a broad avenue, centred on the Anglican chapel, and bisecting a circular road. But this geometry was not apparent from the entrance gate – the avenue began well within the grounds – so that the visitor was

[8] Loudon (1843), 69, and figs 42 and 43. [9] Curl (2000*e*), 42-3. [10] Blair (1857), Pagan (1847), Strang (1831), all *passim*. [11] See Etlin (1984*a*), 240 and *passim*. [12] Eighteenth-century aesthetic category associated with ideas of awe, intensity, power, ruggedness, terror, and vastness. [13] For a background to the revival of formal design, *see* Elliott (1986), *passim*. *See also* Select Bibliography for relevant Loudon items. [14] Elliott (1986), 57, 117-118, for avenues.

greeted by the more familiar ambience of the landscape garden. In its early days, when there were as yet few tombstones in its acres of lawn, the cemetery would have seemed redolent of the spirit of John Nash, the presiding genius of Regency town-planning and landscaped schemes. This influence is not surprising, since, in September 1831, as has been described earlier, Nash's pupil, Thomas Liddell, presented the committee with a sketch 'drawn up under the eye of Mr Nash', with the tempting prospect that, if Liddell were chosen by the Committee, Nash would give his supporting services gratuitously. The Provisional Committee, however, asked John Griffith of Finsbury to furnish a working plan.[15] Neither this nor Liddell's sketch appears to have survived, so it is not possible to determine at what point the Nash influence was established, nor whether Liddell's proposals were significantly reflected in the subsequent design stages.

For the supply of trees, the Committee went to the prominent nurseryman, Hugh Ronalds of Brentford (1759-1833), best known today as an authority on fruit, but, like many suburban nurserymen, prepared to engage in landscape contracting.[16] While Sir John Dean Paul was discussing the plans in Ronalds's office that November, a visitor joined the conversation, criticising the plans and offering his own assistance. The interloper proved to be Richard Forrest (*fl.* 1820s-40s), head gardener to the Duke of Northumberland at Syon Park. Forrest prepared an alternative or amended plan; its nature is not known, but while its details were criticised by the Committee, it was sufficiently impressive for Pugin and Griffith to meet Forrest, and adopt his modified proposals. Ronalds was to supply plants and act as contractor; £300 was allowed for initial planting in November 1831.[17]

At the time, Forrest was just beginning to make his name as a landscape gardener. At Syon Park, he had been responsible for the creation of a rock-garden (since scattered), and he had also worked for Lord Grosvenor (created 1st Marquess of Westminster in 1831) at Eaton Hall in Cheshire; in the 1830s he was to design the Cheltenham, Bristol, and Manchester Zoological Gardens. By 1836, Loudon was claiming that 'As a garden architect, we know of no man to be compared with Mr Forrest', and that he had 'more experience in laying out zoological gardens and arboretums than any other artist'. In the late 1830s he ran a nursery in Kensington and after it closed in the early 1840s he moved to the north of England; his date of death has not yet been traced.[18] He is last heard of in connection with Kensal Green in 1846, when he wrote to the *Gardeners' Chronicle*, which had attributed the design of the cemetery's landscape to Ronalds, indignantly asserting his authorship of the layout.[19] However, as has been outlined earlier, Liddell, Griffith, and others had started constructing the paths, etc., before Forrest became involved at all.

The Company's relations with Ronalds were not always smooth, marked on the one side by complaints about the rate of planting and the quality of the trees, and on the other by demands for payment. Hugh Ronalds died in 1833, and his son Robert (*c.*1799-1880) continued the contract, but the Directors were evidently receptive to alternative proposals. David Ramsay (*fl.* 1810s-1850s), a Brompton nurseryman,[20] had already

[15] Minutes of the Provisional Committee of the General Cemetery Company (20 September and 4 October 1831). [16] For Hugh Ronalds (1759-1833), *see* Loudon (1829), 736-7. Ronalds was best known as the author of *Pyrus Malus Brentfordiensis* (London: Longman, Rees, Orme, Brown, & Green, 1831), possibly the most beautifully illustrated of all English fruit books; most of the subsequent literature on Ronalds deals with this book rather than with his nursery career. On his death in 1833 he was succeeded by his son Robert Ronalds (*c.*1799-1880), who continued the planting of the cemetery into 1834. [17] Minutes of the Provisional Committee (25 November, 12 and 22 December, 1831). [18] For Richard Forrest, *see Gardener's Magazine*, **i** (1826), 349; **ii** (1827), 107-8; **xii** (1836), 622-4, 696; **xiii** (1837), 185; and for his career as a nurseryman in Kensington in the late 1830s-40s, *see* Willson (1982), 32-34. [19] Anon., Untitled editorial on Kensal Green cemetery, in *Gardeners' Chronicle* (1848), 419-20; Richard Forrest: 'Kensal Green Cemetery', letter in ibid., 437. [20] There is little documentation about David Ramsay (born *c.*1796). *See* Willson (1982), 87-88, for what is known about the Ramsay nursery. He was succeeded by 1851 by David Allan Ramsay (*c.*1822-73); Willson erroneously suggests that the two Ramsays may have been the same person. The younger Ramsay later 'pursued a chequered career as a builder on the Ladbroke estate in Northern Kensington' (*see* Sheppard [*Ed.*] [1973], 7-8, 221, 225, 232-3, 239, 250, 253-4, 256-7; and Sheppard [*Ed.*] [1983], 139, 247).

approached the Company in December 1831, offering his services for planting, but Ronalds had by then been engaged (Ramsay did, however, supply gravel). In 1835 he approached the Company again, offering general maintenance, continued planting, and grave-digging services, and hoping to 'add to the repose beauty and solemnity of the place', though in his interview he admitted that the grounds were already in good order; he was granted a year's contract, effectively succeeding Ronalds's firm. He made a loss within the first six months, grumbled for the next six, and his association with the cemetery came to an end in March 1836.[21] The Directors decided that the experiment of contracting out maintenance and grave-digging had not been a success (however Ronalds continued to supply plants at further intervals).

Equal problems were encountered in the search for gardening staff and supervisors. Frederick Humphrey (or Humphries), the cemetery's first directly employed gardener, was sacked in 1840 for illicitly receiving fees.[22] But Robert Maconochie (d. 1858), one of the Directors of the Company, also proved to be a gardener of sufficient skill and probity to be able to assume control and give orders directly to operatives for the planting and weekly running of the cemetery. It was Maconochie, working closely with Paul and Griffith, who arranged for the planting, and who saw to the management of staff, the duties of which went beyond the digging and planting of graves. In order to ensure that some income was generated, the cemetery was grazed by sheep, and ground not yet allocated for burial was planted for potatoes and other market-crops.

Such was the sequence of people involved in the layout of the cemetery. What was actually achieved by the time of the official opening and Consecration in 1833? The earliest surviving plan (as far as is known) is a 'Proposed Picturesque Arrangement of Cemetery Ground', drawn by Thomas Allom and published in Henry Kendall's 1832 volume of proposals (**3.19**). Lacking Liddell's and Forrest's plans, it is not possible to say to what extent the Kendall layout followed either or both of theirs: Kendall's design was, in any case, not realised. But the plan shows a grand avenue, not in a direct line from the entrance, leading to the chapel and bisecting a circular road (features which bespeak the influence of Nash), and work had already begun on laying drains by the time Kendall was awarded his premium. It is possible, however, that the Kendall layout as illustrated was largely based on the existing plans; its most significant differences from what emerged on the ground lay primarily in the complexity of the circle and the curvature of the paths west of the chapel.

Until the drainage system was completed, planting was confined to the periphery; a line of shrubbery (later reduced to accommodate graves) was planted along the north wall to exclude noise from the Harrow Road. A watercolour, probably dating from 1832, now in the Museum of London (**Frontispiece**), shows a view looking west toward the Anglican chapel, along the line of the grand avenue; periphery planting is concentrated near the entrance gate, and the further stretches of ground inside the wall look bare. There are fewer shrubberies than the comments in the Committee Minutes would suggest. But one feature very clearly shown is an avenue of cedars along the principal road. Work on the central areas, including the planting of the cedars, began in the summer of 1832: the age of the trees is not indicated in the Minutes, but if they were as mature as shown in the watercolour one would have expected some comment on the costs of transplanting them. Flower-beds were not planted until just before the public opening in 1833.

[21] For Ramsay's dealings with the Committee, *see* Minutes of the Provisional Committee (12 December 1831; 5 and 11 January 1832; 14 January, 10 February, 30 September, 30 December 1835; 27 January, 10 and 24 February, 20 March, and 27 April 1836). [22] Minutes of the Proceedings of the Directors (30 March 1836, 28 March 1838, and 26 February 1840) for Humphrey.

Why cedars? The English were already noted for a passion for conifers in the mid-1820s, and by 1850 conifers had became the mainstay of new garden planting.[23] The cedar of Lebanon (*Cedrus libani*), however, had been introduced to England by the mid-17th century, so already had a weight of tradition behind it: Lancelot 'Capability' Brown (1716-83) had used cedars in some of his landscaped gardens, so it was a tree that had recognised links to large-scale landscape-planning. Cedars used to line avenues were more novel, in view of the prejudice against avenues that was only beginning to die away in the 1820s. But the choice of large conifers quickly proved unsuitable for ground so waterlogged that, as in the case of the Ducrow funeral, a grave could be filled with water by the time mourners arrived. The cedars were already failing by 1834, and although Maconochie rearranged the avenues in the summer of 1837, the remaining cedars were killed by frost in 1838. The coniferous theme was continued by initially replanting with silver firs (*Abies alba* – a more fastigiate form, but again one widely familiar in landscape-planting), but by 1842 the decision was taken to abandon conifers and plant the central avenue with horse-chestnuts and other deciduous trees.[24] It is this planting, with subsequent *ad hoc* replacements, that can be seen today (and much of it is nearing the end of its natural life).

The cemetery was initially hailed for the handling of its landscape. By 1836 Loudon was proclaiming that 'Kensall Green, near London, is in a highly prosperous state; and, independently of its use as a burying-ground, it is rapidly becoming a school of improvement in architectural taste, and of knowledge in trees and shrubs'.[25] Loudon was a proponent of coniferous planting, as will be seen below, and his initial enthusiasm may have been stimulated by the cedars. In 1848 the *Gardeners' Chronicle*, the leading gardening newspaper, was able to praise the tasteful planting of the flowerbeds and the ingenuity of the design, noting that 'when so much of that space must be reserved for the purposes of interment, the field on which the designers could exercise their skill was very limited indeed'.[26] However, by this time standards of taste were moving on, and Loudon in particular had created a demand for completely geometric design; in his last year (1843) he had published a series of articles on cemeteries in his *Gardener's Magazine*, which were published in book form late in 1843 as *On the Laying Out, Planting, and Managing of Cemeteries*.[27] In this volume he outlined a new aesthetic for cemeteries as a distinctive form of landscape design: laid out on a grid pattern, with its trees – preferably conifers, and again preferably fastigate forms – arranged in rows or as specimens, it could not be mistaken for anything other than a cemetery. Anyone who has travelled in southern Europe, especially Italy, and seen the unmistakable view of a cemetery behind white walls topped by rows of cypresses, will have an idea of the intended effect. The first approximation to this ideal was the West London and Westminster cemetery at Brompton (opened 1840), with its long axial avenue from the entrance to the Anglican chapel. The most rigidly geometric coemeterial landscape in London, Brompton signalled a new taste, which was set to spread throughout the country in the 1850s as local authorities found themselves obliged to create cemeteries, but fortunately had Loudon's manual to provide instructions, suggestions for planting, and much else.

Loudon himself was buried in the General Cemetery at Kensal Green (**5.9**): he had had much to say about the cemetery and various aspects of its management in his book (published in the year of his demise), but the enthusiasm for its sculptures and trees that he had expressed in 1836 was strikingly diminished in 1843. His ideas had become firmer

[23] *See* Elliott (1986), 115-118, for the popularity of conifers. [24] Minutes of the Proceedings of the Directors (26 November 1834; 28 June 1837; 28 March and 25 April 1838; 26 October and 30 November 1842; 27 August and 24 September 1845). [25] Loudon (1836), 613-638, and especially 621. [26] Anon., Untitled editorial in *Gardeners' Chronicle* (1848), 419-20. [27] Loudon (1843), *passim*.

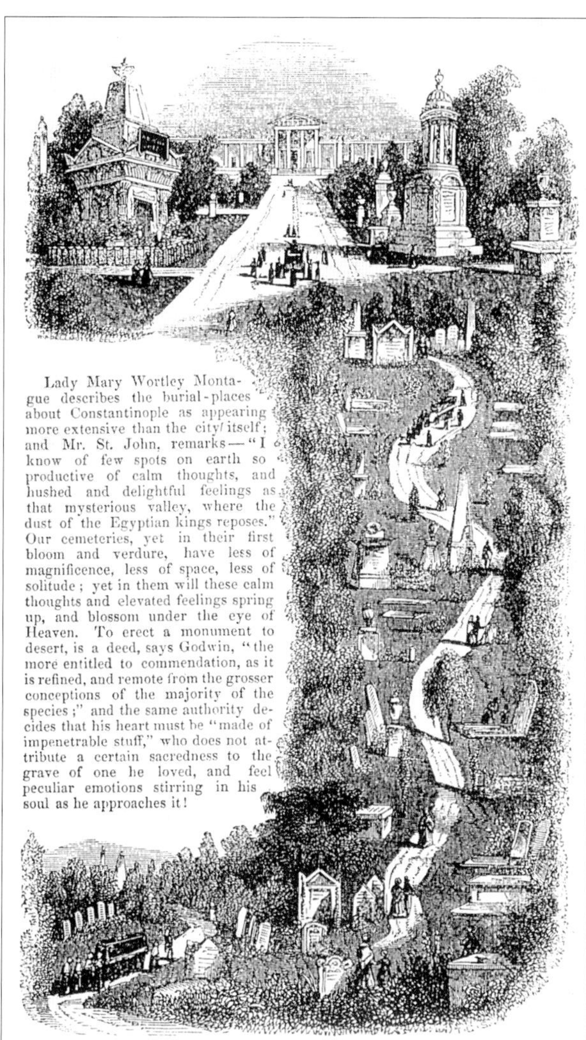

Lady Mary Wortley Montague describes the burial-places about Constantinople as appearing more extensive than the city itself; and Mr. St. John, remarks—"I know of few spots on earth so productive of calm thoughts, and hushed and delightful feelings as that mysterious valley, where the dust of the Egyptian kings reposes." Our cemeteries, yet in their first bloom and verdure, have less of magnificence, less of space, less of solitude; yet in them will these calm thoughts and elevated feelings spring up, and blossom under the eye of Heaven. To erect a monument to desert, is a deed, says Godwin, "the more entitled to commendation, as it is refined, and remote from the grosser conceptions of the majority of the species;" and the same authority decides that his heart must be "made of impenetrable stuff," who does not attribute a certain sacredness to the grave of one he loved, and feel peculiar emotions stirring in his soul as he approaches it!

13.1 Composite view of Kensal Green and some of its monuments, from *Ainsworth's Magazine* for 1842. *See* Blanchard (1842), 178-88.

as a result of his own experiments in cemetery design, and there was no indication that Kensal Green was to be exempted from his grumbles about the London cemeteries as a whole. Relevant complaints were: the planting of strips or belts of trees around the periphery; trees planted in clumps, taking up space that would one day be required for graves; pointlessly serpentine roads and unnecessarily complicated road-systems; the failure to provide adequate foundations for headstones and memorials, so that they tilted as the earth subsided; and the planting of flowers on graves. He specifically complained about Kensal Green's drainage: 'to be convinced of the bad effects of the neglect of surface drainage in a cemetery, it is only necessary to walk on the grass of that at Kensal Green during winter or spring'.[28]

In 1843, Loudon's adverse criticisms represented a minority viewpoint: press-coverage in that decade treated some of the failings he observed as points to be praised. Laman Blanchard published an illustrated article about Kensal Green in *Ainsworth's Magazine* in 1842, delighting in the 'evergreens and flowers, broken with small clumps of trees', and concluding it with an engraving showing, as two contrasting views, the straight avenue to the chapel, and the serpentine perimeter road – the degree of curvature rather exaggerated to make it even more suggestive of Hogarth's 'line of beauty' than was the real path[29] (13.1). This juxtaposition of formal and informal was very much to the public's taste of the 1830s and 1840s, but by 1860 a more rigid geometrical approach to landscape-design had triumphed, and the chorus of praise for Kensal Green cemetery's landscape gradually diminished during the second half of the century. In various ways, however, the landscape had altered during that period, and not only by the replanting of the central avenue. In 1842, only 6,000 interments had taken place in some 46 acres (over 18 hectares), and the cemetery's general appearance was that of a lawn, graced with shrubberies and studded with monuments. Over the decades, the monuments greatly increased in number, and the shrubberies were progressively cut back to make room for more burials. By the 1890s, Mrs Basil Holmes had little to say of Kensal Green's trees or shrubs, but plenty of negative comment on the memorials, their numbers, their qualities, and their costs.[30]

Loudon's emphasis on the grid-plan was in part a response to the difficulty of locating graves in ground that is divided by curving roads, where only the outer rows of graves follow the curvature, and the inner portions of the ground are organised in straight rows that abut those outer rows at an angle. This phenomenon was quickly observed on the sloping ground of West Norwood and Highgate cemeteries. Searching for graves in the General Cemetery of All Souls at Kensal Green is not as difficult as in

[28] Ibid., 20, 68, 28, 21, and 16, respectively, for these complaints. [29] Blanchard (1842), 178-88. [30] She was particularly critical about 'waste' and the expense of erecting tombstones.

either of the foregoing, but, especially if they are not on the main road, it can be time-consuming enough to make Loudon's viewpoint more than understandable. Peter Mackenzie, the Scots gardener, published a note in the *Gardeners' Chronicle* in 1852, describing his failure to locate Loudon's grave,[31] despite the size, severity, and power of the monument that stands over it (**5.9**).

Blanchard exulted over 'that verdant wide expanse, studded with white tombs of infinite shapes, and stone-marked graves covered with flowers of every brilliant dye!' The anonymous leader-writer of the *Gardeners' Chronicle* also called his readers to 'Only observe ... with what taste, at intervals on the side of the paths, beds of shrubs and flowers are placed'.[32] The Board encouraged the planting of individual graves in order to keep the grounds presentable, and there is little indication in the Company's Minutes of conflicts with grave-owners on this issue (apart from some unedifying episodes in which employees of the General Cemetery Company sold plants from graves to the public or to nurseries). In 1857 the Board ruled that a grave-owner could provide his own shrubs for planting so long as they did not exceed the height of the railings around the grave. The more usual problem, however, was the gradual (or not so gradual) falling-off in family attendance on the grave: this is often perceived as a late 20th-century problem, but it is clear it was a phenomenon of the Victorian period as well. Dickens quoted the clerk's observation: 'all melancholy enthusiasm at the funeral; flowers ordered and the company engaged to keep them in order, at the regulation charge of a guinea a year. Two years generally find enthusiasm cooled down, and the guinea discontinued. For ten guineas the company undertake to keep the flowers for ever; and I agree [...] that, the weakness of human nature considered, that is the best plan'.[33]

To meet the need for flowers on graves, a conservatory was built in 1862, to be augmented in 1866 with an additional building. The conservatory complex was rebuilt in 1896, by which time it was offering a purely ornamental display of tropical plants (supplied by Sander of St Albans, the orchid specialists, who had been providing the conservatory's planting since the 1870s) (**13.2**). Gardening under glass could compensate for some of the problems encountered outdoors: the *Gardeners' Chronicle* referred to 'the difficulties that attend plant-culture there, owing principally to the presence of several very large gasometers',[34] but it was not the 'gasometers', but the pollution from the production of gas that caused problems for those trying to rear plants and maintain buildings and memorials. The rôle of the conservatory diminished in the second half of the 20th century: the decline in cemetery-visiting and the fall from fashion of conservatories militated against its purely ornamental function, while the increasing use of gravel chippings as a labour-saving form of treatment of graves, together with the increase of garden-centres, reduced the General Cemetery Company's activities in providing families with plants for their graves. The glasshouses survived into the 1990s, deteriorating in condition: having long since been abandoned as a means of providing ornamental displays, attempts to raise funds for their restoration proved unsuccessful, and they were demolished in 1993.

Conclusion

The 20th century's major addition to the landscape of Kensal Green cemetery was the design of the precincts of the crematorium. In 1938, on the advice of the Royal

[31] Mackenzie (1852), 198. [32] Blanchard (1842), 178; Anon., untitled editorial in *Gardeners' Chronicle* (1848), 419-20. [33] Dickens (1863), 93-6. [34] Minutes of the Proceedings of the Directors (27 August 1862 *et seq.*, 25 July 1866). Anon., 'Flowers at Kensal Green Cemetery', *Gardeners' Chronicle*, **xxi** (1897), 140-1. For Sander's firm, *see* Swinson (1970), *passim*.

13.2 'A group of miscellaneous plants grown in the summer of 1896 in a greenhouse at Kensal Green Cemetery' from the *Gardeners' Chronicle*, **xxii** (27 February 1897), 141-2 (*Royal Horticultural Society, Lindley Library*).

Horticultural Society, the Company hired Edward White[35] (*c*.1873-1952 – President of the Institute of Landscape Architects [1931-3]) to design the garden of remembrance. White was the director of Milner, White, and Son, a firm that had originally grown out of the practice of Edward Milner (1819-84), Sir Joseph Paxton's (1801-65) former assistant and the designer of cemeteries in Halifax and Bath. White was experienced in the genre: he had recently designed the Stoke Poges Memorial Gardens, Buckinghamshire, a vast axial complex of small formal gardens in hedged enclosures culminating in a large parterre.[36] White furnished drawings for a rectilinear garden in an Arts-and-Crafts style, with a terrace and a quadrangular sunken panel with stone retaining-walls, flower-boxes, and flower-beds with kerbs. His plans envisaged a central canal and banks of clipped yews: this was amended to a central path and grass verges.

Work began in 1939, with the firm of J. Burley and Sons as contractors for the construction. The garden was planted with shrubs purchased from Walter Slocock of Knap Hill, and perennial flowers from Ryder of St Albans.[37] Significant among the latter were Russell lupins, which had only been launched on the commercial market the year before. The shrubs largely reflected the interest in deciduous and Spring-flowering subjects that had begun in the late 19th century as a reaction against Loudon's conifers: they included whitebeams, silver birch, standard thorns, philadelphus, lilacs, forsythias (but also hollies, aucubas, and yews). Part of the first shrub-planting had to be quickly replaced, suffering from soil compaction: the wall of the garden had cracked and bulged by May 1939, and had to be rebuilt. The garden of remembrance was opened by Lord Horder on 6 July 1939, but planting continued into 1940[38] (*See* Chapter VI).

During the second half of the 20th century, pressure for extra grave-space began to further erode the landscape: peripheral roads were narrowed to accommodate additional rows of graves, and suffered from waterlogging as their original drainage gullies were silted up; roadside verges that had previously been maintained as ornamental lawn were encroached upon; and even more damaging was the location of new graves within the circular road in the 1980s, effacing part of the original geometries of the planned layout (13.3). The original Board of Directors would never have countenanced such management policies, for it was determined to attract its clientele by appealing not only to security, but to quality and beauty too: erosion of aesthetics can have a deleterious effect on desirability.

35 White had been managing director of the Royal International Horticultural Exhibition (1912), which was held in the grounds of the Royal Hospital, Chelsea, and probably played a major part in laying it out. It was because the 1912 Exhibition was such a success, and that the grounds of the Royal Hospital proved to be such a good locus for a flower-show, that the Royal Horticultural Society moved its Great Spring Show, formerly held in The Temple Gardens, to the Royal Hospital grounds. 36 For White, *see* Anon., 'Mr E. White, V.M.H.', *Gardeners' Chronicle*, **lxxi** (1922), 146, and obituary, ibid., **cxxxi** (1952), 28; Leigh (1985), 9-13. For Stoke Poges, see the promotional brochure by Milner, White & Partners (*c*.1937). 37 For the firm of Slocock of Knap Hill, *see* Street (1960), 378-9. For Ryder and Sons, *see* Key (2000), *passim*. 38 Minutes of the Proceedings of the Directors (16 and 19 August, 24 and 27 October 1938; 1 April, 31 May, and 17 November 1939; 27 March 1940).

As new burials declined in the older areas, the cemetery began to suffer from reduced maintenance and overgrowth of vegetation, and for this very reason attracted sympathetic attention from naturalists.[39] During the 1980s the more overgrown parts of the cemetery began to be managed for wildlife benefit in consultation with the London Wildlife Trust. With the establishment of the Friends of Kensal Green Advisory Committee (later the Advisory Council) at the end of the decade, plans for increased maintenance and a partial restoration of the landscape were set in motion. Guidelines were drawn up in 1988 for the treatment of the landscape, which emphasised the importance of overhauling the drainage system: the need for planting to improve security and reduce intrusion by vandals; the necessity for a more sensitive approach to those portions of the circular road encroached upon by graves so as to keep them visually distinct from surrounding areas; the use of plants for ground-cover to reduce maintenance; and the importance of a partial restoration of the central axis of the cemetery to a well-groomed condition, while allowing ecological planting in peripheral areas. The Friends of Kensal Green Cemetery instituted an 'Ivy League' to help cut back the encroachment of ivy on monuments. Work has begun, but there is vast amount of work still to do before improvements will be apparent. Many of the trees need to be replaced, not least to avoid the danger of falling boughs causing further damage to monuments. London's earliest great metropolitan cemetery not only has buildings that are recognised as of architectural and historic importance and many monuments that deserve to be listed: it possesses the remnants of a landscape of great interest, and one that really ought to be restored with expert care to set off the historic buildings and funerary architecture to the best advantage (**13.4**).

13.3 Photograph of a sector of the circular road in the 1990s, showing the insertion of recent graves (*Brent Elliott*).

13.4 Photograph looking east down Centre Avenue, 1990s (*Brent Elliott*).

39 Latham (1984), 53-67.

CHAPTER XIV

The Land Use History and Flora and Fauna of Kensal Green Cemetery

TIMOTHY H. FREED

The Landscape and Local History: (i) The Middle Ages to 1832; (ii) The Period after 1832; (iii) The Present Situation; ***The Habitats and Their Flora and Fauna; The Habitats:*** (i) Grassland: *Management; Wildflowers; Invertebrates; Grave-plots; Birds and Mammals;* (ii) Stonework: *Ferns, Mosses, Lichens, and Flowering Plants; Invertebrates*; (iii) Wooded Areas: *Trees and Shrubs; Butterflies; Birdlife; Fungi;* (iv) Formal Landscaped Areas: *Gardens and Flowerbeds; Lawns;* (v) The Canal-Side Reserve and Canal; (vi) Ivy: *Ivy Ecology; Ivy in the Historic Cemetery;* ***Conclusion***

> The valley on the north is laid down with grass, and the whole of the district appears to have undergone but little alteration, in respect to culture and division of the land, for several ages; although the distance from London is scarcely three miles, yet the traveller may imagine himself to be embosomed in the most sequestered part of the country, and nothing is heard to interrupt the course of his meditations, but the notes of the lark, the linnet, or the nightingale.

THOMAS FAULKNER (1777-1855):
History and Antiquities of Kensington, with Biographical Anecdotes of Royal and Distinguished Personages, and a Descriptive Catalogue of the Pictures in the Palace from a Survey taken by the late Benjamin West, P.R.A., by Command of His Majesty
(London: Printed by D. Jacques, Chelsea, for T. Egerton, 1820), 590.

The Landscape and Local History

(i) The Middle Ages to 1832

During the Middle Ages much of the land around Kensal Green was covered by the expansive Middlesex Forest. A view from the Thames would have revealed a discontinuous belt of deciduous woodland rising to Willesden Green in the north. The lower part of Kensington was founded on underlying deposits of River Terrace and Flood Plain gravel and sand. These were covered by River Brickearth in the middle of the borough, and in the north at Kensal Green, London Clay was exposed with its characteristic heavy, waterlogged soil.[1]

An important farm existed to the immediate south of the pre-cemetery plot. This was Notting Barnes Manor, owned by the de Vere family (who became Earls of Oxford) between the 11th and 15th centuries.[2] The manor-house stood just over half a mile (0.9 km) south of Kensal Green. The farm underwent various exchanges of ownership between the Crown, the Earls of Oxford, and the Marquis of Berkeley. By the end of the 15th century it amounted to '400 acres of land fit for cultivation, 5 acres of meadow and 140 acres of wood'.[3] In 1524, an account in the will of Robert Fenrother stated that it consisted of '40 acres of land, 140 acres of meadow, 200 acres of wood, 20 acres of moor, and 20 acres of furze and heath'.[4] The extensive common lands of Wormholtwood and Old Oak Common lay to the west of Notting Barnes on the far side of Counter's Creek[5] (the stream which originated on Honeypot Hill and defined the boundary between Hammersmith and Fulham on the west, and Kensington and Chelsea on the east). In 1590, Old Oak Common (then known as Old Holt Wood) comprised an estimated 200 acres of oak and hawthorn scrub.[6] Both commons were used for grazing cattle and pigs. Woodland also existed at Kensal New Town. The estate exchanged hands between various landlords including Henry White, The Crown, William Cecil Lord Burghley, and the Anderson family:[7] many were absentees and the manor was occupied by their various tenants.

The following centuries saw much woodland felled, and arable, meadow, and pasture lands replaced it. Wheat was grown extensively, especially on land to the west in Ealing. As material demands of the expanding capital-city increased, more hay was required for horses, and livestock for meat and dairy-production. On a visit to England in 1748, Per Kalm (1716-79), an eminent Swedish botanist and pupil of the great Carolus Linnaeus (1707-78), was struck by the intensity of dairy-cattle grazing and hay-production in the fields between Paddington and Willesden. From his observations he recorded intense application of manure on fields to increase yields of grass for hay and grazing.[8] In addition, fields were being sown with meadow foxtail grass (*Alopecurus pratensis*) and white clover (*Trifolium repens*) from imported Dutch seed. Great quantities of manure were carted out from the stables and privies of London to the surrounding 'zone of cattle pastures' to be applied to fields in September and October. It became possible to obtain three crops of hay from fields thus treated: one in May, a second in July, and a third in September.[9]

John Rocque's map (*c*.1745), *A New and Accurate Survey of the Cities of London and Westminster, The Borough of Southwark, with the country about ...*,[10] includes a number of significant landmarks around Kensal Green (**14.1**): the names 'Red House', 'Kensel Green', and 'Harrow Road' are clearly printed, and a farmhouse is shown in the region of what is now the entrance to the cemetery; Notting Barnes farm (unnamed on the map) occurs directly to the south of this. Rocque's field boundaries, however, though firm and definite, are regarded as unreliable by modern historians.

[1] Archer and Keech (1993), 3-4. [2] Gladstone (1924), 5-8. [3] Ibid., 9. [4] Faulkner (1820), 591. [5] Barton (1992), 44-7; Trench and Hillman (1993), 45-6. [6] Game *et al.* (1991), 6. [7] Lysons (1811), 502; Gladstone (1924), 11-20. [8] Bull (1975-6), 4. [9] Ibid., 4. [10] KCLSL (*c*.1745).

14.1 John Rocque's map of the London area, *c*.1745 (*RBKC*).

14.2 *Thomas Milne's Land Use Map of London & Environs in 1800;* extract from Plates I and IIII (*By courtesy of The London Topographical Society*).

During the High Farming period in the late 18th century, the agriculturalist, John Middleton, proposed that further enclosure of common fields would increase the economic prosperity of livestock farming and hay production. Old strip fields were amalgamated and enclosed into pastures.[11] About this time Kensington comprised *c*.860 acres of meadow and pasture, 460 acres of arable for corn, 230 acres of market-gardens, 260 acres cultivated for corn and garden crops, and 100 acres of nursery ground.[12]

Between 1795 and 1799, the cartographer, Thomas Milne, made detailed surveys of an area *c*.240 square miles surrounding London. *Thomas Milne's Land Use Map of London and Environs in 1800* was then the most accurate of its kind (**14.2**), even excelling the Ordnance Survey drawings made by William Hyett between 1799 and 1808.[13] The map showed 12 different types of land use, implementing a system of lettering and tinting for individual enclosed plots.

The Paddington Branch of the Grand Junction Canal, which was being built at this time, was omitted by Milne. Red House and the farmstead on the pre-cemetery site were indicated, but not named. The land which comprised the initial purchase was divided into four fields. To the west, across the borough boundary, lay the plot acquired for the

11 Game *et al.* (1991), 5-6. 12 Lysons (1811), 499. 13 Bull (1975-6), 2.

expansion of the cemetery in the 1850s. Two more fields further west became St Mary's Roman Catholic cemetery in 1858. Notting Barnes and Porto Bello farms lay to the south and south-east respectively. The hachuring[14] shows the pronounced sloping of the pre-cemetery site in a south-easterly direction, and a small 'm' in each of the fields destined to become cemeteries informs us that they were being used for pasture and/or meadow.

It may be helpful here to define the terms 'meadow' and 'pasture'. Traditionally, 'meadow' refers to grassland which is primarily managed for hay-production. It is usually closed to grazing stock during late spring and summer. After the hay is cut (between mid-June and early August depending on conditions), the 'aftermath' or 'fog' is grazed. 'Pasture' describes grassland which is used solely for grazing. This favours low-growing plants which tend to survive grazing. Sometimes there is alternation between the two regimes.[15]

Something of the pastoral nature of the landscape may be gleaned by studying the *genre* paintings and engravings of George Morland (1763-1804), the celebrated artist who spent much of his short life in and around Kensal Green. *Children Nutting* (1783) was one of his most famous pictures. Much of his subject-matter was inspired by the surrounding countryside and frequently portrayed Middlesex landscapes (for example, *Travellers Reposing* [1790], and *The Turnpike* [1796]).[16] During the 1780s he came to live in the Harrow Road at the house of his friend, the engraver William Ward (1766-1826), who mezzotinted many of his pictures. The latter's famous brother, James Ward (1769-1859), was subsequently elected to the Royal Academy; he is buried in the cemetery (15560/90/3]. Morland married James and William's sister, Anne (Nancy), in 1786, and Morland's sister Maria, married William in the same year.

George Morland was an industrious artist. It is recorded that he could make two paintings a day, and in his lifetime produced an estimated four thousand pictures. Unfortunately, he had a weakness for drink, which, combined with an extravagant life-style, led to his death, at the age of 42, in a sponging-house[17] in Eyre Street Hill, Coldbath Fields.[18] His close association with the then 300-year-old *Plough* in Kensal Green was such that it was known as 'The Morland Retreat'. There has been much debate over the exact location of this historic tavern since, at one time, two public houses, the *Old Plough* (now *The Paradise By Way of Kensal Green*) and the *Plough* (demolished in 1996) existed within yards of each other. The latter, which lay closest to the cemetery, was generally accepted as 'The Morland Retreat' until recently, when new research by a local historian identified, almost beyond doubt, the *Old Plough* in Kilburn Lane as the true site.[19] This is the tavern referred to by Faulkner in *History and Antiquities of Kensington*.[20] Many of Morland's original artworks are housed in the Print Room of the British Museum, and prints of his pictures still turn up in secondhand bookshops and elsewhere.

In July 1801 the Paddington Canal opened. Its course cut across fields in the northern part of the Notting Barnes farm. Where the canal curved northwards, it incised the fields of the pre-cemetery land. Several bridges were built to transport local traffic across the new barrier: Scrubs Bridge carried Scrubs Lane; another bridge carried the footpath from Kensal Green to Notting Barnes and Porto Bello farms; and a third smaller bridge was built roughly where the old canal-gate in the Eastern Division exists today (square [20]). This was to give the farmer of the pre-cemetery plot access to his 7.67 acres (3.1 ha) south of the watercourse.

To the west of Counter's Creek lay Red House farm. Three of its fields became cemetery land: House, Upper, and Lower Mitre Meadows. They covered 51.54 acres

[14] Lines used as shading in maps to indicate rising ground. [15] Hopkins (1990), 202-3. [16] Baily (1906), 67, 72. [17] A house kept by a bailiff or sheriff's officer as a place of confinement for debtors. [18] Baily (1906), 45. [19] Johnston (1998), 6-7. [20] Faulkner (1820), 589.

(20.8 ha). The site where the farmhouse stood roughly equates with the present position of houses on the north side of Alma Place. Of the farm's tenure it is recorded that Augustine Mead, who succeeded Mrs Blake, resided there until 1778, when Thomas Bramly and Bright Hemming leased the farm for the next 21 years.[21] Three names reappear in farm deeds after this time: Mr Greenfield, Mr George Fillingham, and Mr Thomas Harrison. It is evident that much sub-letting and changes of occupancy occurred. In 1800, Fillingham was the registered licensed victualler of the *Mitre Tavern*[22] (built beside the Scrubs Bridge in the south-west corner of the farm), and lived at Mitre Cottage prior to his death in *c.*1836.[23] In 1829 Harrison lived at the Red House, and owned the farmland in 1831.[24]

In 1815, Farmer Salter was the tenant at Notting Barnes farm. Several Salters farmed in the area at this time and one, whose herd grazed fields along the north side of Upper Mitre and House Meadows, had a dairy near what is now (2001) the main entrance to the cemetery.[25] In 1839 John Salter the elder and younger occupied these fields (see **14.4**). Starling's parish-map of 1822 shows a reduction from four to three fields for the pre-cemetery plot. It is likely that the fields were being manured at this time, and that the grassland was managed as pasture for dairy-cattle and sheep. In November 1831, Sir John Dean Paul, Bart., made his historic purchase of the farm on behalf of the General Cemetery Company, the full history of which is related in Chapters II to VI.

The initial purchase (**4.3**) included the 7.67 acres (3.1 ha) south of the canal (this was subsequently sold to the Western Gas Company). According to this plan, the total acreage for the site was *c.*54.08 acres (*c.*21.88 ha). In the Middlesex Land Register there are three indentures involving the purchase: the first between The Revd. Frederick William Gray of Castle Carey and Sir John Dean Paul of the Strand; the second between John Hawke of the City of Bath and Charles Broughton Bowman of Milk Street in the City of London; and the third between John Nicoll of Willesden and Sir John Dean Paul.[26] In the deeds, Mr Knight is cited as the occupant of the farm with its 'barns, stables, outhouses, edifices, buildings, yards, orchards and gardens … meadows or pasture'. The land here was commonly known as 'Our Lady Fields of Kilbourn Abbey or Wormleaze'. Woodland also existed on the site.[27] Thomas Darby, of Notting Barnes farm, still retained parcels (totalling 0.875 acres [0.35 ha]) in the south-east and south-west corners of the Kensal Green plot: these were subsequently purchased by the General Cemetery Company in 1833. The discovery of pig bones by grave-diggers in the former suggests that a piggery may have existed there.[28] The plan of 'The Ground of the General Cemetery Company' (1831)[29] indicates a small stream which had its origin on the north side of the Harrow Road, and flowed along the west side of the farmstead where it adjoined a cattle pond (see **4.3**). The farmstead stood on ground to the immediate west of the present Company offices. Remarkably, some of these 'lost' features appear to be indicated today by the presence or absence of certain flora: in spring there is a dearth of primrose (*Primula vulgaris*) and cow parsley (*Anthriscus sylvestris*) east of the culverted stream but a proliferation to the west. This could reflect previous land-use differences. Soapwort (*Saponaria officinalis*), an old garden favourite, grows on the site of the

[21] HFALHC (1778), DD/21/10. [22] HFALHC (1800), ND/3/7. [23] HFALHC (1836), DD/14/108; (1837*a*) DD/14/1972. [24] HFALHC (1829), PAH/1/158/1. [25] Gomershall (*c.*1916), 17. [26] LMA (1832), Middlesex Land Register (1832/3/169; 170; 171). The *first indenture* (169) was between Gray and Paul (24/25 November 1831), and involved a lease between Gray and Nicoll, and Sir John Dean Paul. It mentions £4,500 paid to Gray by Paul and then a further £3,400, and two sums of £500 on 5 March 1829. The *second indenture* (170) was between Hawke and Bowman (25 November 1831), and involved Hawke, Gray, Nicoll, Paul, and Bowman (of Milk Street, City of London), a Trustee named and appointed on behalf of Paul (lease of one year between Gray and Nicoll, and Paul). The *third indenture* (171) was between Nicoll and Paul (9/10 December 1831), signed and dated 4 April 1832, so the land was not fully legally acquired until the last date. Bowman is identified as a solicitor on the indentures, and Edward Foss, solicitor, of 36 Essex Street, Strand, was also a witness of Paul's signatures. [27] Denny (1993), 119. [28] S. Meah pers. comm. [29] GCCA (*c.*1831).

farmhouse garden (squares **22** and **23**]. The lather produced by boiling its roots and leaves was used for washing wool. Interestingly soapwort does not grow anywhere else in the cemetery.

(ii) The Period after 1832

Immediately after the cemetery opened, a prodigious planting programme was undertaken, the history and details of which are described above. It is understood that some farming continued: sheep were retained to keep the extensive lawns cropped and potatoes were cultivated.[30] No evidence exists proving that any trees which may have been on the site before the purchase are still extant; however the status of the black-poplar (*Populus nigra*) in square [**78**] is debatable.[31] Farmer Salter's dairy-herd grazed a 4.86-acre (1.96-ha) field (now the entrance driveway to St Mary's Roman Catholic cemetery), situated to the west of the Red House.[32] This land was rented from the Revd. Edward Grinfield of Notting Hill. A little further up Harrow Road was Kensal Lodge where the novelist Harrison Ainsworth (1805-82) came to live with Mrs Touchett and Miss Buckley in 1835.[33] Later he moved to nearby Kensal Manor House, staying there between 1841 and 1853. Dickens, Thackeray, and other literary greats were frequent guests, and it is recorded that 'it was no uncommon thing for the guests at the Manor House to be serenaded by nightingales on their way back to town'.[34] Sadly, one would have to travel to sites as far away as Bookham Common or Hainault Forest to hear the nightingale (*Luscinia megarhynchos*) sing today.

Within a decade of the cemetery's Consecration, changes took place which irreversibly altered the genius of old Kensal Green. Two railway-lines were constructed within a stone's throw of the boundary: the London and Birmingham by Stephenson in 1837; and the Great Western by Brunel in 1838. The Birmingham, Bristol, and Thames Junction Line was built to the west on the far side of Red House farm in 1839, joining the two other rail-lines with the Thames Basin.

The fields of Red House farm (also known as the Fillingham estate) appear to have been dug for brickearth between 1835-50, this being far more lucrative than grazing livestock. Traditionally, brickearth was dug from River Brickearth which overlay the Thames River Terrace gravels and sands to the south. Bricks were also manufactured from clay and clay mixtures[35] which would have been the case on the Fillingham estate. An undated plan of 'Red House Farm' (*c*.1835-38) shows brickearth plots numbered 4-27 with a schedule of acreages (**14.3**).[36]

Mr Harrison lived at the *Mitre Tavern* with the adjoining Mitre Meadow in 1837, and his subtenant was Mr Rieve.[37] A counterpart lease of 25 May 1839 involving the use of House and Upper Mitre Meadows by Richard Fisher, Revd. Edward William Grinfield, and John Salter, the elder and younger, gives the rent as £154 per annum, plus £500 for every acre dug for brickearth and £40 per annum for every acre converted into arable or garden ground.[38] A plan in the lease shows the field where the Salter's dairy-herd grazed. Mr Isaac Riviere (Harrison's subtenant 'Rieve'?) was the occupant of Lower Mitre Meadow (**14.4**). Fillingham, who lived at Mitre Cottage, died in late 1836 or early 1837.[39]

The fact that much, if not all, of this land was dug for brickmaking partly explains why relict flora in the cemetery proliferates east of the borough boundary, but is scarce or absent in the west. In one sense the former constitutes unimproved grassland, and the latter semi-improved. Boundary stones marking the course of the culverted Counter's Creek still stand between Oxford and Cambridge Avenues.

30 B. Elliott pers. comm. 31 J. Latham pers. comm. 32 Gomershall (*c*.1916), 17. 33 Ibid., 13. 34 Ibid. 35 Cawthorne (1994), 31-5. 36 HFALHC (*c*.1835), DD/21/11. 37 HFALHC (1837*b*), DD/15/2, 61. 38 HFALHC (1839), DD/21/12/1. 39 HFALHC (1836), DD/14/108.

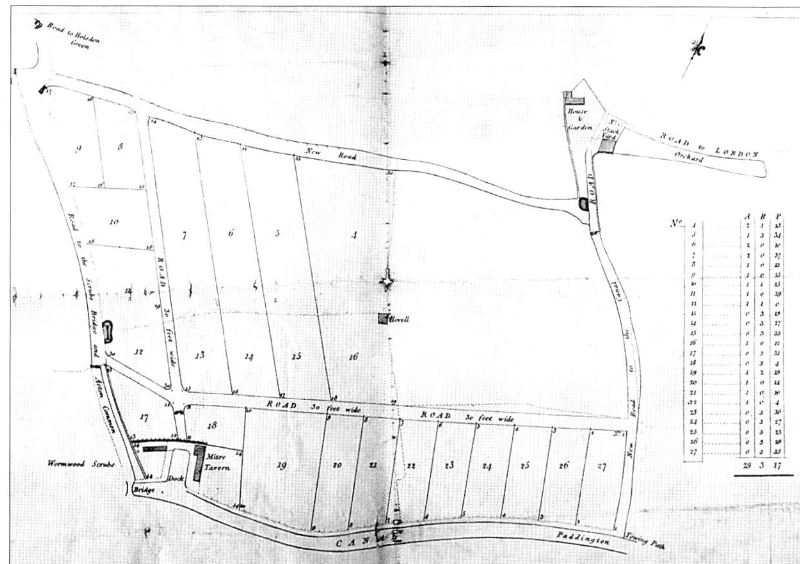

14.3 Plan of 'Red House Farm' showing brickearth plots numbered 4-27 with schedule of acreages. No date given; *c.*1835 (*HFALHC*).

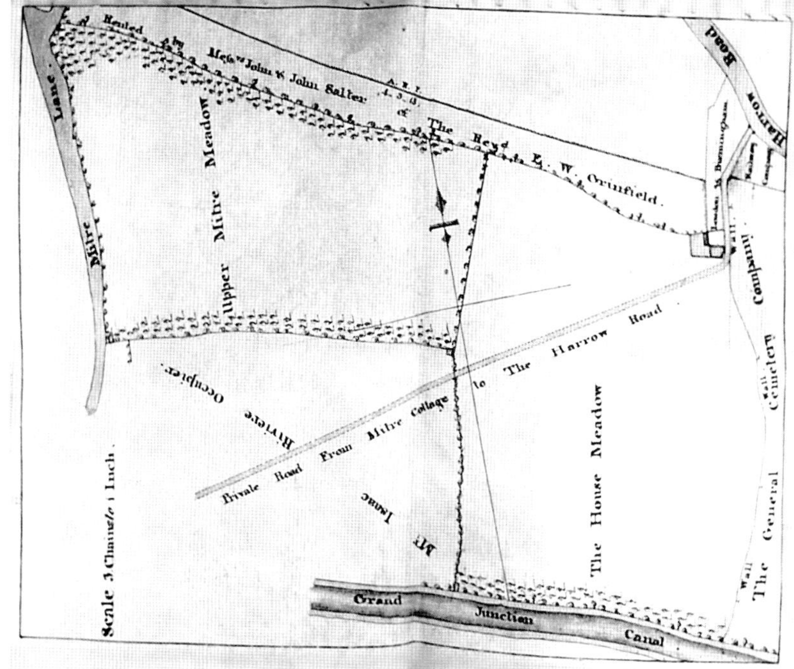

14.4 Plan accompanying counterpart lease for House Meadow and Upper Mitre Meadow of Red House Farm, 1839 (*HFALHC*).

To the south of the canal, the wealthy St Quintin family had acquired the Notting Barnes estate. In the 1844 Tithe Award, when Edward Salter was the farmer, its meadow, pasture, and arable land covered 188.43 acres (76.2 ha).[40] Footpaths across the farmland had always been a favourite walking-place for Londoners. 'An Old Inhabitant', reminiscing in 1882 of life in the area 38 years earlier, wrote:

> ... no wonder that this pleasant lane was the favourite walk not only of the inhabitants of Notting Hill but also of many from the great city.
>
> From west to north, from north to east scarcely a house was to be seen. Cornfields and meadow land on every side, the quiet only broken by the occasional passing of a train on the Great Western Railway at Kensal Green. It seems almost impossible to realise the fact, but it is a fact that during this 38 years the thousands of houses which are now to be seen from Ealing to Hampstead, Hampstead to Edgeware Road have been built.[41]

In 1845 the Western Gas Company constructed gasholders on land purchased from the Talbot estate south of the canal. Some years later, more gasholders were built on the adjacent 7.67-acre (3.1-ha) plot owned by the General Cemetery Company which had never been used for burial. In the early 1850s fields were purchased to the west of the

40 KCLSL (1844), a/c 912. 41 'An Old Inhabitant' (1882), 19.

cemetery increasing it by 22.54 acres (9.12 ha). The additional land comprised the House Meadow and a portion of the Upper and Lower Mitre Meadows. This now gave an overall acreage of *c.*71.9 acres (*c.*29.1 ha); (the erroneous addition of this figure to the 7.67 acres [3.1 ha] from the south, produces an often quoted but fallacious larger acreage for the cemetery (*See also* Appendices 2 and 3).

House- and road-building continued apace, and the northwards extension of Ladbroke Grove between Notting Barnes and Porto Bello farms in the 1850s gave direct access to Kensal Green from the south. Today, the junction of Chesterton Road and St Quintin Avenue marks the site of the old Notting Barnes manor house.[42] Porto Bello farm, which had been purchased by Charles Henry Talbot in 1755, was finally bought by the Little Sisters of the Poor in 1864. The urbanisation of North Kensington was truly underway by the 1880s, although large open spaces still remained around Wormwood Scrubs and Old Oak Common as can be seen from Ordnance Survey maps of 1894.[43]

The main events which influenced and shaped the cemetery landscape through the 19th and 20th centuries have been described in preceding chapters and it is not necessary to elaborate on them here. However, some points of ecological significance should be mentioned: pollution from gasholders near the Eastern Division has damaged flora and fauna as well as memorials. Smoke and sulphur-dioxide emissions, which peaked in the latter half of the 19th century, adversely affected vegetation causing the disappearance of certain lichens, stunted tree-growth, deciduation and death of many evergreens, and aberrations in leaf colouration. Since the passage of the Clean Air Act[44] of 1956, smoke and sulphur-dioxide emissions from domestic fires and small factories considerably decreased. Conversely, acid-rain pollution has increased dramatically: sulphur-dioxide from power-stations and the huge rise in nitrogen oxides from motor-vehicles have resulted in increased ozone which is formed in hot sunny weather.[45] Gilbert gives further information about the effects of air-pollution and exhaust-emissions on flora and fauna.[46]

During the 1939-45 war, the concentration of transport-routes, industry, and high-density housing made Kensal Green a prime target for enemy attack (as outlined in Chapter VI). Several bombs fell in the grasslands leaving areas devoid of wildflowers. The relaxation of ground maintenance led to a fairly rapid increase in scrub and secondary woodland around the borders. Aerial photographs taken between 1938 and 1992[47] show the development of woody habitats, and, by the 1980s, features such as the old or north terrace colonnade became obscured. Mature trees in the borders and Circle produced a mass of self-seeded saplings and suckers, and a dense pole-stage succeeded these, eliminating most of the grassland flora in these areas. Ivy and bramble thrived in the absence of control. The Copse [squares **134**, **147**, and **148**] became a veritable oasis for birds, and foxes (*Vulpes vulpes*) reared their cubs in the Circle. The development of secondary woodland also provided windbreak and shelter. The General Cemetery Company sought to redress the loss of potential burial-space caused by development of woodland. In the 1980s operations commenced which would remove virtually all scrub and secondary woodland by the end of the century.

Limited maintenance kept the grasslands open and free from encroachment of scrub during a period when many other cemeteries became totally neglected. Although much of the grassland has not been improved like neighbouring green spaces, it has sustained considerable disturbance due to the excavation of *c.*65,000 or so grave-plots. Each grave can receive up to four burials and an estimated 250,000 burials have taken place in the cemetery (an additional *c.*3000+ plots occur in the catacombs).[48] Each year, *c.*350 new

42 Denny (1993), 94. 43 Godfrey (1984 *a*, *b*). 44 4 & 5 Eliz. II, c. 52. 45 Ashmore (1987), 1-3. 46 Gilbert (1991), 32-40, 147-50. 47 Aerial photographs for the following years were reviewed in the Royal Borough of Kensington and Chelsea Central Library (1938; 1944; 1946 [OS]; 1971; 1985 [OS]); and in Hammersmith and Fulham Archives and Local History Centre (1980; 1992). 48 D. Burkett pers. comm.

graves are dug and a further *c.*150 interments take place in existing plots. The Western Lawns will eventually be used for burial and new spaces are being created by 'in-fill' and 'banking-up'. The former uses footpaths, verges, and other areas of virgin ground to squeeze in additional grave-plots; the latter involves laying soil over existing but disused grave-plots to provide new plots above the old ones. Neither method enhances the ecology nor the original landscaping of the cemetery (in fact they achieve quite the reverse). However, the considerable pressure exerted by the acute shortage of burial-space in London has deemed such practices legitimate.

(iii) The Present Situation

Today, the flora of Kensal Green cemetery comprises introduced exotic species and mixtures of planted and naturally occurring native types. The latter include species which existed here before the cemetery's formation. The landscape and vegetation have been powerfully influenced and controlled by man: regular maintenance has arrested the development of scrub and woodland over much of the site, allowing the grasslands to remain open. This condition is typical of many cemetery landscapes.[49]

A brief summary of the present layout and topography is as follows: the cemetery is situated on London Clay rising to a maximum *c.*44 m (144.3 ft) on the north boundary (a little east of the west gate), and gradually declining to *c.*29.9 m (98 ft) at the canal and Eastern Division. All but a few local areas have a southerly to south-easterly aspect. An elevated area running south of the Anglican chapel between Cambridge and Terrace Avenues declines relatively steeply on its east, south, and west sides. An expansive brick wall *c.*4-4.5 m high separates the cemetery from Harrow Road to the north, and from Ladbroke Grove to the east. The west boundary lies adjacent to St Mary's Roman Catholic cemetery from which it is separated by shrubberies and low wall. The south side is bounded by railings and a section of brick wall. A narrow strip of land entrusted to the care of the London Wildlife Trust abuts this and the Grand Union Canal with its far-side towpath. Much of the cemetery's grassland is open and covered by burial-plots, except for the Western Lawns and other formal lawns and flowerbeds. Grassy meadow-pathways transect the grasslands. Tree-lined avenues occur in parts with greater frequency in the south-western section. Mature trees also occur around the borders and in the Circle. Small areas of secondary woodland still exist in one or two places along the borders and in the Copse. A tarmacadamed road links the main entrance gateway and the west gate to the centrally located Anglican chapel and to the West London crematorium and garden of remembrance in the west. Several tracks adjoin this road leading to other parts including the Dissenters' chapel in the south-east corner. At present most new graves are being dug in the north-western section and Eastern Division. 'In-fill' graves have been dug along some meadow-pathways and verges. 'Banking-up' has taken place in part of the Eastern Division, the south-west corner, and is currently proceeding along the south border eastwards from square [**82**].

The Habitats and Their Flora and Fauna

The view from the Anglican chapel in Springtime, with its fine row of ancient hollies (*Ilex aquifolium*) in front of the terrace, fills one with a sense of serenity and well-being: before lies the Circle with its dark evergreen oaks (*Quercus ilex*). The horse-chestnuts (*Aesculus hippocastanum*) along Junction Avenue, with their bright green leaves newly burst, sweep away to the north and south across meadow grassland covered with primroses and an apparently endless array of tombs: pedestals, crosses, angels, and obelisks, some

49 Gilbert (1989), *preface*.

whitish, some dark. Southwards and over the canal, lies Kensington and beyond. A gentle breeze, the elevated view, and above all, the absence of traffic and people tempt one to forget for a moment that this is in metropolitan London.

The diversity of wildlife in the cemetery is remarkable. Within the last twenty years, surveys of plants, moths and butterflies, amphibians, reptiles, birds, and mammals have been carried out. Their results are exceptional for a site only 5.25 miles (8.45 km) west of St Paul's Cathedral, and which partly occurs within the 'Inner London' zone defined by the London Natural History Society. Several nationally and locally rare species have been recorded. An extensive survey of the flora carried out by the botanist John Latham between 1981 and 1989 identified 349 flowering and 146 non-flowering species of plants in Kensal Green cemetery.[50] In 1981, 69 moth species were recorded during a three-month survey.[51] The butterfly population was regularly surveyed between 1989 and 1997; 23 species were noted, of which 19 bred at the site.[52] Although no reptiles or amphibians were found in the cemetery during a survey of 1995,[53] at least three species have been recorded nearby.[54] Bird surveys carried out between 1984-6[55] identified 79 species in the cemetery and environs, with 33 species breeding; by 1988, an amazing 106 species had been seen.[56] However, following large-scale clearances, recent annual bird-surveys by Graham Giddens have recorded a huge decline in numbers, species, and breeding pairs.[57] The survey of 2000 found 29 species of which only 17 were definitely breeding.[58] A survey of mammals recorded seven species in 1997,[59] and at least another three have been seen in the recent past. There are numerous casual records of molluscs, spiders, damselflies, dragonflies, grasshoppers, bush-crickets, bugs, beetles, flies, hoverflies, ants, wasps, and bees. Additional flora and fauna are recorded each year.

The rich diversity of wildlife is due to five main factors: the cemetery's large size (approximately 71.9 acres [29.1 ha]); its proximity to three 'green corridors' – the Grand Union Canal and towpath, the Great Western Railway and London & North Western Railway (with their cuttings and sidings); its southerly aspect; the large proportion of archaic, unimproved grassland which has survived; and its diversity of habitats.

The Habitats

The cemetery's habitats may be broadly divided into the following:
(i) unimproved and improved neutral grassland;
(ii) stonework, including memorials, walls, and buildings;
(iii) wooded areas, including mature evergreen and deciduous trees planted singly or in avenues, rows, and groupings; also, a few remaining areas of secondary woodland with undergrowth situated around the borders;
(iv) formal landscaped lawns with flower-beds and shrubberies;
(v) canal-side reserve occupying a narrow strip of land between the southern boundary and the Grand Union Canal;
(vi) ivy (*Hedera helix*), which occurs in most habitats (but treated separately here due to its overall significance in the context of the historic cemetery).

(i) Grassland

Neutral grassland on London Clay covers *c.*70 per cent of the total cemetery area. It includes old, unimproved, species-rich grassland which was damp pasture in 1831 (land east of the borough boundary), semi-improved grassland purchased in the 1850s (land

[50] Latham (1984), 53-67; (1989), 15-24. [51] Plant (1983), 122. [52] Freed (1992), 88; (1997). [53] LARG (1996), 12-3. [54] Langton (1991), 97-123. [55] Cross and Holloway (1986), 1-4. [56] NWLP (1988), 7. [57] Giddens (1996-2000). [58] Giddens (2000), 20-1. [59] Aybes *et al.* (1997), 3.

14.5 View across species-rich grassland towards the 'Copse' from square [108] (*THF*).

west of the boundary), semi-improved grassland purchased in the 1850s, now converted to lawn (Western Lawns) or banked-up with spoil from railway excavations (north-western section). Other areas have been converted to small formal lawns in and around the garden of remembrance and at the entrances.

Anthills of the yellow meadow ant (*Lasius flavus*) occur in all but the north-western section, the Western Lawns, formal lawns, banked-up areas, and heavily shaded grassland. They are indicators of unimproved pasture, and are larger and more numerous in the oldest species-rich grassland. Anthills are nearly always built on or beside gravestones and several may occur together, merging into one large sprawling nest. Their pH is slightly higher than that of the surrounding soil, and they provide substrate for less competitive flora, which would otherwise be shaded out by the sward. A recent pH analysis from plots all over the cemetery gave a mean average pH of 5.35.[60] The lowest value, 4.5, was recorded in the south, where several relict species grow (e.g. squares [**96**] and [108]) (**14.5**). The highest value, 6.5, came from the north-western section. Weathering of calcareous monuments locally increases pH. Elevated sites along the north side are drier than southern sides which were once prone to severe flooding.[61] Recent improvements to the drainage system have rectified this.

Many factors contribute to the present distribution and diversity of wildflowers. The important distinction between old pasture and 'improved' grassland has already been noted. Verges and meadow-pathways are generally more species-rich than inner areas. The effects of shading from trees, dampness and humidity, shelter from prevailing south-westerly winds, pollution from gasholders near the Eastern Division, and the grassland management regime, have all been influential.

Management

Prior to the advent of the strimmer in 1980,[62] the grasslands were hand-scythed, and it took between two to three months to cut the entire site.[63] Problematic areas were burnt

60 Freed (1997), II. 61 J. Burthom pers. comm. 62 Gilbert (1991), 228. 63 D. Burkett pers. comm.

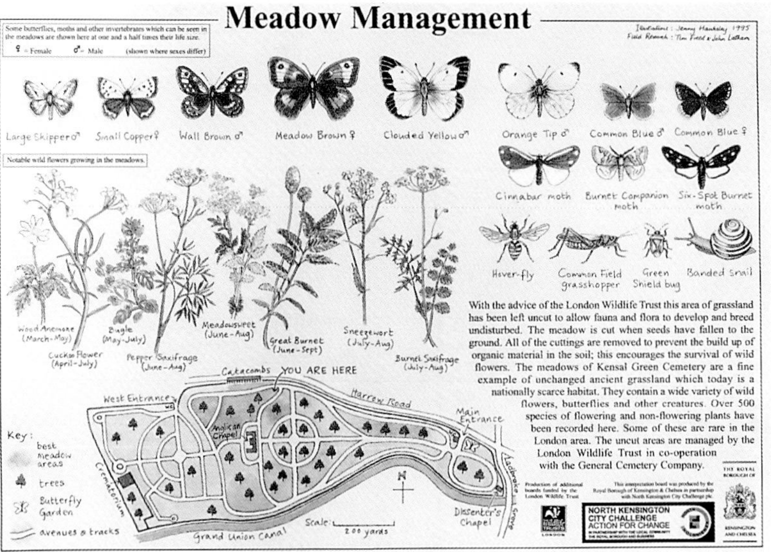

14.6 'Meadow Management' interpretation-board illustrated by Jenny Hawksley. Funded by North Kensington City Challenge plc in association with RBK&C (*RBKC*).

or sprayed with herbicides. Nowadays grass-cutting is carried out by a team of groundstaff using Husquarna 244 RX motorised strimmers. The main grasslands are cut between two and four times per year with the cuttings left *in situ*. New burial-sites and formal lawns receive many more cuts. The frequency and timing of cutting is carried out on an *ad hoc* basis between May and October. Climate influences sward-growth, as well as the seasonal appearance of flowers and creatures. A combination of strimming, climate, and life-cycles is critical in determining what is likely or unlikely to be seen in a particular part of the cemetery.

In recent years, the General Cemetery Company has been advised on changes to the standard strimming regime for specific areas of wildlife interest.[64] This has increased certain wildflowers, butterflies (especially skippers and common blues [*Polyommatus icarus*]), and other organisms which benefit from a taller sward and less disturbance. A recent example was the appearance of a bee orchid (*Ophrys apifera*) along the edge of an uncut area (square [96])in June 1998. A further specimen was found a year later in the Eastern Division. At selected sites, cuttings have been raked off by volunteers to encourage less competitive flora and reduce fertility. The Company presently allows two areas to grow tall until the late autumn, and an interpretation-board positioned beside one of these explains the purpose of leaving the section uncut (**14.6**). It has been found that mowing the verges around such areas gives an impression of deliberate maintenance.[65]

The change-over to strimming in the 1980s led to increased frequency of cutting. This is thought to have caused subtle alterations to the abundance of sensitive species such as sneezewort (*Achillea ptarmica*), which has declined considerably since Latham's surveys began in 1981. Other locally rare plants like hairy St John's-wort (*Hypericum hirsutum*), common valerian (*Valeriana officinalis*), and rough hawkbit (*Leontodon hispidus*) are now considered extinct.[66] In contrast, a beneficial development is the reduction of herbicide use in recent years. The same cannot be said for the neighbouring St Mary's Roman Catholic cemetery where financial and staff constraints led to intense herbicide spraying in 1983-4; this policy has continued ever since.[67] The 29-acre (11.7-ha) site once boasted relict species, but today the grassland has been reduced to a wilderness of coarse,

[64] Freed (1992), 60-7; (1997), II. [65] Brooks *et al.* (1989), 103. [66] J. Latham pers. comm. [67] J. Guerin pers. comm.

straw-coloured tussocks in all but one small area. Amazingly, some butterflies still persist here, feeding on the few wildflowers which have survived. This cemetery receives one cut in spring followed by heavy applications of Altodox, Weedazol, and Diuron. It is hard to imagine that mowings from here were sold as hay a little over a century ago.[68]

14.7 Wood anemones (*Anemone nemorosa*) and primroses (*Primula vulgaris*) (*THF*).

Wildflowers

An outstanding feature of Kensal Green cemetery is the persistence of relict plant communities in old grassland. Some of these are extremely rare, or rare in central London. The London Ecology Unit (now Greater London Authority) recently stated 'It is astonishing to find grassland of this quality so near the heart of London'.[69] Great burnet (*Sanguisorba officinalis*) flourishes in several sites, and burnet saxifrage (*Pimpinella saxifraga*), pepper saxifrage (*Silaum silaus*), wild basil (*Clinopodium vulgare*), and sneezewort all occur more locally. Vegetative parts of common bistort (*Persicaria bistorta*) develop annually but fail to produce flowers due to heavy shading. Other species characteristic of unimproved, damp pasture include cuckooflower (*Cardamine pratensis*), meadowsweet (*Filipendula ulmaria*), meadow crane's-bill (*Geranium pratense*), zigzag clover (*Trifolium medium*), pignut (*Conopodium majus*), common fleabane (*Pulicaria dysenterica*), hoary ragwort (*Senecio erucifolius*), and grey sedge (*Carex divulsa*).

Extensive patches of wood anemone (*Anemone nemorosa*), primrose, and bluebell (*Hyacinthoides non-scripta*), which flower at Eastertide in open grassland, indicate that oak woodland and hedgerow once existed here (**14.7**). The latter two species were no doubt also introduced as grave-plantings in the past, but the former is almost certainly entirely relict. Primroses have hybridised with polyanthi from grave-plantings, producing large clumps of variously tinted flowers. The distribution of wood anemone follows the contour of the southern, western, and north-western boundaries of the 1831 grassland but is totally absent from the 1850s section.[70] The same is true of great burnet which grows in a few locations in more central areas, and along the course of the culverted Counter's Creek. Primrose is very sparse in the 1850s part, but abundant east of the borough boundary. Other woodland and hedgebank flora include bugle (*Ajuga reptans*), common dog-violet (*Viola riviniana*), and early dog-violet (*V. reichenbachiana*). Two patches of sweet violet (*V. odorata*) are almost certainly long-established introductions.

Amongst the commoner grasses are red fescue (*Festuca rubra*), rough meadow-grass (*Poa trivialis*), smooth meadow-grass (*P. pratensis*), cock's-foot (*Dactylis glomerata*), false oat-grass (*Arrhenatherum elatius*), Yorkshire-fog (*Holcus lanatus*), and meadow foxtail. Tall fescue (*F. arundinacea*) forms extensive swards in a few sites. Some of the common and widespread wildflowers include: meadow buttercup (*Ranunculus acris*), common sorrel (*Rumex acetosa*), tufted vetch (*Vicia cracca*), common vetch (*V. sativa*), meadow vetchling (*Lathyrus pratensis*), great willowherb (*Epilobium hirsutum*), rosebay willowherb (*Chamerion angustifolium*), cow parsley, hogweed (*Heracleum sphondylium*), field bindweed (*Convolvulus arvensis*), large bindweed (*Calystegia silvatica*), ribwort plantain (*Plantago lanceolata*), common toadflax (*Linaria vulgaris*), spear thistle (*Cirsium vulgare*), creeping thistle (*C. arvense*), common knapweed

[68] Ibid. [69] Archer and Keech (1993), 37. [70] Freed (1997), II.

(*Centaurea nigra*), yarrow (*Achillea millefolium*), oxeye daisy (*Leucanthemum vulgare*), hoary ragwort, and Oxford ragwort (*Senecio squalidus*).

Wildflowers such as creeping buttercup (*Ranunculus repens*), creeping cinquefoil (*Potentilla reptans*), common bird's-foot-trefoil (*Lotus corniculatus*), white clover, and red clover (*Trifolium pratense*) are especially abundant along meadow-pathways and verges. Red bartsia (*Odontites vernus*), which is rare in inner London, grows uncommonly along some southern meadow-pathways. These tracks also form vital microhabitats for many insects, and they should not be paved or gravelled.

14.8 Common blues (*Polyommatus icarus*) pairing on great burnet (*Sanguisorba officinalis*) (*THF*).

14.9 Meadow brown (*Maniola jurtina*) feeding on sneezewort (*Achillea ptarmica*) (*THF*).

14.10 Long-tailed blue (*Lampides boeticus*); female on broad-leaved everlasting-pea (*Lathyrus latifolius*) in Kensal Green cemetery, August 1990 (*THF*).

Invertebrates

Butterflies breeding in the grassland include the small skipper (*Thymelicus sylvestris*), Essex skipper (*T. lineola*), large skipper (*Ochlodes venata*), small copper (*Lycaena phlaeas*), common blue (**14.8**), meadow brown (*Maniola jurtina*) (**14.9**), and gatekeeper (*Pyronia tithonus*). The last was first sighted in July 1994 near the canal reserve, by which it probably arrived in the cemetery. This butterfly has since increased and spread not only in the cemetery but to other parts of central London. The reverse is true of the wall brown (*Lasiommata megera*) which was abundant until the early 1990s but thereafter declined rapidly until it was last sighted here in May 1995. The deterioration was synchronised in colonies across the south of England.

Over one hundred years ago a lepidopterist named Godwin collected at Old Oak Common just under a mile (*c*.1.5 km) to the south-west of the cemetery.[71] Amongst the butterflies he recorded were the silver-spotted skipper (*Thymelicus acteon*), grizzled skipper (*Pyrgus malvae*), green hairstreak (*Callophyrs rubi*) (one), and chalkhill blue (*Lysandra coridon*) (one). None of these breeds in Middlesex today, although two green hairstreak colonies persisted in North Ealing until the late 1980s,[72] and all except the chalkhill blue have declined nationally in recent years. Godwin may well have been inspired in his pastime by the beautifully illustrated entomological books of Henry Noel Humphreys (1810-79), who is buried in the cemetery [17708/135/2]. One of the finest was *British Butterflies and their Transformations* (1841) which he co-wrote with J. O. Westwood (1805-93).[73]

The small white (*Pieris rapae*), green-veined white (*P. napi*) and orange-tip (*Anthocharis cardamines*) visit flowers in the grassland. Their females lay eggs on cruciferous plants such as charlock (*Sinapis arvensis*), hoary cress (*Cardaria draba*), hedge mustard (*Sisymbrium officinale*), and garlic mustard (*Alliaria petiolata*), growing in the open and within the woody borders. The brimstone (*Gonepteryx rhamni*) is occasionally seen in May though it cannot breed here due to the absence of its hostplant, buckthorn (Rhamnaceae).

Towards the end of the stiflingly hot summer of 1990, the long-tailed blue (*Lampides boeticus*), an extremely rare migrant from southern Europe (**14.10**), made a surprise appearance in the cemetery.[74] Up until 1987, only 16 specimens had been recorded in the London area since 1893.[75] On 22 August a colony of about 11 individuals was discovered flying around broad-leaved everlasting-pea (*Lathyrus latifolius*) in grassland west of the north terrace or old catacomb colonnade. Unfortunately, the area was strimmed a few days later, and breeding was impossible. Other long-tailed blues were observed in south-east England in the latter part of August;[76] an estimated 25 were recorded during the initial influx. At Gillespie Park, Islington, they bred on bladder senna (*Colutea arborescens*).[77] Other migrants include clouded yellow (*Colias croceus*), large white

[71] Cockerell (1891), 30-3. [72] Plant (1987), 74. [73] Humphreys and Westwood (1841). Humphreys (1858); (1859). [74] Freed (1992), 47-50. [75] Plant (1987), 84. [76] Chalmers-Hunt and Skinner (1992), 211-2. [77] Wurzell (1990), 254-6.

(*Pieris brassicae*), small white, red admiral (*Vanessa atalanta*), and painted lady (*Cynthia cardui*) (**14.11**).

The day-flying six-spot burnet (*Zygaena filipendulae*), narrow-bordered five-spot burnet (*Z. lonicerae*), and burnet companion (*Euclidia glyphica*) moths are common. From late June to the end of July, the red and green burnet moths can be seen flying lazily from flower to flower; common knapweed and tufted vetch are favoured. Six-spot burnet larvae feed on common bird's-foot-trefoil, and narrow-bordered five-spot burnet on red clover and meadow vetchling. The larvae crawl high up grass stalks in late May, prior to forming their distinctive cocoons. The equally attractive cinnabar moth (*Tyria jacobaeae*), also seen in daytime, displays scarlet and dark-green wing colourings. In July and August its black-and-yellow larvae feed on ragworts (*Senecio* spp.), often in the company of meadow browns and red soldier beetles (*Rhagonycha fulva*).

A three-month moth-trapping survey between July and September 1981 recorded 69 kinds of macromoths, including local and uncommon species in London such as the chevron (*Eulithis testata*), privet hawk-moth (*Sphinx ligustri*), and dusky-lemon sallow (*Xanthia gilvago*).[78] Two day-flying moths of damp meadowland, the grass rivulet (*Perizoma albulata*) and chimney sweeper (*Odezia atrata*), both very local in London, once flew here. Shaded broad-bar (*Scotopteryx chenopodiata*) is still present and may be found where vetches and clover are abundant. An interesting recent discovery was a full-grown larva and adult specimen of the emperor moth (*Pavonia pavonia*) in 2000.[79] The larva was found in an uncut grassland plot (square [**96**]) and the adult female was recovered from the canal-towpath near Sainsburys. A recent report for Brompton cemetery recorded 201 species of moths.[80] A similar survey in Kensal Green cemetery is likely to produce equally interesting results.

During the summer several kinds of Odonata visit the grassands to feed, bask, and take up territories. The delicate blue-tailed damselfly (*Ischnura elegans*) is easily overlooked, but large and noisy dragonflies such as southern hawker (*Aeshna cyanea*) and migrant hawker (*A. mixta*) are highly apparent as they chase butterflies and other prey, or patrol up and down the North Avenue on late Summer afternoons.

Grasshoppers are abundant, and often bask on gravestones. Three species have been found: common field (*Chorthippus rufus*), meadow (*C. parallelus*), and common green (*Omocestus viridulus*). Bush-crickets are more wary, but may be located with patience. They include: speckled (*Leptophyes punctatissima*), oak (*Meconema thalassinum*), Roesel's (*Metrioptera brachyptera*), and dark (*Pholidoptera griseoaptera*) bush-crickets.

[78] Plant (1983), 122. [79] M. Joseph pers. comm. [80] Freed (2000), 1-39.

The long-winged conehead (*Cononcephalus discolor*) occurs in the Scrubs grassland across the canal and is probably also present in the cemetery.[81]

The cemetery is an excellent place for spiders. *Dysdera crocata*, *Xysticus cristatus*, *Euophrys frontalis*, *Pardosa pullata*, *Pisaura mirabilis*, *Araneus diadematus*, and *Linyphia triangularis* are common. There is opportunity for a detailed survey to be undertaken. A report on spiders and beetles in Brompton cemetery (1994-5) recorded 53 and 43 species respectively, including two new spider records for London, and other rare and Nationally Notable Species.[82] At Scrubs Wood, 24 kinds of spiders and 54 of beetles and weevils were found in 1984.[83]

14.11 *Painted Lady, Skippers, Browns and Burnet moths* – watercolour by Timothy Freed showing butterflies benefiting from areas of uncut grassland. 20 x 14 cm (*By courtesy of The Natural History Museum, London*).

Grave-plots

The grave-plot is an interesting microhabitat, often the source of naturalised cultivars, aliens, and adventives which are characteristic of many old cemeteries' flora. Shrubs like evergreen spindle (*Euonymus japonicus*), spotted-laurel (*Aucuba japonica*), and privet (*Ligustrum* spp.) were popular grave-plantings in Victorian times and are widespread.[84] Two-flowered everlasting-pea (*Lathyrus grandiflorus*) occurs in one location, whilst broad-leaved everlasting-pea is common in the north. Another type of grave-plot comprises loose marble or granite chippings strewn across a solid stone base and enclosed by kerbstones. This creates a habitat for xerophytic plants such as house leek (*Sempervivum tectorum*), Caucasian-stonecrop (*Sedum spurium*), reflexed stonecrop (*S. rupestre*), biting stonecrop (*S. acre*), white stonecrop (*S. album*) and silver ragwort (*Senecio cineraria*). Where bases have cracked, plants like common bird's-foot-trefoil may grow. Popular grave-plantings include thrift (*Armeria maritima*), snow in summer (*Cerastium tomentosum*), oxalis (*Oxalis* spp.), violets and pansies (*Viola* spp.), pinks (*Dianthus* spp.), forget-me-nots (*Myosotis* spp.), bellflowers (*Campanula* spp.), wallflowers (*Erysimum* spp.), polyanthi (*Primula* spp.), lavenders (*Lavendula* spp.), hedge veronicas (*Hebe* spp.), marigolds (*Tagetes* spp.), and daffodils (*Narcissus* spp.); columbine (*Aquilegia vulgaris*) and Himalayan crane's-bill (*Geranium Himalayense*) are more unusual. Many provide nectar for insects when the grass has been cut. 'Keep-neat' grave-plots are maintained by the Company. A selection of butterfly and bee plants for these might include: rock-rose (*Helianthemum* spp.), arabis (*Arabis caucasica*), aubretia (*Aubretia deltoidea*), phlox (*Phlox paniculata*), thymes (*Thymus* spp.), lavenders, hedge veronicas, small scabiouses (*Scabiosa* spp.), and small erigerons (*Erigeron* spp.).

Birds and Mammals

The green woodpecker (*Picus viridis*) is often seen on the ground probing anthills with its long sticky tongue. Kestrels (*Falco tinnunculus*) perch on obelisks, scanning cut grass for rodents. Jays (*Garrulus glandarius*), magpies (*Pica pica*), and, occasionally, cuckoos

[81] N. Anderson, pers. comm. [82] Milner (1995), 1-26. [83] LWTHFG (1984), 32-5, 41-3. [84] Gilbert (1991), 225, 229-30.

(*Cuculus canorus*) may also be seen on memorials. The considerable expanse of grassland in this and St Mary's Roman Catholic cemetery attracts migrating birds in October, and again from March-May. Interesting examples include: red kite (*Milvus milvus*) (in 1958), hobby (*F. subbuteo*), red-legged partridge (*Alectoris rufa*), common snipe (*Gallinago gallinago*), turtle dove (*Streptopelia turtur*), barn owl (*Tyto alba*), short-eared owl (*Asio flammeus*), nightjar (*Caprimulgus europaeus*), sand martin (*Riparia riparia*), yellow wagtail (*Motacilla flava*), black redstart (*Phoenicurus ochruros*), ring ouzel (*Turdus torquatus*), pied flycatcher (*Ficedula hypoleuca*), and brambling (*Fringilla montifringilla*).[85]

The following mammals have been recorded since 1985: hedgehog (*Erinaceus europaeus*), rabbit (*Oryctolagus cuniculus*), grey squirrel (*Sciurus carolinensis*), bank vole (*Clethrionomys glareolus*), field vole (*Microtus agrestis*), wood mouse (*Apodemus sylvaticus*), common rat (*Rattus norvegicus*), fox, and weasel (*Mustela nivalis*). Pipistrelle bats (*Pipistrellus pipistrellus*) were once a common sight over the canal, but their present status is unknown. Noctule (*Nyctalus noctula*) and brown long-eared bats (*Plecotus auritus*) may roost here. A mammal survey of 1997 (not including bats), found seven species in the cemetery, which had the highest diversity of mammals in the Royal Borough of Kensington and Chelsea.[86] The most extraordinary record was of a weasel which was seen and photographed on 6 October 1997 in square [**58**]. This species is rarely reported in Greater London, the majority of observations coming from outer boroughs. The sighting represents the closest western record of a weasel to central London, and its presence is doubtless due to the large extent of habitat present together with the proximity to green corridors. The provision of cover, and hence rodent prey, is of the highest priority if the weasel is to be retained here.[87] Foxes reared cubs in the circle until 1990, when the area was cleared of secondary woodland, but hedgehogs have been seen here at night.[88]

(ii) Stonework

The multitude of horizontal and vertical surfaces of varied composition, texture, and aspect, together with countless cracks and crevices, suit the specific requirements of different kinds of plants and animals. Limestone memorials, old brickwork, and lime-based mortar are important refuges for calcicolous plants and molluscs. Flowerless plants found here include algae, mosses and liverworts, ferns, and lichens. Several flowering plants also adapt well to the xerophytic conditions of some stonework structures, and spiders and insects hunt, dwell, and bask here too. Surveys conducted between 1981-89 recorded 34 mosses, three liverworts, 31 lichens, and six horsetails and ferns growing in the cemetery;[89] many were associated with stonework, and additional species have been added in recent years. Over 500 lichen species have been recorded in churchyards, about 29 per cent of all species occurring in Britain.[90] In the London area a little over thirty ferns have been found;[91] churchyards and cemeteries are important refuges for some of the rarer ones. A recent bryophyte survey in north-west Middlesex produced a list of 112 species and varieties of moss and 22 of liverworts.[92]

Ferns, Mosses, Lichens, and Flowering Plants

Mural Aspleniaceae (wall ferns) are some of the most beautiful plants to be found on memorials, mausolea, and walls. They are highly sensitive to pollution, due to their dependence on direct precipitation. The curled leaves of hart's-tongue (*Phyllitis scolopendrium*) are familiar to most, less so the delicate fronds of black spleenwort

[85] Cross and Holloway (1986), 3-4. [86] Aybes *et al.* (1997), 3. [87] Ibid., 10-11. [88] J. Humpage pers. comm.
[89] Latham (1984), 61; (1989), 22-4. [90] Dennis (1993), 234. [91] Burton (1983), 1-5. [92] Wiltshire (1995), 46-53.

(*Asplenium adiantum-nigrum*), maidenhair spleenwort (*A. trichomanes*), and wall-rue (*A. ruta-muraria*) which grow in a few sites. Hart's-tongue, black spleenwort, and wall-rue also grow nearby on an old brick wall to the south of the canal towpath near Mitre Bridge.[93] Recent surveys have shown an increase in wall ferns in central London where they were previously considered rare.[94] This is thought to be directly related to gradual reduction in sulphur-dioxide pollution since the introduction of the Clean Air Act in 1956. It is also possible that increase in concentration of active nitrogen has been beneficial. More robust ferns of other habitats include bracken (*Pteridium aquilinum*) and male-fern (*Dryopteris filix-mas*) which grow around the Anglican chapel and Centre Avenue. Lady-fern (*Athyrium filix-femina*) and broad-buckler fern (*D. dilatata*) occur in single locations.

Mosses differ in their ability to tolerate pollutants. The following toxitolerant species are found in the cemetery: *Bryum argenteum*, *B. capillare*, *Ceratodon purpureus*, *Funaria hygrometrica*, *Leptobryum pyriforme*, and *Tortula muralis*. Lichens are particularly interesting because of their associations with the history of atmospheric pollution in the area. A case in point is the relict lichen *Caloplaca decipiens* (rare in London) which is restricted to a few limestone memorials in squares [118] and [131]. It occurs mostly on memorials of the 1860s and is extinct by *c*.1900 when the increasing atmospheric pollution in London inhibited its spread.[95] Other *Caloplaca* spp., *Collema* spp., *Lecanora* spp., and *Physcia* spp. also grow here. *Xanthoria parietina* is common on both basic and siliceous gravestones and, like other nitrophilous species, it thrives on stonework which has become encrusted with bird droppings. Lichens, preferring acidic substrate, include some *Candelariella* spp. and *Lecidea* spp.. *Lecanora conizaeoides*, *Parmelia sulcata*, and *L. dispersa* are typical toxitolerant lichens of urban areas; the first two live on wood, the last on stone. *Cladonia* spp. and *Peltigera* spp. form associations with *Bryum* mosses growing on nutrient poor substrate such as marble chippings.[96]

These flowerless plants can be easily overlooked and damaged by excessive cleaning and tidying up of memorials as well as by indiscriminate and overzealous use of herbicides. Further fieldwork in the cemetery is likely to reveal many new species. Laundon *et al.* gives more information on lichens on memorials and in churchyards generally.[97]

Several flowering plants inhabit niches in stonework where humus has collected allowing them to develop a roothold. Xerophytes were noted earlier in the section dealing with grave-plots. Creeping cinquefoil, willowherbs, ivy-leaved toadflax (*Cymbalaria muralis*), common toadflax, dandelion (*Taraxum officinale* agg.), and Oxford ragwort are examples of species typically found here.

Invertebrates

Slugs and snails thrive in the moist, lime-rich environment provided by the memorials and their accompanying cracks and crevices. Here they graze on fungi, lichens, and algae. At Highgate cemetery, a survey carried out by the Conchological Society in 1972 revealed 13 snail and nine slug species including the local tree slug *Limax marginata* and the rare *Arion owenii*.[98] At Scrubs Wood in 1984, nine species of snail including the rare *Oxychilus draparnaudi* were discovered.[99] A survey in the cemetery is likely to produce interesting and unusual species.

Spiders such as *Amaurobius similis* and *Salticus scenicus* dwell in cracks and crevices of memorials. Spider predators include the quick moving spider-hunting wasps (Pompilidae) which are occasionally glimpsed as they dash across ledger-stones in pursuit

93 Archer and Keech (1993), 28. 94 Edgington (2000), 51-4. 95 Latham (1989), 17. 96 Ibid. 97 Laundon (1984). Brightman and Laundon (1994), 10-11. 98 Brooks *et al.* (1989), 83. 99 LWTHFG (1984), 44.

of their prey. Solitary wasps (Sphecidae) also hunt around memorials, and excavate their burrows on grave-plots. Other invertebrates seen on stonework include dragonflies, grasshoppers, and butterflies (see *Grassland* section above); here they bask and absorb heat radiating from the stone. Butterflies also probe the surfaces with the proboscises in search of mineral salts. Those observed on gravestones include: large skipper, small copper, common blue, red admiral, peacock (*Inachis io*), comma (*Polygonia c-album*), and speckled wood (*Pararge aegeria*). The abundance of mosses and lichens on stonework provides ideal habitat for a number of moths, the larvae of which feed on them. They include species from the Psychidae, Tineidae, Oecophoridae, Gelechiidae, Totricidae, Pyralidae, Geometridae, Arctiidae, and Noctuidae. The pyralids *Scoparia ambigualis, S. basistrigalis, Eudonia truncicolella, E. angustea,* and *E. mercurella* may be expected here. The footman moths (Arctiidae, Lithosiinae) have lichen-feeding larvae. The common footman (*Eilema lurideola*) and, possibly, others breed in the cemetery. The wing colouration of the marbled beauty (*Cryphia domestica*) resembles lichen, and its larvae feed on *Xanthoria parietina, Lecidea confluens,* and others.

(iii) Wooded Areas

The planting and subsequent evolution of wooded areas has been discussed elsewhere. It is estimated that about 16 per cent of the total area of the cemetery was wooded in the 1980s. Following large-scale clearance, the extent of wooded parts is now about 6 per cent, representing a loss of some 6.9 acres (2.8 ha). Large-scale clearances have taken place in the Circle, and the north and south borders. The latter involved a 402 m x 9 m (439 yd x 9.8 yd) strip of scrub and undergrowth constituting prime bird-nesting habitat.

Trees and Shrubs

Many of the cemetery's trees have overmatured, becoming vulnerable in high winds. Victims of the recent storms include a splendid weeping purple beech (*Fagus sylvatica* 'Purpurea pendula') in 1997, and Lombardy-poplars (*Populus nigra* 'Italica') in 1998. Interestingly, none of these trees was infested with ivy.

Trees have been planted in avenues and rows in the grasslands. Others exist as solitary specimens adding variety to the landscape. Among the species are: swamp cypress (*Taxodium distichum*), yew (*Taxus baccata*), oriental plane (*Platanus orientalis*), purple beech (*Fagus sylvatica* f. 'purpurea'), sweet chestnut (*Castanea sativa*), Turkey oak (*Quercus cerris*), Lucombe oak (*Q.* x *pseudosuber*), evergreen oak, sessile oak (*Q. petraea*), silver birch (*Betula pendula*), hornbeam (*Carpinus betulus*), lime (*Tilia* x *vulgaris*), grey poplar (*Populus* x *canascens*), black-poplar (*P. nigra*), Lombardy-poplar, hybrid black-poplar (*P.* x *canadensis*), false-acacia (*Robinia pseudoacacia*), holly, horse-chestnut, manna ash (*Fraxinus ornus*), ash (*F. excelsior*), and Indian bean (*Catalpa bignoniodes*). Several occur as single specimens.

Stands of self-seeded saplings and suckering growth still persist in one or two places around the borders. They have originated principally from English elm (*Ulmus procera*), Turkey oak, sycamore (*Acer pseudoplatanus*), and ash. Until recently, introduced shrubs like cotoneasters (*Cotoneaster* spp.), spotted laurel, evergreen spindle, privets, hedge veronicas, laurustinus (*Viburnum tinus*), and snowberry (*Symphoricarpos albus*) could be found here as well as native hedgerow plants like wych elm (*U. glabra*), goat willow (*Salix caprea*), brambles (*Rubus fruticosus* agg.), dog-rose (*Rosa canina*), blackthorn (*Prunus spinosa*), hawthorn (*Crataegus monogyna*), holly, elder (*Sambucus nigra*), and guelder-rose (*V. opulus*). Many are now lost from the site or severely reduced. Ivy and bramble are common in the understorey where it exists, and woodland and hedgerow plants like traveller's-joy (*Clematis vitalba*), lesser celandine (*Ranunculus ficaria*), garlic

14.12 *Holly Blues in the Springtime, South Circle* – watercolour by Timothy Freed. 20 x 15.5 cm (*By Courtesy of Mr and Mrs David Unwin*).

14.13 Green-veined white (*Pieris napi*) resting on cow parsley (*Anthriscus sylvestris*) (*THF*).

mustard, bugle, lords-and-ladies (*Arum maculatum*), bluebell, and black bryony (*Tamus communis*), grow in parts of the remaining woody borders (e.g. squares [170, 171, 183]).

Butterflies

Butterflies inhabiting woody places include purple hairstreaks (*Quercusia quercus*) which fly in July around the canopies of evergreen and Turkey oaks, using both for egg-laying. The double-brooded holly blue (*Celastrina argiolus*) (**14.12**) flies along the north border and adjacent grassland seeking holly in Spring, and ivy in Summer for egg-laying. Speckled woods dwell in semi-shaded woodland where they can be seen between April and October. About ten years ago this species was confined to the Copse (squares [147] and [148]). Following clearances in the Circle it spread there, as well as to other parts. It is one of few British butterflies which are currently expanding their national range.

Small white, green-veined white (**14.13**), and orange-tip were common along the north border, but the recent clearances may have destroyed their breeding habitat. They can still be seen around the Copse during May, together with holly blue, speckled wood, and occasional Brimstone (*Gonepteryx rhamni*). Comma (*Polygonia c-album* f. *hutchinsoni*) take up territories here in July. This is one of the most pleasant places (**14.14**) to observe nature in the cemetery. Sir Winston and Lady Clementine Churchill's daughter, Marigold, is buried close by [47020/160/PS]. Sir Winston was a keen lepidopterist. After the 1939-45 war he actively bred and conserved butterflies at Chartwell, having a special breeding-house constructed for this task.[100] He delighted in releasing hundreds of butterflies on his estate. It is said that he spent long hours at Marigold's graveside. Perhaps it is fitting to think that the abundance of butterflies in this spot helped restore his grieving spirit.

[100] Newman (1967), 43, 168-73.

14.14 View from inside the 'Copse'. Marigold Churchill's grave [47020/160/PS] is close by (*THF*).

Birdlife

The loss of many birds following clearances is deeply regrettable. It is difficult to believe that in 1988 the cemetery was described as 'one of the best areas for birdwatching in central London.[101] The decline is highlighted in the recent surveys referred to earlier,[102] and represents a loss of over 50 per cent of the breeding species. Warblers and finches have been the worst affected: lesser whitethroat (*Sylvia curruca*), garden warbler (*S. borin*), willow warbler (*Phylloscopus trochilus*), spotted flycatcher (*Muscicapa striata*), chaffinch (*Fringilla coelebs*), linnet (*Carduelis cannabina*), and bullfinch (*Pyrrhula pyrrhula*) are no longer seen, nor do they breed here anymore. Whitethroat (*S. communis*), chiffchaff (*Phylloscopus collybita*), greenfinch (*C. chloris*), and goldfinch (*C. carduelis*) have declined alarmingly; the last were once so common that boys used to net them in the southern grasslands. Whilst these declines reflect the national situation, the main reason in this instance is undoubtedly local habitat destruction. The breeding by a pair of sparrowhawks (*Accipiter nisus*) in the cemetery since 1994, and of green woodpecker and great spotted woodpecker (*Dendrocopus major*), are causes for optimism. The nationally declining song thrush (*Turdus philomelos*) still breeds here (although only one pair in 2000 compared with six in 1985). Blue tit (*Parus caeruleus*) and great tit (*P. major*) have been greatly helped by the erection of bird-boxes. Wren (*Troglodytes troglodytes*), dunnock (*Prunella modularis*), robin (*Erithacus rubecula*), blackbird (*Turdus merula*), and greenfinch are highly reliant on bushy ivy for nesting.

Clearances have also been carried out on neighbouring land, namely Scrubs Wood and the British Rail marshalling yards across the canal. The 20-acre (8-ha) site was renowned for birds, several rare plants, and animals which included slow-worm (*Anguis fragilis*), and a colony of *c.*500 common lizards (*Lacerta vivipara*). The 'Save Scrubs

101 NWLP (1988), 7. 102 Giddens (1996-2000).

Wood Group' and others mounted an heroic attempt to halt the clearance before the Channel Tunnel Act of 1987 allowed British Rail to develop an international depot on the site.[103]

Fungi

The cemetery has an interesting collection of fungi including some which are nationally rare and uncommon. Approximately 71 species have been identified[104] and about two thirds of these are associated with wood. Fallen branches and twigs, cut stumps, buried rotting wood, boles of trees, living wood, and leaf-litter all provide niches for different species. (The 14 or so fungi found on the Western Lawn are dealt with in the section on formal landscaped areas.)

The best conditions in which to observe fungi are damp, misty Autumn days. In dry years several types can be found on wood; some of these, such as bracket fungi, are apparent throughout the year. Examples are the rare *Lenzites betulina* and artist's fungus (*Ganoderma applanatum*) which grow on dead and standing trunks. *Tremella foliacea* is common in the cemetery though nationally rare. The intriguing stag's horn (*Xylaria hypoxylon*) and dead man's fingers (*X. polymorpha*) grow on stumps in one or two wooded sites. A search around the borders and Centre Avenue (especially its southern verge) should be productive. Amongst leaf-litter beneath horse-chestnut trees grow the uncommon clouded agaric (*Clitocybe nebularis*), wood blewit (*Lepista nuda*), and *Agaricus silvaticus*. Similarly, beneath evergreen oaks the uncommon club foot (*C. clavipes*) and blewit (*L. saeva*) may be found. Other leaf-litter species include tawny funnel cap (*C. flaccida*) and shaggy parasol (*Macrolepiota rhacodes* var. *hortensis*). Velvet shank (*Flammulina velutipes*) and sulphur tuft (*Hypholoma fasciculare*) are common on stumps, but *Pholiota squarrosa* is restricted to a single site at the base of an ash (square [**22**]). Fawn pluteus (*Pluteus cervinus*) grows on a hollow stump. Uncommon, delicate fungi include *Mycena polygramma* on decaying wood, and *Psathyrella gracilis* which grows along waysides. The attractive little Japanese umbrella toadstool (*Coprinus plicatilis*) and fairies' bonnets (*C. disseminatus*) are also common. In the Eastern Division the spectacular toadstools of fly agaric (*Amanita muscaria*), are occasionally seen beneath silver birch. The blusher (*A. rubescens*) grows nearby with *Russula* spp.. Along mossy, gravelled paths in the western part, the fittingly named weeping widow fungus (*Lacrymaria velutina*) may be found.

Fungi are highly sensitive to atmospheric pollution which is regarded as a far greater threat to their well-being than collecting for culinary purposes. Much opportunity exists for further fungal surveys in the cemetery, with new species being found each year. The recent use of wood chippings to cover some tracks and meadow pathways introduced new and possibly alien species, but smothered flora and invertebrate habitat. Mercifully the mulch was later removed. Dead wood and stumps left *in situ* in the cemetery provide valuable habitat for fungi. Approximately 20 per cent of the British invertebrate fauna is directly or indirectly dependent on dead and decaying wood and associated fungi.[105]

(iv) Formal Landscaped Areas

Formal lawns, flower-beds, and shrubberies are sited at the main entrance, west gate, Anglican chapel, West London crematorium and gardens of remembrance, and in a small memorial garden (squares [**195**] and [**196**]). Together they comprise about four per cent of the cemetery.

[103] Eliz. II, part II, c. 53. [104] Latham (1989), 23-4. [105] A. Halstead pers. comm.

Gardens and Flowerbeds

The gardens of remembrance are particularly attractive, with a fine avenue of hornbeams and beds of roses (*Rosa* spp.). The southern end abuts undergrowth providing habitat for birds and butterflies. Shubberies here and in other parts of the cemetery contain a wide variety of evergreen and semi-evergreen species such as phillyrea (*Phillyrea* spp.), osmanthus (*Osmanthus heterophyllus*), cotoneasters, firethorns (*Pyracantha* spp.), spotted-laurel, evergreen spindle, holly, privets, and laurustinus. They give valuable nesting and roosting cover, berries for food, and shelter from winter gales. Flower-beds are planted with traditional seasonal annuals chosen for ornament, and as such, have a limited usefulness for insects.

The Butterfly and Bee Garden (**14.15**), a flower-bed with an ecological ethos, exists just inside the main entrance. This was created at the suggestion of the General Cemetery Company to compensate for habitat destruction in other parts,[106] and the garden was

14.15 The Butterfly and Bee Garden, July 1995. The garden attracted 18 species of butterflies between 1994 and 1996 (*THF*).

designed and prepared in 1992. It comprises a triangular-shaped flower-bed area of 36.5 m^2 situated on a south-facing lawn. The cost of planting was met by the Company, which also agreed to undertake maintenance.[107] Wildflower seed was sown prior to introducing butterfly- and bee-attracting herbs and hardy perennials. These included garlic mustard, dame's-violet (*Hesperis matronalis*), aubretia, butterfly stonecrop (*Sedum spectabile*), garden cat-mint (*Nepeta* x *faassenii*), marjorams (*Origanum* spp.), bergamot (*Monarda didyma*), lavender (*Lavandula* x *intermedia* 'Munstead' – planted as a continuous border), and butterfly bush (*Buddleja davidii* 'Black Knight'). In the centre, honeysuckle (*Lonicera* spp.) climbed a wooden frame creating a pyramidal effect. Following its initial success, additional funding of £2,000 was given by North Kensington City Challenge plc, allowing for further enlargement and planting. A new design and list of hardy perennials were provided. Two flower-beds for annuals were added at the sides. The plants were chosen to provide continuous flowering from early Spring to late Autumn and included: heathers (*Erica* spp.), Japanese spiraea (*Spiraea japonica* 'Anthony Waterer'), purple crane's-bill (*Geranium* x *magificum*), sea-holly (*Eryngium oliverianum*), caryopteris (*Caryopteris* x *cladonensis*), sages (*Phlomis* spp.), thymes, koromiko (*Hebe salicifolia*), variegated hedge veronica (*H.* x *franciscana* 'Variegata'), scabious (*Scabiosa caucasica*), globe-thistle (*Echinops humilis*), goldenrod (*Solidago* 'Golden Mosa'), Michaelmas-daisies (*Aster novi-belgii*), erigeron (*Erigeron speciosus*

106 Freed (1992), 74-5. 107 Freed (1997), III.

'Darkest of All'), achillea (*Achillea filipendulina*), and sneezeweed (*Helenium* x *hybrida* 'Magnificum'), among others. Work was carried out in November 1993 when some 300 plants of 28 species were planted. The funding also provided for two interpretation-boards, both admirably illustrated by Jenny Hawksley. One was placed beside the garden, the other was erected at a grassland site which had been left uncut by arrangement with the Company (see **Grassland**, *Management* section, **14.6**). Additional plants were donated by Malcolm Newland of Butterfly Conservation, and the London Wildlife Trust funded replacement interpretation-sheets. By 1997, 38 types of nectar plants were established in the garden, and 18 butterfly species had been recorded using them. This represented 78 per cent of the total number seen in the cemetery, and an increase of seven species in the Eastern Division.

14.16 Holly blue (*Celastrina argiolus*) feeding on Michaelmas-daisy (*Aster novi-belgii*) in the Butterfly and Bee Garden (*THF*).

Somewhat surprisingly, the butterfly-bushes attracted very few butterflies. Lavender was easily the favourite being visited by small, Essex, and large skipper, small and green-veined white, common and holly blue (**14.16**), small tortoiseshell and meadow brown. Between 1994 and 1996, 421 butterflies were recorded in the garden on 85 monitoring visits.[108] The most frequent was meadow brown with 299 observations; this butterfly also had the most catholic tastes visiting no less than 15 different kinds of flower. These figures require more interpretation than can be given here; nevertheless they broadly demonstrate that butterflies can be attracted to a part of the cemetery where they were previously lacking, and that certain species are prepared to fly significant distances from their breeding habitats to find nectar. Butterflies also visited the garden for nectar when strimming in local grassland removed wildflowers. The results suggest that introducing butterfly- and bee-attracting plants to other parts of the cemetery would be highly beneficial for these and other insects.

Lawns

Formal lawns are important feeding habitat for pied wagtail (*Motacilla alba*), blackbird, thrushes, and others. Lawns are also a good place to see fungi. The Western Lawns are presently kept neatly mown and are bordered by white poplars (*Populus alba*). Many fungi have been recorded here including the nationally rare *Leccinum duriusculum* which forms a mutually dependent association with white poplar. Its fruiting body appears in August. Other species found on the lawn include: brown roll-rim (*Paxillus involutus*), parrot toadstool (*Hygrocybe psittacina*), *Camarophyllus virgineus, Clitocybe dealbata*, the uncommon *C. rivulosa*, the fairy ring mushroom (*Marasmius oreades*), the uncommon *Mycena flavo-alba*, *M. leptocephala*, the uncommon *Cortinarius cinnamomeus*, poison pie (*Hebeloma crustuliniforme*), and *Inocybe fastigiata*.

(v) The Canal-Side Reserve and Canal

This narrow strip of land, 5-6 m (16.4-19.6 ft) wide, lies between the cemetery's southern boundary and the Grand Union Canal. By agreement with the General Cemetery Company and British Waterways Board, the London Wildlife Trust maintains this area as a nature reserve. The canal, its towpaths, and the adjacent railway sidings and cuttings

[108] Freed (1997), III.

form an important green corridor along which flora and fauna can move between built-up areas, as well as linking sites like Horsenden Hill and Perivale Wood with the cemetery. Access to the reserve is by a locked gate at the west end of the new British Waterways moorings.

The vegetation has been left unmanaged to compensate for loss of scrub and undergrowth in the cemetery, and the extensive bramble thickets provide nesting habitat for many birds. Bat- and bird-boxes have been erected on the site. A wide variety of trees and shrubs may be found including wych elm, English elm, Turkey oak, silver birch, grey poplar, crack willow (*Salix fragilis*), goat willow, hawthorn, horse-chestnut, sycamore, and ash. The waterside flora is impressive in parts where the concrete-and-steel piling of the canal wall has crumbled or is absent (e.g. square [82]). Hemlock water-dropwort (*Oenanthe crocata*), marsh woundwort (*Stachys palustris*), gipsywort (*Lycopus europaeus*), orange balsam (*Impatiens capensis*), water mint (*Mentha aquatica*), London bur-marigold (*Bidens connata*), and yellow iris (*Iris pseudocorus*) grow here. Amongst other canal-side flora noted during a survey in October 1992 were greater pond-sedge (*Carex riparia*), common reed (*Phragmites australis*), and water dock (*Rumex hydrolapathum*). Hops (*Humulus lupulus*) grow on and near the old canal-gate in the Eastern Division (square [20]).

The damselflies and dragonflies seen in the cemetery breed where emergent vegetation has been able to grow. They are often encountered in the grassland and along the North Avenue. Blue-tailed damselfly, southern hawker, migrant hawker, brown hawker (*Aeshna grandis*), and common darter (*Sympetrum striolatum*) have been recorded here. A swan mussel (*Anodonta cygnaea*) was netted from the canal in October 1992, suggesting that the water is not badly polluted. Further evidence is the presence of at least eight species of fish including roach (*Rutilus rutilus*), perch (*Perca fluviatilis*), bream (*Abramis brama*), carp (*Cyprinus carpio*), pike (*Esox lucius*), tench (*Tinca tinca*), eel (*Anguilla anguilla*), and gudgeon (*Gobio gobio*).[109]

Birdlife has fared better along the canal than in the cemetery due to the persistence of adequate bankside vegetation. Regularly noted species include: cormorant (*Phalacrocorax carbo*), grey heron (*Ardea cinerea*), mute swan (*Cygnus olor*), Canada goose (*Branta canadensis*), mallard (*Anas platyrhynchos*), tufted duck (*Aythya fuligula*), moorhen (*Gallinula chloropus*), coot (*Fulica atra*), black-headed gull (*Larus ridibundus*), and lesser black-backed gull (*L. fuscus*). A pair of common tern (*Sterna hirundo*) were seen fishing here in 1997.[110] It is necessary to travel about four miles westward to have a good chance of seeing the kingfisher (*Alcedo atthis*).

(vi) Ivy

Ivy Ecology

Ivy on monuments, walls, and trees provides valuable habitat for a great diversity of wildlife. It is ecologically important in two specific ways: ivy is one of the last major plants to flower, providing nectar and pollen for invertebrates in the Autumn, and its evergreen foliage is used by fauna for feeding, basking, nesting, roosting, and hibernating. The highly nutritious berries provide food for birds and other vertebrates during the winter. Large growths create substantial shelter throughout the year.

A project begun in the cemetery,[111] and still proceeding, produced a preliminary list of 261 species of fauna which associate with ivy in Britain: 238 invertebrates (several Red Data Book species included) and 23 vertebrates were recorded, and many more species are anticipated. In the cemetery, 59 invertebrates and 12 vertebrates were recorded associating with ivy. Many other inhabitants are potential additions. Included were 10

[109] Archer and Keech (1993), 31. [110] Giddens (1997), 10. [111] Freed (1997), IV.

species of butterfly which visited the flowers, the most frequent being holly blue, red admiral, small tortoiseshell (*Aglais urticae*), comma (**14.17**), and speckled wood. The holly blue's second brood, in almost all instances, is dependent on ivy flowerbuds for egg-laying and larval development. The first brood utilises the flowerbuds of holly and several other shrubs. The holly blue is frequently abundant in old churchyards and cemeteries due to the prevalence there of its hostplants.[112]

14.17 Comma (*Polygonia c-album*) feeding on ivy flowers; one of many species to utilise this versatile plant in Kensal Green cemetery (*THF*).

Ivy flowers are visited by moths at night, and, in turn, bats prey on these and other nocturnal insects. 66 kinds of moth (mostly geometrids and noctuids) have been recorded on ivy flowers, and at least 14 moth larvae feed on the leaves.[113] Several butterflies and moths also hibernate amongst the foliage. The flowers have a great attraction for vast numbers of hoverflies (Syrphidae). A list of 32 species has been produced for hoverflies noted on ivy in Britain; 19 of these were recorded in the cemetery.[114] Some of the more unusual species for inner London were: *Chrysotoxum cautum*, *Volucella pellucens*, and *Metasyrphus latifasciatus*. For honey bees (*Apis millifera*) and bumble bees (*Bombus* spp.), the flowers are excellent providers of nectar and pollen, and the last important source of nectar before winter arrives.[115]

Bushy ivy is a valuable habitat for birds: the following are known to have nested amongst its foliage in the cemetery: wren, dunnock, robin, blackbird, song thrush, blackcap (*Sylvia atricapilla*), spotted flycatcher, house sparrow (*Passer domesticus*), chaffinch, and greenfinch. Tawny owl (*Strix aluco*), mistle thrush (*Turdus viscivorus*), goldcrest (*Regulus regulus*), and other irregular visitors also utilise ivy. During recent surveys in the cemetery it was estimated that 80 per cent of all blackbird, dunnock, robin, and a large percentage of wren's nests were situated amongst ivy.[116] The maximum annual number of nests for each species was: blackbird 20+, robin 12+, dunnock eight, and wren eleven.[117] Birds which feed on ivy berries include: woodpigeon (*Columba palumbus*), robin, blackbird, fieldfare (*T. pilaris*), song thrush, redwing (*T. iliacus*), mistle thrush, blackcap, and starling (*Sturnus vulgaris*).

It would be fitting here to draw attention to a beautiful illustration by Henry Constantine Richter (1821-1902) of a family of robins with their nest amongst ivy foliage (**14.18**).[118] The plate appears in *Birds of Great Britain*, Vol. II by John Gould FRS (1804-81), the renowned ornithologist, taxidermist, and publisher, who is buried in the cemetery, together with his wife, Elizabeth, and sister; his two sons are commemorated on the grave-slab [3149/90/PS]. Elizabeth was an accomplished artist, drawing and lithographing many of the plates for Gould's *Birds of Europe*. She predeceased him in 1841, aged 37. Gould travelled extensively in Australia, and produced 41 illustrated folios on birds from many continents. The bicentenary of his birth is due in 2004.

Until recently ivy occurred on walls, trees, and memorials situated around the borders. Virtually all this has been removed in the last ten years. Ivy still occurs on individual memorials and groups of memorials in the grasslands, Circle, and on some trees. It is of concern that much of the remaining ivy is retained since its value for wildlife

112 Willmott (1999), 3, 15. 113 Freed (1997), IV. 114 Ibid., IV. 115 Howes (1979), 160-1. 116 Giddens pers. comm. 117 Giddens (1996-2000). 118 Gould (1866), Plate 48.

14.18 'Robin or Redbreast, *Erythacus rubecula*'. Painting by H. C. Richter; Plate 48 in *Birds of Great Britain*, **ii**, by John Gould FRS (1804-81) (*By courtesy of The Natural History Museum, London*).

cannot be overestimated. Even small flowering growth on solitary headstones can be utilised by species such as holly blue for egg-laying.[119] Indeed, a well-established growth of flowering ivy may be regarded as an ecosystem in its own right.

Ivy in the Historic Cemetery

Ivy was frequently used in 18th-century horticultural schemes to cover walls and buildings. John Claudius Loudon recommended 'seven varieties, all beautiful' of *Hedera helix*, the common Ivy,[120] for planting as climbing shrubs on walls in cemeteries.[121] In 1868, writing in *La Belgique Horticole*,[122] M. Delchevalerie, Chef de Culture au Fleuriste de la Ville de Paris, recommended that 'le lierre d'Irlande' – Irish Ivy (*Hedera hibernica*) – should be planted in Parisian squares and beds. His influence can still be seen today, especially so in the Cimetière du Père-Lachaise where the elite of France from Chopin and Maréchal Ney to Edith Piaf, rest, surrounded by stone and *hibernica*.[123] Ivy has great aesthetic value giving relief and enhancement in what would otherwise be a monotonous landscape of stone. Few subjects complement fine sculpture so aptly as its dark green foliage. Ivy is synonymous with churchyard and cemetery landscape and evokes a sense of antiquity, solemnity, and continuity with the cemetery's past. Many poets and authors have honoured the plant, including Pliny the Elder and Younger, Euripides, Virgil, Cato, Horace, Byron, Keats, Tennyson, and Dickens:[124] several examples are given in *The Ivy* by Shirley Hibberd (1872).

Occasionally the issue of ivy becomes a source of conflict between differing groups. Some wish to retain it for ecological and aesthetic reasons, others sometimes wish to expose monuments having particular historical or sculptural significance. There is also a need to clear ivy for the provision of burial-space. The struggle to resolve these differences requires compromise and understanding. As Brooks *et al.* recognised:

> there will be occasions, however, when important habitats need to be safeguarded, when areas of particular naturalist interest need to be preserved, or, indeed, when it will be appropriate actually to establish such resources.[125]

The Friends' Ivy League and Granite Group carries out monthly tasks including selective ivy clearance in keeping with wildlife concerns. The removal of ivy is carefully planned and executed. Total and hasty clearance is unnecessary and undesirable, often causing more damage to memorials than the ivy itself.

119 Freed (1997), IV. 120 Loudon (1842), 497. 121 Loudon (1981), 107. 122 Delchevalerie (1868), 51-63. 123 Rose (1996), 126. 124 Ibid., 11-2, 15, 20-1. 125 Brooks *et al.* (1989), 109.

It would be useful to clarify some points concerning the biology of ivy. Much of the following information has been extracted from Peter Rose's authoritative works on ivies,[126] and from the Department of the Environment's Arboriculture Research Note:[127] ivy is NOT parasitic, and its adventitious rootlets do not have penetrative powers nor do they absorb food or water. It feeds only via its main ground roots. Concerning ivy on trees, if a tree is healthy ivy growth does it no harm. However, on sick or dead trees ivy will take over. It is possible that ivy roots may compete with a support tree for moisture and nutrients; however no information exists proving such interaction. Dense ivy-foliage can obscure cavities, defects, and fungal fruit-bodies on support trees making structural assessment difficult. Kirby considered that 'The deliberate removal of ivy from trees on any conservation site is an inexcusable act of vandalism'.[128] Concerning walls and buildings, a covering of ivy can actually prolong the life of stone and brickwork. Stonework which has been covered over a long period will be seen, when the ivy is removed, to be fresh and unscathed if compared with adjacent areas that have been exposed to the elements. On old walls where mortar is weak, it is possible that ivy shoots will take root in gaps between bricks, but on walls where brickwork and mortar are sound, ivy will do no harm. Rose recommended biennial clipping of ivy on walls in early Spring before birds begin nesting. Brooks *et al.* gave advice on the management of ivy in historic cemeteries including the main problems created by neglected ivy growth and the correct procedures for its removal.[129]

In the cemetery the following observations were made during recent research into the effects of ivy on stonework: most memorials are fashioned from sandstones and limestones. Many have been severely degraded by weathering and pollution. In addition, ferrous clamps and dowels, once commonly used in construction, have rusted and expanded, cracking surrounding stonework. Many brick-lined graves have collapsed due to subsidence and the proximity of grave-plots. Stonework has been dislodged, and at worst, memorials have disintegrated. In many cases this has happened without any evidence of ivy on them. However, it is inevitable that ivy will exacerbate memorials so damaged. Its creeping shoots enter cracks and gaps and, in time, their thickening stems force stonework apart. Although ivy may not initiate a memorial's demise, its subsequent invasion gives the impression that it has done so. Table- and chest-tombs are particularly prone to ivy damage, and roofs of mausolea can crack under its weight. Free-standing statuary (e.g. crosses and urns) with bushy ivy growth can become unstable in strong winds. In some instances, where moisture persists beneath the foliage, corrosive acids form, causing damage to memorial surfaces. Those least likely to be damaged incorporate few component parts and have durable surfaces: obelisks, pedestals, polished granites, and slates fare extremely well. This is clearly demonstrated when ivy is removed from them.

There is a strong argument for retaining ivy on memorials due to the protective quality of its evergreen foliage. The majority of memorials and walls which had been cleared of ivy appeared to have benefited considerably when compared with those which were unprotected from weathering and pollution. Another advantage is the concealing nature and thereby protective capacity of its foliage: several valuable memorials recently exposed following ivy removal have been stolen or vandalised. This situation is unfortunately being repeated in burial-grounds throughout the country. The cost of ameliorating such vandalism can run into thousands of pounds.

Conclusion

Whilst the provision of burial-space is the function of cemeteries and churchyards, it is significant that many have evolved into exceptional places for a broad diversity of

[126] Rose (1990; 1996). [127] White and Patch (1990). [128] Kirby (1992), 26. [129] Brooks *et al.* (1989), 109-12.

wildlife.[130] Kensal Green cemetery is an outstanding example and due consideration for its flora and fauna was recently given by the London Ecology Committee who designated it as a Site of Metropolitan Importance in 1994, therefore having the highest priority for nature conservation. Although the General Cemetery Company recognises the wildlife value of the site, its main concern is to provide burial-space. However, this may be difficult to reconcile with several sections of the recent draft Conservation Area Proposals Statement (CAPS), produced by the Royal Borough of Kensington and Chelsea, which relate to ecological issues in the cemetery; appraisal of the effects of maintenance programmes on wildlife and habitats and the development of an ecological management plan are given high priority. Preserving the diversity of habitats, and establishing regular meetings between the Company and those concerned with ecology, will also be essential if progress is to be made.

Numerous problems may be encountered in managing historic cemeteries arising from the diversity of interests at stake, and care and foresight are required in formulating workable management plans. An issue currently exerting immense pressure is the acute shortage of burial-space. An acceptable and imaginative way of partially easing the problem is the provision of new cemeteries in urban fringes. Combining burial-grounds with nature conservation is an idea which has been gaining in popularity. Woodland burial-sites and nature-reserve burial-grounds now exist throughout the country, and are listed with their details in *The New Natural Death Handbook*;[131] there are currently 103 and about thirty more in the late planning stage.[132] A more controversial scheme, but one likely to provide a significant solution to the problem of shortage, is the re-use of old graves. This idea is explored in depth in *Reusing Old Graves*[133] and further investigated in *Planning for Burial Space in London*.[134] The London Planning Advisory Committee (LPAC) is presently (2001) carrying out consultations in order to formulate a future policy for the re-use of graves. In 1997, LPAC predicted that Inner London boroughs had, on average, only seven years' supply of burial-space left, and Outer London boroughs, 18 years.[135] However a number of variances could affect these figures. A concern which immediately springs to the ecologist's mind is the potential damage to flora and fauna associated with long-established and undisturbed grave-plots: in Kensal Green cemetery, for example, several locally rare wildflowers (e.g. round-leaved crane's-bill [*Geranium rotundifolium*] and shining crane's-bill [*G. lucidum*]), are restricted to a few graves. Therefore it is important that such sites are identified in a management plan should re-use occur here. This problem is alluded to in LPAC's report and in its burial policy proposals 8 and 9, which refer to the need for surveys of, and avoidance of damage to, natural habitats and biodiversity.[136]

In some historic cemeteries management is controlled by groups of Friends and in such circumstances ecological plans can achieve their full potential. The Living Churchyard and Cemeteries Project[137] provides much literature which is useful in creating such plans.[138] Recent research by Dunk and Rugg[139] showed that about seventy per cent of a functioning cemetery is disused burial-ground which can no longer accommodate new burials; this portion has great amenity potential which is suitable for ecological management.[140] Clearance is the more usual option chosen by cemetery managers who generally equate nature conservation with untidiness and abandonment of management; but this need not be the case.[141] At Tower Hamlets cemetery, London,

[130] E.g. Greenoak (1985); Goode (1986), 105-14; Brooks *et al.* (1989), 81-7; Fry and Lonsdale (1991) 187-9; Gilbert (1991), 218-38; Dennis (1993), 230-41; Meller (1994), 51-4. [131] Albery and Wienrich (2000), 190-227. [132] N. Albery pers. comm. [133] Davies and Shaw (1995). [134] LPAC (1997), 11-13. The matter was also given consideration in 2000-1 by a Committee of Members of Parliament. [135] Ibid., 7-10. [136] Ibid., 3, 17. [137] The Arthur Rank Centre, Stoneleigh Park, Warwickshire, CV8 2LZ. [138] E.g. Goodfellow (1994); Hand and Morfitt (1994); Robinson (1994); Willmott and Clarke (1994). [139] Dunk and Rugg (1994), 15. [140] Ibid., 16, 23, 25-6, 35-6. [141] Ibid., 47, 54-8.

management is planned by the Friends in partnership with the local council.[142] Here, all grass-cutting is carefully controlled, and butterfly numbers, for example, have escalated, with 2,446 of 19 species being recorded during monitored transect walks in 1999;[143] the results included the highest totals for four species from 62 transect sites in Hertfordshire and Middlesex, and four new species were recorded in 2000.[144] Lists of flora and fauna for other old London cemeteries are equally impressive when compared with surrounding habitats and even small sites such as St John's Wood churchyard, London, which was designated as a statutory Local Nature Reserve in 1997, have great value. At York cemetery an ecological management plan was formulated following the purchase of the site in 1987 by the York Cemetery Trust.[145] One of the projects initiated was the development of a Butterfly Walk measuring 150 m x 5 m (164 yd x 5.46 yd). This involved at least 16 voluntary groups, many of whom were schoolchildren. By 1994, about twenty-one species of butterflies had been seen there.

Since the mid-1980s the London Wildlife Trust has been invited by the General Cemetery Company to advise on ecological matters. Its members have carried out practical conservation work, and provided the Company with details of important wildlife areas and lists of suitable trees, shrubs, and herbaceous plants for replacement planting schemes. Local naturalists have arranged nature walks and given illustrated talks. Conservation work has been carried out where it might be effective but the insecure circumstances concerning long-term stability of many habitats has discouraged a more enthusiastic approach, and there have been instances where trees and shrubs specially planted for wildlife have been destroyed during clearance work. Specialists have carried out surveys (see *The Habitats and Their Flora and Fauna*), but populations of many other groups of fauna still need to be evaluated: slugs and snails, spiders, harvestmen, and a host of insects, including bugs, beetles, wasps, and bees should also be included. The results would enhance the cemetery's value and give further inspiration, for they would surely reveal more rare and interesting species. An up-dated botanical review and moth-trapping report would also be useful. It is interesting to note that the survey of Scrubs Wood in 1984 (referred to earlier), involved at least 26 individuals including specialists from the Natural History Museum, London.[146]

The co-operation of the Company has been welcomed and appreciated in several respects: making adjustments to the grass-cutting schedule in selected areas to benefit wildflowers and butterflies; suggesting that a butterfly-garden could be created; and giving its approval to a programme of ecological enhancement for the cemetery to be funded by the North Kensington City Challenge plc. This resulted in the production of wildlife leaflets, two interpretation-boards, planting tree whips and shrubs, erection of bird- and bat-boxes, and the production of an Environmental Education Pack.[147] The British Trust for Conservation Volunteers and the Kensington & Chelsea Conservation Volunteers have been involved with some of these projects, including autumnal grass-raking at selected sites.

Recognition of the cemetery's potential as an educational resource for all levels of study especially in the arts, biology, botany, ecology, geology, history, and zoology has not yet been fully realised, and there is much to be learnt from cemeteries such as York where numerous trails and enterprising conservation projects involving schools and the local community are well established. The beginnings of this approach have been initiated at Kensal Green and further co-operation would be welcome. It is sincerely hoped that the beauty and diversity of Nature (which inspired numerous great works by many who now lie at rest in the cemetery), are given rightful consideration in the future.

[142] T. Lyle pers. comm. [143] Murray and Souter (2000), 10-11. [144] T. Lyle pers. comm. [145] YCT (1994).
[146] LWTHFG (1984), 59-60. [147] RBKC (1996).

CHAPTER XV

Burial at Kensal Green Cemetery

JULIAN LITTEN

Introduction; Funerals, Funeral Furnishings, and Undertakers; Hygienic Treatment of the Body; Shrouds and Coffin Linings; Coffins; Epilogue

The most sensible motive to abate the passions is death. The tomb is the best course of morality. Study avarice in the coffin of a miser: this is the man who accumulated heap upon heap, riches upon riches; see, a few boards enclose him, and a few square inches of earth contain him! Study ambition in the grave of that enterprising man: see his noble designs, his extensive projects, his boundless expedients, are all shattered and sunk in this fatal gulf of human projects! Approach the tomb of the proud man, and there investigate pride: see the mouth that pronounced lofty expressions condemned to eternal silence; the piercing eyes that convulsed the world with fear, covered with a midnight gloom; the formidable arm that distributed the destinies of mankind, without motion or life! Go to the tomb of the nobleman, and there study quality: behold his magnificent titles, his royal ancestors, his flattering inscriptions, his learned genealogies, are all gone, or going to be lost with himself in the same dust! Study voluptuousness at the grave of the voluptuous; see his senses are destroyed, his organs broken to pieces, his bones scattered at the grave's mouth, and the whole temple of sensual pleasure subverted from its foundations.

The Cottager's Friend, and Guide of the Young For the Year 1840, iv/8 (August 1840), (London: John Mason), 119-20.

Introduction

The 19th-century undertaker was the victim of his own success. The ever-increasing amount of varied merchandise on offer to the trade, from the abundance of funeral-furnishing warehouses, gave rise to an excess of accoutrements: plumes, both feathered and ruched,[1] hat-bands of various sizes (depending on the mourner's relationship to the deceased), black scarves and gloves, elaborate appliqué metalwork fittings for the coffin, and coffin-linings of various quality and materials, from cotton to satin and sarsnet[2] to silk. The result was that by the middle of the 19th century the trade had perfected a complex differential between the funerals of the poor and those of the middling sort: the higher one was in the social scale, the more elaborate one's funeral would be. However, by the 1860s and 1870s the middling classes were no longer willing to withstand such excesses, and began to demand a simpler ritual, albeit with a maintenance of the prevailing dignity. Consequently, the funeral became a less elaborate affair for the wealthy, which the lower classes took as an opportunity to adopt a street panoply previously denied to them on account of their low social status.

Conversely, the funerals of the nobility during the 19th century saw little change, and the sight witnessed at Kensal Green cemetery in April 1842 by the reporter from *The Illustrated London News* covering the funeral of HRH Augustus Frederick, Duke of Sussex, proves the point:

> by courtesy of the Directors, at an early hour we were allowed to take a view of the preparations that had been made in the chapel and catacombs, for the impressive ceremony about to take place. The walls of the chapel, the reading desk, chairs, forms, &c., were entirely covered in black cloth. At the back of the reading desk was an emblazoned escutcheon of the royal arms. The vault in which the remains of his late Royal Highness are deposited, until a suitable mausoleum can be erected, is situated about the middle of the catacombs, on the right of the chapel. It is a plain vault, containing two wooden trestles, on which the coffin of his late Royal Highness has been deposited. Immediately on the conclusion of the ceremony, the masons were employed to build a strong wall in front, closing in the remains of his late Royal Highness.[3]

Thus the journal reported on the exequies, declaring that 'all the arrangements were in excellent taste'.[4] *The Pictorial Times* also waxed lyrical on 'the gorgeousness of grief'.[5] What is more, the entombment of the Duke was an event that established the place as a desirable spot in which to be buried (**15.1** and **15.2**).

The Duke's relatively public funeral at Kensal Green cemetery, rather than in the more private surroundings of St George's chapel in Windsor Castle favoured by the majority of the royal family, was the result of personal choice on the part of the deceased. In selecting so public a location, the Duke's obsequies afforded the populace the glimpse of a superior quality funeral as supplied by the Crown undertaker, Banting of St James's, although they would not have seen the coffin because, until the introduction of the glass-sided hearse in the 1870s, such items were conveyed in closed hearses. Furthermore, the Directors of the General Cemetery Company were unsuccessful in their attempts to view the coffin, for there was insufficient room in the chapel to accommodate them, on account of the number of official guests present.

The General Cemetery of All Souls at Kensal Green witnessed its first interment, that of Margaret Gregory, on 31 January 1833. The cemetery had been slow to attract custom

[1] With a pleated frilling: to trim with ruche. [2] Also spelled *sarsenet*, or *sarcenet*, it is a thin tissue of fine stuff, usually silk. [3] *The Illustrated London News*, ii/53 (6 May 1843), 301. [4] Ibid. [5] *The Pictorial Times* (6 May 1843). *See also* Bland (1986), 152-4.

15.1 Funeral-procession of the Duke of Sussex 'in Kensal-Green Cemetery' from *The Illustrated London News*, ii/53 (6 May 1843), 306 (*GLCL*).

15.2 Funeral of the Duke of Sussex in the Anglican chapel, Kensal Green cemetery, 1843. The decoration of the chapel and catafalque was organised by the Crown undertakers, Messrs. Banting of St James's, from *The Illustrated London News*, ii/53 (6 May 1843), 307 (*GLCL*).

at first, and even the massive, secure walls, gates, and railings, the handsome dignified Classical buildings, and the landscaped grounds seemed relatively unsuccessful in dissuading the mass of the populace from patronage of the overcrowded, dismal, and nasally unpleasant City churchyards. The anonymous author of an article entitled 'Kensall-Green Cemetery' in the *Penny Magazine* for 1834 was to observe that there was

> not much in the first view to inform a person of the purposes to which the place is devoted. The ground was only opened in the early part of 1833, and since then we are informed that 193 interments have taken place; but many of these are in the subterranean catacombs; and those in the open ground are so dispersed that the monuments are by no means the first objects to attract the eye.[6]

However, the burial of the Duke of Sussex was a fillip for the cemetery, which gradually acquired a *cachet* as a society burial-ground, though not at the expense of accepting the remains of less exalted mortals. Since the date of the Duke's interment, the cemetery's 250,000 'permanent residents' include more than three hundred with entries in the *Dictionary of National Biography*, over five hundred members of the titled nobility, and two adult children and one adult grandson of King George III. For more than one hundred and sixty years the heavy triple coffins of the aristocratic and upper-middle classes have been deposited on mausoleum shelves, in catacomb *loculi*, or in private vaults and brick graves throughout the cemetery, though most of those buried in

6 *The Penny Magazine*, iii/150 (2 August 1834), 299.

the cemetery's approximately sixty-nine acres (about twenty-eight hectares)[7] are single-shell deposits in earth graves.

As has been established earlier, The General Cemetery Company was incorporated by Act of Parliament 2 & 3 Will. IV., c.110, or, in layman's terms, during the second and third years of the reign of King William IV, i.e. 1832-33. The full title of this was *An Act for Establishing a General Cemetery for the Interment of the Dead in the Neighbourhood of the Metropolis*. Paragraph XLIII of the Act of Incorporation outlines the types of plot for sale:

> XLIII. And be it further enacted, That it shall be lawful for the said Company, and they are hereby authorized and empowered, from Time to Time and at all Times, from and after the passing of this Act, to sell and dispose of, to any Person or Persons who may be willing or desire to purchase or acquire the same, and at or for such Price or Prices or Sum or Sums of Money, and under such Regulations and Restrictions, and subject to such Conditions as the said Company shall think proper to require, the exclusive Right of Burial or Interment, either in Perpetuity or for a limited Period, as may be agreed upon, in all and every or any of the Vaults, Catacombs, Arches, Brick Graves, Graves, and Places of Burial which may be from Time to Time or at any Time erected, made, or built by the said Company within the said Cemetery or any Part thereof; and also the Right and Privilege of erecting and making of any Family or other Vault, Catacomb, Brick Grave, or Place of Burial within the said Cemetery, with the exclusive Right of Burial or Interment therein, either in Perpetuity or for a limited Period; and also the Right or Privilege of single Interment in any of the Vaults, Catacombs, Arches, Brick Graves, Graves, or other Places of Burial made or constructed by the said Company, or in the open Ground of the said Cemetery; and also the Right and Privilege of erecting and placing any Monument or Cenotaph in the said Cemetery, or any Monument, Tablet, or monumental Inscription on or against the Walls of the said Chapel, or other Place appropriated by the said Company for the Reception of Monuments, Tablets, or monumental Inscriptions; and also the Right and Privilege of placing any Grave Stone or Slab of Stone or Marble or other Material or Foot Stones or Head Stones, upon it to any Grave in the said Cemetery; and every such Purchaser or Purchasers of the exclusive Right of Interment or Burial, whether in Perpetuity or for a limited Period, in any such Catacomb, Vault, or Burial Place, his or her Heirs, Executors, Administrators, or Assigns, shall, and he, she, or they is and are hereby required, immediately upon the Completion of such Purchase, to close the Entrance of each such Catacomb, Vault, or Place of Burial with good and substantial Doors, to the Satisfaction of the said Company, under the Penalty of Ten Pounds.[8]

The Act further allowed for the conveyance of the exclusive right of burial in all vaults, catacombs, brick graves, and earth graves to be bequeathed, given, or sold to a second party, whilst Paragraph XLVI assured the purchaser/s of catacomb space beneath either the Anglican or Dissenters' chapels that the upkeep and repair of those buildings would be a charge against the income of the Company.

7 The original purchase of land was 46.41 acres (18.78 hectares) with 7.67 acres (3.1 hectares) south of the canal, making 54.08 acres (21.88 hectares). Two more parcels of land (0.5 and 0.375 acres respectively) were purchased from the St Quintin estate in 1833 as well as another two (*c*.2 and *c*.0.1 acres) formerly belonging to the 'Manor of Abbots' in Kensington. A further 22.54 acres were added in the 1850s, but the 7.67 acres south of the canal were sold to the gas-works. The final total acreage was therefore *c*.71.9 acres (29.1 hectares).

8 General Cemetery Company (1833), 32-33.

Of the cemetery's approximately 71.9 acres about five (2.0235 hectares) were set aside for the burial of Dissenters (4.3, 4.5). This was an innovative move on the part of the Company, as is emphasised in Paragraph XLII of the Act:

> XLII. And whereas it is expedient that some Part of the said Cemetery should be set apart and appropriated for the Interment of Foreigners and other Persons, for whom, as not being Members of the Church of *England*, no Place of Burial is by Law appropriated; be it therefore enacted, That it shall be lawful for the said Company, and they are hereby authorized and empowered, to set apart a Portion of the intended Cemetery as a Place of Burial or Interment for Foreigners and other Persons, not being Members of the Church of *England* and *Ireland* as by Law established; and such Portion of the said intended Cemetery shall not be consecrated, but the same shall nevertheless be for ever set apart and appropriated and exclusively used for the Interment of the Dead; and it shall be lawful to inter the Bodies of the Dead in such unconsecrated Part of the said Cemetery in such Manner and in all respects as the Friends and Relatives of the Person or Persons so to be interred shall think fit; and in default of any Direction by the Friends or Relatives of the Person or Persons so to be interred, then in such a Manner as the said Company shall think fit and appoint: Provided always, that every such Burial shall be conducted in a decent and solemn Manner, and under such Regulations and Restrictions as the said Company shall think fit to impose.[9]

Here, then, was a departure from the norm, whereby Dissenters, and those of no conviction, could be buried with or without the formalities of their sect, a recognition withheld by the Church of England apropos its churchyards until the introduction of the *Burial Laws Amendment Act 1880*,[10] passed following an unpleasant law-suit resulting from an incumbent's refusal to allow a Baptist minister to perform a graveside service for one of his deceased congregation in the churchyard at Akenham, Suffolk.[11]

Whilst the permutation of burial types available in the Dissenters' ground replicated that in the much larger consecrated area, no mausolea or vaults were built, and brick graves tend to be the exception rather than the rule, limited to about twenty brick graves in front of the chapel, and a further fifty or so at the western boundary of the sector.

Mindful of the need to provide a cemetery which was both commodious and sanitary, the Company specified the quality of coffin for those requiring anything other than earth burial in Paragraph L of the Act:

> L. And it be further enacted, That it shall not be lawful to bury any Corpse within any Vault under the said Chapel, or within any Vault or Catacomb which may be erected within the Cemetery, unless the same shall be enclosed in a Coffin of Lead, or otherwise enclosed in Pitch of Half an Inch in Thickness between an interior and exterior Coffin of Wood.[12]

The Company extended the use of lead coffins to the purchaser 'of the privilege of interment in perpetuity in an entire brick grave or common grave'[13] for those requiring something more substantial than wood. To avoid any confusion, the *Bye-Laws* stated:

> XXXI. A Plan or Ground Plot of the Cemetery shall be made upon a scale sufficiently large to show the place and situation of each and every vault, grave, and place of burial which shall or may be made therein; and all such Vaults, Graves, and Places of Burial shall be numbered, and such Numbers shall be

[9] Ibid., 31-32. [10] 43 & 44 Vict., c. 41. [11] R. Fletcher (1974), *passim*. [12] General Cemetery Company (1833), 39. [13] Ibid., 95.

> entered in a Book, to be kept for that purpose, which shall contain the names and description of the several persons interred in such vaults, graves, and places of burial: the said Plan and Book shall be kept by the Clerk of the Company, and shall be open to the inspection of every Proprietor without fee or reward.[14]

Funerals, Funeral Furnishings, and Undertakers

Burials were not allowed to take place in Kensal Green before 7.00 a.m. between Lady Day and Michaelmas,[15] or before 8.00 a.m. between Michaelmas and Lady Day,[16] or after sunset, without special permission of the Board of Directors, in writing, and an additional fee was payable on all funerals taking place before 3.00 p.m. or after sunset.[17] Consequently, prime time was considered to be between 7.00 or 8.00 a.m. and 3.00 p.m., a fact known to most undertakers in the area, and any enterprising funeral-furnisher asked to officiate at Kensal Green would be able to advise his client that mid-day was by far the 'best' time to select.

In being a *general* cemetery, Kensal Green was not solely dependent on local trade, and accepted burials from any part of the Kingdom and the world. Reading the inscriptions on the larger monuments along Centre Avenue it is evident that several mausolea and vaults were constructed by and for people who never lived in London; some, indeed, never lived in England. For example, Edward Molyneux (1798-1864), for some time Consul for Georgia, was a solicitor practising in Liverpool.[18] Similar instances exist elsewhere in the cemetery. Sir Richard Graves MacDonnell K.C.M.G. (1814-81), who lies buried on South Branch Avenue, served as Governor of the British Settlements on the Gambia (1847-52), Governor of St Lucia (1852-3), Administrator and Captain-General of St Vincent (1853-5), Governor of South Australia (1855-62), Lieutenant-Governor of Nova Scotia (1864-5), Governor of Hong Kong (1865-72), and died at Hyères, France, in 1881.[19] General Sir William Casement (1780-1844) spent his latter years in India, died there, and is buried there: his splendid monument is therefore a cenotaph to his memory, although other members of his family are entombed there.[20]

The grander monuments were usually associated with brick graves, or substantial vaults, and coffins deposited therein were required to be of the triple-case variety stipulated by the General Cemetery Company's regulations. Undertakers in 19th-century London able to provide such merchandise were few, and a brief over-view of the undertaking trade in the metropolis at that time will explain the situation.

The funeral trade had three branches: coffin-making, undertaking, and funeral-furnishing. The coffin-maker performed the craft of making coffins, and might also occasionally perform funerals, but not necessarily so. The undertaker usually bought coffins from the coffin-maker, dressed and furnished them, and performed the funeral. At the upper end of the trade was the funeral-furnisher, usually a cabinet-maker more used to supplying his clients with luxury furniture: his workshops made, dressed, plumbed, and upholstered coffins, and performed funerals. This, then, was the hierarchy of the trade. A coffin-maker required the custom of the undertaker and respected the funeral-furnisher; and the undertaker relied on the coffin-maker whilst also respecting the funeral-furnisher; whereas the funeral-furnisher, whilst at times relying on the coffin-maker during moments of workshop stress, would have had no dealings with the undertaker.

Mr Sowerberry, the undertaker in Charles Dickens's *Oliver Twist* (1837-8), was in the middle rank of this funeral hierarchy, albeit at the lower end (for he only catered for

[14] General Cemetery Company (1833), 95. [15] 25 March to 29 September. Bye-Law XXXII. [16] 29 September to 25 March. Bye-Law XXXII. [17] Bye-Law XXXII. *See* General Cemetery Company (1833), 95. [18] Plot number [19607/56 & 65/RS]. [19] Plot number [27709/83/RS]. [20] Plot number [5400/56/RS]. *See The Bengal Obituary*(1848), 273.

parish funerals, which is to say those emanating from the Workhouse[21] or those in receipt of the Overseers'[22] outdoor relief). His shop would have been situated in a back street, probably in the same run-down part of the town where his clients lived; furthermore, Sowerberry himself lived only just above the bread-line. Undertakers such as he may have had trade at Kensal Green, but only in connection with the paupers' graves in the poor ground on the western boundary of the cemetery.

Mr Mould, the undertaker in Charles Dickens's *Martin Chuzzlewit* (1843-4), who was at the upper end of the middle rank of the trade, was of the opinion that his more prestigious clients knew that, in dealing with a well-conducted establishment (where everything was performed upon the very best scale), they were able to secure four horses to each vehicle, velvet trappings, drivers in cloth cloaks and top-boots, ostrich-plumes dyed black, and any number of attendants, all dressed in the latest funereal *haute couture*. Mould's type would have been seen frequently at Kensal Green, though performing rather more earth-burials than those associated with brick graves, vaults, and mausolea.

At least two 'society' funeral-furnishers and two Crown undertakers of the 19th century are themselves buried at Kensal Green. Thomas Dowbiggin (d. 1854) was an upholsterer, cabinet-maker, and society funeral-furnisher,[23] trading in partnership with the furniture-maker and funeral-furnisher William Holland (1779-1856).[24] William Banting (1826-1901)[25] was the Crown undertaker responsible for carrying out the practical aspects of the obsequies of Prince Albert (d. 1861); his son, William Westbrook Banting (1857-1932),[26] did the same for the funerals of Prince Leopold, Duke of Albany (d. 1884), Prince Albert Victor, Duke of Clarence (d. 1892), Queen Victoria (d. 1901), and Edward VII (d. 1910).

The Banting ledgers for the period 1900-1910[27] provide an insight not only into the complexities of the trade performed by the Crown undertaker but also of the fees charged by the General Cemetery Company. The account of the funeral of Mrs H. L. Fladgate (d. September 1900), of 53 Onslow Gardens, South Kensington,[28] came to £65 4s. 3d. (£65.21),[29] made up as follows:

Foreman to measure -		5*s.*	6*d.*
A stout Elm Coffin, lined & ruffled with fine Cambric muslin. A patent craped fine Cambric Muslin sheet, ruffled pillow and tufted mattress bed -	£5	4*s.*	0*d.*
A stout Lead Coffin soldered all around -		10*s.*	9*d.*
A Lead plate of Inscription engraved -		10*s.*	6*d.*
Foreman & 6 men with the above Coffins to 53 Onslow Gardens -	£1	1*s.*	0*d.*
Conveyance for ditto (Sunday) -		10*s.*	0*d.*
Plumber & man making up and soldering down Lead Coffin, used bran and fine wadding[30] -	£1	15*s.*	6*d.*

[21] House established for the provision of work for the unemployed poor of a parish; later, an institution administered by the Guardians of the Poor, in which paupers were lodged and the able-bodied set to work. Under 4 & 5 Will. IV, c. 76, several parishes were united or incorporated together under one Board of Guardians for the administration of the Poor Laws, and the 'Union Workhouse' was usually quite a large institution, much hated and feared by the mass of the population. [22] Overseers of the Poor were parish officers appointed to perform various duties connected with relief of the poor. The office was created by 43 Eliz. I, c. 2, and they were responsible for causing able-bodied paupers to work; giving relief to the disabled poor; putting poor children to work, apprenticing them, etc.; and raising by rate the necessary funds for these purposes. [23] Plot number [11241/77/RS]. [24] Plot number [13191/100/PS]. [25] Plot number [38565/128/PS]. [26] Ibid. [27] Litten Collection. [28] Banting Ledger 1900-1903, 7a-8a. [29] The comparison with £65.21 in 2001 is meaningless, as £65 was the best part of an annual wage for a clerk in 1900. For realistic comparisons of the value of money, see Munby (1996). [30] When the body was not embalmed the coffin was filled with bran and fine wadding to absorb the liquids and mask the odours associated with decomposition.

A stout Oak Outer Coffin, made of 1½ inch Oak with a chamfered plinth round the bottom edge and a chamfer on the edge of the lid & French polished, 8 solid brass Crescent handles with octagon loops and back plates, gilt and highly burnished & 8 solid brass headed long screws to secure lid, the inside of coffin lined stout white calico -	£14	10*s*.	0*d*.
A stout brass plate of Inscription engraved -	£2	4*s*.	0*d*.
Foreman & 6 men in with outer Coffin and moving down Remains -	£1	4*s*.	6*d*.
Conveyance for case -		10*s*.	0*d*.
Funeral Car & pair to bury at Kensal Green Cemetery -	£3	3*s*.	0*d*.
8 men as Bearers – 1st part of Service at St Peter's, Cranley Gardens & then to Kensal Green Cemetery @ 7/-	£2	16*s*.	0*d*.
Manager conducting Funeral -	£1	1*s*.	0*d*.
Foreman assisting -		10*s*	6*d*.
3 Cloth Hatbands and gloves for Coachmen of Private Carriages -		9*s*.	0*d*.
Cash Payments			
Usual allowances to men in with Coffins, to Plumber's closing Lead coffin, and to men in with the Oak Case.		(Blank)	
Ditto to Foreman & 8 men & Hearsemen & 3 Coachmen on day of Funeral -	£1	13*s*.	10*d*.
Cemetery Fees – Kensal Green -	£8	14*s*.	0*d*.
St Peter's Church fees -	£5	0*s*.	0*d*.
Verger & Cleaner		7*s*.	6*d*.
Cemetery Chaplain & Clerk as usual -	£1	11*s*.	6*d*.
Chapel Keeper, Sexton, & Vaultmen -		8*s*.	6*d*.
Usual to Manager, Foreman, Hearseman & 8 men in lieu of fittings[31]	£5	18*s*.	6*d*.
Messrs Wolfe & Son's account for 3 Brougham & pairs[32] -	£4	8*s*.	6*d*.
Cab for Bearers to Cemtery & sundry Cab fares, omnibus hire, & incidental expenses, making the necessary arrangements -		16*s*.	8*d*.
TOTAL	**£65**	**4*s*.**	**3*d*.**

The payment in this instance to the General Cemetery Company was £10 14s., comprising the cost of opening the vault, the officiating minister's fee, the clerk's fee, and the fees to the chapel caretaker, the sexton, and the men required to place the coffin within the vault. Whilst Kensal Green had its own Anglican chaplain, this did not stop the relatives of the deceased bringing their own minister with them should they have preferred to do so, but this had to be arranged beforehand.

In January 1901 Bantings' were again at Kensal Green, this time to officiate at the funeral of Master Charles Luke Russell, the infant son of C. E. Russell of 10, Cleveland

31 The 18th-century practice of allowing the attendants to keep their scarves, hatbands, and gloves had been superseded in the 19th century by gratuities. In this instance, a margin note records the manager and foreman as receiving £1 4s. each, and the hearseman and eight bearers 10s 6d. each.

32 Three coaches, each drawn by two horses. Wolfe & Son were 'black job masters' of St. James's. A 'black job master' hired out black horses, coaches, etc., specifically for funerals. Thus the 'black job master' ran a special type of livery-stable, with extras.

Place, St James's. From the description in the ledger,[33] the child's coffin was a miniature version (though without the lead shell) of that provided in the previous year for Mrs Fladgate, and cost £8 6s.; Messrs Wolfe of St James's again provided the horse-drawn carriages; the officiating minister and clerk received £1 11s. 6d.; the Chapel Keeper 5s., and the grave-maker 2s. 6d.; whilst the fee to the General Cemetery Company for the grave was £9.

Very few 19th-century undertakers had large establishments; consequently there was the need to contract out for the hire of bearers and attendants, drawn from a pool of itinerants who made themselves available to the trade. Similarly, most large towns had their own 'black job masters',[34] from whom funeral-cars, mourning-coaches, and horses could be hired. Consequently, the delay between death and burial resulted not only on the availability of the minister to officiate at the burial, and the work already in hand by the undertaker, but also the availability of the itinerants and the 'black job master' to come together at one and the same time. As far as Kensal Green cemetery was concerned, they were able to reduce any delay occasioned by the minister in providing their own officiating clerk-in-holy-orders. Furthermore, many undertakers relied on funeral-furnishing warehouses and wholesalers to provide on hire those items for which they had little reason to carry as stock, such as the more expensive velvet palls and horse-plumes. One such supplier was J. Turner of Farringdon Street, London, a 'Coffin Maker, Plate Chaser, Furnishing Undertaker and Funeral Featherman', whose 11-page catalogue of *c.*1838 contains a wealth of merchandise, even for the most discerning client.[35] In it he lists 30 coffin types, with each style available in one of four finishes; 20 sizes of shroud, each available in four qualities of material; and 15 types of ruffling, together with winding-sheets, mattresses, coffin-furniture, and palls. His was a large establishment, serving the eastern quarter of the City of London. Mindful of the newly-established cemeteries of Kensal Green, West Norwood, and Highgate, and their distance from central London, Turner was also able to offer on hire funeral-cars, coaches, and horses, both for town and country.

Turner was typical of a number of funeral-furnishing warehouses, operating in London during the first half of the 19th century. Taking items from Turner's catalogue at random, for 17s.[36] the undertaker was able to buy a 'good inch elm Coffin, smoothed, oiled, and finished with one row round of black or white nails, a plate of inscription, four handles, lined and a pillow' – indeed, the type of coffin generally used for earth burial at Kensal Green cemetery well into the third quarter of the 19th century – while for £9 he could secure Turner's finest item: '1½ inch Oak Case, covered with superfine cloth, finished with three rows all round, and six ornamented diamonds, with best nails, lead or brass plate, glory and urn, four pairs of cherub handles, and four dozen rays or stars'. This, together with an inner 'Elm Shell, covered with 4lb lead, lined, ruffled, and pillow', would provide a coffin suitable for brick graves, catacomb-shelves and mausolea at Kensal Green. That they could be bought from the stock of such warehouses as Turner of Farringdon meant that few undertakers were unable to provide even their most discerning clients with a funeral of quality.

The amount required on the part of the undertaker to equip a middle-class funeral from Turner's catalogue can, therefore, be assessed at £12 19s. 2d., made up as follows:

Elm shell, covered with 4lb lead, lined, ruffled, and pillow.	£3 10*s.* o*d.*
1½ inch Oak Case, covered with superfine cloth,	£5 10*s.* o*d.*
finished with three rows all round, and six ornamented	

[33] Banting Ledger 1900-1903, 18-18a. [34] See footnote 32. [35] Trade catalogue of J. Turner (*c.*1838), *passim.*
[36] 17 shillings was almost a weekly wage for an unskilled labourer in the 1830s.

diamonds, with best nails, lead or brass plate, glory and urn, four pairs of cherub handles, and four dozen rays or stars.	
Best quality pall.	3*s*. 6*d*.
2 mutes' gowns, staves, bands, and gloves.	12*s*. 0*d*.
Four cloaks, crape bands, and gloves.	5*s*. 8*d*.
Hearse and coach, pairs; velvets for ditto.	£2 11*s*. 0*d*.
2 cloaks, and bands.	1*s*. 6*d*.
6 pages, bands, gloves, truncheons, wands.	5*s*. 6*d*.
Total	**£12 19*s*. 2*d*.**

With the exception of the coffin and its fittings, all other items were to be returned to Turner's warehouse. Even so, the high-street undertaker would be selling the funeral on with a mark-up of between 100 per cent and 150 per cent above his own outlay, thus presenting his client with a bill of between £38 17s. 6d. and £25 18s. 4d.

Turner also maintained his own coach-house and livery-stable, thereby serving as a 'black job master' in addition to that of funeral-furnishing warehouseman. His *c*.1838 catalogue concluded with the following information:

> Licensed one and two horse hearses for removals, in town or Country, at the following low prices: – Hearse and pair. At 1*s*. 6*d*. per Mile. – Coach and pair, 1*s*. 6*d*. per mile. – Hearse and one horse, at 1*s*. per mile, to and from any part of the Kingdom, including driver and all expenses, except turnpikes.
>
> J. T. flatters himself that every satisfaction will be given respecting safety, good carriages, and careful drivers.
>
> The object of this mode of conveyance is to enable persons being removed at a moderate expense.
>
> Any article in the funeral business may be sent at the same time, if required.
>
> All orders, in town or country, attended to with punctuality and dispatch, for ready money.[37]

By the middle of the 19th century, with an efficient railway network and telegraph system in place, road transport was no longer relied upon to effect a quick and efficient service from the funeral-furnishing warehouse to undertakers' parlours. In Birmingham, Messrs Ingall, Parsons, & Clive had established a nation-wide service via telegraph, and by *c*.1908 Messrs Dottridge Bros. Ltd., of Dorset Works, East Road, City Road, London, had perfected an efficient ordering system:

> MEMORANDA
>
> **Telegraph and Special Orders** can be received at all hours of the night, as there is always an assistant in attendance. For the convenience of our Customers wanting goods on **SUNDAY** we make arrangements to supply them at **12.30** p.m. All goods are charged at a slightly advanced price, especially those requiring labour, as that has to be paid for at higher rates.

[37] J. Turner (*c*.1838), 11.

> **We deem it of the utmost importance that our Customers should be again reminded that we always keep in Stock SHELLS and CASES in ELM and OAK of all ordinary sizes.**
>
> **The Coffins and Cases are polished, and on receipt of Telegram stating Style of FINISH can be sent away**
>
> WITHIN THREE HOURS.
>
> It is presumed that all our Customers have by them our **Illustrated Coffin Furniture List.** This will enable them to see exactly the Furniture described in the Coffin List. In addition, should they wish any other pattern of Handle or Ornament than that described, they have merely to note the price it is estimated at and that which they prefer in order to see the difference in cost.
>
> It is a common error to imagine that in all cases when death takes place the body should be immediately coffined. The deceased should be laid out, and then allowed to remain undisturbed till the body is rigid. This is the best way to keep an ordinary corpse; to disturb the body when it is scarcely cold, only tends to hasten the decomposing process. This fact explained to the friends would often prevent the needless haste to send in a coffin immediately, especially when the death takes place on a Sunday.
>
> **Telegraphing.** – In wiring anything do not omit including your name at the end of the message, otherwise we are at a loss to know from whom it comes.
>
> **Regd. Telegraphic Address: "Funeral, London."**
>
> **Telephone Nos.: 85 London Wall and 123 Dalston.**[38]

Every assistance was provided by Dottridge Bros., to inform clients of their efficiency:

> DELIVERY OF COFFINS.
>
> TO TOWN AND SUBURBAN CUSTOMERS.
>
> We advise customers as far as possible to arrange and send for their Coffins and Cases. In Suburban districts, if necessary, an arrangement can easily be made with a local man to run into town, whereas it is often most difficult for us to provide economical conveyance. Delivery by train should also be remembered, it being both cheap and expeditious.
>
> TO COUNTRY CUSTOMERS.
>
> All Coffins being listed at Warehouse prices, as usual, a charge of ***2s. 6d.*** will be added to every Adult Coffin (except where two are dispatched together) for the **Special Delivery** to the Station. For Children's Coffins the charge will be from ***1s.*** *to* ***2s.***, according to size.
>
> These charges do not apply to Coffins ordered for stock, which do not need *special* delivery.

[38] Dottridge Brothers Limited (*c.*1908), 5.

LETTER BOXES IN MAIL TRAINS.
These are now affixed to all mail trains in which sorting duty is performed. The letter box is suspended outside the sorting carriage at each station at which the train stops, and the letters must bear an extra fee of ½*d.*, prepaid by stamp.
With this assistance, should you require to send an order after the regular time your box closes, you can post a letter at the station up to the time of the arrival of the mail.[39]

Whilst the mid-19th-century funeral was, for the middle classes, a lavish, complex, and expensive cavalcade of pomp, few undertakers were aware of the significance of the many trappings provided, and doubtless the same ignorance was maintained by those attending funerals at Kensal Green. The following embarrassing conversation ensued between Edwin Chadwick and Mr Wild, a London tradesman:

Chadwick — Are you aware that the array of funerals, commonly made by undertakers, is strictly the heraldic array of a baronial funeral, the two men who sand at the doors being supposed to be the two porters of the castle, with their staves, in black; the man who heads the procession, wearing a scarf, being a representative of a herald-at-arms; the man who carries a plume of feathers on his head being an esquire, who bears the shield and casque, with its plume of feathers; the pall-bearers, with batons, being representatives of the knights-companions-at-arms; the men walking with wands being supposed to represent gentlemen-ushers, with their wands: – are you aware that this is said to be the origin and type of the common array usually provided by those who undertake to perform funerals?

Undertaker — No; I am not aware of it.

Chadwick — It may be presumed that those who order funerals are equally unaware of the incongruity for which such expense is incurred?

Undertaker — Undoubtedly they are.[40]

During the first half of the 19th century, the profundity of pomp and panoply of the cortège depended on the social status of the deceased, and it was the undertaker who judged what was considered correct in any given situation. He alone decided on the style and quality of the funeral. Faced with this seemingly necessary charade there was little interference on the part of the client, the usual instruction being 'to provide what is customary'. Unfortunately, the word 'customary' was frequently misinterpreted, and many undertakers went to excess. It is not unreasonable to say that in certain parts of the country, particularly the East End of London, the trade perpetuated a meaningless and elaborate ritual well into the first decade of the 20th century, after it had long been abandoned by the middle and upper classes.

Guidance to the populace on funeral expenses was given in a section entitled 'Death in the Household' in *Cassell's Household Guide to every Department of Practical Life* of 1869-71,[41] where eight classes of funeral offered by a large London undertaking firm were described, ranging from £3 5s. (£3.25) to £53:

Funeral costing £3 5s. – Patent carriage, with one horse; smooth elm coffin, neatly finished, lined inside, with pillow, &c.; use of pall, mourners' fittings, coachman, with hat-band; bearers; attendant with hat-band, &c.

39 Dottridge Brothers Limited (*c.*1908), 8. 40 Chadwick (1843), 49. §45. 41 Cassell & Co. Ltd., (1869-71), *passim.*

Funeral costing £5 5s. – Hearse, with one horse; mourning coach, with one horse; stout elm coffin, covered with fine black, plate of inscription, lid ornaments, and three pairs of handles, mattress, pillow, and a pair of side sheets; use of velvet pall; mourners' fittings; coachmen with hat-bands and gloves; bearers; attendant with silk hat-band, &c.

Funeral costing £6 6s. – Hearse, with pair of horses; mourning coach and pair; strong elm coffin, covered with black, plate of inscription, lid ornaments, and three pairs of handles, mattress, pillow, &c.; use of velvet pall, mourners' fittings; coachmen with hat-bands and gloves; bearers; attendant with silk hat-band, &c.

Funeral costing £8 15s. – Hearse and pair of horses; mourning coach and pair; velvet covering for carriages and horses; strong elm coffin, covered with fine black, plate of inscription, lid ornaments, three pairs of cherub handles and grips, and finished with best black nails, mattress, pillow, and side sheets; use of silk velvet pall; two mutes with gowns, silk hat-bands, and gloves; four men as bearers, and two coachmen with cloaks, hat-bands, and gloves; use of mourners' fittings; and attendant with silk hat-band.

Funeral costing £14 14s. – Hearse and pair of horses; mourning coach and pair; fifteen plumes of black ostrich feathers and complete velvet coverings for carriages and horses; stout inch elm coffin, with inner lid, covered with black cloth, set with two rows all round of best black nails; lead plate of inscription; lid ornaments, four pairs of handles and grips, all of the best improved jet and bright black; tufted mattress, lined and ruffled, and fine cambric winding-sheet; use of velvet pall; two mutes with gowns, silk hat-bands, and gloves, eight men as pages and coachmen, with truncheons and wands, crape hat-bands, &c., use of mourners' fittings; and attendant with silk hat-band, &c.

Funeral costing £23 10s. – Hearse and four horses, two mourning coaches, with pairs, nineteen plumes of rich ostrich-feathers, and complete velvet covering for carriages and horses; strong inch elm shell, covered with black; tufted mattress, lined and ruffled with cambric and pillow; fine cambric winding-sheet, inch elm case to receive the above, covered with fine black cloth; lead plate of inscription, lid ornaments, four pairs of shield handles and grips, and furnished with two rows all round of best nails; use of silk velvet pall; two mutes with gowns, silk hat-bands, and gloves; eleven men as pages; and coachmen with truncheons and wands, crape hat-bands, &c., use of mourners' fittings; and attendant with silk hat-band, &c.

Funeral costing £30. Hearse and four horses, two mourning coaches, with pairs, nineteen plumes of rich ostrich-feathers, complete velvet covering for carriages and horses, an esquire's plume of best feathers; strong elm shell, with tufted mattress, lined and ruffled with superfine cambric, and pillow; full worked fine cambric winding-sheet; outside lead coffin, with inscription plate and solder complete, stout inch elm case, covered with superfine black cloth, set with three rows round, and lid panelled with best black nails; registered lead plate of inscription, lid ornaments to correspond, and four pairs of handles, and grips all of the best imperial black; use of the best silk velvet pall; two mutes with gowns, silk hat-bands, and gloves &c.; twelve men as pages, feathermen, and coachmen, with truncheons and wands, silk hat-bands, &c., use of mourners' fittings; and attendant with silk hat-band, &c.

Funeral costing £53. Hearse and four horses, two mourning coaches with fours, twenty-three plumes of rich ostrich-feathers, complete velvet covering for carriages and horses, and an esquire's plume of best feathers; strong elm shell, with tufted mattress, lined and ruffled with superfine cambric, and pillow; full worked glazed cambric winding-sheet; stout outside lead coffin, with inscription plate and solder complete; one-and-a-half inch oak case, covered with black or crimson velvet, set with three rows round, and lid panelled with best brass nails; stout brass plate of inscription, richly engraved; four pairs of best brass handles and grips, lid ornaments to correspond; use of the silk velvet pall; two mutes with gowns, silk hat-bands, and gloves; fourteen men as pages, feathermen, and coachmen, with truncheons and wands, silk hat-bands, &c., use of mourners' fittings; and attendant with silk hat-band, &c.[42]

In the main, most mid-19th-century funerals at Kensal Green would have been of the quality of £8 15s. and above, with those of the £30 category being considered standard practice for brick-grave, vault, catacomb, and mausoleum deposit. Most of the coffins in the catacomb beneath the Anglican chapel are of the £30 category, whilst those of John Fitzgibbon, 2nd Earl of Clare (1792-1851)[43] and the Rt. Hon. William Pole Tylney Long-Wellesley, 4th Earl of Mornington (1788-1857)[44] are of the £53 category.

By the middle of the 19th century a few of the more enterprising London undertakers had expanded their business to exclude their dependency on coffin-makers and black-job masters. With their own carpenters and coffin-dressers (who doubled-up as bearers) and their own horses, hearses, and mourning carriages, they were now in a position to equip all qualities of funeral from their own establishments, trading as 'funeral-furnishers' rather than 'undertakers'. It was William Banting, who held the royal warrant as funeral-furnisher to Queen Victoria, who provided the role-model for the aspiring funeral-furnisher. Even so, Banting was not averse to sub-contracting some of his work to Messrs J. D. Field of London.[45]

The handing-down of jobs from the busy high-street funeral-furnisher was ably described in 1843 in a conversation between Edwin Chadwick and Mr Dix, one of the more successful London undertakers performing upwards of eight hundred funerals a year:

Dix — I frequently perform funerals three deep: that is, I do it for one person, who does it for another who does it for the relatives of the deceased, he being the first person applied to.

Chadwick — The people then generally apply to the nearest person?

Dix — Yes, they do. Everybody calls himself an undertaker. The numerous men employed as bearers become undertakers, although they have never done anything until they have got a job. I have known one of these men get a new suit of clothes out of the funeral of one decent mechanic.[46]

Unfortunately, not all undertakers were strictly honest in their dealing with clients, frequently disobeying the instructions for a simple funeral by providing one in accordance with *their* opinion of the social status of the deceased. To a great extent this arrogance in 'kicking over the traces' of the client's specific commands contributed to

[42] Cassell & Co. Ltd., (1869-71), iii, 292. [43] **Catacomb B**/Private Vault. Fitzgibbon had been a friend of Byron, and was Governor of Bombay (1830-4). [44] **Catacomb B**/Vault 65/Compartment 15. His obituary in *The Morning Chronicle* stated he 'was redeemed by no single virtue, adorned by no single grace'. *See Gentlemen's Magazine* (1857), ii, 215. [45] When William Westbrook Banting died in 1932, J. D. Field endeavoured to secure the royal warrant as Crown Undertaker. George V was not content with this suggestion, and the warrant was given to J. H. Kenyon of Westbourne Grove, London. [46] E. Chadwick (1843), 51, §46.

funeral reform. A request for a funeral exhibiting propriety without excess panoply was made in 1859 by a Mr Robey, sail-maker, of Shadwell, London, when he placed an order for his late wife's funeral with the undertakers, Field of Charlotte Street, Shadwell.[47] Negotiations between Robey and Field settled on the provision of a £50 funeral for £25. The bill came to £22, but Robey, dissatisfied with the services provided by Field, was only willing to pay £20. Consequently, Field took Robey to court to secure the outstanding £2. The judgement was in Field's favour. However, the court received more than £2 in entertainment:

> COURT OF EXCHEQUER: before Mr Baron Channell.[48]
>
> *An Undertaker's Bill – Field* v. *Robey*. This action was to recover £22, the amount of an undertaker's bill. The defendant had paid £20 into the court and had denied his liability to the £2. The plaintiff is an undertaker carrying on his business in Charlotte Street, St George-in-the-East, and the defendant is a sail-maker. On the 21st March last (1859) the defendant met the plaintiff in Watney Street and informed him of his wife's death and gave directions to make a case for his wife's leaden coffin and conduct the funeral. After the funeral the defendant expressed his satisfaction at what had been done and desired him to send his bill the next morning and he would give him a cheque for the amount. In a conversation with the defendant the plaintiff, who has a peculiarly solemn cast of countenance, said he smiled and told the defendant the funeral would cost £50. Defendant replied, 'I did not think half of it', upon which plaintiff said, 'Well, it will be about £25'. The plaintiff said his charges were fair and reasonable. In his cross-examination by Mr Huddlestone, the plaintiff said he did not publish handbills headed 'Respects to the departed', 'Decency and pomp combined for £10', with 'a hearse, prancing horses, &c.' (*laughter*). He had charged £5 for the elm shell, which was French polished. He presented the minister with silk band and gloves, which he informed Mr Robey was usual at respectable funerals, and the defendant said he did not object to it. He had charged half-a-guinea for himself attending the funeral with silk fittings (*laughter*). He had charged for six horse hearse velvets, three hammer cloths, and two mourning coaches, and for ten men including two mutes, described in the bill as 'two porters with robes and silk fittings'.
>
> Mr Morsley and Mr Adam Springfield were called to prove the charges were fair and reasonable. In cross-examination the latter said that there were prices for mutes (*laughter*). Mr Huddlestone – What is the usual charge for a mute with a dark, good melancholy physiognomy? (*laughter*). Mr Springfield – 'There are various prices. It depends on whether he is a good-looking fellow' (*laughter*). Mr Baron Channell – 'Then you charge according to their looks?' Mr Springfield – 'Yes, certainly' (*laughter*). Mr Baron Channell – 'When returning from a funeral they are generally merry-looking fellows?' Mr Huddlestone –'They are then off duty; and, as my friend near me, Mr Hawkings, observed, they are no longer mutes, but liquids' (*laughter*). To witness – 'What is the fair price for a good melancholy mute?' Mr Springfield – 'That depends entirely how he looks (*laughter*). Mr Huddlestone – 'That is when he has got a white choker on, and well pulls down the corner of his mouth? (*laughter*). Mr Springfield – 'Yes, just so' (*renewed laughter*). 'The ordinary price of a mute is three halfcrowns. I have never heard of them being had for a sovereign' (*laughter*). Several other undertakers

[47] This Field is not to be confused with Banting's sub-contractor, J. D. Field. [48] Sir William Fry Channell (1804-73) was appointed to succeed Baron Alderson at the Court of Exchequer in 1857.

were called, who proved that the charges were fair and reasonable, some of them were too small, none of them too high. Mr Huddlestone said that his action was defended on principle, the plaintiff having supplied many of the articles against the defendant's consent, and that some of the charges were too high. The defendant was called. He denied the conversation as spoken to by the plaintiff. Instead of ten men and two mutes, as charged for, being at the funeral, there were but eight men and two mutes. He objected to the minister's scarf and gloves, informing the plaintiff that having many bills to pay in consequence of his wife's illness, he must be just before he was generous, and could not afford to give anything to the parson; at the same time he objected to all pomp and foolery, and told the plaintiff it should be a plain funeral. He particularly told him he would have no mutes, and if he had not been prevented they would not have remained long at the door (*laughter*). When the plaintiff was making the coffin, he (defendant) called at this shop, and seeing what he was about, told him he would not have a parcel of ornaments about it – angels and such trash (*laughter*). Several witnesses were called to show the charges were high, one of them, Mr Holley, in his cross-examination, said it was usual for undertakers to charge according to the condition in life of the parties who employed them. The evidence with reference to the actual order was conflicting. Mr Baron Channell, in summing up, left it to the jury to say whether, under all the circumstances, they considered the funeral was conducted in a decent manner without pomp.

The jury returned a verdict for the plaintiff and the amount claimed.[49]

Whilst attendance at Victorian funerals rarely came to more than a dozen or so relatives and close friends, those of well-known personalities tended to attract large numbers of sight-seers. At Kensal Green the funerals of William Makepeace Thackeray (d. 1863), Anthony Trollope (d. 1882), William Wilkie Collins (d. 1889), and Émile Blondin (d. 1897),[50] attracted crowds by the thousand, thronging the avenues from the main gate to the chapel, and from the chapel to the graveside.[51] The funeral of the department-store proprietor, William Whiteley (1831-1907), drew an excessively large crowd on account of his having been murdered (shot) in his office by Horace George Rayner, who claimed to be his illegitimate son.[52]

It can be argued that the anticipation of these crowds influenced some undertakers to provide just a little more than would otherwise have been expected by the client. However, it seems probable that the amount of pomp and panoply attending Andrew Ducrow's funeral at Kensal Green on Saturday, 5 February 1842 had more to do with the inflated importance the former proprietor of Astley's Amphitheatre had adopted during his lifetime:

At half past noon on 5 February 1842, Andrew Ducrow set out on his final journey. For several hours previously the streets in the vicinity of his residence in York Road had been crowded with eager spectators, while six mutes stood conspicuously before the house door. Some among this vast throng were accommodated in temporary booths erected for the occasion; others occupied windows or jammed into coaches and stood on carts to obtain a better view. Nor did the great press of people diminish much along the long route to Kensal Green,

49 *The Moufussilite* (Meerut), New Series, **xiv**/1415 (26 July 1859), 462, quoting *The Weekly Dispatch* (5 June 1859). 50 His real name was Jean-François Gravelet. 51 Such crowds were there as spectators rather than participants, consequently they were not expected to attend the service in the chapel. 52 Rayner's mother had been Whiteley's mistress, though at the time of the murder it appears Whiteley had transferred his affections to Rayner's aunt.

> with traffic consequently brought to a halt in all the adjacent streets and thoroughfares through which the procession passed ... Preceded by a vanguard of policemen to clear the way, the procession was led by an undertaker on horseback, followed by the mounted porters and pages on foot carrying plumes of sable ostrich feathers. Then came three of Ducrow's highly trained steeds – Vienna, Pegasus, and Beauty – each led by two grooms and costumed in velvet, feathers, and crape head-dresses... but the "favourite horse" mentioned in the will was lamentably absent: John Lump, whose sturdy back had supported his master's dazzling impersonations for the past seventeen years, had died of old age a few days before the funeral. The hearse, drawn by six horses with postillions and accompanied by pages, came next. The outer coffin was of oak, covered with purple velvet[53] and studded with silver-gilt nails, and bearing an allegorical plate showing Genius weeping over the ashes of her favourite son.[54] This in turn was followed by eleven mourning coaches, also accompanied by pages, bearing Ducrow's family, close friends, and colleagues. Additional mourners on horseback and in private carriages brought up the rear... At the cemetery Louisa Ducrow, supported by Ducrow's old friend William Bunn and William D. Broadfoot, entered the mausoleum to spend a few minutes with her husband and to strew his casket with *immortelles*[55] ... Then the iron door clanged shut, and Ducrow's greatest spectacle was over.[56]

Had Ducrow died two years earlier, the ladies attending the funeral might have had difficulty securing suitable mourning-dress in the nine days between the great circus-performer's death and his burial. Fortunately, Messrs Jay's of Regent Street, London, had opened their doors in 1841, with the boast of being able to dress an entire family and their servants in full mourning livery from their stock. The *History of Mourning*, published by Jay's *c.*1889, outlined the establishment of the firm:

> The ingenious idea of the *Magasin de Deuil*, or establishment exclusively devoted to the sale of mourning costumes and of the paraphernalia necessary for a funeral, has long been held to be exclusively French; but our quick-witted neighbours have, to speak the truth, originated few things; ...*The Magasin de Deuil* is but a brilliant and elaborate adaptation of the old *Mercerie de lutto* which has existed for centuries, and still exists, in every Italian city, where people in the haste of grief can obtain in a few hours all that the etiquette of civilisation requires for mourning ... Continental ideas are slow to reach this country, but when they do find acceptance with us, they rarely fail to attain that vast extension so characteristic of English commerce. Such development could scarcely be exhibited in a more marked manner than in Jay's London General Mourning Warehouse, Regent Street, an establishment which dates from the year 1841, and which during that period has never ceased to increase its resources and to complete its organisation, until it has become, of its kind, a mart unique both for the quality and nature of its attributes. Of late years the business and enterprise of this firm has enormously increased, and it includes not only all that is necessary for mourning, but also departments devoted to dresses of a more general description, although the colours are confined to such as could be worn for either full or half mourning. Black silks, however, are pre-eminently a speciality of this house, and

53 This in itself was an arrogance, as use of purple velvet was traditionally reserved for the coffins of monarchs, their consorts, and the episcopacy. 54 This inference was to be repeated on the tomb's inscription: 'Within this tomb, erected by Genius for the reception of its own remains...'. 55 A name for various composite flowers of papery texture which retain their colour after being dried. 56 Saxon (1978), 352-4.

15.3 A cortège outside the Dissenters' chapel shown in a watercolour, *c.*1860 (GCC. © *English Heritage [NMR]. Photographic Library*, K970179, April 1997).

> the Continental journals frequently announce that "*la maison Jay de Londres a fait des forts achats*". Their system is one from which they never swerve. It is to buy the commodity direct from the manufacturer, and to supply it to their patrons at the very smallest modicum of profit compatible with the legitimate course of trade. The materials for mourning costumes must always remain virtually unchangeable, and few additions can be made to the list of silks, crapes, paramattas, cashmeres, *grenadines*, and *tulles* as fabrics. They and their modifications must be ever in fashion so long as it continues fashionable to wear mourning at all; but fashion in design, construction, and embellishment may be said to change, not only every month, but well-nigh every week.[57]

Without doubt the funerals of the noble and middle classes at Kensal Green during the 19th century were majestic affairs, especially those performed by such society funeral-furnishers as W. W. Banting, France & Sons, or Dowbiggin & Holland. Their equipage was particularly lavish, the number of attendants a spectacle in itself, the cortège being preceded by two mutes in deep mourning, then the plumed hearse drawn by four velvet-clad horses, flanked by eight coffin-bearers, the whole followed by as many mourning-coaches as were required.

Most cortèges arrived at the main gate off the Harrow Road at the east end of the cemetery, and either went left to the Dissenters' chapel (15.3) or right to the Anglican chapel. For those going left, the journey was a short one, whereas the Anglican chapel was approached via Centre Avenue, North Branch Avenue, and Terrace Avenue, it not being possible to gain vehicular access via Centre Avenue itself owing to the podium steps at its western termination. Both chapels were equipped with a catafalque, bench-seating against the (liturgical) north and south walls, and a double-decker pulpit for the minister and clerk against the (liturgical) east wall. On arrival at the portico, and whilst the coffin was being made ready for removal from the hearse, the mourners were shown to their seats.

If the funeral took place in the Dissenters' chapel its format would follow the service book of the sect of the deceased, be he Baptist, Methodist, or Hindu. Humanists had no

57 Davey (*c.*1889), 95.

formal service, rather their obsequies were attended by secular readings and eulogies. If earth or brick-grave burial was to follow, the coffin was carried out of the chapel at the conclusion of the service to the grave for the committal. Should the coffin be destined for the catacomb, it was lowered on webbing through the trap-door in the floor and on to the shoulders of the coffin-bearers below, who had previously descended during the service via a staircase next to the vestry at the back of the chapel.

Funerals in the Anglican chapel had a set liturgy, performed in accordance with *The Order for the Burial of the Dead* from the 1662 *Book of Common Prayer*, and, whilst the Cemetery Company had its own bound pew copies of the 1662 funeral-service, it was not unusual for families to request the funeral-furnisher to provide copies of the service, generally as 4 x 3-inch (101 x 76mm) booklets, bound in leather or black buckram, the cover usually impressed with a gilt cross or the IHS Sacred Monogram, and containing on the inside end-paper a memorial-card to the deceased giving the plot-number and, if not specifically requested otherwise, the name of the officiating funeral-furnisher.

Meeting the coffin at the door, the minister would proceed the bearers into the chapel whilst reading the Sentences, during which the coffin would be placed on to the catafalque (**15.2**). At the conclusion of the 20-minute service[58] the coffin was made ready for disposal. If it were to be given an earth burial, or deposited in a brick-grave, vault, or mausoleum within the cemetery, the top deck of the catafalque was revolved through 180 degrees (**7.32, 7.33**) and the coffin carried out of the chapel to be placed back into the horse-drawn hearse for the short journey through the cemetery to the place of deposit. If deposit were to take place in the catacomb, an hydraulic action was used whereby the catafalque slowly descended through the floor to the vaults beneath (**7.28**), the bearers having previously descended via a flight of stone steps adjacent to the boiler room at the (liturgical) west of the chapel (see Chapter VII). Whilst the committal was taking place, the hearse would drive back to the funeral-furnisher's premises, leaving the mourning-coaches to transport the family of the deceased back to their homes.

The funeral reform championed by Edwin Chadwick in the 1840s took about thirty years to come to fruition, and it was not until the 1870s that the middle classes were asking for a less convoluted panoply whilst at the same time maintaining a dignity of performance. In London, it was difficult to curb the enthusiasm of some funeral-furnishers, who now turned their attention to the lower orders (**15.4**). The result was the establishment of the 'East End' funeral, a crude mockery of that previously performed for those of more exalted rank. Writing in *The London Tradesman* in 1747, R. Campbell said, 'The last Trade I shall mention is the Undertaker, a Set of Men who live by Death, and never care to appear but at the End of a Man's Life, they may properly enough serve to bring up the Rear of our Trades;[59] similarly, the down-selling of the grand Victorian funeral to the lower classes was seen as the rear-end of the craft. The success of funeral reform lay in the hands of the middle class; consequently those on its fringes were able to satisfactorily embrace change without the fear of social stigma. In 1923 the popular household-management book, *Enquire Within*, whilst acknowledging the social differentials, contained the following useful tips on organising funerals:

> *Funerals* – It is always best to place the discretion of a funeral under a respectable undertaker, with the precaution of obtaining his estimate for the expenses, and limiting him to them. He can best advise upon the observances to be attended to, since the style of funerals differs with the station of the deceased's family, and is further modified by the customs of particular localities, and even by religious

[58] It was not until 1910 with the funeral of Edward VII that hymns for congregational singing were incorporated within the Burial Service. [59] Campbell (1747), 329.

15.4 Funeral of a London shopkeeper, photographed in 1901 by Sir Benjamin Stone, MP (1838-1911). Writing to his friend, Dr Dan McKenzie, of Leytonstone, London, Stone commented: 'The pictures you have been able to secure will, I am sure, be of interest to future historians of the morals and manners of the nineteenth century'. The cortège is shown standing outside Cumberland Terrace, Regent's Park, with the chapel of the Royal Foundation of St Katharine of 1826-8 (designed by Ambrose Poynter [1796-1886]) in the background (*Birmingham Library Services*).

views. He will also make the necessary arrangements at the cemetery or place of interment.

Mourning – The dressmaker will advise upon the "degree" of mourning to be worn, which must be modified according to the age of the deceased, and the relationship of the mourner. The undertaker will advise respecting the degree of mourning to be displayed upon the carriage, horses, &c.

In the Funeral Cortège the nearest relatives of the deceased occupy the carriages nearest the hearse. The same order prevails in returning. Only the relatives and most intimate friends of the family should return to the house after the funeral; and their visit should be as short as possible.

In Walking Funerals it is considered a mark of respect for friends to become pall-bearers. In the funerals of young persons, the pall should be borne by their companions, wearing white gloves. It is a pretty and effecting sight to see the pall over the coffin of a young lady borne by six of her female friends. Flowers may be placed upon the coffin, and over the grave.

Funeral Expenses – As funerals in England, conducted in the ordinary way, with the usual display of hearse, mourning carriage, and costly mourning, are attended with considerable expense, societies have been formed in many parishes with the view of reducing the outlay resorted to on these occasions, and at a time perhaps when it would be better in many cases to observe the strictest economy. The members of these societies agree among themselves to do all that is possible to reduce the expenditure at funerals, and to render the accompaniments of the sad ceremony as inexpensive as possible. Instead of going into mourning, many now content themselves with wearing a simple band of cloth on the left arm. This is done by women as well as by men.[60]

60 Anonymous (1923), 223-4.

The trade abhorred the cultural revolution, and their dissatisfaction was not disguised. In *c.*1908 Dottridge Brothers of London thinly veiled their displeasure between the lines of the following advertisements:

MEN'S PAY FOR ATTENDING FUNERALS

> Now that so many funerals take place without the use of hat-bands, the principle upon which men's pay has always been regulated is interfered with. We think, therefore, the fairest way to arrive at their pay is by the number of coffins used, that being, as a general rule, a fair index to the position of the family.
>
> If the principle on which the ... prices is regulated be thought peculiar in these days of Funeral Reform, we have only to say that it is a very difficult matter for us to attempt to alter without the general agreement of the Trade, as when a number of men are required they are obviously extra to our own shopmen. And even were one price agreed upon, it would not be so favourable as at present for common work.[61]

ASSISTANTS' DRESS

> Customers will please note in making up their order for the Funeral that they can now have Assistants dressed alike.
>
> We need scarcely remind you that the diversity in Men's dress has always been the greatest defect in a Funeral Cortège, and as in these days Feathers, Mutes, and a good deal of paraphernalia are curtailed, it is absolutely necessary to have the little that is supplied in the best of taste.[62]

Hygienic Treatment of the Body

In addition to the public spectacle of the cortège, the funeral-furnisher was also responsible for the preparation of the body. The standard treatment for the dead is for the bowels to be emptied, the corpse to be washed, the hair combed, and finger-nails cleaned prior to dressing the remains in a shroud. Chemical hygienic treatment, commonly known as 'embalming', was introduced from America in the 1890s;[63] even so it was rarely practised, being limited to the bodies of those dying in London whose remains were destined for repatriation abroad. The standard technique in the 19th century, and that concerning almost all the corpses destined for Kensal Green, was for cotton wadding, bran, and sawdust packed beneath the fitted base-sheet within the coffin, to absorb the seepage of body-fluids. In some instances, the space remaining once the body had been coffined was filled with bran as an additional sanitising precaution.[64] Where the body was mutilated – as frequently resulted from death by fire, suicide, road or rail accident, or death by violent hands – and there was the risk of profound nasal offence, the space within the coffin once the body had been cased was filled with charcoal. It was unusual for corpses to be subjected to full evisceration. In such cases, the soft tissues were removed and separately cased, and the corpse seared and sluiced with aromatic spices and balsam. The only known example at Kensal Green of this drastic form of preparation is Howe Peter Browne, 2nd Marquess of Sligo (1788-1845), the

[61] Dottridge Brothers (*c.*1908*a*), 53. [62] Ibid., 62. [63] The first embalming fluid to be patented was in 1856 in America, consisting of white arsenic and pyroligenous acid injected into the body and controlled by an electric charge passed through the corpse until the body-liquids and tissue congealed. The first commercial use of arterial embalming fluid with a formalin base occurred in America in 1906. [64] Litten (1991), 85-118.

friend of George IV, Byron, and de Quincey, whose coffin and encased viscera rest in the brick grave beneath his sarcophagus-tomb on Centre Avenue.[65]

The leading campaigners for the introduction of American techniques of arterial hygienic treatment were Messrs Dottridge Brothers of London, though it was not until the 1920s that this system of temporary preservation began to be accepted amongst the funeral fraternity. Dottridge Bros., in an attempt to promote the process, eulogised hygienic treatment in their trade catalogue of *c.*1908:

> It is now becoming a generally acknowledged fact that the Undertakers in England have too long neglected the importance of sanitation as applied to their own profession. No doubt the neglect has been due to the absence of knowledge in dealing with these matters, and the ignorance of the right methods and necessary articles for use ... We all know the prehistoric method of treating the dead, which obtain even today in the less enlightened parts of the country – the body hurriedly placed in the coffin, the packing with sawdust, and the necessary precipitate screwing down of the lid. We know, too, the frequent results of such crude precautions, the often painful unpleasantness – to use a mild term – which results from putrefaction, and which the undertaker assures the family is "quite inevitable". Happily we believe that such indecencies have seen their day, and that the effective methods of preserving the body, which are universally adopted in the United States, will soon rob the death chamber in England, too, of everything unhealthy and offensive. For years past we have endeavoured to press these views upon the Trade, and the rapidly increasing resort to the practice induced a member of the firm to cross the Atlantic and become proficient in the latest and most perfect methods in use. The wholesale mutilation of the body by which the early embalmers did their work is a thing of the past; and now a small incision in the arm, followed by the injection of antiseptics, is sufficient to destroy the germs of corruption, decomposition is arrested, and the flesh retains its natural colouration ... Where no process of preservation is resorted to it frequently happens that relations from a distance are debarred, whereas when the body has been prepared by the Operator it keeps its appearance of life for an indefinite period, and the last look remains a pleasant remembrance for their friends.
>
> In view of the increasing favour with which the process is being met in this Country we have made such arrangements that on receipt of a telegram a qualified Operator can be immediately despatched to any part of the Kingdom. Where burial is to take place within the walls of a church or in a vault, the preservation of the body is most desirable, and that the public is awakening to this fact is evident from the protests which were raised when the widow of a distinguished statesman was recently interred in Westminster Abbey,[66] when the precautions which science has found absolutely necessary to the public health were neglected.[67]

It is not possible to ascertain the early success-rate of Dottridge Brothers's advertising campaign, nor the numbers buried at Kensal Green during the period of, say, 1900 to 1925, whose remains were subjected to hygienic treatment. Dottridge's main trade was within Greater London, the area from which the majority of the bodies at Kensal Green came and, as they maintained an aggressive marketing approach, it is reasonable to suggest that some of their more prestigious customers availed themselves of the services of Dottridge's 'qualified Operator'.

65 [4867/101/3]. 66 Mrs W. E. Gladstone (d. 1900). 67 Dottridge Brothers Limited (*c.*1908), 11-12.

Shrouds and Coffin Linings

Dressing the corpse for presentation to those who desired to view the body was an important part of the funeral trade; the better the presentation, the better the chance of further trade from the family. The majority of 19th- and 20th-century grave-clothes or 'shrouds' (to use the common terminology), were produced in the textile towns of Lancashire and Yorkshire.[68] The repeal of the *Act for the Burial in Woollen*[69] in 1815 had opened up the market to a variety of textiles for burial purposes: alpaca, calico, cambric, cashmere, etamine,[70] flannel, Holland (linen), muslin, poplin, satin, serge, and silk for shrouds, and calico, flannel, linen, satin, silk, and swansdown[71] for linings and ruffles.

Most of the soft furnishings were provided as complete 'coffin sets', a 'set' comprising of the lining for the inner sides of the coffin, a ruched ruffle along the top edge of the coffin to mask the pins used to fit the lining, a base sheet, a shroud, and a face-cloth. Furthermore, the majority of coffin-makers supplied their coffins to the trade already dressed with 'coffin sets', holding in reserve pillows and coffin-shaped mattresses for the more discerning client. One way of dispensing with the shroud was to have the coffin fitted with side sheets: these cloths, the width of the coffin itself, were tacked to the base and tucked over the corpse once it had been coffined.

A description of the standard style of grave-clothes in use at the time of Kensal Green's establishment can be found in *The Workman's Guide* of 1838:[72]

> A SHROUD
>
> Is composed of a peculiar kind of flannel, woven on purpose, and called shrouding flannel; it is made of a breadth and a half, full length, so as to cover the feet; one seam is sewed up, leaving the other open behind, like a pinafore; slits are cut for arm-holes, and plain long sleeves, without gussets set in; the front is gathered at the waist, and drawn up into a narrow piece; this is twice repeated, at intervals of three nails[73] down the skirt. Upon each of these gatherings, round the neck and at the wrists, a kind of border of the same flannel, punched at the edge in a pattern, is plaited, and an edging of the same is made at the bottom.
>
> For men the shroud is made exactly the same as the above for women, excepting that there is no gathering at the front.
>
> CAP
>
> If the usual cap is not put on, the following is made for a man:– it is of flannel, cut exactly like an infant's foundling cap. A quilling of the punched flannel is put round the face, and a band of it laid on behind, and across the top of the head, strings of the same, are also sewed in.
>
> CAP FOR A WOMAN
>
> This is of flannel: the found part is plaited up to form the front, and a quilling of the bordering put on, a band of the same is also laid on at the back, and strings.

In the same year, 1838, J. Turner's Farringdon, London, funeral-furnishing warehouse was advertising 20 lengths of shrouds, in a price range of 9d. for a child's 'common quality' shroud of 1ft. 8ins. (509mm), to 6s. 6d. for an adult's 'superior rose, full trimmed' shroud of 6ft. 3ins. (1,905mm), and 19 lengths of winding-sheets from 1s.

[68] R. Jannaway, 'An introductory guide to textiles from 18th and 19th century burials', in Cox (*Ed.*), (1998), 17-32.
[69] 30 Car. II, c. 3 and 36 Car. II, c.1. [70] Also *estamin*, an open woollen fabric, or some type of silk fabric, presumably also of open texture. [71] A thick cotton cloth with a nap on one side, also called *Canton* or *cotton flannel*. [72] Anonymous (1838), 124. [73] A measure of length for cloth; 2¼ inches (57mm), or the 16th part of a yard.

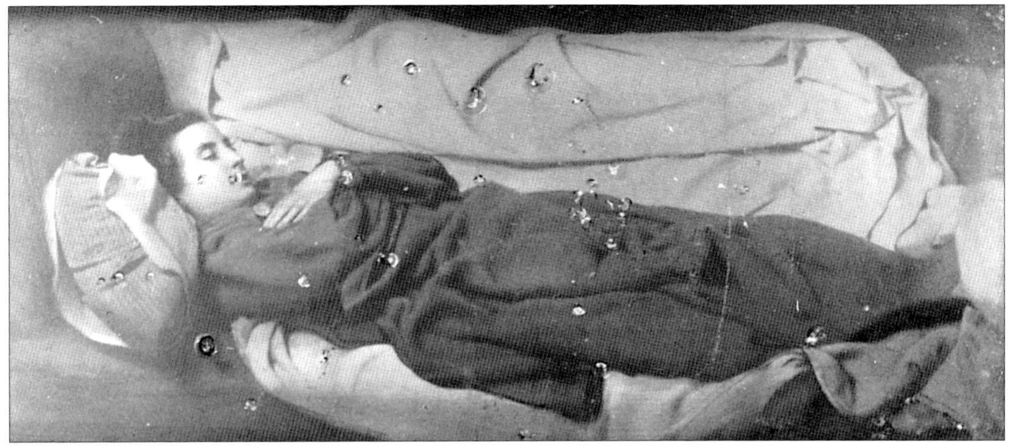

15.5 John Garmston Hopkins, laid out in a serge shroud. Positive collodion by F. C. Earl of Worcester, 1871 (*By courtesy of the Vicar and Churchwardens of St John in Bedwardine, Worcester, Worcestershire*).

for a child's 'common quality' sheet at 1ft. 10ins. (559mm), to 10s. 6d. for an adult's 'superfine quality' sheet of 6ft. 3ins (1,905mm).[74]

By the third quarter of the 19th century, the soft-furnishing side of the funeral industry was selling direct to the wholesale funeral warehouses, coffin-makers, and the larger funeral-furnishing establishments. The shroud was beginning to adopt its own *couture*, with distinct styles for boys and girls, men and women. Materials such as swansdown and cashmere were replacing silk, though flannel and calico continued to account for the majority of the market. There was a wider choice in colour, with purple or lilac cashmere for women, though off-white remained the predominant colour. The 13-year-old John Garmston Hopkins (d. 22 January 1871), the only child of the Worcester hop-merchant, Thomas Hopkins, was in a cashmere shroud when his remains were photographed for his parents by Francis Charles Earl of Broad Street, Worcester (**15.5**). Shrouds of this quality would have been considered standard for grave-clothes of the middle class being buried at Kensal Green throughout the period 1860-85.

Few early 20th-century trade catalogues for the funeral-furnishing trade survive; but two, one of 1922 and the other of 1924, give an indication of the range of shrouds, robes, and coffin sets available. Dottridge Brothers, of London, illustrated nine shrouds and robes (**15.6**), from cotton to cashmere,[75] and coffin sets, traded as 'inside sets' in flannel, swansdown, 'silkette', cashmere, satin, and silk (**15.7**).[76] Almost identical wares were available from Ingall, Parsons, Clive & Co. Ltd., of Birmingham, London, Manchester, Liverpool, Bristol, Glasgow, and Leeds. Their trade catalogue of 1924[77] illustrates 10 swansdown shrouds, from a child's robe at 1s. 6d. to an adult's gown at 9s., 12 patterns of 'side sets' from 2s. 9d. in swansdown to 17s. in silk, and 11 styles of frillings, in calico, cambric, cashmere, lace, lawn, satin, and swansdown, ranging in price from 1s. 1d. per dozen yards in cambric, to 13s. per dozen yards in cashmere.

Coffins

The pride of the society funeral-furnisher was in his most important component of the funeral, the coffin itself. Swathes of forest must have been felled to provide the oak, elm, and mahogany for the coffins in the numerous mausolea, vaults and brick-graves at Kensal Green, though it is today only from the coffins in the catacomb beneath the Anglican chapel that an indication can be gained of the high quality of the merchandise.

74 Trade catalogue of J. Turner (*c*.1838). 75 Dottridge Brothers, *Catalogue of Funeral Furnishing Supplies*, London (1922), 38. 76 Ibid., 37. 77 Ingall, Parsons, Clive, Co. Ltd., (1924), *passim*.

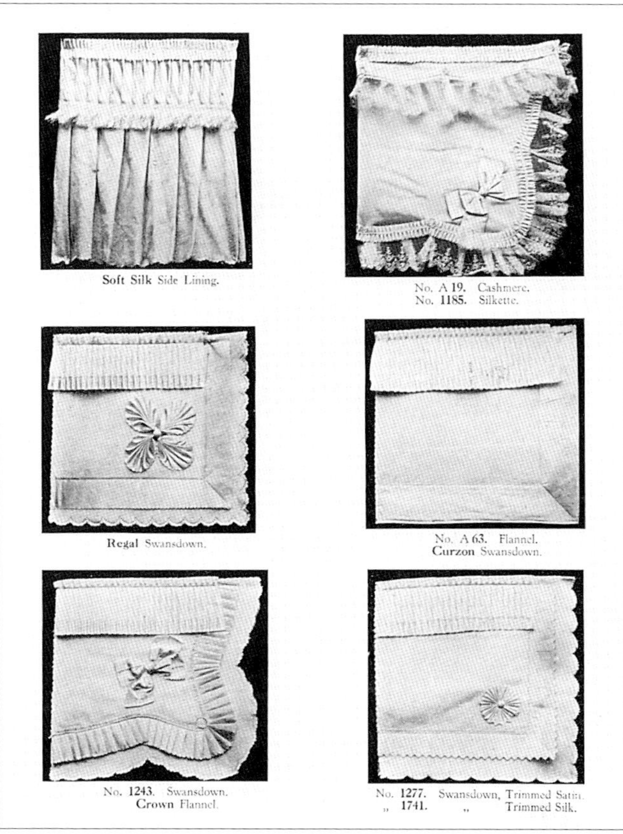

15.6 Shrouds and robes, from Dottridge Brothers's 1922 Catalogue (*J. Litten*).

15.7 Coffin-linings, known as 'inside sets', from Dottridge Brothers's 1922 Catalogue (*J. Litten*).

The triple-coffins destined for the Kensal Green catacomb shelves in the 1830s and 1840s had outer cases of elm or oak, usually covered with black serge, and studded with one, two, or three rows all round of upholstery pins, with japanned tin-dipped sheet-iron coffin-furniture, though there are few examples of this date where the outer cases had been covered in black Utrecht velvet. For the nobility, the standard practice was to cover the outer case in scarlet Genoese velvet, with coffin-plates and handles of cast brass, gilt; three-dimensional funerary coronets are rare at Kensal Green, there being only 10 examples amongst the many coffins of the nobility in the catacomb. In general, most coffins appear to be rather plain; nevertheless the thickness of the wood, and the cabinet-making skills required for their construction, render the majority of today's coffins as poor imitations.

The post-1840s coffins are of polished oak, butt-jointed, with simple mouldings, tapered brass name-plates, and cast-brass gilt handles in a 'gothic' or 'crescent' design. In some instances, an additional name-plate has been affixed to the head-end of the coffin. Among the more unusual designs of coffin to be found in the catacomb are three versions of the *Manila*, manufactured and retailed by Dottridge's in the 1880s and 1890s (**15.8**).

A careful examination of the outer cases show that they were made with more attention to detail than is manifest today. For example, they are deeper at the head-end than at the foot, thus allowing for the introduction of a pillow. The head-end is lightly angled at about six degrees, whilst the foot-end is angled at around twelve degrees; in some instances the lid is as much as two inches (51mm) wider than the base, consequently its sides appear to be tapered from top to bottom. This bespoke treatment of cabinet-making is a far cry from the mass-produced machine-made coffin of the 20th century, of which examples can be seen in the catacomb under the Anglican chapel.

15.8 The *Manila* coffin, manufactured by Ingall, Parsons, Clive, & Co. Ltd., of Birmingham in the 1880s and 1890s. From Ingall, Parsons, Clive, & Co. Ltd.'s trade catalogue of *c.*1890 (*J. Litten*).

Coffins for mausoleum, catacomb, vault, and brick-grave deposit are of the 'coffin, shell, and case' model. The 'coffin' is the inner wooden construction, usually of 1½in. (38mm) elm, into which was placed the shrouded body; the 'shell' is the intermediary lead coffin, fashioned from 4lb. lead,[78] between the inner coffin and the outer case;[79] the 'case' is the heavy butt-jointed outer wooden coffin, constructed from single planks of wood varying from 1 in. (25mm) to 2 in. (50mm) in thickness, and on to which the metal coffin-furniture is affixed. In its complete state, coffins of this nature could weigh up to four hundredweight.[80] Most coffins in the catacomb are raised from their shelves by means of wooden wedges, to facilitate the circulation of air as a means of preventing dry rot. In the knowledge that these outer wooden cases would eventually decay, an additional name-plate was soldered to the lead shell.

To understand the complexity of an upper-middle-class funeral at the end of the Victorian era, reference needs to be made to the ledgers of the society funeral-furnisher, Banting of St James's, London. The 1901 arrangements for Monsieur Gustave E. Michaelis, whose remains are interred in a brick grave on Centre Avenue, are typical of the type of service expected:

Dr. to the Executors of the late Mons. Gustave E. Michaelis,
To his Funeral

A large size and stout elm coffin, lined and ruffled with fine cambric muslin. A patent craped fine cambric muslin sheet, ruffled pillow and tufted mattress bed	£5	4*s*.	0*d*.
A large size and stout lead coffin soldered all round	£10	9*s*.	0*d*.
A lead plate of inscription engraved		10*s*.	0*d*.
Plumbers and man making up and soldering down lead coffin. Used bran and fine wadding.	£1	15*s*.	0*d*.

[78] Lead weighing 4lb. per square foot. [79] Lead remains the more popular material for the shell, though zinc is occasionally used. [80] Avoirdupois weight equal to 112 pounds, abbreviated to cwt. It was a 20th part of a ton, equivalent to 50.80 kg.

A large size and stout outer coffin of 1½ inch thick oak with a chamfered plinth round the bottom edge and a chamfer on the edge of the lid, French polished, 8 solid brass crescent handles with octagon loops and backplates gilt and highly burnished, and 8 solid brass headed long screws to secure the lid, the inside lined with stout white calico.	£16 10*s*. 0*d*.
A stout brass inscription plate, highly burnished	£2 5*s*. 0*d*.

At a cost of £36 13s. 0d., Michaelis's coffin accounted for almost two-thirds of the £59 1s. 3d. charges invoiced to his executors.[81]

Banting's ledgers are particularly useful in that they give not only the cost to the client but also the wholesale cost paid for the merchandise. For example, Michaelis's executors were charged £16 10s. for the outer case with its brass fittings, whilst the cost to Banting's was £8 6s. In 1908 a similar case with identical fittings was available from Dottridge Brothers at the wholesale price of £10 18s. 6d.,[82] or from Ingall, Parsons, Clive, & Co. Ltd. at £11 7s. 6d.[83] in 1924.

Most of the triple-shell coffins arriving for deposit at Kensal Green during the second half of the 20th century were supplied by the coffin-makers Henry Smith (Wandsworth) Ltd., using coffin-furniture manufactured by Newman Brothers (Birmingham) Ltd., and there was very little difference between their merchandise and that available a century earlier from Banting's. Newman Brothers went out of business in 1996/7, since when the supply of high-quality solid cast-brass coffin-furniture ceased.

It would be false to say that all funerals taking place at Kensal Green cemetery between 1833 and 2000 involved such supreme coffins as those provided by Messrs Banting. Both Dottridge Brothers and Ingall, Parsons, Clive, & Co. Ltd. manufactured an extensive range of coffins and caskets: of the 88 coffins retailed by Dottridge Brothers in 1908, the cheapest was the *Admiralty*, a 1 in. (25mm) polished plain elm shell with a chased brass or nickel name-plate, lid ornaments, four pairs of handles, and closing screws, the inside lined with calico, side sheets, ruffle, and pillow, at £1 9s. 6d., and the cheapest of the range of 30 designs available from Ingall, Parsons, Clive, & Co. Ltd. in 1924 was the *Alcester*, a polished English elm coffin, lined and fitted complete, at £3 15s.

The *c*.1908 Dottridge Brothers trade catalogue also offered perishable coffins and wicker coffins:[84]

PERISHABLE COFFINS
(Earth-to-Earth System.)

This make of Coffin, although very light and perishable, is constructed to meet all Sanitary requirements up to the time of Burial, and is finished in two qualities, as under:-

Adult Coffin, covered Black or Violet, finished with Iron Handles, Black Clips, White Metal Breast Plate, trimmed with Calico and Set of Swansdown, lined throughout with Waterproofing, "Seymour"	£3 5*s*. 0*d*.
Ditto ditto finished with Brass, "Haden"[85]	£5 5*s*. 0*d*.

[81] Banting Ledger 1900-1903, 27-8. [82] Dottridge Brothers (*c*.1908*b*), 42. [83] Ingall, Parsons, Clive, & Co. Ltd. (1924), 68. [84] Dottridge Brothers (*c*.1908*b*), 49. [85] The trade names 'Seymour' and 'Haden' are a play on Sir Francis Seymour Haden (1818-1910), who advocated a natural 'earth to earth' burial, which he effected by his invention of a *papier-mâché* coffin.

WICKER COFFINS

Adult size in White Wicker, close Mesh, lined with Swansdown and Waterproof,	£2 10*s*. 0*d*.
Ditto ditto ditto with Superior Quality lining, and Brass Handles,	£3 15*s*. 0*d*.

Doubtless some of the interments at Kensal Green involved *papier-mâché* and wicker coffins; a few continue to do so, as witnessed by the writer in the Autumn of 2000.

Whilst there was no crematorium at Kensal Green until 1939, there are some early cremation caskets in sundry mausolea, vaults, brick graves, and in the catacomb beneath the Anglican chapel. Cremation was, at first, more favoured by the middle and upper classes, but it was also seen as a convenient means of conveying remains over long distances, which may be the reason for the large number of deposits of cremated remains in the mausolea and vaults, the freehold owners of which resided outside London. In 1892, seeing the possible financial gain to be made by offering space at Kensal Green cemetery for cremated remains, the ever-innovative Board of the General Cemetery Company constructed a columbarium within the Monumental Chambers between the north wall of the Anglican chapel and the north colonnade.[86] Coffins for cremation differed from those destined for earth burial or mausoleum, catacomb, vault, and brick-grave deposit. To begin with, there was no need for any inner wooden or metallic coffin; only a single-shell coffin was required. Dottridge Brothers reproduced a colour illustration in their 1908 catalogue[87] of the *Woking*[88] pine cremation coffin, 'Covered grey Velvet, with gilt panelling, finished with 3 pairs brass handles, and lined', at £5 5s., and the Willesden, with a slightly less elaborate finish, at £2 15s. 6d.

Epilogue

Most of the 250,000+ burials that have taken place at Kensal Green cemetery since its opening in 1833 have been attended by some form of liturgy and ritual. In today's London, its colourful and varied multi-cultural and multi-faith complexion has been embraced by the General Cemetery of All Souls. Nowadays, the graves of Christians, Hindus, Buddhists, Moslems, Jains, Sikhs, and those of no faith, may be seen side by side. Gone is the strict division between 'consecrated' and 'un-consecrated' land – albeit in flagrant contradiction to Paragraph XXVI of the Company's 1832 Act:

> and be it further enacted, That so much and such Part of the said Land or Ground so as to be purchased as aforesaid shall be set apart for the Interment of the Dead according to the Rites and Usages of the United Church of *England and Ireland*, when consecrated by the Bishop of the Diocese for the Time being, shall 'for ever thereafter be set apart and be used and applied exclusively for the Purpose of Christian Burial'.[89]

and the headstones tell, in various languages, of the love of the living for the deceased. In the hectic daily round of a busy cosmopolitan city, Kensal Green cemetery remains a haven of rest for London's international dead. On a quiet summer's evening, as the sun begins to set, there is no more beautiful place to be than in *the* necropolis of the metropolis.

86 Stephenson (July 2000), 10-11. The columbarium was damaged during the 1939-45 war and demolished in *c*.1950-54; the caskets of cremated remains were translated to the catacomb where they continue – 2001 – to be stored. 87 Dottridge Brothers (1908*b*), 48B. 88 Named after England's first crematorium at St John's, Woking, opened in 1885. 89 General Cemetery Company (1833), 23-4. Editor's quote marks.

CHAPTER XVI

The Friends of Kensal Green Cemetery

ANDRÉ DAVIES & HENRY VIVIAN-NEAL

Brief History; Tours; The Ivy League and Granite Group; Lecture Series; Exhibitions; The Catafalque; The Magazine; The Future

The dead have few friends.

ROBERT MANNYNG (ROBERT DE BRUNNE) (*fl.* 1288-1338):
Handlyng Synne (1303), 6302.

(i) on the foundation of the Friends;
(ii) on the need for working parties;
(iii) on the London Wildlife Trust; and
(iv) on the launch of the Friends.

The announcement on working parties was in itself a brave move on Litten's part, for it was without the knowledge of the Advisory Committee, and was putting the Secretary of the Friends in a delicate position. It read:

> WORKING PARTIES MONUMENTS, LANDSCAPE AND GUIDES
> Volunteers are needed to establish three specialist working parties:
> Monuments Working Party to clear ivy and weeds from prominent monuments;
> Landscape Working Party - to redefine pathways; and
> Guides Group - to establish weekend tours (hopefully four on Saturdays and two on Sundays) between April and September 1991.
> All offers of help should be addressed primarily to the Secretary. Hands-on training will be given so please do not think that the impossible will be asked of the courageous. All equipment and tools - apart from protective clothing – will be provided by the FOKGC. For insurance reasons it is regretted that we are unable to accept volunteers under 18 years of age for the Monuments Working Party.

As it transpired, there was little need to fear from anybody under 18 years of age, or from anyone else, for, during the period April to July 1991, monument maintenance was undertaken by the four officers of the Friends Committee, and all guiding was done by three volunteers, though after a fortnight tours were reduced to one tour on Saturday and Sunday afternoons.

The 17 December 1990 Advisory Committee was joined by Dr Martin Cherry, Miss Hermione Hobhouse, MBE,[17] and Mrs Isobel Sinden (Secretary, FOKGC). Restoration of the chapels was the main item on the agenda. Mrs Freeman was able to report grants totalling £5,100 towards the investigation of the decorative scheme of the Anglican chapel, and an 80 per cent English Heritage grant towards the restoration of the Dissenters' chapel.[18] The General Cemetery Company also reported on a 25 per cent grant from English Heritage towards the restoration of the Listed Grade II* main gate.

Vandalism to the recently-listed Gregory[19] monument was reported.[20] However, the improvement in landscape maintenance in accordance with the Elliott scheme was to be welcomed. On the recommendation of Professor Curl, Mr Litten was asked to pursue the possibility of the Friends being registered with the Charities Commission.[21] In April 1991, the second *Newsletter* was issued. Under the same production and distribution as the first, it was a larger publication, being twice the size of its predecessor. A report on a spate of vandalism reported damage to the Cooke monument[22] and to the Birkbeck mausoleum,[23] and two attacks on the Huth mausoleum,[24] though this was partially offset by a report on the outstanding clearance of dense vegetation to the south of Centre Avenue, bringing to light a fine group of unrecorded monuments.[25]

[17] Secretary of the Victorian Society (1976-82), General Editor of the *Survey of London* (1983-94), and author of works on *Prince Albert: His Life and Work* (1983), and *Thomas Cubitt, Master Builder* (1971 and 1995). [18] The 20 per cent shortfall was eventually taken up by a CAT (1983) (Community Action Trust) grant. [19] [4031/48/RS]. [20] The iron doors had been broken, displaying the coffins inside. [21] This overture failed. The Commissioners' opinion being that the Friends' work would only improve the cemetery to the advantage of the Board, making it a more attractive place for burial leading to increased profits for the shareholders; charitable funds could not be used to advance private enterprise. [22] [11719/76/PS]. [23] [19470/76/RS]. [24] [2735/77/IC]. The iron entrance-doors had been forced open, and coffins tampered with. [25] To the sculptor Joseph Durham (1814-77); the composer Sir John Goss (1800-80); the Hambro Banking family; the watercolourist George Price Boyce (1826-97); and Sir Walter Scott's daughter, Anne (1803-33).

The gift of a series of memorial-cards, funeral-service books, and photographs relating to several significant monuments was also recorded, as was the announcement of the Patron of the Friends, HG the Duke of Grafton, KG, the appointment of Miss Mary Giles, MBE, to the Advisory Committee, and of Mr André Davies[26] as Treasurer of the Friends. The main item related to the Friends' launch:[27]

LAUNCH PAD - THE OFFICIAL OPENING

It may appear to those who are already members that the Friends of Kensal Green Cemetery (FOKGC) have been going for some time. Not so. Our membership stands at a little over one hundred, and most of you joined as the result of articles in the national press in October and December last year. When the Advisory Committee formed in 1989 it was the intention that most of the monies required for the restoration of the Chapels should be raised before the official launch thereby releasing all contributions made by the Friends for the restoration of the monuments. The Advisory Committee, together with the Board of the General Cemetery Company, have agreed that SATURDAY 6 JULY 1991 should be the day for the Official Launch of the Friends of Kensal Green Cemetery. Further details will be sent out nearer the time. The outline for the day has already been agreed upon and will be as follows:

14.00 CEMETERY OPENS. Please enter via the ROYAL GATE[28] (the green gate on the Harrow Road to your left as you come out of Kensal Green BR/Underground station). Cars should also come in through this gate where they will be directed to the car park.

15.00 TOUR OF THE CEMETERY AND VISITS TO THE GRAVES OF THE FAMOUS. There will be two tours - each lasting about forty-five minutes. One to begin outside the Anglican Chapel, the other by the Main Gate.

16.00 SPEECH OF WELCOME FROM THE PRESIDENT. REPLY BY THE CHAIRMAN OF THE ADVISORY COMMITTEE VOTE OF THANKS FROM THE DIRECTOR OF THE FOKGC. These will take place on the podium behind the Anglican Chapel.

16.15 REFRESHMENTS. To be served in the Anglican Chapel Colonnade.

17.30 DEPART During the afternoon please feel free to wander through the Cemetery at will; there is no need to join an organised tour for an annotated map giving the location of over fifty famous graves will be available.

Messrs T Cribb & Sons of Rathbone Street, Canning Town London E16 1JQ, will be displaying their unique team of Friesian black horses and glass-sided funeral car outside the Anglican Chapel. After the Speech of Welcome this team will parade along the Main Avenue affording an opportunity for photography. The horses, which are in use daily, will be sporting their velvets and black plumes and, unlike similar teams, still prance, a dressage performed by no other funeral horses today. A Guided Tour of the Catacombs will take place after the Speeches, and both the Anglican and Dissenters' Chapels will be open. The Advisory Committee and the

[26] *See* biographical note at the beginning of this book. [27] Excerpt from the Friends' *Magazine*, 2 (April 1991), 4.
[28] Although called the royal gate, it should be known as the upper gate: the legend that it was constructed especially to admit vehicles containing the Royal Family has no basis in fact.

Officers of the FOKGC will be present throughout the afternoon's proceedings and will be recognisable by their badges. Do please feel free to approach them with any query you might have. A little before 15.00 the President, Director, and Secretary of the FOKGC will be laying a wreath on the grave of George Carden, the founder of the Cemetery. Should you wish to place a tribute on the grave of a particular 'hero', please feel free to do so. NB: THE AFTERNOON IS GRATIS. IT IS INCLUDED WITHIN YOUR ANNUAL SUBSCRIPTION. HOWEVER, THERE WILL BE A PAY BAR IN THE ANGLICAN COLONNADE.

The Advisory Committee meeting on 12 June 1991, three weeks before the Open Day, saw Dr Thomas Cocke[29] and Mr Davies join that Committee. Mrs Freeman was able to report that Dr Bristow had completed his examination of the paint surfaces in the Anglican chapel, and on her site-meeting with English Heritage and Mrs Margaret Davies[30] regarding the restoration of the Dissenters' chapel. Mrs Sinden outlined the events for the Open Day on 6 July, adding that the Mayors of Brent, Hammersmith & Fulham, and Kensington & Chelsea had agreed to attend, together with representatives of the national press, radio, and television. Kilburn Skills[31] gave much assistance during 1991, and indicated they would be willing to work in three specific areas within the cemetery:

clearance of ivy and other foliage (in consultation with London Wildlife Trust);
raking-out and re-pointing damaged brickwork and masonry on monuments;
and re-defining and re-gravelling of the original pathways.

Kilburn Skills provided and paid for the labour costs whilst the Friends of Kensal Green Cemetery paid for tools and materials.

Slowly, with Kilburn Skills' assistance, the late 19th-century plan of the cemetery re-emerged, and, with it, some fine and handsome monuments. The particularly successful clearance of 'scrub' within the 'inner circle paths' took place in the early part of 1991. The most successful repair and refurbishment carried out by Kilburn Skills was on the Ducrow[32] mausoleum on Centre Avenue. The liaison with Kilburn Skills was a fruitful one which lasted until 31 December 1994.[33]

Dr John Physick succeeded Mr Ashley Barker as Chairman of the Advisory Committee in 1992. The years 1993/4 saw a consolidation of the work of both Committees at the cemetery. The Friends' Secretary, Mrs Sinden, resigned her post in 1993 to become Events Organiser. Her place was filled for approximately eighteen months by Miss Deborah Dear and then from 1995 onwards by Mr Henry Vivian-Neal.[34] Mr Litten proposed that Mr David Taylor-Pescod should succeed him as Secretary to the Advisory Committee, and this was unanimously agreed. Mr Taylor-Pescod continued to act as Secretary from March 1993 until December 1995,[35] when Mr Vivian-Neal took over. Professor Curl resigned as Director due to pressure of work on his *Oxford Dictionary of Architecture*[36] and the fact that he was to move to live for part of the year in Northern Ireland.[37] He remained an active member of the Advisory Committee.[38]

At the meeting of the Advisory Committee on 14 June 1994, Mrs Freeman, Chairman of the Fabric Committee, proposed that the Dissenters' chapel be acquired on a long lease by the recently-established (1993) Historic Chapels Trust (HCT), of which she had been

29 Secretary, Council for the Care of Churches. 30 Of The Conservation Practice, Architects. 31 Kilburn Skills, founded some eight years previously, trained unskilled school-leavers in basic trades such as woodworking and bricklaying. 32 [820/76/RS]. 33 Help from that source came to end due to the cessation of vital funding. 34 *See* biographical note at the beginning of this book. 35 When he was obliged to resign through ill-health.
36 Commissioned to write the *Oxford Dictionary of Architecture* in 1993, he had to give up most of his time to this task. The book was published in 1999. *See* Curl (1999, 2000*a*) *passim*. 37 Where he had been commissioned to write the history of *The Honourable The Irish Society, 1608-2000* (published in 2000), and was later appointed Professor of Architectural History and Senior Research Fellow at The Queen's University of Belfast. 38 Re-named the Advisory Council in 1995.

appointed Director. HCT was a registered charity established to take into care redundant Nonconformist chapels and other places of worship of outstanding architectural interest. The Dissenters' chapel fitted the HCT criteria, and this fact unlocked an enhanced level of grant aid for repairs from English Heritage (EH) which offered £200,000 to match City Challenge funding of the same sum. £100,000[39] was still to be found, the Friends having paid all the professional fees on the project to date. Mr David McDonald of RBK&C indicated that City Challenge funding would be available in 1995-1996 and confirmed that formal approval would be sought at a meeting held at Kensington and Chelsea Town Hall on Thursday 28 July: Sir Edward Ford,[40] Mr Litten, and Mr Davies were to represent the Friends.

During 1995, British Waterways, working with RBK&C and City Challenge, made significant improvements to the canal tow-path which runs along the southern perimeter of the cemetery. Improvements included upgrading the materials of the towpath to granite setts, canal-side planting including the cemetery boundary (to enhance wildlife value), providing interpretative information-boards, making general improvements to access-points and to boundary-walls, and the granting of permanent mooring-sites. The enclosure of the cemetery by boundary-walls along the Harrow Road made the canal corridor the most public frontage. Lack of adequate maintenance and continued vandalism to the boundary over the years reflected badly on the rest of the cemetery.[41] British Waterways and RBK&C were of the opinion that the cemetery and the canal should be seen as a coherent whole, as they dated from the same period and both were considered as resources of both historic, wildlife, and landscape interest. A Sub-Committee[42] was set up comprising members of the Advisory Committee, the GCC, RBK&C, and British Waterways to monitor the impact on the cemetery during the improvements. Works to the canal towpath were completed in 1996.

Security and vandalism still continued to trouble the cemetery in the mid-1990s and were the cause of protracted discussions at the meeting of the Advisory Council in June 1996. Mr Litten advised that thefts had taken place since the previous meeting and that certain monuments had been taken into storage, particularly the Paul Rosin lion. Dr Elliott asked about the possibility of marking all movable statuary. The Committee felt that, as it was not known where the items were sold on or ended up, there was little point in doing so, but Professor Curl dissented, and agreed with Dr Elliott that markings might help to recover stolen goods. Dr Eric Robinson[43] reported that the Princess Sophia monument[44] was being used as a target for air-gun users in the northern part of the cemetery, which had caused some damage. A suggestion was adopted that random checking of all vehicles entering the cemetery would be carried out and an access-barrier operated by the gate-keeper would be fitted to the west entrance (the main entrance being for pedestrians only).

Dr Roger Bowdler[45] advised the Committee that he had been giving consideration to proposals for further listing of the monuments at the General Cemetery of All Souls at Kensal Green. Having worked on the monuments at the South Metropolitan, West Norwood, and St James's, Highgate, cemeteries, he was of the opinion that Kensal Green was significantly the biggest and finest of the early London cemeteries and should therefore have more listed monuments than any other. In response to a question relating

[39] This was achieved by a successful application to the Heritage Lottery Fund (HLF) securing £85,445 in further grant aid. An additional grant of £35,000 from HLF was made in 1996/7 with an extra small grant from the Metropolitan Public Gardens Association. [40] Sir Edward William Spencer Ford, GCVO, KCB, ERD, DL, joined the Advisory Council at that time. [41] As is made clear in Lady Freeman's Chapter VII, the boundary-walls, -railings, and gates are an important part of the cemetery's historic fabric, and are themselves not without distinction. [42] Mr M. Nodes and Mr R. Callard (GCC), Miss Hobhouse, Mr Richard Cook, Mr Litten (Advisory Committee FOKGC), Mr Robin Gray and Ms Frances Read (British Waterways), Mr David McDonald (RBK&C), and Prof Curl to advise on any design technicalities. [43] *See* biographical note at the beginning of this book. [44] [8028/114/PS]. [45] In attendance from English Heritage. *See* biographical note at the beginning of this book.

to listing criteria Dr Bowdler indicated that he would be looking at various categories, such as the architectural/artistic merits of the monuments and the historical importance of the persons commemorated. A likely date for announcing the listings could not be given at that time, as the schedule had to be submitted to the Department of National Heritage and approved by the Minister.

Mrs Freeman was able to report that works to the Dissenters' chapel had commenced on site in February 1996. Catacomb-related work had been completed, with large amounts of spoil, and access had been possible without the need for precautionary smallpox vaccinations or the donning of special suits: coffins had all been enveloped in sealed plastic sheeting, the chapel had been re-roofed, and the remaining stonework had been taken to the contractors' works for sorting. English Heritage had carried out extensive analysis of the decorative schemes at the chapel (the original 1830s scheme and the 1860s scheme in the style of, or, possibly, by, Owen Jones[46] [1809–76]). She went on to indicate that it was the intention to restore the 1860s scheme: the 1830s scheme would remain covered, although there would be a small illustrative display of it in the chapel. After the works to the Dissenters' chapel were completed in May 1997 (a major success-story that won many admirers and accolades), the Friends spent most of 1997/8 settling in to the new accommodation. Interest in tours had grown due to increased coverage in the national press and on television as a result of the careful and professional restorations of the Dissenters' chapel and catafalque in the Anglican chapel.

The need for a useful reference-book, giving details of the 'Great and the Good' interred in the cemetery, resulted in the first (ring-bound) edition of *Paths of Glory*[47] being published in 1997. This 100-page volume, compiled by Mr Vivian-Neal, carried all grid-references of graves, as well as line-drawings by Mr John and Mrs Karen Humpage[48] depicting the significant monuments. Mrs Claire Aston, who had been Director of the Friends (after Professor Curl relinquished the post in 1994), stepped down in 1998, and Mr Davies took over as Director. The then vacant post of Treasurer was taken on by Mr Ian Johnson. Dr John Physick retired as Chairman of the Advisory Council in June 2000 after eight years and Miss Hobhouse agreed to take over.

At the meeting of the Advisory Council on 13 June 2000, it was decided to revive the idea of a projected scholarly and comprehensive book on the cemetery (first mooted in 1989),[49] and in due course Professor James Stevens Curl was invited to research the history of the cemetery and was appointed Editor. This arrangement was formalised in the Autumn of 2000 and the new Editor immediately set in motion a programme of photography of documents, buildings, and monuments: at the same time he began a systematic trawl through the Minute-Books and other material. With the assistance of Mr Martin Charles,[50] the bulk of the documentary photography was completed in September 2000, and work on recording the buildings and monuments began.[51] After the Advisory Council meeting of 12 December 2000 it was agreed that the Editor should instruct Mr Charles to take all necessary photographs to illustrate the papers by Drs Physick and Robinson, as well as all others essential for the book. The Editor made his own extensive collections of pictures available, and provided the bulk of his photographic survey of 1967-97 for use in the projected volume.

[46] Owen Jones, architect and decorator – published works include *The Grammar of Ornament* (1856). [47] *Paths of Glory* (*see* Vivian-Neal [1999], *passim*) was reprinted and perfect-bound in 1998-9, and a new, enlarged edition is (2001) in preparation. [48] Active members from the start of the Friends, Mr Humpage has been prominent as a Guide, and Mrs Humpage has contributed many of her drawings for the FOKGC notepaper and for *Paths of Glory*. She has also exhibited her water-colours in the Dissenters' chapel. [49] Although some draft contributions had been written, the project did not advance. [50] The well-known professional architectural photographer. [51] Although the National Monuments Record had recorded numerous monuments, and Professor (then Dr) Curl had instigated earlier photographic surveys in the 1960s, 1970s, and 1990s, a tailor-made programme for the book was necessary to augment material already available.

By this time, it had been decided to raise money by subscription in order to publish the book, and the Editor wrote suitable copy and obtained illustrations, which he provided for Phillimore & Co. Limited, publishers, of Chichester, the firm selected to bring out the book. At a meeting with Mr Noel Osborne of Phillimore on 13 December 2000, 2000 copies of the approved leaflets inviting subscriptions were delivered to the Friends, and the Editor and Friends undertook to distribute these.[52] It was agreed that a Limited Edition of 1,000 numbered copies would be offered and that the delivery-date of the complete typescript, disks, and illustrations would be 30 April 2001.

By March 2001, the Editor had completed his researches and writing, had compiled the Bibliography, had edited and agreed most of the contributions, and had collated all the illustrations, and by 24 March the target of 300 subscriptions had been exceeded. The Editor was able to report that this book would be delivered on time, and it was, in the first week of May.

Tours[53]

Following the success of the launch-date in July 1991, during which tours of the cemetery (and especially of the catacomb) proved most successful, three Friends undertook to give weekend tours when possible. This obviously was an unsatisfactory affair, placing a great burden on a few devoted members.

The Secretary of the FOKGC, Mrs Isobel Sinden, wrote to the membership requesting those interested in becoming guides to contact her. Some 20 people offered their services but mentioned that they would require training. All were invited to attend a Tour Guiding Day in the Anglican chapel led by Mrs Sinden and Mr Litten, which turned out to be a cold, frosty morning in October. Mrs Sinden expressed the hope that the day's meeting would be of help for those wishing to become guides, and that it would be possible for the Friends to offer regular guided tours. Mr Litten gave a detailed account of the history of the cemetery. This was followed by a lengthy tour, during which he discussed many of the important monuments and gave brief biographical details of those interred.

The following week Mr David Taylor-Pescod[54] offered to train guides and co-ordinate tours: the FOKGC Main Committee appointed him Guide Supervisor and trainer, and he was also invited to become a member of the Main Committee.[55] The Supervisor undertook to collate information received from the Friends, guides, and other sources. This was used to produce a short historical account of the cemetery and its buildings, guiding details, brief biographical notes, and indicative maps showing suggested routes through the cemetery, which could form the basis for a variety of different tours, both long and short.

Regular weekend tours commenced, but lack of publicity still meant that visitors were few or non-existent. However such times were put to profitable use. The new guides planned various routes through the cemetery according to interest (e.g. architectural, artistic, scientific, the nobility, and the eccentrics), discovered long-forgotten monuments, and were able to add further biographical notes for individual and general use.

Mr Taylor-Pescod organised a meeting in January 1992 for the guides to share their experiences of giving tours: among the topics discussed then was the problem of how best to advertise those tours. Many guides offered to place details in local shops, churches,

[52] In fact, a further 1000 leaflets were printed and distributed by the Editor and Friends. [53] This section has been kindly provided by Mr David Taylor-Pescod. [54] Fellow of The Linnean Society of London. [55] And, as previously noted, was Secretary to the Advisory Committee from March 1993 until December 1995.

and libraries. The Supervisor mentioned that he and Mr Litten had asked the General Cemetery Company's Secretary, Mr David Burkett, to grant public access to Catacomb B. By late January permission had been given for one visit on the first Sunday of each month. Official tours effectively started on the first Sunday in February 1992 when the catacomb was open to the public. In December 1992 the Saturday morning tour – never a popular time for visitors – was cancelled.[56] As the weeks went by so did the number of visitors increase. The opportunity of visiting the catacomb proved immensely attractive to the public: there were often well over a hundred visitors attending the first Sunday tours.

In addition to their weekend activities, the guides gave tours throughout the year to various societies, schools, and other organisations (including the Canal Society, The Linnean Society of London, Camden Historical Society, the City Rambling Club, Paddington & Maida Vale Waterways Society, and Edward Wilson Primary School). Visitors also included individuals and groups from abroad. The largest group to visit Kensal Green cemetery came from Japan and consisted of 200 Japanese women who came to pay homage to the memory of Freddie Mercury (1946-91) at the place where his body had been cremated – the West London Crematorium – in the autumn of 1991.[57]

By January 1993 tours of this great necropolis had helped to place it well and truly on the map thanks, in part, to the commitment and dedication of the guides. All Souls Cemetery, Kensal Green, had become for many tourists one of *the* places to visit. The training of new guides is, therefore, of great importance, in order to ensure a continuing high standard of tours for visitors (the number of which topped three thousand in the year 2000). Contributions from tours did, and still do, supply the FOKGC with substantial funds, and indeed these constitute a large part of the income of the Friends, although since 1998 the Dissenters' chapel has generated income from its use as an exhibition-gallery. All these monies are used to help achieve the aims and objectives of the organisation.

Mr Taylor-Pescod resigned as Guide Supervisor in December 1995.[58] His successor, Mr John Humpage, continues as the Supervisor of 15 guides, each of whom gives his or her time freely, every weekend without fail, to ensure visitors receive a unique insight into the special qualities of the cemetery.

The Ivy League and Granite Group

So dramatic was the effect of the work carried out by Kilburn Skills under the guidance of the Friends and the General Cemetery Company that the urgent need for regular clearance and recording of the obscured monuments *over and above* the day-to-day maintenance became very apparent. The Friends decided to tackle this in an imaginative way by first advertising in its quarterly *Magazine* for helpers to assist Ms Godden in the recording and photographing of interesting monuments. Mr Litten went somewhat further and established the Ivy League and Granite Group to deal with the more labour-intensive activities. The first meeting took place on 3 July 1993, a glorious hot Summer's day: despite the fact that only nine people turned up, it proved to be very productive. Dr Robinson was in attendance: he gave advice on the care and cleaning of the many varied monuments to be found in the cemetery. He also enlightened the group on the different types of granite and other materials at Kensal Green, and expatiated on their composition, peculiarities, and places of origin.

[56] A Sunday morning tour was considered, but abandoned after a month's trial. [57] Born Farrokh Bulsara in Zanzibar, died in London 24 November 1991. [58] Due to ill-health, and, as previously noted, he also resigned as Secretary to the Advisory Council at the same time.

The Ivy League and Granite Group still exist today. Continued efforts in the cemetery have uncovered many different monuments including that of the eminent railway engineer Joseph Locke (1805-60).[59] In addition, the two groups seek to maintain sections of the routes taken on tours.

Lecture Series

Lectures have formed an important educational / and informing rôle as well as complementing the Friends' other activities. The list of public lectures (at first organised by Mrs Sinden, and since 1995 by Mr Robert Stephenson) is given below:

Venue:	St John's church-hall, Kilburn Lane, Kensal Green
1991	
22 October	'To Paradise by Way of Kensal Green' by Julian Litten
1992	
5 June	'Embalming and Presentation' by Mark Bowis
Venue:	The Linnean Society of London, Burlington House, Piccadilly[60]
1993	
5 March	'The Architecture of Kensal Green Cemetery' by Jennifer Freeman
2 June	'Transport of the Dead 1450 to 1900' by Julian Litten
20 October	'Methods of Disposal of the Dead' by David Taylor-Pescod
1994	
23 February	'Italian Cemeteries: Florence, Genoa, and Venice' by John Ashby
13 April	'A Hundred Years of Burning the Dead – Cremation' by David Taylor-Pescod
12 October	'Embalming' by David Taylor-Pescod[61]
7 December	'Church Monuments: from Coffin Lids to Weeping Widows' by Isobel Sinden
1995	
15 March	'The Butterflies of Kensal Green' by Tim Freed
12 April	'Gone but not Forgotten: Famous People of the Past' by June Firkins
12 June	'Extraordinary Epitaphs' by Nigel Rees
20 September	'Prehistoric Burial Sites' by Robert Stephenson
18 October	'Post-Mortem Movements and the Rise of the Vampire' by David Taylor-Pescod
13 December	'The Treatment of Post-Industrial Corpses' by David Taylor-Pescod
1996	
3 April	'The Notorious Earl of Mornington and his Wanstead Connections' by Peter Lawrence
29 May	'Brookwood Cemetery and its Railway' by John Clarke
2 October	'Church Monuments and the Gothic Revival' by Thomas Cocke
6 November	'Frogmore Mausoleum and the Royal Burials at St George's Chapel, Windsor' by Leslie Grout
27 November	'Preserved Corpses' by David Taylor-Pescod
1997	
19 March	'Vampires' by David Taylor-Pescod[62]
23 April	'The Monuments of Kensal Green and their Stylistic Development' by Roger Bowdler
21 May	'Mount Auburn Cemetery – America's First Garden Cemetery' by Stephen Jerome
17 September	'Eric Gill's Monuments at Kensal Green and Elsewhere' by David Peace

[59] [6866/99/PS]. [60] The Linnean Society of London, Burlington House, Piccadilly, became the regular meeting place and lecture venue of the Friends until the completion of the restoration of the Dissenters' chapel, Kensal Green, in 1997. The first lecture to be given in the Dissenters' chapel was on 18 March 1998. [61] A lecture by Robert Flanagan on Norwood cemetery scheduled for 13 July 1994 was cancelled because of the London Underground strike. [62] This replaced the talk scheduled to be given by the indisposed J. Thomson.

15 October 'The Prehistoric Iceman' by David Taylor-Pescod
12 November 'The Life, Death, Burial, and Resurrection Company' by Ruth Richardson
Venue: The Dissenters' chapel, Kensal Green cemetery, Ladbroke Grove

1998
18 March 'Frederick Salmon and St Mark's Hospital' by James Thomson
15 April 'The 5th Duke of Portland and his Burrowing Career' by Roger Morgan
20 May 'Death and the Victorians' by Robert Stephenson
16 September 'Burial Vaults of the Aristocracy' by Julian Litten
21 October 'Spontaneous Human Combustion' by David Taylor-Pescod

1999
21 April 'Excavating the Crypt of Christ Church, Spitalfields' by Jez Reeve
19 May 'The Cult of the Ruin' by Christopher Woodward
16 June 'The Surgeon, the Cadaver, and the Resurrectionist' by Karen Howell
15 September 'The Landscape of Kensal Green Cemetery, its Inspiration and Planting' by Brent Elliott
20 October 'From Victoria to Diana: Changing Attitudes to Death' by Tony Walter
17 November 'Well Hung in London: the City's Execution Sites' by Robert Stephenson[63]

2000
19 April 'West Norwood Cemetery' by Bob Flanagan
17 May 'A History of the Mausoleum' by Robert Stephenson[64]
21 June 'Thackeray: The Road to *Vanity Fair*' by David J. Taylor
20 September 'The Royal Mausolea at Frogmore' by Hermione Hobhouse
18 October 'Tombstones' by John Physick
18 November 'Funerary Symbolism' by Don Bianco

Lectures scheduled for 2001 are given below.[65] The variety of the topics covered and the academic standards achieved by all guest speakers over the years have made the Friends of Kensal Green Cemetery Lecture Series an important contribution to social and historical research. It is intended to carry on this tradition.

Exhibitions

The completion of the restoration of the Dissenters' chapel and its re-opening by Sir Jocelyn Stevens, CVO, Chairman of English Heritage, on 7 May 1997 enabled the Friends to use the chapel and adjacent meeting / events-room for exhibitions and displays: this was in addition to its daily use as administrative offices, and up-to-date visitor facilities include a meeting / lecture space and small souvenir shop. Previously, the Friends had to make use of a small, disused waiting-room in the Anglican chapel as a base for all their activities within the cemetery.

The Dissenters' chapel gallery has proved to be one of the successful and lucrative ventures that the Friends have embarked on in recent years. It serves to complement the educational and outreach activities which were among the major requirements in securing funding / support for the restoration of the chapel in the first place from the Heritage Lottery Fund (HLF), City Challenge, and the Royal Borough of Kensington & Chelsea. Exhibitions to date are listed below:

[63] This replaced the lecture scheduled to be given by David Taylor-Pescod, who was indisposed. [64] This replaced a lecture scheduled to be given by M. Kirby, who was indisposed. [65] 'Disposal of the Dead in the Hindu Kush' by David Taylor-Pescod (17 April 2001); 'Music Hall Artistes buried at Kensal Green and other London Cemeteries' by Terry Lomas (16 May 2001); 'The Work of the Friends of War Memorials' by Maggie Goodall (20 June 2001); 'Burial before Undertakers: Death in Early Modern England' by Clare Gittings (15 August 2001); 'The Bravo Murder Mystery' by Nicholas Reed (19 September 2001); and 'Sir Marc Brunel: the Forgotten Genius' by Michael Bennett (17 October 2001).

May to July 1998	'Exposed' by Rowena Jackson. A series of oil paintings depicting the Suffering and Frailty of the Human Body
October to December 1998	'Elysian Fields' by Karen Humpage. Architectural Watercolour Studies of Monuments and Mausolea
April to May 2000	'Louisa Fairbrother - Romantic Ballerina and Royal Bride' by Keith Cavers. The exhibition was opened by Diana FitzGeorge-Balfour[66]
June to August 2000	'Elements' by Lucy O'Meara. A photographic study into weather, water and texture
September to October 2000 and	'Architectural Cemetery Sculpture' by Karen Humpage. A series of watercolour studies
November to December 2000	'Stations of the Cross – Westway' by Mark Cazelet, paintings depicting religious iconography

Revenue from exhibitions also helps to support the objectives of the Friends of Kensal Green Cemetery.

The Catafalque

1997 also saw the completion of another long-standing refurbishment project, the full restoration of the catafalque in the Anglican chapel. On 31 May 1997 a dedication was made by the Revd Royston Beal of St John's church, Kensal Green, before the catafalque gracefully descended from the chapel through the floor and into the catacomb below.

The early mechanism for the catafalque was installed in the Anglican chapel around 1837 by Mr A. Smith of Princes Street, Leicester Square, London. It was replaced by a much superior hydraulic mechanism by Bramah & Robinson, installation of which was completed in December 1844.[67] The original catafalque itself had been in constant use until the early 1960s but by 1990 was in poor condition. The restoration was commenced in 1994 by Dorothea Restorations Limited after considerable grant aid was secured from various charitable trusts and English Heritage. The Friends were also able to donate funds to top up the total required to just over £50,000.

The Magazine

From the start, members of the Friends have been kept abreast of developments and news through the Friends' *Magazine*, a formal journal in A4 size recording activities, events, etc., which is also an organ for the publication of research into the cemetery, its environment, occupants and so on. From a humble start as a couple of sheets of stapled A4 paper, the *Magazine* is now a more substantial publication.

The Future

The Friends of Kensal Green as a body has a loyal and growing membership which, it is hoped, will continue to support the aims and objectives set out in the Constitution. No voluntary group, however, can survive without the dedication and sheer determination of its members to make it work and endure for the future.

The purpose of the Friends is clear: the group continues to exist in order to ensure the continuing care, restoration, and conservation of the unique landscape and buildings

[66] Great-great-grand-daughter of H.R.H. The Duke of Cambridge and Louisa Fairbrother, and was attended by other members of the family. [67] *See* Lady Freeman's Chapter VII, and, especially, Pepper (2000), 7-10. As is clear from the Minutes of the General Cemetery Company the mechanism Smith had installed was unsatisfactory from the start.

at Kensal Green cemetery. To achieve this, the Friends, its Committee, and Advisory Council are fully committed to:

informed and engaging education for all age-groups;
continuing dialogue with the General Cemetery Company;
and
activities such as guiding, publishing, exhibitions, lectures, the annual open day, and other fund-raising initiatives and events.

Efforts over the next few years will concentrate on restoration of the Anglican chapel, including its catacomb, colonnades, and loggias, and it is also intended to conserve the old, north, or terrace colonnades which, inevitably, will involve work on the catacomb below. Attention will also be given to the boundary-walls, railings, and gates, and in due course the landscape and planting will require a major programme of conservation and judicious renewal based on scholarly research and historical precedent. It is intended to expand the exhibitions and schools education programmes to embrace requirements within the national curriculum, stages two and three. This should help the Friends to re-open discussions with the Charities Commission in relation to the acquisition of charitable status.

Commitment to an informed sustainable regime of conservation and 'best practice' at the cemetery to secure it for future generations will be continued through 'The Conservation Area Proposals Statement' and 'Management Plan', currently (2001) being written in collaboration with the Friends of Kensal Green Cemetery, the Historic Chapels Trust, English Heritage, The General Cemetery Company, and the Royal Borough of Kensington & Chelsea. Without the help and support of such allies, the Friends of Kensal Green Cemetery would cease to exist.

Conclusion

Jennifer M. Freeman
& James Stevens Curl

But see! the well-plum'd herse comes nodding on,
Stately and slow; and properly attended
By the whole sable tribe, that painful watch
The sick man's door, and live upon the dead,
By letting out their persons by the hour,
To mimic sorrow, when the heart's not sad.
How rich the trappings, now they're all unfurl'd,
And glittering in the sun! triumphant entries
Of conquerors, and coronation-pomps,
In glory scarce exceed. Great gluts of people
Retard th' unwieldy show: whilst from the casements
And houses' tops, ranks behind ranks close wedg'd
Hang bellying o'er. But! tell us, why this waste?
Why this ado in earthing up a carcass
That's fall'n into disgrace, and in the nostril
Smells horrible? – Ye undertakers! tell us,
Midst all the gorgeous figures you exhibit,
Why is the principal conceal'd, for which
You make this mighty stir? 'Tis wisely done:
What would offend the eye in a good picture,
The painter casts discreetly into shades.

ROBERT BLAIR (1699-1746): *The Grave* (1743), 156-76.

Many aspects of the General Cemetery of All Souls at Kensal Green have been outlined above. The illustrations, though generous, cannot provide a *comprehensive* record of the architectural and monumental riches to be found in one of London's most remarkable sites, but they can give a *flavour* of what an extraordinary and very significant place the cemetery actually is.

Like many other 19th-century British cemeteries, Kensal Green has suffered greatly from many problems described in the foregoing Chapters, and it is abundantly clear that this great necropolis urgently needs massive and urgent help. In March 2001 the Environment, Transport, and Regional Affairs Committee of the House of Commons published an important *Report* on *Cemeteries*[1] which is heartening and a glimmer of hope for those who have urged the necessity of conserving such places, but whose voices and arguments, it seemed, had not been heard and were ignored.

In its *Summary of Conclusions and Recommendations* the Committee expresses its belief that

> it is *essential*[2] that the Government address *immediately*[3] the lack of basic information on the number, condition, and operational viability of the country's cemeteries.[4]

Furthermore, it is clear that the Committee's investigations were wide-ranging and gratifyingly comprehensive. Although the *Report* is mainly concerned with the diminishing amounts of land available for burial, and, very properly, draws attention to the appalling condition of many cemeteries, it also mentions the needs of the bereaved,[5] the cultural value of cemeteries,[6] their historical, environmental, and amenity value,[7] the place of the cemetery in the 'urban renaissance',[8] and other matters that should have been the concerns of officialdom long ago, had not a utilitarian ethos prevailed.

The *Report* urges that a cemeteries survey should be undertaken, and that English Heritage and English Nature 'should work together to formulate special assessment procedures for cemeteries which encourage cooperation between those seeking to protect the built and natural heritage value which they represent'.[9] Although the *Report* concentrates mainly on cemeteries in public ownership, many of the conclusions are relevant to the privately-owned General Cemetery of All Souls at Kensal Green (as well as to historic cemeteries generally), and they should be strongly supported. In particular, Parliament is urged to bring in new legislation to re-regulate burial and cemetery management in a way that will transform the economics of running and maintaining cemeteries. The *Report* rightly emphasises the importance of cemeteries in terms of their environmental, historic, and cultural significance: moreover, it points to the role that public policy can play in securing their protection and viability, and in arresting the devastating 'spiral of decline' that has been responsible for so much damage. It refers to 'unsafe, littered, vandalised, unkempt' cemeteries that 'shame all society in their lack of respect for the dead and the bereaved'.[10] Quite so, and it is high time this problem was officially recognised. The Government's 'hands-off' approach to cemetery provision is implicitly criticised as having given local authorities *carte blanche* to 'treat cemeteries as the lowest of low priorities'.[11]

Recommendations in the *Report* to include cemeteries firmly within the Government's 'vision for an urban renaissance' are to be welcomed, as is recognition that problems 'facing cemeteries should be addressed and their contribution appreciated when developing urban policy'.[12] Particularly laudable is the firm statement that cemeteries

[1] House of Commons Environment, Transport, and Regional Affairs Committee (2001), *passim*. [2] Ibid., i, xlviii, § (a). Editor's italics. [3] Ibid. [4] Ibid. [5] Ibid., § (b) – (d). [6] Ibid., § (e) – (f). [7] Ibid., § (g) – (j). [8] Ibid., xlix, § (k) – (l). [9] Ibid., **xlviii**, § (j). English Heritage is to undertake a survey of cemeteries. [10] Ibid., **xlix**, § (m). [11] Ibid., § (p). [12] Ibid., § (k).

'require special consideration as a particular kind of landscape',[13] something that the contributors to this volume have been arguing for many years.

There is a sound plea for all-inclusive management-plans to be drawn up for 'cemeteries which pull together the various competing demands on the cemetery',[14] reconciling their operational, conservation, and national heritage values.[15] There is also warm support for the formation of voluntary bodies and local Friends' Groups (such as the Friends of Kensal Green Cemetery). Friends' Groups are to be encouraged to make applications to the Heritage Lottery Fund for grant-support. Money should be made available from the Lottery's New Opportunities Fund to make cemeteries 'a specific funding commitment'.[16]

English Heritage's positive role with respect to historic cemeteries is underlined, and proposals that EH should produce guidance-notes on their conservation receive positive backing. There is a powerful case for additional resources to be made available to ensure that the historic environment, including cemeteries, is properly protected. In particular, concern is expressed for 'unsafe' monuments in cemeteries: the *Report* unequivocally states that 'the Government should make available specified funds for selected programmes of renovation of unsafe memorials'. Access to these funds should be conditional on the development of detailed management plans 'for the site in question'.[17]

Interestingly, although the *Report* recognises the 'importance of ensuring that unsafe memorials do not cause any further deaths or serious injuries', it believes the Health and Safety Executive 'could act with greater sensitivity towards the *historical* and *cultural significance* of such memorials'.[18] This is undoubtedly true, and it is greatly encouraging that the authors of the *Report* have taken the views they have, including recommending 'that local authorities pay more attention to the *cultural significance* of their cemeteries'.[19]

However, contributors to the *Report*, like those to the present volume, recognise that 'the primary purpose of the cemetery, as a place for the service of the bereaved, must be paramount', and historical, educational, and amenity uses 'conducted with all due sensitivity'.[20]

Cemeteries are of great importance to our towns and cities:[21] indeed, it was widely perceived during the 19th and early 20th centuries that no town or city could function properly without provision of a cemetery or cemeteries, appropriately laid out, planted, and managed. 'The value of the nineteenth-century cemeteries today ... in large urban conurbations is enormous. The trees are now mature (indeed, many are at the end of their lives and need to be replaced); graves, monuments, and mausolea have taken on the patina of age; and a wonderful quality has evolved that could all too easily be ruined. The reminders of death ... in the cemeteries laid out [in the 19th century] convey an ever-present visual memorial to our collective past without which we [can] have no [cultural] memory'.[22]

In landscapes as evocative as that of the General Cemetery of All Souls at Kensal Green, where gracious monuments were once enhanced by comely planting, it is possible to perceive the cemetery as a place where a reticent people poured out feelings into the selection of sites, botanical embellishments, and architectural and sculptural ornamentation. There, death might be considered with resignation: perhaps, if this book proves to be a catalyst for the cemetery's restoration, it may once more be a necropolis of dignified regret and heartfelt beauty.

[13] Ibid., § (l). [14] Ibid., **lviii-xlix**, § (j). [15] The Friends of Kensal Green Cemetery and the General Cemetery Company have already taken steps to commission a Conservation Management Plan for Kensal Green. This should be available late in 2001. [16] House of Commons Environment, Transport, and Regional Affairs Committee (2001), **i**, l, § (u) –(x). [17] Ibid., § (ll). [18] Ibid., § (kk). Editor's italics. [19] Ibid., **xlviii**, § (f). Editor's italics. [20] Ibid., **xlix**, § (j). [21] Ibid., § (k). [22] Curl (2000*e*), 266.

As it is, one is left with the feeling that

> Death is fortunate for the child, bitter to the youth,
> far too late for the old[23]

but perhaps, as Sir Thomas Browne (1605-82) observed, 'the long habit of living indisposeth us for dying'.[24]

[23] Publilius Syrus (first century BC): *Sententiæ*, 402 (*Mors infanti felix, iuveni acerba, nimis sera est seni*).
[24] *Hydriotaphia* (1658), v.

APPENDIX I

Chairmen of the General Cemetery Company

Henry John Chetwynd Talbot, Viscount Ingestre, later (1849) 3rd Earl Talbot and (1856) 18th Earl of Shrewsbury and Earl of Waterford (1803-68)	1832-4
Sir John Dean Paul, Bart. (1775-1852)	1834-51
Charles Lushington (1785-1866)	1852-64
John Griffith (1796-1888)	1864-79
George R. Bengough	1879-82
James Augustus Cotter Morison (1832-88)	1882-88
F. Kendall Glover (*c.*1820-98)	1888-98
Robert Willey (*c.*1835-1918)	1898-1918
Robert John Stannard (*c.* 1855-1936)	1918-36
John Dorrofield Hardy	1936-42
Alfred Kendall Glover (1881-1949)	1942-49
Wilfrid Bristowe Paton (1902-64)	1949-64
Kirtley John Nodes (1902-77)	1964-77
Aubrey Edward Gough (1902-86)	1977-86
Donald Owen Roberts (1916-)	1986-88
Michael John Kirtley Nodes (1928-)	1988-

APPENDIX 2

Abstract[1] of Indenture (Deed of Transfer/Conveyance) dated 19 September 1832
This is a Transfer of the land etc (*described in italics below*) at 'Kensall Green' by **Sir John Dean Paul to the General Cemetery Company –**

Which first recites the land, etc., had already, in effect, been transferred on 9 and 10 December 1831 for a consideration of £9,400 by John Nicoll (the previous owner) to Sir John Dean Paul as Trustee for The General Cemetery Company which had been set up by an Act of Parliament passed in the second and third years of the reign of William IV.

And then goes on to transfer/convey to the General Cemetery Company (for the sum of Five Shillings paid by the General Cemetery Company to Sir John Dean Paul) *the barns, stables, outhouses, edifices, buildings, yards, orchards, and gardens 'at a place called Kensall Green in the parish of Kensington' (formerly in the occupation of Mr Knight) and also several freehold closes or parcels of meadow or pasture ground thereunto belonging, also formerly in the occupation of Mr Knight, containing by estimation 53 acres, 3 rods and 38 perches, as shown on the attached plan, known by the name of Our Lady Fields of Kilbourn Abbey, and also the piece or parcel of freehold land on the South side of the Harrow Road and on the South West side of land formerly in the possession of Abraham Adams and at the west end on the land formerly in the possession of Miss Nicoll and afterwards of John Nicoll, abutting on the east side upon a piece of waste ground formerly in the possession of Miss Nicoll and afterwards of John Nicoll containing in length 75 rods and in width at each end thereof 4.5 (four and a half) rods and also the freehold land fronting the Harrow Road on the South side of the said Road and lying between the land of the said John Nicoll and the said road containing in length about 175 feet and in the extreme depth about 27 feet all which land was formerly Copyhold 'holden' of the Manor of Abbotts Kensington but afterwards enfranchised as shown in the plan drawn 'in the margin' of this document together with all the buildings etc on the said land 'with water rights and privileges of common of every kind',*

and the said Sir John Dean Paul declared (in effect) that he had not done anything to interfere with or spoil the title to the land now vested on the GCC.

Signed etc.

1 This Abstract was prepared by Dr Timothy Freed, with the assistance of Mr Alasdair Black. The Editor acknowledges with gratitude their help in this matter, and also that of Mr Martin Charles, who photographed the Indenture, thus enabling the Editor to prepare this version for publication. Permission of the General Cemetery Company was granted to copy and reproduce this material.

APPENDIX 3

Abstract[1] **of Indenture of two smaller plots of land dated the** day of 1833 (the blanks appear on the conveyance)

The transfer/conveyance is by **William St Quintin**[2] of Scampston Hall in the County of York to **The General Cemetery Company**

Which first recites that the land (both plots) was, with other land, previously transferred to Wm St Quintin on the 1st and 2nd days of July 1822, and that Wm StQ had agreed to sell the two plots of land to the GCC for £250.

And then, for the consideration of £250 it transfers:

(*a*) *The plot of land on the north side of the Grand Junction Canal at Kensall Green in the Parish of Kensington containing 2 roods plus the messuage, or tenement and building on it, bounded on the south and west by the canal and on the north by land belonging to the GCC, and on the east by [blank space] as shown on the plan in the margin;*

and

(*b*) *The plot of land on the north side of the canal containing 1 rood and 20 perches bounded on the south and east side by the canal and on the north by land of the said company* [GCC] *and on the west side by land then or lately belonging to Thomas Harrison Esq as shown on the plan in the margin.*

Plus, as to both plots of land, all ways, paths, passages, rights, privileges, easements and appurtenances,

Wm St Q also appears to have received five shillings for some reason – there are three or four lines, in a bracketed section about half way down the Deed, referring to a bargain and sale made by an indenture between the same parties the day before the Deed itself. There is also reference to a statute which is presumably the one referred to in the Indenture relating to the other land and which enabled the GCC to acquire land. This section is unclear.

The remainder of the Deed consists of covenants by Wm StQ to do whatever else might have been necessary to complete or perfect the title he had transferred as well as to indemnify the GCC against the possibility of anyone making any adverse claims against the GCC through his former title/ownership.

Signed etc

1 This Abstract was prepared by Dr Timothy Freed, with the assistance of Mr Alasdair Black. The Editor acknowledges with gratitude their help in this matter, and also that of Mr Martin Charles, who photographed the Indenture, thus enabling the Editor to prepare this version for publication. Permission of the General Cemetery Company was granted to copy and reproduce this material. 2 The Manor or Lordship of Notting Barns was the property of William Darby of Sunbury in 1767, in which year Darby conveyed it to William St Quintin of Scampston Hall, Yorkshire, to whom he was related by marriage (*see* Middlesex Land Register [1767/6/70-1]. St Quintin inherited a Baronetcy, but on his death (1795) this became extinct, and the London estate passed to William Thomas Darby, who assumed the surname St Quintin: on *his* death (1805), the property passed to his eldest son, William St Quintin (d. 1859) (*see* Middlesex Land Register [1802/2/663], Public Record Office, PROB 11/1426, f. 384, and Principal Probate Registry [1859], f. 687). For the St Quintin family, *see Walford's County Families of the United Kingdom* (1909 edition). There are others mentioned in the indenture: they include General John Calcraft; Arabella, widow of William Thomas St Quintin; Major-General Matthew Chitty Darby Griffith, of Padworth, Berkshire; John Darby, late of Addiscombe, Surrey, and then of Great George Street, Westminster; The Revd. George Wyld, of Newbury, Berkshire; and George ?Tharfrah Lambert, of Bedford Row, Middlesex. (*Editor's note*.)

APPENDIX 4

Constitution of the Friends of Kensal Green Cemetery

Registered address:

c/o The General Cemetery Company
Harrow Road
Kensal Green
LONDON W10 4RA

1.00 NAME

The Society shall be known as THE FRIENDS OF KENSAL GREEN CEMETERY (hereinafter called 'the Friends').

2.00 OBJECTS

The Friends are established for the public benefit, to promote the historic interest of Kensal Green Cemetery, Harrow Road, Kensal Green, LONDON W10 4RA (otherwise known as All Souls' Cemetery, Kensal Green) by associating the General Cemetery Company (hereinafter called 'the Company'), and local and national statutory and voluntary amenity societies in a common cause to promote the Cemetery's architectural, sculptural, landscape, ecological and historical interest and to provide such facilities as required for the furtherance of social welfare, education, recreation and leisure-time occupation.

3.00 POWERS

In furtherance of the foregoing objectives, but for no other purpose, the Friends shall be subject to the provisions of the Acts 2 & 3 William IV Chap CX and 2 Victoria Chap V and the Bye Laws, Rules and Orders made from time to time by the Company thereunder and have power to do all things as are lawful and as shall be conducive to the attainment of those objects.

4.00 MEMBERSHIP

4.01 Full membership of the Friends shall be open to all persons who wish to subscribe to its objects.

4.02 Members shall pay such subscriptions and fees as are due from time to time as determined by the Main Committee of the Friends.

4.03 The Main Committee shall have power to reject, suspend or terminate the membership of any individual for good and sufficient reason.

4.04 The title 'Friends' embraces the Main Committee, the Sub-Committees and their working parties, the Advisory Council and the subscribing members of the society.

5.00 MAIN COMMITTEE

5.01 Subject to the limitations set out elsewhere in this CONSTITUTION the affairs of the Friends shall be managed by the Main Committee assisted by five Sub-Committees, each of which is answerable to the Main Committee, and shall meet not less than twice and not more than four times a year.

5.02 The MAIN COMMITTEE shall consist of:

a) The DIRECTOR;

b) the honorary officers of the Friends as elected in accordance with the Rules governing officers;

c) not less than FIVE and not more than TEN members of the Friends elected in accordance with the Rules governing the Annual General Meeting;

d) not more than FOUR members (or one half of the number elected of the Main Committee as above defined, whichever is the less) may be co-opted by the Main Committee, though they will not have the power to vote;

e) a SECRETARY elected from its membership; and

f) a MINUTES SECRETARY elected from its membership.

The Main Committee shall be responsible for all matters dealing with the servicing of the ordinary members of the Friends, guiding, lectures, organised tours, Open Day/s, publicity and marketing.

All members of the Main Committee shall sit for three years and retire at the close of the Annual General Meeting but two following their election or co-option, but shall be eligible for re-election or further co-option.

5.03 The five Sub-Committees shall be:

FABRIC COMMITTEE; FINANCE COMMITTEE; IVY LEAGUE; LAPIDARY COMMITTEE; and PUBLICATIONS COMMITTEE.

5.04 The FABRIC COMMITTEE will be drawn from the membership of the Advisory Council and will be responsible for organising the repair and conservation of the listed Chapels and their contents, the Main Gate, the North Terrace Catacomb, the Sepulchral monuments, mausolea, the perimeter boundary walls/railings/gates and the landscape. The work will only be carried out after full consultation with the Company and after consent in writing signed by two Directors of the Company shall have been obtained.

In accordance with the candidature of the Advisory Council, the members of the Fabric Committee will sit for five years and retire at the end of their quinquennial appointment, but shall be eligible for re-appointment.

5.05 The FINANCE COMMITTEE will be drawn from the membership of the Main Committee and the Advisory Council and will be responsible for all matters relating to the funding of the objectives of the Friends.

The Honorary Treasurer will be a member of the Finance Committee but cannot be appointed Chairman. In accordance with their candidature of the Main Committee and the Advisory Council, the members of the Finance Committee will sit for either three or five years and retire at the end of their quinquennial appointment, but shall be eligible for re-appointment.

5.06 The IVY LEAGUE will be drawn from the membership of the Friends and will be responsible for the on-going programme of vegetation management on monuments.

It will appoint a CONVENOR from its membership. In accordance with the candidature of the Main Committee, the members shall sit for three years and retire at the close of the Annual General Meeting but two following their appointment, but shall be eligible for re-appointment.

5.07 The LAPIDARY GROUP will be drawn from the membership of the Friends and will be responsible for the continuing recording/cleaning of stones evident within the Cemetery for sepulchral purposes.

In accordance with the candidature of the Main Committee, the members shall sit for three years and retire at the close of the Annual General Meeting but two following their appointment, but shall be eligible for re-appointment.

5.08 The PUBLICATIONS COMMITTEE will be drawn from the membership of both the Advisory Council and the Friends Committee and will be responsible for all matters relating to the production of publications.

In accordance with the candidature of the Advisory Board, the members shall sit for five years and retire at the close of their quinquennial appointment, but shall be eligible for re-appointment.

5.09 A written report on the year's activities of each Sub-Committee shall be submitted to the Secretary to the Advisory Council by the 1st Tuesday of NOVEMBER in each year.

6.00 ADVISORY COUNCIL

6.01 An Advisory Council of not less than **TEN** and no more than **FIFTEEN** shall be drawn from such historians, conservators, national/local amenity/advisory concerns with an acknowledged interest and expertise in the cemetery movement.

6.02 The Advisory Council shall meet twice a year, on the second Tuesday in JUNE and on the second Tuesday in DECEMBER with the Board of the General Cemetery Company to report the year's progress and to set the forward plan for the ensuing year.

6.03 The Advisory Council shall select from their membership a CHAIRMAN who will enjoy the post for five years as chairman of the said Council and retire at the close of their quinquennial appointment but shall be eligible for re-appointment.

6.04 The Main Committee shall select from its membership an HONORARY SECRETARY to the Advisory Council who will enjoy the post for five years and be responsible to the Chairman for servicing the Advisory Council and for the day-to day implementation of the Council's aims. The Secretary will retire at the close of the appointment, but shall be eligible for re-appointment.

6.05 All members of the Advisory Council shall sit for five years and retire at the close of their quinquennial appointment, but shall be eligible for re-appointment.

6.06 The Patron, President, Vice-President/s and honorary officers are *ex officio* members of the Advisory Council.

6.07 Members of the Advisory Council will be subscribing members of the Friends of Kensal Green Cemetery.

7.00 HONORARY OFFICERS

The honorary officers shall be appointed by the Main Committee and shall comprise a Treasurer and the Secretary to the Advisory Council and any other such officer/s as may from time to time be determined by the Advisory Council.

Each honorary member shall sit for five years and retire at the close of the quinquennial appointment, but shall be eligible for re-appointment.

8.00 PATRON

It shall be the responsibility of the Advisory Council to nominate the Patron of the Friends.

9.00 PRESIDENT

It shall be the responsibility of the Advisory Board to nominate a President of the Friends, such a person having exhibited a unique contribution to the objects of the Friends of Kensal Green Cemetery.

10.00 VICE-PRESIDENT/S

It shall be the responsibility of the Advisory Council to nominate, if required, a Vice-President/s, such person/s having made an outstanding contribution as a former member/s of the Advisory Council.

11.00 ANNUAL GENERAL MEETING

Once in each year, on the first Saturday in DECEMBER, the Secretary of the Main Committee shall convene an Annual General Meeting at which all paid-up members shall be entitled to vote on any question for the primary purpose of:

a) electing members of the Friends to serve on the Main Committee in accordance with the Rules governing the Friends Committee;
b) taking note of the Main Committee's appointment of honorary officers;
c) receiving the approved Statement of Accounts in accordance with the Rules governing finance;
d) receiving the Annual Reports of the Sub-Committees; and
e) any other business.

The Agenda will be compiled by the Secretary having had reference to the Director and will be distributed **four weeks** prior to the date of the meeting.

12.00 SPECIAL GENERAL MEETING

12.01 The Director of the Main Committee may, with the approval of the Chairman of the Advisory Council, convene a Special General Meeting of the Friends.

12.02 A Special General Meeting shall **only** consider such business as may be set out in the notice of the meeting given in accordance with Rule 13.04 of the Rules governing Procedure.

12.03 Thirty full members (or one fifth of the membership entitled to vote, whichever is the less) may in writing and giving good reason/s request the Chairman of the Advisory Council to instruct the Director of the Main Committee to convene a Special General Meeting.

13.00 PROCEDURE

13.01 VOTING: Subject to the provisions of the Rule relating to Alterations, all matters at any meeting shall be determined by a simple majority of votes cast by members present and voting thereat; each member shall have one vote saving that in the event of an equality of votes the Director/Chairman may exercise a second, or casting, vote.

13.02 QUORUM: One half of the membership shall form a quorum at meetings of the Advisory Council, one half of the elected members shall form a quorum at meetings of the Friends Committee, and thirty members of the Friends (or one fifth of the members entitled to vote, whichever is the less) shall form a quorum at an Annual General Meeting.

13.03 MINUTES: Minutes shall be kept of all Advisory Council and Main Committee meetings and the appointed officer/s shall enter therein a record of all proceedings and resolutions.

13.04 NOTICE: The period for due notice of an Annual General Meeting and any

Special General Meeting shall be **SIXTY DAYS**; and for a Main Committee meeting, **TWENTY-ONE DAYS.**

13.05 VACANCIES: The Main Committee shall have power to appoint a member of the Friends to any casual vacancy amongst the officers of the Committee, howsoever arising, and such person/s shall sit until the next Annual General Meeting.

13.06 NOMINATIONS: Proposed and seconded WRITTEN nominations for candidates for election to the Main Committee, and bearing the consent of the nominee to stand, shall be received by the Minutes Secretary not less than FOURTEEN DAYS before the Annual General Meeting, provided that if no such nominations are received for a particular vacancy nominations made and seconded from the floor will be valid.

13.07 SUB-COMMITTEES: The Main Committee shall have the power to appoint sub-committees with such powers as it may from time to time determine provided that all such acts and proceedings of such sub-committees shall be reported back to the Main Committee via copies of the Minutes as soon as possible after their scheduled meetings.

14.00 REGULATIONS

The Advisory Council shall have power to make, adopt and issue rules and/or Standing Orders for the conduct of the Friends and of all the meetings provided that they shall not be inconsistent with the provisions of this Constitution or the Acts and Bye Laws, Rules and Orders referred to in clause 3.00 of this Constitution.

15.00 FINANCE

15.01 All monies raised by or on behalf of the Friends shall be applied to further its objects and for no other purpose whatsoever.

15.02 The Honorary Treasurer shall keep proper accounts of the finances of the Friends and shall present a written report to each meeting of the Main Committee and the Advisory Council.

15.03 The accounts shall be approved at least once a year by a qualified book-keeper.

15.04 A bank account shall be opened in the name of the Friends of Kensal Green Cemetery into which all monies shall be paid and the signatories of which shall be the President, the Chairman of the Advisory Council, the Chairman of the Fabric Committee, the Secretary of the Friends and the Honorary Treasurer for the time being.

15.05 The financial year of the Friends of Kensal Green Cemetery shall run from the first day of JANUARY to the last day of DECEMBER in any one year.

16.00 TRUSTEES

The title of all any real property which may be acquired by or for the purposes of the Friends shall be vested in not less that THREE and not more than FOUR Trustees who shall be appointed by the Advisory Council, two of which at least shall be members of the Advisory Council, and who shall enter into a Deed of Trust setting out the purposes and conditions upon which the said property is held in trust for the benefit of the Friends.

17.00 DISSOLUTION

17.01 If the Advisory Council, by a simple majority at any time, resolve that it is necessary or advisable to dissolve the Friends it shall call a Special General Meeting in accordance with the provisions in this Constitution.

17.02 If a motion for the dissolution is carried by a simple two thirds majority of members present and eligible to vote at such a meeting the Advisory Council shall have power to dissolve the Friends and to receive any assets held by or for the Friends which, after full satisfaction of all proper debts and liabilities towards the society, it shall apply all assets remaining towards such charitable purposes similar to those of the society.

18.00 ALTERATIONS

18.01 Any proposal to alter this Constitution shall be delivered in writing to the Secretary of the Main Committee not less than TWENTY-EIGHT days before the second Tuesday in June to be considered by the Advisory Council and the Board of Directors of the Company on the second Tuesday in June.

THIS CONSTITUTION WAS ADOPTED AS THE CONSTITUTION FOR THE FRIENDS OF KENSAL GREEN CEMETERY BETWEEN THE COMPANY AND THE ADVISORY COUNCIL AT A DULY CONVENED MEETING AT THE REGISTERED OFFICE OF THE COMPANY ON TUESDAY 10 DECEMBER ONE THOUSAND NINE HUNDRED AND NINETY SIX.

SIGNED:

....

MICHAEL JOHN KIRTLEY NODES, GENERAL CEMETERY COMPANY
For and on behalf of the General Cemetery Company

....

JOHN PHYSICK, CHAIRMAN, ADVISORY COUNCIL OF THE FRIENDS OF KENSAL GREEN CEMETERY
For and on behalf of the Friends of Kensal Green Cemetery

Select Bibliography

Books are sepulchres of thought.

HENRY WADSWORTH LONGFELLOW (1807-82):
'The Wind Over the Chimney', in *Tales of a Wayside Inn* (1863), 8.

This Select Bibliography does not have any spurious claims to comprehensiveness, but is intended to assist the reader with recommendations for further explorations of the background to the subject, and backs up the Chapter notes. The Editor acknowledges with gratitude the assistance of Mrs Julie Bunyan, Mr Anselm Kersten, Mrs Karen Latimer, Mr Robert Moulder, Mr Patrick Perratt, Mrs Ann Perry, Mr Roger Towe, and Mr Henry Vivian-Neal in its compilation.

ACT OF PARLIAMENT (1832), reprinted 1833, with subsequent Act [1839]: *An Act for Establishing a General Cemetery for the Interment of the Dead in the Neighbourhood of the Metropolis.* 2 & 3 Will. IV, c. 110, 11 July 1832 (London: Eyre & Spottiswoode for H.M.S.O.).

——— (1838a): *An Act for Establishing a Cemetery for the Interment of the Dead, Southward of the Metropolis, to be called 'The South Metropolitan Cemetery'.* 6 & 7 Will. IV, c. 129, 28 July 1836 (London: Eyre & Spottiswoode for H.M.S.O.).

——— (1838b):

An Act for establishing Cemeteries for the Interment of the Dead, Northward, Southward, and Eastward of the Metropolis, by a Company to be called 'The London Cemetery Company'. 6 & 7 Will. IV, c. 136, 17 August 1836 (London: Eyre & Spottiswoode for H.M.S.O.).

——— (1839): *An Act for enabling the General Cemetery Company to raise a further Sum of Money; and for amending the Act relating to the said Cemetery.* 2 Vict., c. 5, 14 May 1839 (London: George E. Eyre & Andrew Spottiswoode).

All the private cemeteries run by joint-stock Companies were founded by similar Acts of Parliament to the three cited above.

ALBERY, JAMES (1939): *The Dramatic Works of James Albery*, edited by WYNDHAM ALBERY (London: Peter Davies).

ALBERY, NICHOLAS, EVANS, STEPHEN, and WIENRICH, STEPHANIE (1998): *Natural Death and Woodland Burial* (London: The Natural Death Centre).

ALBERY, NICHOLAS, EVANS, STEPHEN, and WIENRICH, STEPHANIE (2000): *The New Natural Death Handbook* (London: Rider).

ALISON, ARCHIBALD (1811): *Essays on the Nature and Principles of Taste* (Edinburgh: Bell & Bradfute; Archibald Constable & Co.; London: F. C. & J. Rivington; Constable Hunter Park & Hunter).

ALLEN, F. D. (1822): *Documents and Facts, showing the Fatal Effects of Interments in Populous Cities* (New York: F. D. Allen).

ALLOM, THOMAS (1832): *See* KENDALL, HENRY EDWARD.

ANDALUCÍA, JUNTA DE, CONSEJERÍA DE OBRAS PÚBLICAS Y TRANSPORTES - DIRECCION GENERAL DE ARQUITECTURA Y VIVIENDA (1993): *Una Arquitectura para la Muerte. Actas. I Encuentro Internacional Sobre los Cementerios Contemporaneos* (Seville: Junta de Andalucía).

ANDREWS, WILLIAM (1889): *Curious Epitaphs Collected from the Graveyards of Great Britain and Ireland, with Bibliographical, Genealogical, and Historical Notes* (London: William Andrews & Co.).

ANGELOS, CHRISTINE WALSH (1982): *See* PADDOCK, SHIRLEY MACDONALD.

AN OLD INHABITANT (1882): *Kensington, Notting Hill, and Paddington, with Remembrances of the Locality 38 Years Ago* (London: Griffiths & Co., *Paddington Mercury* office, 58 Porchester Road, W. London).

ANONYMOUS (1811): *Documents relative to an Investigation of the Manner in which the Funeral of the Late Matthew Boulton, Esq. was furnished* (Birmingham: printed by R. Jabet).

——— (1825): *The Life, Death, Burial, and Resurrection Company* (London: s.n.).

——— (1848*a*): *The Cemetery. A brief appeal to the feelings of society in behalf of Extra Mural Burial* (London: William Pickering).

——— (1848*b*): Untitled editorial on Kensal Green cemetery in *Gardener's Chronicle* (1848), 419-20.

——— (1850): *Extramural Burial. The Three Schemes. I: the London Clergy Plan; II: The Board of Health or Erith Plan; III: The Woking Necropolis Plan. With General Remarks* (London: Effingham Wilson).

——— (1868): *Monumenta, or, Designs for Tombs, Wall-Monuments, Head-Stones, Grave-Crosses, &c.* (London: J. Hagger).

——— (1880): *The Burials Question further examined from a Layman's Point of View. Is there a Grievance?* (London: W. J. Johnson).

——— (1838): *The Workwoman's Guide* (New York: Bloomfield – reprint of 1975).

——— (1897): 'Flowers at Kensal Green Cemetery' in *Gardener's Chronicle*, **xxi** (1897), 140-1.

——— (1923): *Enquire Within Upon Everything*, 113th Edition (London: Herbert Jenkins).

——— (1968): *The Royal Mausoleum, Frogmore* (Windsor: printed by Oxley & Son [Windsor] Ltd.).

ARCHER, JOHN (1991): *See* GAME, MEG.

———, and KEECH, DANIEL (1993): *Nature Conservation in Hammersmith and Fulham. Ecology Handbook 25* (London: London Ecology Unit).

ARIÈS, PHILIPPE (1974): *Western Attitudes Towards Death: from the Middle Ages to the Present* (London: Marion Boyars).

——— (1983): *The Hour of Our Death* tr. HELEN WEAVER (Harmondsworth: Penguin Books Ltd).

——— (1985): *Images of Man and Death* (Cambridge, Mass.: Harvard University Press).

ASHMORE, M. (1987): 'Acid Rain. Its effect on the flora and fauna in and around London' in *The London Atalanta*, Newsletter of the London Natural History Society. Ecology and Entomology Section, **i** (January), 1-3.

ATKINS, WILLIAM (1997): *See* AYBES, CHARLOTTE.

ATTICUS (1838): *Hints on the Subject of Interment Within the City of Philadelphia: Addressed to the Serious Consideration of the Members of Councils, Commissioners of the Districts, and Citizens Generally* (Philadelphia: William Brown).

AUDIT COMMISION REPORT (1988): *The Competitive Management of Parks and Green Spaces* (London: H.M.S.O).

AUSTIN, EDWIN (1907): *Burial Grounds and Cemeteries: A Practical Guide to Their Administration by Local Authorities* (London: Butterworth & Co. and Shaw & Sons).

AUSTRALIAN DICTIONARY OF BIOGRAPHY (1966): In 14 volumes (Melbourne: Melbourne University Press).

AYBES, CHARLOTTE, ATKINS, WILLIAM, and HERBERT, CLIVE (1997): Mammal (excluding bats) Borough Survey: 1997 (A report prepared for Ecology and Leisure Services, Royal Borough of Kensington and Chelsea).

BACKER, BARBARA, HANNON, NATALIE, AND RUSSELL, N. A. (*Eds.*) (1982): *Death and Dying: Individuals and Institutions* (New York and Chichester: Wiley).

BADHAM, PAUL (1976, 1978): *Christian Beliefs about Life after Death* (London: Macmillan and S.P.C.K.).

BAILEY, BRIAN (1987): *Churchyards of England and Wales* (London: Robert Hale Ltd.).

BAILY, J. T. HERBERT (1906): *George Morland – a Biographical Essay* (London: Otto).

BAILEY, CONRAD (1975): *Famous London Graves* (London: George Harrap & Co.).

BAKEWELL, JOAN, and DRUMMOND, JOHN (1977): *A Fine and Private Place* (London: Weidenfeld & Nicolson).

BALTHAZAR, HERMAN (*Ed.*) (1999): *Een introductie tot de zorg voor het Funerair Erfgoed. Verlagsboek.* Acts of the Colloquium held at the Prometheuscentrum, Antwerp, (20-21 March 1999) (Brussels: Vlaamse Contactcommissie Monumentenzorg).

BARCLAY, D (1983): *Interpretation of the Environment* (Dunfermline: Carnegie U.K. Trust).

BARKER, B. ASHLEY (1969): *See* GLADSTONE, FLORENCE, M. (1924).

BARKER, FELIX, and GAY, J. (1984): *Highgate Cemetery: Victorian Valhalla* (London: John Murray [Publishers] Ltd.).

BARKER, G. M. A. (1977): *Wildlife Conservation in the Care of Churches and Churchyards* (London: Council for Places of Worship of the General Synod of the Church of England).

BARKER, THE REV THOMAS BURGESS (*c.*1869): *Abney Park Cemetery: A Complete Descriptive Guide to Every Part of this Beautiful Depository of the Dead* (London: Houlston & Wright).

BARNARD, SYLVIA (1990): *To Prove I'm Not Forgot. Living and Dying in a Victorian City* (Manchester: Manchester University Press).

BAROZZI, JACQUES (1990): *Guide des Cimetières Parisiens* (Paris: Éditions Hervas).

BARRECA, REGINA (*Ed.*) (1990): *Sex and Death in Victorian Literature* (Basingstoke: Macmillan & Co. Ltd.).

BARRELL, J. (1980): *The Dark Side of the Landscape* (Cambridge: Cambridge University Press).

BARTON, NICHOLAS (1992): *The Lost Rivers of London* (London: Historical Publications).

BASSETT, S. (1993): *Death in Towns* (Leicester: Leicester University Press).

BATSFORD, HERBERT (1916): *English Mural Monuments and Tombstones.* With an introduction by WALTER W. GODFREY (London: B. T. Batsford Ltd.).

BEATY, NANCY LEE (1970): *The Craft of Dying: a Study in the Literary Tradition of the 'Ars Moriendi' in England* (New Haven and London: Yale University Press).

BEESLEY, IAN (1991): *see* JAMES, DAVID.

BELLASIS, A. F. (1868): *An Account of the Old Tombs in the Cemeteries of Surat* (Bombay: The Education Society's Press, Byculla).

BENDANN, EFFIE (1930): *Death Customs: An Analytical Study of Burial Rites* (London: Kegan Paul & Co.).

BENGAL OBITUARY, THE (1848): *The Bengal Obituary, or A Record to Perpetuate the Memory of Departed Worth, being a compilation of tablets and monumental inscriptions from various parts of the Bengal and Agra Presidencies. To which is added Biographical Sketches and Memoirs of such as have pre-eminently distinguished themselves in the History of India, since the formation of the European Settlement to the Present Time* (Calcutta: Holmes & Co.).

BERCHTOLD, COUNT LEOPOLD VON (1791): *Projet pour prévenir les Dangers Très-Fréquens des Inhumations Précipitées* (Paris: Berchtold).

BERNARDIN DE SAINT-PIERRE, JACQUES-HENRI (1784): *Études de la Nature* (Paris: P. F. Didot).

BERRY, JAMES (1987): *The Glasgow Necropolis Heritage Trail* (Glasgow: City of Glasgow District Council).

BIGELOW, JACOB (1860): *A History of the Cemetery of Mount Auburn* (Boston and Cambridge, Mass.: James Munroe & Co.).

BLAIR, GEORGE (1857): *Biographic and Descriptive Sketches of Glasgow Necropolis* (Glasgow: Maurice Ogle and Thomas Murray & Son).
BLAIR, ROBERT (1826): *The Grave* (Edinburgh: Stirling & Kenney; and London: Longman Rees Orme Brown & Green).
BLAKE, WILLIAM (1973): *William Blake's Illustrations to* [Blair's] *The Grave* (London: Wildwood House).
BLANCH, WILLIAM (1875): *Ye Parish of Camberwell: A Brief Account of the Parish of Camberwell, its History, and Antiquities* (London: E. W. Allen).
BLANCHARD, LAMAN (1842): 'A Visit to the General Cemetery at Kensal Green' in *Ainsworth's Magazine*, **ii**, 178-88.
BLAND, OLIVIA (1986): *The Royal Way of Death* (London: Constable & Co. Ltd.).
BLOCH M. (*Ed.*) (1989): *Ritual, History, and Power* (London: Athlone Press).
BLOCH, M., and PARRY, J. (*Eds.*) (1982): *Death and the Regeneration of Life* (Cambridge: Cambridge University Press).
BLOM, ERIC (*Ed.*) (1966): *Grove's Dictionary of Music and Musicians* (London: Macmillan & Co. Ltd.).
BLORE, EDWARD (1826): *The Monumental Remains of Noble and Eminent Persons, comprising the Sepulchral Antiquities of Great Britain* (London: Harding, Lepard, & Co.).
BLOXHAM, MATTHEW HOLBECHE (*c.*1841): *Fragmenta Sepulchralia. A Glimpse of the Sepulchral and early Monumental Remains of Great Britain* (Oxford: Oxford University Press).
——— (1882*a*): *Companion to the Principles of Gothic Ecclesiastical Architecture* (London: George Bell & Sons).
——— (1882*b*): *The Principles of Gothic Ecclesiastical Architecture* (London: George Bell & Sons).
BLUNDELL, JOE WHITLOCK, and PHYSICK, JOHN (1989): *Westminster Abbey: The Monuments* (London: John Murray [Publishers] Ltd.).
BOASE, FREDERIC (1965): *Modern English Biography, containing many thousand concise memoirs of persons who have died between the years 1851-1900* (London: Frank Cass & Co.).
BODE, WILHELM ARNOLD VON (1928): *Florentine Sculptors of the Renaissance* (London: Methuen & Co.).
BOGLE, JOANNA (1989): *Who Lies Where?* (London: Lamp Press).
BOND, FRANCIS (1913): *An Introduction to English Church Architecture from the Eleventh to the Sixteenth Century* (London: Humphrey Milford for Oxford University Press).
——— (1916): *The Chancel of English Churches* (London: Humphrey Milford for Oxford University Press).
BOND, PETER BERNARD (1967): 'The Celebration of Death: some thoughts on the design of crematoria' in *The Architectural Review*, **cxli**/842 (April), 303-4.
BONDESON, JAN (2001): *Buried Alive: The Terrifying History of Our Most Primal Fear* (New York and London: W.W. Norton & Company, Inc.).
BOUTELL, CHARLES (1849*a*): *Christian Monuments in England and Wales: An Historical and Descriptive Sketch of the Various Classes of Sepulchral Monuments which have been in use in the Country from about the Era of the Norman Conquest to the Time of Edward the Fourth* (London: George Bell).
——— (1849*b*): *The Monumental Brasses of England* (London: George Bell).
BOWKER, ADAM & SON (1876): *In Memoriam, or Funeral Records of Liverpool Celebrities* (Liverpool: Bowker & Son).
BOWKER, J. (1991): *The Meanings of Death* (Cambridge: Cambridge University Press).
BOYLE, A., *ET AL.* (1985): *Ruins and Remains: Edinburgh's Neglected Heritage* (Edinburgh: Memento Mori).
BRIDGMAN, HARRIET, and DURY, ELIZABETH (*Eds.*) (1982): *The Last Word* (London: Andre Deutsch).
BRIGGS, ASA (1968): *Victorian Cities* (Harmondsworth: Penguin Books Ltd.).
BRIGHTMAN, F. H., and LAUNDON, JACK R. (1994): 'Lichens in Churchyards' in *The Friends of Kensal Green Cemetery's Quarterly Magazine*, **xiii**, 10-11.
BRINDLEY, WILLIAM, and WEATHERLEY, W. SAMUEL (1887): *Ancient Sepulchral Monuments containing Illustrations of over Six Hundred Examples from Various Countries and from the Earliest Periods down to the End of the Eighteenth Century* (London: printed for the Authors by Vincent Brooks Day & Son).
BRISCOE, JOHN POTTER (1883): *Gleanings from God's Acre: being a Collection of Epitaphs* (Edinburgh: Oliphant & Co.).
BRITISH ASSOCIATION FOR CEMETERIES IN SOUTH ASIA (B.A.C.S.A.) (1986): *The South Park Street Cemetery, Calcutta*, edited by MAURICE SHELLIM (London: B.A.C.S.A.).
——— (1992): *South Park Street Cemetery, Calcutta: Register of Graves and Standing Tombs* (London: B.A.C.S.A.).
——— (from 1977): *See CHOWKIDAR.*
BRITTON, JOHN (1836): *Cathedral Antiquities: Historical and Descriptive Accounts, with 311 Illustrations, etc.* (London: Longmans Rees Orme Brown Green and T. Longman jun.).
BRONFEN, ELISABETH (*Ed.*) (1993): *See* GOODWIN, SARAH WEBSTER.
BROOKFIELD, CHARLES and FRANCES (1905): *Mrs Brookfield and her Circle* (London: Sir Isaac Pitman & Sons Ltd.).
BROOKS, CHRIS (1999): *The Gothic Revival* (London: Phaidon Press Ltd.).
BROOKS, CHRISTOPHER, with ELLIOTT, BRENT, LITTEN, JULIAN, ROBINSON, ERIC, ROBINSON, RICHARD, and TEMPLE, PHILIP (1989): *Mortal Remains: The History and Present State of the Victorian and Edwardian Cemetery* (Exeter: Wheaton Publishers Ltd.).
BROWN, JAMES (1867): *The Epitaphs and Monumental Inscriptions in Greyfriars Churchyard, Edinburgh* (Edinburgh: J. Moodie Miller).
BROWNE, SIR THOMAS (1893): *Hydriotaphia. Urn Burial; with an Account of Some Urns found at Brampton in Norfolk* edited by SIR JOHN EVANS (London: Charles Whittingham & Co. at The Chiswick Press).
——— (1912): *The Works of Sir Thomas Browne* edited by CHARLES SAYLE (Edinburgh: John Grant).
BRYAN'S DICTIONARY OF PAINTERS AND ENGRAVERS (1964): Fifth edition of *Bryan's Biographical and Critical Dictionary of Painters and Engravers* (Port Washington, New York: Kennikat Press Inc.).

BUILDER, THE (1842-1966): Published in London, this architectural periodical is an invaluable source for material.

BULL, G. B. G. (1975-6): *Thomas Milne's Land Use Map of London and Environs in 1800* (London: London Topographical Society).

BUNNING, JAMES BUNSTONE (1839): *Designs for Tombs and Monuments* (London: John Williams Library of Art).

BURGESS, FREDERICK (1963): *English Churchyard Memorials* (London: Lutterworth Press).

BURGESS, J. (1987): *See* HARRISON, C.

BURMAN, PETER, and STAPLETON, THE REV. HENRY S. L. (*Eds.*) (1988): *The Churchyards Handbook* (London: Church House Publishing).

BURTON, RODNEY M. (1983): *Flora of the London Area* (London: London Natural History Society).

BUSHWAY, ROBERT (1982): *By Rite: Custom, Ceremony, and Community in England, 1700-1880* (London: Junction).

BYRON, LORD (1967): *Poetical Works of Lord Byron* (Oxford: Oxford University Press).

CAMPBELL, R. (1748): *The London Tradesman* (London: T. Gardner).

CANNADINE, DAVID, and PRICE, SIMON (*Eds.*) (1987): *Rituals of Royalty: Power and Ceremonial in Traditional Societies* (Cambridge: Cambridge University Press).

CANSICK, FREDERICK TEAGUE (1869): *A Collection of Curious and Interesting Epitaphs, copied from the Monuments of Distinguished and Noted Characters in The Ancient Church and Burial Grounds of Saint Pancras, Middlesex* (London: J. Russell Smith).

——— (1872): *A Collection of Curious and Interesting Epitaphs, copied from the Existing Monuments of Distinguished and Noted Characters in The Cemeteries and Churches of Saint Pancras, Middlesex* (London: J. Russell Smith).

——— (1875): *A Collection of Curious and Interesting Epitaphs copied from the Existing Monuments of Distinguished and Noted Characters in The Churches and Churchyards of Hornsey, Tottenham, Edmonton, Enfield, Friern Barnet, and Hadley, Middlesex* (London: J. Russell Smith). Also three volumes in the Large Paper Edition of the same year.

CARLYLE, THOMAS (1882): *Collected Works*, 31 vols. (London: Chapman & Hall).

CARROGIS, LOUIS (1779): *Jardin de Monceau, près de Paris, appartenant.... à... M. le duc de Chartres* (Paris: Delafosse).

CARROTT, RICHARD G. (1978): *The Egyptian Revival: its Sources, Monuments, and Meaning, 1808-1858* (Berkeley, Los Angeles, and London: University of California Press).

CASSELL & CO. LTD. (1869-71): *Cassell's Household Guide to Every Department of Practical Life* (London: Cassell & Co. Ltd.).

CAWTHORNE, W. A., and FULLER, J. G. C. M. (1994): 'James Mitchell's *Brickmaking* – an early nineteenth-century study in economic geology' in *London Naturalist*, **lxxiii** (November), 31-5.

CEMETERY AND CREMATORIA SUPERINTENDENTS, NATIONAL ASSOCIATION OF (1935): *The Joint Conference of Cemetery and Cremation Authorities* (Folkestone: National Association of Cemetery and Crematoria Superintendents).

CHADWICK, EDWIN (1843): *A Supplementary Report on the Results of a Special Inquiry into the Practice of Interment in Towns* (London: W. Clowes & Sons for Her Majesty's Stationery Office).

CHADWICK, OWEN (1966): *The Victorian Church* (London: S.C.M.P.).

CHALMERS-HUNT, JOHN M., and SKINNER, BERNARD (1992): 'The Immigration of Lepidoptera to the British Isles in 1990' in *Entomologists' Record*, **civ** (15 July), 211-2.

CHAPPLE, CHRISTINE E. (1987): *Undercliffe Cemetery: Bradford's Great Heritage in Stone* (Bradford: The Bradford Undercliffe Cemetery Company).

CHARTERED INSTITUTE OF PUBLIC FINANCE AND ACCOUNTANCY (Annual): *Cemetery Statistics* (London: C.I.P.F.A.).

CHERRY, BRIDGET, and PEVSNER, NIKOLAUS (1991): *London 3: North West* in *The Buildings of England* Series (London: Penguin Group).

CHOWKIDAR (from 1977): Journal of the British Association for Cemeteries in South Asia (B.A.C.S.A.), edited by ROSIE LLEWELLYN-JONES (London: B.A.C.S.A.).

CHURCH MONUMENTS (from 1985): *Journal* of The Church Monuments Society.

CLARK, BENJAMIN (1843): *Hand-Book for Visitors to the Kensal Green Cemetery* (London: Joseph Masters). A second, revised edition was published in 1864.

CLARK, D. (*Ed.*) (1993): *The Sociology of Death* (Oxford: Blackwell).

CLARK, KENNETH MACKENZIE (1962): *The Gothic Revival: An Essay in the History of Taste* (London: John Murray).

CLARKE, BASIL FULFORD LOWTHER (1969): *Church Builders of the Nineteenth Century. A Study of the Gothic Revival in England* (Newton Abbot: David & Charles Reprints).

CLARKE, JOHN M. (1988): *The Brookwood Necropolis Railway. Locomotion Papers*, **cxliii** (Oxford: The Oakwood Press).

——— *ET AL.* (1992): *An Introduction to Brookwood Cemetery* (Brookwood, Surrey: Necropolis Publications).

CLARKE, R.S.J. (*Ed.*) (1991): *See* MERRICK, A.C.W.

CLARKE, SUSAN A. (1994*a*): *Wildlife in Churchyards – Management to Attract Butterflies & Other Animals* (Salisbury: 'Derwent', SP5 2RB).

——— (1994b): *See* WILLMOTT, KENNETH J.

——— (1995): *Wildlife in Churchyards Management Planning* (Salisbury: 'Derwent', SP5 2RB).

CLAUSSEN, HORST (*Ed.*) (1995): *See* SCHUCHARD, JUTTA.

CLEAVELAND, NEHEMIAH, and WALTER, CORNELIA (1847): *Green-Wood and Mount Auburn* (New York: s.n.).

COCKERELL, T. D. A. (1891): 'A preliminary list of the insect fauna of Middlesex', 2, in *The Entomologist*, **xxiv**/332 (January), 29-33.

COHEN, KATHLEEN (1973): *Metamorphosis of a Death Symbol* (Berkeley: University of California Press).
COHN-SHERBOK, D., and LEWIS, C. (1995): *Beyond Death* (Basingstoke: Macmillan).
COLE, HUBERT (1964): *Things for the Surgeon: a History of the Resurrection Men* (London: Heinemann).
COLLINSON, HUGH (1975): *Country Monuments: Their Families and Houses* (Newton Abbot: David & Charles).
COLLISON, GEORGE (1840): *Cemetery Interment: Containing a Concise History of the Modes of Interment Practised by the Ancients; Descriptions of Père la Chaise, the Eastern Cemeteries and those of America; the English Metropolitan and Provincial Cemeteries, and More Particularly of Abney Park Cemetery, at Stoke Newington; with a Descriptive Catalogue of its Plants and Arboretum* (London: Longman Orme Brown Green & Longman's).
COLLOCOTT, T. C. (*Ed.*) (1984): *See* THORNE, J. O.
COLVIN, HOWARD (1991): *Architecture and the After-Life* (New Haven and London: Yale University Press).
——— (1995): *A Biographical Dictionary of British Architects 1600-1848* (New Haven and London: Yale University Press).
CONNER, PATRICK (*Ed.*) (1983): *The Inspiration of Egypt. Its Influence on British Artists, Travellers, and Designers, 1700-1900* Catalogue of an Exhibition held at Brighton Museum, 7 May-17 July 1983, and at Manchester City Art Gallery, 4 August-17 September 1983 (Brighton: Brighton Borough Council).
CONNOR, ARTHUR BENTLEY (1970): *Monumental Brasses in Somerset* (Bath: Kingsmead Reprints).
CONTEMPORARY REVIEW, THE (1874): January issue.
COOK, ELIZA (1870): *The Poetical Works* (London: Henry Frowde).
COONES, PAUL (1987): 'Kensal Green Cemetery: London's First Great Extramural Necropolis' *in Transactions of The Ancient Monuments Society*, **N.S. xxxi** (London: A.M.S), 48-76.
——— (1994): *Kensal Green Cemetery. A Concise Introductory Guide & Select List of Notable Monuments Together with a Plan* (London: Friends of Kensal Green Cemetery).
COOPER, JEREMY (2000): *No Fun Without U* (London: Ellipsis).
COOPER, ROBYN (1982): 'The Crowning Glory of Pisa' in *Italian Studies*, **xxxvii**, 72-100.
CORNFORD, STEPHEN (*Ed.*) (1989): *See* YOUNG, EDWARD.
CORPORATION OF LONDON: *See* REED, CHARLES.
COURT DE GÉBELIN, ANTOINE (1776): *Monde Primitif, anlaysé et comparé avec le monde moderne* (Paris: Court de Gébelin).
COUSSILLAN, AUGUSTE ANDRÉ (1958): *See* HILLAIRET, JACQUES.
COUTTS, J. (1992): 'Kensal Green' in *History Today*, **xlii** (July), 62-3.
COX, M. (*Ed.*) (1998): *Grave concerns: death and burial in England 1700-1850* (York: Council for British Archaeology).
CRAIG, MAURICE, and CRAIG, MICHAEL (1999): *Mausolea Hibernica* (Dublin: The Lilliput Press Ltd.).
CREMATION SOCIETY OF ENGLAND, THE (1877-1912): *Transactions.*
——— (1909): *Crematoria in Great Britain. The Modern Cremation Movement* (London: The Cremation Society).
CRICHTON, IAN (1976): *The Art of Dying* (London: Peter Owen).
CROFT, H. J. (1867, 1881): *Guide to Kensal Green Cemetery* (London: J. Howell).
CROOK, JOSEPH MORDAUNT (1972): *The Greek Revival. Neo-Classical Attitudes in British Architecture 1760-1870* (London: John Murray).
——— (1981): *William Burges and the High Victorian Dream* (London: John Murray).
CROSS, COLIN and HOLLOWAY, LESTER (1986): 'Kensal Green Bird Report, 1984-85' (London: London Wildlife Trust).
CROSSLEY, FRED H. (1921): *English Church Monuments A.D. 1150-1550. An Introduction to the Study of Tombs and Effigies of the Mediaeval Period* (London: B. T. Batsford Ltd.).
CROYDON WEEKLY STANDARD (1865): 25 November issue.
CULBERTSON, JUDI, and RANDALL, TOM (1991): *Permanent Londoners. An Illustrated Guide to the Cemeteries of London* (London: Robson Books Ltd.).
——— (2000): *Permanent Londoners: An Illustrated Biographical Guide to the Cemeteries of London* (London: Robson Books Ltd.).
CUNNINGTON, PHYLLIS, and LUCAS, CATHERINE (1972): *Costume for Burials, Marriages, and Deaths* (London: A. & C. Black).
CURL, JAMES STEVENS (1968): 'Highgate: a great Victorian cemetery' in *RIBA Journal*, **lxxv** (April), 179-83.
——— (1971*a*): 'Works of Art in Memoriam. 19th-Century Sepulchral Monuments' in *Country Life* (9 September), 634-5.
——— (1971*b*): 'Taking the Waters in London I' in *Country Life* (2 December), 1534-8.
——— (1972): *The Victorian Celebration of Death* (Newton Abbot: David & Charles [Publishers] Ltd.).
——— (1973): 'XIXth Century Funerary Architecture' in *The Architect* (February), 49-52.
——— (1974*a*): 'Scotland's Spectacular Cemeteries' in *Country Life* (3 October), 950-4.
——— (1974*b*): *The Cemeteries and Burial Grounds of Glasgow* (Glasgow: City of Glasgow District Council Parks Department).
——— (1975*a*): 'Saving a Victorian Burial-Ground. Nunhead Cemetery, South London' in *Country Life* (17 July), 146-8.
——— (1975*b*): 'The Architecture and Planning of the Nineteenth-Century Cemetery' in *Garden History. The Journal of The Garden History Society*, **iii/3** (Summer), 13-41.
——— (1976*a*): 'The Plight of Highgate Cemetery' in *Country Life* (1 April), 848-50.
——— (1976*b*): 'Taking the Waters in London. Old Spas, Wells, and Baths' in *Country Life* (18 November), 1386-90.
——— (1976*c*): 'Spas on the City's Fringes' in *Country Life* (18 November), 1499-1502.
——— (1977*a*): 'Nunhead Cemetery, London. A History of the Planning, Architecture, Landscaping, and Fortunes of a Great Nineteenth-Century Cemetery' in *Transactions of The Ancient Monuments Society*, **N.S. xxii** (London: A.M.S.), 28-89.

——— (1977*b*): 'Europe's Grandest Cemetery? The Staglieno, Genoa' in *Country Life* (15 September), 700-1.
——— (1978*a*): 'Scotland's Cities of the Dead' in *The Architect* (January), 20-2.
——— (1978*b*): 'An Urban Necropolis. The Cemetery of Père-Lachaise, Paris' in *Country Life* (25 May), 1511-3.
——— (1978*c*): *Mausolea in Ulster* (Belfast: Ulster Architectural Heritage Society).
——— (1978*d*): 'Built in Remembrance. Mausolea in Ulster' in *Country Life* (13 July), 126-7.
——— (1980*a*): *A Celebration of Death. An Introduction to some of the Buildings, Monuments, and Settings of Funerary Architecture in the Western European Tradition* (London: Constable & Co. Ltd.). Revised Edition London: B. T. Batsford Ltd. 1993*a*.
——— (1980*b*): 'Irlande: une Architecture de la Mort' in *Connaissance des Arts*, **cccxlv** (November), 102-7. Also published in English in the same journal (U.S. No. 10), 92-7.
——— (1981*a*): 'The Historical Problems of Designing Crematoria' in *Pharos: The Official Journal of The Cremation Society of Great Britain*, **xlvii**/2 (April-June), 45-51.
——— (1981*b*): 'Northern Cemetery under Threat. Jesmond, Newcastle upon Tyne' in *Country Life* (2 July), 68-9.
——— (1981*c*): 'Funereal Fantasy. The Mortuary Chapel, Arbroath' in *Country Life* (10 September), 875-6.
——— (1981*d*): 'Requiem for a Graveyard: Undercliffe Cemetery, Bradford' in *Bradford Telegraph and Argus* (17 November), 10.
——— (1982*a*): *The Egyptian Revival as a Recurring Theme in the History of Taste* (London: George Allen & Unwin [Publishers] Ltd.).
——— (1982*b*): 'Neo-Classical Necropolis in Decay. York Cemetery' in *Country Life* (28 January), 235-8.
——— (1982*c*): 'The Architecture and Landscapes of Death in Hampshire' in *Hampshire: The County Magazine*, **xxii**/7 (May), 55-8.
——— (1982*d*): 'Cemeteries and Planning History' in *Planning History Bulletin*, **iv**/1, 19-22.
——— (1982*e*): 'Suggestion of Permanence. Funerary Architecture in the Classical Tradition - I' in *Country Life* (9 September), 756-60.
——— (1982*f*): 'Language of Rationalism. Funerary Architecture in the Classical Tradition - II' in *Country Life* (16 September), 827-30.
——— (1983*a*): 'Twilit world where Bonapartist Hopes came to an End' in *Hampshire: The County Magazine*, **xxiii**/9 (July), 36-9.
——— (1983*b*): 'John Claudius Loudon and the Garden Cemetery Movement' in *Garden History: The Journal of The Garden History Society*, **xi**/2, (Autumn), 133-56.
——— (1983*c*): *The Life and Work of Henry Roberts (1803-76), Architect: The Evangelical Conscience and the Campaign for Model Housing and Healthy Nations* (Chichester: Phillimore & Co. Ltd.).
——— (1984*a*): 'Southampton Cemetery: one of the County's Treasures' in *Hampshire: The County Magazine*, **xxiv**/6 (April), 55-8.
——— (1984*b*): 'The Design of Early British Cemeteries' in *Journal of Garden History*, **iv**/3 (July-September), 223-254.
——— (1986*a*): 'Architecture for a Novel Purpose. Death and the Railway Age' in *Country Life* (12 June), 1716-7.
——— (1986*b*): *The Londonderry Plantation 1609-1914: The History, Architecture, and Planning of the Estates of the City of London and its Livery Companies in Ulster* (Chichester: Phillimore & Co. Ltd.).
——— (1988): 'The Design of Historical Gardens. Cultural, Magical, Medical, and Scientific Gardens in Europe' in *Interdisciplinary Science Reviews*, **xiii**/3 (September), 264-81.
——— (1989): 'The West of London and Westminster Cemetery at Brompton', Final Report and Survey (1 September) for English Heritage.
——— (1990): *Victorian Architecture* (Newton Abbot: David & Charles plc).
——— (1991): *The Art and Architecture of Freemasonry. An Introductory Study* (London: B. T. Batsford Ltd.).
——— (1992): *Classical Architecture. An Introduction to its Vocabulary and Essentials, with a Select Glossary of Terms* (London: B. T. Batsford Ltd.). *See* the new edition of 2001.
——— (1993*a*): *See* CURL, JAMES STEVENS (1980*a*).
——— (1993*b*): *Georgian Architecture* (Newton Abbot: David & Charles Publishing plc).
——— (1994*a*): 'Young's *Night Thoughts* and the Origins of the Garden Cemetery' in *Journal of Garden History*, **xiv**/2 (Summer 1994), 92-118.
——— (1994*b*): *Egyptomania: The Egyptian Revival as a Recurring Theme in the History of Taste* (Manchester: Manchester University Press).
——— (1995): *The English Heritage Book of Victorian Churches* (London: B. T. Batsford Ltd.).
——— (1997): 'Gardens of Allusion' in *Interdisciplinary Science Reviews*, **22**/4 (December), 325-42.
——— (1999): *The Oxford Dictionary of Architecture* (Oxford: Oxford University Press). Also published (2000*a*) as part of the Oxford Paperback Reference Series.
——— (2000*a*): *See* previous item (1999) above.
——— (2000*b*): *The Honourable The Irish Society and the Plantation of Ulster, 1608-2000. The City of London and the Colonisation of County Londonderry in the Province of Ulster in Ireland. A History and Critique* (Chichester: Phillimore & Co. Ltd.).
——— (2000*c*): 'Egypt in Rome – an introductory essay. I: Isis, obelisks, and the Isaeum Campense' in *Interdisciplinary Science Reviews*, **25**/1 (Spring), 53-64.
——— (2000*d*): 'Egypt in Rome – an introductory essay. II: The Villa Adriana and the beginnings of Egyptology' in *Interdisciplinary Science Reviews*, **25**/2 (Summer), 123-35.
——— (2000*e*): *The Victorian Celebration of Death* (Thrupp, Stroud: Sutton Publishing Ltd.).

CURLL, EDMUND (1717): *The Inscriptions upon the Tombs, Grave-Stones, &c. .in the Dissenters Burial-Place near Bunhill-Fields* (London: Edmund Curll). *See* REED, CHARLES.

CUTTS, EDWARD LEWES (1849): *A Manual for the Study of the Sepulchral Slabs and Crosses of the Middle Ages* (London and Oxford: John Henry Parker).

DAGLEY, RICHARD (1827): *Death's Doings: consisting of numerous original compositions, in prose and verse...* etc. (London: J. Andrews W. Cole).

DALLETT, FRANCIS JAMES (1959): 'John Notman, Architect', in *The Princeton University Library Chronicle* (Spring), 130-1.

DALY, CÉSAR (1871): *L'Architecture funéraire contemporaine* (Paris: Duchet).

DAVEY, RICHARD (*c.*1889): *A History of Mourning* (London: printed by McCorquodale & Co. Ltd. for Jay's Mourning Warehouse).

DAVIES, DOUGLAS, and SHAW, ALASTAIR (1995): *Reusing Old Graves – a Report on Popular British Attitudes* (Crayford: Shaw & Sons).

DAVIES, J. (1994): *Ritual and Remembrance: Responses to Death in Human Societies* (Sheffield: Sheffield Academic Press Ltd.).

DEARBORN, NATHANIEL S. (1852): *Guide through Mount Auburn, for the benefit of strangers desirous of seeing the clusters of monuments with the least trouble* (Boston: Dearborn).

DELCHEVALERIE, M. (1868): 'Les squares et les marchés de Paris' in *La Belgique Horticole*, **xviii**, 51-63.

DELILLE, ABBÉ JACQUES (actually JACQUES MONTANIER, *called*) (1782): *Les Jardins, ou l'art d'embellir les Paysages* (Paris: Didot).

DELVES, H. C. (1952): 'The Disposal of the Dead' in *Journal of the Town Planning Institute*, **xxxviii** (September-October), 261-5.

DENNIS, EVE (1993): 'The Living Churchyard – Sanctuaries for Wildlife' in *British Wildlife*, **iv**/4, 230-41.

DENNIS, GEORGE (1883): *The Cities and Cemeteries of Etruria* (London: John Murray).

DENNY, BARBARA (1993): *Notting Hill and Holland Park Past* (London: Historical Publications).

DEPARTMENT OF THE ENVIRONMENT (1991): *Competitive Tendering for Local Authority Services: Initial Experiences* (London: H.M.S.O.).

DESMOND, RAY, with ELLWOOD, CHRISTINE (1994): *Dictionary of British and Irish Botanists and Horticulturalists including Plant Collectors, Flower Painters, and Garden Designers* (London: Taylor & Francis and The Natural History Museum).

DICKENS, CHARLES (1846): *The Adventures of Oliver Twist; or, the Parish Boy's Progress* (London: Bradbury & Evans).

——— (1850*a*): *The Personal History of David Copperfield* (London: Bradbury & Evans).

——— (1850*b*): 'City Graves' in *Household Words. A Weekly Journal*, **ii**/38 (14 December), 277 (London: Household Words).

——— (1855): 'An Enemy's Charge' in *Household Words. A Weekly Journal*, **xii**/291 (20 October) 265-70 (London: Household Words).

——— (1863): 'Kensal Green' in *All the Year Round*, **x**, 93-6.

D. N. B. (1917 – *Dictionary of National Biography*), edited by SIR LESLIE STEPHEN and SIR SIDNEY LEE (London: Geoffrey Cumberlege for Oxford University Press).

DIÉGUEZ PATAO, SOFÍA, and GIMÉNEZ, CARMEN (*Eds.*) (2000): *Funeral Art and Architecture (XIX-XX); Dublin, Genova, Madrid, Torino* (Madrid: Electa and Comunidad Económica Europea).

DOTTRIDGE BROTHERS LTD. (*c.*1908*a*): *Funeral Requisites Catalogue* (London: Dottridge).

——— (*c.*1908*b*): *Wholesale Net Coffin List* (London: Dottridge).

——— (1922): *Catalogue of Funeral Furnishing Supplies* (London: Dottridge Brothers).

——— (1924): *Catalogue of Funeral Furnishing Supplies* (London: Dottridge Brothers).

DOWNING, A.J. (1849-50): 'Public Cemeteries and Public Gardens' in *The Horticulturalist and Journal of Rural Art and Rural Taste*, **iv**, 9-11.

DRABBLE, MARGARET (*Ed.*) (1995): *The Oxford Companion to English Literature* (Oxford: Oxford University Press).

DRUMMOND, JAMES (1881): *Archaeologia Scotica. Sculptured Monuments in Iona and the West Highlands* (Edinburgh: Society of Antiquaries of Scotland).

DRUMMOND, JOHN (1977): *See* BAKEWELL, JOAN.

DUFFY, EAMON (1992): *The Stripping of the Altars. Traditional Religion in England c.1400-c.1580* (New Haven and London: Yale University Press).

DUNK, JULIE, and RUGG, JULIE (1994): *The Management of Old Cemetery Land. Now and the Future. A Report of the University of York Cemetery Research Group* (Crayford: Shaw & Sons Ltd.). *See also* RUGG, JULIE.

DURY, ELIZABETH (*Ed.*) (1982): *See* BRIDGMAN, HARRIET.

DYER, J. (*Ed.*) (1985): *Archaeology and Death* (London: Council for British Archaeology).

DYOS, H. J., and WOLFF, MICHAEL (*Eds.*) (1973): *The Victorian City: Images and Reality* (London: Routledge & Kegan Paul).

EASSIE, WILLIAM (1875): *Cremation of the Dead: its History and Bearings upon Public Health* (London: Smith Elder).

EATON, HUBERT (1954): *The Comemoral. The Cemetery of the Future* (Los Angeles: Interment Association of California).

EBERT, JOHANN ARNOLD (1753): *Dr Eduard Youngs Klagen, oder Nachtgedanken über Leben, Tod, und Unsterblichkeit* (Brunswick and Hildesheim: Ludwig Schröders Erben).

ECCLESIOLOGIST, THE (1841-88): *Especially see* 1845.

EDGINGTON, JOHN (2000): 'Aspleniaceae and Polypodiaceae in London' in *London Naturalist*, **lxxix** (December), 51-4.

EDWARDS, JAMES *ET AL.* (1843): *Health of Towns: An Examination of the Report and Evidence of the Select Committee; of Mr. MacKinnon's Bill* [sic] *and of the Acts for Establishing Cemeteries around the Metropolis* (London: J. Snow).

EISLER, BENITA (1999): *Byron: Child of Passion, Fool of Fame* (London: Hamish Hamilton).
ELIAS, N. (1985): *The Loneliness of the Dying* (Oxford: Blackwell).
ELLIOTT, BRENT (1986): *Victorian Gardens* (London: B. T. Batsford Ltd).
———— (1989): *See* BROOKS, CHRISTOPHER.
ELLIS, L.T. (1995): *See* WILTSHIRE, ELINOR.
ELLWOOD, CHRISTINE (1994): *See* DESMOND, RAY.
EMMETT, A. MAITLAND, and HEATH, JOHN (1989): *The Moths and Butterflies of Great Britain and Ireland*, **vii**, Part 1 (Colchester: Harley Books).
———— (1991): *The Moths and Butterflies of Great Britain and Ireland*, **vii**, Part 2 (Colchester: Harley Books).
ENGLISH HERITAGE (1988): *Visitors Welcome: A Manual on the Presentation and Interpretation of Archaeological Excavations* (London: H.M.S.O.).
ENRIGHT, D. J. (*Ed.*) (1983): *The Oxford Book of Death* (Oxford: Oxford University Press).
ERNST, J. (1991): 'Land for the Living? – The land use and conservation of urban cemeteries and churchyards' in *Local Government Policy Making*, **17**, 14-21.
ESDAILE, KATHARINE A. (1946): *English Church Monuments 1510 to 1840* (London: B. T. Batsford Ltd.).
ETLIN, RICHARD A. (1982): 'The Architecture of Death' in *Progressive Architecture* (May), 134-7. The same issue contains other articles on cemeteries and mausolea.
———— (1984*a*): *The Architecture of Death. The Transformation of the Cemetery in Eighteenth-Century Paris* (Cambridge, Mass.: The M.I.T. Press).
———— (1984*b*): 'Père-Lachaise and the Garden Cemetery' in *Journal of Garden History*, **iv**/3 (July-September), 211-222.
EVANS, STEPHEN (1998, 2000): *See* ALBERY, NICHOLAS.
FAIRLEY, WILLIAM (1875): *Epitaphiana: or, the Curiosities of Churchyard Literature* (London and Aylesbury: Fairley).
FALK, STEVEN J. (1996): *See* STUBBS, ALAN E.
FAULKNER, THOMAS (1820): *History and Antiquities of Kensington, with Biographical Anecdotes of Royal and Distinguished Personages, and a Descriptive Catalogue of the Pictures in the Palace from a Survey taken by the late Benjamin West, P.R.A., by Command of His Majesty* (London: T. Egerton).
FELLEMAN, HAZEL (1936): *Best Loved Poems of the American People* (Garden City, N.Y.: Doubleday & Co. Inc.).
FELSTEAD, ALISON, FRANKLIN, JONATHAN, and PINFIELD, LESLIE (*Compilers*) (1993): *Directory of British Architects 1834-1900* (London: Mansell Publishing Ltd.).
FENNER, BRYAN G. (1985): 'The History of Woking Crematorium' in *Pharos International*, **li**, 85-91.
FIELD, D., HOCKEY, J., and SMALL, N. (*Eds.*) (1996): *Death, Gender, and Ethnicity* (London: Routledge).
FISCHER, CHRISTOPH, and SCHEIN, RENATE (*Eds.*) (1987): *'O Ewich is so Lanck': Die Historischen Friedhöfe in Berlin-Kreuzberg. Ein Werkstattbericht* (Berlin: Nikolaische Verlagsbuchhandlung Beuermann GmbH).
FISK, WILBUR (1838): *Travels in Europe* (New York: Harper & Brothers).
FITZGERALD, EDWARD (1871): *A Hand Book for the Albany Rural Cemetery, with an Appendix on Emblems* (Albany: Van Benthuysen Printing House).
FLAXMAN, JOHN (1865): *Lectures on Sculpture* (London: Bell & Daldy).
FLETCHER, R. (1974): *The Akenham Burial Case* (London: Wildwood).
FLETCHER, R. F. (1975): The History of the Leeds General Cemetery Company 1833-1965. Unpublished MPhil Thesis (University of Leeds).
FOREST LAWN MEMORIAL PARK ASSOCIATION (1956): *Pictorial Forest Lawn* (Glendale, Calif.: Glendale).
FORREST, RICHARD (1848): 'Kensal Green Cemetery' in *Gardeners' Chronicle*, 437.
FORSTER, HAROLD (1986): *Edward Young. The poet of the Night Thoughts 1683-1765* (Alburgh, Harleston: Erskine Press).
FRANKLIN, JONATHAN (*Compiler*) (1993): *See* FELSTEAD, ALISON.
FREED, TIMOTHY H. (1992): The Butterflies of Kensal Green Cemetery (Unpub. M.A. thesis, Royal College of Art).
———— (1997): Butterfly Ecology in an Urban Cemetery; four illustrated projects researched at Kensal Green Cemetery (Unpub. Ph.D. thesis, Royal College of Art). This contained studies of four projects: I – A Pictorial Introduction to the Butterflies and their Habitats; II – the Effects of Strimming on Butterflies and their Host- and Nectar-Plants, with particular emphasis on Small Skipper (*Thymelicus sylvestris*), Essex Skipper (*T. lineola*), and Large Skipper (*Ochlodes venata*); III – The Butterfly Garden; and IV – Ivy Ecology and the Historic Cemetery.
———— (1998): Holland Park Lepidoptera Survey Report 1997-1998 (Royal Borough of Kensington and Chelsea).
———— (2000): Brompton Cemetery Moth Survey Report 1997-1998 (London: Royal Parks Agency).
———— (2001): Habitat Management for Butterflies in Brompton Cemetery (London: Royal Parks Agency).
FREEMAN, ALBERT CHAMBERS (1906): *Crematoria in Great Britain and Abroad* (London: St Bride's Press).
———— (*c.*1909): *Antiquity of Cremation and Curious Funeral Customs* (London: The Undertakers' Journal).
FRENCH, S. (1974): 'The Cemetery as Cultural Institution: The Establishment of Mount Auburn and the "Rural" Cemetery Movement' in *American Quarterly*, **xxvi**, 37-59.
FRITH, MATTHEW (1991): *See* GAME, MEG.
FRY, REG, and LONSDALE, DAVID (1991): *Habitat Conservation for Insects – a neglected Green Issue* (Colchester: Amateur Entomological Society).
FUENTE, BEATRIZ DE LA, and NOELLE, LOUISE (*Eds.*) (1987): *Arte Funerario. Coloquio Internacional de Historia del Arte* (Mexico City: Universidad Nacional Autonoma de Mexico).

FULLER, J.G.C.M. (1994): *See* CAWTHORNE, W.A.

GAME, MEG, ARCHER, JOHN, and FRITH, MATHEW (1991): *Nature Conservation in Ealing. Ecology Handbook 16* (London: London Ecology Unit).

GAME, MEG (1993): *See* WAITE, MICHAEL.

GANDY, JOHN P. (1852): *See* GELL, SIR WILLIAM.

GARDEN HISTORY, JOURNAL OF (from 1981): *See* HUNT, JOHN DIXON, AND SCHUYLER, DAVID (*Eds.*).

GARDENERS' CHRONICLE (1848): Untitled editorial on Kensal Green cemetery in *Gardeners' Chronicle*, 419-20.

———— (1897): 'Flowers at Kensal Green Cemetery' in *Gardeners' Chronicle*, **xxi**, 140-1.

GAY, J. (1984): *See* BARKER, FELIX.

GCCA (*c.*1831): *See* GENERAL CEMETERY COMPANY.

GEARY, STEPHEN (1840): *Cemetery Designs for Tombs and Cenotaphs* (London: Tilt & Bogue).

GÉBELIN: *See* COURT DE GÉBELIN.

GELL, SIR WILLIAM, and GANDY, JOHN P. (1852): *Pompeiana: The Topography, Edifices, and Ornaments of Pompeii* (London: Henry G. Bohn).

GENERAL BURIAL-GROUNDS ASSOCIATION (1825): *Prospectus* (London: The Association).

GENERAL CEMETERY COMPANY (GCCA= General Cemetery Company Archive) (1830): *Prospectus* (London: The Company).

———— (from the 1830s): Minutes of the Provisional Committee (1830-2) and Minutes of the Proceedings of the Directors of the Company, from 1833, still held in the Company's offices on the Harrow Road, London. During the 19th century the Company had offices at 95 Great Russell Street, Bloomsbury, London. *See also* Minutes of General Meetings, Memorabilia, and other items held in the archives.

———— (*c.*1831): Plan of the 'Ground of the General Cemetery Company'.

———— (1832): Catalogue of Designs for a Chapel &c.

———— (1833): *The General Cemetery Company Incorporated by an Act of Parliament 2 & 3 William IV. c. 110, 1832. The Act of Incorporation. The Bye-Laws Passed at the Annual General Meeting held on the 13th June, 1833. Lists of the Directors and Officers. With an Index* (London: Printed for the Company by Charles Frederick Cock).

———— (1833 onwards): Proceedings and Minutes of the Directors.

THE GENTLEMAN'S MAGAZINE (1830): **c/1**.

———— (1832): **cii/2** (September).

GESSNER, SALOMON (1756): *Idyllen von dem Verfasser des Daphnis* (Zurich: S. Gessner).

———— (1762): *Idylles et Poëmes champêtres de M. Gessner* (Lyons: J. M. Bruyset).

GIDDENS, GRAHAM (1996): Borough Bird Survey 1995-1996 (Royal Borough of Kensington & Chelsea).

———— (1997): Borough Breeding Bird Survey 1997 (Royal Borough of Kensington & Chelsea).

———— (1998): Borough Breeding Bird Survey 1998 (Royal Borough of Kensington & Chelsea).

———— (1999): Borough Breeding Bird Survey 1999 (Royal Borough of Kensington & Chelsea).

———— (2000): Borough Breeding Bird Survey 2000 (Royal Borough of Kensington & Chelsea).

GIFFORD, JOHN (1996): *Dumfries and Galloway*, in *The Buildings of Scotland* Series (London: Penguin Books Ltd.).

GIFFORD, JOHN, MCWILLIAM, COLIN, AND WALKER, DAVID (1984): *Edinburgh* in *The Buildings of Scotland* Series (Harmondsworth: Penguin Books Ltd.).

GILBERT, OLIVER L. (1989): *The Ecology of Urban Habitats* (London: Chapman & Hall).

———— (1991): *The Ecology of Urban Habitats* (London: Chapman & Hall).

GILLON, EDMUND V., JR. (1972): *Victorian Cemetery Art* (New York: Dover Publications).

GIMÉNEZ, CARMEN (*Ed.*) (2000): *See* DIÉGUEZ PATAO, SOFÍA.

GIRARDIN, RENÉ-LOUIS, MARQUIS DE (1777): *De La Composition des Paysages, ou Des Moyens d'embellir la Nature autour des Habitations* (Geneva and Paris: P. M. Delaguette).

GIRARDIN, STANISLAS-CÉCILE-XAVIER-LOUIS, COMTE DE (also VICOMTE D'ERMENONVILLE) (1788): *Promenade ou Itinéraire des Jardins d'Ermenonville*, illustrated by Mérigot Fils (Paris and Ermenonville: Mérigot, Gattey, Guyot, and Murray).

GIROUARD, MARK (1971): 'Restoring Highgate Cemetery' in *Country Life* (5 August), with illustrations by JAMES STEVENS CURL, 334-6.

GITTINGS, CLARE (1984): *Death, Burial, and the Individual in Early Modern England* (Beckenham: Croom Helm).

———— (*Ed.*) (1999): *See* JUPP, PETER C.

GLADSTONE, FLORENCE M. (1924): *Notting Hill in Bygone Days* (Re-edited by ASHLEY BARKER and republished by A. Bingley in 1969) (London: Anne Bingley).

GLASER, S., and STRAUSS, A. (1965): *Awareness of Dying* (Chicago, Ill.: Aldine).

———— (1968): *Time for Dying* (Chicago, Ill.: Aldine).

GLOAG, JOHN EDWARDS (1970): *Mr Loudon's England. The Life and Works of John Claudius Loudon, and his influence on architecture and furniture design* (Newcastle upon Tyne: Oriel Press Ltd.).

GODFREY, ALAN (1984*a*): *Willesden Junction 1894, Old Ordnance Survey Maps, London Sheet 46* (Gateshead: Alan Godfrey).

———— (1984*b*): *Kensal Green & Queen's Park 1894, Old Ordnance Survey Maps, London Sheet 47* (Gateshead: Alan Godfrey).

GODWIN, WILLIAM (1809): *Essay on Sepulchres: or, a Proposal for erecting Some Memorial of the Illustrious Dead in all Ages on the Spot where their Remains have been interred* (London: Godwin).

GOETHE, JOHANN WOLFGANG VON (1774): *Die Leiden des jungen Werthers* (Leipzig: Weygand). See also the translation (1989) as *The Sorrows of Young Werther* by MICHAEL HULSE (London: Penguin Group).

———— (1809): *Die Wahlverwandschaften* (Tübingen: Cotta). See also the translation (1971) as *Elective Affinities* by R. J. HOLLINGDALE (Harmondsworth: Penguin Books Ltd.).

GOMERSHALL, Rev. W. J. (*c.*1916): *A Short History of Old Kensal Green and its Parish Church*. Being a reprint from the *Willesden Chronicle* (London: North-Western Printing and Publishing Association, Ltd.).
GOODE, DAVID (1986): *Wild in London* (London: Michael Joseph).
GOODFELLOW, PETER (1994): *Birds in Churchyards* (Stoneleigh: Church and Conservation Project).
GOODWIN, SARAH WEBSTER, and BRONFEN, ELISABETH (*Eds.*) (1993): *Death and Representation* (Baltimore, Md.: The Johns Hopkins University Press).
GORDON, ANNE (1984): *Death is for the Living* (Edinburgh: Paul Harris).
GOUGH, RICHARD (1786): *Sepulchral Monuments of Great Britain applied to illustrate the History of Families, Manners, Habits, and Arts, at the Different Periods from the Norman Conquest to the Seventeenth Century* (London: J. Nichols for the Author).
GOULD, JOHN (1866): *Birds of Great Britain*, ii/10, **48** (published in 5 vols., 1862-1873) (London: John Gould).
GRANT, MAURICE HAROLD (1953): *A Dictionary of British Sculptors* (London: Rockcliff).
GRAVES, ALGERNON (1905): *The Royal Academy of Arts: A Complete Dictionary of Contributors and their work from its foundation in 1769 to 1904* (London: Henry Graves & Co. Ltd., and George Bell & Sons).
GREENOAK, FRANCESCA (1985): *God's Acre* (London: Orbis/W.I. Books).
GREEN-WOOD CEMETERY (1891*a*): *Green-Wood Illustrated* (New York: Photo-Engraving Co.).
——— (1891*b*): *Exposition of the Plan and Objects of Green-Wood Cemetery, an Incorporated Trust Chartered by the legislature of the State of New York* (New York: Green-Wood Cemetery Trust).
GREENWOOD, DOUGLAS (1982): *Who's Buried Where in England* (London: Constable & Co. Ltd.).
GREIFF, CONSTANCE, M. (1979): *John Notman, Architect, 1810-65* (Philadelphia: The Athenaeum of Philadelphia).
GREVILLE, CHARLES C. F. (1875): *The Greville Memoirs: A Journal of the Reign of King George IV and King William IV*, edited by HENRY REEVE (*London: Longman, Green, & Co.*).
GRINDON, L.H: *See* TRUTH-SEEKER.
GRISCOM, JOHN (1823): *A Year in Europe Comprising a Journal of Observations in England, Scotland, Ireland, France, ...etc. ... in 1818 and 1819* (New York: Collins & Co.).
GRONOW, REES HOWELL (1862): *Recollections and Anecdotes of the Camp, the Court and the Clubs, at the Close of the Last War with France* (London: Smith Elder & Co.).
GULLIVER, R. (1980): 'Green Oases in Concrete Jungles' in *Country Life* (3 April), 1044-7.
GUNNIS, RUPERT (1968): *Dictionary of British Sculptors 1660-1851* (London: Abbey Library).
HADDON, ARCHIBALD (1935): *The Story of the Music Hall, from Cave of Harmony to Cabaret* (London: Fleetway Press).
HAESTIER, RICHARD EMILE (1934): *Dead Men Tell Tales. A Survey of Exhumations from Earliest Antiquity to the Present Day* (London: John Long).
HAINES, HERBERT (1970): *A Manual of Monumental Brasses*, originally published 1861 (Bath: Adams & Dart).
HAKEWILL, ARTHUR WILLIAM (1851): *Modern Tombs, Gleaned from the Public Cemeteries, of London. Measured drawn and etched by Arthur William Hakewill, Archt.* (London: Longman, Brown, Green, and Longman).
HALE, C. H. (1858): *The Graves of our Fathers* (London: Hamilton, Adams, & Co.).
HALLAM, ARTHUR (*Ed.*) (1905-8): *The Burial Reformer, a quarterly journal devoted to the scientific investigation of trance and the various forms of suspended animation.* Continued as (1909-14) *Perils of Premature Burial* (London: Hallam).
HAMMERSMITH & FULHAM ARCHIVES & LOCAL HISTORY CENTRE (HFALHC) (1778): Red House Farm: Details of Counterpart Lease. 8 September 1778 (DD/21/10).
——— (1800): Licensed Victuallers 1800: George Fillingham – Mitre (ND/3/7).
——— (1829): Red House, stable and garden, Wormholt, Thomas Harrison 1829 (PAH/1/158/1).
——— (*c.*1835): Plan printed; endorsed, MS, 'Red House Farm'. Showing plots numbered 4-27 with schedule of acreages. No date given, *c.*1835-8 (DD/21/11).
——— (1836): Records of the homage jury of the manor of Fulham, 1810-1929: Encroachment of Mr Fillingham on Wormholt Scrubbs. 20 November 1836 (DD/14/108).
——— (1837*a*): Records of the homage jury of the manor of Fulham, 1810-1929: Call for settlement over land claimed on Wormholt Scrubbs by representatives of the late Mr Geo Fillingham (DD/14/1972).
——— (1837*b*): Minute book of courts leet and baron; indexed. April 1831-December 1850. Relate to Plans and transactions of land by Railway Companies *c.*1836-38, p.61 (DD/15/2).
——— (1839): Hammersmith: House Meadow, Upper Mitre Meadow. Counterpart lease for 7 years with plan of fields. 25 May 1839 (DD/21/12/1).
HAMON, FRANÇOISE, and MACCALLUM, CHARLES (*Eds.*) (1991): *Louis Visconti 1791-1853* (Paris: Délégation à l'Action Artistique de la Ville de Paris). *See* 'L'Architecture Funéraire' (162-7).
HAND, KEVIN, and MORFITT, DAVID (1994): *Trees and Hedges in Churchyards* (Stoneleigh: Living Churchyards Project).
HANNON, NATALIE (*Ed.*) (1982): *See* BACKER, BARBARA.
HARE, AUGUSTUS JOHN CUTHBERT (1856): *Epitaphs for Country Churchyards* (Oxford: J. H. & J. Parker).
——— (1896): *The Story of my Life*, **i** (London: George Allen).
HARE, TONY (1988): *London's Meadows and Pastures. London Ecology Unit Handbook 8* (London: London Ecology Unit).
HARFIELD, ALAN (various dates): *Records of various cemeteries of the former British Empire* (London: B.A.C.S.A.).
HARRISON, C., LIMB, M., and BURGESS, J. (1987): 'Nature in the city – popular values for a living world' in *Journal of Environmental Management*, **25**, 347-62.
HARRISON, J. (1984): 'Grave Problems' in *Journal of Planning and Environmental Law* (February), 77-80.
HART, HENRY (1892): *Burning or Burial* (London: The Author).
HARTLAND, FREDERICK D. (1856): *Tapographia, or A Collection of Tombs of Royal and Distinguished Families. Collected during a tour of Europe in the Years 1854 and 1855* (Privately printed for the Author).

HAVERGAL, FRANCIS TEBBS (1881): *Monumental Inscriptions in the Cathedral Church of Hereford* (London: Simpkin Marshall & Co.).
HAWEIS, HUGH REGINALD (1875): *Ashes to Ashes – A Cremation Prelude* (London: Daldy Isbister & Co.).
HAYWOOD, WILLIAM (1855): *Plans of the City of London Cemetery at Little Ilford in the County of Essex* (London: Day & Son).
——— (1856): *Plans and Views of the City of London Cemetery at Little Ilford in the County of Essex formed under the direction of the Commissioners of Sewers of the City of London and under the Superintendence of William Haywood, Architect* (London: Day & Son).
HEATH, CHARLES (1829-31): *See* PUGIN, AUGUSTUS CHARLES.
HEATH, JOHN (1989): *See* EMMETT, A. MAITLAND.
HEATHCOTE, EDWIN (1999): *Monument Builders: Modern Architecture and Death* (Chichester: Academy Editions).
HER MAJESTY'S STATIONERY OFFICE (1999): *See* H.M.S.O.
HERBERT, CLIVE (1997): *See* AYBES, CHARLOTTE.
HÉRICART-FERRAND: *See* THURY.
HEWITT, JOHN (1876): *See* STOTHARD, C. A.
HFALHC (1778, 1800, 1829, *c.*1835, 1836, 1837*a*, 1837*b*, 1839): *See*: HAMMERSMITH & FULHAM ARCHIVES & LOCAL HISTORY CENTRE.
HIBBERD, SHIRLEY (1872): *The Ivy* (London: Groombridge).
HIBBERT, CHRISTOPHER (*Ed.*) (1984): *Queen Victoria in her Letters & Journals* (London: John Murray).
HIBBERT, H. G. (1916): *Fifty Years of a Londoner's Life* (London: Grant Richards Ltd.).
HICK, J. (1976): *Death and Eternal Life* (Glasgow: Collins).
HIGGS, MALCOLM (1990): *See* WILLIAMSON, ELIZABETH.
HILLAIRET, JACQUES (pseudonym of COUSSILLAN, AUGUSTE ANDRÉ) (1958): *Les 200 Cimetières du vieux Paris* (Paris: n. s.).
HILLMAN, ELLIS (1993): *See* TRENCH, RICHARD.
HIRSCHFELD, CHRISTIAN CAJUS LORENZ (1779-85): *Theorie de Gartenkunst*, also published at the same time as *Théorie de l'art des Jardins* (Leipzig: M. G. Weidmanns Erben und Reich).
H.M.S.O. (1999): *Chronological Table of the Statutes 1235-1996* (London: H.M.S.O.).
HOBHOUSE, HERMIONE (1983): *Prince Albert: His Life and Work* (London: Hamish Hamilton Ltd.).
HOCKEY, J. (1990): *Experiences of Death* (Edinburgh: Edinburgh University Press).
——— (*Ed.*) (1996): *See* FIELD, D.
HOLLIS, T. and G. (1840-2): *The Monumental Effigies of Great Britain* (London: Hollis).
HOLLOWAY, HAROLD (1986, 1992): *The South Park Street Cemetery, Calcutta* (Calcutta Association for the Preservation of Historical Cemeteries in India).
HOLLOWAY, LESTER (1986): *See* CROSS, COLIN.
HOLMES, MRS. BASIL ISABELLA (1896): *The London Burial Grounds. Notes on their History from the Earliest Times to the Present Day* (London: T. Fisher Unwin).
HOOD, THOMAS (1869-73): *The Works*, 10 vols. (London: E. Moxon, Son, & Co.).
HOPKINS, JOHN J. (1990): 'British Meadows and Pastures' in *British Wildlife*, i/4 (April), 202-13.
HOUGHTON, WALTER E. (1957): *The Victorian Frame of Mind 1830-1870* (New Haven and London: Yale University Press).
HOULBROOKE, RALPH (*Ed.*) (1989): *Death, Ritual, and Bereavement* (London: Routledge & Kegan Paul).
——— (1998): *Death, Religion, and the Family in England, 1480-1750* (Oxford: Clarendon Press).
HOUSE OF COMMONS ENVIRONMENT, TRANSPORT, AND REGIONAL AFFAIRS COMMITTEE. SESSION 2000-2001 (2001): *Cemeteries. Report and Proceedings of the Committee, together with the Minutes of Evidence taken before the Environment sub-committee. Ordered by The House of Commons to be printed 21 March 2001* (London: Published by Authority of The House of Commons by The Stationery Office Ltd.).
HOWARTH, GLENNYS, and JUPP, PETER C. (*Eds.*) (from 1996*a*): *Mortality* (Abingdon: Carfax Publishing Co.).
——— (1996*b*): *Contemporary Issues in the Sociology of Death, Dying, and Disposal* (Basingstoke: Macmillan Press Ltd.).
——— (*Ed.*) (1997): *See* JUPP, PETER C.
HOWES, FRANK NORMAN (1979): *Plants and Beekeeping* (London: Faber & Faber).
HUMAN, B. (1982): 'St Giles's Cemetery' in *Cambridgeshire, Huntingdon, and Peterborough Life* (July), 36-7.
HUMBERT, JEAN-MARCEL (*Ed.*) (1996): *L'Égyptomanie à l'épreuve de l'archéologie* (Brussels: Éditions du Gram, and Paris: Musée du Louvre).
HUMPHREYS, HENRY N., and WESTWOOD, J. O. (1841): *British Butterflies and their Transformations* (London: Smith).
HUMPHREYS, HENRY N. (1858): *The Butterfly Vivarium or, Insect Home* (London: Lay).
——— (1859): *The Genera and Species of British Butterflies* (London: Paul Jerrard & Son).
HUMPHREYS, SALDY C., and KING, HELEN (*Eds.*) (1981): *Mortality and Immortality: The Anthropology and Archaeology of Death* (London: Academic Press).
HUNT, JOHN DIXON, and SCHUYLER, DAVID (*Eds.*) (1984): *Journal of Garden History*, **iv**/3 (July-September 1984). Special issue on cemeteries.
HUNT, LEIGH (1844): *Rimini and Other Poems* (Boston: William D. Ticknor).
HUNTINGTON, R., and METCALF, P. (1987): *Celebrations of Death: The Anthropology of Mortuary Ritual* (Cambridge: Cambridge University Press).
HUTTON, JAMES (1795): *Theory of the Earth* (Edinburgh: Printed for William Creech; and London: printed for Messrs. Cadell Jr. & Davies).
ILLUSTRATED HISTORIC TIMES (1849): 'Extra-Mural Interments, All Souls' Cemetery, Kensal-Green', 148-9.
ILLUSTRATED LONDON NEWS (various years).
INGALL, PARSON, CLIVE, & CO. LTD. (1924): *Everything for the Undertaker* (Birmingham: Ingall, Parsons, Clive, & Co. Ltd.).

JALLAND, PAT (1996): *Death in the Victorian Family* (Oxford: Oxford University Press).

JAMES, DAVID, and BEESLEY, IAN (1991): *Undercliffe: Bradford's Historic Victorian Cemetery* (Halifax: Ryburn Publishing Ltd.).

JAMIESON, JOHN (1818): 'On the Origin of Cremation, or the Burning of the Dead' in *Transactions of the Royal Society of Edinburgh*, **viii**, 83-127.

JANEWAY, THE REV. J. (1844): *A Token for Children: being an account of the Conversion, Holy and Exemplary Lives and Joyful Deaths of Several Young Children* (London: S. Allman).

JENKINS, HERBERT (1923): *See* ANONYMOUS (1923).

JERVIS, SIMON (1983): *High Victorian Design* (Woodbridge: The Boydell Press).

JOHNSTON, IAN (1998): 'Ploughing Through Archival Paradise' in *Out of the Archives*, **xiv**, 6-7 (Summer 1998) (London: Brent Archive).

JOINT CONFERENCE OF BURIAL AND CREMATION AUTHORITIES (Various Years): *Conference Reports*.

JOLIMONT, FRANÇOIS-GABRIEL-THÉODORE BASSET DE (1821): *Les Mausolées Français. Recueil des tombeaux les plus remarquables par leur structure, leurs epitaphs, ... dessinés d'après nature* (Paris: Firmin Didot).

JONES, BARBARA (1967): *Design for Death* (London: Andre Deutsch).

JONES, OWEN (1856): *The Grammar of Ornament. Illustrated by Examples from Various Styles of Ornament* (London: Day & Son).

JONES, P. HERBERT, and NOBLE, GEORGE A. (*Eds.*) (1931): *Cremation in Great Britain* (London: Cremation Society of Great Britain).

JONES, RICHARD A. (1997): *The Butterflies of Nunhead Cemetery: a visitor's guide to the many species likely to be seen in this beautiful Victorian Cemetery* (London: Friends of Nunhead Cemetery).

JOWETT, JANE (n.d.): *On Burial, Death, and Resurrection* (Sold in Leeds: Jane Jowett; and London: W. & F. G. Cash).

JOYCE, PAUL (1984): *A Guide to Abney Park Cemetery* (London: Save Abney Park Cemetery in association with the London Borough of Hackney).

JUPP, PETER C. (1993): The Development of Cremation in England, 1820-1990: a sociological account (University of London: unpublished PhD thesis).

————, and HOWARTH, GLENNYS (*Eds.*) (1997): *The Changing Face of Death. Historical Accounts of Death and Disposal* (Basingstoke: Macmillan Press Ltd.).

————, and GITTINGS, CLARE (1999): *Death in England: an Illustrated History* (Manchester: Manchester University Press).

———— (*Ed.*) (1996*a* and *b*): *See* HOWARTH, GLENNYS.

JUSTYNE, WILLIAM (*c.*1858): *Illustrated Guide to Kensal Green Cemetery* (London: The Author).

———— (*c.*1864): *Guide to Highgate Cemetery* (London: Printed for the Author by J. Moore).

KCLSL (*c.*1745 and 1844): *See* KENSINGTON & CHELSEA LOCAL STUDIES LIBRARY.

KEARY, CHARLES FRANCIS (1898): *The Journalist* (London: Methuen & Co.).

———— (1923): *The Posthumous Poems of C. F. Keary* (Oxford: Basil Blackwell).

KEECH, DANIEL (1993): *See* ARCHER, JOHN, and WAITE, MICHAEL.

KEELING, DENIS F. (1969/70): 'The City of London and Tower Hamlets Cemetery' in *East London Papers*, **xii**, 118-28.

KELKE, W. HASTINGS (1851): *The Churchyard Manual: intended chiefly for Rural Districts* (London: Cox).

KELLER, FAMILY (1876): *Atti della Cremazione di Alberto Keller* (Milan: C. Civelli).

KEMP, BRIAN (1980): *English Church Monuments* (London: B. T. Batsford Ltd.).

KEMPE, ALFRED JOHN (1876): *See* STOTHARD, C. A.

KEMPNER, FRIEDERIKE (1856): *Denkschrift über die Nothwendigkeit einer Gesetzlichen Einführung von Leichenhäusern* (Breslau: Korn). Another edition was published in 1867.

KENDALL, HENRY EDWARD, and ALLOM, THOMAS (1832): *Sketches of the Approved Designs of a Chapel and Gateway Entrances intended to be erected at Kensal Green for the General Cemetery Company* (London: J. Williams).

KENSINGTON & CHELSEA LOCAL STUDIES LIBRARY (KCLSL) (*c.*1745): *A New and Accurate Survey of the Cities of London and Westminster, The Borough of Southwark, with the country about ...* Atlas of 16 sheets drawn by John Rocque 1741-5 (London: John Rocque) (copied from negative no: C/6102).

———— (1844): Tithe commissioners for England and Wales *Map of the titheable lands in the parish of Kensington ... Middlesex*. Photocopy of original map in the GLC Record Office (912 [1844]).

KENSINGTON AND CHELSEA ROYAL BOROUGH OF (1999): *See* MCCOY ASSOCIATES.

KERNEY, M. (1987-8): 'Polished Granite in Victorian Architecture' in *Victorian Society Annual*, 20-22.

KEY, PETER (2000): *Samuel Ryder: the Man behind the Ryder Cup* (Weymouth: Wright Press).

KIND, JOHN LOUIS (1906): *Young in Germany* (New York: Macmillan).

KING, HELEN (*Ed.*) (1981): *See* HUMPHREYS, SALDY C.

KINGSLEY, CHARLES (1889): 'The Three Fishers' in *Poems* (London: Macmillan & Co.).

KIRBY, P. (1992): *Habitat management for invertebrates: a practical handbook* (Sandy: Royal Society for the Protection of Birds).

KNIGHT, CHARLES (*Ed.*) (*c.*1870): *London*. Revised and Corrected by EDWARD WALFORD (London: Virtue & Co. Ltd.).

KNIGHT, DAVID B. (1973): *Cemeteries as Living Landscapes* (Ottawa: Ottawa Genealogical Society, Ottawa Branch).

KNIPSEL, FRANZ (1982): *Zur Geschichte des Bestattungswesen in Wien* (Vienna: Wiener Stadtwerke Städtische Bestattung).

KOK, H. L. (2000): *Funerair Lexicon* (Maastricht: Stichting Crematorium Limburg).

KOONTZ, DEAN (1996): *See* ROBINSON, DAVID.

KRYGER, KARIN (1985): *Allegori og Borgerdyd. Studier i det nyklassicistiske gravmæle i Danmark 1760-1820* (Copenhagen: Christian Ejlers' Forlag).

——— (1999): 'Kirkegårde og gravminder i Tranquebar-realiseringen af et projekt' in *Kirkegårdskultur 1999*, edited by Anne-Louise Sommer, Gunver Vestergaard, and Leif Arffmann (Copenhagen: Foreningen for Kirkegårdskultur).

KSELMAN, THOMAS A. (1993): *Death and the Afterlife in Modern France* (Princeton, N.J.: Princeton University Press).

LABORDE, ALEXANDRE-LOUIS-JOSEPH, COMTE DE (1808-15): *Descriptions des Nouveaux Jardins de la France et de ses Anciens Châteaux, mêlée d'observations sur la vie de la campagne et la composition des Jardins* (Paris: Delance).

LABOUCHARDIERE, BASIL (1983): *The French Cemetery, Calcutta* (London: B.A.C.S.A.).

LADY'S NEWSPAPER, THE (1849): Article and illustration of 'Intramural Burials' (16 September 1849), 145.

LAMB, CHARLES (1852): *The Works of Charles Lamb, his Letters, and a Sketch of his Life by THOMAS NOON TALFOURD* (New York: Harper & Brothers).

LANE, CHARLTON (1854): *To the Parishioners of Kennington, Stockwell, and South Lambeth: How to Meet the Cholera* (London: Lane).

LANGLEY, BATTY (1747): *Gothic Architecture improved by Rules and Proportions in many Grand Designs of Columns, Doors, Windows, Chimney-Pieces, Arcades, Colonnades, Porticos, Umbrellos, Temples and Pavilions, &c.* (London: Millan).

LANGTON, TOM (1991): 'Distribution and Status of Reptiles and Amphibians in the London Area' in *London Naturalist*, **lxx** (November), 97-123.

LARG (1996): *See* LONDON AMPHIBIAN and REPTILE GROUP.

LASSALLE (n.d.): *See* MARTY.

LATHAM, JOHN B. (1984): 'A Survey of the Flora of Kensal Green and St Mary's Cemeteries, 1981-1983' in *London Naturalist*, **lxiii** (November), 53-67.

——— (1989): 'Further Studies of Plant Groups in Kensal Green and St Mary's Cemeteries, 1983-1989' in *London Naturalist*, **lxviii** (November), 15-24.

LAUGHLIN, C. J. (1948): 'Cemeteries of New Orleans' in *The Architectural Review*, **ciii**/614 (February), 47-52.

LAUNDON, JACK R. (1986): *Lichens* (Aylesbury: Shire Publications Ltd.).

——— (1994): *See* BRIGHTMAN, F.H.

LBTH (*c*.1988): *See* LONDON BOROUGH OF TOWER HAMLETS.

LEATHLEAN, HOWARD (1997): 'Loudon's *Gardener's Magazine* and the Morality of Landscape' in *Ecumene*, **iv** (1), 86-107.

LEEDS CIVIC TRUST (1984): *The Beckett Street Cemetery: A Report* (Leeds: Leeds Civic Trust).

LEIGH, I. W. (1985): 'Milner White and Partners' in *Landscape Design*, **clvi**, 9-13.

LEPAGELET and DE LUSSI (LUSSY) (1790): *Tableau Pittoresque de la Vallée de Montmorency, un des séjours le plus agréable des Environs de Paris* (Paris: Lepagelet & Lussi).

LERICI, CARLO MAURILIO (*Ed.*) (1962): *Italia Sepolta* (Milan: Lerici Editore).

LEVY, HERMANN (1938): *See* WILSON, SIR ANDREW.

LEWIS, C. (1995): *See* COHN-SHERBOK, D.

LEWIS, R. A. (1952): *Edwin Chadwick and the Public Health Movement* (London: Longmans).

LEWIS, THOMAS (1721): *Seasonable Considerations on the Indecent and Dangerous Custom of Burying in Churches and Churchyards, with Remarkable Observations historical and philosophical. Proving that the Custom is not only contrary to the Practice of the Antients, but fatal, in case of Infection* (London: A. Bettesworth).

LIGHT, ALFRED W. (1913): *Bunhill Fields* (London: C. J. Farncombe & Sons Ltd.).

LIMB, M. (1987): *See* HARRISON, C.

LINDEN-WARD, BLANCHE (1989): *Silent City on a Hill: Landscapes of Memory and Boston's Mount Auburn Cemetery* (Columbus: Ohio State University Press).

LINDLEY, KENNETH ARTHUR (1972): *Graves and Graveyards* (London: Routledge & Kegan Paul).

LINSTRUM, DEREK (1999): *Towers and Colonnades: The Architecture of Cuthbert Brodrick* (Leeds: The Leeds Philosophical and Literary Society Ltd.).

LISCOMBE, RHODRI WINDSOR (1980): *William Wilkins, 1778-1839* (Cambridge: Cambridge University Press).

LITTEN, JULIAN W. S. (1989): *See* BROOKS, CHRISTOPHER.

——— (1991): *The English Way of Death: The Common Funeral Since 1450* (London: Robert Hale).

LLEWELLYN, NIGEL (1991): *The Art of Death. Visual Culture in the English Death Ritual c.1500-c.1800* (London: Reaktion Books in Association with the Victoria and Albert Museum).

LLOYD, JOHN HARRY (1888): *The History, Topography, and Antiquities of Highgate, in the County of Middlesex* (Highgate: The Author).

LMA (1832): *See* LONDON METROPOLITAN ARCHIVE.

LONDON AMPHIBIAN and REPTILE GROUP (LARG) (1996): Amphibian and Reptile Borough Survey 1995 (A report prepared for the Royal Borough of Kensington & Chelsea).

LONDON BOROUGH OF TOWER HAMLETS (LBTH) (*c*.1988): *Tower Hamlets Cemetery Park*. Poplar Neighbourhood Information Service, leaflet 6 (London: Poplar Press Office).

LONDON CEMETERY COMPANY (from *c*.1860): Minutes of the Company. Apparently only parts survive, and are held by the London Borough of Southwark.

LONDON, CORPORATION OF: *See* REED, CHARLES, *ET AL*.

LONDON METROPOLITAN ARCHIVE (LMA) (1832): Middlesex Land Register (1832/3.169; 170; 171).

LONDON PLANNING ADVISORY COMMITTEE (LPAC) (1997): *Planning for Burial Space in London* Ref.: CON69 (London: LPAC).

LONDON WILDLIFE TRUST, HAMMERSMITH & FULHAM GROUP (LWTHFG) (1984): 'The Wildlife of Scrubs Wood' (London Wildlife Trust: London).

LONSDALE, DAVID (1991): *See* FRY, REG.

LOUDON, JOHN CLAUDIUS (*Ed.*) (from 1826): *The Gardener's Magazine and Register of Rural and Domestic Improvements*. The 1843 volume contains *On the Laying Out, Planting, and Managing of Cemeteries and on the Improvement of Churchyards* in serial form as part of *The Gardener's Magazine* (New Series) of 1835-43.

——— (1829): 'The Brentford Nursery' in *Gardener's Magazine*, **v**, 736-7.

——— (1834): *An Encyclopaedia of Cottage, Farm, and Villa Architecture and Furniture* (London: Longman Rees Orme Brown Green & Longman).

——— (1836): 'A Summary view of the progress of gardening ... during the year 1836' in *Gardener's Magazine*, **xii**, 613-38.

——— (1842): *An Encylopaedia of Trees and Shrubs, being the Arboretum et Fruticetum Britannicum abridged, containing the hardy trees and shrubs of Britain, native and foreign, scientifically and popularly described, with their propagation, culture, and uses in the arts, and with engravings of nearly all the species* (London: Longman, Brown, Green, & Longman).

——— (1981): *On the Laying Out, Planting, and Managing of Cemeteries and on the Improvement of Churchyards* with an *Introduction* by JAMES STEVENS CURL (Redhill: Ivelet Books Ltd. A facsimile of the edition of 1843).

LPAC (1997): *See* LONDON PLANNING ADVISORY COMMITTEE.

LUCAS, CATHERINE (1972): *See* CUNNINGTON, PHYLLIS.

LUCAS, EDWARD VERRALL (1905): *The Life of Charles Lamb* (London: Methuen & Co.).

LUSSI, DE (1784): *Vues des Monumens construits dans les jardins de Franconville-la-Garenne, appartenans à Madame la Comtesse d'Albon gravés d'après ses dessins et ceux de M. de Lussi* (Paris: de Lussi).

LWTHFG (1984): *See* LONDON WILDLIFE TRUST, HAMMERSMITH & FULHAM GROUP.

LYSONS, DANIEL (1811): *Kensington* in *The Environs of London*, **ii**, *County of Middlesex* (2nd edition) (London: T. Cadell).

MACCALLUM, CHARLES (*Ed.*) (1991): *See* HAMON, FRANÇOISE.

MCCOY ASSOCIATES (1999): *Brompton Cemetery: Conservation Area Proposals Statement* (London: Royal Borough of Kensington & Chelsea).

MACREADY, WILLIAM CHARLES (1875): *Macready's Reminiscences and Selections from his Diaries and Letters*, edited by SIR FREDERICK POLLOCK, Bart. (London: Macmillan & Co.).

MCDOWELL & PARTNERS (1976): *Victorian Catacombs, Nunhead Cemetery, Southwark. Building Surveys and Structural Report* (Claygate, Esher: McDowell & Partners).

MACKECHNIE, A. (1988): 'Walter Newall, Architect in Dumfries' in *Transactions of the Dumfriesshire & Galloway Nat. Hist. & Antiq. Soc.*, 3rd Series, **lxiii.**

MCKENDRY, JENNIFER (1995): *Weep Not For Me. A Photographic Essay and History of Cataraqui Cemetery* (Kingston, Ontario: The Author).

MACKENZIE, PETER (1852): 'Loudon's Tomb' in *Gardeners' Chronicle*, 198.

MCMANNERS, J. (1981): *Death and the Enlightenment: Changing Attitudes to Death among Christians and Unbelievers in Eighteenth-Century France* (Oxford: The Clarendon Press).

MCWHIRTER, NORRIS, and MCWHIRTER, ROSS (*Eds.*) (1972): *The Guinness Book of Records* (19th Edition) (Enfield, Middlesex: Guinness Superlatives Ltd.).

MCWHIRTER, ROSS (1972): *See* MCWHIRTER, NORRIS.

MCWILLIAM, COLIN (1984): *See* GIFFORD, JOHN.

MACKLIN, THE REV. HERBERT W. (1905): *Monumental Brasses* (London and New York: Swan Sonnenschein).

MAETERLINCK, MAURICE POLYDORE MARIE BERNARD (1911): *Death* (London: Methuen & Co.).

MAGNUSSON, MAGNUS (*Ed.*) (1994): *Chambers Biographical Dictionary* (Edinburgh: Larousse).

MALCHOW, H. L. (1985): 'Public gardens and social action in late-Victorian London' in *Victorian Studies*, **xxix**, 97-124.

MANNING, E. (1905): *Guide to Birmingham General Cemetery* (Birmingham: The Author).

MANNING, ROBERT (1880): *History of the Massachusetts Horticultural Society, 1829-1878* (Boston: The Society).

MARIE LOUISE, PRINCESS (1956): *My Memories of Six Reigns* (London: Evans Brothers Ltd.).

MARION, JOHN FRANCIS (1977): *Famous and Curious Cemeteries* (New York: Crown Publishers Inc.).

MARKLAND, J. H. (1843): *Remarks on English Churches, and on the Expediency of Rendering Sepulchral Memorials Subservient to Pious and Christian Uses* (Oxford: John Henry Parker; London: G. F. and J. Rivington; and Bath: Simms & Son Pocock and Collings).

MARSHALL, JOHN (1975): *The Guinness Book of Rail Facts and Feats* (Enfield: Guinness Publications).

——— (1978): *Biographical Dictionary of Railway Engineers* (Newton Abbot: David & Charles).

MARSHALL, T.K. (1975): *See* POLSON, C.J.

MARTIN, MAJOR THOMAS (1864): *Specification of a 'Cinerator' for the Use of Brahmins and other Hindoo Castes* (Poona: The Author).

MARTY (*Author*), with LASSALLE (*Lithographer*) and ROUSSEAU (*Architect*) (n.d.): *Les Principaux Monuments Funéraires Du Père-Lachaise, de Montmartre, du Mont-Parnasse et autres Cimetières de Paris* (Paris: Amédée Bédelet).

MAXWELL, INGVAL, NANDA, RATISH, and URQUHART, DENNIS (2001): *Conservation of Historic Graveyards. Guide for Practitioners*, 2 (Edinburgh: Historic Scotland).

MAY, TREVOR (1996): *The Victorian Undertaker* (Princes Risborough: Shire Publications Ltd.).

MELLER, HUGH (1981): *London Cemeteries: an Illustrated Guide and Gazetteer* (Amersham: Avebury). *See also* the 1994 edition published in Godstone by the Scolar Press.

MERRICK, A. C. W. (*Compiler*), and CLARKE, R. S. J. (*Ed.*) (1991): *Old Belfast Families and the New Burying Ground from Gravestone Inscriptions, and Wills and Biographical Notes* (Belfast: Ulster Historical Foundation).

METCALF, P. (1987): *See* HUNTINGDON, R.

METZE, ERNO (1981): *See* PEGG, PATRICIA F.

MILLER, THOMAS (1852): *Picturesque Sketches of London Past and Present* (London: Office of the National Illustrated Library). Contains an early description of Highgate Cemetery.

MILLWARD, A., and MOSTYN, B. (1988): *People and Nature in Cities* (London: Nature Conservancy Council).

MILNER, J. EDWARD (1995): 'Report on a spider survey in Hyde Park, Kensington Gardens, and Brompton Cemetery, 1994-1995 (Unpublished report, London: Central Royal Parks Agency).

MILNER WHITE & PARTNERS (*c.*1937): *Stoke Poges Gardens of Remembrance* (np: s.n.).

MITFORD, JESSICA (1963): *The American Way of Death* (London: Hutchinson).

——— (1998): *The American Way of Death Revisited* (London: Virago Press).

MOGRIDGE, GEORGE (*alias* OLD HUMPHREY) (1846): 'The Cemeteries of London' in *Old Humphrey's Walks in London* (London: Religious Tract Society).

MONTANIER, JACQUES (1782): *See* DELILLE, ABBÉ.

MORFITT, DAVID (1994): *See* HAND, KEVIN.

MORGAN, G. (1991): *A Strategic Approach to the Planning and Management of Parks and Open Spaces* (Reading: Institute of Leisure and Amenity Management).

MORLEY, JOHN (1971): *Death, Heaven and the Victorians* (London: Studio Vista).

——— (*Ed.*) (1970): *Death, Heaven & The Victorians.* Catalogue of an Exhibition held at Brighton Art Gallery and Museum 6 May-3 August 1970 (Brighton: Brighton Art Gallery and Museum).

MORNING CHRONICLE (1830): 12 April, 10 June.

——— (1833): 25 January.

MORRIS, R. J. (1976): *Cholera 1832: the Social Response to an Epidemic* (London: Croom Helm).

MOSTYN, B. (1988): *See* MILLWARD, A.

MOUFUSSILITE, THE (Meerut) (1859): New Series, **xiv** 1415 (26 July).

MULLER, HELEN (1994): *Jet Jewellery and Ornaments* (Princes Risborough: Shire Publications Ltd.).

MUNBY, LIONEL (1996): *How Much Is That Worth?* (Chichester: Phillimore for B.A.L.H.).

MUNCEY, R. W. (1930): *A History of the Consecration of Churches and Churchyards* (Cambridge: W. Heffer & Sons Ltd.).

MURRAY, HUGH (1991*a*): 'Philosophers in the Cemetery' in *Annual Report of the Yorkshire Philosophical Society*, 62-72.

——— (1991*b*): *This Garden of Death. A History of the York Cemetery* (York: Ebor Press).

MURRAY, JOHN B., and SOUTER, ROB (2000): *Hertfordshire and Middlesex Butterfly and Moth Report for 1999* (Dedham: Butterfly Conservation).

MYTUM, HAROLD (1989): 'Public Health and Private Sentiment: The Development of Cemetery Architecture' in *World Archaeology*, **xxi**, 283-97.

NANDA, RATISH (2001): *See* MAXWELL, INGVAL, NANDA, RATISH, and URQUHART, DENNIS.

NATIONAL PHILANTHROPIC ASSOCIATION (1850): *Sanatory Progress: being the Fifth Report of the National Philanthropic Association* (London: Hatchard & Son).

NATURAL DEATH CENTRE (1996): *Woodland Burial & Nature Reserve Burial Grounds in the United Kingdom* (London: Natural Death Centre).

NEWMAN, JOHN (1976): *West Kent and the Weald* in *The Buildings of England* Series, edited by NIKOLAUS PEVSNER (Harmondsworth: Penguin Books Ltd.).

NEWMAN, L. HUGH (1967): *Living with Butterflies* (London: John Baker).

NICHOLS, JOHN GOUGH (1838): *Description of the Church of St Mary, Warwick, and of the Beauchamp Chapel and the Monuments of the Beauchamps and Dudleys: also of the Chantry Chapel of Isabella, Countess of Warwick, in Tewkesbury Abbey* (London: J. B. Nichols).

NICOL, ROBERT (1985): *The Victorian Way of Death* (Flinders: University of South Australia).

——— (1994): *At the End of the Road* (St Leonard's, N.S.W.: Allen & Unwin).

NILSSON, STEN (1968): *European Architecture in India 1750-1850* (London: Faber & Faber Ltd.).

NOBLE, GEORGE A. (*Ed.*) (1931): *See* JONES, P. HERBERT.

NOELLE, LOUISE (*Ed.*) (1987): *See* FUENTE, BEATRIZ DE LA.

NORFOLK, HORATIO EDWARD (1866): *Gleanings in Graveyards: A Collection of Curious Epitaphs* (London: J. R. Smith).

NORMAND FILS (LOUIS-MARIE NORMAND [1789-1874]) (1832): *Monumens Funéraires choisis dans les Cimetières de Paris et des Principales Villes de France* (Paris: Normand Fils).

NORTH WEST LONDON PRESS SERIES G (NWLP) (1988): 'Birdwatchers gather at Cemetery' (Thursday 17 March), 7.

NWLP (1988): *See* NORTH WEST LONDON PRESS SERIES G.

O'CONNOR, H. W. (1919): 'The Narcissa episode in Young's *Night Thoughts*', in *Publications of the Modern Language Association*, **xxxiv**, 130-49.

O'DONOGHUE, D. G. (1912): *The Poets of Ireland: A Biographical and Bibliographical Dictionary of Irish Writers of English Verse* (Dublin: Hodges, Figgis & Co.).

OLD HUMPHREY (1846): *See* MOGRIDGE, GEORGE.

OLD INHABITANT, AN (1882): *See* AN OLD INHABITANT.

PADDOCK, SHIRLEY MACDONALD, and ANGELOS, CHRISTINE WALSH (1982): *Symbols in Stone* (Northbook, Ill.: Print Post).

PAGAN, JAMES (1847): *Sketches of the History of Glasgow, Embellished with Twenty Three Plates, and A Map of the City* (Glasgow: Robert Stuart & Co.).

PALLISER, FANNY BURY, and PALLISER, M. A. (1892): *Mottoes for Monuments, or Epitaphs Selected for Study or Application* (London: J. May).

PANOFSKY, ERWIN (1938): '"Et in Arcadia Ego" et le tombeau parlant' in *Gazette les Beaux-Arts*, **i**, 305-6.

——— (1964): *Tomb Sculpture. Its changing aspects from ancient Egypt to Bernini* (London: Thames & Hudson).

PAPWORTH, WYATT ANGELICUS VAN SANDAU (*Ed.*) (1852-92): *The Dictionary of Architecture* (London: The Architectural Publication Society).

PARLIAMENTARY PAPERS (1842): *Effect of Interment of Bodies in Towns*, **x**, 349-618.

——— (1843): *The Practice of Interment in Towns*, **xii**.

——— (1850): *Report on a General Scheme for Extra-Mural Sepulture*, **xxi**.

——— (1851): *General Scheme of Extra-mural Sculpture for County Towns*, **xxiii**, 1348.
PARRY, J. (*Ed.*) (1982): *See* BLOCH, M.
PARSONS, BRIAN (2001): *The London Way of Death* (Thrupp, Stroud: Sutton Publishing Ltd.).
PATCH, D. (1990): *See* WHITE, J.E.J.
PATMORE, COVENTRY (1909): *Poems* (London: George Bell & Sons).
PEACE, DAVID (1994): *Eric Gill: The Inscriptions. A Descriptive Catalogue* (London: Herbert Press).
PEGG, PATRICIA F., and METZE, ERNO (1981): *Death and Dying: a Quality of Life* (London: Pitman).
PEGGS, JAMES (1840): *A Cry from the Tombs: or, Facts and Observations on the Impropriety of Burying the Dead among the Living* (London: John Snow for the Author).
PELLING, M. (1978): *Cholera, Fever, and British Medicine* (Oxford: Oxford University Press).
PENNY, NICHOLAS (1974): 'The Commercial Garden Necropolis of the Early Nineteenth Century and its Critics' in *Garden History: The Journal of the Garden History Society*, **ii**/3 (Summer), 61-76.
——— (1977): *Church Monuments in Romantic England* (New Haven and London: Yale University Press for the Paul Mellon Centre for Studies in British Art).
——— (1981): *Mourning* (London: H.M.S.O.).
PENNY MAGAZINE, THE, OF THE SOCIETY FOR THE DIFFUSION OF USEFUL KNOWLEDGE (1834): **iii**/150 (2 August 1834).
PEPPER, EDWARD (2000): 'The Mechanical Catafalque' in *The Magazine of the Friends of Kensal Green Cemetery*, **xxv** (March), 7-10.
PETTIGREW, THOMAS JOSEPH (1857): *Chronicles of the Tombs. A Select Collection of Epitaphs, preceded by an Essay on Epitaphs and Other Monumental Inscriptions, with Incidental Observations on Sepulchral Antiquities* (London: H.G. Bohn).
PEVSNER, NIKOLAUS (1976): *See* NEWMAN, JOHN.
——— (1991): *See* CHERRY, BRIDGET.
PFISTER, RUDOLF (1948): 'Die Kultur des Friedhofes' in *Baumeister*, **xlv**/3 (March), 49 and 64, and 97-8.
PHYSICK, JOHN (1969): *Designs for English Sculpture, 1680-1860* (London: Victoria & Albert Museum).
——— (1973): *Five Monuments from Eastwell* (London: Victoria & Albert Museum).
——— (1982): *The Victoria and Albert Museum. The History of the Building* (Oxford: Phaidon-Christie's Ltd.).
——— (1989): *See* BLUNDELL, JOE WHITLOCK.
PICKLES, JOHN D. (1993): *The Victorian Cemetery. An Illustrated Exhibition* (Cambridge: Cambridge University Library).
PIGMAN, G. W. (1985): *Grief and English Renaissance Elegy* (Cambridge: Cambridge University Press).
PINFIELD, LESLIE (*Compiler*) (1993): *See* FELSTEAD, ALISON.
PLANT, COLIN W. (1983): 'A review of the Lepidoptera of the London area for 1981 and 1982' in *London Naturalist*, **lxii**, 122.
——— (1987): *Butterflies of the London Area* (London: London Natural History Society).
——— (1993): *Larger Moths of the London Area* (London: London Natural History Society).
POLLOCK, SIR FREDERICK (*Ed.*) (1875): *See* MACREADY, WILLIAM CHARLES.
POLSON, C. J., and MARSHALL, T. K. (1975): *The Disposal of the Dead* (London: English Universities Press Ltd.).
PONTIN, JOHN (1996): 'Ants Nests, Sun and Shade – their measurement and significance for invertebrate conservation' in *British Wildlife*, **viii**/1, (October), 21-7.
POTTERTON, HOMAN (1975): *Irish Church Monuments 1570-1880* (Belfast: Ulster Architectural Heritage Society).
POWELL, KENNETH (1980): 'Vandals in Valhalla' in *Country Life* (27 November), 2011-2
PREVETTE, KENNETH G. C. (1975): *The Cremation Society Handbook and Directory of Crematoria* (Maidstone: The Cremation Society).
PRICE, SIMON (*Ed.*) (1987): *See* CANNADINE, DAVID.
PRICKETT, FREDERICK (1842): *The History and Antiquities of Highgate, Middlesex* (London: The Author).
PRIOR, L. (1989): *The Social Organisation of Death* (Basingstoke: Macmillan Press Ltd.).
PUCKLE, BERTRAM S. (1926): *Funeral Customs: Their Origin and Development* (London: T. Werner Laurie).
PUGIN, AUGUSTUS CHARLES, and HEATH, CHARLES (1829-31): *Paris and its Environs Displayed in a Series of 200 Picturesque Views from Original Drawings taken under the Direction of A. Pugin Esq. The Engraving executed under the Superintendence of Mr C. Heath* (London: Jennings & Chaplin).
PUGIN, AUGUSTUS WELBY NORTHMORE (1836): *Contrasts; or, a Parallel between the Noble Edifices of the Fourteenth and Fifteenth Centuries, and Similar Buildings of the Present Day; Shewing the Present Decay in Taste* (London: Printed for the Author, and Published by Him).
——— (1841*a*): *The True Principles of Pointed or Christian Architecture: set forth in Two Lectures delivered at St. Marie's, Oscott, by A. Welby Pugin, Architect, and Professor of Ecclesiastical Antiquities in that College* (London: John Weale). *See also* the edition of 1853 (London: Henry G. Bohn).
——— (1841*b*): *Contrasts: or, a Parallel between the Noble Edifices of the Middle Ages, and Corresponding Buildings of the Present Day; Shewing the Present Decay of Taste* (London: Charles Dolman) *See also* the facsimile edition of 1973 with extra material (Leicester: Leicester University Press). An earlier version, with a slightly different title, came out in 1836 (*See above*).
——— (1843): *An Apology for the Revival of Christian Architecture in England* (London: John Weale).
PULLIN, ANDREW S. (1995): *Ecology and Conservation of Butterflies* (London: Chapman & Hall in association with British Butterfly Conservation Society).
QUARTERLY REVIEW (1819): **xxi**.
——— (1842): **xliv**.
RAGON, MICHEL (1983): *The Space of Death: a Study of Funerary Architecture, Decoration, and Urbanism* (Charlottesville, Va.: University of Virginia Press).
RANDALL, TOM (1991): *See* CULBERTSON, JUDI.

RAVENSHAW, THOMAS FITZ-ARTHUR TORIN (1878): *Antiente Epitaphes (from A.D. 1250 to A. D. 1800) Collected & Set Forth in Chronologicall Order* (London: Masters & Co.).
RAWLINSON, H. G. (1920): *British Beginnings in Western India, 1579-1657. An Account of the British Factory of Surat* (Oxford: Clarendon Press).
RAWNSLEY, STUART, and REYNOLDS, JACK (1977): 'Undercliffe Cemetery, Bradford' in *History Workshop: a Journal of Socialist Historians*, **iv**, 215-21.
RBKC (1996): *See* ROYAL BOROUGH OF KENSINGTON & CHELSEA.
READ, BENEDICT (1982): *Victorian Sculpture* (New Haven and London: Yale University Press for the Paul Mellon Centre for Studies in British Art).
REED, CHARLES, *ET AL.* (1867): *Proceedings in Reference to the Preservation of the Bunhill Fields Burial Ground* (London: Benjamin Pardon for the Corporation of London). This fascinating volume contains an 'exact reprint' of EDMUND CURLL's rare tract of 1717.
REEVE, HENRY (*Ed.*) (1875): *See* GREVILLE, CHARLES C.F.
REID, MAYNE (1852): *The Scalp Hunters, or Romantic Adventures in Northern Mexico* (London: Simms & McIntyre).
REVETT, NICHOLAS (1762-1816): *See* STUART, JAMES.
——— (1769-97): *The Antiquities of Ionia* (London: Society of Dilettanti).
REYNOLDS, JACK (1977): *See* RAWNSLEY, STUART.
RICHARDSON, EDWARD (1843): *The Monumental Effigies of the Temple Church with an Account of their Restoration, in the Year 1842* (London: Longman Brown Green & Longman's).
RICHARDSON, RUTH (1987): *Death, Dissection, and the Destitute* (London: Routledge & Kegan Paul).
——— (1993): 'La Compañía de la Vida, la Muerte, el Entierro y la Resurrección: el entierro metropolitano en el Reino Unido, 1800-1900' in *Una Arquitectura para la Muerte: I Encuentro Internacional sobre Los Cementerios Contemporaneos, Sevilla 4/7 Junio 1991. Actas* (Sevilla: Junta de Andalucía), 73-87, also translated as 'The Life, Death, Burial and Resurrection Company: UK metropolitan burial 1800-1900' in the same publication, 577-83. *See* ANDALUCÍA (1993) cited above.
RICHES, ANNE (1990): *See* WILLIAMSON, ELIZABETH.
RIMMER, ALFRED (1875): *Ancient Stone Crosses of England* (London: Virtue & Co.).
ROBINSON, DAVID, and KOONTZ, DEAN (1996): *Beautiful Death. Art of the Cemetery* (New York and London: Viking Penguin and Penguin Books).
ROBINSON, J. ERIC (1989*a*): 'Opening Unknown Doors' in *Country Life* (11 May), 166-8.
——— (1989*b*): *See* BROOKS, CHRISTOPHER.
——— (1994): *Geology in the Churchyard* (Stoneleigh: Living Churchyard Project & Geologists' Association).
ROBINSON, RICHARD (1989): *See* BROOKS, CHRISTOPHER.
ROBINSON, W. (1883): *God's Acre Beautiful or The Cemeteries of the Future* (London: John Murray; and New York: Scribner & Welford).
RODRÍGUEZ BARBERÁN, FRANCISCO JAVIER, *ET AL.* (1990): *Los Cementerios en la Sevilla del Siglo XIX* (Seville: Obra Cultural/Monte de Piedad y Caja de Ahorras de Sevilla).
——— (1994): *Cementerios de Andalucía. Arquitectura y Urbanismo* (Seville: Junta de Andalucía, Consejería de Obras Públicas y Transportes - Direccíon General de Arquitectura y Vivienda).
ROGERS, THE REV. CHARLES (1871-2): *Monuments and Monumental Inscriptions in Scotland* (London: Charles Griffin & Co. for The Grampian Club).
RONALDS, HUGH (1831): *Pyrus Malus Brentfordiensis* (London: Longman, Rees, Orme, Brown, & Green).
ROSE, PETER Q. (1980): *Ivies* (London: Blandford [2nd ed. Revised 1990]).
——— (1996): *Ivies* (Newton Abbot: David & Charles).
ROSENTHAL, ERIC (1966): *South African Dictionary of National Biography* (London: Frederick Warne & Co.).
ROUSSEAU (n.d.): *See* MARTY.
ROUSSEAU, JEAN-JACQUES (1761): *La Nouvelle Héloïse, ou Lettres de deux amans, habitans d'une petite ville au pied des Alpes* (Paris: Duchesne).
ROWELL, G. (1974): *Hell and the Victorians* (Oxford: Oxford University Press).
——— (1977): *The Liturgy of Christian Burial* (London: Alcuin Club/S.P.C.K.).
ROWSE, A. L. (1971): 'Holywell Cemetery: Victorian Oxford' in *Contemporary Review*, **ccxix**, 93-9.
ROYAL BOROUGH OF KENSINGTON & CHELSEA (RBKC) (1996): Kensal Green Cemetery and North Kensington Environmental Pack (RBK&C Ecology Service/North Kensington City Challenge).
RUGG, JULIE (1992): The Rise of Cemetery Companies in Britain, 1820-52. Unpublished PhD thesis (University of Stirling).
——— (1994): *See* DUNK, JULIE.
———, and DUNK, JULIE (1994): 'Conserving Cemeteries' in *Landscape Design*, **235** (November).
——— (2000): 'Defining the place of burial: what makes a cemetery a cemetery?' in *Mortality*, **5**/3, 259-75.
RUSHEN, PERCY C. (1910): *The Churchyard Inscriptions of the City of London* (London: Phillimore & Co.).
RUSSELL, N.A. (*Ed.*) (1982): *See* BACKER, BARBARA.
SAGUAR QUER, CARLOS (1994): 'Arquitectura funeraria Neomedieval en la Europa del Siglo XIX' in *GOYA Revista de Arte*, **241-2** (July-October), 91-102.
——— (1996): 'La Egiptomania en la España de Goya' in *GOYA Revista de Arte*, **252** (May-June) 367-81
——— (1997): 'Egiptomania y Arquitectura en España (1840-1940)' in *GOYA Revista de Arte*, **259-60** (July-October), 386-406.
SAINT-A, M. P. (1816): *Promenade aux Cimetières de Paris, aux Sépultures Royales de Saint-Denis, et aux Catacombes* (Paris: C.-L.-F. Panckoucke).
SAINT JOHNS, ADELA NORA ROGERS (1959): *First Step up towards Heaven. Hubert Eaton and Forest Lawn* (Englewood Cliffs: Prentice-Hall).

SAXON, A. H. (1978): *The Life and Art of Andrew Ducrow & the romantic age of the English Circus* (Hamden, Conn: Archon Books).
SCHEIN, RENATE (*Ed.*) (1987): *See* FISCHER, CHRISTOPH.
SCHOR, ESTHER (1994): *Bearing the Dead. The British Culture of Mourning from the Enlightenment to Victoria* (Princeton, N. J.: Princeton University Press).
SCHUCHARD, JUTTA, and CLAUSSEN, HORST (*Eds.*) (1985): *Vergänglichkeit und Denkmal: Beiträge zur Sepulkralkultur* (Bonn: Bouvier).
SCHUYLER, DAVID (1984): 'The Evolution of the Anglo-American Rural Cemetery: Landscape Architecture as Social and Cultural History' in *Journal of Garden History*, **iv**/3 (July-September), 291-304.
——— (*Ed.*) (1984): *See* HUNT, JOHN DIXON.
SCOTT, GEORGE GILBERT (1854): *Consecration versus Desecration. An Appeal to the Bishop of London against the Bill for the destruction of City Churches and the sale of Burial Grounds* (London and Oxford: G. Bell, J. B. Nichols & Sons, and J. H. Parker).
——— (1995): *Personal and Professional Recollections*, with new material and a Critical Introduction by GAVIN STAMP (Stamford: Paul Watkins).
SCOTT, N. A. JR. (*Ed.*) (1967): *The Modern Vision of Death* (Richmond, Va.: John Knox Press).
SCULPTURE CENTRE, THE (1937, 1938): *Sculptured Memorials and Headstones Designed and Carved in Sculptors' Studios in British Stones* (London: The Sculpture Centre).
SELECT COMMITTEE ON IMPROVEMENT OF THE HEALTH OF TOWNS (1842): 'Report .... together with the Minutes of Evidence – Effect of Interment of Bodies in Towns' in *Parliamentary Papers*, **x**, 349-618.
SELWYN, BERNARD (1988): *The Brompton Cemetery* (London: Friends of Brompton Cemetery).
SEYMOUR, THE REV. WILLIAM WOOD (1898): *The Cross In Tradition, History, and Art* (London: G. P. Putnam's Sons; and New York: The Knickerbocker Press).
SHAW, ALASTAIR (1995): *See* DAVIES, DOUGLAS.
SHELLEY, HENRY CHARLES (1914): *The Lives and Letters of Edward Young* (London and New York: I. Pitman & Sons).
SHELLIM, MAURICE (*Ed.*) (1986): *South Park Street Cemetery, Calcutta* (London: B.A.C.S.A.).
SHEPPARD, F. H. W. (*Ed.*) (1956): *Survey of London*, **xxvi**: *The Parish of St Mary Lambeth* (London: Athlone Press).
——— (1973): *Survey of London*, **xxxvii**: *Northern Kensington* (London: Athlone Press). *See especially* 335-9.
——— (1975): *Survey of London*, **xxxviii**: *The Museums Area of South Kensington and Westminster* (London: Athlone Press).
——— (1983): *Survey of London*, **xli**: *Southern Kensington: Brompton* (London: Athlone Press).
SIMO, MELANIE LOUISE (1988): *Loudon and the Landscape. From Country Seat to Metropolis* (New Haven and London: Yale University Press).
SINGLETON, C. C. (1960): 'The Rookwood Cemetery Line' in *Australian Historical Railway Society Bulletin*, **268** (February), 17-24.
SKINNER, BASIL (1977): 'Entering Heaven Politely: The Georgian Way of Death' in *Country Life* (3 February), 258-9.
SKINNER, BERNARD (1992): *See* CHALMERS-HUNT, JOHN M.
SKOTTOWE, P. F. (1969): 'Thomas Talfourd and David Copperfield' in *The Dickensian*, **lxv** (January), 30.
SLIGGERS, BERT (1988): *Westerveld: van buitenplaats tot begraafplaats 1888-1988* (Haarlem: De Vriesborch).
SLOANE, DAVID C. (1991): *The Last Great Necessity: Cemeteries in American History* (Baltimore: The Johns Hopkins University Press).
SLONIMSKY, NICOLAS (*Ed.*) (1994): *Baker's Biographical Dictionary of Musicians* (New York: Schirmer Books).
SMALE, D. (1993): *Davies's Law of Burial, Cremation, and Exhumation* (Crayford: Shaw & Sons).
SMALL, N. (*Ed.*) (1996): *See* FIELD, D.
SMILES, SAMUEL (1862): *Lives of the Engineers, with an Account of their Principal Works; comprising also a History of Inland Communication in Britain*, 3 vols. (London: John Murray).
——— (1905): *Self-Help. With Illustrations of Conduct and Perseverance.* Popular Edition (London: John Murray).
SMITH, E. E. F. (1979): 'The South Metropolitan Cemetery, West Norwood and its Memorials' in *Transactions of the London and Middlesex Archaeological Society*, **xxx**, 152-6.
SMITH, R. A. (1847): *Guide to Laurel Hill, near Philadelphia* (Philadelphia: C. Sherman).
SNOW, WILLIAM (1817): *Sepulchral Gleanings; or, a Collection of Epitaphs, Ancient, Modern, Curious, Instructive, and Moral; As actually and accurately taken down from various parts of England; including those in the vicinity of London and Westminster, forming a complete Mirror of Mortality, and calculated (in an unusual degree) to promote the cause of Virtue and Religion; the whole collected, digested, and alphabetically arranged* (London: William Snow).
SOUTER, ROB (2000): *See* MURRAY, JOHN B.
SOUTHEY, CAROLINE (1841): *Chapters on Churchyards* (Edinburgh and London: William Blackwood & Sons).
STACE, CLIVE A. (1995): *New Flora of the British Isles* (Cambridge: Cambridge University Press).
STAGLIENO CEMETERY (*c.*1910): *Souvenir du Cimitière de Gênes: 37 Vues* (Genoa: A. P.) Later revised and updated (n.d.) as *Camposanto di Genova: 50 Vedute* (Milan: Edizioni A. Serocchi; and Genoa: V. Lichino & Figlio).
STAMP, GAVIN (1995): *See* SCOTT, GEORGE GILBERT.
STANLEY, ARTHUR PENRHYN (1882): *Historical Memorials of Westminster Abbey* (London: John Murray).
STANNARD, D. E. (*Ed.*) (1975): *Death in America* (Philadelphia: University of Pennsylvania Press).
——— (1977): *The Puritan Way of Death: A Study of Religion, Culture, and Social Change* (New York: Oxford University Press).

STAPLETON, THE REV. HENRY S.L. (*Ed.*) (1988): *See* BURMAN, PETER.

STEPHENSON, MILL (1926): *A List of Monumental Brasses in the British Isles* (London: Headley Bros.).

STEPHENSON, ROBERT (2000): 'The Lost Columbarium at Kensal Green' in *The Magazine of the Friends of Kensal Green Cemetery*, **26** (July 2000), 10-11.

STEVENSON, ROBERT LOUIS BALFOUR (1924): *Further Memories* (London: William Heinemann, Ltd., Tusitala Edition).

STEWART, AUBREY (1897): *English Epigrams and Epitaphs* (London: Chapman & Hall).

STOKES, GWYNETH (*Ed.*) (1988): *Nunhead Cemetery. An Illustrated Guide* (London: The Friends of Nunhead Cemetery).

STONE, MRS. ELIZABETH (1858): *God's Acre: or, Historical Notices relating to Churchyards* (London: John W. Parker & Son).

STOTHARD, C. A. (1876): *The Monumental Effigies of Great Britain*, with descriptions by ALFRED JOHN KEMPE, edited by JOHN HEWITT (London: Chatto & Windus).

STRAIN, ROBERT WILLIAM MAGILL (1961): *Belfast and its Charitable Society. A Story of Urban Social Development* (London: Oxford University Press).

STRANG, JOHN (1831): *Necropolis Glasguensis; with Osbervations* [sic] *on Ancient and Modern Tombs and Sepulture* (Glasgow: Atkinson & Co.).

STRAUSS, A. (1965): *See* GLASER, S.

STREET, FREDERICK (1960): 'A great nurseryman' in *Gardeners' Chronicle*, **cxlvii**, 378-9.

STUART, JAMES, and REVETT, NICHOLAS (1762-1816): *The Antiquities of Athens* (London: Haberkorn, etc.).

STUBBS, ALAN E., and FALK, STEVEN J. (1996): *British Hoverflies* (Reading: British Entomological and Natural History Society).

STYAN, KATE E. (1902): *A Short History of Sepulchral Cross-Slabs, with Reference to Other Emblems found thereon* (London: Bemrose & Sons).

SUDNOW, D. (1967): *Passing On: The Social Organization of Dying* (Englewood Cliffs, N. J.: Prentice-Hall).

SULZER, JOHANN GEORG (1771-4): *Allgemeine Theorie der schönen Künste in einzeln, nach alphabetischer Ordnung der Kunstwörter auf einander folgenden. Artikeln abgehandelt* (Leipzig: M. G. Weidmanns Erben und Reich).

SUMMERSON, JOHN (1978): 'Sir John Soane and the Furniture of Death' in *The Architectural Review*, **clxiii**/973 (March), 147-55. also published in SUMMERSON, JOHN (1990): *The Unromantic Castle* (London: Thames & Hudson), 121-2.

SUMNER, A. (*Ed.*) (1995): *Death, Passion, and Politics* (London: Dulwich Picture Gallery).

SURGEONS, A MEMBER OF THE ROYAL COLLEGE OF (1857): *Burning the Dead, or Urn Sepulture* (London: George Philip & Son).

SWINSON, ARTHUR (1970): *Frederick Sander: the Orchid King* (London: Hodder & Stoughton).

TATE GALLERY (1996): *Tate Gallery. Illustrated Catalogue of Acquisitions 1986-88* (London: Tate Publishing).

TAYLOR, JOSEPH (1816): *The Danger of Premature Interment, Proved from Many Remarkable Instances of People who have recovered after being laid out for dead, and of others entombed alive, for want of being properly examined prior to Interment. Also a Description of the Manner the Ancient Egyptians, and other Nations, Preserved and Venerated their Dead, and a Curious Account of their Sepulchral Ever Burning Lamps and Mausoleums. Likewise the pernicious effects of burying in the body of Churches, and confined Church-Yards pointed out, whereby many valuable lives have been lost to the Public, and their Friends. Selected from Historical Records* (London: Simpkin & Marshall).

TAYLOR, LOU (1983): *Mourning Dress: A Costume and Social History* (London: George Allen & Unwin).

TAYLOR, NICHOLAS (1970): 'Norwood Victorian' in *The Architectural Review*, **cxlvii**/876 (February), 93-7.

TEGG, WILLIAM (1876): *The Last Act: being the Funeral Rites of Nations and Individuals* (London: William Tegg & Co.).

TEMPLE, PHILIP (1989): *See* BROOKS, CHRISTOPHER.

TENENTI ALBERTO (1952): *La Vie et la Mort à travers l'art du XVe Siècle*, etc. (Paris: Cahiers des Annales 8).

——— (1957): *Il Senso della Morte e l'Amore della Vita nel Rinascimento* (Turin: Studi e ricerche 5).

TENNYSON, ALFRED (1850): *In Memoriam A. H. H.* (London: Macmillan & Co.).

THOMAS, WALTER (1901): *Le Poète Edward Young, 1683-1765; étude sur sa vie et ses oeuvres* (Paris: Hachette).

THOMPSON, C. J. S. (1928): *Mysteries of History* (London: Faber & Gwyer).

THOMPSON, SIR HENRY (1891): *Modern Cremation: its History and Practice. With information relating to the recently improved arrangements made by the Cremation Society of England* (London: Kegan Paul & Co.).

THORNBURY, WALTER (*c.*1875): *Old and New London: a Narrative of its History, its People, and its Places*, **i-ii** (London: Cassell Petter & Galpin).

THORNE, J. O., and COLLOCOTT, T. C. (*Eds.*) (1984): *Chambers Biographical Dictionary* (Edinburgh: Chambers).

THURY, LOUIS-ÉTIENNE-FRANÇOIS HÉRICART-FERRAND, VICOMTE DE (1815): *Descriptions de Catacombes de Paris* (Paris: Bossange & Masson).

TIMBS, JOHN (1867): *Curiosities of London exhibiting the most Rare and Remarkable Objects of Interest in the Metropolis with nearly Sixty Years' Personal Recollections* (London: Virtue & Co. Ltd.).

TIMES, THE (1830s and 1840s): *See* PALMER'S *Index* to *The Times*. *See also The Times* obituaries 1800-2000.

TOURNEUR, PIERRE LE (1769): *Les Nuits d' Young* (Paris: Chez Lejay).

TOYNBEE, ARNOLD, *ET AL.* (1968): *Man's Concern with Death* (London: Hodder & Stoughton).

TRENCH, RICHARD, and HILLMAN, ELLIS (1993): *London under London* (London: John Murray).

TRENDALL, EDWARD W. (1850): *A New Work on Monuments, Cenotaphs, Tombs, and Tablets, etc., etc., with their details drawn to a large scale, by which the Workman can erect each design with facility* (London: Atchley & Co.).

TREUHERZ, JULIAN (1987): *Hard Times. Social Realism in Victorian Art* (London: Lund Humphries Publishers Ltd.).

TROLLOPE, EDWARD (1858): *Manual of Sepulchral Memorials* (London: Piper Stephenson & Spence).

TRUTH-SEEKER, A. (i.e. LEO H. GRINDON) (1874): *Cremation considered in reference to the Resurrection* (London: s.n.).

TURNER, JANE SHOAF (*Ed.*) (1996): *The Dictionary of Art and Architecture* (London: Macmillan).

TURNER, J. (*c.*1838): *Trade Catalogue of J. Turner, Coffin Maker, Plate Chaser, Furnishing Undertaker* (London: Cunningham & Salmon).

TYACK, THE REV. GEORGE S. (1900): *The Cross in Ritual, Architecture, and Art* (London: William Andrews & Co.).

URBAIN, JEAN-DIDIER (1989): *L'archipel des morts: le sentiment de la mort et les dérives de la mémoire dans les cimetières d'Occident* (Paris: Plon).

URQUHART, DENNIS (2001): *See* MAXWELL, INGVAL, NANDA, RATISH, and URQUHART, DENNIS.

VAES, GUY (1978): *Les Cimetières de Londres* (Brussels: Jacques Antoine).

VALLANCE, AYMER (1933): *Old Crosses and Lychgates* (London: B. T. Batsford Ltd.).

VICKERY, MARGARET (1998): *Gardening for Butterflies* (Colchester: Butterfly Conservation).

VICTORIA and ALBERT MUSEUM (1971): *Victorian Church Art* (London: H.M.S.O.).

VILLENEUVE (1787): *Vues pittoresques, plans, &c., des principaux jardins anglois qui sont en France, fidelement dessinées d'après nature* (Paris: Simon & Guillot).

VINCENT, WILLIAM THOMAS (1896): *In Search of Gravestones Old and Curious* (London: Mitchell & Hughes).

VIVIAN-NEAL, HENRY (1999): *Paths of Glory; or, A Select Alphabetical and Biographical List, Illustrated with Line Drawings of their Monuments, of Persons of Note Commemorated at the Cemetery of All Souls at Kensal Green* (London: The Friends of Kensal Green Cemetery).

VOVELLE, MICHEL (1983): *La Mort et l'Occident de 1300 à nos Jours* (Paris: Gallimard).

WAITE, MICHAEL, KEECH, DANIEL, AND GAME, MEG (1993): *Nature Conservation in Camden. Ecology Handbook 24* (London: London Ecology Unit).

WAKE, HENRY THOMAS (1878): *All the Monumental Inscriptions in the Graveyards of Brigham and Bridekirk, near Cockermouth, in the County of Cumberland, from 1666 to 1876* (Cockermouth: D. Fidler).

WALFORD, EDWARD (*c.*1870): *See* KNIGHT, CHARLES.

———— (*c.*1875): *Old and New London: a Narrative of its History, its People, and its Places*, **iii-vi** (London: Cassell Petter & Galpin).

———— (*c.*1880): *Greater London: a Narrative of its History, its People, and its Places*, **i-ii** (London: Cassell & Co. Ltd.).

———— (*Ed.*) (originally published in 1860, but *see* 1909 edition): *Walford's County Families of the United Kingdom, or Royal Memorial of the Titled and Untitled Aristocracy of England, Wales, Scotland, and Ireland* (London: Spottiswoode, Ballantine, & Co. Ltd.).

WALKER, DANIEL PICKERING (1964): *The Decline of Hell. Seventeenth-Century Discussions of Eternal Torment* (London: Routledge & Kegan Paul).

WALKER, DAVID (1984): *See* GIFFORD, JOHN.

WALKER, GEORGE ALFRED (1839): *Gatherings from Grave-Yards, Particularly those of London, with a concise History of the Modes of Interment among different Nations, from the earliest Periods: and a Detail of dangerous and fatal Results produced by the unwise and revolting Custom of inhuming the Dead in the midst of the Living* (London: Longman etc.).

———— (1843): *Interment and Disinterment* (London: Longman & Co.).

———— (1847): *A Series of Lectures on the actual conditions of the Metropolitan Graveyards* (London: Longman & Co.).

WALL, JAMES CHARLES (1891): *The Tombs of the Kings of England* (London: Sampson Low & Co.).

WALTER, CORNELIA (1847): *See* CLEAVELAND, NEHEMIAH.

WALTER, TONY (1966): *The Eclipse of Eternity: A Sociology of the Afterlife* (Basingstoke: Macmillan Press Ltd.).

———— (1990): *Funerals and How to Improve Them* (London: Hodder & Stoughton Ltd.).

WATERFIELD, GILES (*Ed.*) (1996): *Soane and Death* (London: Dulwich Picture Gallery).

WATKIN, DAVID (1974): *The Life and Work of C. R. Cockerell* (London: Zwemmer).

———— (*Ed.*) (2000): *The Age of Wilkins. The Architecture of Improvement* (Cambridge: The Master and Fellows of Downing College).

WAUGH, EVELYN (1948): *The Loved One: an Anglo-American tragedy* (Boston, Mass.: Little Brown & Co.; and London: Chapman & Hall).

WEATHERLEY, W. SAMUEL (1887): *See* BRINDLEY, WILLIAM.

WEAVER, LAWRENCE (1915): *Memorials and Monuments Old and New: Two hundred subjects chosen from seven centuries* (London: Country Life and George Newnes Ltd.; and New York: Charles Scribner's Sons).

WEBER, F. PARKES (1914): *Aspects of Death in Art and Epigram* (London: T. Fisher Unwin and Bernard Quaritch).

WEEVER, JOHN (1631): *Ancient Funerall Monuments within the United Monarchie of Great Britaine and Ireland, and the Islands adjacent, with the dissolved Monasteries therein contained* (London: Tho. Harper).

WEIDENMANN, JACOB (1888): *Modern Cemeteries. An Essay upon the Improvement and Proper Management of Rural Cemeteries* (Chicago: Monumental News).

WELCH, D. (1991): *The Management of Urban Parks* (Harlow: Longman).

WEST OF LONDON AND WESTMINSTER CEMETERY COMPANY (from the 1830s): Minutes, now in the Public Record Office (P.R.O. WORK 6/65, 6/66, 6/67, 38/146).

WESTWOOD, J.O. (1841): *See* HUMPHREYS, HENRY N.

WHALEY, JOACHIM (*Ed.*) (1981): *Mirrors of Mortality: Studies in the Social History of Death* (London: Europa Publications).

WHEELER, MICHAEL (1990): *Death and the Future Life in Victorian Literature and Theology* (Cambridge: Cambridge University Press).

WHINNEY, MARGARET D. (1964): *Sculpture in Britain 1530 to 1830* (Harmondsworth: Penguin Books Ltd.).

WHITE, HENRY KIRK (1850): *The Works of Henry Kirk White, containing his Life, Poems, and Melancholy Hours* (London: Charles Daly).

WHITE, J. E. J., and PATCH, D. (1990): *Ivy – Boon or Bane? Arboriculture Research Note* (Farnham: Department of the Environment Arboricultural Advisory & Information Service).

WHITE, LESLEY (1987): *Monuments and Their Inscriptions* (London: Society of Genealogists).

WHITTICK, ARNOLD (1965): 'The First Great Modern Cemeteries: Père-Lachaise and Kensal Green' in *Commemorative Art*, **xxxii**, 251-65.

WICKER, CECIL VIVIAN (1952): *Edward Young and the Fear of Death; a Study in Romantic Melancholy* (Albuquerque, New Mexico: University of New Mexico).

WIEBENSON, DORA (1969): *Sources of Greek Revival Architecture* (London: Zwemmer).

WIENRICH, STEPHANIE (1998, 2000): *See* ALBERY, NICHOLAS.

WILKINSON, THEON (1976*a*): *Two Monsoons* (London: Duckworth).

——— (1976*b*): 'Crumbling Monuments of the Raj. European Cemeteries in India' in *Country Life* (2 September), 606-8.

——— (1976*c*): Letter in *Country Life* (23 September), 810.

——— (1984): 'British Cemeteries in South Asia: an Aspect of Social History' in *Asian Affairs*, **xv**, 46-54.

WILLIAMSON, ELIZABETH, RICHES, ANNE, and HIGGS, MALCOLM (1990): *Glasgow*, in *The Buildings of Scotland* Series (London: Penguin Group).

WILLIAMSON, R. P. ROSS (1942): 'Victorian Necropolis: the Cemeteries of London' in *The Architectural Review*, **xcii**/550, 87-96.

WILLMOTT, KENNETH J. (1999): *The Holly Blue Butterfly* (Colchester: Butterfly Conservation).

——— , and CLARKE, SUSAN (1994): *Discovering Butterflies in Churchyards* (Colchester: British Butterfly Conservation Society).

WILLSON, E. J. (1982): *West London Nursery Gardens* (London: Fulham & Hammersmith Historical Society).

WILLSON, THOMAS (*c.*1830 or *c.*1831): *The Pyramid. A General Metropolitan Cemetery to be Erected in the Vicinity of Primrose Hill* (London: The Author).

WILSON, SIR ANDREW, and LEVY, HERMANN (1938): *Burial Reform and Funeral Costs* (Oxford: Oxford University Press).

WILSON, J. B. (n.d.): 'The Story of Norwood'. Unpublished MSS. formerly in the Members' Library, County Hall, London.

WILTSHIRE, ELINOR, and ELLIS, L. T. (1995): 'John Benbow (1821-1908) and the bryophytes of north-west Middlesex' in *London Naturalist*, **lxxiv** (December), 21-53.

WINTER, GORDON (1975): *A Cockney Camera* (Harmondsworth: Penguin Books Ltd.).

WOLFF, MICHAEL (*Ed.*) (1973): *See* DYOS, H.J.

WOLFSTON, PATRICIA S. (1985): *Greater London Cemeteries and Crematoria* (London: Society of Genealogists).

WOOD, SIR H. T. (1913): *A History of the Royal Society of Arts* (London: John Murray).

WOODHAM-SMITH, CECIL (1972): *Queen Victoria* (London: Hamish Hamilton).

WOOLLACOTT, RON (1976): 'Brief Guide to Nunhead Cemetery' in *Newsletter of the Peckham Society*, **iv** (February-March).

——— (1984): *Nunhead Notables* (London: Friends of Nunhead Cemetery).

WORDSWORTH, CHRISTOPHER (1874): *On Burning the Body, and on Burial* (Lincoln: s.n.).

WRIGHT, GEOFFREY NORMAN (1972): *Discovering Epitaphs. Being a collection of some of the most curious epitaphs and memorials gathered together* (Aylesbury: Shire Publications).

WURZELL, BRIAN (1990): 'The Long-tailed blue, *Lampides boeticus*, breeding in North London' in *Bulletin of the Amateur Entomologists' Society*, **xlix**/373 (December), 254-6.

YCT (1994): *See* YORK CEMETERY TRUST.

YORK CEMETERY TRUST (YCT) (1994): Ecological Land Management Plan (York: York Cemetery Trust).

YOUNG, EDWARD (1989): *Night Thoughts*. Edited by STEPHEN CORNFORD (Cambridge: Cambridge University Press).

Index *compiled by Frances Mather*

Page references in **bold** refer to plates.